W9-BCZ-138

The
Robert Frost
Encyclopedia

Courtesy of Lesley Lee Francis

The
Robert Frost
Encyclopedia

Edited by
Nancy Lewis Tuten
And
John Zubizarreta

GREENWOOD PRESS
Westport, Connecticut • London

Library of Congress Cataloging-in-Publication Data

The Robert Frost encyclopedia / edited by Nancy Lewis Tuten and John Zubizarreta.
   p. cm.
  Includes bibliographical references and index.
  ISBN 0–313–29464–X (alk. paper)
  1. Frost, Robert, 1874–1963—Encyclopedias. 2. Poets, American—20th
century—Biography—Encyclopedias. I. Tuten, Nancy Lewis. II. Zubizarreta, John.
  PS3511.R94Z459 2001
  811'.52—dc21   00–025146
  [B]

British Library Cataloguing in Publication Data is available.

Library of Congress Catalog Card Number: 00–025146
ISBN: 0–313–29464–X

First published in 2001

Greenwood Press, 88 Post Road West, Westport, CT 06881
An imprint of Greenwood Publishing Group, Inc.
www.greenwood.com

Printed in the United States of America

The paper used in this book complies with the
Permanent Paper Standard issued by the National
Information Standards Organization (Z39.48–1984).

10 9 8 7 6 5 4 3 2

Copyright Acknowledgments

The editors and publisher are grateful to the following for permission to reprint from their sources:

"In White" and excerpts from Frost poems cited in "Uncollected Poetry" reprinted by permission of the Estate of Robert Lee Frost.

Selections from *Complete Poems of Robert Frost 1949*, copyright 1916, 1923, 1928, 1930, 1934, 1939, 1943, 1945, 1947, 1949, © 1967 by Henry Holt and Co., copyright 1936, 1942, 1944, 1945, 1947, 1948, 1951, 1956, 1958, 1962 by Robert Frost, and copyright 1964, 1967 by Lesley Frost Ballantine. *In the Clearing,* copyright 1942, 1948, 1950, 1951, 1952, 1953, 1955, 1956, 1958, 1959, 1960, 1961, 1962 by Robert Frost and copyright © 1970 by Lesley Frost Ballantine. Reprinted by permission of Henry Holt and Co.

Contents

Preface

Whenever he had the chance, Robert Frost warned his readers of what he called in his essay "*Caveat Poeta*" the "danger of too much analysis." Earlier, in the essay "Poetry and School," he wrote that "poems are not meant to be read in course any more than they are to be made a study of":

One of the dangers of college to anyone who wants to stay a human reader (that is to say a humanist) is that he will become a specialist and lose his sensitive fear of landing on the lovely too hard. (With beak and talon.)

Rather than have critics tell us what to think of his poems, Frost wanted us to delight in his verses on our own, to "settle down ... and make ourselves at home among the poems, completely at our ease as to how they should be taken." Perhaps for Frost the most important word in his comment is *taken*, one form of a verb that reappears often in both his poetry and prose and that carries the sense of active participation in the construction of meaning, a vigorous act, as he suggests elsewhere, not unlike our giving ourselves over to love. Certainly, such *taking* of poetic meaning is not the result of relying passively on criticism.

We can probably guess, then, what Frost would think about a book entitled *The Robert Frost Encyclopedia*. The presumption suggested in such a title is that somehow in one volume we have captured the essence not only of his poetry but of his life as well. The Greek roots of the word *encyclopedia* remind us, however, that a text like this one provides merely a general education, an overview—a place to begin one's discovery, by no means an end in itself.

As we compiled and edited the volume, we were guided by the philosophy that the entries should provide readers with a starting point. Unlike scholarly journal articles that often seek to advance a particular literary theory or thesis about a particular work or aspect of a life, the entries here serve as introductions to the poems, helping readers to place them in the larger context of Frost's life and work and, when possible, providing them a map of earlier readings. Making certain that each entry accomplished such goals was just one of the many challenges we faced as editors of the volume.

The initial challenge, of course, was in deciding which people, places, ideas, and events warranted treatment as separate entries. For example, while we decided to include an entry on every collected poem, we opted for a single entry on Frost's poetics rather than a separate entry on each of his prose statements. All of the uncollected poetry is treated in one entry, as are all the Georgian poets, and plays appear in the entry on drama. Exceedingly difficult was deciding which of Frost's poetic and intellectual forebears or personal friends deserved individual treatment. Another complex issue was how to treat the Frost family; we chose to include an entry only on Frost's wife, Elinor, and let all references to other family members remain as integral but unhighlighted pieces of many entries. In making these and other difficult decisions, we relied heavily on the counsel of our editorial board members, each of whom is a Frost scholar. Readers who cannot find a particular subject addressed in a separate entry should check the index for references to that subject in other entries. Cross-references have been indicated in **boldface** upon their initial appearance in an entry.

With over a hundred contributors—each of whom writes in a unique voice— perhaps the most daunting task was that of editing the manuscript to achieve a fair amount of consistency in tone and style. Recognizing, however, the impracticality—and, in fact, the undesirability—of reducing these many talented voices to a single articulation, we did not strive to erase all evidence that the volume is the combined effort of many points of view. We view the encyclopedia as a celebration of the rich, multiple, sometimes opposing perspectives that continue to define the emerging state of scholarship on Frost. The diversity of critical approaches and readings, combined with enduring *takes* on Frost's work, confirms the current vitality of Frost studies. To the extent possible, we shaped the entries to provide readers with a starting place for scholarship on a particular aspect of Frost's life and works. The "References and Further Reading" sections that follow the entries in this volume guide the reader to more in-depth discussions.

We have assumed that readers of entries on individual poems will have a copy of the poem, and entries were edited with that assumption in mind; extensive quotations from the poems were avoided to make room for additional analysis. Quotations from either poems or prose by Robert Frost are from Poirier and Richardson's Library of America edition (1995) with acknowledgments to Holt and the Frost estate. The bibliography compiles all the sources quoted throughout the volume and noted in the "References and Further Reading" sections.

The final challenge came in deciding how to incorporate the work of Jay Parini in his recent biography entitled *Robert Frost: A Life*. Long awaited by serious Frost scholars, Parini's work appeared in 1999, just as *The Robert Frost Encyclopedia* was about to enter production. Our contributors, of course, had relied solely on earlier biographies—namely, Lawrance Thompson's three-volume tome, which remained the most factually accurate and reliable biography despite its distortion of Frost as a "selfish, egomaniacal, dour, cruel, and angry man" (Parini, *A Life* 452). What, then, were we to do with a completed manuscript in one hand and Parini's important biography in the other? Eager for the *Encyclopedia* to gain from Parini's balanced presentation of both the life of Frost and the connections between his life and his work, we decided to add *Robert Frost: A Life* to the "References and Further Reading" section following entries on subjects with which Parini deals at some length. Thus, although our contributors were unable to refer to Parini's insights as they wrote, our readers can make use of those ideas as they move from these introductory studies toward more comprehensive readings.

In the Afterword to *Robert Frost: A Life*, Jay Parini recalls a note Frost wrote to Sidney Cox in 1932: "To be too subjective with what an artist has managed to make objective is to come on him presumptuously and render ungraceful what he in pain of his life had faith he had made graceful." Parini notes that Frost's biographers "must tremble slightly" when reading these words. We, too, tremble—perhaps more than slightly—faced with the knowledge that any single study runs the danger of reducing a poem to one limited reading or of providing a singular perspective on each person, event, and place. We had to come to terms with the fact that this book would surely omit important ideas, figures, events, and points of view. We were also mindful of the 1997 Holt CD-ROM on Frost and its contribution in a different medium to critical resources available to students and teachers of Frost. However, we continue to believe in the value of an encyclopedia devoted to the life and works of Robert Frost, a place where both first-time readers and seasoned scholars can find useful information—useful but not exhaustive and certainly not the final word. In a 1955 lecture at Bread Loaf, once again critical of readers who "strike too hard" at a text, Frost asserted, "Let them have their say and then take it your own way." Perhaps our readers would do well to heed Frost's advice.

No project this large could reach fruition without the support of many people. We are indebted to Columbia College for granting us sabbatical leave time to work on the manuscript and for underwriting clerical costs. Especially we are grateful to June Mullinax and Lori Yates for their administrative assistance at various (often tedious) stages of the project. Jennifer Davis, Suzanna Edson, Amanda Holling, and Ginger Vroblesky, all outstanding undergraduate English majors at Columbia College, contributed their skills as researchers and copyeditors. We thank our editor at Greenwood Press, George Butler, for patiently guiding us through the process of preparing the manuscript. Peter Gilbert generously granted permission for us to publish quotations from unpublished Frost material, and the Henry Holt Company allowed us to include excerpts from the published works.

We owe our greatest debt of gratitude to members of the Editorial Advisory Board, all eminent Frost scholars: Donald J. Greiner (University of South Carolina), Katherine Kearns (Yale University), George Monteiro (Brown University), Judith Oster (Case Western Reserve), Mark Richardson (Western Michigan

University), Donald G. Sheehy (Edinboro University), Peter Stanlis (Rockford College, Professor Emeritus), and Earl Wilcox (Winthrop University). In addition to contributing entries of their own, they tirelessly read multiple versions of the manuscript and provided us with detailed feedback. Their insights, suggestions, and encouragement were invaluable.

Chronology

1874	Born Robert Lee Frost, 26 March, San Francisco, California. Parents: William Prescott Frost, Jr. and Isabelle Moodie.
1876	Sister, Jeanie Florence, born 25 June, Lawrence, Massachusetts.
1881	Baptized in Swedenborgian church attended by mother.
1885	Father dies of tuberculosis, 5 May, and family moves to Lawrence.
1889	Develops friendship with Carl Burell and begins lifelong interest in botany and other sciences.
1890–1891	"La Noche Triste," Frost's first published poem, and, later, "The Song of the Wave" and "A Dream of Julius Caesar" printed in Lawrence High School *Bulletin*. Meets Elinor Miriam White.
1892	Valedictorian honor shared with Elinor at Lawrence High School graduation. Engaged to Elinor and enrolls at Dartmouth College but withdraws prematurely. Acquires Frances Turner Palgrave's *Golden Treasury of Songs and Lyrics*.
1894	Publishes "My Butterfly: An Elegy" for $15 in the 8 November issue of *The Independent* and begins influential correspondence with the magazine's editor, Susan Hayes Ward. Prints two copies of *Twilight* and plunges into depression after he appears unexpectedly at St. Lawrence University to offer himself and one copy of *Twilight* to Elinor, but she sends him away.
1895	Marries Elinor, 19 December.
1896	Son Elliott born, 25 September.
1897–1899	Enrolls at Harvard College, strongly influenced by ideas of William James, but eventually withdraws amidst worries over his own health, Elinor's pregnancy, and his mother's illness. Daughter Lesley born, 28 April.

1900	Elliott dies of cholera, 8 July. Family moves to grandfather's farm at Derry, New Hampshire. Mother dies, 2 November.
1902	Son Carol born, 27 May.
1903	Daughter Irma born, 27 June.
1905	Daughter Marjorie born, 28 March.
1906	Takes position as English teacher at Pinkerton Academy, Derry.
1907–1908	Daughter Elinor Bettina born, 18 June, and dies 21 June. Continues at Pinkerton and befriends student John Bartlett.
1911	Moves to Plymouth, New Hampshire, to teach at Plymouth Normal School.
1912	Moves to England, 23 August, and rents cottage north of London in Beaconsfield, Buckinghamshire.
1913	Attends opening of Harold Monro's Poetry Bookshop in Kensington. Meets Frank S. Flint and Ezra Pound and eventually other figures such as William Butler Yeats, T. E. Hulme, the Georgian group of poets, and Edward Thomas. *A Boy's Will* published, 1 April, by David Nutt and Company.
1914	Moves to Dymock, Gloucestershire. *North of Boston* published, 15 May, by David Nutt and Company.
1915	Leaves England from Liverpool, 13 February, and arrives in New York, 23 February. *North of Boston* published in America by Henry Holt and Company, 20 February. Buys farm in Franconia, New Hampshire, and befriends Louis Untermeyer.
1916	*Mountain Interval* published, 27 November, by Henry Holt. Takes position at Amherst College.
1920–1921	Leaves Amherst, learns of sister Jeanie's worsening mental illness, and moves to the Stone Cottage in South Shaftsbury, Vermont, to farm apples. Begins long affiliation with Bread Loaf School of English and moves to Ann Arbor to take a fellowship position at University of Michigan.
1923	*Selected Poems* published, 15 March, by Henry Holt. Returns to Amherst College. Son Carol marries Lillian LaBatt. *New Hampshire* published, 15 November, by Henry Holt.
1924	Pulitzer Prize for *New Hampshire*. Grandson William Prescott Frost born to Carol and Lillian.
1925–1926	Returns to University of Michigan in fall 1925 but by spring agrees to return to Amherst College. Daughter Irma marries John Paine Cone.
1927	Grandson Jack born to Irma and John.
1928	Daughter Lesley marries James Dwight Francis. Visits France, England, Scotland, and Ireland, seeing Yeats and meeting T. S. Eliot. *West-Running Brook* published, 19 November, by Henry Holt.

1929	Granddaughter Elinor Frost Francis born to Lesley and James. Sister Jeanie dies in Augusta, Maine, mental hospital, 7 September.
1930	*Collected Poems* published in November by Henry Holt.
1931	Pulitzer Prize for *Collected Poems*. Granddaughter Lesley Lee Francis born to Lesley and James.
1933	Daughter Marjorie marries Willard Fraser.
1934–1935	Granddaughter Marjorie Robin Fraser born to Marjorie and Willard in March, but mother Marjorie dies, 2 May. Elinor suffers angina attack and Frosts winter in Key West, Florida, where Frost meets Wallace Stevens, and in Miami.
1936	Accepts Charles Eliot Norton Professorship in Poetry at Harvard University. Befriends Theodore and Kathleen Morrison. *A Further Range* published, 20 May, by Henry Holt.
1937	Pulitzer Prize for *A Further Range*. Returns to Amherst; winters in Gainesville, Florida.
1938	Elinor dies, 20 March, and Frost remains in Gainesville in deep depression. After Elinor's memorial at Amherst College, leaves Amherst; returns to South Shaftsbury; proposes unsuccessfully to Kathleen Morrison, who becomes his permanent assistant and companion; and takes an apartment in Boston.
1939	Enlarged edition of *Collected Poems* published, 17 February, by Henry Holt. Accepts Ralph Waldo Emerson Fellowship in Poetry at Harvard University and buys Homer Noble Farm in Ripton, Vermont.
1940	Grandson Harold born to daughter Irma and John. Son Carol dies by suicide, 9 October.
1941	Begins pattern of summers in Ripton and winters in "Pencil Pines" property in South Miami.
1942	*A Witness Tree* published, 23 April, by Henry Holt.
1943	Pulitzer Prize for *A Witness Tree*. Accepts George Ticknor Fellowship in the Humanities at Dartmouth College.
1945	*A Masque of Reason* published, 26 March, by Henry Holt.
1947	*Steeple Bush* published, 28 May, by Henry Holt. Daughter Irma committed to Concord, New Hampshire, mental hospital. *A Masque of Mercy* published, November, by Henry Holt.
1949	Returns to Amherst as Simpson Lecturer in Literature. *Complete Poems of Robert Frost 1949* published, 30 May, by Henry Holt.
1952–1954	Daughter Lesley's second marriage to Joseph W. Ballantine. Awarded Fellowship of the Academy of American Poets; invited to White House under Eisenhower's presidency; travels to South America with Lesley as delegate to the World Congress of Writers in Brazil.
1957	Returns to England and Ireland for nostalgic visit and various honors.

1958   Plays instrumental role in securing release of Ezra Pound from federal mental hospital where Pound was imprisoned for treason. Named as Consultant in Poetry to the Library of Congress and receives Emerson-Thoreau Medal of the American Academy of Arts and Sciences.

1961   Invited to read poem at inauguration of President John F. Kennedy. Travels to Israel and Greece as emissary of U.S. State Department. Named Poet Laureate of Vermont.

1962   Hospitalized with pneumonia in South Miami. *In the Clearing* published, 26 March, by Holt, Rinehart and Winston. Receives congressional Gold Medal of Honor and is invited by President Kennedy to travel as emissary of U.S. State Department to Soviet Union, where Frost meets with Premier Nikita Khrushchev. On 10 December, undergoes prostate and bladder cancer surgery at Peter Bent Brigham Hospital in Boston and suffers pulmonary embolism on 23 December.

1963   Awarded Bollingen Prize for Poetry, 3 January. After another pulmonary embolism on 7 January, dies late at night on 29 January; ashes buried in the Frost family plot in the Old Bennington Cemetery in Old Bennington, Vermont.

𝒜

"ACCEPTANCE" first appeared in *West-Running Brook* **(1928)** as the final poem in the first section. It is a **sonnet** rhymed as three quatrains and a couplet, and the quatrains are syntactically interconnected. The title suggests an attitude toward nature expressed by a bird at dusk and apparently characteristic of all natural elements. The bird at dusk is said to "murmur . . . quiet" or "twitter softly," an expression of natural (stoic?) acceptance of the light's passing: "Let what will be, be." Unlike **"Spring Pools,"** which opens this section of poems, "Acceptance" presents no subtle struggle for dominance in the natural order. Instead, the unity of nature seems complete, the bird voice confirming the rightness of the sunset. No human voice is directly heard in the poem, but the personification of the "waif" bird suggests a possible human response to recognition of limits: quiet acceptance.

References and further reading: Pritchard, *Literary Life*; Thompson, *Triumph*.

Douglas Watson

"ACCIDENTALLY ON PURPOSE." *See* **"Cluster of Faith."**

"ACQUAINTED WITH THE NIGHT," published in *West-Running Brook* **(1928)**, appeared initially as the final poem in a series entitled *Fiat Nox*, a title that refers ironically to *fiat lux* ("Let there be light," Gen. 1:3). Critics have speculated that the poem has debts to Shakespeare's *Hamlet*, Baudelaire's *Les Fleurs du Mal*, and Dante's *Inferno*. Issues of most interest to critics include the poem's form, the sources and meanings of its "luminary clock," its placement in *Fiat Nox*, and its night's transcendental meaning.

Judith Oster notes that Frost borrows his stanza from Shelley's "Ode to the West Wind" but modifies the ending, a tactic that helps him blend the **sonnet**'s compact quality with the circularity—enhanced by the repetition of words—of

Dante's doomed characters, "as if . . . the speaker is going in circles bound at once by his particular circle of torment and by his inability to get anywhere even within it." The resonance of the terza rima form may be one reason the poem has been set to music at least six times.

The critical debate that surrounds the "luminary clock against the sky" is important not only because it seeks to find the actual inspiration for this line but because it determines whether we will locate "Acquainted with the Night" in a purely urban wasteland or whether we see it as a poem of cosmic, even astrological darkness. The "night" yields up its meaning readily; Laurence Perrine calls it "a symbol for sorrow, loneliness, evil, desolation, isolation, at the personal, sociological, and cosmic levels." Many critics, including Perrine, argue that the poem's urban context makes plain that the clock is a literal one.

As a real clock, which "proclaimed the time was neither wrong nor right," the image suggests the arbitrariness of human assertions of meaning in a world that nevertheless has no natural moral guideposts or "clocks." Whatever its source, this image lends the poem a haunting sense of alienation (*"unearthly height"*); for the man-made clock, which has displaced the steeple as the town's moral and temporal center, all value is arbitrary.

Given the poem's placement in *Fiat Nox*, the choice of Dante's distinct meter is important. The poems in the series are not only dark but violent, and many are narrated by an unsettling speaker who might say with Milton's Satan, "I myself am hell." Taken together, the poems create the apocalyptic mood of the end of history, when "God's last *Put out the Light* [*fiat nox*] was spoken." But they also provide us with a narrator who has "no one left but God"—haunted, depressed, and disturbingly in tune with this mood. The final poem in the series, "Acquainted with the Night" reads more like denouement than climax, stranding the protagonist not within but just after an unspecified apocalyptic moment. The walker of the poem is also a transgressor, a border crosser, as Frost makes clear by his use of "outside" locators: "out," "outwalked," "furthest," "passed by," "far away," "further still"; the speaker passes beyond society's meaning-making apparatus without a specific destination.

References and further reading: Martin; Oster, 98, 278; Parini, *A Life*, 245–47; Perrine, "Frost's 'Acquainted.' "

Mary Adams

ADDRESSES (PUBLIC SPEECHES). Robert Frost's best-known public appearance was at the inauguration of President John F. Kennedy in 1962, during which the poet recited **"The Gift Outright"** from memory after being unable to read the poem he had written for the occasion because of the glare of the January sun (*see* **"For John F. Kennedy His Inauguration"**). Frost was accustomed to reciting his poems ("saying" them, as he liked to call the practice) at the many talks and readings he gave each year for high school, college, university, literary society, and international audiences. Such public addresses are significant in several ways. First and foremost, they were an experimental form of thinking for the poet. Second, in tape-recorded form, they provide a record of Frost's comments on his own poems. Last, they offer insights into Frost's character and ideas.

Frost usually introduced his public readings with a loosely interrelated series of anecdotes, serious observations, joking comments, and literary, historical, and political allusions that centered on a theme or an idea about which he had recently been thinking. Sometimes the ideas would later appear in a poem. In fact, in 1938 Frost described his public talks and readings as being his "inner world of raw material," saying that "their chief value for me is for what I pick up from them when I cut across them in a poem under emotion." During his lectures Frost was thinking on his feet, very much aware of his audience, so much so that, as the poet Robert Francis says, "when Frost spoke from the platform, one felt that it was the audience's wordless response on which Frost depended for his next word." The public talks were experimental in the sense that Frost was trying out ideas, developing them before a series of audiences year after year. The ideas were not limited to his theories about poetry. They ranged widely, including ideas about originality, American democracy, the significance of historical figures such as the Greek general Epaminondias, and the contributions scientific inquiry can make to human life.

In addition to offering extended meditations on a variety of subjects during his public talks, Frost recited and, in some cases, read his poems aloud. The poems he chose to recite and read included many of his best-known, such as **"The Death of the Hired Man," "The Road Not Taken," "Birches,"** and **"Stopping by Woods on a Snowy Evening."** However, Frost also recited poems such as **"Etherealizing"** and **"One More Brevity"** or ones that were less popularly known, such as **"Provide, Provide," "The Silken Tent,"** and a comic poem he used to demonstrate how to recognize good rhymes, **"Departmental"** (if we can't tell which word of the rhyme pair the poet thought of first, then it is a good rhyme, he would say). Between poems Frost would usually comment briefly on the poem's meaning, background, or form. For example, in a reading at the University of California, Berkeley, in 1953, Frost recited "The Silken Tent," then noted that the poem is "one figure, sustained through one sentence into a whole **sonnet**. That's the free spirit." Recordings of Frost's comments about his poems are valuable resources: With them we can better understand the complexities of what can sometimes be mistaken as simple work.

Not only do Frost's talks offer useful correctives to misreadings of his poems, but they also provide insights into his ideas and his character. Though most of Frost's recorded talks remain unpublished and so still unavailable to general readers, several of his public addresses were published in his lifetime, revised by the poet himself as essays. (Several more were published after his death.) Talks that Frost revised and published as essays include "Education by Poetry: A Meditative Monologue," "On Emerson," and "Speaking of Loyalty," all of which can be studied to good purpose. The most interesting of the transcribed addresses, one of Frost's last, given 27 November 1962, is "On Extravagance: A Talk." In it, Frost explores one of poetry's most essential characteristics. He takes great pleasure in the quality of "*Abandon*" he finds in good poetry, a quality of serious playfulness so extreme that by sheer daring it hits on some truth about human experience. His admiration of this quality in poetry suggests by implication an essential quality of his own character, namely, how necessary playfulness is to his thinking.

The essentially experimental quality of Frost's public addresses is itself playful in the best sense. Frost entertained his audiences with the play of his thought for a span of nearly fifty years. His public talks and readings continue to entertain and teach us about his work and character.

References and further reading: R. Francis, 3; R. Frost, *Selected Letters*, 461. An excellent collection of transcribed talks by Frost, demonstrating the wide range of Frost's ideas, is R. Cook's *Living Voice*. For a short, lively account of the significance of Frost's public addresses, see Ridland. "On Extravagance: A Talk," "Education by Poetry: A Meditative Monologue," "On Emerson," "Speaking of Loyalty," and others of Frost's addresses may be found in R. Frost, *Collected*. Parini, *A Life*, 302–5, discusses Frost's Norton Lectures at **Harvard**.

Lisa Seale

"AFTER APPLE-PICKING," first published in *North of Boston* (**1914**), could have been subtitled "After the Fall." **Ralph Waldo Emerson** says in "Experience" that after the Fall we see only "mediately," as through a distorting lens, never really knowing where or even *what* we are. Everything has been for us like a dream, which is only to say that we see as the speaker of Frost's poem sees: as through an imperfect lens of ice ("through a glass darkly," as St. Paul says, in a passage Frost may have in mind). Memory and sensation are confused in "After Apple-Picking"; concept and percept begin to blend. Grammatically, we cannot say whether the lines following the reference to "dreaming" in line 17 refer to the day's labor or to the memory of it.

The form of this strange poem is especially important. There are twenty endrhymes for forty-two lines; about twenty-five of the forty-two lines are more or less in iambic pentameter, allowing for liberties native to the form in English. The poem thus wanders in and out of structure, working in a place between control and relinquishment. The twilight balance of control against release mirrors the speaker's state of mind.

Another consequence of the Fall is that we labor, and Frost's poem suggests that even the most commonplace human endeavor—apple-picking, for example—is inescapably steeped in larger significances. The experience described in "After Apple-Picking" and the language used to describe it perfectly combine "the actual" and "the mythological." In fact, "After Apple-Picking" shows us just how difficult it is sometimes to separate these two modes of thinking about and experiencing the world. As Richard Poirier points out, "After Apple-Picking" depends upon words that suggest transcendental possibilities—"the great harvest," "essence of winter sleep"—but at the same time never really privileges them. The language of "After Apple-Picking" is in this way very Emersonian: Every word of any significance at all in the poem is a kind of "fossil poetry," alive with sleeping metaphors.

Frost's language often slides from the commonplace into a much more resonant key, as when, after several colloquial lines, we fall into this remark: "But I am done with apple-picking now. / Essence of winter sleep is on the night." Here, "sleep" is (figuratively) "seasonal" in significance: The reference is to winter. But by the poem's end "sleep" begins to work much more mysteriously, as it does in **"Stopping by Woods on a Snowy Evening,"** and we ask, *"Will we be awakened by the renewals of spring?" See also* **Nature Poet and Naturalist**.

References and further reading: Brower, 23–27; Condor; J. Ferguson; Fleissner, "Frost as Ironist"; Monteiro, "Frost's 'After Apple-Picking' "; Poirier, *Knowing*, 290–301; Scheele; Stein.

Mark Richardson

"AFTERFLAKES," probably written in 1932 in California, was first published in the *Yale Review* (Autumn 1934) and first collected in the second section ("Taken Singly") of *A Further Range* **(1936)**. This neglected lyric has an unusual rhyme scheme (*xabba*), which Frost used in only one other poem, the uncollected "Flower Guidance" (1912–15).

"Afterflakes" is also noteworthy for being one of several poems written throughout his career in which the poet puns on his last name: "And the thick flakes floating at a pause / Were but frost knots on an airy gauze." In other poems, "frost" tends to represent an elemental ornament that kills or at least threatens to; in "Afterflakes," it is used playfully in a gaudy name for the last, indifferent snowflakes of a storm. It is also a potential metaphor for the craft of poetry fashioned from the elements.

In the context of the poem's lyrical philosophizing, the word *frost* also forces a sly pun on "knots": The "afterflakes" are "not" Frost, not the poet provoked by strange weather to Neoplatonic querying. The poem relies on a number of oppositions recalling Plato's allegory of the cave in Book VII of *The Republic*: light–shadow; opacity–transparency; up–down; form–shapelessness. However, the issue of inherent "darkness," also figured as being "swarthy," is related to later Christian questions regarding the body and the soul. The conspicuous metaphor and pun of the penultimate line also suggest that the poem is considering the source of poetry, behind the decoration, as a fundamental purity. Ending a poem with a prepositional adverb is a rare syntactical move in poetry; in this example, it is appropriately delicate and remote from the line's dominating noun. For a related rhyme, see the final couplet of **"Looking for a Sunset Bird in Winter."**

References and further reading: Marcus, *Explication*.

Gary Roberts

"AIM WAS SONG, THE," was first published in *The Measure* (Mar. 1921) and later included in *New Hampshire (1923)*. It describes how, in still uncivilized times, the wind coarsely blew itself by rubbing against every obstacle it could find. Humans came to teach it how to blow harmoniously, keeping wind in mouth long enough to transform the frozen northern atmosphere into a warm southern scene. Humans modulated the wind through lips and throat, following a measure that turned the wind's rough sound into song.

The most likely interpretation of "The Aim Was Song" is that it represents the civilizing action of human art and, particularly, that it is a self-reflexive discourse on the process of poetic writing. Within this figurative context, the wind is a metaphor for pure sound, the raw material of which both oral speech, music, and poetry are made. Frost likens the sounds of poetry to the human voice: To reach the form of a poem, the sounds of poetry must be molded by a measure in the same way as the human voice must be modulated to produce song. Thus, song becomes a metaphor for the completed poem.

In "The Aim Was Song," Frost also possibly hints at his favorite theory of the superimposition of speaking intonation on the metrical scansion of verse, or—as he would have said—of the "sentence sounds" on the "regular accents of meter." This would be the meaning of the identification in the poem of "measure" with "word and note"—that is, with a melody that originates from speech.

In accord with its content, "The Aim Was Song" is written in fairly regular iambic tetrameters, alluding to the "measure" by which the individual's artistic skill—and the poet's craft—tries to tame the wind's unruly blowing. The strict observance of a very simple rhyme scheme (*abab*) in all its four quatrains reinforces the effect of a strong cadence.

In the case of "The Aim Was Song," as in many others, Frost's strategy in reading the poem aloud supports one possible interpretation of it. Frost's recitations of the poem seemed to imitate the two "voices" of the wind and of the individual. He attributed to the wind a more clearly perceptible monotone cadence that was emphasized by the use of an even pitch, particularly in the first stanza and at line 14, where the wind's original behavior and imitative intentions are described. By contrast, he modulated his voice into an intonation contour that was characterized by a flowing rhythm in the third stanza, descriptive of the individual's subsequent and creative activity.

References and further reading: R. Frost, *Frost in Recital* (audiorecording) and *Selected Letters*, 111, 128; Richardson, *Ordeal*, 169–70.

Paola Loreto

"ALL REVELATION" first appeared in 1938 as "Geode" in the the *Yale Review*. It was subsequently collected under its present title in *A Witness Tree* **(1942)**. "All Revelation," the fifth poem contained in the collection, has been described by Brower as Frost's "most symbolist" poem due to its "radiating overlapping meanings." Its debt to the Emersonian view of the individual's relationship with nature has been widely cited. Dorothy Hall calls it a poem "riddled with ambiguity." Together with such nearly uniform recognition of the poem's puzzling ambiguity and difficulty, "All Revelation" has received positive comment. In attempting to unravel its complex metaphors and decipher its meaning, critics have consistently suggested that the poem represents the individual's efforts to connect to the universe and to give it meaning and order, once that connection has been made. Critics disagree, however, about the manner or method of such connection.

In his study of Frost, Poirier suggests that "All Revelation" concerns "man's efforts to penetrate the stuff of life—to discover life through the pleasure of genitalia," "the probings of science," or "the faculties of vision." Opting for the last interpretation, Marcus asserts that the mysteries of the poem are best understood by "visionary" experiences, much in the same manner that the "ray cathode" penetrates the geode, illuminating the crystals contained therein. For Marcus, "all revelation" is, in fact, a product of our own minds.

Similarly, D'Avanzo sees the poem as an assertion that the mind's search for meaning in nature is "our highest pursuit." The poem explores the individual mind's "quest for insight into the ultimate mystery: the meaning, purpose, origins and ends of nature," reflecting Frost's lifelong interest in **Emerson**.

Hall adds another level of experience to "All Revelation," seeing the poem as a "rhetorical enactment of the difficulty of correspondence between man and the universe—and also, between poet and reader, for both of whom . . . Frost wanted every poem to be a 'revelation.' "

Finally, a more literal interpretation is provided by Hays, who suggests that the poem is actually "an attack on those who take their knowledge of nature indirectly from television" or other "mechanical medium" as opposed to actual firsthand experience. Citing extensive press coverage of television appearing as early as 1936 and the advent of limited network broadcasting as early as 1937, Hays argues that Frost would have had ample opportunity to be exposed to this new medium when the poem was composed in 1938.

References and further reading: Brower, 139; D'Avanzo, *Romantics*, 26, 29; D. J. Hall, *Contours*, 73–79; Hays, "Frost and the Critics"; Kearns, 118–20; Marcus, *Explication*, 167; Poirier, *Knowing*, 20; Pritchard, *Literary Life*; Thompson and Winnick.

John C. Bradley, Jr.

"AMERICA IS HARD TO SEE" first appeared as "And All We Call American" in the *Atlantic Monthly* (June 1951) and was later collected in *In the Clearing* **(1962)**. The poem depicts the speaker's deliberating in smooth iambic tetrameter the plight of Columbus, suggesting throughout the fourteen stanzas of the poem that the explorer's failure to find the riches he had promised his Spanish queen was due to a lack of perspicacity. Columbus did not discover the proper way to the plentiful East and lacked insight enough to appreciate the enormous possibilities associated with his findings. In retrospect, of course, events seem more well defined. The speaker's age (he is past his youth), poetic sensibility, and twentieth-century situation allow him to put into better context Columbus's feats.

In "America Is Hard to See" Frost explores the issue of colonialism. With the innocence of childhood, the speaker admits, he might mistakenly have "had Columbus sung / As a god who had given us / A more than Moses' exodus." But with the wisdom of his years he has come to realize that in fact Columbus in his probings unwittingly, perhaps even ironically, was a model for the deplorable actions of many later generations. Columbus's ignorance has yet to be eliminated in our twentieth-century society. Indeed, what constitutes America and its people is still far from evident, even centuries after Columbus arrived on the rough coast. Part of what obstructs the view is too much ambition: "High purpose makes the hero rude." If Columbus (or his ghost) were in the twentieth century to start anew, the speaker muses, he would "find that Asiatic state / Is about tired of being looted / While having its beliefs disputed." The Asiatic state to which he refers is China (Cathay), a reference in part conditioned by the fact that in 1951, when the poem was written, Americans were fighting the Chinese army in Korea.

References and further reading: O'Donnell, "Frost at Eighty-eight."

Sabine Sautter-Leger

AMERICAN ACADEMY OF POETS AWARD. *See* **Awards, Honors, and Prizes**.

AMHERST COLLEGE. Although several times interrupted and not without its difficulties, Frost's relationship with Amherst College—a private liberal arts college founded in Amherst, Massachusetts, in 1821—was the most significant of his academic career. The affiliation divides into four periods: 1917–1920; 1923–1925; 1927–1938; 1949–1963. In 1917, at the urging of Stark Young, poet and faculty member, President Alexander Meiklejohn appointed Frost to the regular English faculty. The poet, however, grew restive under teaching obligations and resentful of Meiklejohn's academic and political liberalism, and he resigned in 1920. After Meiklejohn's removal in 1923, Frost returned to Amherst from the **University of Michigan** at the invitation of President George Daniel Olds but remained only two years before returning to Michigan as a Fellow in Letters. The pull of family concerns brought Frost back to Amherst in 1927 when the college offered a full professorship that required one semester in residence and no regular teaching. For the next decade, the college and its increasingly prominent poet-in-residence enjoyed a mutually beneficial relationship. During the period of emotional turmoil that followed **Elinor Frost**'s death in 1938, Frost again resigned, insisting that President Stanley King had questioned the value of his presence. After three years as Emerson Fellow and Fellow in American Civilization at **Harvard** and six years as Ticknor Fellow at **Dartmouth**, Frost was persuaded by President Charles Woolsey Cole—a former favorite student of the poet—to return to Amherst in 1949 as Simpson Lecturer in English. The appointment stipulated one month in residence and one public reading annually and provided a retirement allowance after 1954. During a visit by Frost in 1962, President Calvin Plimpton announced plans for the Robert Frost Library. At the dedication in October of 1963, nine months after the poet's death and weeks before his own, President John F. Kennedy paid tribute to Frost as "an artist and an American." The Robert Frost Library houses today one of the finest collections of Frost manuscripts, letters, photographs, and first editions. *See also* **Teacher**.

References and further reading: T. Rodman; Sheehy, " 'To Otto as of Old' "; Thompson, *Triumph*; Thompson and Winnick.

Donald G. Sheehy

"ANSWER, AN," first published in *A Witness Tree* **(1942)**, is a single heroic couplet containing the ambiguous reply of a father to his son on the subject of human happiness. If we take the key word "blessèd" as meaning happiness, contentment, or pleasure, then most likely, the son has asked his father whether or not true happiness is possible in this life, or perhaps, less philosophically, he has actually requested of his father a bestowal of prosperity or happiness. In either case, the son is not to be satisfied, as the adversative "But" tells us at the poem's inception. Frost, uncertain in his own life about answers to such philosophical questions, opening as they do on so many possible answers, once wrote a friend: "I am neither optimist nor pessimist. I never voted either ticket." "Islands of the Blessèd," the perfect paradise of ancient Greek thought, suggests strongly that the father can neither bestow blessing upon his son nor say where happiness may be found. It is beyond us all, Frost seems to say; the real condition of the world is such that one is not likely to live an undisturbed, contented life. The reply of the speaker has both classical and biblical overtones. Frost balances the classical and biblical in a *ploce*, a device of rhetoric in which a word is repeated (here "Blessèd" / "bless" / "blessèd") with a new signification after intervening words. The classical implications of the poem spring from "Islands of the Blessed," a phrase Frost would have come across in his readings of Homer, Hesiod, and especially Plato. These happy islands are for Frost a physical representation of the whole problem of happiness considered as a philosophical concept. Using the islands to address a metaphysical concept is typical of Frost, who called himself a "Synecdochist" and liked to go from the physical to the spiritual or metaphysical, and vice versa. Thus, the Islands of the Blessèd are a synecdoche that Frost uses ironically to deny the possibility of happiness. The biblical connotations of the poem stem from the phrase "bless you, son," which echoes Esau's sad plea to his father Isaac to give him a good bestowal of property and prosperity as he had already done to Esau's brother Jacob: "Do

you have only one blessing, my father? Bless me, even me also, O my father."
But Isaac cannot reverse his pronouncement and so regretfully tells his son,
"Your brother came deceitfully, and has taken away your blessing" (Gen.
27:38).

References and further reading: Frost's remark about optimism may be found in R.
Frost, *Selected Letters*, 462. D. J. Hall is an excellent source for discussion of Frost's
metaphysics. Thompson, *Triumph*, 693–94, discusses Frost's use of synecdoche to establish metaphysical meaning.

Larry R. Isitt

"ANY SIZE WE PLEASE" first appeared in *Steeple Bush* **(1947)**. While the
Italian **sonnet** form usually dictates a shift in thought between the octave and
sestet, this poem's rhetorical break occurs halfway through line 7, at the exact
midpoint. Formally, then, it mirrors the shift in cosmology that occurred during
Frost's lifetime. For those who resisted the basic tenets of scientific naturalism,
one of the most fortuitous developments in the battle against late nineteenth-
century despair was the revolution in modern physics, which was welcomed by
many as a strong rebuttal to the mechanistic determinism that had so dominated
the third quarter of the nineteenth century. Developments in relativity and quantum mechanics would not have been possible, however, without the corresponding revolution in geometry that occurred nearly seventy years earlier. In
particular, the development of the first non-Euclidean geometry by Lobochevsky
and Bolyai in the 1830s not only served as the basis for Einstein's theories but
also challenged the epistemological status of all scientific conclusions. In the
wake of the new geometry, philosophers and scientists began to ask themselves
how it was possible for reality to conform equally well to two different geo-
metrical models. Either one model was correct and the other incorrect, or both
models were merely projected conventions that served as useful guides through
the flux of sensory experience. In either case, it was clear that Euclidean geometry was not a literal transcript of reality.

Frost's "Any Size We Please" challenges the nineteenth-century belief in scientific omniscience along similar epistemological lines. The first half of the
poem is clearly indebted to the seventeenth century's unquestioned acceptance
of Euclid's parallel postulate—a theorem that led not only to an unquestioned
acceptance of infinite space and absolute time but also to Newton's belief in the
intricate order of God's "clockwork" universe. Here, the speaker, feeling insignificant about one's place in the natural order, holds arms out "parallel" in
"infinite appeal" to a universe that refuses to respond. In the second half of the
poem, the speaker, finding such lack of response "hell," immediately draws arms
around in an effort to contain the immense size of the universe. The imaginative
gesture, clearly indebted to Einstein's curved space–time dimension, allows the
speaker to transform the universe into a more manageable size. The speaker's
subsequent assertion that his **science** needn't "get him so unnerved" issues from

his knowledge that scientific models, like poetic forms, are merely projected explanatory guides—metaphors, as Frost calls them in "Education by Poetry"— that are subject to radical revision and collapse. Since we alone are the sole authors of meaning and consolation ("And hugged himself for all his universe") and since projected models are not literal transcripts of reality, Frost ultimately suggests that we have nothing to fear from science's more disturbing conclusions.

References and further reading: Abel, "Instinct"; R. Frost, *Selected Letters*; Rotella, "Comparing." *See also* Jeremy Bernstein, *Einstein* (New York: Viking, 1973), 147–59.

Robert Bernard Hass

"ARMFUL, THE," first appeared on 8 February 1928 in *The Nation* and was collected in **West-Running Brook** later the same year. It is a twelve-line poem of couplets that depict a semicomic scene and reveal Frost's tendency to hint at moral lessons learned from common human experiences. The persona is walking along, trying to balance a number of objects in his arms, but when one object slips away, the attempt to recover it leads to further slippage and further attempts at recovery. Contorted in his attempt to retain the uncertain collection, the poet finally has to "drop the armful in the road" and reorder them into a more manageable load.

One plausible application is that Frost is recalling the frustration of balancing diverse personal responsibilities (as father and husband) while wishing for unencumbered attention to his poetry. The situation is perhaps borrowed from Frost's grocery shopping trips for his family while at South Shaftsbury, Vermont, in 1927. The "lesson" of the poem illustrates a folksy wisdom found often in Frost: It is sometimes better to stop and build anew than to adjust constantly and readjust a situation that resists balance. As with "bottles" and "buns," so with activities and commitments, and so with ideas of individuals and God and nature. Such tension of objects and ideas and words is present in numerous poems of *West-Running Brook* but nowhere treated more playfully than in "The Armful."

References and further reading: Thompson, *Triumph*, 307–8.

Douglas Watson

"ASSURANCE," first published in *A Witness Tree* (**1942**), takes the measure of an individual attitudinizing about one's own power to defy the forces of nature that can destroy the self. The one-word title means not so much "a firm persuasion," "full confidence," "trust," or "freedom from doubt" but an excess of boldness, an unwarranted sense of security. What great store of confidence or, perhaps, sheer impudence impels one to feel safe in a ship while looking (or sleeping) behind glass, less than an inch thick, that stands as a flimsy barricade to the ever-present dangers posed by nature? It is as if such an individual bases an overall defiance of nature on a pane of glass that permits one to look out at nature, even at the most dangerous times. Held fast by a "double ring of fitted brass," the porthole gives countenance to such defiance. Indeed, how double the individual's brassiness when exhibited by impudent confidence in mere human-made devices contrived in defense against the forces of nature. Notice, too, that the speaker has had the temerity to anthropomorphize nature. It is "danger," perceived to be beyond the porthole, that, as the speaker tells us, feels "properly defied."

References and further reading: Marcus, 183.

George Monteiro

"ASTROMETAPHYSICAL," appearing first in the *Virginia Quarterly* (1946) and then in the collection *Steeple Bush* (**1947**), is one of many poems Frost wrote throughout his life, featuring heavens, stars, and the poet's intensely self-isolating probings of an uncertain universe. Victor Reichert, in a passing reference to poems reflective of Frost's spirituality, says that "Astrometaphysical" shows "Frost's steadfast spiritual purpose." We may agree with this pronouncement yet doubt that Frost was as steadfast in his soul as he was in his purpose, for his poems are never self-confident assertions of theological trust in a God who is actually out there. The poem has generally been ignored by critics who have no doubt seen in it a rehashing of familiar Frostian metaphysical themes far more powerfully set in previous poems such as **"Design"** and **"Desert Places."** In form it is a mock prayer, playful yet darker in tone than the prayer **"Forgive, O Lord"** and not at all the exultant offering to God that is **"A Prayer in Spring."** Frost mistrusted prayer generally and said in a letter to Lawrance Thompson that he never prayed except on occasion to be polite in public with recitation of the Lord's Prayer. Frost's praying narrator in "Astrometaphysical" comes to God hesitantly, yet somehow also defiantly.

At first the speaker appears to be a genuinely humble seeker after God's favor. But in stanza three humility evaporates into chiding as he presses God, insisting he should be "rewarded" for his love of the heavens (all seven of them) over which the Lord has "lorded" (as a tyrant). In stanza four, chiding turns to skeptical rejection of the traditional Christian hope of heaven after death. "Hope," in traditional Christian usage, refers to confident expectation that upon death one will be "translated" or taken up to heaven. But the speaker's hesitant faith can only vaguely point him to the stars among which he hopes to be "constellated." Frost's narrator loses his buoyant confidence in stanza five and offers God a compromise. "That" refers to the rejection of hope and confidence made in the previous stanza. If his rejection of traditional Christian hope is unfavorable in God's sight, at least this blemish on his soul should not be viewed so seriously as to cancel his chances of translation altogether.

References and further reading: Angyal, "Swedenborg to James," 76; D. J. Hall, *Contours* and "Mystic Lens," provide discussions of Frost's metaphysics; Reichert, 421; Frost's comment on prayer is in R. Frost, *Selected Letters*, 530.

Larry R. Isitt

"AT WOODWARD'S GARDENS" was first published in April 1936 in *Poetry* and was collected that same year in *A Further Range*. It is a poem named for an estate in San Francisco that had at its center a zoo visited by Frost when he was a youth living in that city. Subtitled "Resourcefulness Is More Than Understanding," the poem narrates a confrontation, a kind of utilitarian duel, between human and simian intellects. A boy, repeatedly presumptuous, uses a "burning-glass" to torment two caged monkeys. The creatures experience first singed noses, then knuckles. As the speaker remarks near the midpoint of the poem, had the boy not "presumed too close and long," the only story would be how a glass once again confirmed through experiment its ability to focus the rays of the sun to a single pinpoint. And, of course, as the boy knew already, the earth was still far from being a planet of the apes. However, the monkeys do turn the tables, and they abruptly snatch the magnifying glass from their seemingly more evolved adversary. Spiriting the glass away and eventually burying it in their bed of straw, perhaps with an eye toward future amusement, the monkeys disturb the narrator's fundamental notions of *understanding*.

Marcus argues that the monkeys' "knowledge of what to do with it was better than [the boy's]," but when Frost concludes, "It's knowing what to do with things that counts," he means both boy and monkeys. The magnifying glass was used no more properly by the boy to sting the monkeys' "purple little knuckles" than by the monkeys themselves, who bite and break the apparatus. The poem is also one of revelation and epiphany. Frost's revelations are subtle: The monkeys do not evolve suddenly, enabling a novel understanding of the glass. Rather, the speaker finally determines that mere understanding is not at all the point, anyway. Indeed, "Who said it mattered / What monkeys did or didn't understand?" Resourcefulness in the poem entails a specific sort that Frost frequently explores. Thompson suggests that the resourcefulness "can make a comprehensible little world within an incomprehensibly big world."

References and further reading: Faggen; Marcus, *Explication*, 146; Parini, *A Life*, 13; Thompson, *Fire and Ice*, 207.

Eric C. Brown

"ATMOSPHERE," first published in *Ladies' Home Journal* (Oct. 1928) as "Inscription for a Garden Wall," was included that same year in the first edition of *West-Running Brook*, originally divided into six sections. *Spring Pools*, the title of the first section, included "Atmosphere" as the fifth of eleven poems. "Atmosphere" is connected to the other poems in this grouping both in theme and tone; it is related most closely to **"Spring Pools," "The Cocoon,"** and **"Acceptance"** in that Frost considers in each a moment when elements coalesce to generate a feeling of endurance as opposed to the potential for destruction. In "Atmosphere," Frost highlights dampness, earthiness, and the sense of a place being passed over or covered. As in "Cocoon," man-made walls deflect and/or make something beautiful out of nature. In the case of "Atmosphere," the wall makes possible a kind of fertility, actualized by the promise of new life growing in a sheltered garden. The aesthetic values implicit in its construction are also suggested: A sunny garden wall, diverting the wind and absorbing the rays of the sun like a human cheek, creates its own climate below, where time—"the hours of daylight"—becomes a contained, tangible, and beautiful entity. *West-Running Brook* as a whole was received less enthusiastically than Frost's previous collections; critics pointed to trivial poems unworthy of inclusion, yet "Atmosphere," in spite of its brevity, remains an indication of Frost's continuing interest in human attempts, however modest, to grapple with nature's power. Frost's judicious use of spondees in verse that is largely iambic pentameter accommodates the lines that sound like spoken voice to the strong qualities he admires in a garden wall: While "Winds blow" is quite strong, equally strong is the sequence of spondee followed by iamb in "too toppling weak," which suggests that the wall, like the wind, is a force to be reckoned with. The second line also suggests the power of a human-made boundary. The most obvious meaning is that the wall itself is sun-burned, yet the use of the active verb *burns* implies self-generated power on behalf of the wall to initiate destructive force, intensifying the sense of a battle being waged between wind and edifice, the outcome of which is the pleasurable, moist atmosphere generating the fertility so eloquently implied.

References and further reading: see Deutsch for critical reception of *West-Running Brook*; C. Lyons discusses boundaries and walls in Frost's poetry.

Susan Burns

"AUSPEX" appeared first in Elizabeth Shepley Sergeant's *Robert Frost: The Trial by Existence* (1960) and was collected in *In the Clearing* **(1962)**. The poem narrates an eagle's attack on a terrified small boy and his parents' light-hearted and literary reaction. The speaker interprets the experience in terms of two ancient Roman religious approaches to the problem of fate versus free will. The title is the Latin word for a sign of divine approval of a planned undertaking. The auspex, in traditional Roman religious practice, was indicated by birds' flight patterns as interpreted by specially appointed priests. The boy's parents refer to the story of Ganymede, who was carried off by an eagle, symbol of Jupiter, to be cupbearer to the gods. The story is retold in both Ovid (*Metamorphoses* 10.155) and Virgil (*Aeneid* 5.250). The two classical references and the speaker's "resentful" reaction to them indicate his rejection of limitations on personal freedom either by an impersonal fate or by a personal god yet acknowledge the possibility of such restrictions.

References and further reading: D. J. Hall, "Frost and Bergson"; Parini, *A Life*, 13, suggests that this poem alludes to Frost's childhood excursions into the California countryside; Potter, 69–84.

Nanette Cumley Tamer

AWARDS, HONORS, AND PRIZES. With four Pulitzer Prizes, the Bollingen Prize for Poetry, numerous Phi Beta Kappa Poet awards, forty-four honorary degrees, and appearances on the covers of *Time* and *Life*, Frost is one of the most acclaimed writers in American history. Only the Nobel Prize, which he desired most, escaped him. On both his seventy-fifth and eighty-fifth birthdays, the U.S. Senate adopted formal resolutions extending felicitations to him. The honors awarded to Frost culminated in his being asked to participate in the inauguration of President John F. Kennedy in 1961, where he recited *"The Gift Outright"* (*see also* **"For John F. Kennedy His Inauguration"** and **Addresses**).

Despite all the adulation he received throughout his career, Frost's attitude toward honors and awards remained ambiguous. At some points, he appeared indignant of the praise; at others he seemed grateful and incredulous. One cause attributed to this ambiguity involves the fact that he received all of the awards after he was forty years old; the honors and awards supposedly never made up for the years he spent in ignominy. Another cause rests with Frost's self-image and his relation to academics. Frost clearly states his attitude: "I'm imperfectly academic and no amount of association with the academic will make me perfect. . . . I may be wrong in my suspicion that I haven't pleased **Harvard** as much as I have the encompassing barbarians." Frost as the people's poet collides with his own need to be accepted by the academy. Knowing his insecurity about the academy makes it ironic, then, that Frost received as many honorary degrees as he did in his life.

Awards and honors include the following: Pulitzer Prize for *New Hampshire*, 1924; *Collected Poems*, 1931; *A Further Range*, 1937; *A Witness Tree*, 1943. American Academy of Poets Award, 1953; Bollingen Prize in Poetry, 1963; Boston Arts Festival "First Annual Poetry Award," 1958; Book of the Month Club (*A Further Range*), 1936; Congressional Gold Medal, 1962; Dickinson College, $1,000 award, 1959; Emerson-Thoreau Medal (American Academy of Arts and Sciences), 1958; Gold Medal for Poetry (National Institute of Arts and Letters), 1939; Gold Medal (Holland Society of New York), 1957; Gold Medal (Limited Editions Club), 1949; Gold Medal (Poetry Society of America), 1941, 1958; Golden Rose Trophy (New England Poetry Club), 1928; Huntington Hartford Foundation Award, 1958; Levinson Prize (*Poetry* magazine), 1922; Russell Loines Poetry Prize (National Institute of Arts and Letters), 1931; Edward MacDowell Medal, 1962; Medal of Honor (New York University), 1956; Medal for Achievement in the Arts (Harvard University), 1958; New Hampshire Education Association, Citation for Distinguished Service to Education, 1954; Signet Society, Harvard, Medal for Achievements in the Arts, 1958; Theodore Roosevelt Society medal, 1954; Vermont Legislature designates Ripton "Robert Frost Mountain," 1955, names Frost "Poet Laureate of Vermont," 1961; Phi Beta Kappa Poet, Columbia University, 1932; Harvard University, 1916, 1941; Tufts University, 1915, 1940; College of William and Mary, 1941. Elected to National Institute of Arts and Letters, 1916; American Academy of Arts and Letters,

1931; American Philosophical Society, 1937. Charles Eliot Norton Professor of Poetry, Harvard University, 1939; Ralph Waldo Emerson Fellow in Poetry, Harvard University, 1939. Consultant in Poetry for the Library of Congress, 1958. Honorary degrees from **Amherst College**, M.A. 1918, Litt.D. 1948; Bates, L.H.D. 1936; Boston University, Litt.D. 1961; Bowdoin, Litt.D. 1926; California, LLD. 1947; Cambridge, England, Litt.D. 1957; Cincinnati, LL.D. 1954; Colby, LL.D. 1956; Colgate, Litt.D. 1950; Colorado, L.H.D. 1939; Columbia, Litt.D. 1932; **Dartmouth**, Litt.D. 1933; LL.D. 1955; Detroit, L.H.D. 1962; Duke, Litt.D. 1948; Durham, England, Litt.D. 1951; Florida, LL.D. 1960; Harvard, Litt.D. 1937; Hebrew Union, L.H.D. 1960; Ireland, Litt.D. 1957; Kenyon, Litt.D. 1945; Massachusetts, Litt.D. 1951; Marlboro, Litt.D. 1950; **Michigan**, M.A. 1922, LL.D. 1962; Middlebury, Litt.D. 1924; Miami (Florida), LL.D. 1961; Miami (Ohio), L.H.D. 1959; New Hampshire, Litt.D. 1930; North Carolina, Litt.D. 1953; Ohio State, L.H.D. 1957; Oxford, England, Litt.D. 1957; Pennsylvania, L.H.D. 1936; Princeton, Litt.D. 1941; Rhode Island, Litt.D. 1955; St. Lawrence, L.H.D. 1936; Syracuse, Litt.D. 1959; Tufts, Litt.D. 1959; Vermont, L.H.D. 1923; Wesleyan, L.H.D. 1931; Williams, L.H.D. 1932; Windham, Litt.D. 1961; Yale, Litt.D. 1924.

References and further reading: R. Frost, *Letters to Untermeyer*, 277. Most studies of Frost mention, at least in passing, his many honors and awards. Lawrance Thompson's official three-volume biography of Frost is a valuable source of detailed information.

Eric Leuschner

"AWAY!" was written when Frost was in his eighties and was first published in booklet form as Frost's 1958 **Christmas poem**. It later appeared in Frost's last volume, *In the Clearing* **(1962)**. **Louis Untermeyer** calls the poem "a kind of enlarged epitaph that served as a premature leave-taking" and says it shows "Frost in his most whimsical mood." Joseph Kau notes that the poem's "saucy tone . . . masks the persona's apprehension" about death.

The narrator's anxiety is linked to his uncertainty about the existence of God, his solitude in the universe, and the question of free will. The angst about such issues is cloaked in the poem's casual, punning tone. In saying, "There is no one I / Am put out with / Or put out by," the narrator may mean that he is on bad terms with no one or that he is leaving alone (being put out with—in the company of—no one) and that there is no one—no God—to put him out. In other words, he is totally alone, and his destiny is determined only by his free will. In the next stanza, however, he questions the existence of his free will, suggesting that instead of choosing he is instinctually obeying the "urge of a song: / I'm—bound—away!" As Kau notes, being "bound" may mean either that he is voluntarily headed for a destination or that he is restrained like a prisoner who has no choice but to go. In a final effort to profess his control over his destiny, the narrator says that he "may return / If dissatisfied / With what I learn / From having died."

Jeffrey Cramer notes that the song referred to in line 19 is from the chorus of the folksong "Shenandoah," which Frost admired. Frost quoted the same sentence from that song in line 172 of *A Masque of Mercy* (see **Drama**).

References and further reading: Cramer, *Frost among His Poems*, 161; Kau; Untermeyer's comments are in R. Frost, *Enlarged*, 280.

Claudia Milstead

"A-WISHING WELL" is a late poem, published originally in booklet form as Frost's **Christmas poem** for 1959 and subsequently collected in *In the Clearing* **(1962)**. One should notice first that the title does not consist of a participial adjective and noun as in the common parlance of a well into which one throws a coin and makes a wish but rather of a gerund modified by an adverb. The poem has to do with making good wishes and as such was appropriate as a Christmas sentiment. The playfulness of the title continues all through the poem, which is full of obscure allusions and what seem to be inventions posing as allusions.

A. R. Ferguson has identified the poet to whom Frost refers in the first line as Edward Rowland Sill, an American whom Frost read as a boy and whom he once called a "neglected and noble poet." Ferguson asserts that Sills's "one thing more," in wishing for a better world, was the extinction of ego and pride, allowing a perfect union between humanity and nature. Frost's wish, however, is more concrete, if equally unlikely. He wishes for a second moon. Since he often uses heavenly bodies to suggest the human race's imaginative capacity to dream and establish high ideals for itself (compare **"Choose Something Like A Star"** or **"Bond and Free,"** for example), we may assume that the substance of the speaker's wish is for a world that provides more inspiration and stimulation to the human spirit.

This thought, however, leads Frost to raise a question about the source of new moons, at which point he interjects an aside about the bizarre stories he makes up in response to questions about the origin of his poems. He then proceeds to tell an equally bizarre story, which he attributes to the Arcadians, about the origin of the moon. Although the Arcadians were believed to be the original people, born of oak trees (which, perhaps, led Frost to the idea of a plant—"silphion"—that could not be uprooted), and although Greek and Latin literatures contain references to a "pro-selene" (pre-moon) people in Arcadia, who witnessed the birth of the moon, the particular legend seems to be Frost's invention. In any case, in contrast to the wish for a "better sky" in the first part of the poem, the legend presents people desperately clinging to earth. Hence, the poem contains Frost's characteristic opposition of spirit and matter, heaven and earth, ideal and mundane realities. Unlike poems such as **"Birches,"** however, "A-Wishing Well" does not work toward a balance or reconciliation of such opposites. Instead, it moves by way of more allusions (references to Plato's "demiurge" and Noah after the flood on Mount Ararat) to an affirmation of human continuity and rebirth, an idea certainly in keeping with the Christmas spirit.

References and further reading: A. Ferguson.

Todd Lieber

"AX-HELVE, THE," first appeared in the *Atlantic* (Sept. 1917) and was later collected in **New Hampshire (1923)**. The narrative poem details an enigmatic encounter with a country neighbor. Frost examines the theme of individual autonomy amidst an increasingly invasive American culture.

"The Ax-Helve" also broaches the subject of art and poetry. According to Marjorie Borroff, Frost implies through Baptiste's craft that mere skill, whether that of carving an ax-helve or crafting a poem, is not sufficient to attain perfection in one's discipline; a necessary corollary to skill is the greater sensibility of perception. Borroff sees a correspondence between the wood craftsman's skill of carving "native to the grain" and the poet's work with "sentence sounds."

The poem further establishes the relationship between humans and perfect craft. Baptiste's expertise is immediately evident when he catches the speaker's ax at midswing, timing it perfectly to apprehend it at the moment of least resistance. Such passion for a particular labor is, as Borroff notes, "ideally expressive; and 'expression' requires the existence of a reality against which 'pressure' can be brought to bear." Borroff's claim indicates a central issue underlying the poem, that of humanity's relationship to the outside world. The reality against which Baptiste brings pressure is society itself, the society that expects him to send his children to public school. Baptiste asserts his right to define the nature of his children's education. The speaker comes to represent the very society against which Baptiste is reacting, and the latter demands that this representative agree that he has the right to oversee his children's education. (It is worth noting here that Frost home schooled his children.) The crafting of the ax-helve becomes, in this reading, both what Squires calls the "basis for understanding" between the two individuals and the symbol of Baptiste's competency and qualifications for taking charge of his children's education.

References and further reading: C. Anderson; Borroff, "Frost: 'To Earthward,' " 34–35; Kjørven, 77, provides a structuralist reading of the poem, focusing on the breakdown of language that occurs as a result of Baptiste's struggle to communicate in English; Monteiro, "Redemption"; Parini, *A Life*, 187–88; Potter, 72, argues that the ax-helve is transformed into "a symbol of man's knowledge" and explores the subjectivity involved in the phenomenological construction of one's reality; Squires, 71.

Gavin Schulz

ℬ

"BAD ISLAND—EASTER, THE," first published in the *Times Literary Supplement* (17 Sept. 1954), appears in *In the Clearing* **(1962)**. Easter Island, one of the most remote islands on earth, is over 2,000 miles from the nearest population center. A Dutchman, Admiral Roggeveen, came upon the island on Easter Day 1722. Frost puns on the name: "(Perhaps so called because it may have risen once)." The poem is about the people's and the island's downfall—not its rising—as one might expect at Easter. The "Woes of the past" refer to the transformation the island has undergone since the time the natives (Rapa Nui) first arrived when the island was heavily forested and food was in surplus. To celebrate their generous gods, the native inhabitants made quarried stone figures called Moai; eventually over 600 statues were on the tiny island. Later, social order declined into a bloody civil war when resources declined.

Frost is puzzled by the scornful expression on the stone face and questions why the frown is there. Were the people scornful because they had been born there? Were they scornful because of the way they had been governed? Frost asserts that they became "overtaxed" in every way and began to "wane" as their life under rule was brought to ruin. Perhaps "kultur" implies a society where the individual has been subordinated to the state, a possibly veiled suggestion that the welfare state in America would mean subordination to the system.

References and further reading: R. Cook, "Frost on Frost," 42. See also Easter Island Home Page (Apr. 1997), http://www.netaxs.com/~trance/rapanui.html

Sarah R. Jackson

BARTLETT, JOHN THOMAS (1892–1947). When John Bartlett died in 1947, he had been a friend to Frost for nearly forty years. The friendship extended to their families (including two of Frost's grandchildren) and owed its value for Frost partly to its origin "back then when none of us was anybody," as Frost wrote to John's wife Margaret in 1949. Frost's sense of an innocent past shared with Bartlett may have helped to keep the relationship free of the hurts that clouded others of his long-term associations. However, while Frost's public life seems not to have affected his friendship with Bartlett, Bartlett's friendship played a significant role in Frost's life as a poet.

The two men met at **Pinkerton Academy** in Derry, New Hampshire, where in 1907 Bartlett was a new student and Frost had returned to teaching when life on the **Derry** farm refused to support his growing family. Bartlett, shy by his own report, was gratified when Frost "observed . . . that I was a fellow who had ideas" and took "several times the interest in me that other teachers had" (quoted by Anderson).

Begun over books, their friendship soon took them through many subjects and over the local terrain, for both were avid **naturalists** and walkers as well as talkers and readers. Like Frost, Bartlett had an educated, literate mother with a strong improving streak. And like Frost, who had married his high school sweetheart, Bartlett fell deeply in love with a Pinkerton classmate, Margaret Abbott, who, like Frost's **Elinor White**, would be valedictorian of his graduating class before she was his wife. As Frost encouraged his young friend's love along with his education, the friendship soon grew to include the women, as it would for the rest of their lives.

John entered Middlebury College in the fall of 1910; by winter, suffering equally from bronchial asthma and life without Margaret, he had returned to Derry. (Like Frost, he would never complete a college degree.) The following year, he and Margaret, now married, went west to British Columbia, where John began work as a journalist in rapidly developing Vancouver. Regaled by their friends' reports of the area's beauty and economic opportunity, the Frosts considered a move to British Columbia before settling on **England** as the place where Robert, in the fall of 1912, would stake all he had to establish himself as a poet.

Even 6,000 miles away, Bartlett played a part in this critical phase of Frost's poetic life. It was he who had sent Frost, while still in America, copies of *T. P's Weekly*, a popular London literary journal through whose offices the Frosts found, in September 1912, the Beaconsfield cottage in which they lived for the next eighteen months. It was the same member of the *Weekly* staff who soon led Frost, with the manuscript of *A Boy's Will*, to **David Nutt**, Ltd., who published it in March 1913. That fall, apparently sharing Frost's pride if not his sense of bruised merit, Bartlett prepared, from reviews Frost sent him, an article for *The Derry News* to announce the success of Pinkerton's prodigal son—or, as Frost jokingly wrote Bartlett in June 1913, "to bother the enemies we left behind in Derry."

More significant was Bartlett's indirect contribution to Frost's ideas on prosody—or what he called "the sound of sense." Frost's most absorbing aim during his "English" years was to perfect a metrical verse that captured genuine "sentence sounds"—the voice patterns of actual speech that give life to a poetic line.

While working on the poems for *North of Boston*, his second book, Frost attempted to define—in conversations with English poets and in letters to friends at home—the principles behind the work, the vision within his craft.

Chief among the letters are those to John Bartlett in July 1913 and February 1914, in which Frost called his ideas on English prosody "the most important thing I know" and suggested that Bartlett save Frost's "discourse" "for an essay or two I am going to write some fine day (not far distant)." Walsh believes that during this time Frost planned a preface to his forthcoming volume. But while he never wrote the preface, these letters gave Frost the invaluable chance to validate his artistry of the vernacular—the conscious craft behind his poetic voice—which, as he had learned, was easily mistaken for something artless and naive. Here, Bartlett's proven admiration can only have aided the growing assurance that Frost's ideas take on in this intense period of poetic realization. As he writes out for Bartlett phrases that show the voice how to "posture *specially*," we glimpse the former **teacher** dramatizing his thought before a star pupil.

As another literate lover of farms, Bartlett may also have represented something of an earlier self with which Frost in England strove to stay in touch. He was, at the least, a crucial link to the rural New England they had known and delighted in together—a fellow exile from the soil and culture from which Frost's poems had sprung. "You are about all I saved from the years I spent in Derry," Frost wrote Bartlett in November 1913. This link could only have become more important as Frost perceived that the public recognition now within reach must take him further from that former life, grown all the more precious in retrospect. As a trusted and respected friend with his own connection to these poetic sources, Bartlett was just the sort of audience to help Frost articulate ideas that were critical to his future yet rooted in his past.

By August 1914, *North of Boston*, published in London that May, found itself gathering good reviews in a country suddenly at war. And so, in February 1915, Frost took his family (and future prospects) back across the Atlantic, already dangerous with German submarines, docking in New York to the news that an American edition of his second volume had just been published by **Henry Holt**. The European war that brought Frost home to the American public also brought the Bartletts back from Vancouver, as the Canadian periodicals no longer had funds to buy his agricultural articles. Though both families were soon in New Hampshire, the different pressures on each established a pattern for the years ahead, in which their friendship was maintained by letters (especially Frost's) with only occasional personal visits. Throughout the correspondence one senses Frost's gratitude for a relationship free from ulterior motives, as the newly celebrated poet writes in August 1915: "I know I need you or someone like you dating back to the days when my friends were those who had had brains enough to judge me for themselves. . . . I long for something old and sure to cling to" (quoted by Anderson).

In 1917 John, chronically asthmatic, led Margaret, weak with tuberculosis, and their two children to Fort Collins, Colorado, where they pieced together a living from freelance writing on agriculture, business, and household management. Within ten years, they had established the Bartlett Syndicate Service and developed two profitable business periodicals, while John had published his first of three books on retail business practice. Through the 1930s and 1940s, Bartlett, now established in Boulder, became active in civic and business organizations as well as electoral politics, though never running for office himself.

Visits with the Frosts increased with the establishment in 1931 of the Rocky Mountain Writers' Conference, which brought Rob and Elinor to Boulder each summer through 1935. These arrangements encouraged them to send their daughter Marjorie, recovering from tuberculosis, to a sanitorium in Boulder, where the Bartletts were a second family through her long convalescence and her courtship by Willard Fraser, a student at the University of Colorado. In the spring of 1934, the Bartletts rushed to Billings, Montana, to offer their support when Marjorie contracted childbed fever weeks after delivering her first child, Robin. (Marjorie died on 2 May 1934, at the Mayo Clinic in Rochester, Minnesota.) Frost came again to Boulder in 1935, and John saw him in Denver in 1939—the last meeting between the two men.

John Bartlett died of a coronary thrombosis in January 1947. Shortly after that, Margaret asked Frost's permission to use his letters, along with Bartlett's notes on their Colorado visits, in a book about their friendship with the Frosts, which she and John had hoped to write together. Frost's response in December of that year—"write anything you please about me but put off publishing it till I am dead and gone"—did not change even when Margaret, dying of cancer, again asked in 1949. While expressing "deep mourning" and admiring Margaret's courage, Frost could not let her "make a publisher's venture of the letters I wrote you and John in the simplicity of the heart." As a result, the task was left, as Frost had suggested, to their daughter, Margaret Bartlett Anderson.

Frost's answer reached Margaret in November 1949, five days before she died. But it was his 1947 letter that came nearer the keynote of their friendship. There, he recounted his daughter Irma's commitment to a mental hospital, the freshest of his griefs since Elinor's death in 1938 and Carol's suicide in 1940. "But . . . I have things to be thankful for," Frost closed. "I have friends for instance. I have had you and John."

References and further reading: The single most complete account of Bartlett's relationship to Frost is found in M. Anderson, 11, 97, which adds to the documentary record a daughter's knowledge of characters and events. Frost's *Selected Letters* illuminates the friendship in a different way simply by placing the letters to Bartlett among those to other correspondents: 75, 81, 97, 113, 528, 539, 540. Readers especially interested in the 1912–1914 period, when Frost was in England, should see chapter 3 of Pritchard, *Literary Life*, and Walsh (esp. chapters 6, 7, and 9).

David Sanders

"BEAR, THE," inspired by what Frost called a "descent of bears" in New Hampshire in summer 1925, was written in 1927 and first appeared in *The*

Nation on 18 April 1928. It became the last poem in the original edition of *West-Running Brook* (**1928**) until Frost added **"The Egg and the Machine"** to the 1930 edition of *Collected Poems*.

The poem frames in couplets what could be expected from a poet–educator once honored as the best **teacher** in the state of New Hampshire. The poem is a satirical mix of contrasts such as learning and teaching, theory and practice, caged (humanity) and uncaged (nature), microscope and telescope, Hellenistic extremes, appearance and reality.

Yvor Winters makes an example of "The Bear" in his castigation of Frost as a shallow, dangerous thinker, arguing that the poem venerates the impulsive over the reasoning individual. Citing Hart Crane and **Ezra Pound** as "tragic examples" of the impulsive life, Winters chides Frost for "irresponsible foolishness." Marcus counters that Winters "neglects the bear's mindless roughness" and misses the satirical pose of "Frost's moody frustration with the human situation."

References and further reading: Marcus, *Explication*, 134; Squires, 62, 64; Thompson, *Triumph*, 312–13; Winters.

Andy Duncan and Roland H. Lyford

"BEARER OF EVIL TIDINGS, THE," was first published in the Winter 1936 issue of the *Yale Review*. It was collected in *A Further Range* that same year and placed in a grouping called "The Outlands" with **"The Vindictives"** and **"Iris by Night."** "The Bearer of Evil Tidings" was then subtitled "The Himalayas," reflective of the poem's setting. As Jeffrey Cramer indicates, a possible inspiration, according to a statement Frost made to Louis Mertins in 1932, was the ancient practice of a general's sending to his ruler a messenger with news of a losing battle. The messenger was killed as soon as he delivered the bad news. Pritchard admires the poem, noting that it reveals Frost's sense of play and mischief in relating the tale of the fated and legendary bearer of evil tidings who finds himself suddenly an ordinary fellow.

References and further reading: Cramer, *Frost among His Poems*, 118; Pritchard, *Literary Life*, 210–12.

Mark Sutton

"BEECH" is one of two short verses used to introduce *A Witness Tree* (**1942**), in which it first appeared. Taken with its companion, **"Sycamore,"** borrowed from *The New England Primer*, "Beech" establishes the poetic and thematic tension of the volume—a range between the limitation of a boundary marker and the freedom of an elevated vantage point. Whereas "Sycamore" restates the *Primer*'s version of short Zaccheus climbing a tree to see Jesus pass nearby—an act that led to recognition, fellowship, repentance, and redemption—"Beech" serves as the poet's reminder of "being not unbounded" in "a world of doubt."

The poem consists of three statements—two descriptive and one a moral conclusion. The first tells of an iron spike supported by a pile of rocks; the second tells of the beech tree "impressed as Witness Tree" and its function for the poet. The final three lines draw from the presence of remembered boundaries a moral conclusion: Truth is "established" amid dark and doubt, as order is defined amid apparent chaos. Similar to **Wallace Stevens**'s "Anecdote of the Jar" in its demarcation of order amid the "wild," "Beech" illustrates Frost's difference from Stevens in the natural, given quality of his boundary marker. Stevens's jar is placed arbitrarily and is separate from nature. Frost's beech tree is accepted where it stands, though "wounded" by its function.

The land marked by the tree is the Homer Noble farm near Ripton, Vermont. The cited source of the poem, *The Moodie Forester*, is a fictitious device by which the poet refers to his mother, whose maiden name was Moodie.

Metrically, the poem is not complicated but reflects Frost's typical care. The twelve iambic tetrameter lines consist of a couplet (*aa*), a quatrain (*bccb*), another couplet (*dd*), and another quatrain (*beeb*). The echoing rhyme emphasizes key terms in the poem's drama: "founded," "wounded," "unbounded," "surrounded."

References and further reading: Pritchard, *Literary Life*, 229–31; Thompson and Winnick, 92–93.

Douglas Watson

"BEREFT" was first published in the *New Republic* (9 Feb. 1927) and was collected in **West-Running Brook (1928)**. It was written, however, in 1893—twenty years before the publication of his first collection—in response to his wife **Elinor**'s return to college at St. Lawrence after they had spent the summer together taking care of Elinor's older sister, Ada, at a country home in Salem, New Hampshire.

The poem details the emotions and thoughts of a man who suddenly finds himself alone in his house at the onset of a storm. Frost's speaker is in psychological peril as he faces the demons of loneliness. Leaves, personified as a snake, hiss and strike at the speaker who, in turn, reads the malevolent actions of the leaves as a sign that the storm knows his secret: He is alone and afraid.

Traditional readings of the poem see the speaker and the storm enacting Frost's theme of the individual in conflict with nature. In this case, the storm acts to terrorize and mock the speaker as he stands in the doorway. However, critics disagree on the outcome of the poem: some read the last line as a call of faith to God, whereas others see only empty words offering little strength or resource. Frank Lentricchia argues that the poem expresses the dangers of psychological imbalance, asserting that the speaker's psychological well-being seems threatened "as the self is wholly overcome, strangled by the malevolent fictions of a sick mind that projects the world as an actively hostile force." The speaker's house represents the loneliness and isolation of his identity, whereas the woods represent all the external forces that act to destroy that identity. The speaker's imagination overworks itself, and the poem suggests that the speaker, alone and in need of some outside strength, may be destroyed by his fear that the world is working against him.

References and further reading: Lentricchia, *Modern Poetics*, 95; Oster; Thompson, *Early Years*, 153.

Jeannette E. Riley

"BEYOND WORDS" first appeared in *Steeple Bush* **(1947)**. One reading ac- . knowledges the playfulness of the gutter/utter rhyme, which mimics the gutteral timbre of anger expressed both in words and in nonlinguistic expressions, such as growls. Written to some extent in a schoolyard idiom, it is the sort of poem a child might enjoy.

Yet the poem also recalls a serious and dark poem, **"Home Burial,"** wherein the character Amy repeats a word four times in reaction to the unbearable mention of her child's grave: "Don't, don't, don't, don't," she cries. Thirty years later, in "Beyond Words," Frost repeats the word *you* four times. In a 1915 letter to **Louis Untermeyer**, Frost described the movement from words to aggression: "To fight is to leave words . . . Sometimes I have my doubts of words altogether . . . unless they amount to deeds as in ultimatums and war crys." The poem "Beyond Words" issues an ultimatum; it goes beyond words into aggression. In the first two lines, the speaker articulates icy hate, developing the "hate . . . destruction . . . ice" theme of Frost's poem **"Fire and Ice,"** a parallel noted by George Monteiro. The third and final lines move "beyond words" into the inarticulate four "yous" and the adjective "utter." And then, for lack of a sufficiently condemnatory noun, the speaker uses words to carry him or her beyond words into a belligerent promise of action: "You wait!" The irony, of course, is that a poem entitled "Beyond Words" actually exists very comfortably within words; characteristically, Frost has disciplined seemingly unruly utterance to meter and rhyme.

References and further reading: R. Frost, *Letters to Untermeyer*, 10, *Selected Letters*, 79–81; Monteiro, *New England*, 73.

Gerard Quinn

BIOGRAPHERS OF ROBERT FROST. Frost's life has provoked as much commentary as his poetry; the hagiographic impulse has been as strong as the critical in Frost studies. Frost once remarked, "Trust me on the poetry, but don't trust me on my life. Check up on me some" (Thompson xiv); he could just as easily have urged us to trust the poems and not the lives or biographies.

Friends and associates of Frost turned out memoirs from early on. Sidney Cox's *Robert Frost: Original "Ordinary Man"* (1929) is among the earliest, and Cox's *A Swinger of Birches: A Portrait of Robert Frost* (1957) was published five years after Cox's death; the posthumous volume records the forty-year relationship between the two men that began in 1911 when Cox started teaching at Plymouth High School. The Cox/Frost relationship, as well as the

John Bartlett/Frost relationship, has occasioned further commentary; William R. Evans has edited *Robert Frost and Sidney Cox: Forty Years of Friendship* (1981), whereas Margaret Bartlett Anderson memorializes the friendship of her father and Frost in *Robert Frost and John Bartlett: The Record of a Friendship* (1963).

Anderson's memoirs were the first to appear following Frost's death in 1963, although others followed quickly. Daniel Smythe's *Robert Frost Speaks* appeared in 1964; Louis Mertins charts thirty years of friendly association in *Robert Frost: Life and Talks-Walking* (1965); **Reginald Cook**, longtime director of the Middlebury College **Bread Loaf School of English**, whose association with Frost extends back to the late 1920s, published two critical studies: *The Dimensions of Robert Frost* (1958) and *Robert Frost: A Living Voice* (1974). The latter is of particular importance because it abundantly quotes Frost in context and includes transcripts of twelve major addresses by Frost at Bread Loaf. In 1972 Robert Francis, another friend, weighs in with *Frost: A Time to Talk*.

Formal biographies are equally numerous. As much as Frost distrusted the biographical project, he had an eye for, and was careful in planning, his own memory: "I want to be perpetuated: I want the world told about me," Frost writes Richard H. Thornton, his editor at **Holt**, in 1937; however, Frost would always be ill at ease with those friends or associates who, formally or informally, presumed to tell the world about his life. In 1928 he pointedly chided Sidney Cox in a letter, "I never chose you as a Boswell." Nonetheless, during the same years, Frost encouraged—or at least did not take action against—Robert Newdick, a professor of English at Ohio State University, who began a project that was to become a proposed biography. Newdick died unexpectedly, however, in 1939; in 1976 William A. Sutton edited his protobiography of thirteen minichapters as *Newdick's Season of Frost: An Interrupted Biography of Robert Frost*. Within two weeks of Newdick's death, and despite his announced distaste for biography, Frost invited a newly appointed Princeton professor of English named Lawrance Thompson to write his biography. Frost had known Thompson since 1925, when Thompson was an undergraduate at Wesleyan University. Thompson's interest in Frost increased until Thompson became, in his own curious words, a "Frost addict." Frost mentored the young man through a Columbia dissertation on Longfellow, and their relationship continued to deepen; Thompson eventually served as an honorary pallbearer for **Elinor Frost** when she died in 1938.

Probably, Frost thought Thompson would be an acceptable biographer because he, as Newdick before him, was suitably in awe of his subject, even though Newdick's "zeal" had seemed "excessive" to Frost, as he says in a letter to poet John Holmes; Thompson's adulatory devotion, in the role of authorized biographer, would leave Frost room to maneuver out of other offers of biography. Frost was sixty-five when he invited Thompson to be his biographer in 1939; he would live another quarter century, and the long relationship between the two men was frequently strained, and increasingly so in the later years. In the first place, Frost distrusted the basis on which the relationship came to be centered—biography—and in addition, Thompson's eager—to Frost, too eager—pursuit of a truth narrowly defined as fact did not set well with the Frost who had written to Cox in 1932, "I have written to keep the over curious out of the secret places of my mind both in my verse and in my letters to such as you." The relationship was further strained as Frost increasingly distrusted Thompson's often rigid interpretation of events as well as attitudes; in particular, Frost thought Thompson ill-equipped to handle the complexity of his spiritual-religious thought. Distrust deepened on both sides until finally, hearing that the poet lay near death in Peter Bent Hospital, Boston, Thompson, as Stanley Burnshaw reports, writes, "The truth of the matter is that I really don't care whether I ever see him again, alive or dead."

Last, a contributing factor to the tension between the two was, ironically, Thompson's loyalty to Frost. Frost stipulated that no biography would appear in his lifetime (even Cox's *Swinger of Birches*, published after Cox's death, was still problematic for Frost). Thompson honored the agreement, while other biographers did not. As a result of the various tensions between the two men, Thompson concluded that Frost turned to other biographers. For example, although he initially declined, Frost later grudgingly accepted the task of writing a preface for Cox's book, and he openly cooperated with Elizabeth Shepley Sergeant, whose *Robert Frost: The Trial by Existence* (1960) seemed to Thompson a direct move by Frost to repudiate, by anticipating, Thompson's biography. There is even indication that Frost encouraged his longtime friend **Louis Untermeyer** to write some form of memoir. Stanley Burnshaw, Frost's editor at Holt, reports Frost's telling him during this period of time—the last six years of Frost's life—"I am counting on you to save me from Larry. Remember!"

Within seven months of Frost's death, Untermeyer complied, in a sense, with Frost's wish; his edition of *The Letters of Robert Frost to Louis Untermeyer* (1963) appeared, arranged and edited to be something of a biography itself. Jean Gould's *Robert Frost: The Aim Was Song* (1964) is the first full-length biography to appear after Frost's death, but it is largely derivative, depending upon Sergeant's earlier portrait of Frost. In his edition of *Selected Letters of Robert Frost* (1964), Thompson collects 466 letters to and from Frost, and some from Elinor; in his introduction Thompson writes that the letters will permit an "imaginative reader to 'roll his own' biography." The volume was to be a testing of the waters, as it were, for Thompson's forthcoming biography of Frost. Thompson had told Al Edwards at Holt that his edition of the letters would "dispel or at least modify" Frost's "mythic image." Unfortunately, Thompson was as good as his word. Thompson's edition of the letters—and then the later ham-handed, irony-proof biography—prompted a series of reverberating outcries. Reviews by important or at least well-known voices in notable venues alternately repudiated Thompson's method while, in essence, accepting his portrait uncritically. For instance, in a *New York Times Book Review* piece on *The Years of Triumph*, Helen Vendler calls the biography "intellectually superficial"; nonetheless, calling Frost a "monster of egotism," she accepts without demur Thompson's biases and conclusions. John W. Aldridge's review in *Saturday Review* likewise was influential; its headline reads "Frost Removed from Olympus." Despite the public clamor about the book, the volume won for Thompson the Pulitzer Prize for Biography.

Thompson had spent a quarter century waiting to undertake the biography, but he died with the third volume barely sketched out. Under his guidance, a graduate student, R. H. Winnick, finished the third volume from Thompson's notes. Burnshaw reveals that Winnick later reflected that in working with the dying Thompson, he was "struck" by "Thompson's evident animus toward his subject." Thompson died on 15 April 1973, and after Winnick completed and published *The Later Years* (1976), the stage was set for the various revisionist Frost lives. Some reacted directly to Thompson, whereas others studied specific periods in Frost's life. Some appeared before Thompson's biography was complete. In 1969 Lesley Frost published *New Hampshire's Child: The Derry Journals of Lesley Frost*. In 1972 Arnold Grade's edition of *The Family Letters of Robert and Elinor Frost* appeared, with an introduction by Lesley Frost; two years later **Kathleen Morrison**—secretary and companion to Frost for almost the last quarter of his life—published *Robert Frost: A Pictorial Chronicle* (1974). The complicated—and contested—relationships between Morrison and Frost and between Morrison and Thompson become gratuitously the focus of Jeffrey Meyers's largely salacious *Robert Frost: A Biography* (1996).

In 1981 Edward Connery Lathem edited and condensed Thompson's three volumes, trimming Thompson's almost 2,000 pages down to fewer than 550. The attempt to correct, at least partially, Thompson's distortions in some ways left matters worse off, since Thompson had consigned to his notes sources, documentation, and, often, anecdotal material. Thus, without the notes, one lacks vital facts as well as much of the actual color of Frost's life. Two years later, William H. Pritchard published *Frost: A Literary Life Reconsidered* (1984); as his title suggests and as Pritchard directly argues in his introduction, his biography is intended to revise Thompson's portrait of Frost. As Pritchard states, "As a writer [Thompson] was not adequate to that subject." In particular, Pritchard addresses what Thompson most egregiously does not: the poetry itself and Frost's ironic and nuanced voice. Thompson rarely addresses the poetry *as poetry*, maintaining that it was not of biographical interest. Notwithstanding, he was capable of an odd sort of exegesis, using poems—famously **"Stopping by Woods on a Snowy Evening"**—to buttress his determinedly psychological interpretations of Frost's life. Otherwise, Frost's voice, either in poem or quotation, is rarely in evidence. On the other hand, Pritchard moves "back and forth between life and art, often blurring the distinctions in the interest of telling a story of a literary life."

Burnshaw's *Robert Frost Himself* (1986) is at times more about Burnshaw than Frost, but such can be said about many of the Frost hagiographies. Burnshaw was Frost's editor at Henry Holt during a crucial period—the years immediately preceding and following Frost's death—enabling him to examine, with dispassion and clarity, "The Fabrication of the 'Monster' Myth" (in the words of a chapter title). John Evangelist Walsh's *Into My Own: The English Years of Robert Frost, 1912–1915* (1988) also takes oblique aim at Thompson. The well-researched and intelligent account of Frost's three-year life in **England** demonstrates how Frost set out to make himself up from scratch as a New England poet. Walsh shows how such "classic" New England poems as **"Mending Wall"** were actually written far away, while Frost lived in England. Frost was thirty-eight when he traveled to England; by carefully detailing the early years, Walsh's portrait is the retrieval of the young poet from Thompson's curmudgeon, since many of the horror stories detailed by Thompson, even if true, occur in the last, troubled years of the poet's very long life. In 1988 Sandra Katz adds her biography of Elinor, *Elinor Frost: A Poet's Wife*, which in the main explicitly follows Thompson's biography on Elinor and Frost's relationship.

When Thompson died, he left an account of his complicated relationships with Frost and the writing of the biography; his typescript notes of more than 2,000 pages, with some omissions, extend back to 1939. The "Notes from Conversations with Robert Frost" are available for review in the Alderman Library, University of Virginia at Charlottesville.

The account of Thompson's biography is still not settled, as indicated by two other biographical works, one a rich and warm testament of Frost's complex family life and labors to succeed as a poet, the other a self-proclaimed effort to "add a significant layer" to those biographies already in existence. Lesley Lee Francis, Frost's granddaughter, examines the Frost family's early years in *The Frost Family's Adventure in Poetry: Sheer Morning Gladness at the Brim* (1994). Francis handles the Frosts' poignant struggles and triumphs during the **Derry** years and the years in England while Frost established and developed his considerable reputation in modern letters. Jay Parini's biography *Robert Frost: A Life* appeared in Great Britain late in 1998 and even later in America and was, thus, unavailable to most contributors to this encyclopedia (*see* Preface). In Parini's words, his biography offers "a comprehensive reading of the poet's life and work" and "presents Frost as a major poet who struggled throughout his long life with depression, anxiety, self-doubt, and confusion" but who was, at the same time, "a man of immense fortitude, an attentive father, and an artist of the first order who understood what he must do to create a body of work of lasting significance." Most valuable is Parini's "Afterword" in which he explains why he believes "Frost has generally not been well served by his biographers." In Parini's view, the poet emerges as neither saint nor villain but as fully human.

References and further reading: All biographies discussed in the entry are listed in the bibliography. Specific quotations come from Burnshaw, 6, 217, 222; R. Frost, *Selected Letters*, viii, 351, 385, 447, 449; Parini, *A Life*, xi, 449–58; Pritchard, *Literary Life*, xiii, xviii; Thompson, *Early Years*, xiv. Bober's "story" of Frost is aimed at young readers; for critical examinations of the Thompson Notes in the Alderman collection and of

Thompson's biography of Frost, see Sheehy, "Neurotic," and W. A. Sutton, "Biography." The following is a ready-reference list of selected reviews not included in the bibliography:

Francis

Calhoun, Richard J. *South Carolina Review* 28 (1995): 177–79.

Kirby, David. *Library Journal* 1 May 1994: 104.

Klausner, Lewis. *American Literature* 68 (1996): 255–56.

Monteiro, George. *Robert Frost Review* (Fall 1994): 106–10.

Publishers Weekly 4 Apr. 1994: 65.

Rotella, Guy. *New England Quarterly* 68 (1995): 156–59.

Times Literary Supplement 15 Sept. 1995: 32.

Meyers

Kakutani, Michiko. *New York Times* 23 Apr. 1996, late ed.: C16.

Keller, Joanna. *Antioch Review* 55 (Winter 1997): 115.

Seymour, Miranda. *New York Times Book Review* 19 May 1996: 8.

Stanlis, Peter J. *Robert Frost Review* (Fall 1997): 80–86.

Vendler, Helen. *London Review of Books* 4 July 1996: 3+.

Parini

Benfey, Christopher. *New York Times Magazine*. http://www.nytimes.com/books/99/04/25/reviews/990425.25benfyt.html (30 Apr. 1999).

Updike, John. *The New Yorker* 15 Mar. 1999: 84–91.

Pritchard

Corn, Alfred. *New Republic* 4 Feb. 1985: 39–41.

Poirier, Richard. *New York Review of Books* 25 Apr. 1985: 26.

Sheehy, Donald G. *New England Quarterly* 58 (1985): 320–23.

Vendler, Helen. *New York Times Book Review* 14 Oct. 1984:1.

Thompson, Vol. 1.

Dickey, James. *Atlantic Monthly* Nov. 1966: 53–56.

Poirier, Richard. *New York Times Book Review* 6 Nov. 1966: 4+.

Untermeyer, Louis. *Saturday Review* 5 Nov. 1966: 32–33.

Thompson, Vol. 2

Aldridge, John W. *Saturday Review* 15 Aug. 1970: 21–23+.

Vendler, Helen. *New York Times Book Review* 9 Aug. 1970: 1+.

Thompson and Winnick, Vol. 3

Bedient, Calvin. *New Republic* 5 Mar. 1977: 37–40.

Bromwich, David. *New York Times Book Review* 16 Jan. 1977: 4.

Spencer, Benjamin Townley. *American Literature* 49 (1977): 447–49.

Edward J. Ingebretsen

"BIRCHES" was written in 1913–1914 while Frost was living in England. The poem first appeared in the *Atlantic Monthly* (Aug. 1915). It was then chosen for the 1915 edition of *Anthology of Magazine Verse* and appeared in Frost's third book, **_Mountain Interval_ (1916)**.

Frost claimed that he wrote "Birches" quickly, in a rush of inspiration, but worksheets show that in fact he labored over the poem. Whatever the reality of composition, the poem does give a sense of spontaneity and impulsiveness. Among other themes, "Birches" deals with the question of how to reconcile impulse and carefulness, spontaneity and structure—a crucial tension in Frost's thought. The characteristic Frost response is to express them in a form that requires control and skill, whether it be a technique of climbing and swinging or an act of writing. Either is a balancing act, and the same is true in the living of a life.

"Birches" shows Frost's metaphorical thinking at its richest. Early in the poem Frost gives a sharp description of what ice storms do to birch trees. He introduces the idea that a boy's swinging might "bend them down to stay," which he says is his preferred explanation. But first he deals with the real cause, the ice. Alive with words like "click," "breeze," "cracks and crazes," "crystal shells," the lines show Frost's brilliance as a describer of the physical world. They also show his love of sound, as he plays the music of *s*'s, *z*'s, and *c*'s. He then says of the shattered ice on the ground, "You'd think the inner dome of heaven had fallen." Through the metaphor of the dome, the poem about birch trees and ice storms takes on, almost casually, a metaphysical dimension. And since the image is of a structure that has collapsed, it reverberates with a loss of faith as well.

At the conclusion of his description, Frost compares the trees to girls on hands and knees with their hair thrown in front of them to dry in the sun, recalling, perhaps, the maenads, female members of the orgiastic cult of Dionysus. Frost's poem **"Wild Grapes,"** written as a companion piece for "Birches," contains striking echoes of the *Bacchae* of Euripides, which features both maenads and tree climbing, as the classicist Helen Bacon has pointed out. Frost, who knew the classics, surely realized that the traditional ecstatic gesture of the maenads was shaking their hair by throwing back the head.

One need not be a Freudian to see a phallic metaphor in the poem's assertion that the boy rode the trees "Until he took the stiffness out of them, / And not one but hung limp." Even if used unconsciously, those stiff and drooping birches, and the joy of riding them "over and over," are a triumph for Frost's earthiness, as well as for his metaphoric richness and slyness.

There are other poems of Frost that link tree climbing and spiritual vision— for example, **"After Apple-Picking,"** with its ladder pointed "toward heaven," and the little poem **"Sycamore."** Thus, "Birches" emerges as a poem about tree-climbing, one that through its metaphors is also about reaching higher states, whether of physical excitement, emotional abandon, or spiritual vision; it is a poem that for all its resonances remains deeply and wonderfully a poem about birch trees, ice storms, tree climbing, and swinging. *See also* **Nature Poet and Naturalist** and **Pastoral Poetry**.

References and further reading: Bacon, "For Girls." In a sketch of Frost's work Robert Bly discusses Frost's strategy and tone in "Birches": "Frost talks of ordinary birches and boys who climb them though he was well aware that shamans once climbed birches to the spiritual world. If you ask him: 'Do you visit the other world?' he would answer, 'I wouldn't tell you if I did.' " For a Freudian reading of this poem, see Ellis, "Types of Belief." Randall Jarrell, though one of Frost's most eloquent advocates, says, "We begin to read Frost, always, with the taste of 'Birches' in our mouth—a taste a little brassy, a little sugary" (*Poetry* 41). William Pritchard identifies "Birches" as the poem that "signals the beginning of Frost's use of the Yankee as wise spokesman about all matters" (*Literary Life* 155). See also Hadas; Lentricchia, *Modern Poetics*; Monteiro, *New England*, 99– 111; Oster; Parini, *A Life*, 135–38.

Howard Nelson

"BIRTHPLACE, THE," was first published in *The Dartmouth Bema* (June 1923) and was collected in *West-Running Brook* **(1928)**. Katherine Kearns suggests that Frost associates order with masculinity and "barrierlessness," chaos, and insubordination with femininity. She concludes that for Frost "the work of manhood" is "to urge control on the uncontrollable, to impose upon its own 'femaleness'—that which embodied in women seems to be randomly destructive—moderation and orderliness." Kearns helps us see how the conflict in Frost's poetry between insubordinate natural forces and the forms he imposes on them is always also, indirectly and residually, a conflict between the feminine and the masculine: To speak for order and culture is to speak as the Father; to speak for insubordination and nature is to speak as Woman. Such concerns certainly enter into "The Birthplace." Most remarkable is what "The Birthplace" omits or fails to mention, as Kearns has pointed out, the mother that presumably had something to do with "bringing" a "dozen" girls and boys "to pass." The poem concerns instead—and this quite literally—the Founding Father. "The Birthplace" seems written out of the dispensation Simone de Beauvoir describes in *The Second Sex*: "With the advent of patriarchal institutions, the male laid eager claim to his posterity. It was still necessary to grant the mother a part in procreation, but it was conceded only that she carried and nourished the living seed, created by the father alone." Still, the name of the mother is repressed only inefficiently in "The Birthplace," as Frost acknowledges. In fact, her role is not so much repressed as *displaced* onto the mountain itself (gendered feminine in the poem), which the father "husbands" and makes fertile, rather like the man in **"Putting in the Seed"**: The mountain "pushes" the children off her "knees" once they have grown. The displacement of the mother issues from a certain apprehension: That is what the quietly sardonic "something" in the "smile" of the mountain-mother is meant to suggest. She is enigmatic and only temporarily subject to mastery. This homestead is an enclave of patriarchal order imposed on an unruly but nonetheless potentially productive "feminine" landscape. Moving to a higher level of abstraction we can see that the feminine, as "The Birthplace" implies, is only partly and ephemerally susceptible to masculine orders that would "subdue" it. The "stay" against wilderness figured in "The Birthplace" is but "momentary," a quality that associates it with "the figure a poem makes" in Frost's well-known formulation (*see* **Poetic Theories**). The father of this poem is therefore, at least provisionally, also a "father-poet." So far as the father-poet is concerned, to bring a life to pass and to bring a poem to pass are cognate endeavors: Both entail "a momentary stay against confusion." And as always in Frost *something* escapes the father's government.

References and further reading: Simone de Beauvoir, *The Second Sex* (New York: Vintage, 1989), 8; Kearns, 1–31.

Mark Richardson

"BLACK COTTAGE, THE," was published in *North of Boston* **(1914)** and exists in two manuscript versions. One from 1905, when Frost was in **Derry**, New Hampshire, reflects his late Romantic sensibility, whereas the other, more typical and far more nuanced version dates from 1913. This second version was composed while Frost was in **England**, and, according to John Kemp, it reflects the influence of the **Georgian poets** on Frost's poetics. Despite the various biographical sources that may exist for the poem, its major source is textual and can be found in William Wordsworth's "Ruined Cottage," which Frost would have known as *The Excursion* Book I. Like Frost's poem, Wordsworth's also tells the story of a recently dead woman and takes place directly outside of an abandoned cottage. Also, Wordsworth's poem is told as a **dramatic monologue** by the poet who records what he is told about the obstinate woman who once lived in the now-ruined cottage.

Still one of the most underrated and little studied of Frost's poems, "The Black Cottage" explores such typically Frostian themes as skepticism, the pastoral imagination, and interpersonal relations by telling multiple stories. The first, a framing narrative, describes a poet's and a minister's two approaches to the cottage and the sudden appearance of bees that chase the two men away. In the second story—the minister's tale—we learn about a stubborn woman, now dead, whose convictions, both political and spiritual, continue to trouble the minister.

John Kemp believes that Frost represents two philosophies—the woman's absolutism and the minister's doubts—and makes the poet mediate between the two in order not to take a stand one way or the other. Other critics look at the specific philosophical influences in the poem. Reuben Brower, for example, thinks that the "minister is made to sound like a young man who has swallowed William James too hastily." By contrast, Lewis H. Miller, Jr. uncovers in the poem a sophisticated engagement with James's philosophy. Frank Lentricchia sees a modern conflict between stability and flux that gives the poem a modernist philosophy of the sort we associate with **T. S. Eliot**. Margaret V. Allen focuses on the poem's discussion of "Jeffersonian equality." This is a concept the now-dead female inhabitant of the cottage believed fully but in which the minister has doubt. Allen tells us that "the poem itself is Frost's tribute to the strength of that ideal, and an expression of his own uncertainties about it." *See also* **Pastoral Poetry**.

References and further reading: M. Allen, 228; Brower, 78–80; Kemp, 119–20; Lentricchia, *Modern Poetics*, 78–80; Miller, "William James"; Walsh, 47, n.263, notes the Wordsworthian connection.

Jonathan N. Barron

"BLUE RIBBON AT AMESBURY, A," was first published in April 1936 in the *Atlantic Monthly* and was included later that same year in *A Further Range* with the subtitle "Small Plans Gratefully Heard Of." The secondary title may provide some clue to the significance of the poem. The poem's subject is the beautiful, prizewinning female pullet. The emphasis shifts away from the physical beauty of the bird to qualities of character that can be likened to those of humans. The pullet is "almost perfect," much like, but not quite, the human who was created in perfection. She is strong, proud, independent, and resourceful, much in the image of the Yankee farmer. In this we find a typical downward comparison of human to beast that exists in many of Frost's poems. Yet here we encounter another shift in emphasis, a second level of comparison of God to human; the breeder is godlike in his scheming. As a higher being capable of design, the breeder has a responsibility to plan. Humans are empowered not only to be artists and creators of a living beauty but also to use our ingenuity to be nurturers and guardians of that beauty. The last lines of the poem echo the idea, and the practical human goal to avoid aimless wandering in a purposeless existence, the "dark and wind and cold" from which the breeder shelters his prize pullet, becomes in itself a "plan" set down by the poet in metaphor for the reader to hear gratefully.

Reference and further reading: Kemp further discusses Frost's use of the voice of the Yankee farmer.

John R. Woznicki

"BLUEBERRIES" first appeared in *North of Boston* **(1914)**. In a dialogue between two individuals alternately figured as "pickers" and "trolls," the poem explores a familiar Frost topic: the nature of borders. At first brisk and playful, the poem finally becomes almost melancholic in the nostalgia shared by the two speakers, probably husband and wife. The blueberries are flourishing in a pasture owned by Mr. Patterson, a man who, according to one voice, "won't make the fact that they're rightfully his / An excuse for keeping us other folk out." The poem focuses largely on such "other folk," including a family—the "chattering Lorens"—who apparently subsist exclusively on wild berries. The nearly ludicrous portrait of the Lorens, "Just taking what Nature is willing to give" while simultaneously pursuing Nature's bounty with a possessive ardor, wavers between jocularity and condemnation. (Doyle calls it "a poem of hilarious mood.") Loren is "thrifty" and a "rascal," an amusingly ingenious if eccentric survivalist, a panjandrum of the berry fields. But he and his clan, according to the primary speaker, "won't be too friendly" to those whom they mistakenly "look on as having no right / To pick where they're picking." As Nitchie wonders of Loren, "Are we to admire or despise [this man]?" A great many such carefully constructed ambivalences enrich the layering of the poem. Apparent contrasts between the characters (the magnanimous Patterson and the selfish Lorens, for instance) can alternately be seen as grave similarities—in this case, as an utter disregard for others. The speakers implicate themselves in the same problematics. They do not need the berries, as the Lorens do, nor do they own them. They hope to pick in the pasture only "for a whim," and they alone seem at times to exist outside the natural system altogether, as when they disturb the bird from its nest near the close of the poem. In the final lines, "two kinds of jewels"—both the berries and their glitter after the rain—depict "a vision for thieves." The identity of those thieves is perhaps the question that lingers longest after the reader has finished this poem.

Expressing a view similar to Doyle's, Marcus feels this poem to be "the slightest and lightest-hearted poem" in all of Frost's *North of Boston*. Not all critics see such whimsy. Goede staunchly proposes that "Blueberries" should be considered a major work, deserving of deeper readings than it has generally received, and suggests the poem may be illuminated by an understanding of Ernest Hemingway's "code hero."

References and further reading: Doyle, *Poetry*, 100; Goede; Marcus, *Explication*, 49; Nitchie, 93.

Eric C. Brown

"BLUE-BUTTERFLY DAY" is an early masterpiece written between 1896 and 1900, first published in the *New Republic* (16 Mar. 1921), and collected in *New Hampshire* **(1923)**. Frost recited the poem in an interview with Paul Waitt (*Boston Traveler*, 11 Apr. 1921) as an example of the appealing nature of spring when thawing starts. In a much later interview with Milton Bracker (*New York Times Magazine*, 30 Nov. 1958), Frost was asked about his "incredible exactness with words" in this poem, to which Frost responded: "That's what I live for. . . . [The exactness of poetry] cuts a little edge across your feelings."

The eight-line lyric, ending in the mud of April, is deceptively prosaic. A speaker is first made audible by the use of "here" and "these," which both allude to physical presence at an ostensibly real occasion. At the end of the poem, however, human absence is signaled by "now," such that the initial spatial experience is replaced by a temporal one. Alliteration, repetition, and parallelism order the poem's tandem narratives: Butterflies move from the air "down" to the ground, and a poetic vision moves from fanciful figuration to precise observation. The nonchalance of this move from the poetic transformations of the butterflies to their literal description is buoyed by the dominant rhyme sequence that, with its final word, mimics the concluding change in the poet's imaginative priorities. Part of its quiet pathos depends on the unremarked change in the look of the wings of the "blue-butterflies," which are colored only when they are open; wings "closed over" are drab.

Although the stanza break and the conjunction "but" at the start of the second stanza begin to qualify the exuberance of the "blue-butterfly day," the most important transition occurs at the run-on from line 7 to line 8, which allows the butterflies to hang on to the edge of the poem as it focuses away from them to "freshly sliced" tracks. (For a different but related use of "freshly," see the later butterfly poem **"Pod of the Milkweed."**) The last line cuts across several of the poem's interests, the most significant of which is the sexual "desire" of newborn beings. The play of "ridden out" against the "wheels" and the potential pun in "ridden" ("written") confirm the tacit equation between poetry and procreation and extend the psychological relevance of the beautiful, vulnerable, and trivial butterflies. As in his other "butterfly" poems, Frost revises the romantic communing of Wordsworth's "To a Butterfly" with a Blakean correction of innocence by experience. His difference from both poets, however, is seen in his morbid aesthetic materialism. To rhyme "desire" with "mire," instead of with "aspire" as Blake does in "Ah! Sun-Flower," is to defeat the vanity of "flowers that fly" by reducing them to litter on the unvariegated mud of an earth marked only by the passage of time. *See also* **Nature Poet and Naturalist**.

References and further reading: R. Frost, *Interviews*, 33, 187.

Gary Roberts

"BOEOTIAN" first appeared in *A Witness Tree* (1942). The title refers to an ancient Greek district, namely Boeotia, which, as Cramer suggests, was known proverbially for its dull inhabitants. The lyric poem subscribes to a certain Platonism: the speaker considers that *ideas*, not merely physical facts, should have their apt reality. Such a switch back from Aristotle's presumed improvement over Plato (as then converted by the medieval Church through the use of Thomistic thought to represent dogmatic Christian philosophy) to an idea-oriented way of life can be easily thought of as, in essence, romantic, for it lends itself readily to subjective interpretation, which appealed to the romantic sensibility and to Frost.

The poet, in other words, feels that he has a certain prerogative to follow his own conscience and not bow to the dictates of a *prescribed* orderly universe, that which is thereby merely "systematic." In this respect, he was no doubt also bringing out his basic puritan convictions, his stress upon the individual conscience and not on some imposed order of things. The poem may thus be correlated with longer efforts in the same direction, such as his **"After Apple-Picking."**

References and further reading: Cramer, *Frost among His Poems*, 141; Fleissner, *Road Taken*; Pritchard, *Literary Life*.

Robert F. Fleissner

BOLLINGEN PRIZE IN POETRY. *See* **Awards, Honors, and Prizes**.

"BOND AND FREE" first appeared in Frost's third book, **Mountain Interval (1916)**, where it precedes **"Birches."** Like the more famous "Birches," it concerns the relationship between the physical/emotional and artistic/intellectual dimensions of life, associating the former (identified here as "Love") with earth and the latter ("Thought") with heaven. As in "Birches" where Frost claims "Earth's the right place for love," so this poem begins, "Love has earth to which she clings." Love, by being bound, achieves not only physical and emotional satisfaction but a degree of safety as well ("Wall within wall to shut fear out"). Thought, on the other hand, is fearless and soars toward the unknown, achieving the satisfactions of invention and new knowledge. In describing the "smell of burning on every plume" as Thought returns from his flight to the heavens, Frost invokes the mythological figure of Icarus, son of Daedalus, who, despite his father's warning, soared too high, too close to the sun, melted his wax wings, and fell to his death in the sea.

The poem's last stanza asserts that the discoveries of love and thought, and the significance of them, equal each other, but we note that in the allegorical abstractions of the poem Frost makes the domesticated and bound "Love" feminine and the liberated, daring "Thought" masculine in keeping with the gender stereotypes of his day and with the general representation of male and female throughout his poetry.

"Bond and Free" is written in iambic tetrameter five-line stanzas, rhyming *abbaa*, but Frost skillfully varies the meter at crucial points in the poem. For instance, he adds additional unaccented syllables occasionally to complement "Thought's" free motion and escape.

References and further reading: Marcus, "Frost's 'Bond and Free' "; S. Cox's *Swinger* provides a book-length study focused on the alternation Frost describes in "Bond and Free" and "Birches."

Todd Lieber

"BONFIRE, THE," was first published in *The Seven Arts* (Nov. 1916) and was collected that same year in *Mountain Interval*. The poem perhaps had its origins in **Derry** in the spring of 1905 when a fire that Frost and his children set to a pile of dead leaves and branches got out of control. Only Frost's heroic efforts saved their house. Frost completed the poem in 1916 and read it that year, along with **"The Ax-Helve,"** at a Phi Beta Kappa Day dinner held at **Harvard**. According to Mertins, Frost considered it one of his "ostensible war poems," yet in a letter he claimed it was "more of New England than of what is going on over yonder."

"The Bonfire," which paints an explicit portrait of war as it develops and is an attempt to explain how and why war continues, points to several paradoxes. The first occurs because older generations believe it is important to prepare younger ones for the real possibility of having to deal with destructive impulses within themselves. Unfortunately, during that preparation, the young are often beguiled by those very impulses. The second concerns the benefits of fires. Often they are both good ("bon") and necessary, providing for renewal, but once set, they can easily get out of control, turning destructive.

Frost's poem also depicts a very genuine excitement that human beings experience in war. The excitement caused by fire is not unlike the "lonely impulse of delight" that **Yeats** talks about in his poem "An Irish Airman Foresees His Death."

References and further reading: Abel, "Frost's 'Range-Finding' "; R. Frost, *Selected Letters*, 220; Mertins and Mertins, 44; Monteiro, *New England*, 70–72; Thompson, *Early Years*, 301.

James M. Dubinsky

"BOUNDLESS MOMENT, A," first appeared in the *New Republic* (24 Oct. 1923) and was collected in *New Hampshire* **(1923)**. The poem presents a human being stumbling upon a facet of nature in order to contemplate wider human experience, which, in this case, is the human tendency to project false hopes onto a clearly declining situation, represented here by nature in winter.

The dramatic situation of the poem consists of two people walking through a woods in March. One of them stops because he sees something "Far in the maples, pale" and wonders if it is a ghost. His companion says that it is but "Paradise-in-Bloom," a floral portent of spring, but since it is only March and "Such white luxuriance" is more typical of May, he has to convince both himself and his companion.

The poem's final stanza clarifies the significance of the event. The speaker states that they both have stood for a moment "in a strange world," realizing that they have not really beheld the flower and breaking the silence to reveal that they have actually witnessed "A young beech clinging to its last year's leaves," a clear sign that nature is still deep in winter.

Frost uses the encounter with nature to comment on the human tendency toward self-delusion in reaction to a hopeless situation. The man accompanying the speaker at first perceives a ghost, a symbol of anything frightening. The speaker deceives himself into believing that he is observing the flower, a symbol of the rejuvenation of spring. However, the speaker finally admits that what he has, in fact, seen is the beech tree's trying to avoid the inevitable by preserving its beauty instead of moving naturally into winter. Instead of lingering in the past, the speaker, on the other hand, seems overly eager to move into the future, looking for the Paradise-in-Bloom before its time. Still, both the speaker and the tree delude themselves by refusing simply to exist in winter, one clinging to the pleasant past with fear of the future and the other longing in vain for a more hopeful future.

References and further reading: Poirier, *Knowing.*

Melissa Simpson

BOY'S WILL, A (1913) was Frost's first commercially published book of poetry. It was preceded only by the privately printed *Twilight* **(1894).** Published in London by **David Nutt** in 1913, an American edition was not published until 1915 when **Henry Holt and Company** of New York issued it simultaneously with the American publication of Frost's second book, *North of Boston* **(1914).** The book was dedicated to Frost's wife, **Elinor Miriam Frost**.

The title was taken from the refrain of Henry Wadsworth Longfellow's poem "My Lost Youth": "A boy's will is the wind's will / And the thoughts of youth are long, long thoughts." Longfellow was a favorite poet to whom Frost paid tribute in the uncollected poem "The Later Minstrel," in which he wrote of Longfellow as "one knocking at your heart, / With perfect songs to sing" (*see* R. Frost, *Collected*, 511–12, for text of the poem).

After having settled in **England** in 1912, Frost went through the packet of poems he had brought with him to see if he had enough to put together as a small volume. Sorting through them, he tossed some in the fireplace, but with others, particularly the early lyrics, he began to see a unifying theme, that of a youth who progresses from solitude toward fellowship, from a fear of life to love. After adding one or two new poems, he found enough self-confidence to approach a publisher.

Being directed to the office of David Nutt and Company on Bloomsbury Street, he made an appointment. When he returned, he met with the widow of Nutt's son, who had taken over the business after the death of her husband. Frost did not feel in any way encouraged after the interview, but nonetheless he left his manuscript with Mrs. Nutt. A week later he received a letter from her with a proposal that the firm have first right to his next four books, verse or **prose**, and a few months later, on or about 1 April 1913, *A Boy's Will* was published.

Frost originally divided the book into three numbered sections, and each poem, with the exception of **"Going for Water"** and **"Reluctance,"** was glossed in the table of contents. The gloss for **"Into My Own,"** for example, read, "The youth is persuaded that he will be rather more than less himself for having forsworn the world"; for **"Ghost House,"** the gloss read, "He is happy in society of his choosing"; for **"My November Guest,"** "He is in love with being misunderstood"; and so forth. Frost liked to tell stories about how he somewhat haphazardly spread out his manuscripts on the floor and picked some, almost at random, to create his first book. He then added the glosses to give the poems a more connected look than they may have originally had. The glosses were first conceived of in the first person, but Frost later hoped to mask the deeply personal aspect of the poems by hiding behind the mythic third-person "youth" of the glosses. The glosses were omitted from later editions of *A Boy's Will*.

Frost appears, however, to have put a much greater effort into the creation of a particular type of book, representative of one aspect of his poetic output, than he would later admit. Such intentionality is made apparent when one looks at the poems that were written or begun prior to the publication of his first book. In Cramer's *Robert Frost among His Poems*, one can find a detailed list of poems from each of Frost's books from his second to his last that could possibly have been included in *A Boy's Will*; additional bibliographical information is also available, charting the complex development of Frost's first volume.

Although the earliest reviews of Frost's first book were disappointing, important reviews soon began to appear. In England, Flint commented, "I have tried to find in these poems what is most characteristic of Mr Frost's poetry, and I think it is this: direct observation of the object and immediate correlation with the emotion—spontaneity, subtlety in the evocation of moods, humour, an ear for silences." Abercrombie wrote that the effect of each poem "burns out, as a rule, rather quickly; but while it is burning, substance and fire are completely at one, and at the end we are not left with embers, but with the sense of a swift and memorable experience." Back in America, **Pound**'s review revealed his scorn of American editors and contained his judgment of *A Boy's Will* as "a little raw," but he offered much praise that helped bring Frost's work to the forefront.

References and further reading: The texts of the poems omitted from *A Boy's Will* appear in R. Frost, *Collected*, 524–26, and in Cramer, *Frost among His Poems*, 227–30. See also Abercrombie; Flint; R. Frost, *Poetry and Prose*, 244–57; Parini, *A Life*, 119–22; Pound, Rev.; Richardson, *Ordeal*, 104–9; Thompson, *Early Years*, chap. 29; Walsh.

Jeffrey S. Cramer

"BRAVADO." *See* **"Five Nocturnes."**

BREAD LOAF SCHOOL OF ENGLISH AND WRITERS' CONFERENCE. The Bread Loaf Graduate School of English was founded by Middlebury College in 1920, in the Green Mountains of Vermont; in 1926 the Bread Loaf Writers' Conference, the first of its kind in the United States, was added to the summer program. The school is in session from late June to mid-August; the Writers' Conference runs during the last two weeks of August. Both institutions were among Frost's favorite organizations for sound education and writing experience, and he contributed much to the purposes and spirit of the school and conference.

Frost's first contact with Bread Loaf was in 1921, when he was scheduled to speak to the graduate students of English on "The Responsibilities of Teachers of Composition." During the next forty-two summers Frost attended thirty-nine sessions of the school, missing only those in 1922, 1926, and 1932. His presence, personality, and educational philosophy shaped the spirit and curriculum of the Bread Loaf School of English, with special emphasis upon American literature and writing courses. Each summer early in July he gave a poetry reading in the Little Theatre, and he often spoke informally in the Barn at Bread Loaf to the students, most of whom were high school teachers of English. Following the death of **Elinor Frost** in 1938, a scholarship in her honor was established at the Bread Loaf School.

When Theodore Morrison became director of the Bread Loaf Writers' Conference in 1932, Frost assumed a major role in molding its essence and objectives in promoting good writing. For over thirty summers Frost was the literary lion at Bread Loaf. The poet's love of Bread Loaf led him in 1939 to buy the Homer Noble Farm, almost within shouting distance west of the Bread Loaf campus. Thereafter, he was not merely a visiting lecturer but a resident of Bread Loaf and spent about six months each year, from May through October, on his farm. For the last twenty-three years of his life Frost was a living presence on the Bread Loaf campus. On his farm he received a steady stream of famous literary figures and visitors from Europe and the United States, and on occasion faculty members and students at the Bread Loaf School talked with him in his cabin. Each summer he attended literary lectures, concerts, and plays at the school, and his frequent presence at the Writers' Conference raised its prestige as the model for many other such conferences. Frost enjoyed excellent relationships with two directors of the School, H. G. Owen (1938–1942) and **Reginald L. Cook** (1944–1963), and with directors of the Writers' Conference, Theodore Morrison (1932–1955) and John Ciardi (1955–1963).

Both the School of English and the Writers' Conference were important to Frost. Better than any other academic institutions with which Frost was connected, they fulfilled his strong beliefs of what constitutes good education in literature and sound pedagogical methods in teaching writing. The informal atmosphere at Bread Loaf, the friendly personal relationships between teachers and students, realized completely Frost's ideal of "education by presence" and resulted in a direct humanistic and aesthetic approach to literature as "a living tradition," free from the stultifying apparatus of research and the dry-as-dust techniques of scientific scholarship. Amid its mountain ranges the spirit of Bread Loaf created a magical sense of community that often penetrated to the bones of its faculty, students, and writers, stimulating them to their best efforts in literary studies and writing, causing many to return summer after summer, as Frost did for thirty-nine years. *See also* **Untermeyer, Louis**.

References and further reading: G. K. Anderson; Bain and Duffy; T. Morrison, *Bread Loaf*; Stanlis, "Acceptable" and *Frost at Bread Loaf.*

Peter J. Stanlis

"BROKEN DROUGHT, THE," first published in the *Atlantic Monthly* (Apr. 1947) with the more revealing title "But He Meant It," appears as the penultimate poem in *Steeple Bush* **(1947)**, one of a dozen poems labeled "Editorials" in the book's last subdivision.

The **sonnet** tells a story of an interrupted jeremiad but seems to conclude that persistent naysayers are undaunted by signs of hope. The drama is simple: A "prophet of disaster," declaiming the terrible future of his drought-stricken country, is interrupted by the sound of rain outside; he grows silent in confusion, then spits, "As Shakespeare says . . . / Good orators *will* do when they are out" (*As You Like It* IV.i.75–76). But the prophet's theory is unchanged, though his voice is silent: "Earth would soon / Be uninhabitable." Though the poem may be a simple mockery of the foiled prophet, the last two lines suggest that Frost does not so certainly intend to separate himself from the final questioning about earth's uninhabitability.

References and further reading: Marcus, *Explication*; Maxson; Nitchie; Parini, *A Life.*

Douglas Watson

"BROOK IN THE CITY, A," is a twenty-four-line poem written in iambic pentameter. The poem first appeared in the *New Republic* (9 Mar. 1921) and was subsequently published in *New Hampshire* **(1923)**. Frost laments a pastoral scene engulfed by urban expansion. A farmhouse and its surrounding land have been converted to fit with the new cityscape. While "the farmhouse lingers," it must now "wear / A number." The other changes seem more severe: "the meadow grass" has been "cemented down" and apple trees have been "sent to hearth-stone flame." However, to some extent, such occurrences have precedent and can be accepted. But the swiftness and permanence of change seem to shock Frost, who has seen the transformation within his lifetime. If urbanization is to be regarded as progress, one must reconcile oneself to such change. Yet the fate of the brook is something that Frost cannot accept. His memories of the waterway are nostalgic: It once affectionately "held the house as in an elbow-crook." Indeed, Frost had engaged in friendly compromise with nature. While placing his hand in the water, he made the brook "leap my knuckle," but he remained subject to the power of its currents. The subjugation of the brook to the city undermines its natural properties. The "fetid darkness" in which the water is forced "to live and run" underlines its bleakness. The new equilibrium between the city and nature is uneasy, indeed. Frost asks whether the "thoughts" of the stifled brook might "not have risen" to "keep / This new-built city from both work and sleep." *See also* **Nature Poet and Naturalist**.

References and further reading: For brief but useful identification of references and sources, see Cramer, *Frost among His Poems*, 82.

Craig Monk

"BROWN'S DESCENT (OR THE WILLY-NILLY SLIDE)" was read by Frost as "The Story of Brown and the Winter Wind" at Abbot Academy in January 1916 before its original publication in **Mountain Interval** that same year, according to Lawrance Thompson. A poem in iambic tetrameter quatrains, the semicomic narrative and the poet's reflections on it reveal one of *Mountain Interval*'s several Yankee "characters." The story of the icy slide " 'Cross lots, 'cross walls, 'cross everything' " is based on an actual incident told to Frost by his friend George H. Browne, and the title memorializes Browne rather than the person who actually experienced the "descent" years earlier.

The story is told in a straightforward tone, though the dimensions of events seem somewhat exaggerated. Brown, who farms on a hillside above a town, was caught by the wind between barn and house on an icy night, and he began to slide downward on the icy crust that covered everything. Frost supposes that persons in the town below saw Brown's lantern, like a slowly falling star, mark the path of his descent. He describes the farmer's early struggle to halt his slide, but by the time it was ended, two miles below his house, Brown had both preserved his light and so "reconciled" himself to the slide that he came down the latter portion of the hill "like a coasting child." Finally at bottom, Brown "bowed with grace to natural law" and started back toward home by a longer, less direct route than his downward one.

The tension between event and reason makes this more than a simple narrative. As the early subtitle says, Brown's slide is a "willy-nilly" affair, utterly unintended and uncontrolled. His early attempts to check the slide are frustratingly unsuccessful, but his reconciliation to it comes as a relief; he accepts a return home by an indirection that he can control as a counter to a natural intervention that he cannot. Such stoic determinism and good humor are essential to Frost's Yankee. He even acknowledges that to invest Brown "with reasons" for his actions accomplishes nothing but to keep him "standing in the cold." Thus, the poem successfully resists a moralistic interpretation and remains a sort of regional tall tale. Brown is not an unthinking victim of nature, but he is a victim nonetheless.

References and further reading: Thompson, *Triumph*, 536–37.

Douglas Watson

"BUILD SOIL—A POLITICAL PASTORAL" first appeared in print in *A Further Range* (1936), but a note included in that book indicated that the poem had been written sometime before spring of 1932 and "delivered at Columbia

University" in May of that year. Also in May 1932 in a letter to **Louis Unter-meyer**, Frost discussed some of the themes of the poem but did not refer to it directly. Frost resisted what he felt were the socialistic tendencies of the times, and he felt the antidote to misguided political policies lay in keeping close to the land. By the time of its appearance in print, in the final year of Franklin Roosevelt's first term, the poem had become even more timely. (*See also* **Politics**.)

The poem is in the form of a dialogue modeled on Virgil's First Eclogue, written around 40 B.C. An eclogue generally involves a conversation or singing contest between shepherds, usually on rural or rustic themes but often (in Virgil, at least) with allusions to politics. In the First Eclogue, a farmer and a poet (who also farms, but apparently not out of economic necessity) discuss the hard times that afflict both the countryside and the city. From Virgil, Frost borrows the context and the names of the two conversants, Tityrus and Meliboeus.

The subtitle, "A Political Pastoral," gives us a clue to Frost's purpose. **Pastoral poetry**—celebrating the land, nature, and the values supposedly inculcated in those who live close to the land—usually steers clear of overt political themes, and Frost's choice to follow Virgil's model in mixing politics with rusticity arises from his strong belief that politics and economics, anathema to life on the land, were encroaching on a way of life that had previously provided a refuge from them.

Tityrus, the farmer–poet, tells his old acquaintance Meliboeus, a poverty-stricken potato farmer, that the socialistic reforms are more of a threat than a deliverance. Meliboeus believes the times are "revolutionary bad," but Tityrus disagrees—or changes the subject to poetry. Eventually it becomes clear that Tityrus means to compare poetry to farming, as activities that require patience and solitude, and where one needs to preserve one's means of production even at the cost of lower production. From this arises the poem's central metaphor: To build soil is to fold organic material back into the dirt. He tells his friend to plow his crops under until his soil is too rich to benefit from any more. He says he will do the same with poetry, refusing to rush to market with his first thought or even his second; he will hold back until unable to do so any longer.

Frost develops the theme of holding back in various ways. One is that we withhold ourselves and our thoughts from the "market," always cautious lest we be corrupted. We must remain local, particular; we must allow ourselves to mature in the direction of our own natural development. Even the speech of another person can lead us unwittingly out of our own course, as the dialogue form of the poem dramatizes.

Here Frost shows the influence of two important philosophers. William James, in his *Psychology: Briefer Course* (1892), which Frost studied at **Harvard**, talks about "the stream of consciousness" and posits it as being identical with our individuality. The twists and turns, pauses and rushes of the stream are what make us who we are. Implicit (and made explicit by Frost, not by James) is the idea that we are most ourselves when we are most isolated, least influenced by the words and the very speech-rhythms of others.

Frost saw a parallel between James's ideas and those of Francis Bacon in *Novum Organum* (1620). Bacon wrote that we must resist the urge to generalize, that we learn the most about the world by remaining in the realm of particulars and of sense experience. We also make mistakes when we are subject to what he called "the idols of the tribe" and "the idols of the marketplace," very probably the phrase that inspired Frost's cautions about the danger of the market.

By "idols of the marketplace" Bacon means language itself as it is used in the community at large—the "marketplace." We are deluded into thinking something exists merely because there is a word for it; we are deluded by names that are vague, confused, misapplied. Most dangerous is the false generalization, and it is this that Frost means by "socialism": combining particulars into one vast generality. His example in "Build Soil" is love: Tityrus tells Meliboeus that there is no general "love" but only specific feelings, such as those between friends, between parent and child, and so on. (James himself may have pointed Frost in the direction of Bacon's philosophy when, in *Pragmatism*, he refers to the belief in absolute truth as "that typical idol of the tribe.")

Like Frost's few other didactic poems (for example, **"To a Thinker,"** which immediately follows "Build Soil" in *A Further Range*), "Build Soil" sacrifices lyricism for philosophy. Compare either poem with the sonnet **"Unharvested,"** also in *A Further Range*, with its much more lyrical treatment of the theme of holding back from market.

However, when read as a drama that enacts its theme, "Build Soil" comes off better than a cursory reading would suggest. By the end it is clear that Tityrus has influenced Meliboeus's thinking, just as he has warned him that the market would do, but he has also succeeded in making Meliboeus aware of the influence and has thus, in a sense, saved him—or taught him to save himself. The course of the conversation has taught Meliboeus the truth of Tityrus's claims, and in the final lines it is Meliboeus who expresses caution about Frost's broadly construed "socialism": "We're too unseparate. And going home / From company means coming to our senses." In his essay "On Taking Poetry" Frost discusses his ideas about the stream of consciousness and the importance of solitude in keeping that stream on its course.

References and further reading: Francis Bacon's *Novum Organum* is usefully synopsized in *Masterpieces of World Philosophy*, ed. Frank N. Magill (New York: Harper-Collins, 1990); William James's *Psychology: Briefer Course* is included in *William James: Writings, 1878–1899* (New York: Library of America, 1992); *Pragmatism* is included in *William James: Writings, 1902–1910* (New York: Library of America, 1987), and James's indirect reference to Bacon is on page 591; Virgil's First Eclogue in Latin with facing-page English translation appears in *Virgil: The Eclogues* (London: Penguin, 1984); Frost's essay "On Taking Poetry" is reprinted in R. Frost, *Collected*; see also R. Frost, *Letters to Untermeyer*, 222; Parini, *A Life*, 278–82.

Richard Wakefield

"BURSTING RAPTURE" first appeared in *Steeple Bush* **(1947)**. The poem finds **science** to blame for the loss of a simpler time and for the possibility of the complete destruction of humanity. In this Italian **sonnet** Frost uses the octave to pose the problem. The content is parallel to the form in that the speaker is presenting his problem to a physician: He can't stand the strain of the growing body of science overtaking everything, even farming. At the turn of the sonnet the physician begins speaking in glibly reassuring tones, explaining that what the patient feels is common and that all who suffer from this ailment will find relief in one final burst, that of the bomb.

The sestet also introduces a sexual connotation in humanity's passionate grappling for **science**. The title, as well, suggests a comparison between the atom bomb and sexual release. While Frost often pits science against nature, here he seems to be pairing the two in terms of orgasmic rush. That this comparison is a patronizing appeasement from the knowledgeable physician to the simple farmer suggests how the common man might easily fall victim to the seductive elements of technology.

References and further reading: Barry, 79–98; O. Evans; Rood.

Belinda D. Bruner

"BUT GOD'S OWN DESCENT" is an excerpt from **"Kitty Hawk"** (lines 219–24 and 246–57, joined as one segment without intervening white space) that Frost used to introduce his 1962 collection of poems *In the Clearing*. Apart from its context in "Kitty Hawk," we may wonder why Frost chose these lines especially to introduce his last volume of poetry. The answer would seem to lie in a parallel Frost undoubtedly intended between what God did in limiting Himself by becoming a man and what a poet does in the act of composition (the charge of "the soul's ethereal / Into the material"). In both acts there is great descent and great risk. "But God's own descent / Into flesh" is parallel to "risking spirit / In substantiation" and may be taken as the key thought behind the whole poetic act as Frost conceived it. Further, Frost intends another parallel that overlaps the first, namely, that a poet, in working out a poem's thought and forms, is like one flying, a new Wright brother, as it were, soaring at a Kitty Hawk of the mind. Both parallels taken together, God and Kitty Hawk, make us appreciate that Frost conceived of all poetic thought, before it appears on a blank page, as unconstrained and soaring flight in the unlimited regions of the mind of the poet. But he realizes that to become a poem thoughts cannot remain thoughts unformed and continuously varying permutations on ideas and images. Eventually, the poet must risk his thought, transforming it, confining it to permanent form (its "substantiation") on paper in a great descent—one as majestic as was God's own descent into human flesh. To strike a parallel between God and a poet is not an act of blasphemy in Frost's mind but an act of worship. All of his poetry was an offering to God, as Frost wrote to one of his religious friends, G. R. Elliot (1947): "My fear of God has settled down into a deep inward fear that my best offering may not prove acceptable in his sight." A year later, in a letter to Lawrance Thompson, he specifically calls his poetry an offering: "[Prayer] might be an expression of the hope I have that my offering of verse on the altar may be acceptable in His sight Whoever He is." That Robert Frost should begin his last book of "offerings" to the Lord by excerpting a passage from "Kitty Hawk" is unorthodox but fully in keeping with Frost's essentially private theology.

References and further reading: R. Frost, *Selected Letters*, 525, 530, contains the letters by Frost to Elliot and Thompson; *Letters*, 555–56, records the correspondence between Frost and Rabbi Victor E. Reichert in which Frost searches for the source of the final lines of *A Masque of Mercy*: "May my sacrifice / Be found acceptable in Heaven's sight."

Larry R. Isitt

"[BUT OUTER SPACE]," originally titled "The Astronomer," was first published in *A Remembrance Collection of New Poems* (1959), a commemorative chapbook published for Frost's eighty-fifth birthday gala at New York's Waldorf-Astoria. Subsequently, it appeared in Frost's final volume, ***In the Clearing* (1962)**.

To Mordecai Marcus, the poem suggests the limitations of the successes of space travel, and Walter Stiller, noting the tension in much of Frost between the yearning for order and the yearning for discovery, offers comments useful in appreciating Frost's short lyric.

References and further reading: Marcus, *Explication*; Stiller.

Andy Duncan

C

"CABIN IN THE CLEARING, A," written about August 1950, was Frost's 1951 **Christmas poem** and was first published in booklet form. Cramer notes that the poem was later published with a dedication to Frost's friend and publisher Alfred Edwards and appears in Frost's last collection, *In the Clearing* **(1962)**, lending the collection its title.

Reginald Cook notes that Frost once described the poem as being "about knowing ourselves," a point that Richard Wilbur also raises in his review of *In the Clearing* in the 25 March 1962 *New York Herald Tribune*. According to Linda Wagner, Wilbur refers to "A Cabin in the Clearing" as a "charming" conversation between the chimney smoke and garden mist, the result of which is a philosophical "clearing": "a little area of human coherence" and "clarification." As the smoke and mist eavesdrop on the conversation between the couple in the cabin, they realize, however, that the people in the cabin have not clarified their existence, but rather, through their talk and unrest, they continue to probe the mystery of who and where they are. Any clarification the people acquire, then, is gradual, gained through their continual learning and by asking "anyone there is to ask" and driven by their "fond faith" that "accumulated fact / Will of itself take fire and light the world up."

Even if they do come to know who they are, and thereby discover where they are, the smoke argues that "who they are is too much to believe." The mist, however, has the last word, admiring the fact that the people continue to talk in the dark even after turning out the light: "Putting the lamp out has not put their thought out." The value of this continual searching is a theme that Frost seems to keep returning to and one that also informs earlier poems such as **"Neither Out Far Nor in Deep."** Coming late in his career, Frost's "A Cabin in the Clearing" perhaps represents his acceptance of the prevailing mist and smoke that cloud our vision and veil our access to complete knowledge about ourselves and the world, as well as his appreciation for those rare moments of clearing.

References and further reading: R. Cook, *Living Voice*, 190; Cramer, *Frost among His Poems*, 161; Pritchard, *Literary Life*, 238, 257; Wagner cites reviews of *In the Clearing* that discuss the strengths of "A Cabin in the Clearing," 245, 265.

Gary Totten

"CANIS MAJOR" was first published as "On a Star-Bright Night" in the Books Section of the *New York Herald Tribune* (22 Mar. 1925). The poem was later published in *West-Running Brook* (1928). Critical attention has focused on the poem's debt to **Emerson**. Noting the hierarchical division between the speaker as the "poor underdog" and the sublime "great Overdog," readers have been divided about where Frost stands with regard to the imagined union of the individual and nature. Modernist writers generally denied Transcendentalism's claim that the world's mysteries could be apprehended through a mystical union with nature. The universe was too immense to understand, and it was more appropriate to deal with the world impersonally. Some critics find the whimsical use of metaphor in "Canis Major" to be modern in this respect. Others, however, believe Frost continues Emerson's idea that we are able to redeem our identity in an industrialized world because we, as humans, are part of nature. Clearly, in this poem Frost wrestles with the human's situation in the face of modernism.

References and further reading: Lentricchia, in *Modern Poetics*, explains Frost's comic tone with regard to the redemption of the self through imagination; Nitchie reviews critical commentary on Frost's use of metaphor; see also Waggoner, "Humanistic Idealism" and *American Poets*, particularly the chapter "The Strategic Retreat," where he outlines Frost's Emersonian heritage.

John R. Woznicki

"CARPE DIEM" first appeared in the *Atlantic Monthly* (Sept. 1938) and was collected in *A Witness Tree* (1942). According to George Bagby, Frost deviates from the traditional notion that one ought to "seize the day" in terms of its association with the immediate present. As Reginald Cook notes, the poem suggests that the present is often supersaturated with life and therefore must be looked upon with retrospective distance in order that one can glean meaning from the otherwise stultifying immediacy of the moment. The poem suggests that only with age is one able to appreciate life. In this way, the narrator of "Carpe Diem" takes care to designate a dwelling place for life in time: "It lives less in the present," the poem reads, "Than in the future always, / And less in both together / Than in the past." Reuben A. Brower points out that the present can be contained only when seen as a possession of the past. That is why "Age" knows not whether the "two quiet children" are going "homeward, / Or outward from the village, / Or . . . churchward." Significantly, he waits until they can no longer hear him to bid them, "Be happy, happy, happy, / And seize the day of pleasure," suggesting that only when the children's present day has aged will they be able to "seize" it. In other words, the present moment must first be experienced before its meaning can be fully appreciated.

References and further reading: Bagby, *Nature*, 97; Brower, 227; R. Cook, *Living Voice*, 293.

Alex Ambrozic

"CASE FOR JEFFERSON, A," first appeared in *Steeple Bush* **(1947)**. Written in couplets with an extra eleventh line, the poem is an outcry against the political intellectualism that Frost thought was changing the country (*see also* **Politics**). Frost's disdain of the social attitudes (Freudian) and the political leanings (Marxist) of "Harrison" in the poem is heightened because the man is a fellow Yankee. To Thomas Jefferson, such would indeed be a case of democracy gone wrong. Even though the poet admits that Harrison loves the country too, he believes this new Democrat is supporting destructive programs and labels the man's intellect as merely adolescent.

Reginald Cook reports that Frost singled out "A Case for Jefferson" as "dated": "See, that's the period poem. That's what they call dated. . . . I said to a person high up in the government lately, I said, 'As long as all my educated friends and Mrs. Roosevelt think that socialism is inevitable and can't be avoided and has got to come that way, why don't you and I join in and hurry it up and get it over with? It couldn't last. . . . I wouldn't favor that policy.' " Selden Rodman notes that in a public lecture at **Harvard** in 1948 Frost criticized "A Case for Jefferson": "My, that's bad. I don't ever want to write like that again!"

References and further reading: R. Cook, *Living Voice*, 125; S. Rodman, 44.

Sarah R. Jackson

"CENSUS-TAKER, THE," was published first in the *New Republic* (6 Apr. 1921) and subsequently in *New Hampshire* **(1923)**. In this monologue in blank verse, Frost describes the actions and thoughts of a census-taker whose job it is to count people. Upon arriving at an abandoned logging camp, the census-taker sees only an empty house. Through the description of the house, now fallen into ruin, and the description of the forest that surrounds it, Frost examines what Potter calls "the vulnerability of man in an empty universe."

For both the house and the universe surrounding the logging camp, only the memories of the past are left. The poem's conclusion is seen by critics to reflect the ineffectuality of humanity in an empty universe.

References and further reading: Doreski; Potter, 112; Stott.

Chris-Anne Stumpf

"CHOOSE SOMETHING LIKE A STAR," also published with the title "Take Something Like a Star" in *Selected Poems* **(1963)**, first appeared in *Come In and Other Poems* (1943), compiled by **Louis Untermeyer**, and then in "An Afterword" to *The Complete Poems of Robert Frost 1949*. A serious purpose finds playful expression in the poem, which, as Frost explained in a short statement for *Poet's Choice*, "mingle[s] science and spirit" while "playing the words."

The poem is related to earlier poems, such as **"On Looking Up by Chance at the Constellations"** and **"The Most of It,"** in which Frost confronts his version of the pathetic fallacy. The tone here is difficult to follow because it is mixed. The apostrophe of the opening line invokes the conventional attitudes of reverence, query, and supplication associated with that device, but there is condescension in the lines following. The digressive qualification of lines 4–5 at first seems deferential, but then, as the grammar unfolds, the poet asserts the right to speak through the witty (and gratuitous) explanation of line 5, which recalls the sixteenth- and seventeenth-century poetic penchant for "Metaphysical" intellectualization. The joke in line 11 also relies on the wit of Tudor lyric poetry: The imploring turns momentarily desperate and demanding; the star's response echoes the clichéd hyperbole of "burning" desire in courtly love poems, but this response's "taciturn" matter-of-factness, which results from both the plainness that "something" lends to it and the literalization of the courtly simile, undercuts the intensity of the human speaker's need. The scientific bent of the poem's middle further complicates the tone of the whole, since it seems slightly incongruous (though typically Frostian), given the archaic poetics of the opening.

The plain vagueness of "something" is crucial to the poem. Richard Poirier stresses that the word "is not simply an affectation of country talk to cover an uncustomary bookishness," but he misreads its meaning slightly when he claims that "something" is synonymous with "anything, any kind of work done by anyone that can extend the capability of human dreaming." Frost probably does not extend to us an invitation to such relativism, since "something," after all, is of "a certain height." This use of "something" is related to the provisional "something" in **"The Exposed Nest,"** which stands for a protective fiction "interposed between[. . .] sight / And too much world at once." Like "some obscurity of cloud," "something like a star" (but not a star itself) stands in the way of our domination by bare fact and brute power. Elizabeth Shepley Sergeant suggests that the last line contains "a direct reference" to the beginning of Isaiah 26, an allusion that is in stark contrast to the direct reference to Keats's **sonnet**, which longs for eternal erotic gratification. We should remember that Keats rejects the meaning of the star as a remote, godlike watcher (a "sleepless eremite") and tries to make it a paradoxical emblem of passionate human constancy. For Frost to compare his bright star to this one is potentially counter to his ostensible intention to invoke the authority of Keats, leaving us to decide whether the biblical and Romantic allusions work together or in conflict.

The poem also had a range of private meanings for Frost. He explained several of these in his talk "On Extravagance," and in an interview with Richard Poirier, Frost alluded to the poem when asked his opinion of the Beat Poets. Such comments suggest that Frost regarded the poem as a statement of literary criticism in addition to all of its other purposes.

References and further reading: Frost's "On Extravagance" can be found in R. Frost, *Collected*, 902–26; Poirier, *Knowing*, 300; Sergeant, 382–83.

Gary Roberts

CHRISTMAS POEMS. In 1929, as Joseph Blumenthal of the Spiral Press was setting the type for Robert Frost's *Collected Poems* **(1930)**, it occurred to him that the poem **"Christmas Trees"** would make an attractive greeting if printed in a handsome typeface on specially made paper. Upon receiving permission from the publisher, **Henry Holt and Company**, Blumenthal printed 275 copies of the poem, retaining 75 and sending 200 to the Holt firm and two of its executives. Frost later became so intrigued with the venture that he requested 6 copies for himself (which Blumenthal had to retrieve from recipients). The next such poem, **"Two Tramps in Mud Time,"** was not issued until 1934. The edition was expanded to 775 copies and the number of senders to six (each of whose names was printed on the title page of all the allotted copies). Thus was launched an unbroken succession of thirty-four imprints that continued through Frost's last Christmas. (In some years more than one greeting was produced.)

In the context of Robert Frost's poetic oeuvre, the term "Christmas poem" is somewhat misleading. Only two of these thirty-five special printings bear any direct relevance to Christmas itself. Two are actually prose extracts, one a section from an unfinished play. All but one appear elsewhere (usually in one of the collected editions). However, these imprints, consisting of beautifully designed text on carefully selected paper, and running up to twenty pages in length, highlighted the Christmas seasons of roughly the final three decades of the poet's life (excepting the Depression years, 1930–1933).

Twenty-five of the total—by far the majority—were printed at the Spiral Press by Blumenthal (who, beginning with *Collected Poems*, 1930, became the principal designer of Frost titles issued by Holt). Other Christmas poems were either private press imprints or else were printed at the direction of Frost **collectors** (e.g., Earle J. Bernheimer, Clifton Waller Barrett). What distinguishes the Blumenthal imprints, aside from their typographic design, are the graphic images that adorn the poems. **J. J. Lankes** was one of the eleven well-known artists who produced these designs, but the list included Thomas Nason, whose woodcuts Blumenthal greatly admired, and others such as Leonard Baskin and Fritz Eichenberg.

Although much admired and avidly sought, the Christmas poems pose formidable challenges for any collector intent upon assembling a complete set of all thirty-five titles. This is mainly because some of the poems were printed in small editions (e.g., **"Two Leading Lights,"** 1944, 52 copies; "The Falls," 1947, 60 copies) and are thus quite scarce. Also, the list of senders grew very rapidly over the years. For instance, the 9,155 copies of **"Away"** (1958) were divided among twenty-two entities. Therefore, a full set of this printing of the poem would constitute twenty-two variants, each containing the name of a different sender on its title page. The total number of variant sender pages of all thirty-five poems runs into the hundreds. The size of the editions also grew to mammoth proportions, finally reaching 17,055 in 1962 (the final Christmas of Frost's life) with "The Prophets Really Prophesy as Mystics / The Commentators Merely by Statistics."

References and further reading: The Christmas poems are given detailed bibliographic treatment in a separate chapter of Crane's *Descriptive Catalogue*; Blumenthal discusses them in more general terms in *Spiral Press* and *Frost and His Printers*.

Welford Dunaway Taylor

"CHRISTMAS TREES: A CHRISTMAS CIRCULAR LETTER" is the second poem in **Mountain Interval (1916)**, where it was first published. An epistle, the poem belongs to a time when the holiday memory of a stocking with an orange inside would last a lifetime. The relentless market forces, personified by the stranger in the poem, will return, perhaps as developers ready to cut roads, not just trees. Meanwhile, the farmer, after his epiphany, plans to enjoy the beauty of his firs, and he wishes he could enclose his trees in envelopes, along with Christmas greetings. Sergeant records that in 1915 Frost and the children did send the original poem, with a sketch by Lesley. "Christmas Trees" has been published as a children's picture book.

References and further reading: L. Frost, *Derry Journals*; R. Frost, *Christmas Trees*; Sergeant, 177.

Nancy Vogel

"CLEAR AND COLDER" was originally printed in *Direction* in 1934. Following its debut, the poem was subsequently revised by Frost for inclusion in *A Further Range* **(1936)**. It is perilously easy to confuse this poem with another uncollected work bearing almost the same title: "Clear and Colder—Boston Common," one of Frost's earliest compositions. The speaker is a witchlike woman reading a recipe for autumn that has been dictated to her by "Wind" in her "Weather Primer." According to her playful prescription, one must travel great distances in order to gather just the right ingredients: a pinch of summer and a drop of "leftover winter"; yet despite the seeming lightness of its tone, the poem presents more than a fanciful honorarium to fall. Richard Poirier discusses "Clear and Colder" in the context of other poems by Frost in which human beings attempt, through the use of recipes, witches brews, and designs, to effect a momentary control over the accidents of life.

References and further reading: Poirier, *Knowing.*

Susan M. Stone

"CLIFF DWELLING, A," was published first in *Steeple Bush* **(1947).** It is similar to **"A Missive Missile"** and **"To an Ancient"** in that in each poem the speaker raises the question of the possibility of sending messages into the future, of leaving something behind with the capacity to endure. Frost deals in this poem specifically with archeology and ancient ruins.

In "A Cliff Dwelling" the narrator stands at a distance from the ancient caves of the New Mexico cliff dwellers and at first seems uncertain of what he sees. The "golden sky" and "sandy plain" seem to merge into one another. But closer scrutiny is rewarded with a series of more acute observations that grow in intensity until they are swallowed up in wonder.

At first "No habitation meets the eye," but then the reader is stopped by the word "Unless," which changes the course of the poem. The narrator notices that the "spot of black" is not merely a "stain" against the sandstone cliffs but a "cavern hole" where someone lived out the struggle for existence. In line 10, "I see" speaks of the message that is being passed down to the speaker. What is seen is not merely the sole of the laborer's foot but also the callus, which represents the necessary labor and effort of raising a family and surviving. That labor and effort are necessary for survival is a theme found throughout Frost's work and is the essence of the message that is passed on.

References and further reading: Hadas; Poirier, *Knowing.*

Wm. Thomas Hill

"CLOSED FOR GOOD" is a poem with an unusual textual history. It first appeared in booklet form as Frost's 1948 **Christmas poem.** In *The Complete Poems of Robert Frost 1949*, a section entitled "An Afterword" appeared between the poems of *Steeple Bush* **(1947)** and "A Masque of Reason" (*see* **Drama**). "An Afterword" consisted of a trio of previously published poems: **"Choose Something Like a Star," "Closed for Good,"** and **"From Plane to Plane."** "An Afterword" continued to appear as a section in the 1954, 1955, and 1963 editions of the selected poems but contained only two poems: "Closed for Good" and "Choose Something Like A Star" (retitled "Take Something Like a Star" for the 1963 edition).

In 1962, a revised version of "Closed for Good" was published as part of *In the Clearing* **(1962).** In the earlier location the poem seems to make a comment on a "complete" poetic system, a system now closed for good. But in its second location the poem is part of a book about Frost's poetry: It is one of the "letters to you in verse" addressed personally to his readers, helping them to understand his poetry. This final book of letter-verse is about seeing down into the clouded water of his poetry; the caption explains, "And wait to watch the water clear, I may," suggesting that the title *In the Clearing* could be read "In the Clarifying."

That Frost uses the poem in these two locations suggests that it deals with the clarifying of his *Complete Poetry* by readers after Frost is finished writing it.

In its 1948 first edition, "Closed for Good" was six stanzas; the form was maintained for the collected and selected editions of 1949, 1954, and 1955. In 1958, Frost told Elizabeth Shepley Sergeant that he was "trying out a new version of four stanzas and changing one word" during his public appearances. When the poem appeared in *In the Clearing*, the first stanza (lines 1–6) was deleted, and two word changes occurred: the word "And" became "They" in line 7 and the word "brush" became "spread" in line 24. When Edward Connery Lathem's edition of *The Poetry of Robert Frost* was published in 1969, the poem was presented in five stanzas and the words "And" and "brush" were restored.

Although "Closed for Good" has not received much critical attention, the poem stands as a commentary on Frost's inheritance from the past and his legacy to the future. Frost credits the poets of the past with having "cut this road to last." Rather than claiming a place for himself on that literary road, Frost pays homage to his predecessors and then notes his own "slowness," which we might read as his careful observation of nature, his advancing age, or even his worries about his poetic powers. In the poem's final stanza, Frost envisions the "winter" of his life, subsuming his identity into the natural image of the animal footprint, remaining true to the natural world he has gone to such pains to document. His legacy is left for any traveler (and reader) to find. Whether his tracks will be noticed is irrelevant, but they will be there.

References and further reading: Crane, *Descriptive Catalogue*, 88, provides an invaluable reference guide with complete bibliographic information on the extensive Barrett collection of Frost documents; Doyle, *Poetry*, examines structural and poetic principles in Frost's poetry, 17; Lentricchia and Lentricchia, 19–29; Richardson, "Frost's 'Closed,' " presents a detailed textual history of the poem.

Diane N. Hulett and Gerard Quinn

"CLOUD SHADOW, A," first published in *A Witness Tree* (1942), is a brief, playful, relatively unknown narrative poem that examines the relationship between art, nature, and the human imagination. Apparently set in winter, the poem depicts an encounter between a melancholy speaker and a personified, sportive breeze that disturbs the pages of the speaker's open book. Imagining that the breeze rustles the pages in search of a poem about spring, the speaker denies that such a poem can exist. Entrenched in the present moment, he is unable to imagine either the return of spring or the poet who would write about it. The breeze, however, is annoyed at the speaker's doubts, and a cloud shadow passes over her face.

Although the speaker does not reflect on the meaning of the incident, apparently nature influences his understanding of himself and his art. The breeze is perhaps a projection of the speaker's own desire for renewal as a poet. And although the breeze reproaches him for his pessimism, the speaker seems to be seeking inspiration in the wisdom of the natural world.

References and further reading: Marcus, *Explication.*

Audra Rouse

"CLUSTER OF FAITH": "ACCIDENTALLY ON PURPOSE"; "A NEVER NAUGHT SONG"; "VERSION"; "A CONCEPT SELF-CONCEIVED"; "FORGIVE, O LORD." Each of these poems from *In the Clearing* **(1962)** considers the individual's dilemma of understanding and expressing the possible connection between life on earth and a purposeful God. If there is a consistent statement of faith in them, it is that human reason is insufficient to comprehend existence fully.

In "Accidentally on Purpose" (originally published as Frost's 1960 **Christmas poem**), theories of blind evolution are debunked. "Never believe it," the poet implores: There *was* a purpose in the development of the universe, even if the "scientific wits" cannot precisely state it. Instinct and experience of "love at [first] sight" are enough to show that there is in Creation "intention, purpose, and design."

In "A Never Naught Song," the target is another scientific theory, the "big bang" of Creation. Frost deconstructs the image of an "atomic One" exploded into cosmic separation by reversion to a more primitive, more natural figure, the Norse myth of the Yggdrasill, a great ash tree that holds together heaven, earth, and hell with its roots and branches. This tree's purpose and potential, according to Frost, are contained in the tree's tiny seed. Thus, in the "infra-small" source of all life, posited by atomic scientists, there is no less a purpose or design than in the larger, expanding universe. There was "never naught" but "always thought." As in "Accidentally on Purpose," a unity of all life seems no less real to Frost because human reason cannot conceive it.

"Version," as Cramer notes, was first published incompletely in *In the Clearing*. It is the most oblique of the poems in the group. Interpretation is made even more problematic by Edward C. Lathem's reconstruction and lengthening of the poem from manuscript evidence. Once again Frost seems to debunk a form of modern thinking about the nature of the universe, this time borrowing the figure of an "Archer" who shoots an arrow into what he presumes to be nothingness. In the longer version of the poem, the stated target of the arrow is the "non-existence / Of the Phoenix pullet," but the arrow is "blunted," even "splattered" by what turns out to be "matter." Frost's argument against nonbeing is both mythological and philosophical. The Phoenix, though it may appear to be nothing in destruction, is always capable of regeneration; and Plato's argument regarding nonbeing, a rebuttal to Parminides's categories of being and nonbeing, is that there is really no such thing as nonbeing. Perhaps the Archer is a reference to Apollo, perhaps to the kindly centaur Chiron, transformed into the constellation Sagittarius (both labeled as Archer in various myths and each with its attraction to Frost); in either case, the shooting of the arrow has a comic end, for it surprises the shooter by finding a target presumed not to exist. Thus Frost has his revenge against those who would deny the importance of materiality.

"A Concept Self-Conceived" criticizes the modernist idea that the unity of the universe is a product only of human reason. Against this rationalistic oneness, Frost again argues for a simpler, more primitive creed or catechism. Better than leave the oneness of God to human choice, he prefers simply to posit unity: "never give a child a choice."

"Forgive, O Lord," a two-line prayer-promise, was originally published under the title "The Preacher" in *A Remembrance Collection of New Poems* (New York, 1959). The brevity and whim of the individual's bargaining forgiveness with God should not obscure Frost's sense of life's ironies that undergirds the poem. Our "little jokes" on God might be the various rational theories treated in the previous four poems, but God's "great big" joke on us must be that we were created with reason and vision but without real power to understand life completely.

References and further reading: For useful commentaries on most of the poems in the "Cluster," set in the context of Frost and Darwin, see Faggen.

Douglas Watson

"COCOON, THE," first appeared in the *New Republic* (9 Feb. 1927) and was subsequently collected in ***West-Running Brook* (1928)**. It is a poem in which Frost explores the implications of human isolation. Thematically similar to **"The Vantage Point,"** the poem is founded upon issues of perspective, and Frost positions himself carefully. The speaker's point of vantage in "The Cocoon" is vague, specified only by the opening phrase, "As far as I can see." The speaker's vision is an internal gaze, located within the realm of his own imagination, which effectively isolates him from the world that he views. From this location he can observe and meditate upon human community while maintaining his own protective isolation.

Thematically, Frost emphasizes the inhabitants' unnatural isolation. They keep themselves "close," a word oddly appropriate in its emphasis of a suspicious rejection of humanity, and thus they fail to interact with the society that Frost so often deemed central to a truly humane existence. As Philip Gerber notes, "Frost saw man as achieving little so long as he considers only himself, isolated from those around him." The implications are clear: A balance must be struck between the individualism that Frost advocates and the stagnation caused by a rejection of the outside world. The imagined inhabitants of the house embrace the latter tendency, and it is this refusal to interact imaginatively with the world that turns the cocoon that they are weaving into a shroud. The image of a cocoon hints of the final transformation humanity must face in death and thus creates for the inhabitants of the house a life-in-death.

References and further reading: W. French, 394; Gerber, *Frost*, 146; on the significance of vantage, see Lentricchia, *Modern Poetics*, 35–37; Stamper.

Gavin Schulz

"CODE, THE," appeared as "The Code—Heroics" in *Poetry* (Feb. 1914), after Frost took up residence in **England**. Later included in *North of Boston* **(1914)**, it was reprinted so often that Frost remarked, "It has been reprinted rather more than its share." A dramatic narrative with humorously ironic undertones, "The Code" describes how a city-bred farmer, working alongside two hired hands, unknowingly violates the unwritten code of the New England farmer, causing one of the men to stop working suddenly and leave. Attempting to explain the man's behavior, the remaining farmhand describes an earlier event involving a former employer who likewise disturbed the code. **Ezra Pound** comments in his review of *North of Boston* that the poem "has a pervasive humor, the humor of things as they are, not that of an author trying to be funny. . . . It is a great comfort to find someone who tries to give life, the life of the rural district, as a whole, evenly, and not merely as a hook to hang a joke on." Mark Richardson and James Dawes offer readings that comment on what the poem reveals about Frost's perspectives on gender and work.

References and further reading: Dawes; Feaster writes that the poem is a consideration of the socioeconomic relationship between owner and worker; R. Frost, *Selected Letters*, 233; Monteiro's "Frost's Hired Hand" suggests that an essay in the *Atlantic Monthly* (1894) entitled "The Hired Man" influenced Frost's writing of "The Code" and **"The Death of the Hired Man"**; Pound, "Modern Georgics," 130; Richardson, *Ordeal*.

Eric Leuschner

***COLLECTED POEMS* (1930, 1939).** *Collected Poems* was published by **Henry Holt and Company** on 1 November 1930. (There was also an English edition, published by Longmans, Green, in London.) The publication of the volume was one promise made to Frost during the contract negotiations for *West-Running Brook* in 1928; it contains the poems from Frost's first five books of poetry. Only minor modifications were made prior to publication: Frost removed three poems from and added one poem to the section for *A Boy's Will* **(1913)**, added two poems to the section for *Mountain Interval* **(1916)**, and added three poems to the section for *West-Running Brook*. Even before receiving and approving of his copy of *Collected Poems*, Frost was worried about its public appearance. He believed this publication might be a turning point in his career, depending on reviews. In addition, Frost was worried that critics might echo some of the attacks made against *West-Running Brook*. Although some Marxist critics, such as Granville Hicks, did repeat and elaborate upon the attacks made against *West-Running Brook*, many critics, such as Frost's friend Genevieve Taggard, published favorable reviews of the volume, and the publication became the major victory for which Frost had hoped. *Collected Poems* won the Pulitzer Prize on 2 June 1931 for being the best volume of poetry published during 1930 by an

American author (Frost's second Pulitzer). Furthermore, Frost's election to membership in the American Academy of Arts and Letters on 13 November 1930 was possibly related to the appearance of *Collected Poems* (*see also* **Awards, Honors, and Prizes**). Years later, Elizabeth Shepley Sergeant would suggest that the 1930 *Collected Poems* "stands today as a landmark, a sort of division between the poet's earlier and later work." Indeed, Frost was not finished producing poetry and would go on to publish four more major volumes of poetry and several other works.

   Collected Poems of Robert Frost (reissued from 1930) was published by Holt on 16 February 1939. (There was also an English edition published by Longmans, Green, in London.) Before this volume was published, Frost was considering leaving Holt for another publisher due to internal turmoil at Holt. Holt executives, however, convinced Frost to stay with the firm by offering a new, more lucrative contract and by persuading Frost that Blue Ribbon Books would publish a cheap reprint edition of the forthcoming *Collected Poems*, thereby increasing his earnings. The volume contains the poems from Frost's first six volumes of poetry. In addition, William M. Sloane III, from Holt, specifically asked Frost to write a special preface for this volume to distinguish the Holt edition from the Blue Ribbon Books edition. Frost, seeing the logic of the request, rose to the occasion and wrote "The Figure a Poem Makes," which also appeared in all later collections of his work, except for the Lathem edition, *The Poetry of Robert Frost* **(1969)**. The reviews of *Collected Poems* were positive. Sloane's telegram to Frost the day after publication, in part an alteration of a quotation from Horace—"You have erected a monument more lasting than bronze"—perhaps summarizes best Frost's accomplishment. In addition, on 18 January 1939, shortly before the publication of *Collected Poems*, Frost was awarded the Gold Medal for Poetry from the National Institute of Arts and Letters.

References and further reading: Sergeant, 306–7; Van Egmond, *Reception*, contains excerpts of reviews of *Collected Poems* (1930) and *Collected Poems of Robert Frost* (1939); Wagner contains full-length reprints of original reviews of *Collected Poems* (1930) and *Collected Poems of Robert Frost* (1939). Lentricchia and Lentricchia provide a list of specific poems included in each of the above entries of *Collected Poems*.

                                                                 Scott Robert Stankey

COLLECTORS AND COLLECTIONS. When Frost remarked, in a May 1916 letter to **Louis Untermeyer**, that he had "become his own salesman," for the most part he spoke figuratively. But twenty years later, when he entered into formal arrangements with the collector Earle J. Bernheimer to transform scraps of paper, notebooks, manuscripts, and inscribed books into outright commodities, he might have said much the same thing and meant it *literally*. He had managed to sell his charisma *as such*. It is an interesting case of what the German philosopher Walter Benjamin called the *aura* of uniqueness that surrounds such objects—manuscripts of printed works, signed books—in an age of mechanical reproduction. Frost pushed the effect of this aura to its limit by formalizing the means by which it is generated: In return for Bernheimer's monthly check for $150, he sent along, at more or less regular intervals, parcels of manuscripts and signed books. He even undertook on several occasions— always at the request of collectors—to copy out certain of his works again in manuscript when the "original" manuscripts no longer existed to be sold, a curious act of self-forgery whereby the "literary" value of the artifact is super- seded almost entirely by the "charismatic" value of its aura.

Frost was canny about such things. He wrote Lawrance Thompson in June 1948 about the "rarity" of his signed letters and the "value" they may or may not have "on the market at auction." This is a charming way to apologize for epistolary delinquency. Frost does his correspondents a fiscal good turn by *ne-glecting* their letters and cards. How could they not be grateful?

In a tribute read at a banquet celebrating Percy MacKaye's fiftieth birthday, Frost observed of his fellow poet: "Everybody knows how he has spread himself over the country, as with two very large wings, to get his fellow poets all fellowships at the universities." Apparently Frost's mischievous idea is that something like a quid pro quo is involved in such "tribute" banquets as these. The literati constantly bestow favors on one another, so who can trust the mo- tives of their affection and praise? It is a home truth delivered in such a forum as this. The irony, for Frost, is deft and personal. He had himself enjoyed the favors of Percy MacKaye, who helped secure his two "fellowships" at the **Uni- versity of Michigan** in the early 1920s. In other words, he, too, was "paying his tribute" to MacKaye, a writer for whom he had little respect as an artist. And we can consider Frost's relationship to Earle Bernheimer in light of this tribute to MacKaye. The ironies of that "tribute" turn on the word *fellowship*, with its various—and, in this context, wryly opposed—meanings of *camara- derie* and *stipend*. The often hearty inscriptions Frost entered into books and documents given to Bernheimer in return for his monthly check press something of the same point upon us: Such inscriptions pointedly ignore, as the playful 1948 letter to Thompson pointedly does not, the pecuniary function they serve, a fact to which Frost was undoubtedly sensitive, as the tribute to MacKaye suggests.

All ironies aside, Frost was in any case better "collected" than most twentieth- century American poets, undoubtedly because of his generosity and celebrity. But the demand for Frost's work is due also to the way his poetry was published. Many of his volumes are distinguished by fine book-making, beginning with his 1923 collection *New Hampshire*, which featured wood-cuts by the artist **J. J. Lankes**. Subsequent collections always appeared in both "trade" and more ex- pensive "limited" editions, the latter signed and numbered by Frost himself, again in an effort to make them as "rare" as possible. The poet also for a great many years issued finely printed Christmas cards, each with a poem and, typi- cally, a little illustration. These were circulated gratis to a number of friends and collectors, many of whom maintained "complete" collections of the cards.

Several aficionados undertook privately to collect Frost. In addition to Earle Bernheimer, one might name Louis Mertins, Clifton Waller Barrett, and Lawrance Thompson. Barrett's rich private collection is housed now at the University of Virginia's Clifton Waller Barrett Library. The collection is described in Joan St. C. Crane's remarkable *Descriptive Catalogue*. Thompson's papers are held now at the University of Virginia and at Princeton University's Firestone Library.

Libraries with which Frost had long-standing personal affiliations assiduously collected his manuscripts and published works. Chief among these are the **Dartmouth College** Library, the **Amherst College** Library, and the Jones Library in Amherst, Massachusetts. The Dartmouth collection, the largest single collection in existence, includes a wealth of manuscript and published materials that it would be impossible even to outline here. Scholars may search its contents, which are impeccably and thoroughly catalogued, via Dartmouth College's computer network. Two major collections are held in Massachusetts: at Amherst College, in the Robert Frost Memorial Library; and at Amherst's town library, the Jones. Both collections are of great value.

A number of other significant collections bear mentioning here: the Huntington Library's collection of Frost's early poetry; the William B. Ewert Robert Frost Collection and the **Elinor M. Frost**–Robert Frost Archive, Dimond Library, University of New Hampshire; the John Holmes Robert Frost Collection, Wessell Library, Tufts University; the Frost collection at the McCain Library, Agnes Scott College; the Frost collection at the Watkinson Library, Trinity College; the Frank P. Piskor Collection of Robert Frost at the Owen D. Young Library, St. Lawrence University, and the Frost materials in the Parkman Dexter Howe Collection, University of Florida Library.

Much of Frost's business correspondence with **Henry Holt and Company** resides now in the Holt archive at the Firestone Library, Princeton University. His extensive, fascinating correspondence with poet and critic **Louis Untermeyer** is held at the Library of Congress, in the James Madison Building. Some years ago, Frost's eldest daughter, Lesley Frost, donated the poet's personal library to New York University (NYU), where it resides to this day. Here, scholars may browse through Frost's own collection of books and examine as well the marginalia he occasionally inscribed in them. A finding list of the contents of this collection is available at NYU's Bobst Library.

References and further reading: Blumenthal, *Frost and His Printers*; Byers; Clarke; Crane, *Descriptive Catalogue*; Lancaster. For Frost's tribute to MacKaye, see R. Frost, *Collected*, 711; for letter to Thompson, see R. Frost, *Selected Letters*, 529.

Mark Richardson

"COME IN" was first printed in the *Atlantic Monthly* (Feb. 1941) and included in *A Witness Tree* **(1942)**. As in many of Frost's lyrics, a speaker journeys out into nature to register a typically ambiguous sign from an encounter there. In "Come In" the journey is significantly only to the edge of the darkening woods—no further. Frost soon added the poem to his poetry-reading repertoire, recognizing that it displays the conversational directness of his best poetic voice, running contrary to the expected regularity and lyricism of the dominantly anapestic meter.

At his public readings Frost would use "Come In" to declare his objections to the grimness of modernist wasteland verse, occasionally suggesting that this poem might express his rejection of invitations to gatherings of modern poets. Private comments and letters at this time reveal disdain for "the **Pound-Eliot**-Richards gang" and the "world's end whimper of T. S. Eliot." Frost believed that his quarrel with the literary establishment was well known by the 1940s, and any invitation would not be sincere.

"Come In" is rich in image and in symbol, evoking a world of woods, twilight, sunset, song, stars. Frost knew the appeal of oneness with nature but also recognized the ultimate separateness mandated by a nonhuman "otherness" there. "Come In" is, consequently, a twilight poem of contrasts exploring the differences between a bird's song and imaginative human response to something portentous—the "last of the light of the sun." The bird "still" has the expressiveness of song, but it is "still," immobile, "*slight* of wing" (italics mine), not able in the dark even "to better its perch." The response of the human listener is an existential choice to use the light that remains and not to enter the dark. The dark is strikingly described as "pillared," suggesting something monumental like the pillars of a temple but also, perhaps, suggesting a pillory, something punishing. Whether the song is a "call" or not, a simple invitation or a predetermined event, remains ambiguous. All that can be said is that "it is almost like a call." His choice is determined by his being "out for stars," suggesting either that he can act under the lesser light of starlight or, in ordinary language usage, that he may seek the impossible, the stars themselves. The word "out" also suggests the response of an outsider, not a joiner.

Frost is not a poet of pathetic fallacies, a provider of human voice or purpose for nature's creatures. Human consciousness is autonomous, able to interpret ambiguity and to act on that interpretation. The rejection is neither ambiguous nor ambivalent but a strongly asserted choice of will. He "would not come in . . . not even if asked." And he concludes with self-assurance, "I hadn't been."

References and further reading: Brodsky, 9–18; Pritchard, *Literary Life*, 228; Thompson and Winnick, 231.

Richard J. Calhoun

COMPLETE POEMS OF ROBERT FROST 1949, THE. Frost's revised 1948 contract with **Henry Holt and Company** gave the publisher the right to decide when to bring out new books of his poems, but Frost was eager for a redesigned and up-to-date collection at this point in his career, while his reputation was continuing to grow. Since the publication of the *Collected Poems* in 1939, Frost had published *A Witness Tree* **(1942),** *A Masque of Reason* (1945), **Steeple**

Bush **(1947)**, and *A Masque of Mercy* (1947), but at seventy-four, he still looked forward to years of further productivity. Consequently, while he reluctantly agreed to the title *Complete Poems* for the new book, he insisted on adding to it the year of publication. In every way, this was a carefully designed volume that represented the achievement of half a century, a volume that helped to secure Frost's reputation as a national figure, the "greatest living American poet."

At 642 pages, *The Complete Poems of Robert Frost 1949* had impressive weight and bulk. The poems are arranged by volume, with each poem beginning on a new page. The volumes follow in chronological order except the masques, which are placed together at the end, after a new section entitled "An Afterword," consisting of three miscellaneous poems: **"Choose Something Like a Star"** (which had appeared in *Come In and Other Poems*, 1943), **"Closed for Good"** and **"From Plane to Plane."** The prefatory essay that Frost had written for *Collected Poems* (1939), "The Figure a Poem Makes," was reprinted, and once again **"The Pasture"** was positioned on page one and omitted from the Table of Contents.

Opposite the title page, a new head and shoulders photograph by Clara E. Sipprell showed Frost, wizened and snowy-haired, in an open collar shirt and smock. The book was handsomely designed by Maurice Serle Kaplan; bound in green cloth with gold lettering on the spine and Frost's signature embossed in gold on the front cover, it was priced at $6.00. This was the last major collected poems that Frost himself would supervise. As editor of the 1969 collection ***The Poetry of Robert Frost***, Edward Connery Lathem introduced a number of controversial emendations to the poems. Nevertheless, the later and more comprehensive collection has become a popular text.

Frost had already won four Pulitzer Prizes, and the new collection gave readers an opportunity to reassess Frost's place in the American canon. Most reviewers were warmly appreciative; many remarked on the darker aspect of Frost's work, as opposed to the Yankee regionalism of so much early comment. While several criticized the didacticism and "glibness" of some of the later poems, they were inclined to celebrate the lifework as a whole rather than to dwell on evidence of recent decline. And they perceived the need for still closer study: As an anonymous reviewer in *Time* declared in 1949: "Frost's reputation has been secure for 35 years, he is America's most popular living poet of the first rank; but only lately, and to the keenest readers, has he begun to seem as subtle, as haunting and hurting a poet as in truth he is."

The book sold well; in 1950, Frost's royalties ($1.20 a copy) exceeded $10,000. The volume was reissued in two volumes by the Limited Editions Club (Sept. 1950) and given its Gold Medal as the book "most likely to attain the stature of a classic" of those published in the previous five years. It also helped Frost to secure a nomination by the American Academy of Arts and Letters for the 1950 Nobel Prize for Literature. The nomination was unsuccessful, but in March 1950, the U.S. Senate passed a unanimous resolution extending felicitations to him, thereby recognizing his substantial contribution to American literature.

References and further reading: Daiches presents a perceptive survey of Frost's work as represented by the *Complete Poems*; Humphries provides a balanced, sensitive review; "The Intolerable Touch," an anonymous piece in *Time*, is a representative review in a major newsweekly; Thompson and Winnick, 178–86, include a detailed discussion of the circumstances surrounding the publication of Frost's volume.

Matthew Parfitt

"CONCEPT SELF-CONCEIVED, A." *See* **"Cluster of Faith."**

CONGRESSIONAL GOLD MEDAL. *See* **Awards, Honors, and Prizes**.

"CONSIDERABLE SPECK, A," first appeared without the subtitle "Microscopic" in the *Atlantic Monthly* (July 1939) and was later collected in *A Witness Tree* **(1942)**. One of Frost's most self-effacing and playful poems, "A Considerable Speck" is described by Philip Gerber as "beautifully conceived and wrought." The poem follows a microscopic mite as it scurries madly and wildly—and yet with some inscrutable purpose—across the page of a freshly written manuscript on which the speaker is working. The mite pauses suspiciously at a line of wet ink. It turns away, only to flee again in "loathing" from another line. It runs in "terror" across the page, faltering and cowering in desperation. Frost ultimately invests the mite with considerable intelligence in the closing quatrain.

"A Considerable Speck" was written at the height of Frost's successful and triumphant middle years. *A Witness Tree* was awarded the Pulitzer Prize, Frost's fourth—an unprecedented feat (*see* **Awards, Honors, and Prizes**). Coming at a time of great optimism, renewed energy, and growing public acclaim, it may be entirely fitting that Frost could afford to confess his self-absorption by writing a sympathetic poem about an intelligent critic (a mite!) who slights Frost's writing (of course, we hear Frost's comic irony in the overwrought encounter).

Then again, maybe the mite is just afraid and running for its life. Frost's first instinct is to aim his pen in the air like a dart and bring it down on the mite. Far from being an exercise in humility, the poem may then be read as a celebration of personal righteousness, an ode to Frost's magnanimity and mercy. Instead of wiping out the terrified and defenseless mite, Frost allows "it [to] lie there till I hope it slept," making it absolutely clear in a decidedly polemical and unpoetic aside, however, that his sparing of the mite's life is not prompted by political conscientiousness or any "tenderer-than-thou / Collectivistic regimenting love / With which the modern world is being swept."

Eminent writers and poets of Frost's generation—notably Archibald MacLeish, John Dos Passos, John Steinbeck—argued forcefully and publicly that literary figures should become active agents in social and political reform or grievances, a calling to which Frost, as Gerber points out, was completely un-sympathetic. Frost spares the mite out of a sense of decency not because it is the right thing to do in terms of any ideological litmus.

More significantly, as Greiner hints, Frost, typically playful and coy, also allows us to read his gesture as profound and complex respect for "Mind when I meet it in any guise," for the tension between the presumed power of imagi-nation and nonhuman otherness, a major theme in all of Frost.

References and further reading: Faggen; Gerber, *Frost*, 41, 81; Greiner, *Poet and His Critics*; Parini, *A Life*, 352; Thompson collects anecdotes of Frost's reputed antireformist views throughout *Triumph*.

David D. Cooper

CONVERSATIONALIST. Frost was justly famous for his brilliant and pro-found conversations, which reflected his audacious literary imagination, his pow-erful intelligence, and remarkable erudition. Even his ordinary casual talk was frequently peppered with fresh images and metaphors. His high-spirited gnomic wit; his constant, joyful, and irrepressible sense of verbal "play for mortal stakes"; his anecdotal, dry, and often serious humor and mischievous irony; his love of gossip for its dramatic tone; his fanciful and whimsical spoofing and teasing; his puns and verbal gymnastics; his sudden inversion of words and phrases and muted eloquence; his beguiling meditative shifts in voice tones; his swift reversals of dramatic situations between the whole range of comedy and tragedy, so filled with the wildness of hyperbolic images and metaphors or the pathos of understatement—all of these lyrical, narrative, or dramatic qualities fired and filled his literary imagination and provided the spontaneous intuitions or rational arguments in his conversation. Frost simply reveled in the felicities of the English language. He was always at his best in one-to-one talks with his friends. His comments during poetry readings fall far short of his private con-versations.

As **Kathleen Morrison** notes in *Robert Frost: A Pictorial Chronicle*, Frost had "a formidable mind—constantly active, skeptical, believing, joking, probing, mocking, sometimes giving offense, sometimes warmly genial, the delight of wonder of visitors from every-where. . . . To encounter Robert Frost was to en-counter one of the notable minds of a generation, a mind with restless curiosity seeking the truth unfettered by second-hand opinions and moving to its target swiftly as an arrow. Many witnesses could testify to the range of his intellectual force." Frost's conversation has vital affinities with his aesthetic theory and his insistence on "the sound of meaning and the meaning in sound" in his voice tones in poetry. Frost regarded his poems as the highest form of conversation.

References and further reading: There is no scholarly study of Frost as a conversation-alist. Specimens of his talk are found in the following works: R. Cook, *Living Voice*; R. Francis; R. Frost, *Interviews*; Mertins; Stanlis, "Acceptable."

Peter J. Stanlis

COOK, REGINALD L. (1903–   ). A graduate of Middlebury College (1924) and Rhodes Scholar at Oxford (1926–1929), Reginald L. Cook was a close personal friend of Frost from 1925 to the poet's death in January 1963. After their first meeting at **Bread Loaf**, when Cook was a graduate student at the school, he recorded Frost's spontaneous and forceful talk about "the idea of progress" in "a continuous meditative monologue," ranging "over a wide territory, historically and ideologically." Frost was highly critical of the assumed claim that "progress" was the inevitable result of the evolutionary process and that through science humanity would in time establish a utopian world order, a skepticism that he retained throughout his life.

Cook took seriously Frost's belief that American literature deserved special treatment apart from English literature, and in 1929 he established the Department of American Literature at Middlebury College and served as its chairman until he became director of the Bread Loaf Graduate School of English from 1946 through 1964.

A well-known **Thoreau** scholar, Cook also published many articles on Frost and compiled a bibliography of the poet. His first book on his friend, *The Dimensions of Robert Frost*, based upon "listening thirty years" to Frost's superb talk, presents the poet's ideas on technique, form, and themes and the relationship between the artist and his work. Cook's own observations are particularly valuable because they "have been picked up directly from the poet."

Cook's greatest contribution to Frost studies is *Robert Frost: A Living Voice*. This book records their warm and unbroken friendship at Bread Loaf, Middlebury, and elsewhere, and it transcribes with annotations twelve major talks given by Frost during the last decade of his life, delivered originally at the Bread Loaf Graduate School of English. Frost's personal beliefs on the craft of poetry, on education, politics, science, and other important subjects, receive from Cook a sympathetic treatment. He records the authentic and profound Frost in a manner that almost literally captures the "living voice" of the poet, and in ten excellent essays he presents Frost in intimate action on the world of New England, poetry, and philosophy. Among many fine studies, this one is most valuable for a personal image of Frost.

References and further reading: R. Cook, *Dimensions* and *Living Voice*.

Peter J. Stanlis

"COURAGE TO BE NEW, THE," first appeared in *Steeple Bush* **(1947)** in a section of whimsical poems called "A Spire and Belfry," which takes a satirical look at **religion** and, in this case, **politics**. According to Lathem, in his notes to *The Poetry of Robert Frost*, the first two stanzas were originally published as a separate poem called "1946," in a broadside produced for dedication ceremonies at a memorial park in Ripton, Vermont, in July of that year. The occasion of the poem was the post–World War II move to found a "Federation of Mankind" that led to the United Nations. While the poem grants the courage of those who would end the "brutality and fighting" that accompanied "the mistakes of ancient men," the additional third and last stanzas portray them as without a firm plan or sense of direction, and Frost, on the whole, seems skeptical about a plan that failed once before (the post–World War I League of Nations), especially one that presumes it is possible to change the basic human nature that has led to war.

The poem is written in quatrains with *abab* rhymes, some of which employ unusual words ("militate" used as a verb to rhyme with "trait") or off-rhymes ("as soon as" / "newness") to heighten the satirical tone. The tone is further developed by the rare (for Frost) use of seven-syllable lines, mixing anapestic and iambic feet.

References and further reading: For an alternate reading, see Marcus, *Explication.*

Todd Lieber

"COW IN APPLE TIME, THE," was written and first published in **England** (*Poetry and Drama*, Dec. 1914) and later was included in *Mountain Interval* **(1916)**. Because the poem was written in Europe in the wake of the Great War, it can be read on one level as a commentary on the modern world. The dawning of the modern age in the new Eden—an imperial British empire that seemingly knows no boundaries—has brought along with it a spirit of transgression. Commentators have noted the Edenic motif of this poem, one complete with the eating of forbidden fruit, the "windfalls" of modernity that ironically are rotten, growing not in a lush garden but in a wasteland, "a pasture withering to the root." This offense brings about a debilitating intoxication, a loss of order, and the ruin of what is natural, emphasized by the cow's shriveled udder. There is little consensus of what one is to make of the speaker's attitude toward the cow's behavior. Readings range from a serious call for human control of animal nature to a tragic yet humorous portrayal of the cow, the comedy perhaps masking the pain of modern existence.

References and further reading: D'Avanzo, *Romantics*, sees the poem as a call for human control of animal nature; Oster comments on the Edenic as well as the tragicomic aspect of the poem; Reed focuses on Frost's use of animals to critique human behavior.

John R. Woznicki

$\mathcal{D}$

DARTMOUTH COLLEGE. Frost's relationship to Dartmouth College was intermittent but lifelong: He matriculated as an undergraduate in the fall of 1892 and returned for his final visit a couple of months before his death in 1963. His brief time as a student at the college (he did not complete his first semester) attests to Frost's ambivalence toward formal education. (He would later attend **Harvard** as an undergraduate for a short time and leave before taking a degree.) Stories conflict about why Frost left Dartmouth. According to Lawrance Thompson, Frost's official **biographer**, he left because he did not believe that Dartmouth was intellectually stimulating; as Frost recalled, the main pursuit at the college was the hazing of freshmen by upperclassmen. Whatever the circumstances surrounding his leaving, Frost did not remain a student at Dartmouth for long; he remains, though, one of its most famous students.

Perhaps the most important moments of Frost's Dartmouth experience are two literary encounters he had there. At a local bookstore, Frost bought Francis **Palgrave's** *Golden Treasury of Songs and Lyrics* (1861), a poetry anthology that he cherished throughout his life and that shaped many of his ideas about the English lyric tradition. Frost also ran across an issue of the New York weekly *The Independent* (17 Nov. 1892) in the college library; the entire first page of that publication was devoted to a new poem by Richard Hovey (himself a recent graduate of Dartmouth) entitled "Seaward: An Elegy on the Death of Thomas William Parsons." The editorial in that issue announced that Hovey's poem was one of the finest elegies ever written in English and set it in the company of Milton's "Lycidas," Shelley's "Adonais," and Arnold's "Thyrsis." Frost's reading of the poem and the accompanying editorial encouraged him to write an elegy of his own, which he sent to **Susan Hayes Ward**, the literary editor of *The Independent*; the poem was published by her as "**My Butterfly: An Elegy**" on 8 November 1894, marking the beginning of Frost's career as a paid published poet.

Frost returned to Dartmouth in 1933 to receive an Honorary Doctorate of Letters and in 1955 to become a Doctor of Laws; the awarding of a second honorary degree was unprecedented in the history of the college. Between these years, Frost taught at Dartmouth as Ticknor Fellow in the Humanities, holding that position from 1943 to 1949. For the last time, he traveled to the college in November 1962 to attend the dedication of the Hopkins Center—a new facility for the performing arts—and gave a talk entitled "On Extravagance," one of his last two public appearances (*see* **Addresses [Public Speeches]**).

References and further reading: Parini, *A Life*, 36, quotes a passage from a 1914 letter by Frost in which the poet acknowledges his curious lack of literary activity while at Dartmouth; Thompson, *Early Years*, 138–46.

Tyler B. Hoffman

"DEATH OF THE HIRED MAN, THE," which first appeared in *North of Boston* **(1914)**, has many of the characteristics one might look for in a Frost poem: a rural New England setting; ordinary people using language that, itself ordinary, has somehow been transmuted to poetry; a certain static view of characterization that holds that people don't really change; and a picture of the universe that could arguably be described as bleak. We also find a typical stress on the value of work and of the ways in which that work defines the life devoted to it. Home for Silas, the "hired man," is where he worked most productively—where, by extension, his life held the most meaning—and it is where he chooses to die. The narrative unfolds largely through the dialogue of the hired man's former employers, a farmer named Warren and his kindly wife Mary. They debate the reasons behind Silas's unexpected reappearance and what to do about it, a device that allows Frost to comment on a wealth of issues ranging from the merits of forgiveness to the ultimate frustration of one man's dreams, from the difference between books and experience to the desire the old feel to pass on their knowledge to the young. Indeed, the poem reveals a great deal about not only its principal characters but the world that has shaped them.

The dialogue, in blank verse, is easy to follow and resembles prose even in its divisions, with a stanza to each speaker and a short line break denoting each change. The speaker is unobtrusive, setting the scene briefly and then breaking in four more times in the long poem to paint a character's action or provide some lyrical counterpoint to the everyday tragedy unfolding. Such brief interludes give us the most overtly poetic moments of the piece, including the alliteration of the opening lines and the symbolic softness of the moonlight in the last half of the poem. Of course, the moon is also cold and distant, an appropriate backdrop to an ending that was inevitable from the very title. We are moved not only by the man's death but by how he dies—alone, his last "great" work (ditching the meadow and clearing the upper pasture) unachieved, his knowledge and experience lost. And yet there is almost a pathetic dignity about him, a pride that can be brought low but never wholly vanquished. The poem is vintage Frost.

Frost has also been notable in his preoccupation with rural New England folk. Radcliffe Squires says that the characters in "The Death of the Hired Man" are "accomplished" and "apparently, incapable of change." Thus, he concludes, they are "incapable of learning" and the poem is "almost meaningless for the reader since it is meaningless for the characters." Such obdurate resistance to change may simply be a reflection of the hard New England country that has shaped them. Mordecai Marcus has a different reading of the poem, recognizing the essential contrast between Warren and Mary: justice and mutual responsibility versus love and acceptance. But he adds that by the poem's end they do in fact merge their outlooks and their feelings. Marcus points out that "the couple's final handclasp, initiated by Warren, implies a bond of love including Silas," a softer view of the characters and by extension Frost's universe. If human beings can be open to change and can learn to accept and forgive, perhaps the death of the hired man is instructive after all.

References and further reading: Lentricchia, *Modern Poetics*, 62–64; Marcus, *Explication*, 44; Richardson, *Ordeal*, 49–50; Squires, 78; Thompson, *Triumph*.

Scott Earle

"DEMIURGE'S LAUGH, THE," which first appeared in *A Boy's Will* (1913), offers an early sample of the relationship between Frost's ideas and those of **Emerson** and **Thoreau**. In Frost's poem, the speaker, happily attempting to pursue the Demon, is made to appear foolish by the elusive creature's mocking laughter. Frost's demiurge is strongly reminiscent of Thoreau's loon on the lake: Frost had high praise for *Walden*, with special admiration for the loon in the "Brute Neighbours" chapter, in which Thoreau chases the elusive loon that suddenly gives an unearthly, demoniac laugh behind him, as if deriding Thoreau's attempts to catch it.

Frost had even higher praise for Emerson, who, in his essay "Nature," presented a number of ideas and phrases that would seem to constitute a common source for both Thoreau's loon and Frost's demiurge. Emerson's text describes a pursuit that does not find its quarry. Oddly enough the pursuer is a blend of scientist and poet, both of them trying to understand nature but finding that it constantly eludes them. Emerson's unusual juxtaposition of poetry and science could account for Frost's strange comment on "The Demiurge's Laugh" in the first edition of *A Boy's Will*: "He resolves . . . to know definitely what he thinks . . . about science."

In "Nature," the poet–scientist finds that nature is a living, evolving thing (*natura naturans*), so that his quest is fated never to find its grail; instead, the disappointed seeker is destined to be nature's fool after being enticed, flattered, and mocked by nature's elusive mysteries. Emerson's passage would seem to be the source for both Melville's "practical joke" of *Moby Dick* (Ch. XLVIII) and Frost's couplet "Forgive, O Lord" (*see* **"Cluster of Faith"**).

It is worth noting that the word *demiurgic* can mean "creative," and the word

Demon need not mean "evil spirit"; it can mean "attendant or indwelling spirit, one's genius."

References and further reading: R. Frost, *Interviews*, 143, and *Selected Letters*, 182.

Gerard Quinn

"DEPARTMENTAL" first appeared in the *Yale Review* (Winter 1936) and was included in *A Further Range* later that same year. An ironic celebration of bureaucratic efficiency, "Departmental" draws critical attention as a model of Frost's humor and satire but often escapes, because of its own insistent objectivity, the deeper analysis given to some of his other creature allegories.

Frost and his wife spent the winter of 1934–1935 on the recently bankrupt Key West and watched its being managed by the federal government through the administrator of public relief, an example of the New Deal's method of addressing the economic depression. "Departmental" obliquely treats such issues in a far more impersonal manner with only slight references by thought or pronoun to the speaker/observer. The forced objectivity of the poem is underscored by the poem's tightly regulated couplets and by seeming almost childlike in tone, description, and language, except for occasionally unusual diction such as "formic," "Janizary," "sepal," and "ichor of nettle" and witty rhymes such as "Jerry/Janizary," "people/sepal," and "atwiddle/middle."

But the surface objectivity is deceptive; this is penetrating foolery. There is reference to a possible "inquiry squad," specialists in divining God and the nature of time and space; there is communication, albeit impersonal; there are lines of authority, formality, even monarchy. The human parallels insist that the poem be treated as commentary on human civilization. And the lines "No one stands round to stare / It is nobody else's affair" echo Frost's commentary in the final lines of **" 'Out, Out—' "** where the observers remain impassive, detached.

In his 1955 commencement address at **Dartmouth**, Frost insisted that "Departmental" was "very objective," but the poem is also an allegory of bureaucratic specialization and departmentalization, emotions related to function, and functions circumscribed.

References and further reading: D'Avanzo, "Frost's 'Departmental' "; Doyle, *Poetry*, 92–99, contains an analysis of the poem's prosody; Faggen; Gerber, *Frost*, 56–57, 104–5; Parini, *A Life*, 293, discusses the poem as a reaction to the New Deal; Sergeant, 338–39.

Stephen D. Warner

DERRY HOMESTEAD (THE ROBERT FROST FARM). In 1900, Robert Frost, his wife **Elinor** and eldest daughter Lesley (born Apr. 1899) moved to a farm on the Londonderry Turnpike at Derry, New Hampshire. The thirty-acre homestead had been purchased for his use by Frost's paternal grandfather for $1,725. Three more children were soon added to the Frost family: Carol (May 1902), Irma (June 1903), and Marjorie (Mar. 1905). The family would move from the farm to Derry Village in 1909, where Frost could continue teaching at **Pinkerton Academy**, and, in 1911, to Plymouth, New Hampshire, for a year of teaching at the **Plymouth Normal School**. A year later the family sailed for **England**, largely on the proceeds from the sale of the farm. (*See* Frost's previously unpublished poem "On the Sale of My Farm" in *Collected*.) It was in England that his first two books, *A Boy's Will* **(1913)** and *North of Boston* **(1914)**, were published, including many poems written on the New Hampshire farm. Frost later would write to a friend of the significance of those years in Derry:

You might be interested to know that during my ten years in Derry the first five of them farming altogether and the last five mostly teaching but still farming a little, I wrote more than half of my first book much more than half of second and even quite a little of my third, though they were not published till later.

I might say the core of all my writing was probably the five free years I had there on the farm down the road from Derry Village toward Lawrence. The only thing we had plenty of was time and seclusion. I couldnt have figured in advance. I hadnt that kind of foresight. But it turned out right as a doctor's prescription.

Although the homestead passed out of the Frost family in 1911, Frost dreamed of reclaiming the property, which had fallen into disrepair as an auto graveyard. It was at the suggestion of Frost's friend Stewart Udall (Secretary of the Interior, 1961–1969) that the state of New Hampshire acquired the property; in 1977, it was dedicated as a National Historic Landmark by the National Parks Service. The rooms had been restored with period pieces and facsimiles—even the wallpaper in Elinor's bedroom; in the kitchen the soapstone sink is original, and the Morris chair whose arms supported the writing board on which the poems were penned is in the living room–parlor. The well and pump are gone, and the barn, now empty of horse, cow, and chickens, serves as a visitor's center. But still it is not difficult to imagine a man or a child setting off across the surrounding pastures in morning dew or evening dusk to lead the cow to barn for milking or to harness the horse Eunice for work or travel into Derry Village or to fetch the little calf or clear the spring or walk as far as Hyla or West Running Brook to gather nuts or flowers.

Taught at home by their father and mother, the Frost children received a remarkable education. Reared on poetry, nurtured on the world of the imagination, and instructed in the art of direct observation, the children created an exceptional body of creative work during this period. Their journals (published in facsimile in *New Hampshire's Child* and described in Francis, *The Frost Family's Adventure in Poetry*) help us understand what motivated the struggling poet in the years just prior to public recognition in England and America. We learn how Frost was constantly enriched by his interactions with his children; how he benefited from the routine activities that allowed him to ruminate on and mull over the constant flow of impressions, to respond in subtle ways to the natural phenomena, and to apply, with all kinds and types of talking and walking companions, his by now carefully thought out philosophical and psychological orientations.

References and further reading: M. Anderson; L. Francis, *Morning Gladness*; L. Frost, *Derry Journals*; R. Frost, *Selected Letters*, 552, and *Stories*.

Lesley Lee Francis

"DESERT PLACES," first published in the *American Mercury* (Apr. 1934), later appeared in *A Further Range* **(1936)**. Questioning the nature and existence of God, Frost describes in the first stanza how one speaker reacts to a snowy field at dusk, and in the three stanzas that follow, the poem meditates on the meaning of "loneliness" itself. According to Frost, loneliness is the negative emotion we associate not just with the absence of other people but also with the absence of God. To a religious sensibility, barren fields should not connote loneliness, for, to the faithful, God is always present. As an existential condition, in other words, loneliness implies an absent God. It is precisely this absence with which "Desert Places" is concerned. In the three meditative stanzas, Frost notes that both philosophy and astronomy offer evidence to support the claim that God is not just absent but does not even exist. And if God does not exist, says Frost, then the world is "A blanker whiteness of benighted snow / With no expression, nothing to express." Frost counters such a view, however, with the fact that he *does* feel and express loneliness. Therefore, loneliness—an emotion contingent on the belief that God exists, yet is unavailable, absent—is, for Frost, an existential condition, a theology of absence made explicit in the theological skepticism of the final stanza.

Frost divided *A Further Range* into six named sections and included "Desert Places" in the second section, "Taken Singly." Its location there suggests that it concerns a unique, singular and especially philosophical issue. The thematic connection is particularly evident when one realizes that other poems of the second section include three that we now associate with the darker, more skeptical Frost: **"Design," "Neither Out Far Nor in Deep,"** and **"Provide, Provide."**

Cleanth Brooks and Robert Penn Warren set the standard for reading "Desert Places." In *Understanding Poetry*, they present the poem not as expression of skeptical views but rather as an attack on skeptical views. In an interpretation reflective of the Great Depression, Brooks and Warren suggest that the poem is an argument on behalf of faith. In the years following their interpretation, scholars have debated its merits by asking if the poem is an argument on behalf of doubt or of faith. Those who argue on behalf of doubt have gone so far as to claim that its skepticism is part and parcel of a New England literary tradition that can be traced back to Hawthorne (Ellis; Stone). Others, such as Reuben Brower, have made a particularly powerful argument on behalf of the poem's skepticism by comparing it to work by the English Romantics. In Brower's comparison Frost's poem proves to be far more modern, ironic, and incredulous than those of his Romantic predecessors. In particular, Brower compares Frost with Wordsworth and notes that "where Wordsworth finds the working of one mighty mind or ennobling strength through discipline and faith, Frost stands alone with the ironic attitude his only resource." Noting the modern sensibility in Frost's skepticism, Frank Lentricchia argues that, in poems such as "Desert Places," "the self finds itself confronting its own dangerous impulses."

Even more recently, critics have begun to read the poem for what it tells us about Frost's faith in poetry, writing, and expression itself. Judith Oster, offering a particularly bleak reading of "Desert Places," writes: "Whereas **'Stopping by Woods'** presented an invitation to the solitude and inertia of snow, ['Desert Places'] presents the attendant fear that once giving in to the self, or going into the self, he will find that the journey has been for nothing. That there is nothing but loneliness, blankness, and absent-spiritedness in the sense of absence of spirit." Alluding to **Wallace Stevens**'s "Snow Man," Oster writes that "there is a difference between" Frost's "nothing to express" and Stevens's "expression of nothingness." That difference is how we measure Frost's skepticism. According to Oster, unlike Stevens's poet figures, Frost's poet is unable to speak in any language, even in the imagined language of a Stevensian Snow Man. Frost's greatest fear is the fear that he may have "nothing to say," that his poem offers no counterimagination, no counterlanguage to the "desert place." In the end, the desert place is the name for the absence of all possibility of language, the panic (as much verbal as philosophic or religious) of the imagination slipping toward what Seamus Heaney calls "the cold tingle of infinity."

The critical record of this poem, then, is the critical record of Frost's ability to speak to his time. In the Great Depression the poem spoke to the need for faith, while in our own postmodern age of doubt, an age obsessed with language, he speaks to our fear that we cannot even begin to speak. *See also* **Nature Poet and Naturalist**.

References and further reading: Brooks and Warren; Brower, 110; Ellis, "Frost and Hawthorne"; Heaney, 70; Lentricchia, *Modern Poetics*, 100; Orlov; Oster, 157–60; Parini, *A Life*, 285–86; Stone.

Jonathan N. Barron

"DESIGN" appeared in its final form in *A Further Range* **(1936)** but had appeared earlier in *American Poetry 1922: A Miscellany*. The poem plays with the theological argument whereby God's benevolent design for the universe can be inferred from created things ("And God saw everything that he had made, and behold, it was very good"—Gen. 1:31). While it is clear that Frost, an inveterate antiromantic, is exploding such an argument, his poem is cagey and ambiguously worded, leaving us uncertain about what sort of universe the poet does imagine.

The action of the poem is simple enough: The speaker finds a white spider preying upon a dead white moth and speculates upon the meaning of the drama, which is staged on a "white heal-all," a flower that ought by rights to be blue. Puzzling over the malevolent force that brought spider, moth, and flower together, the speaker is reduced to a series of unanswerable questions. Simply read, then, the scene undermines the speaker's faith in a benevolent "design," but the poem is not that simple. We must wonder, for instance, whether the poet means that the design is evil or that the designer is absent altogether. Is Frost in earnest, or is "Design" a satire on a kind of smug Emersonian optimism?

Some readers gain clues from the possible sources for "Design." Several critics argue that important sources for the concept of whiteness are Poe's *Narrative of Arthur Gordon Pym* and "The Whiteness of the Whale" chapter from Melville's *Moby-Dick*. Like Frost, Melville never says finally whether the whiteness signifies evil or a neutral atheism. Like "Design," Melville's chapter is structured by questions that have no answers. Others see the poem as a parody of **Emerson**'s "Rhodora" or William Cullen Bryant's "To a Waterfowl." Such influences alone might lead us to believe that Frost asserts the "darkness" of the designer's purpose, or at least that he mocks those who dispense with the reality of evil.

While critics also see affinities with Whitman's "Noiseless Patient Spider" and **Eliot**'s *Waste Land*, the metaphysics of "Design" is, according to Poirier, most frequently attributed to a passage from William James's *Pragmatism*, which Frost was teaching students at **Plymouth Normal School** in New Hampshire in 1912, the year he sent an early draft of the poem to **Susan Ward**. Poirier suggests we look to *Pragmatism*'s Lecture Three, "Some Metaphysical Problems Metaphysically Considered," for the background of "Design."

A second source for uncovering the meaning of "Design" is the process of its composition. Monteiro has made a detailed comparison of the final version of the poem and the first, called "In White" (1912):

> A dented spider like a snow drop white
> On a white Heal-all, holding up a moth
> Like a white piece of lifeless satin cloth—
> Saw ever curious eye so strange a sight?
> Portent in little, assorted death and blight
> Like the ingredients of a witches' broth?
> The beady spider, the flower like a froth
> And the moth carried like a paper kite.
>
> What had that flower to do with being white,
> The blue Brunella every child's delight?
> What brought the kindred spider to that height?
> (Make we no thesis of the miller's plight.)
> What but design of darkness and of night?
> Design, design! Do I use the word aright?

Monteiro has noted the addition of words that connote infants; multileveled words such as "rigid" and "appall"; the shift of questions from the octave to the sestet exclusively, a revision that essentially undoes the platitudes of the octave;

and the inclusion of words such as "steered" and "govern," suggesting external agency. His conclusion is that such changes reveal the poem's fundamental ironies. But perhaps the most important change, according to several critics, is the addition of a first-person voice; from the bookish inversions and anachronisms of the first version (for example, "Saw ever curious eye," "make we no thesis," "aright"), we can infer that Frost had intended the speaker to be conventional and limited, far from the allusive complexity of voice in the revised draft.

The sometimes-overlooked speaker is central to an adequate understanding of "Design." Critics since Lionel Trilling have asserted the "terrifying" implications of "Design," an insight dependent on the role of a speaker confused by his own failed metaphysics of whiteness and darkness. Confronted by an unlikely conjunction of spider, moth, and flower, the speaker resorts, as others have noted, to the language of advertising. Poirier goes so far as to call such a concept of design "packaged." As his system breaks down, the speaker makes a series of trite similes ("like a kite") designed to humanize and make intelligible a relationship that defies human meaning. The speaker's terror, then, stems from the failure of the created world to reveal such meaning. The speaker stands alone in the darkness of his metaphysics. But we must be careful not to attribute such terror to Frost, the poet, personally, whose poem is to the speaker (and reader) what the web is to the moth. Frost actually reveals considerable pleasure in his virtuoso performance, exemplified by his delight in paradox, allusion, and wordplay. "Appall," for instance, suggests "pall," to "make pale," and "impale," and its use reminds us that such multiplicity is a *creation* of language.

Nowhere is such pleasure more apparent than in the poem's form. A Petrarchan **sonnet** with a variant sestet, "Design" is arranged as a logical argument reasoned through in fourteen lines. But the sonnet form overdetermines the argument, mimicking the gulf between the problem's breadth and the speaker's simplicity. Frequently noted is how the questions in the sestet, a place usually reserved for answers, undo the certainties of the octave, circling the problem and finally evading it by suggesting that size ("a thing so small") might be a legitimate factor in the moral equation. Perhaps Reuben Brower's detailed formal analysis of the poem shows best how Frost uses meter and sound to establish a playful, joking tone.

"Design," then, calls attention to its own "design," which is the point. The spider, the moth, and the flower are "kindred"; they have a relationship that cannot be glossed by human oppositions, similes, or systems. The poem makes a web of its own meaning, which is all the meaning we have. *See* **Nature Poet and Naturalist.**

References and further reading: Brower; R. Cook, *Dimensions*; Hiatt, 41; Monteiro, *New England*; Parini, *A Life*, 25, suggests that Frost first encountered the "argument from design" in Richard A. Proctor's *Our Place among the Infinities*; Poirier, *Knowing*. "In White" can be found in Cook, 85; R. Frost, *Collected*; and Monteiro, *New England*.

Mary Adams

"DEVOTION" first appeared in *West-Running Brook* **(1928)**. In the tradition of such Frost "classics" as **"Tuft of Flowers," "Mending Wall,"** and **"Two Look at Two,"** the poem depicts a speaker who uses an observation of the natural world as a stepping-stone to meditate on human relationships.

In the poem's first two lines, Frost sets up his analogy, using the relationship of the shore to the ocean as an example of the greatest devotion possible. In the final two lines, Frost explains the analogy: Although human beings may speak of the tide's coming in and going out, in reality the shore and the ocean are never separated. Frost seems to refer to such a phenomenon when he describes the "curve of one position"—a togetherness that may change appearance as the beach grows larger with a receding tide but is always constant. As the final line reiterates, two entities truly devoted to one another as are shore and ocean may move or change, but they will never truly be separated. Frost reinforces such unity by making the final two lines of the poem metrically identical: a dactyl followed by three trochees.

References and further reading: Gierasch; Poirier, *Knowing.*

Melissa Simpson

DEVOTO, BERNARD (1897–1955), American historian, novelist, biographer, critic, and editor, was born and reared in Utah and remembered primarily for his histories of the American frontier. After graduation from **Harvard** in 1920 and periods of lecturing at Northwestern University and at Harvard, the already controversial author of *Mark Twain's America* (1932) devoted himself full-time to writing. For two decades, 1935–1955, he wrote a monthly column as the editor of *Harper's* "Easy Chair." From 1936 through 1938, he was editor of the *Saturday Review of Literature.* As an essayist and critic, DeVoto assumed the role of "antagonist" with a gleeful belligerence, publishing his iconoclastic "correctives" to prevailing literary, political, and cultural attitudes. In 1948, he was awarded the Pulitzer Prize in History for *Across the Wide Missouri.* Much of his later career was concerned with conservationist causes.

Frost and DeVoto met as colleagues at the University of Miami Winter Institute in 1936. A friendship began when Frost conveyed his admiration for DeVoto's anti–New Deal essays and grew when DeVoto helped to host the Frosts during the poet's Norton Lectures at Harvard later that year. Eager to express his own regard for Frost, DeVoto published "The Critics and Robert Frost" in 1938, a polemical assault on those who had disparaged *A Further Range* from socialist and Modernist perspectives. DeVoto's disapproval of Frost's relationship with **Kathleen Morrison** opened a rift in the friendship in 1938 that was never fully closed despite a reconciliation in 1947.

References and further reading: DeVoto; Stegner, *Frost & DeVoto* and *The Uneasy Chair: A Biography of Bernard DeVoto* (Garden City: Doubleday, 1974); Thompson, *Triumph.*

Donald G. Sheehy

"DIRECTIVE" was published first in the *Virginia Quarterly Review* (Winter 1946) and later appeared in *Steeple Bush* **(1947)**. It is one of the most often anthologized and analyzed poems in the Frost canon. Full of puns, allusions, and "obliquities," it has so challenged readers that they have produced myriad interpretations. Lentricchia calls it "Frost's *summa* . . . the one poem that a critic of Frost must sooner or later confront if he hopes to grasp the poet's commitment to his art as a way of saving himself," whereas Poirier takes the minority view that it is "a tricky and devious poem" and a "prime example of misplaced adulation." Critics have argued that it is a statement of Frost's philosophy, religion, ethics, or aesthetics; that it is his answer to **T. S. Eliot**'s use of the Grail legend in *The Waste Land*; or that it is an example of his making a joke of all solemnities. S.P.C. Duvall has argued that it is a poetic rendering of *Walden*, and John F. Lynen has made a strong case that the poem is about process. Valuable as the scholarship is, the individual reader's interpretation must finally rest on one's perception of the attitude of the persona who issues the directives.

From the very first word Frost's penchant for the double entendre is manifest, making even a summary of the poem open to argument. "Back out of all this now too much for us," we are instructed in the first line. The "back out," in context of the title, suggests that an unnamed speaker is giving an order to someone to turn around and go somewhere. Grammatically, however, the "back" is not really an imperative (a directive) but a modifier of the "house that is no more a house" in line 5. To such spatial interpretations of the word "back" must be added the probability of its being a temporal command—to think back to an earlier or simpler time, which Frost denotes as "this now too much for us." The puzzles of the first line anticipate numerous further perplexities for the reader who puts the words and syntax of the poem under careful scrutiny. But for the one who reads it superficially, the poem is a satisfyingly simple set of directions leading to a cheerfully explicit conclusion.

If the perplexities of syntax and complexities of vocabulary are temporarily set aside, a general description of the poem's progress can be made: A speaker directs a listener/reader to go back to a place familiar to him in an earlier time. While on the journey he will pass by prehistoric rock formations and relatively youthful trees. He is told to discount fears that he is being watched, to make up a song to cheer himself up and imagine others that have used the road in the past. Eventually he will come to a point where he is to make himself at home. There he will find the remains of a house, a tree whose branches once served as the roof of a children's playhouse, a "broken drinking goblet like the Grail," and a brook. Using the goblet he is to "drink and be whole again beyond confusion."

The emphasis on the journey and the activities at the destination demand that the first symbolic construct of the poem is the quest motif, but the unspecified quest is qualified by the prominent religious elements. Frequent allusions to the New Testament have encouraged some critics, such as Dorothy Judd Hall, to find a Christian message in the poem, although she concedes that Frost refuted such an interpretation. Matthew 10:39 is the likely source for the lines "if you'll let a guide direct you / Who only has at heart your getting lost" and "if you're lost enough to find yourself." Mark 4:11–12 is the passage to which Frost refers explicitly when he writes that the goblet is "Under a spell so the wrong ones can't find it / So can't get saved as St. Mark says they mustn't." Mark 10:15, "Whoever does not receive the kingdom of God as a little child will never enter it," is a likely source for the emphasis on the children's playhouse, where the goblet is located. John 4:13–14, with its injunction to drink of living waters, may be the source for the final line, "Drink and be whole again beyond confusion."

The explicit allusion to Mark has attracted considerable attention and speculation about why it is included. Theodore Morrison has reported a conversation Hyde Cox had with Frost about the passage, pointing out that Frost made the connection between people who do not understand parables and those who cannot understand poetry. When Robert Francis asked him why he picked that passage, he told him, "I wanted to say that it was as good a passage as any other people wish were not in the Bible." In an interview in *The Dartmouth* Frost is quoted as saying, "Saint Mark says that these things of Christ are said in parables so the wrong ones won't understand them and then get saved. It seems that people weren't meant to be saved if they didn't understand figures of speech" (7 Dec. 1956). Frost appears to find the passage a joke on people who take the Bible too literally. But he appears to be only half in jest.

John Lynen finds in the oppositions and instabilities the strength of the poem. Citing Heidegger, he offers a reader's response view that with each reading a poem is re-created. It is especially true of "Directive," he says, because the poem is built on an elaborate system of paradoxes. The strategy of the poem is "a series of antitheses so numerous and subtly interlinked that the reader's mind is continually engaged in a process of 'composing' or creatively harmonizing miscellaneous sense data into rational wholes." He finally sees the poem as "an earnest commitment to the Sisyphean task of making sense in the face of chaos." While every reader must decide whether, after all the sly allusions and contradictions, the final directive is a sincere one, this reader finds it so. If the traveler succeeds in returning to his source, whatever that source may be, he will have the opportunity to "be whole again beyond confusion"—or, at least, as Frost so famously defined poetry, he will find "a momentary stay against confusion."

References and further reading: Bagby, *Nature*; Duvall; R. Francis, 5; R. Frost, *Letters to Untermeyer*; D. J. Hall, *Contours*, 108–9; Lentricchia, *Modern Poetics*, 112; Lynen, "Du Cote"; T. Morrison, "Agitated"; Oster; Parini, *A Life*, 361–64; Poirier, *Knowing*, 99–100; Richardson, *Ordeal*, 237–43.

Nancy Carol Joyner

"DISCOVERY OF THE MADEIRAS, THE," which first appeared in *A Witness Tree* (1942), has as its source the late sixteenth-century *The Principal*

Navigations, Voyages, Traffiques and Discoveries of the English Nation by Richard Hakluyt, the English geographer and historian. The basic story, as told by Hakluyt, can be found in Jeffrey Cramer's *Robert Frost among His Poems* (1996). The poem contains an interpolated story told by the captain of the ship, regarding the cruel fate of a pair of slave lovers who are bound naked, facing each other, and thrown into the sea alive. The main story and the interpolated one show two pairs of lovers whose romance ends tragically in death.

This poem about tragic love, written after the death of Frost's wife **Elinor** and during the time of his close relationship with **Kathleen Morrison**, possibly carries with it certain personal reflections that go beyond the mere narrative aspect. In the sadly resigned final couplet to not only this poem but the entire "One or Two" poetic sequence in *A Witness Tree*—a sequence that stands as a coda to Frost's relationship with Elinor as it ranges from such early poetic subjects as **"The Subverted Flower"** to poems written in the immediacy of Elinor's death, **"Carpe Diem"** and **"The Wind and the Rain"**—Frost concludes, perhaps looking forward to his own death and reputation, "And soon it is neither here nor there / Whether time's rewards are fair or unfair."

References and further reading: Cramer, *Frost among His Poems*; Richardson, *Ordeal.*
Jeffrey S. Cramer

"DOES NO ONE AT ALL EVER FEEL THIS WAY IN THE LEAST?" was first published as "Does No One But Me at All Ever Feel This Way in the Least" in booklet form as Frost's 1952 **Christmas poem**; the poem was later published in 1962, when Frost was close to ninety years old, in his final volume *In the Clearing*. Although the volume received mixed reviews, it suggests the poet's coming to terms with the close of his career in remarkable ways. "Does No One at All" consists of seven stanzas of six lines each in iambic pentameter. It is a complaint about the lost possibilities of the sea, exacerbated by American homesickness, to function as a protective boundary that could have defined and ensured the promise of greatness of a "New World." What comes across most powerfully in this poem is the coalition of forces, both human and natural, conspiring to prevent newness. A lost Eden is what Frost mourns, an irrecoverable past and identity whose remoteness is suggested by the inland "baby-school" teacher's failure to "give the class a notion" of the sea "by calling it a pool / And telling them how Sinbad was a sailor," an attempt far short of capturing what Frost asks of the sea. We also note Frost's employment of monologue to dramatize a conflict, a technique he utilizes in much of his work, as well as his continuing fascination with issues of boundaries related to the idea of a special Americanness.

References and further reading: For a discussion of the ways in which Frost deals with themes of isolation, particularly his treatment of the American Adam, see Killingsworth. Mason studies how Frost handles conflict by using a dramatic context. See Vogel, *Frost,*

Teacher, for an examination of Frost's conflicted feelings about the value of schoolteachers and education, especially as related to stanza seven.

Susan Burns

"DOOR IN THE DARK, THE," published first in *West-Running Brook* **(1928)**, was written in June of 1928. Under the title "Speaking of Metaphor," the poem was included as part of a letter dated 21 June from Frost to **Louis Untermeyer**; the last two lines of the poem originally contained a reference to Untermeyer's recent remarriage to his first wife, Jean, soon after divorcing his second wife, Virginia. Frost changed the title and removed the personal allusion when he published the poem in *West-Running Brook*. It is the first poem in the collection's final section, "My Native Simile."

The poem's speaker tells how he hit his head against an open door while wandering in a dark room, having forgotten "to lace / My fingers and close my arms in an arc" as shrewd protection against whatever threats could have been concealed by shadows. The impact scrambles the speaker's common sense and perceptions; his words no longer match what he means. Most critics connect the startled speaker's complaint and comic description of his failed ingenuity to save his face with outstretched arms to Frost's concern over the inability of poetry to create effective, lasting metaphors against the dark. Appropriately, Frost writes to Untermeyer of his ambition to write "a few connections." The anecdote related in the poem, however, creates a paradox, for the entire poem is itself a metaphor, both discomforting and humorous.

References and further reading: Cramer, *Frost among His Poems*; R. Frost, *Letters to Untermeyer*.

Mark Sutton

"DRAFT HORSE, THE," was written around 1920 but not published until Frost's final collection, *In the Clearing* **(1962)**. This dark poem relates a senseless act of violence and the speaker's surprisingly mild reaction to it. In five terse quatrains the speaker tells the story of a couple traveling through woods at night under adverse circumstances ("too frail a buggy" and "too heavy a horse") when a man comes out of the woods and stabs the horse. The horse falls dead, breaking his traces and making the night seem darker and more menacing. The gentle couple, not wishing to interpret the act as an evil one, assume that the horse killer or his boss "Wanted us to get down / And walk the rest of the way." While the stark narrative is more straightforward than most of Frost's poems, it nevertheless lends itself to a variety of interpretations.

Monteiro sees the poem as a companion to the two famous woods poems— **"Stopping by Woods on a Snowy Evening"** and **"The Road Not Taken"**— not only because of the settings but also because in each the speaker has a choice to make. Greiner, in exploring the variations of metaphorical interpretations of woods, sees the poem as an example of woods as a place of terror but observes that the couple's acceptance of the evil they encounter "is tempered by the almost humorous, matter-of-fact expression of their blind fatalism." Some critics make a mythic interpretation; Gwynn equates the slaughter with a primitive religion's ritual act in which the animal is killed as a sacrifice, thereby saving the couple. Dorothy Hall compares the couple to Adam and Eve, or perhaps the poet and his wife, and suggests that their reaction to the death of the horse is Job-like. Others, such as Burrell and Tomlinson, put an existential spin on the poem. Tomlinson compares the couple to the protagonists of Beckett's *Waiting for Godot*: She calls them "absurd heroes," choosing "in defiance of the odds to begin again."

While the actors in such drama may reasonably remind readers of Eve or Estragon, very little is known about them. Critics frequently assume that the two riders of the buggy are a married couple, but there is no evidence in the poem to promote that view over any other pair of people. There is evidence in the poem, however, that the two people do not see the death of the horse as a malevolent act but simply a mysterious one. These people neither rail against their fate nor have hard feelings toward the perpetrator of the disaster.

The title seems incongruous, for the poem appears to be not about the draft horse but about the protagonists' failure to react to its slaughter. Their response to the situation calls for our own reaction to it, leading us either to an appreciation of the irony or to admiration of the stoicism demonstrated. Possibly, the couple, who now must use their own feet to get them to their destination and who do not complain about their lot, become a substitute for the draft horse.

References and further reading: Burrell; Greiner, "Dark Woods," 387; Gwynn; D. J. Hall, *Contours*; Monteiro, *New England*; Tomlinson, 29.

Nancy Carol Joyner

DRAMA. Frost is not generally known as a dramatist despite his lifelong love of the theater and despite the fact that many of his best poems owe a large part of their greatness to their dramatic nature. He published only one "official" play in his lifetime, *A Way Out*, which appeared in *The Seven Arts* in 1917. This fascinating one-act play depicts an encounter between a hermit, Asa, and the Stranger, a murderer who takes over Asa's cabin to hide out from the authorities. Eventually, the Stranger tries to take over Asa's identity as well, and the play becomes pregnant with eerie psychological implications. The enigmatic conclusion—oddly anticipatory of Samuel Beckett—leaves the audience in doubt about which character is which, or if the characters have somehow merged, or if indeed they were ever two separate characters to begin with.

Two other Frost plays have been published since his death, *The Guardeen* and *In an Art Factory*. The first is a five-scene play about a college student hired as "guardeen" of a cabin in order to protect the proprietor's cider and to perform a sociological study of a neighbor girl. The other is a one-act conversation play between a sculptor and a model about the nature of art and the role of the artist. Though neither play is ultimately as satisfying or complete as *A Way Out*, they are both interesting as dramatizations of familiar Frostian tensions: individuality versus community, urban life versus rural life, art for art's sake versus art for an audience, self-reliance versus social activism.

Frost's most important "plays," however, may be his two masques, *A Masque of Reason* (1945) and *A Masque of Mercy* (1947). Though both pieces have been staged, they are best considered as closet dramas in which distinctly human, American, and modern prototypes engage in theological/ideological debate via colloquial blank verse. Both pieces are ironic in tone and satirical in aim, but they also constitute Frost's most serious examination of the individual's relationship to God. In *A Masque of Reason*, Frost dramatizes a confrontation between God, Job, and Job's wife Thyatira. Job and Thyatira press God for an explanation of Job's seemingly unwarranted torture, ultimately eliciting the surprising confession, "I was just showing off for the Devil." God, for His part, is enormously grateful to Job for

>   releasing me
> From moral bondage to the human race.
> The only free will there at first was man's,
> Who could do good or evil as he chose.
> . . . .
> I had to prosper good and punish evil.
> You changed all that. You set me free to reign.

Frost's God runs the risk of sounding smug, cruel, and cavalier, yet he seems to serve as spokesperson for Frost's own philosophy on the relationship between humanity and God. As Peter J. Stanlis observes, "The main thrust of Frost's theme is a criticism of the human error of reading man's own rational nature into God." Stanlis continues, "Where the modern rationalist makes man's reason supreme and simply eliminates God as irrelevant to his temporal or spiritual salvation, Frost exalts the omnipotence of God's arbitrary justice and makes man's reason appear peevish and impotent by comparison." Frost dismisses human reason as finally inadequate to understanding the mysteries of divine justice. He therefore endorses Job's conclusion, "But I don't mind. Let's leave it as it stood. / The point was it was none of my concern. / I stick to that."

If *A Masque of Reason* concerns itself chiefly with the individual's treatment of God, *A Masque of Mercy* focuses more on God's treatment of the individual. Specifically, the masque probes the prophet Jonah's difficulty in reconciling Old Testament justice with New Testament mercy. Jonah believes that, in offering mercy to unbelievers, God is failing to dispense justice properly: "I've lost my faith in God to carry out / The threats He makes against the city evil. / I can't trust God to be unmerciful." The merits of Jonah's position are debated in a contemporary New York City bookstore by Paul the Apostle (the primary author of New Testament mercy) and My Brother's Keeper (a proponent of social justice through "New Deal" programs of wealth redistribution). The unlikely pair actually find a good deal of common ground, agreeing that they would rather see justice "mercy-crossed" than "evil-crossed." Paul states the central concern of the masque most clearly when he concedes,

> Yes, there you have it at the root of things.
> We have to stay afraid deep in our souls
> Our sacrifice—the best we have to offer,
> . . . may not
> Be found acceptable in Heaven's sight.
> And that they may be is the only prayer
> Worth praying. May my sacrifice
> Be found acceptable in Heaven's sight.

Again, Frost emphasizes the limitations of humanity's knowledge of God. Just as human reason is insufficient to understand the mysteries of God's justice, so, too, must God's mercy remain unfathomable. Ultimately, human beings must simply have faith that God dispenses mercy as freely (if inscrutably) as he dispenses justice.

As Frost states in his 1929 preface to *A Way Out*, "Everything written is as good as it is dramatic. It need not declare itself in form, but it is drama or nothing." In keeping with this dictum, many of Frost's greatest poems draw their energy from the dramatic tension between two or more speakers (e.g., **"Home Burial," "The Fear," "Two Witches"**). As further evidence of the essential dramatic nature of his poetry, at least two of Frost's dramatic-dialogue poems were adapted and produced for the stage, **"The Death of the Hired Man"** and **"Snow."** Frost himself frequently attended the theater, produced a series of five plays for **Pinkerton Academy** in 1910, and even intended at one point to follow up *North of Boston* with a book of "out and out plays." Unfortunately, such a collection never came to fruition. But the student of theater will find no shortage of fascinating material to study in Frost's work. Whether it "declares itself in form" or not, Frost's work is full of dramatic potential and power.

References and further reading: Brock; R. Frost, "Preface to *A Way Out*," *Collected*; Parini, *A Life*, 120, 202–3, discusses the dramatic quality of the lyrics in *A Boy's Will* and in **"Two Look at Two"** and, 349–58, discusses the masques, arguing that they have been largely ignored; Sell; Sheehy, "Frost and 'Lockless Door' "; Stanlis, *"Masques"*; Sullivan; Winters.

Graley V. Herren

DRAMATIC MONOLOGUE. The dramatic monologue is a type of lyric poem that flourished in the English Victorian period. Though there is no general agreement on a definition of the genre, nor on its origins, Robert Browning's "My Last Duchess" is commonly considered the first dramatic monologue, while his "The Bishop Orders His Tomb" and "Andrea del Sarto," together with Alfred Tennyson's "Ulysses" and "St. Simeon Stylites," rank among the best examples of the form. The two most authoritative attempts at characterizing the dramatic monologue oscillate between an exclusive and an inclusive definition. In her study, Ina B. Sessions lists seven elements she deems indispensable to the dramatic monologue: speaker, audience, occasion, revelation of character, interplay between speaker and audience, dramatic action, and action that takes place in the present. According to Robert Langbaum, on the contrary, a dramatic monologue is not defined by the presence of a set of objective elements but by the fact that its meaning is conveyed through experience. The monologue involves the reader in a vicarious reliving of the speaker's experience.

After its heyday in Victorian **England**, the dramatic monologue found new fertile ground in America. Among its best craftsmen emerged, as Langbaum has noted, **T. S. Eliot, Ezra Pound**, Edgar Lee Masters, **Edwin Arlington Robinson**, Robert Frost, and Robert Lowell. Eliot and Pound especially contributed to the development of the genre. Eliot's *The Waste Land*, in particular, with its collage of dramatic monologues opened a new path for this century's experimentation with the form. Each of these poets used the dramatic monologue for his own purpose. Robinson and Masters wanted the reader to sympathize with misfits of the American scene; Eliot wrote of asexuality and fear of life; Pound actually made dramatic monologues of his paraphrases from the personal utterances of ancient poets by introducing into them a modern consciousness. Frost used the form to expose aberrations of mind and soul in New England.

A classification of Frost's dramatic monologues can rest on Langbaum's crucial standard and on the most discriminating characteristics in Sessions's list: speaker, auditor, and the revelation of character. With a more flexible definition, other poems that employ variations of monologue and dialogue forms could arguably be included in an analysis of Frost's innovative use of the traditional dramatic monologue, but on this rather restricted but firm basis, two poems in Frost's canon—**"The Pauper Witch of Grafton"** and **"A Servant to Servants"** (*see* **"Two Witches"**)—prove to be strict dramatic monologues.

In "The Pauper Witch of Grafton," in fact, the auditor lacks all characterization. The persona seems almost to be talking to herself in a personal outlet of her feelings. According to Langbaum, though, provided the speaker's attention is directed outward, the poem can be considered a dramatic monologue because the fundamental aim of self-expression is reached anyway. The poem conveys not only the revelation of the speaker's character but also the depiction of a local atmosphere. The woman begins her monologue in the aggressive tone of someone who has been hurt and wants to strike back at the offender. Her narrative gradually reveals the situation. It opens and closes in the present tense, and even when it refers to the past, it does so for the sake of its weight on the present action. The witch of Grafton appears as a woman who is thought to be a witch and for this reason is rejected by two towns in New England, Warren and Wentworth. She starts out playing the witch who plans to add what confusion she can to her neighbors' awkward attempts to clarify her nature and her origins but finally gives in to the sense of decadence and solitude that has come over her life. As in many of Browning's dramatic monologues, Frost's begins with a touch of the picturesque and ends with the ring of a deep and moving, universal note. "The Pauper Witch of Grafton" is linked to the tradition of the dramatic monologue also by its language, which is strongly in the colloquial register and is loosely blank verse in metrical scansion.

"A Servant to Servants" belongs more legitimately to the genre of the dramatic monologue. The auditor has an identity and interacts with the speaker. The latter is a woman who is telling her friend how glad she is to have her camping on her land. Through the projection of her lifestyle against the background of her friend's choices and way of living, the woman realizes her psychological predicament. By way of often unintentional hints, she reveals her unhappiness as the wife of a New England farmer who has devoted his life to hard work and frugality. Her existence, consequently, has consisted of performing a large number of heavy tasks, such as cooking for "a houseful of hungry men." The anxiety to fulfill her duty has now brought her to lose her sense of pleasure—a typical sign of modern neurosis. To the traditional revelation of an individual character, Frost adds the ingredient of a psychological approach. By the end of the monologue, it becomes clear that her problem is her passive nature, which renders her unable to express her feelings. Langbaum points out that "A Servant to Servants" resembles Victorian dramatic monologues also in the incidental quality of the speaker's self-revelation and in the disequilibrium with what she reveals and understands. As in Browning's "My Last Duchess," a slight suggestion of the possibility of the speaker's mental illness adds an intriguing flavor to the reader's involvement in her monologue.

References and further reading: Langbaum, esp. 76–77, 93–94, 146; Sessions.

Paola Loreto

"DREAM PANG, A," first appeared in *A Boy's Will* (**1913**). In this **sonnet**, the speaker struggles with conflicting desires: to be an isolated individual unencumbered by care and responsibility and to be a partner in a conjugal relationship. James Potter recognizes the poem as an intimate love poem to **Elinor**, Richard Poirier uses it to offer subtle insights into Frost's strong association of lovemaking with making poetry, and Ronald Bieganowski reads the poem in the context of Frost's relationship to Henri Bergson and the idea that dreaming, reminiscence, and poetry permit the poet to "span an interval of duration" by helping him appreciate his lover's presence in contrast to her former absence.

References and further reading: Bieganowski, *"A Boy's Will* and Bergson," 11; Poirier, *Knowing*; Potter; Thompson, *Early Years.*

Chris-Anne Stumpf

"DRUMLIN WOODCHUCK, A," first appeared in the *Atlantic Monthly* (Apr. 1936) and was collected in *A Further Range* (**1936**). It has lent its title to a biography of Saul Bellow, who remarked in 1961, "Frost is a different kettle of

woodchuck altogether. Woodchuck I say because he has more exits to his burrow than any man can count" (qtd. in Harris). The drumlin woodchuck penned
by Frost, of course, has for his own burrow but two exits, which suffice to give
the creature a strategic confidence. The woodchuck describes his retreat with
the shrewdness of a skilled real estate agent. He details the benefits of his rock-
solid foyer, his cozy living area, and the quietude of his study; he even begins
by announcing that compared to his den the rest of the neighborhood, while
serviceable, has to get by on "rotting planks." Appearing in the "Taken Doubly"
portion of *A Further Range*, the poem's subtitle—"Be Sure to Locate"—stresses
the importance of finding a suitable niche for one's survival and safety. Indeed,
Frost once said, "I never tire of being shown how the limited can make snug
in the limitless" (qtd. in Thompson, *Fire and Ice*). According to the woodchuck,
the "limitless" in which he must foster his safe-house includes hunters and other
attackers: They are the equivalents of "war and pestilence / And the loss of
common sense." Against all life's tribulation and ruin, really, he has only his
home to protect him. Still, even "As measured against the All," this "crevice
and burrow" do what they must: They allow him to live another day.

Autobiographical parallels in the poem are tempting to draw, especially for
those who deem Frost to be, like the protagonist, "one who shrewdly pretends /
That he and the world are friends." "The drumlin" of the title signifies an elongated hill or ridge of glacial drift, and the poet undoubtedly was influenced by
a specific drumlin near The Gully, his Vermont home. Frost himself felt "A
Drumlin Woodchuck," his "most Vermontly poem," to be a "smug poem" but
"a love poem, too" (qtd. in R. Cook, "Frost's Asides"). The latter point should
not be overlooked. The woodchuck's mate, whom he addresses directly at the
end, becomes an ulterior justification for his tidy fortification. Beyond simply
living another day or year, the drumlin woodchuck is living for his beloved.
After a reading, Frost once suggested that in this poem, especially, the tone is
everything. Whether one finds in it dismissive sarcasm, saccharine ingratiation,
or pure sincerity, the idea remains that the poem concerns not just the connection
between self and surroundings but the relationship between two beings.

The "little whistle" given by those "who prefer to live" hearkens to the animal's nickname of "whistle pig," its regional epithet in the Appalachian Mountains. The creature himself, however, seems at times actually to disappear from
the poem, as if dipping into a subterranean stanza somewhere off the page, only
to resurface "after the hunt goes past." One never gets a physical glimpse of the
woodchuck, only that hint of a whistle and a narration of its stance outside its
home. Such evasive qualities help to link the themes of self and place. Bagby
calls one aspect of this idea "the boundary line of property and selfhood." The
poem is as much, if not more so, about the homey burrow as it is about the
drumlin woodchuck. Indeed, the animal's very name suggests a poetic species
with a kind of residual status: He seems himself a tiny remnant of glacial passage.

References and further reading: Bagby, *Nature*, 64; R. Cook, "Frost's Asides"; Mark Harris, *Saul Bellow: Drumlin Woodchuck* (Athens: University of Georgia Press, 1980), 14; Oehlschlaeger, "Two Woodchucks"; Parini, *A Life*, 293–94; Thompson, *Fire and Ice*.

Eric C. Brown

"DUST IN THE EYES," first appearing as an advertisement for *West-Running Brook* **(1928)**, the volume in which it appears, reads less as a piece of self-promotion than as the poet's acquiescence to charges of "getting overwise." Nonetheless, his willingness to be humbled is made uncertain by his poetic structure and by his Promethean posturing. By setting "as they say" in commas and letting the stress fall on *they*, Frost calls attention to the hint that his need for humiliation was not his idea. Similarly, by characterizing his humiliation as a test in need of "proof," he may be tacitly reminding his readers that an awareness of suffering is central to his wisdom. Like the mythical Prometheus, who was tortured by Zeus for bringing fire to humanity, the poet defies his punishment by invoking the worst, a "blizzard snow for dust." Although he would be humbled, the excess of his punishment would testify to his native endurance. **R. Cook** records that in a 1955 **Bread Loaf** lecture Frost links the Greek world-view to his Puritan sensibility through their shared distrust of pleasure. If his humiliation overwhelms him to the point of blindness and "a standstill," then it offers the poet a grim recompense in the certainty of his pain.

References and further reading: R. Cook, *Living Voice*, 88–105, includes Frost's lecture on Puritanism; Monroe, "Frugal."

Michael Berndt

"DUST OF SNOW" first appeared as "A Favour" in the *London Mercury* (Dec. 1920), was later published in the *Yale Review* as "Snow Dust" (Jan. 1921), and finally appeared in *New Hampshire* **(1923)** under the present title. It belongs to the batch of poems Frost originally placed in his "Grace Notes" section of *New Hampshire*. For such a "small" poem—one sentence spread over eight lines and thirty-four words in total, of which only two are more than one syllable in length—it has undergone many title changes. It has appeared as "Mercy," "A Favour," and "Snow Dust," before finally settling down into "Dust of Snow."

Laurence Perrine suggests that there are only four ways to characterize the crow's behavior: beautifully, animatedly, cheerily, and humorously. Another possibility is to consider that the crow did nothing on purpose; its action has no inherent meaning. Only the man can choose to give the crow's action meaning—to see it as significant. The man's "change of mood" occurs not as a result of "the way a crow" did something but in how he saw, or perhaps misinterpreted, the event as having meaning. The man's delight can be from recognizing such human error in perception.

"Dust of Snow" playfully recasts the interplay between man and bird found in **"The Wood-pile."** In the darker poem, the speaker is wrong to assume what the bird is thinking, and the bird commits the same error of misinterpretation (as seen by the speaker). In the lighthearted and comical "Dust of Snow," the poem is a commentary on the speaker's thinking that the crow has made some commentary about the speaker. The joke is on Frost (in the poem) and on the reader, but it's done in an uplifting way. We get our own little dusting at the hands of Frost. *See also* **Nature Poet and Naturalist**.

References and further reading: Monteiro, *New England*; Oster; Perrine, "Frost's 'Dust of Snow' "; Waggoner, *American Poets*.

Robert W. Scott

E

"EGG AND THE MACHINE, THE," first published in 1928 as "The Walker" in *The Second American Caravan*, became a part of *West-Running Brook* **(1928)** with the publication of *Collected Poems* in 1930. The poem's inclusion in *West-Running Brook* was continued in *Collected Poems* **(1939)** and in *The Complete Poems of Robert Frost 1949*.

"The Egg and the Machine" explores the tension between technology or industry and nature, a frequent theme of Frost's work. A train, with "a roar that drowned the cries," speeds by a subject who does not understand how an object of such power can be created and who attributes the wonder to "the gods in the machine" instead of to the progress of his fellow human beings. Promising to be "armed for war," should the train return, the individual imagines turtle eggs as "Torpedo-like" and takes heart that the next train to return "Will get this plasm in its goggle glass." Frost does not suggest an obvious or easily achieved resolution to the conflict between technology and nature portrayed in his poem and instead seemingly calls upon readers to negotiate the conflict for themselves.

Yvor Winters uses "The Egg and the Machine" as a primary example in his castigation of Frost as a shallow, dangerous thinker, accusing Frost of naive treatment of the conflict between machines and nature. The action of Frost's poem is infantile, Winters argues, and action and poem alike represent "a petulant and self-righteous gesture, a feeble joke."

References and further reading: Cramer, *Frost among His Poems*; Winters.

James A. Inman and Andy Duncan

ELIOT, T. S. (1888–1965), and Robert Frost, although both prominent twentieth-century poets, had very different personalities and philosophies. Eliot was educated at **Harvard**, the Sorbonne, and Oxford. While at the Sorbonne in 1910–1911, he attended the lectures of Bergson and was so greatly impressed by the ideas as to claim that Bergson's mind should be the twentieth-century mind. At almost the same time, Frost was beginning to study Bergson, having read high praise of him in a book by William James (see **Philosophy**). Frost soon placed Bergson with James and **Emerson** at the center of his intellectual life and kept him there: Twenty years later he was still making metaphor inspired by these philosophers. Eliot, however, needed a species of fixed certainty that Bergson's philosophy would not allow, and in 1914 he stood at a crossroads, still speaking of Bergson's relativism but complaining that his interest in Bergson was making it nearly impossible to write the Bradley thesis.

Such a clash reveals a basic difference between Eliot and Frost. Eliot's doctoral thesis was on the British philosopher F. H. Bradley, and Bradley's world is far from Bergson's and far from Frost's. Frost's "best teacher," William James, attacked Bradley's rationalism and absolutism on numerous occasions, for although Bradley was a modern philosopher, in many ways he was pre-Modernist: He put great trust in Plato and in logic; he believed in an Absolute that was a nonliving, rational concept. Eliot's involvement with such philosophy would have drawn him toward the Right in **politics**, further and further from the Modernist pluralism and relativism of Bergson and James.

In 1927, Eliot expressed his predilection for royalist and hierarchic absolutes by becoming a British citizen and an Anglo-Catholic, after which, like **Ezra Pound**, he took a further step into anti-Semitism. As Frost put it, "If I was ever cross with you it was for leaving America too far and Ezra not far enough behind." As Burwick and Douglass note, Eliot rejected the creative evolution of Bergson and gloomily took arms against what he called "the fallacy of progress, which is the Bergsonian fallacy." Typical of Eliot's pessimism is his claim that "Life is death" and his famous description of how the world ends. Frost was cognizant and called him in one letter "world's-end-whimper T. S. Eliot." Furthermore, Frost was upset to hear Eliot dismiss Burns and claim that perhaps the only good poem produced in Scotland was Dunbar's one with the refrain "Timor mortis conturbat me [the fear of death disturbs me]." On another occasion Frost remarked that while he himself played euchre, Eliot played eucharist—a Frostian pun, which, like Joyce's puns, responds to reflection, and a little reflection discovers that Frost's card game is based on risk that Frost loved, whereas Eliot's eucharist is a ritual celebration of death. Going up to Cambridge once to visit Eliot, Frost said, "I have a rendezvous with death." Frost, the Bergsonian, had a different approach to the all and the nothing; he claimed in his "Letter to *The Amherst Student*" that any little form he achieved was "velvet and to be considered for how much more it is than nothing. If I were a Platonist I should have to consider it, I suppose, for how much less it is than everything."

In 1928, Frost visited London and had a meal with Eliot, describing him afterward as affecting an English accent, engrossed in his own affairs, and "a mealy-mouthed snob." In 1932, Frost attended a dinner in Boston in honor of Eliot and later admitted to some disgust as he watched how Eliot patronized his overawed questioners. In 1934 he wrote to his daughter Lesley, "I confess I

have several times forgotten my dignity in speaking in public of Eliot"; he added
that Eliot had even greater learning than Pound. It would seem that much of
Frost's negative criticism of Eliot the man and the poet was prompted by the
view that Eliot was recognized as deep, whereas Frost's own poetry, both erudite
and superficially accessible, was not being read carefully in the universities.
John Zubizarreta has shown how Eliot's difficulty disturbs us in an overt way,
whereas Frost uses internal ironies under an ostensibly simple surface. Frost was
indeed far from simple, and he had some justification for his resentment of the
lionizing of Eliot, the more so when we consider that he had gone very far into
the nature of America, while Eliot had become British.

Nonetheless, in spite of their differences, the two great men eventually began
to treat each other with magnanimity. Burnshaw records that in 1947 Frost had
a surprise visit from Eliot: "Without a warning he knocked at my door . . . 'to
pay his respects.' I welcomed him in, still amazed. And there we sat—in my
front room—soon at ease with each other, talking about everything in the world:
his own writing, mine, the War. . . . I hadn't liked him at all when we'd met
before, twice. . . . Everything changed." And when, ten years later, Frost visited
England in June 1957, he was invited to luncheon at the home of Mr. and Mrs.
T. S. Eliot, where, as Frost reported, "It was all easy, friendly, polite. He seemed
to like to listen more than to speak." Two days later, there was a dinner in his
honor at which T. S. Eliot was toastmaster. Frost had become rather deaf, and
Eliot, sensing this, invited him to sit by his side as he made a speech in his
honor: "Mr. Frost is . . . perhaps, the most eminent, the most distinguished, I
must call it, Anglo-American poet now living. . . . There is another kind [of local
feeling] which can go with universality: the relation of Dante to Florence, of
Shakespeare to Warwickshire, of Goethe to the Rhineland, the relation of Robert
Frost to New England. He has that universality." Frost replied, almost in tears,
"There's nobody living in either country that I'd rather hear that from."

References and further reading: Burnshaw, 133; Frederick Burwick and Paul Douglass,
The Crisis in Modernism: Bergson and the Vitalist Controversy (New York: Cambridge
University Press; 1992), 295–98; R. Frost, *Family Letters*, 160, 233, 567, "Letter to *The
Amherst Student*," *Collected*, 739–40; Anthony Julius, *T. S. Eliot, Anti-Semitism, and
Literary Form.* (New York: Cambridge University Press, 1995); Richardson, *Ordeal*;
Thompson, *Triumph*, 337–38, 402–3, 661; Thompson and Winnick, 243–44; Zubizarreta.

Gerard Quinn

EMERSON, RALPH WALDO (1803–1882), was a major figure in the heyday
of American Transcendentalism, the cultural movement that helped introduce
European Romanticism into New England. A philosopher and a poet, Emerson
had an idealistic, platonic conception of the universe. He saw the Divinity as
immanent in nature and based his theory of knowledge on the conviction that
the human senses are able to perceive in nature signs that are symbols of spiritual
realities. In "Nature" (1836), the best known of his essays and what was later
taken as a key "manifesto" of the Transcendentalist movement, he describes his

moments of insight within nature with the famous words, "I become a trans-parent eye-ball. I am nothing. I see all." Another essay fundamental in its im-portance for later writers was "The Poet," in which Emerson defines his concept of the expressive nature of poetic creation.

As Frost himself declared in the essay "On Emerson," Emerson was one of the earliest and strongest influences in his education, and a lifelong one. Hyatt H. Waggoner writes that together with Walt Whitman, Emily Dickinson, and **Edwin Arlington Robinson**, Frost establishes the direct Emersonian line of descent in American poetry, even though his world "gets its special character-istics from its unique combination of closeness and distance from Emerson's world."

Frost inherited Emerson's conception of the universe and the theory of knowl-edge deriving from it. He also shared with Emerson his notions about the nature of poetic creation. In the purest Romantic tradition, Frost believed in poetic inspiration and thought that poetry was a form of intuitive knowledge. In "The Poet," Emerson had written that "the world is a temple whose walls are covered with emblems, pictures . . . of the Deity." Frost, for his part, called himself a mystic, who believed in symbols. For both poets, a poem is born from an insight that leads to the articulation of its own expression. Other important principles of Frost's thinking that can be traced back to Emerson are his concentration on the individual quest for selfhood, owing much to Emerson's doctrine of self-reliance, and his emphasis on facts as a point of departure for symbolic signif-icance.

Frost expressed his strong admiration for Emerson openly. In his speech "On Emerson" he called him "the poet" and named him as one of the "four greatest Americans"; he also acknowledged Emerson's philosophical blend of poetry as his favorite. In a letter to **Louis Untermeyer**, he wrote that Emerson had "one of the noblest least egotistical of styles." In another one to Lawrance Thompson he declared Emerson an extraordinary poet both in **prose** and verse. Among Frost's favorite poems by Emerson were "Uriel," "Monadnoc," and "Brahama." It is probably "Uriel" to which he refers in A Masque of Reason as "the greatest Western poem yet," and in a conversation with Hyatt Waggoner, Frost com-mented that "Uriel" anticipated "the moral of Einstein." Lawrance Thompson notes that "Monadnoc" seems to have played a relevant role in the development of Frost's theory of "sentence sounds" by providing a convincing example of how verse could catch the speech rhythms of everyday life.

As Parini points out, even when Frost was creating distance between himself and Emerson, it was more by way of extension than contradiction. The main controversial question was that of Emerson's "cheerful" Monism versus Frost's "melancholic" Dualism. According to Emerson, the universe was a perfectly round circle at whose center was God, that is, the principle of Good. According to Frost in "On Emerson," a circle is round only ideally, in thought, while in practice, in nature, the circle becomes an oval that has two centers: Good and Evil. The difference in their opinions, though, was more apparent than real. On the one hand, Frost tended to diminish the importance of such distinctions by wondering whether soundness of reasoning is of the essence. On the other, Emerson himself was aware of the contradictions arising from his philosophical thinking but was inclined to overlook them. As Frost said once in a letter to Thompson, Emerson "could see the 'good of evil born' but he couldn't bring himself to say the evil of good born." Also, Frost distinguished himself from Emerson in the different tone he used both in his life and in his poetry. As a public figure, a semiofficial poet laureate, he wore the mask of a caustic but confident Yankee rustic. As a poet, he often employed irony and humor. Irony, of course, has been the ordinary mode of our century's poetry—a means of keeping a fruitful ambiguity of meaning that Frost was ready to exploit. Waggoner notes that Frost departs from Emerson in his use of humor to make the affirmation seem casual.

Parini concludes that Frost fulfilled the Emersonian goals better than Emerson himself because he was better able to fasten words again to visible things. Waggoner holds that Frost could make "Emerson's points for him in ways that Emerson himself would have recognized as superior." Frost's deep respect for the Emersonian tradition to which he was heir was recognized during his life through the award of the Emerson-**Thoreau** Medal by the American Academy of Arts and Sciences (8 Oct. 1958) and through his appointment as a Ralph Waldo Emerson Fellow in Poetry at **Harvard University** (10 May 1939).

References and further reading: Quotations from Emerson's works are taken from Joseph Slater et al., eds., *The Collected Works of Ralph Waldo Emerson* (Boston: Harvard University Press, 1971); "On Emerson" is the address Frost delivered on the occasion of the award of the Emerson-Thoreau Medal and can be found in R. Frost, *Collected*, 860–66; Parini, "Emerson and Frost," offers an exhaustive, recent study of the weight of Emerson's work on Frost's poetry and poetics; Thompson, *Triumph*, contains factual information about Frost's relationship to Emerson; Waggoner, *American Poets*, 91, 112, 293–327, provides a seminal study of Emerson's influence on Frost; see also R. Frost, *Interviews* and *Selected Letters*, 299, 584.

Paola Loreto

"EMPTY THREAT, AN," with its short lines, provides visual and aural relief in the context of *New Hampshire* **(1923)**, where it first appeared, for it follows many pages of blank verse poems. In many of his poems, Frost imagines other lives; here he imagines an alternative one for himself—a life not taken, as it were. It is a vision of radical solitude, in which there is no one else between the speaker and the North Pole. Contemplating the fur trade, he dreams of purveying something more practical and solid than poems, a dream also of a relationship with simple, hardy, self-sufficient folk like John-Joe the Esquimaux. Perhaps Frost is longing for, as he sketches a correlative of, one of his "desert places." Imagining his way up to Hudson's Bay causes the speaker to turn in the last part of the poem to contemplation of Henry Hudson, a figure who failed radically. Such failure is absolute and final, like the absolute cold of which the speaker dreams as he expresses dissatisfaction with the ceaseless *talk* that clutters his life, the noisy life of small compromises he spurns, but only rhetorically, in the poem's final stanza.

References and further reading: Perrine, "Frost's 'An Empty Threat' "; Pritchard, *Literary Life*; Thompson, *Fire and Ice*.

C. P. Seabrook Wilkinson

"ENCOUNTER, AN," which first appeared in the *Atlantic Monthly* (Nov. 1916) and was included in **Mountain Interval (1916)**, addresses the issue of technology's encroachment upon nature. The speaker of the poem has ventured "out of beaten ways" into a realm where nature has so profusely filled the scene that a clear path is discouragingly difficult to find. The move into such a region of tangled vegetation is ultimately rewarding, however. In Frost's poems, the person who dares to go into unfamiliar territory usually learns a valuable, if subtle, lesson. In this case, the speaker finds out that the land he traverses has been marked to its detriment by modern industrial development. A "resurrected tree," a "barkless specter" that "drag[s] yellow strands / Of wire with something in it from men to men" catches the speaker off guard. The tree-turned-telephone pole is personified in the poem, but it does not have the ability, as the speaker does, to say what it knows. The questions the speaker poses to the "tree" regarding its role in the world and the nature of the "something" it carries from "men to men" remain unanswered. Apparently, the real power of communication stays with those who have a poetic sensibility, not those whose sole power lies in practical, industrial transmissions. "An Encounter" reminds us that good communication is often indirect. Like the speaker whose route is somewhat haphazardly determined (his goal is not perfectly defined: He is "Half-looking for the orchid Calypso"), the wisdom we gain often comes to us in unexpected ways, perhaps even through unanswered questions—that is, in poetry as in life, we often learn serendipitously, when we are half-aware and our thoughts are actually directed elsewhere.

References and further reading: Bagby, *Nature*; Bieganowski, "Frost's 'An Encounter.' "

Sabine Sautter-Leger

"ENDS," appearing first in **In the Clearing (1962)**, suggests love's sad dissolution. Dorothy Judd Hall recalls that in the midst of reading "Ends" aloud Frost once remarked, "Love can't have a happy ending." A particular marriage is the focus of the first verse, but by the end of the poem, we feel the sad dissolution of all promising beginnings in human life. As Hall notes, Frost's poems frequently assert that nothing is salvageable from waste and dwindling in human affairs. We sense the biblical overtones and Edenic corruption lying behind the shouting in the "overlighted house" in the emphatic phrases "Night the first" and "night the last." What once began in bliss for the couple long before is now drawing to an end in blistering recriminations.

From the dissolving marriage of the first two stanzas, Frost abstracts a principle that comments on it and yet goes beyond it to the general condition of all human endeavors. The third stanza insists that in the blindness of our nature, when we argue over love (and other matters), we cannot distinguish easily the past from the present, the small from the large, the inconsequential from the serious. We are apt to misunderstand the dimensions of our problem and so take a small part for the whole and place too much weight upon it until we break the whole. The cause of the confusion in communication, the last two lines suggest, is that some of us say too much without discriminating, whereas others of us speak soberly and to the point.

References and further reading: Dorothy Judd Hall, in *Contours*, writes from the standpoint of personal acquaintance with Frost and with his daughter Lesley and is an excellent source for discussion of Frost's metaphysics, especially 101; Reichert, 422, speaks of two poems reflective of Frost's themes in "Ends": **"Away!"** and **"West-Running Brook"**; Thompson, *Triumph*, 693–94, discusses Frost's use of synecdoche to establish metaphysical meaning.

Larry R. Isitt

ENGLAND. It would be hard to overestimate the importance of Frost's English years, which stretched from September 1912 to February 1915. Frost came to England a thirty-eight-year-old man who had spent many years as a farmer in New Hampshire and a few years as a **teacher**. Although he had published a handful of poems in scattered periodicals, he knew almost nobody in the literary world. He left England just over two years later with two well-received books under his belt and with another nearly finished. He was by now widely admired in English literary circles and had been befriended by many of the leading poets of the day, including **W. B. Yeats** and **Ezra Pound**.

What drove Frost and his family to England in the first place was the poet's overwhelming sense that he must do something drastic to change the course of his career. He needed time to write, and teaching had not been good for this. His days had been utterly absorbed by the work at **Pinkerton Academy** and the **Plymouth Normal School** in New Hampshire.

Frost was able to take his family abroad largely because he had recently come into an inheritance from his paternal grandfather in the form of an annuity. This money—roughly $800 per year—was payable each summer; it was just enough to live on, provided the family did not attempt to live too extravagantly. The family—Frost, **Elinor**, and their four young children—arrived by ship in Glasgow in early September 1912 and traveled by train to London. After a few weeks of searching, Frost found a house in the suburban town of Beaconsfield, in Buckinghamshire. It was called The Bungalow. The family kept to themselves through the fall, while Frost assembled his first collection, *A Boy's Will* **(1913)**.

Frost quickly found a publisher for his work in London. The firm of **David**

Nutt accepted the book within a week of reading it, and they took an option on the next four: an astounding act of goodwill. Now Frost had to get a foothold in British literary society.

The opportunity to do so came on 8 January 1913, at a party for the opening of a new bookshop owned by Harold Monro on Devonshire Street in London. There Frost met several of the leading poets of the day, including F. S. Flint, who in turn introduced him to Ezra Pound, Wilfrid Gibson, and others. With amazing rapidity, Frost was taken in by British literary society. He often attended weekly meetings at the home of W. B. Yeats in London, and he went to similar meetings at the home of T. E. Hulme, a leading theorist of poetry who was closely allied with the Imagist School of poets (which included Ezra Pound and **Amy Lowell**).

His first collection, *A Boy's Will*, was published to brief but mostly respectful reviews in March of 1913. Frost's poetry superficially resembled that of the currently fashionable **Georgian poets**, who wrote simple verses about country things, and he was quickly assimilated as a member of this school. Among the well-known Georgian poets were Rupert Brooke, Wilfrid Gibson, W. H. Davies, Ralph Hodgson, Edmund Blunden, J. C. Squire, and Robert Graves (*see also* **Georgian Poetry**).

David Nutt published Frost's second collection, ***North of Boston***, in the spring of 1914, and the reviews this time were almost uniformly enthusiastic. Frost had won the support of several important poet–critics of the day, including Wilfrid Gibson, Lascelles Abercrombie, and Edward Thomas. Ezra Pound also joined the chorus of praise, reviewing the book enthusiastically in *Poetry*, the Chicago journal founded by **Harriet Monroe**.

Edward Thomas became one of Frost's closest friends in 1914. Thomas was not yet a poet, although he had already published twenty-six books, a miscellany of travel narratives, nature writing, criticism, and biography. Encouraged by Frost, Thomas turned his hand to poetry, writing poems very much in the vein of Frost's work, although Thomas had his own unmistakable voice. When he was killed in the war, a year later, Frost was deeply affected.

The Frosts moved from Beaconsfield to a small village in Gloucester at the suggestion of Wilfrid Gibson. They rented a small house in the Dymock region called Little Iddens—a house that reminded the family of their farm in **Derry**, New Hampshire. Frost entered upon his most productive period there, working on such poems as **"Mending Wall," "After Apple-Picking,"** and **"Birches."** Going to England apparently provoked just enough homesickness in the poet for him to return in his poetry to the landscape and people who most deeply stirred his imagination.

In Gloucestershire, Frost found himself part of a congenial group of writers. He benefited immensely from being part of the Dymock poets—the only such group or school of writers with whom he would ever willingly associate. One catches a glimpse of what these informal gatherings were like in Wilfrid Gibson's "The Golden Room," cited by Lesley Francis:

Do you remember the still summer evening
When in the cosy cream-washed living room
Of the Old Nailshop we all talked and laughed—
Our neighbors from the Gallows, Catherine
and Lascelles Abercrombie; Rubert Brooke;
Elinor and Robert Frost, living awhile
At Little Iddens, who'd brought over with them
Helen and Edward Thomas? In the lamplight
We talked and laughed, but for the most part listened
While Robert Frost kept on and on and on
In his slow New England fashion for our delight,
Holding us with shrewd turns and racy quips,
And the rare twinkle of his grave blue eyes?

We sat there in the lamplight while the day
Died from rose-latticed casements, and the plovers
Called over the low meadows till the owls
Answered them from the elms; we sat and talked—

Now a quick flash from Abercrombie, now
A murmured dry half-heard aside from Thomas,
Now a clear, laughing word from Brooke, and then
Again Frost's rich and ripe philosophy
That had the body and tang of good draught-cider
And poured as clear a stream.

Gibson's portrait of Frost reveals something of the public manner he later perfected on platforms across the United States. His homespun "rich and ripe philosophy" went down well among the Dymock group, and it played well in
England overall, as it would eventually in Frost's own country.

During their last fall in England, in 1914, Frost and his family left Little
Iddens for The Gallows, a thatch-roofed, rambling farmhouse in a neighboring
village that was occupied by Lascelles and Catherine Abercrombie. The Aber-
crombies were traveling through much of the season, and they were happy to
share their house. This was, however, an uncertain time for Frost. The Great
War had broken out the previous summer, and the threat of a German blockade
on British ports made the prospects for a return passage to the United States
less than bright. Frost decided that he must go home, even though he was not
sure what he would do upon his return.

He was deeply unsure of what he might do when he returned, but he was
hesitant to take another grueling teaching job, although he knew this might be
necessary. He dreamed of "a quiet job in a small college where I would be
allowed to teach something a little new on the technique of writing and where
I should have some honor for what I suppose myself to have done in Poetry."
At this point, however, he could not imagine that any college would be willing
to hire him.

The family left from Liverpool on the *St. Paul*, an American liner, on 13 February, taking with them Mervyn Thomas, the fifteen-year-old son of Edward and Helen Thomas. Frost's feelings toward England on the eve of his departure are perhaps best seen in a farewell note to Harold Monro, whose support had been invaluable: "Thanks for everything. I had intended to see you before leaving but at the last moment we go rather precipitously; so that I am scanting duties. Anyway I don't want too much made of my going or I should feel as if I were never coming back. England has become half my native land—England the victorious. Good friends I have had here and hope to keep."

Frost would always look upon the English years as a crucial experience. Although he had already found his voice before setting foot in England, there he would be able to connect to his first real audience. In the supportive atmosphere of English literary society, especially among the Dymock poets, he was able to summon his deepest energies as a writer, and many of his best poems were written in The Bungalow, Little Iddens, and The Gallows.

References and further reading: L. Francis, *Morning Gladness*; R. Frost, *Selected Letters*, 138, 152; Parini, *A Life*; Thompson, *Early Years*; Walsh.

Jay Parini

"EQUALIZER, AN," first appeared in *A Witness Tree* (1942) during a time when Frost did not like the turn he thought the country was taking under Roosevelt and the Democrats. In the poem Frost conveys his view that the new welfare economists of the day would like to see all people made equal financially. He feels such economists actually despise the capitalistic way of life and even view thrift as miserly rather than as virtuous. When the gap between rich and poor gets too wide, the New Deal economist feels he can cure the economy and regain the public health by taking from the rich and giving to the poor, making the poor equal with the wealthy. The medicine the country would have to take in the form of such an "equalizer" would, to Frost, be a bitter pill to swallow. Frost shows his disdain for what he regards as unjust.

In 1947, Frost wrote to **Louis Untermeyer**, "At every commencement I hear young Americans reproach themselves or their country with the indecency of our success and prosperity. I get sick of it. . . . I was born and brought up to our kind of capitalism and I feel as if I might as well not change it to their [Marxists'] form of the same thing." *See also* **Politics**.

References and further reading: R. Cook, *Living Voice*, 106; R. Frost, *Letters to Untermeyer*, 347; Sergeant, 318, 353; Frost, *Selected Letters*, 533, and numerous references to Roosevelt and New Deal.

Sarah R. Jackson

"ESCAPIST—NEVER" was published in the *Massachusetts Review* in 1962, when Frost was eighty-seven years old, and was later included in his final volume, *In the Clearing* (1962). The poem is about restless pursuit; significantly, the last word is "longing." The generalized "He" could represent Everyman, but most critics assume Frost is referring to himself. As Lawrance Thompson points out, Frost grappled with the advantages and disadvantages of running away throughout his career. **"Into My Own,"** for example, describes the allure of "steal[ing] away" into the woods, and much of his work contains similar retreats into nature, causing many readers to see Frost as an escapist. John F. Lynen talks of Frost's "withdrawal from the modern city to an agrarian world that belongs to the past." In the same way, Thompson says Frost "could and did frequently run away to nature, as a means of escape from unpleasantness." Frost himself sometimes buttressed such views, saying, with a smile, "Me for the hills."

Yet more often, he denied he was an escapist, calling himself a "pursuitist" instead. As he told a large audience at **Harvard** in 1936, "We are chasing something rather than being chased." In "Escapist—Never," the emphatic negatives in the title and first three lines reject all charges of escape, and in the remainder of the poem Frost depicts the "He" as a pursuer who "seeks a seeker who in his turn seeks." In such an endless hall of mirrors, the goal is ambiguous and unclear, but the pursuer keeps moving ahead resolutely, with none of the hesitation that Frost displays in earlier poems such as **"The Demiurge's Laugh."** Like the speaker in **"The Onset,"** the pursuer here faces forward, toward the future. His fear is "beside him," an almost positive force helping him to press ahead. The poem presents several paradoxes. Life is "a pursuit of a pursuit forever." While this prospect may give the speaker a sense of yearning at the end, it also seems to offer a certain satisfaction. The pursuit, the not giving up or swerving from the "crooked straightness" of the trail, seems to be a victory and affirmation. The poem shows Frost at the end of his career still forging ahead and delighting in the chase even as he longs for it to be over.

References and further reading: Lynen, *Pastoral Art*, 174–82; O'Donnell, "Frost at Eighty-eight"; Oster, 277, n.24, observes that portions of the poem have origins in an unpublished draft of **"Two Look at Two"**; Potter, 122; Thompson, *Triumph*, 595; Vogel, *Frost, Teacher*, 67.

Christopher Krentz

"ETHEREALIZING" was first published in the *Atlantic Monthly* (Apr. 1947) and subsequently in Frost's *Steeple Bush* **(1947)**. "Etherealizing" offers printed proof that Frost could write not only lyrical and "dark" **sonnets** but also humorous and even satirical sonnets on a subject in which he has a serious interest: **science**.

His attitude is often ambivalent; he can entertain scientific tenets seriously, or he can mock them, especially when it is assumed science is gospel or scientists omniscient. The attitude mocked here is suggested by the word "hard" in the first line. "Hard," in the sense of concrete, real proof, may be positive, but it can also be deleterious to hold theories "hard," with a closed mind that might exclude other explanations. The danger in an age fascinated by ratings lies in a rigidity that leads to a theory's being "rated as a creed." What is mocked severely in this poem is overintellectualizing, valuing mind over body and rejecting the likelihood of soul. Describing the process as "slough" connotes an insect's or reptile's shedding of skin. "Atrophied" carries the degeneration image further, suggesting a wasting away, as if from disease, a shriveling up, from inactivity of the body.

Frost describes an ethereal end as no different from life's beginning—"At evolution's opposite extreme." His darkest humor is saved for the final image of mind as an ill-defined shape without a sound body. The result of such evolution is also imagined as the cessation of all physical work: "We'll lie and dream." The only regret possible is a "vestigial creature wish"—from a primitive, imperfectly developed part of the body—that high tide will occur soon enough to keep future poets' abstract verse (i.e., without concretions) from becoming dry. "Etherealizing" ironically reverts us to the evolutionary stage from which we have come.

References and further reading: Faggen; Gerber, *Frost*, 94–95; Thompson and Winnick.

Richard J. Calhoun

"EVENING IN A SUGAR ORCHARD" appeared in *Whimsies* (**University of Michigan**) in November 1921 and was subsequently collected in *New Hampshire* (**1923**). The poem alludes to a traditional New England evening in early spring; the days are above freezing, while nights still fall below. The sap is running, and while the maples are tapped, the sap, collected in buckets, is boiled down to make maple syrup. In the sugar-house, the "fireman" boils sap in evaporator pans. The "arch" of line 4 is the large wood-fired stove that extends beneath the pans. Above, an open vent or chimney allows the fire's smoke to escape. Note, however, that despite the vivid details of place and work, neither the boiling process nor the actual tapping of the trees is central in the poem. Instead, the speaker's eye is on the fire sparks.

The poem's contemplative tone depends upon its elemental imagery. All four of the ancient substances are here: earth, air, fire, and water. Earthbound trees give up their sap; the "rare / Hill atmosphere" feeds the sparks; snow on "black ground" melts in the brief overlap of spring and winter. Light and dark are also central here. As spring eases winter, so the sparks send light into the darkness, lighting up the sky and the orchard trees. Frost, after an image of moonlight shining on those buckets, turns the focus to the boughs of the trees and the sky beyond. The sparks with their own small light seem satisfied, do not aspire to be the moon. Unified with the light from the stars of three major constellations, the sparks shine beautifully in bare treetops.

The poem further suggests that from work comes benefit—not just the making of the central product but also the by-product, a peripheral beauty burning off the pulse and all parts of that work. And, ultimately, the sparks provide the inspiration for the writing of the poem.

References and further reading: Oster; on the significance of stars in this and other Frost poems, see Gerber, *Frost*, 164–65, and Maynard.

Linda Lovell

"EVIL TENDENCIES CANCEL," first called "Tendencies Cancel," was originally published, with the rest of the original "Ten Mills," in *Poetry* (Apr. 1936) and appeared in *A Further Range* that same year. The six-line poem, composed of three rhymed couplets, asks, "Will the blight end the chestnut?" The answer is probably no, Frost argues, because sooner or later the blight itself will be ended by "another parasite." The chestnut blight, caused by the fungus *Endothia parasitica*, killed millions of mature native American chestnut trees in the years between the world wars, forever changing the rural landscape, especially in New England. Frost's prediction notwithstanding, the blight has endured to the present day.

Frost wrote in 1936: "A philosopher may worry about a tendency that, if run out to its logical conclusion, might ruin all; but he worries only till he can make out in the confusion the particular counter tendency that is going to collide with it to the cancellation of both" (qtd. in Cramer). The collision of opposing tendencies is an abiding theme of Frost's poetry, one most notable, perhaps, in **"West-Running Brook"** but evident in his love of paradox as well.

This poem is not to be confused with a fourteen-line fragment, alternately titled "Tendencies Cancel" or "That's Where the One Comes in," first published in the 27 March 1947 edition of the *Washington Post*.

References and further reading: Cramer, *Frost among His Poems*, 255.

Andy Duncan

"EXPOSED NEST, THE," originally published in *Mountain Interval* **(1916)**, was probably written in 1915. The poem recounts an event probably from the Frost family's early period at the **Derry Homestead** in New Hampshire. The farmer–poet and one of his children are playing in the hay field when the child discovers a nest of young birds in the grass, exposed but "miraculously" spared the mower blade's destruction. First the child and then the father set to work to re-cover the nest, hoping to preserve the babies until the mother bird should return to them. The deed is not performed naively: The rescuers know enough of bird habits to realize that their helpful "meddling" could actually keep the mother bird from coming back to the nest; yet they rebuild the screen "the best [they] could." The poet argues that the deed proves concern but confesses that, as in **"The Road Not Taken,"** their way leads them on and they do not return to test the success of their good intentions.

A curious technique of the poem is an uneven but "woven" scheme of end rhymes. No line is left unrhymed, but some rhymes are tripled or quadrupled, and the pattern resembles more the random weaving of the grasses into the protective screen than any regular stanza. Against this are set the more regular, dominant iambic pentameter lines.

Frost's attitude toward human manipulation of nature here is typical. The problem of the exposed birds results from human interference; resolution is sought by the innocent child who thinks to restore nature, and the conclusion is ambiguous. Perhaps human effort matters; perhaps it does not. Human attention seems brief, almost random, and unsustained. The pattern is set in the early lines, when the parent pretends in a game with the child to reroot the harvested hay but then discovers that the child is engaged in "no make-believe" restoration, an earnest, generous, and sympathetic, if dubious and perhaps harmful, caring for the delicate birds.

References and further reading: Ingebretsen, *Grammar of Belief*; Marcus, *Explication*; Nitchie; Squires.

Douglas Watson

F

"FEAR, THE," is a long narrative poem in blank verse, first published in *Poetry and Drama* (Dec. 1913) and later in ***North of Boston* (1914)**. Most of the poem is in the form of a dialogue between a man and woman who have come home to a farmhouse at night. Tension drives the narrative forward, spurred by the glimpse of a face in the woman's light, a presence somehow ominous on the dark and lonely road. The appearance triggers a deeper tension between the couple themselves. The woman's fear is mixed with a palpable eagerness to confront the stranger and a conviction—fueled by a volatile melange of hope and dread—that he is no stranger at all, rather an old lover (or husband) who "hadn't had enough." Her companion, Joel, tries to rationalize the situation, even hold her back physically from the confrontation she wants. They are both surprised when a voice actually does answer from the dark and a man materializes: a harmless stranger taking his boy on an after-bedtime walk. The woman, trying to justify her feelings, points out, "This is a very, very lonely place." The reader cannot help but agree.

Radcliffe Squires observes an intentional lack of character development in Frost's narrative poems—the characters are "people finished before they are begun"—because Frost himself saw them as "a waxworks allegory." The observation would seem to fit the closing lines of "The Fear," in which little hope appears for an amelioration of the couple's fundamental tensions. Several scholars, including Thompson and Marcus, have pointed out a biographical genesis to the poem, with Frost as the stranger walking his son late and meeting an alarmed woman, a married nurse who had run off with one of her patients. Reading the poem with this story in mind highlights the possibility that what the woman fears most is really her own conscience.

"The Fear" is one of several narratives centered on farm couples. Sometimes problems face them that seem insurmountable, as in **"The Hill Wife"** and **"Home Burial."** But in poems such as **"In the Home Stretch"** the couple manages to surmount their difficulties. Finally, considering the profoundly reflective and tender method of Frost's treatment of couples in his work, one is tempted to read into such poems Frost's attempt to explore his own complex relationship with his wife **Elinor**.

References and further reading: Katz, *Elinor Frost*; Kearns; Lentricchia, *Modern Poetics*; Marcus, *Explication*; Squires, 80; Thompson, *Early Years*.

Scott Earle

"FEAR OF GOD, THE," first appeared as part of the section "A Spire and Belfry" in *Steeple Bush* (**1947**) and can be interpreted as a representative articulation of the poet's public persona. The speaker addresses himself as well as the reader. He enjoins those who succeed to take pains not to let victory turn their heads. "Stay unassuming," the speaker advises.

In spite of the conventional theme of the benefits of humility and the dangers of hubris, a biographical reading of the poem suggests a more complex issue. Frost's early years were fraught with financial uncertainties and depression. Perhaps the speaker's crediting "an arbitrary god" with success reveals a lingering pain from remembered rejections; in the words of Irving Howe, quoted in Waggoner, Frost's work is "antipathetic to the notion that the universe is inherently good or delightful or hospitable to our needs."

References and further reading: For details of the financial and emotional stresses of Frost's early career, see Thompson, *Early Years*; Waggoner, *American Poets*, 294.

Lynn Barrett

"FEAR OF MAN, THE," as Jeffrey Cramer reports, was written before 1944. Manuscripts list "The Common Danger The Fear of Man," and "Her Fear" as earlier titles. Frost first published it in *Steeple Bush* (**1947**) as part of the section "A Spire and Belfry."

Due to its placement in the collection, many critics see the poem as a companion piece to **"The Fear of God,"** different in that "The Fear of Man" shows timidity instead of haughtiness. Critics see the poem as an apology in the form of an extended metaphor. The skittish girl represents Frost's poetry, beautiful but defensive and difficult to comprehend completely. Her fear of a lout's misconstruing her actions parallels Frost's fear of being misinterpreted by casual readers. The streetlamps she races to and from correspond to Frost's recurrent image of light as symbolizing temporary companionship, in opposition to the isolation symbolized by darkness. The light around the safe—possibly a symbol of financial support for a poet—is provided, however, by a biblical "pagan" god. It may be tainted. The final couplet obliquely emphasizes Frost's desire to speak only with readers who are willing to accept the intended challenge of meaning in his work.

References and further reading: Cramer, *Frost among His Poems*; D. J. Hall, *Contours*; Kearns.

Mark Sutton

"FIGURE IN THE DOORWAY, THE," a companion piece to **"On the Heart's Beginning to Cloud the Mind,"** was first published in the *Virginia Quarterly Review* (Apr. 1936) and collected in *A Further Range* that same year with the subtitle "On Being Looked at in a Train." The poem explores two solitudes that briefly touch; the speaker glances into a life he will not enter. Perhaps a hint of self-directed irony exists in the opening lines, for the poet is indeed "riding high" on a passing train, enjoying both fame and fortune; the speaker is fascinated to encounter a figure who does not need either. As lines 11–12 make clear, the latter can do without human society. The speaker contemplates a radical simplification of life, an extreme form of self-reliance. He employs the first-person plural, for he is dining with others on food he has not prepared. He perhaps envies those like the silent figure who does not need the "civilization" he embodies and who grows his own sustenance. The self-sufficiency of the man, who appears to have all he wants, is detailed in lines 15–18 with their emphatic anaphora. The speaker tries to make it a two-way encounter: The man provides entertainment for the passengers, and they *may* amuse him, but the speaker cannot be sure that they do, for although he might wave back, the glimpsed man makes no gesture. The door is open, but apart from the brief glance, the life of the figure in the doorway remains closed to speaker, passengers, and reader.

References and further reading: Parini, *A Life*, 273–75, compares this poem unfavorably to "On the Heart's Beginning to Cloud the Mind"; Poirier, *Knowing*.

C. P. Seabrook Wilkinson

FILMS ON ROBERT FROST. The following selective, annotated list of films on Robert Frost suggests the extent to which the poet has endured as an American cultural icon.

The Afterglow: A Tribute to Robert Frost, issued as both a motion picture (16mm) and videocassette (VHS), features actor Burgess Meredith reflecting on Frost's life and works as he walks through the countryside of the poet's native Vermont.
   Recommended Audience: Grades 9–12, College, Adult
   Director, Producer, Screenwriter: Burgess Meredith
   Distributor: Winterset Productions: Malibu, CA
   Year of Production: 1989, © 1988
   Running Time: 35 min.
   Medium: One VHS videocassette (color) or one 16mm film reel (color)
   Availability: VHS ($195) from Pyramid Media
   LCCN: 89707430 /F (VHS) or 89707429 /F (16mm)

The American Experience in Literature: Poets of the 20th Century, issued as a filmstrip with audiocassettes and teacher's guide, features the works of five major American poets, including Frost, **Carl Sandburg**, Marianne Moore, e. e. cummings, and Langston Hughes. The relationships between the poets' social and biographical backgrounds are discussed and related to their writings.
   Recommended Audience: Grades 9–12

Collaborators: James M. Cox, Herbert Mitgang, Bernard F. Engel, Norman Friedman, and Milton Meltzer
Distributor: Encyclopaedia Britannica Educational Corporation; Chicago, IL
Year of Production: 1976
Medium: 5 rolls: color; 35mm and 5 cassettes (2-track. ca. 84 min.); 5 rolls; color; 35mm and 5 discs (33⅓ rpm. 12 in. ca. 84 min.); Robert Frost (89 frames); Carl Sandburg (113 fr.); Marianne Moore (71 fr.); e. e. cummings (88 fr.); Langston Hughes (90 fr.)
Availability: Film Libraries: Library of Congress
Other: Encyclopaedia Britannica Educational Corporation
LCCN: 76732182 /F

Camera Three [Poems of Robert Frost], issued for television audiences by CBS-TV, features selections of Frost's poetry being read by various personalities. Participants include Mildred Dunnock, William Clemens, Norma Crane, Tim O'Connor, and Rawm Spearman.
Recommended Audience: Grades 9–12, College, General
Director: Anthony Farrar
Producer: John McGiffert
Screenwriter: Clair Roskam
Distributor: Public Affairs Department, WCBS-TV, New York
Year of Production: 1959
Medium: One reel (1080 ft.): black and white; 16mm. kinescope positive
Availability: Film Libraries: Library of Congress
Other: Public Affairs Department, WCBS-TV, New York
LCCN: 97504077 /MP

A Conversation with Robert Frost and Bela Kornitzer, Author is a 1958 interview originally issued under the title *Robert Frost.* Hungarian-born author Bela Kornitzer and Frost discuss the poet's life and career. Frost's experiences as a small-town mill worker, **teacher**, editor, and farmer are considered as the impetus of the Pulitzer Prize–winning poet's career. Frost is also featured reading two of his better-known poems: **"Stopping by Woods on a Snowy Evening"** and **"A Drumlin Woodchuck."**
Recommended Audience: General
Series: Wisdom Series
Director: Unknown
Producer: National Broadcasting Company
Distributor: Zenger Video: Culver City, CA
Year of Production: 1958
Running Time: 30 min. (VHS); 28 min. (16mm)
Medium: One videocassette (30 min.); black and white; issued as U-matic 3/4 in. or Beta 1/2 in. or VHS 1/2 in.; also issued as a motion picture
Availability: Film Libraries: (VHS): MiU and TxU; (16mm): CoU, CU, IcarbS, IdeKN, IU, MBU, NbU, NmPE, NsyU, PSt, TxU, UU, WaPS, WU
Other: Available for sale on VHS from Zenger Video ($70)
ISBN:0–699–06269–1 (VHS); 0–699–25223–7 (16mm)

The Earlier Twentieth Century, featuring selections from **W. B. Yeats**, Wilfred Owen, Edward Thomas, Frost, **T. S. Eliot**, and Auden, focuses on the new "poetic aims" and ideas of these early twentieth-century poets. The cast of performers includes host John

Gielgud, Peggy Ashcroft, Ralph Richardson, and Stacy Keach.
   Recommended Audience: High School and College
   Series: A Survey of English Poetry
   Director: Unknown
   Producer: Unknown
   Distributor: Films for the Humanities and Sciences, P.O. Box 2053, Princeton, NJ
08543–2053; Phone: 1–800–257–5126
   Year of Production: 1997
   Running Time: 28 min. (VHS)
   Medium: One videocassette (VHS); color
   Availability: Available for sale on VHS from Films for the Humanities and Sciences
for $89.95

An Introduction to Robert Frost's Poetry
   Director: Matthew J. Bruccoli and Richard Layman
   Series: The Eminent Scholar/Teachers Series
   Distributor: Omni Graphics
   Year of Production: 1988
   Medium: One videocassette (color)—running time: 57 minutes; 16-page teacher's
guide
   Availability: Viewing copy available in Copyright Collection of the Library of Con-
gress
   LCCN: 89710310 /MP

Norman Rockwell: A Tribute to Robert Frost, a short motion picture, features artist
Norman Rockwell illustrating twelve of Frost's poems.
   Director: Unknown
   Producer: The Franklin Mint
   Distributor: Modern Talking Picture Service, Inc.
   Year of Production: 1974
   Running Time: 14 min.
   Medium: 16mm (color)
   Availability: Film Libraries: Library of Congress
   LCCN: 75700154 /F

The Poetry of Robert Frost features dramatizations of twelve of Frost's best-known
poems. An excellent presentation of Frost's capacity to balance the contrarities of man
and nature, this production closes with a memorable dramatization of **"The Death of
the Hired Man."**
   Recommended Audience: Grades 9–12, College, Adult
   Director, Producer, Screenwriter: Robert Ornstein
   Distributor: Case Western Reserve University, Department of Instructional Support:
Cleveland, OH
   Year of Production: 1977, made 1976
   Running Time: 45 min.
   Medium: Two reels (16mm); color
   Availability: Film Libraries: Library of Congress
   LCCN: 77700022 /F

Reading Poetry: Mending Wall features actor Leonard Nimoy reciting Frost's poem
"Mending Wall" as scenes representative of the poem are shown. The poem is again

repeated with the words of the poem superimposed over different visual effects.
 Recommended Audience: Junior High
 Series: Reading Poetry Series
 Director: Unknown
 Producer: Oxford Films
 Distributor: Oxford Films (out of business)
 Year of Production: 1972
 Running Time: 10 min.
 Medium: 16mm (color)
 Availability: Film Libraries: IU, KU, LU, MBU, NbU, NsyU, OkentU, OkS, WlacU
 Other: Arthur G. Evans, 460 Arroya Parkway, Pasadena, CA 91101
 ISBN: 0–699–18945–4

Robert Frost, a riveting biographical exploration of Frost's development as a poet, delineates the poet's growth as an American icon and elder statesman. Special features
include interviews with Frost as well as readings and personal insights into many of his
most famous poems. Poets Seamus Heaney, Joseph Brodsky, and Richard Wilbur discuss
Frost's individual works as well as the social and biographical factors that influenced his
poetry. Leading scholars and critics such as William H. Pritchard and Richard Poirier
reveal compelling insights into Frost's canon and consider Frost as an "American myth."
Poems discussed and read include **"Mowing," "After Apple-Picking," "Mending
Wall," "The Wood-pile," "Acquainted with the Night,"** and **"Never Again Would
Birds' Song Be the Same."** A moving dramatization of a portion of Frost's **"Home
Burial"** is included to illustrate the underlying pathos of many of Frost's deceptively
simple poems.
 Recommended Audience: High School and College
 Series: Voices and Visions (PBS), program five
 Director: Richard P. Rogers
 Producer and Screenwriter: Jill Janows in association with the New York Center for
Visual History and presented by South Carolina ETV Network (an Annenberg/ CPB
project)
 Distributor: Intellimation, P.O. Box 1922, Santa Barbara, CA 93116–1922
 Year of Production: 1988
 Running Time: 60 min.
 Medium: One VHS videocassette (color) plus one preview guide or one 16mm film
reel (color) plus one preview guide
 Availability: VHS ($19.95) from Mystic Fie Video, 200 Madison Ave., 24th Floor,
New York, NY 10016; Phone: 212–252–7722 or 1–800–999–1319
 ISBN: 0–89776–251–7

Robert Frost opens with footage of Frost reading at the inauguration of President John
F. Kennedy and regresses in time to trace the poet's youth, education, his life in **England**,
and his sudden rise to fame among the American public. The final sequence features
actor Leonard Nimoy reading Frost's **"Mending Wall,"** which is complemented by evoc-
ative scenery and live-action photography.
 Recommended Audience: Junior High
 Series: Poetry by Americans
 Director: Unknown
 Producer: Oxford Films

Distributor: Oxford Films (out of business)
Year of Production: 1972
Running Time: 11 min.
Medium: Motion picture (16mm); color
Availability: Film Libraries: AzU, IU, LU, MBU, NbU, UPB, WlacU
Other: Arthur G. Evans, 460 Arroya Parkway, Pasadena, CA 91101
ISBN: 0–699–25222–9

Robert Frost: A First Acquaintance is used to demonstrate Frost's relationship with children. It features the poet's daughter Lesley Frost and neighboring children interpreting Frost's poetry at the family farm in **Derry**, New Hampshire. The children visit the places that inspired many of Frost's best-known poems and interpret the action of each poem.
   Recommended Audience: Intermediate, Junior High, College
   Director: Harold Mantell
   Producer: Harold Mantell
   Distributor: Films for the Humanities, Inc., P.O. Box 2053, Princeton, NJ 08540
   Year of Production: 1974
   Running Time: 16 min.
   Medium: Motion picture (16mm); color
   Availability: Film Libraries: FTaSU
   Distributors: Films for the Humanities, Inc.,
   ISBN: 0–699–38690-X

Robert Frost: A Lover's Quarrel with the World presents two striking views of Frost—first as the beloved poet and public speaker of the American populace and, second, as intimate thinker. Featuring Frost reading poetry to a large audience at Sarah Lawrence College, **Amherst**, and then at Ripton College, we see the poet as he relates to the public in two very different situations.
   Recommended Audience: High School, College, General
   Director: Unknown
   Producer: Unknown (contact university film library holder for further information)
   Distributor: Holt, Rinehart and Winston, 383 Madison Avenue, New York, NY 10017
   Year of Production: 1967
   Running Time: 40 min.
   Medium: Motion picture (16mm); black and white
   Availability: Film Libraries: FtaSU, InTI, InU, IU, NsyU
   ISBN: 0–699–25224–5

Robert Frost's New England features scenes from Frost in New England. His works are read as images evocative of his poetry are shown. Stone walls, apple trees, woodland roads, autumn foliage, snow, and rain are shown in conjunction with the words of each poem to better illustrate New England's effect on Frost's poetry. As well, the poet is shown at his home, speaking with the easy colloquial manner that infused his poetry.
   Recommended Audiences: High School, College, General
   Director: Dewitt Jones
   Producer: Dewitt Jones Productions
   Distributor: Churchill Films, 662 North Robertson Boulevard, Los Angeles, CA 90069
   Year of Production: 1975
   Running Time: 22 min.

Medium: Motion picture (16mm); color
Availability: Film Libraries: AzTeS, AzU, IaU, InU, IU, LU, MBU, MiU, NmPE, NsyU, OkentU, OkS
ISBN: 0–699–25225–3

Robert Frost's Poems uses various pictures of New England scenes to illustrate the poems.
Recommended Audience: Unknown
Author: Theodore S. Johnson
Producer: Unknown
Distributor: Unknown
Year of Production: 1971
Medium: Slide Set: 22 color slides (2 × 2 in.) with teacher's guide
Availability: Film Libraries: Library of Congress
LCCN: 74733155 /F

Robert Frost's "The Death of the Hired Man" is a 1978 dramatization of one of Frost's best-known poems. It considers the subject of the poem, an aged and no longer productive hired man, who returns to live at a couple's farm, and the apprehension the man's appearance brings to the family concerning his fate.
Director: Jeanne Collachia
Producer: Jeanne Collachia
Distributor: Encyclopaedia Britannica Educational Corporation, 425 North Michigan Ave., Chicago, IL 60611
Year of Production: 1978
Running Time: 22 min.
Medium: Motion picture (16mm); color
Availability: Film Libraries: LU and NbU
ISBN: 0–699–35372–6

Selected Poems by American Writers, narrated by Charles A. Schmidt, features poems by four of America's best-known poets: "Miniver Cheevy" by **Edwin A. Robinson, "Neither Out Far Nor in Deep"** by Frost, "The Chambered Nautilus" by Oliver Wendell Holmes, and "The Snow" by Emily Dickinson.
Recommended Audience: Unspecified
Director: Unknown
Producer: Unknown
Distributor: Educational Filmstrips, Huntsville, TX
Year of Production: 1970
Running Time: 6 min.
Medium: 70 fr. (color); 35mm and phonotape in cassette
Availability: Film Libraries: Library of Congress
LCCN: 73737385 /F/r72

Stopping by the Woods of Mr. Frost features scenes from Frost's native New England and introduces students to the poet's life and works. Narrator Thomas S. Klise offers interpretations of many of his most famous poems.
Recommended Audience: Junior High, High School, College
Director, Producer, Screenwriter: Thomas S. Klise
Distributor: The Company, Peoria, IL

Year of Production: 1985
Running Time: 22 min.
Medium: One filmstrip (98 fr.), 35mm, plus one sound cassette and one teacher's guide
Availability: Film Libraries: Library of Congress
LCCN: PS3511.R94

To Hear Their Voices: Chaucer, Shakespeare, and Frost features Professor Marie Borroff discussing three of the most profound English-language poets, Chaucer, Shakespeare, and Frost. Her lectures explore the ways in which each poet's themes and language have affected our own.
Recommended Audience: College
Series: Yale Great Teachers Series
Director: Bill Heitz
Producer: Brenzel Publishing, Inc., in association with the Association of Yale Alumni
Distributor: Brenzel Publishing, Inc.
Running Time: Unspecified
Medium: Two VHS videocassettes (color)
Availability: Film Libraries: Library of Congress
LCCN: 97512507 /MP

Twentieth Century Poetry One features various performers interpreting well-known poems by popular twentieth-century poets such as **Carl Sandburg**, Frost, and Edna St. Vincent Millay.
Recommended Audience: High School
Director: Unknown
Producer: Bob Cooley
Distributor: Auburn University, Educational Television Department, in cooperation with the Alabama Educational Television Commission: For sale ($150) or rent ($30)
Running Time: 20 min.
Medium: One VHS videocassette (color); one teacher's guide
Availability: Film Libraries: Library of Congress
LCCN: 83706206 /F

References and further reading: The Consortium of University Film Centers and R. R. Bowker Company, *Educational Film Locator*, 2d ed. (New York: R. R. Bowker, 1980); *The Library of Congress*, 12 Aug. 1997.

Marley Nicole Washum

"FIRE AND ICE" appeared in *Harper's Magazine* in December 1920 and later in *New Hampshire* (**1923**). Short, succinct, and accessible, it is frequently anthologized. With simple and straightforward language Frost names his symbols openly: Fire is equated with desire, ice with destruction. The general topic is a familiar one to readers of twentieth-century literature: the end of the world. But if the subject matter is by now perhaps somewhat commonplace, the treatment of the theme remains unmistakably and originally Frost's. Here as in many Frost poems, elements of the natural world are deliberately foregrounded, and the poem's message is contained in relatively smooth iambic meter. The metaphors are simple but not simplistic. Frost promises through the arrangement of the lyric and the careful technical treatment of the subject matter a meaning beyond the superficial.

In nine short lines Frost posits the possibility of two different versions of the same catastrophe. Life as we know it may end because of an excess of sensual appetites, of lust, longing, "desire"; or existence may come to a close due to a surplus of malevolence, rancor, "hate." The speaker of the poem presents the two alternatives as equally plausible scenarios. The fact that the world will end is not questioned; merely the manner of its devastation is deliberated as something yet to be determined. Rumors that circulate regarding the topic are anonymous and impartial, but in the third line the speaker qualifies the opening statement with personal knowledge. Individual experience is introduced in order to prove the initial claims real and of consequence. The speaker insists that "from what I've tasted of desire," fire is more likely as a deadly instrument. At least a fiery end might allow one to derive a certain pleasure or satisfaction from the passion to possess that leads to our ultimate demise. By contrast, hatred leads only too swiftly to destruction. Yet the speaker's wisdom is great enough that he knows that "for destruction ice / Is also great / And would suffice."

Coming after World War I, Frost's lines about "ice" may speak to the calamity and misfortune the world suffered during the period. The reference to "tasting" desire indicates that the poem may also be a testament to private observations of dangerously passionate personal encounters. Certainly the language is large or abstract enough to allow for both possibilities. Indeed, lacking the precise detail that Frost otherwise typically includes in his poems, "Fire and Ice" is somewhat exceptional in Frost's oeuvre. It is almost aphoristic, a contemporary maxim of sorts. In the nine lines of the poem, we make a rare exit from Frost's idyllic New England landscape and enter for a short while a slightly more philosophical world of causes and principles.

The poem's meaning is also tied to its structure. Frost uses the arrangement of the lines to make a subtle but concrete point about his theme. "Fire and Ice," about the destructiveness to which overindulgence leads, contains a lesson regarding the necessity of boundaries. Technically, Frost's verse reminds us that we need limits, confines, in order both to be safe and to make sense. We need rules to govern, to manage, both life and poetry; immoderation, in Frost's view, leads to ruin. Thus the speaker puts forth the ideas about the possible alternatives of our fate in a very regular pattern. The speaker is located at a point in time when the end of the world has not yet taken place, and chaos has not yet won the day. In the poem, as in the world, there is still a pattern to be identified. Each line is somewhat metrically predictable: It has either four beats or two. The number of beats is significant, however. Only three lines have two beats—2, 8, and 9—and these all make reference to ice. Near the end of the poem, as the idea of destruction is rehearsed a second time, it seems to gain intensity. As destruction appears to become more imminent, the lines of the poem describing it are suitably diminished. Lines 8 and 9 are the only successive ones with merely two beats each. As the end of the world appears inevitable, the poem itself loses energy. Hate or ice, the speaker concludes, "would suffice." With such a declaration the poem achieves at least a double, final effect. On the literal level, we learn about the finality of "ice." Technically, this same "ice" ends the world of the poem. The otherwise regular four-beat pattern of the poem is destroyed, and "ice" becomes not only the last image but also the final verbal element: That is, the last three letters of the verse spell "ice."

References and further reading: Beacham offers a detailed analysis of the correlations among rhyme, line length, and meaning; Brower; Lynen, *Pastoral Art*; Oster; Parini, *A Life*.

Sabine Sautter-Leger

"FIREFLIES IN THE GARDEN" first appeared in *West-Running Brook* **(1928)**. Employing a rhyme scheme of *aaabbb*, this six-line **lyric** serves as an example of Frost's ability to use **nature** as a source for metaphor (*see* **Nature Poet and Naturalist**).

Robert T. Fleissner looks at the poem as a lyrical study of the charming attempt and failure of fireflies to be starlike. However, given the growing sense of doom and loneliness various critics have recognized in *West-Running Brook*, a darker meaning might also be possible. If the fireflies are a metaphor for individuals and the stars are a metaphor for God, Frost suggests that on earth humans can make only vain attempts to be godlike. When first they attempt to be starlike, the fireflies "Achieve . . . a very star-like start." Unfortunately, they can never be stars, for they do not have the ability to "sustain the part," perhaps a subtle comment on fleeting poetic accomplishment, for according to Jeffrey Cramer, Frost said in 1938 that poems "are fireflies. They represent our lucid intervals and glow only for a moment."

References and further reading: Cramer, *Frost among His Poems*, 88; Fleissner, "Frost's 'Fireflies.' "

Chris-Anne Stumpf

"FIVE NOCTURNES" is the title of the second section of Robert Frost's eighth poetry collection *Steeple Bush* **(1947)**. Following the title page, Frost devoted a separate page to each poem. The poems were numbered and presented as follows: I. "The Night Light," II. "Were I in Trouble," III. "Bravado," IV. "On Making Certain Anything Has Happened," and V. "In the Long Night." The "Five Nocturnes" range in length from four lines ("Bravado") to sixteen lines ("On Making Certain" and "In the Long Night") and exhibit varied rhythmic and metrical patterns. *Steeple Bush* marks the first appearance of the poems as a group, although they had all been published previously. The first three poems were published in the Autumn 1946 issue of the *Yale Review*. The general title "Nocturnes" indicated the shared form of the poems but not that they should be seen as a collective unit. Two of the poems were retitled for *Steeple Bush*:

"Bravery" became "Bravado" and "Were I in Trouble with Night Tonight" was shortened to "Were I in Trouble." The fourth poem, "On Making Certain," was Frost's **Christmas poem** for 1945. Crane records that 2,600 copies were printed for Frost and his friends by Spiral Press with "Decorations by Armin Landeck," including "a compass chart, a compass instrument, and a star." The fifth poem, "In the Long Night," first appeared in the 1944 edition of *"Dartmouth in Portrait"* (Hanover, NH, 1943), the annual calendar of **Dartmouth College**, where Frost was George Ticknor Fellow in Humanities from 1943 to 1949.

Frost was seventy-three when *Steeple Bush* was published, leading many critics to review the collection with faint praise (showing respect for Frost's reputation) or harsh criticism (citing the poet's failing poetic powers). "**Directive**" found an appreciative audience, but the remaining poems received little critical attention. Despite such lack of recognition, "Five Nocturnes" stands as Frost's "balm of Gilead" to an American public weary from the physical and emotional toll of World War II. Thompson and Winnick see Frost's *Steeple Bush* poems reflecting "more direct cognizance than in previous collections of the issues affecting the contemporary world." Frost's decision to number the poems and to sustain the viewpoint of a consistent poetic persona—the "I" in each of the poems—encourages a reading of them as a cohesive philosophical argument.

"The Night Light" describes a woman who uses a night light to calm her fears. Frost's friend Hyde Cox suggests that the poem was inspired by his cook, Mary Douglas, who left a lamp on nightly because she feared wild animals who approached the rural farmhouse where she was staying with the Cox family. In the poem, the female figure resorts to artificial courage, the mechanical aid of the lamp, but must suffer "bad dreams and broken sleep" as a consequence. The poet calls this a waste of the "good gloom" that he experiences as well but that he will convert to better use.

"Were I in Trouble" offers his alternative strategy. Seeing a distant "blinding headlight" where he can discern "no thoroughfare," the poet imagines the headlight "bounc[ing] down a granite stair / Like a star fresh fallen out of the sky." Connecting to the "unintimate light" satisfies the poet, although he acknowledges that it probably should not, since the driver is too distant to be of any real help in an emergency. The movement to connect is what the poet celebrates—in direct opposition to the denial, or movement away from experience, that the use of the night light represents.

In "Bravado," the poet acknowledges that imaginative enterprises do not eliminate the real danger that we each encounter daily. But, he argues, "it was a risk I had to take—and took." Living is a risk, as is poetic creation, but seeking the light—to mark a territory and conquer the night—must supersede all other concerns. The retitling of the poem from "Bravery" to "Bravado" establishes the primacy of the will to be brave over the act of bravery itself.

Frost continues his argument in "On Making Certain Anything Has Happened." Here, vigilant observation acts as a distraction and partial remedy for distress. There is comfort in activity—such as being a "watcher of the void" who counts falling stars—and it fills up the time that might otherwise be devoted to worrying.

The final poem, "In the Long Night," stands as the fullest and most self-involved expression of the poetic imagination. In a winter fantasy, the poet makes contact with "a solitary friend" (who may, of course, be a fiction). The two pass the time telling stories, watching the Aurora Borealis, and waiting for visits from other travelers—including, perhaps, the two "Esquimaux" Etooka-shoo and Couldlooktoo. The fanciful names accentuate the magical quality of the imagined meeting, but it is also clear that the poet chooses two everyday men who have done extraordinary deeds as his honored guests. In the end, as the poet tells us, you can "rest assured . . . There will come another day." The poet is sustained by the light and warmth he creates with his imagination. As readers, we are encouraged to do the same.

In a "Sermon" that he preached at Rockdale Avenue Temple in 1946, Frost reminded his congregation that "wisdom is better than bravery." For an America weary from its participation in World War II and searching for a source of renewal, the five small poems offer hope and a blueprint for imaginative recovery. Although his powers may have been failing, Frost offered comfort the only way he knew—through the gifts of his imagination.

References and further reading: For an excellent bibliographic source covering the extensive Frost collection at the Barrett Library, see Crane, *Descriptive Catalogue*, 120 (includes the essay "On Collecting Frost," by C. Waller Barrett and a "Bibliographical Introduction" by Fredson Bowers); R. Frost, *Collected*, esp. 792 for "Sermon"; Mertins, 245; Thompson and Winnick.

Diane N. Hulett

"FLOOD, THE," originally published as "Blood" in *The Nation* (8 Feb. 1928), is a **sonnet** that characterizes the human propensity for aggression and violence as a manifestation of nature within us. Choosing words such as "barrier," "releases," and "outlet," Frost impersonalizes the tendency, comparing it to natural processes like flooding or, in a reference to the medieval theory of humors, to the necessity of bleeding an oversanguine body (hence the word "chafe" with its suggestion of skin irritation). Frost's public declaration that "blood will out" offers the grim reassurance that such events are outside the need for moral anxiety. They are displays of an involuntary impulse, which, like other natural processes, cannot be eliminated. Although we may wish to blame individuals and societies for acts of aggression or, as the scale of violence exceeds our comprehension, to say "it is let loose by the devil," such accounts console us only with the illusion of intelligence and purpose behind our dark, inexplicable drives.

References and further reading: Faggen; Kearns; Oster, 177–79, offers a general discussion of Frost's treatment of walling nature in and out; Potter, especially the chapter " 'Acquainted with the Night': The Fearsome World."

Michael Berndt

"FLOWER BOAT, THE," was first published in *The Youth's Companion* (20 May 1909), appeared later that year in *The Pinkerton Critic* (Dec.), and was later collected in **West-Running Brook (1928)**. In a letter to the Curator of Manuscripts at the Huntington Library, Frost identified the actual date of composition as "about 1894 or 5." His description of the retired fisherman who swaps yarns in the barbershop and converts his boat into a flower box is thus remarkable for its perspicacity, having been written by a man barely twenty. Returning to the land and sea imagery of **"Sand Dunes,"** the first poem of the "Sand Dunes" section, "The Flower Boat" continues to set nature against the vital human spirit. The fisherman has survived the dangers of his profession to enjoy a temporary harbor; the dory that once carried cod from Georges Bank now carries flowers. The "Elysian freight" is suggestive of a blessed period in the fisherman's life, and yet, as the narrator acknowledges, "all they ask is rougher weather" and the fisherman, like the delicate flowers, will die. Although the man is "At anchor" only temporarily, Frost creates a tone of positive resignation by depicting the man's death as another search, this time for "the Happy Isles" and a more permanent harbor.

References and further reading: R. Frost, *Selected Letters.*

Michael Berndt

"FLOWER-GATHERING," included as one of the poems originally published in *A Boy's Will* (1913), was apparently first written to **Elinor Frost** in the summer of 1896 to apologize for separations occasioned by Frost's country wanderings near Allenstown, New Hampshire, where they spent a delayed honeymoon. Under the influence of friend **Carl Burell**, an amateur botanist, Frost gleaned much of the knowledge of flowers that was to inform his subsequent poetry. Elinor, seven months pregnant, could not comfortably accompany her husband on his walks, and the poem reflects his regret and attempt to compensate. The speaker in the poem has been gone all day and returns to an uncertain silence. The gift of "faded flowers" is but a remnant of the flower-gatherer's day, and the giver seems to recognize its inadequacy as solace to the separation of this "ages of a day" spent apart. In the original table of contents to *A Boy's Will*, Frost annotated the poem as reflecting a discovery that the "greatness of love lies not . . . in any spur it may be to ambition." The gloss may suggest why the gathered flowers (ambition realized) provide so little satisfaction to the gatherer or to the receiver: They are evidence of ambition's power to separate those who would be together. In form, the poem consists of two eight-lined stanzas with interlocking rhyme patterns: *abcbddeb*. The structure and falling stress at the end of lines 1, 3, 5, and 6 of each stanza reflect both Frost's early experimentation with poetic forms and the emotional uncertainty of the poem.

References and further reading: Thompson, *Early Years.*

Douglas Watson

"FOR JOHN F. KENNEDY HIS INAUGURATION," composed as a preface to **"The Gift Outright"** for the occasion of President John F. Kennedy's inauguration, was not read by Robert Frost on the day of the inauguration due to blinding sun on the podium. Frost did, however, recite "The Gift Outright" from memory. When Frost appeared at the inauguration on 20 January 1961, he was seen and heard by a television audience estimated in excess of 60 million Americans. "For John F. Kennedy His Inauguration" was published as a 42-line dedication under various titles immediately thereafter in the *New York Times* (21 Jan. 1961: 9) and other newspapers. The current 77-line version appeared that March, first in a commemorative leaflet printed by an Israeli airline, then in the *New York Times Magazine* (26 Mar. 1961). The poem's present title and form were established in Frost's final volume, *In the Clearing* **(1962).**

"For John F. Kennedy His Inauguration" appropriately not only celebrates America's "revolutionary and anti-colonial" origins as William O'Donnell's 1962 review of *In the Clearing* suggests but also delineates the "glory" in the evidence of a working democracy in America. John F. Kennedy's victory margin over Richard Nixon was a scant 113,000 out of 68.8 million votes cast. Even though the margin represented much less than 1 percent of the popular vote, Frost points out that it was "sure to be abided by" in order that the youngest president ever to be elected could lead America into the "golden age of poetry and power" that Kennedy's hopeful New Frontier promised. In Frost's poem, Kennedy's youth and bold spirit inspire a pride in the American willingness to risk everything for democratic freedom. O'Donnell notes that, typical of Frost's duality with regard to his beliefs, such exultant praise of America and its history is different in tone from the comic yet bleak picture of America that one finds in **"America Is Hard to See,"** another poem found in *In the Clearing.*

The chain of events leading to the inaugural poem began nearly two years earlier. In a 1959 interview commemorating his eighty-fifth birthday, Frost made front-page news with the comment, "Somebody said to me that New England's in decay—but the next President is going to be from Boston." Kennedy sent Frost a letter of gratitude, and the two men had their first meeting soon afterward at the Library of Congress. Kennedy would quote Frost's poetry throughout the 1960 campaign.

In December 1960, new cabinet appointee Stewart Udall suggested to Kennedy that Frost be part of the inaugural ceremony, to give "a kind of poet's benediction." Kennedy agreed but, fearing Frost would upstage him like "Edward Everett at Gettysburg," cautioned that Frost merely should read a poem and not make a speech. Frost's secretary, **Kathleen Morrison**, suggested to Udall that Frost read "The Gift Outright," and Kennedy agreed, calling that poem "just right."

Only Morrison knew that Frost had decided to write a new dedication poem and read that as well. Udall recalled, "He was still rewriting it and trying to memorize its lines when we picked him up to drive through the snow to the Capitol." As some 60 million people watched via television, Frost attempted to read his new poem but faltered, despite Lyndon Johnson's attempt to shield his paper from the sun. In Udall's words, "The wind, sun, and snow (his collaborators in many verses) robbed him of his sight." Giving up, Frost saved the moment and electrified the audience by powerfully reciting "The Gift Outright" from memory.

Frost felt afterward "like the fellow who fumbles in the big game." That week, after lunch at the White House, Frost gave Kennedy an autographed copy of the dedication poem, having written on it "Amended copy. Now let's mend our ways." Frost's friend **Louis Untermeyer** later told Udall, "It was a good thing he couldn't read the dedication poem—it was the worst thing he ever wrote!"

The public nature of the dedication poem, eventually published as "For John F. Kennedy His Inauguration," has inspired as much commentary as the poem itself. Harold K. Bush, Jr., for example, views the Kennedy inauguration as one of the moments in American literary history when a cultural myth was installed in the public psyche.

Udall suggests that when Frost extolled "a next Augustan age" of "poetry and power," he was not merely praising the president-elect, nor speaking in the realm of myth, but actually envisioning a practical role for himself and other poets on the international political stage. In a letter to Udall that spring, Frost wrote,

That dedication poem goes on being added to in my mind till it threatens to become a history of the United States to rival the one Harry Truman says he is writing. You know one of my missions is to get a secretary of the arts into the President's cabinet but I am as good as in there now with you to talk to. I have been reaching the President through you for some time.

Frost's newfound influence in Washington peaked in 1962, the last year of his life, with his much-publicized, Kennedy-endorsed trip to the Soviet Union, where he had a warm 90-minute meeting with Premier Nikita Khrushchev. But Frost's off-the-cuff remarks to reporters afterward soured Kennedy's enthusiasm for the trip, and the president never spoke to Frost again; indeed, he did not even contact Frost during the poet's well-publicized final illness. Frost thus was reminded on his deathbed that the "golden age of poetry and power" had not yet arrived.

References and further reading: Bush, "Endicott's Ghost"; Cramer, *Frost among His Poems*, includes a detailed publication history; Eberhart, "Clearing"; Fleissner, "A Title," discusses the poem's many variant titles; O'Donnell, "Frost at Eighty-eight," 164; Udall.

Alex Ambrozic and Andy Duncan

"FOR ONCE, THEN, SOMETHING" (initially titled "Well" and then "Wrong to the Light") was written in 1917 while Frost was living in **Franconia**. It was first published in *Harper's Magazine* (July 1920) and later collected in

New Hampshire (1923). The ingeniously ambiguous poem may have been in-spired by an animated discussion between Frost and his wife **Elinor** over **reli-gion**. By focusing on the central dilemma Frost sets up in the poem between transcendental truths and faulty perceptions of truth, the poem can be read as a meditation on the difficulty of seeing beyond human limits to a supernatural or spiritual plane. Other readings reveal the philosophical, humanistic, and moral origins of the ambiguities that drive the poem.

Cast in unrhymed hendecasyllabic meter, the poem presents a speaker kneel-ing at a well, an individual who has been taunted by others for a self-preoccupation that prevents one from ever seeing much beyond "the shining surface picture" of oneself, "godlike." "Once," however, the speaker recalls dis-cerning at the bottom of the well "something white, uncertain . . . and then I lost it." A ripple caused by a drop of water falling from a fern "rebukes" the clear water, and the speaker loses the image in the depths. As Frost ponders the meaning of his fleeting glimpse, he offers a tentative answer to searching ques-tions: "What was that whiteness? / Truth? A pebble of quartz? For once, then, something."

Assuming that the "Truth" alluded to concerns ultimate or transcendental reality, the questions in the final lines can be rephrased less ambiguously: "Is there anything beyond the physical to see? If there is, can a person see it?" Restrained by earthly reality, we are handicapped by our own physical resources; we are allowed only partial glances or oblique glimpses into the supernatural dimension. Without faith or a capacity to believe, perhaps all we can see is the surface of reality, the quotidian plane, "a pebble of quartz."

The poem may also serve as Frost's slight to those critics who complained about the "enigmatical reserve" in his poetry. Frost felt that poetry should prop-erly reflect the same nuances of indirection and even confusion of life itself; "life does not," as he said, "readily yield up its meaning and purpose—indeed, if it has any." The poem's title, repeated as the end, expresses both Frost's frustration at his failure to achieve a final, comprehensive vision and his irrita-tion with those critics who doubt the seriousness of his efforts.

Looked at from a different angle, "For Once, Then, Something" examines the transaction—the interpersonal exchange—between one human being and an-other through a search for language that can refine a person's talent for self-reflection while simultaneously extending his or her capacities for reciprocity. The poem's ambiguity and imprecision, its intentional fumbling for a language appropriate to describing a certain "something" that transcends the boundaries of self-knowing, are less laments over the poet's failed vision than a commentary on a literacy that fails the speaker in his efforts to see beyond his own reflection when interacting with reality. *See also* **Nature Poet and Naturalist**.

References and further reading: Marcus, *Explication*, and Oster stress philosophical and moral implications of the poem; for a discussion of Frost's penchant for speaking in "indirections," see Pack; Potter examines the tension between human limitations and the transcendental sphere; Thompson, *Triumph*, relates the charged conversations between Frost and his wife over religious belief.

David D. Cooper

"FORGIVE, O LORD." *See* **"Cluster of Faith."**

"FOUNTAIN, A BOTTLE, A DONKEY'S EARS AND SOME BOOKS, A," was first published in the October 1923 issue of *The Bookman* and subsequently in Frost's volume *New Hampshire* **(1923)**. The rambling walk and talk depicted in the poem were fondly recalled by Frost's friend Raymond Holden, who said he and Frost made many similar tramps through the mountains of Grafton County, New Hampshire:

Robert often told me of the legend he had heard when he lived in **Derry** to the effect that the Mormons had once built a stone temple in the forest somewhere in New Hampshire, the ruined altar or fount of which was sometimes stumbled upon by hunters. It could be said that Robert and I never took a walk without the sometimes spoken and sometimes tacit understanding that we were looking for that altar. We never found it. (qtd. in Cramer)

Mordecai Marcus calls the poem "an elaborate joke," but the title, like the title of the "Ten Mills" sequence, is suspicious in its assertion of triviality. In fact, the poem may address issues central to Frost's poetics. The poem links the fates of the forgotten poet and the forgotten house, conveying an implied critique of the former through a description of the latter. Sara Lundquist asserts that all of Frost's houses, especially abandoned houses, "serve as analogies for poetic form" as Frost struggles "to write formal poetry amid prevailing skepticism about the traditional and the inherited." The abandoned house and the modern poet, Lundquist argues, both "struggle for definition and form" amid a chaotic universe. Similarly, Walter N. Stiller notes the tension in much of Frost between the yearning for order and the yearning for discovery. In "A Fountain, a Bottle, a Donkey's Ears and Some Books," the roving speaker discovers the confined space of a previous consciousness that was, seemingly, fatally limited.

The poem also fits within the "peripatetic" literary mode identified by Anne Denice Wallace, in which the act of walking, from Wordsworth onward, is depicted as a "cultivating" and "renovating" labor. In Frost, however, the walker's expectations are more often "frustrated or denied." Certainly the forgotten poet's career, if not the house itself, is past "renovating," and the renewing fountain remains elusive.

References and further reading: Cramer, *Frost among His Poems*, 73; Lundquist; Marcus, *Explication*, 101; Stiller; A. D. Wallace.

Andy Duncan

"[FOUR-ROOM SHACK ASPIRING HIGH]," written in 1963 and included in editions of *In the Clearing* only after its initial publication in 1962, is a seven-line poem in mostly iambic trimeter with initial anapests in each line. The rising meter corresponds to the meaning of the poem in an ironic way, for while Frost is concerned with visions from the sky and directs the reader's attention upward to the heavens, such visions are debased. Although the poem seems to be slight at first glance, it gives voice to the poet's interest in the changing nature of the New England countryside by focusing on the antenna atop a house that brings in "visions" from the world outside to the television inside. The value of such visions is satirically characterized in the quip "What you get is what you buy," referring to a purely commercial vision rather than any spiritual one. In contrast to many of Frost's other poems in which a viewer examines the night sky and stars for visions that inspire or generate insight, the visions one receives by virtue of the mast atop the house are paltry and worthless by comparison.

If we compare this poem with ones from his previous volume, *Steeple Bush* **(1947)**—poems such as **"A Steeple on the House,"** in which a spire on the roof is a symbol of a soul springing from flesh, or **"Astrometaphysical,"** in which looking at the night sky sparks the speaker's fancy that when he dies he will be "constellated"—we find that in the poem a mast reaching up into the heavens stands for a kind of modern cynicism; satisfaction with the visions the mast can bring surely will not be lasting, as the last line implies. Frost's interest in the skies and how they are connected to earth finds humorous expression here, although the poem may very well be what critics were referring to when they characterized *In the Clearing* as "oddly light." Yet surely this poem succinctly reflects the feelings of a man at the end of his life who is contemplating the negative consequences of the modern turn from church steeple to television antenna.

References and further reading: Hopkins examines the significance of houses Frost himself inhabited and houses as metaphor; for a discussion of houses in Frost's poetry, see McGavran.

Susan Burns

"FRAGMENTARY BLUE" is the initial poem of the "Grace Notes" section of *New Hampshire* **(1923)**; it first appeared in *Harper's Magazine* (July 1920). The poem consists of iambic pentameter quatrains, with one interlocking rhyme sound. Through synecdoche, Frost addresses the disparity between earth and heaven.

Frost acutely contrasts physical objects—birds, butterflies, flowers, stones, eyes—with metaphysical ideas. Blueness here is both seen and unseen, physical and ethereal. Similar in theme to **"A Passing Glimpse,"** the opening question— "Why make so much of fragmentary blue . . . ?"—is answered by the momentary view it offers of eternal truth. Like the whiteness in the bottom of the well in **"For Once, Then, Something,"** flashes of blue provide the promise of a beneficent eternity, an idea that contrasts sharply with the dour intensity of poems such as **"Design."**

Like **"Fire and Ice,"** which follows in *New Hampshire*, "Fragmentary Blue" shows Frost's playful intellect—teasing **science** and **religion** in line 5—while underscoring his search for meaning. To the physicist, the perception of blue is merely the potential human observation of a spectrum of light; to the believer, such wavelengths are wondrous glimpses of heaven. However, blue does not exist in itself; neither, perhaps, does heaven. Both possibilities are sustained by human perception and longing. As in **"All Revelation,"** objects have meaning only with reference to human cognition, and blue incarnates the lasting truth and beauty of heaven that can give meaning to human experience. Frost recognizes that we cannot see this truth clearly or completely; we see only fragments.

References and further reading: Holland, 16–42; Poirier, "Art of Poetry"; Poole.

Kenneth Rickard

FRANCONIA, NEW HAMPSHIRE (THE FROST PLACE). In 1915, shortly after he returned from **England** in February, Frost purchased a farm in Franconia, New Hampshire, from Willis E. Herbert for, Thompson tells us, $800, a handshake, and "nothing down." He and his family moved into the house in June. The farm, which Frost never worked, had (and has) a fine view of the Presidential Range in the White Mountains. It was a place where the family was glad to settle, though Frost was saddened to be "far from all the literary life I had ever known and in the midst of dirtier little misgoverned towns than I seemed to remember flourished in America" (as he wrote to a friend in Gloucester, England). They had escaped the dangers of wartime England and were relieved to be back in New England. "We are come home," Frost later wrote to the same friend. **Elinor** in particular was glad to be back in the natural world she had missed so much. A mark of the comfort they felt was that the children went to the Franconia schools, their first attendance in public schools since they had lived in Plymouth. In dedicating ***Mountain Interval* (1916)** to Elinor, Frost refers to the Franconia neighborhood where they lived as "this interval of the South Branch under black mountains."

The locale of his close friendship with Raymond Holden, the farm in Franconia was also the place where Frost wrote such poems as **"Good-by and Keep Cold," "A Hillside Thaw," "Two Tramps in Mud Time,"** and **"The Bear."** (He wrote such works on a home-made writing board, attached to his chair, which can still be seen in the house, now part of The Frost Place, a summer writing school and museum.) Later, his daughter Marjorie wrote a privately published book of poems in 1936 entitled *Franconia*.

The Frost family spent their summers in Franconia until 1920, when Frost sold the farm and bought another in South Shaftsbury, Vermont. The move from New Hampshire to Vermont becomes the subtext for one of Frost's most accomplished pieces of comic verse, the title poem of *New Hampshire* **(1923)**.

References and further reading: L. Francis, *Morning Gladness*; Thompson, *Triumph*.

Thomas C. Bailey

"FREEDOM OF THE MOON, THE," was first published in *West-Running Brook* **(1928)** and is a playful, joyous **lyric** about the dance of perception. Placed following **"Spring Pools"**—wherein each pool's location is fixed—the poem celebrates the imagination's freedom to travel and to wonder. Ironically, the moon itself is (relative to earth) stationary; Frost is the traveler, and his perception is what changes. Frost gives the new moon an abstract quality—freedom—grounded in specifically human visions—a jewel, an ornament, a shining moment of new joy—each of which revels in possibilities. The poet has the power to place the moon high or low, to free the moon from "a crate of crooked trees" and take it "over glossy water" just to see what the image might become.

The images of the moon enliven the speaker and the night, leading to wondrous, uncertain futures. Like the moon, the poem itself runs in cycles (as suggested in the first line), so the joy is eternally recurrent, repeating a theme developed in **"Fragmentary Blue"** and elsewhere in Frost.

References and further reading: Bagby, "Promethean."

Kenneth Rickard

"FROM IRON," first published as "The Sage" in *A Remembrance Collection of New Poems* (New York, 1959), appeared in its final form in *In the Clearing* **(1962)**. Dedicated to Ahmed S. Bokhari, an assistant secretary at the United Nations, the couplet is an ironic statement about an enormous lump of iron ore, which the King of Sweden had sent to the United Nations and which ended up enshrined in the Meditation Room. The United Nations, an organization Frost considered naive, was disturbed by Frost's opposition to it, so Mr. Bokhari was sent to visit Frost in Ripton, Vermont. He requested that Frost write a poem celebrating the notion that nations are interdependent. Frost couldn't resist the temptation to challenge what he thought were unrealistic concepts about humanity's ability to resist struggle. In an interview, Frost explained that "when I wrote of that lump of iron in the United Nations building, that stands for unity. But, even as you look at it, it seems to split. You think of tools that can be made of it, and you think of weapons." His transformation of the symbol of peace into a symbol of opposing forces is typical of his belief in the "ultimate irreconcilable [opposites of] . . . peace and strife" in which the "Weapons of war and implements of peace / Are but the points at which it finds its release" (**"The Flood"**), with "it" being the power of blood and the need to release it. (*See also* **"Bursting Rapture."**)

References and further reading: For the background of the poem, see Dolbier; for Frost's comments on the poem, see R. Cook, *Living Voice*.

James M. Dubinsky

"FROM PLANE TO PLANE," a blank verse dialogue, first appeared in *What's New* (Abbott Laboratories, North Chicago, IL) in December 1948 and later as one of three poems (with **"Choose Something Like a Star"** and **"Closed for Good"**) in "An Afterword" to *The Complete Poems of Robert Frost (1949)*. The two field laborers in the poem—Bill Pike, an experienced farmhand, and the younger Dick, a college student—argue as "equals" about the nature of work, rest, and individualism. Most of the poem centers on Pike's and Dick's contrasting impressions of a doctor they see driving in the distance. Pike is unwilling to admit that he may be "on an equality" with the upper-class doctor, though Dick observes similarities between Pike's and the doctor's leisure styles. In the end, the two men consider work in terms of the different "planes" they occupy: Pike discusses his ideas in terms of the sun and Santa Claus, and Dick replies with correlative allusions to Milton's *Paradise Lost* and Shakespeare's *Hamlet*.

References and further reading: Marcus, *Explication*.

Beth L. Diehls

FROST, ELINOR MIRIAM WHITE (1872–1938). Robert Frost told **Louis Untermeyer**, "[Elinor] has been the unspoken half of everything I ever wrote, and both halves of many a thing from **'My November Guest'** to the last stanzas of **'Two Tramps in Mud Time.'** " Frost's poems mirror the more than forty-three years he shared with his wife, and even more important, they reflect her feelings, intelligence, and critical ideas. Sometimes Elinor collaborated on poems by suggesting words, and in several places, Frost incorporated entire sentences that she had spoken. Frost also attempted to understand some of his wife's views that were contrary to his own. The result, at times, produced ambiguities in his work, especially in poems about **religion** and **politics**.

Elinor Miriam White was born in Lawrence, Massachusetts, the youngest of three daughters. Her father, Edwin, left his position as a minister in the Universalist Church and supported his family by working as a cabinet maker. Elinor's socially ambitious mother, Henrietta Ada Cole White, was unhappy as a carpenter's wife and ultimately left her husband. As a young woman, Elinor was slight, about five feet tall, with dark brown hair, fair skin, blue eyes, and cameo features. She was serious and quiet, but she had a sense of humor. She enjoyed drawing and writing, and a few of her poems appeared in the Lawrence High School newspaper—the editor was a classmate and special friend, Rob Frost. Earlier, Elinor had suffered from what was called "slow fever," and for two years she had not attended school. By the end of her senior year, Elinor's grades were the highest in the class; the principal, however, believed that Robert

Frost should deliver the valedictory speech at the graduation of 1892. Elinor delivered the salutatory speech, which she entitled, "Conversation as a Force in Life."

During the summer after graduation, Elinor and Rob conducted a private, unofficial "wedding ceremony" on the banks of the Merrimack River, where the two pledged their love and exchanged rings. In the fall, Elinor attended her father's alma mater, St. Lawrence University, where she had received a scholarship. Late one night, during the winter of 1894, Rob went to see Elinor at a students' boarding house in Canton, New York. He brought with him a copy of *Twilight*, a privately printed book of poems that he had written about their courtship. Embarrassed by his visit, Elinor accepted the gift without comment— to young Frost's mortification. Convinced that she did not really love him, he ran away to the Dismal Swamp in Virginia. The two reconciled, and Elinor accelerated her studies so that she would graduate in three years. They married in December 1895.

In the fall of 1895, Elinor became a teacher in the school that Rob's mother had established in an office building in Lawrence. The following year, Elinor gave birth to the Frosts' first child, Elliott. She was told that, because of a heart condition, it would be dangerous for her to have more children, but two and a half years later, in April 1899, Elinor gave birth to a daughter, Lesley. During the following years, four more children were born: a son, Carol, 1902; and three daughters, Irma, 1903; Marjorie, 1905; and Elinor Bettina (who died shortly after birth), 1907. In 1919, at age forty-three, Elinor suffered a miscarriage; nine years later, she miscarried again.

In July 1900, little Elliott died of cholera on the chicken farm the Frosts were renting in Methuen, Massachusetts. Frost would include Elinor's words, "The world is evil," in **"Home Burial,"** his poem about a husband and wife whose marriage is collapsing after the loss of their child. Elliott's death embittered Elinor, who subsequently lost her religious faith. That fall, the Frosts moved to a farm that Elinor had asked Rob's grandfather to buy for them in **Derry**, New Hampshire. Elinor taught her four surviving children at home until the family moved to Derry Village in 1909, where the children attended public school.

In 1911, the Frosts moved to Plymouth, New Hampshire, where Rob taught at New Hampshire State Normal School for one year. Thompson records that the poem **"Paul's Wife"** includes Frost's angry response when his friend, the president of the college, remarked that someone had said that Elinor was "lacking in personality." A similar incident occurred during the summer of 1921 when Elinor accompanied Robert to **Bread Loaf**. Frost became furious because he thought that the director, Wilfred Davison, and his staff had "ignored and neglected" Elinor.

In 1912, the family decided to leave Plymouth. Elinor wanted to go to the English countryside where they could "live under thatch," but Rob preferred Vancouver. He flipped a coin, and Elinor won. In **England**, Elinor continued to perfect "the art of letting go," as far as housework was concerned, and spent what she later realized were the happiest years of her life. Because of the war, the Frosts left England in 1915. On their return to America, they bought a farm in **Franconia, New Hampshire**. Achieving some fame with the publication of two books in England, Frost began to accept speaking engagements at various college campuses. Elinor was opposed to her husband's "barding around," leaving the family and farm, and wasting time that she thought should be used for writing poetry.

In December 1917, Elinor began a lifelong friendship with Ethel Manthey-Zorn, wife of a German professor. The Manthey-Zorns were neighbors of the Frosts when Robert accepted the position of poet-in-residence at **Amherst College**. Elinor disliked living in Amherst; she resented the intrusions of the students into their home, and she was concerned about her children, who were in poor physical health and socially maladjusted. Elinor became so nervous that she underwent "electric treatments," a common remedy at that time for neurasthenia.

Although she was married to one of the greatest poets in America, Elinor was an unhappy woman. She did not enjoy her husband's fame; rather, she worried about his health and about the effect of his celebrity on the lives of their children. As she grew older, Elinor became more conservative politically. She despised President Franklin Delano Roosevelt and embarked on an "Anti-F.D.R." letter-writing campaign. In 1934, she endured the most profound tragedy of her life, the death of her twenty-nine-year-old daughter Marjorie.

In the fall of 1937, Elinor underwent an operation for breast cancer. The following winter, the Frosts went to Gainesville with their children and grandchildren. One afternoon, Elinor went out with Rob and their son Carol to look at some properties Frost was interested in buying. When they returned home, Elinor collapsed. She had suffered a severe heart attack. During the next three days she had at least seven additional attacks. Rob stood vigil by her bedroom door, but she did not call for him before she died. Most likely, she was too ill to ask for anyone. After her death, she was cremated. Frost knew that she had wanted her ashes to be scattered in Hyla Brook, on their first farm in Derry, but when he went there and saw how rundown the farm had become, he could not do it. That summer, Frost's daughter-in-law discovered the urn with Elinor's ashes hidden on a shelf in his closet. Next to it was a vase with a freshly picked wild orchid.

References and further reading: L. Francis, *Morning Gladness*; R. Frost, *Letters to Untermeyer*, 295–96; Katz, *Elinor Frost*; Parini, *A Life*, Ch. 3, discusses the complexity of Frost's relationship with Elinor; Sergeant, 88; Thompson, *Early Years* (see Index, 613–14, for titles of poems relating to Elinor); unpublished letters of Elinor Frost to Ethel Manthey-Zorn can be found at the Robert Frost Library, Amherst College.

Sandra Katz

FROSTIANA is a set of seven musical compositions for voice and piano. Amherst, Massachusetts, commissioned Randall Thompson to compose music in celebration of the bicentennial of the town's incorporation. Thompson composed the music in Switzerland, and in 1959 Robert Frost heard the first performance in Amherst. The titles in the series are **"The Road Not Taken," "The Pasture," "Come In," "The Telephone," "A Girl's Garden," "Stopping by Woods on a Snowy Evening,"** and **"Choose Something Like a Star."**

References and further reading: Frostiana: Seven Country Songs for Men's, Women's and Mixed Voices with Piano Accompaniment (Words by Robert Frost. Music by Randall Thompson. E. C. Schirmer Music Co., 1959).

Nancy Vogel

FURTHER RANGE, A **(1936).** Although *A Further Range*, Frost's sixth book of poetry, went on to win the Pulitzer Prize, it drew scathing attacks from leftist critics at the time of its publication for its conservative political cast (see **Politics**). Perhaps not surprisingly, the volume came under heavy fire, since Frost makes explicit his foray into "the realm of government"—always a controversial pursuit for an artist in his dedicatory epigraph. When he later recalled the negative critical reaction to *A Further Range*, Frost called attention to its topicality and the firestorm that it provoked: "It has got a good deal more of the times in it than anything I ever wrote before. . . . One well-known paper called me a 'counter-revolutionary' for writing it." The paper to which he refers is *New Masses*, well known for its socialist sympathies. In his review of *A Further Range* in *New Masses*, Rolfe Humphries, a socialist poet, railed: "The further range to which Frost invited himself is an excursion into the field of the political didactic, and his address is unbecoming." He ended his review by noting that *A Further Range* represents a "shrinking" of Frost's poetic talent. Other reviews of Frost's book, many of them by politically liberal critics, similarly sought to diminish Frost's reputation. In *New Republic*, Horace Gregory criticized Frost for his lack of "social responsibility," calling several of the poems in the book "self-defensive" and "ill informed"; he further suggested that Frost's "wisdom may be compared to that of Calvin Coolidge," a U.S. president known for his reactionary social and political views. Disparaging reviews by left-leaning critics also ran in *Partisan Review* and *The Nation*. Although some might discount literary criticism that is so highly politicized, Frost himself was troubled and angered by these attacks.

A *Further Range* includes fifty-one poems and is divided into six parts. The first part, entitled "Taken Doubly," includes fourteen poems, each of which bears two titles (for example, **"A Lone Striker or, *Without Prejudice to Industry*"**). The second title states the theme of each of the poems, in many cases clarifying its moral or political ramifications. The second section of the book, "Taken Singly," is a sequence of twenty lyrics, each of which has only a single title. This section is followed by "Ten Mills," a sequence of eleven epigrams, several of which reflect on the art of poetry; the title "Ten Mills" (ten mills equal one cent) signifies that here Frost is giving a penny's wisdom, adding one tenth of a mill for good measure. Next follows "The Outlands," including three poems about three different mountain ranges. **"Build Soil—A Political Pastoral"** is the title of the fifth part as well as the title of one of the two poems within it; the other is **"To a Thinker,"** a humorous poem about the oscillation between extremes, whether political or aesthetic. Frost ends the book with a section called "Afterthought," which features a poem about the difficulties of interpretation, **"A Missive Missile"**; it is an appropriate conclusion to a book that prompted, and still prompts, competing interpretations.

Some of Frost's best-known lyrics are gathered together in *A Further Range*, and in them he exhibits a wide range of poetic meters and forms not found in his earlier verse. **"Desert Places,"** a poem in quatrains that experiments with a complicated envelope rhyme, invokes a waste land scenario as it figures the falling snow as a terrifying effacement of ego. **"Design,"** a modified Italian **sonnet** that Richard Poirier has shown is influenced by the pragmatist philosophy of William James, questions whether there is any system that governs the operations of the universe. Such poems, as well as **"Neither Out Far Nor in Deep,"** led Lionel Trilling to label Frost "a terrifying poet," not one "who reassures us by his affirmation of old virtues, simplicities, pieties, and ways of feeling." Contrary to Frost's professed interest in sound at the expense of sight in poetry (promoted by his **poetic theory** of "the sound of sense"), many of these poems feature metrical stunts that are as much a function of our seeing as our hearing. **"A Leaf-Treader"** is a poem about the difficulty of overcoming grief and is spoken by someone struggling to keep moving, unsure of being able to stay alive. In imitation of his theme, Frost's seven-stress lines (as measured against an iambic pentameter norm) depict the speaker's long, agonizing trek. **"There Are Roughly Zones"** also features elongated lines; although each line has five stresses, he swells the lines beyond the ten-syllable standard for iambic pentameter (some lines include as many as thirteen and fourteen syllables), illustrating through his formal practice the violation of zones, or boundaries, the subject of the poem.

"Build Soil—A Political Pastoral" is one of Frost's long poems (292 lines), and as he states in the table of contents of *A Further Range*, it was delivered as the Phi Beta Kappa poem at Columbia University on 31 May 1932 "before the National party conventions of that year." Inspired by Virgil's "First Eclogue," Frost's poem is a dramatic dialogue that pits Tityrus, the farm-loving city poet, against Meliboeus, the shepherd–farmer, two characters that appear in Virgil's pastoral; in it, the two men talk about the state of affairs in the city and on the farm, Meliboeus voicing his belief that "the times seem revolutionary bad," while Tityrus reassures. When the question of socialism and its usefulness arises, Tityrus argues against Meliboeus's idea that perhaps more of the world should be socialized. Tityrus satirically dismisses such a notion and espouses a doctrine of laissez-faire (an indirect assault on Roosevelt's activist administration). Exhorting Meliboeus to "build soil," that is, turn the soil over on itself to enrich the earth, Tityrus insists on the importance of self-sufficiency, economic and otherwise. Dismissing the notion of collective political action, Tityrus advocates individual response: "I bid you to a one-man revolution." Such a position is consistent with the speaker's conservative view of organized labor expressed in the opening poem of *A Further Range*, "A Lone Striker."

In light of Frost's seeming hostility toward the New Deal, one reviewer mistakenly read Frost's poem "To a Thinker" as a mean-spirited attack on the president, accusing Frost of intentionally ridiculing Roosevelt's physical disability in his figure of a hobbling man (the "thinker" of the title). However, the poem was written in 1933, before Roosevelt took office. Frost's ideology was in fact more complicated than many of his critics allowed. As Stanley Burnshaw points out, a couple of poems in the book, **"On Taking from the Top to Broaden the Base"** and **"Provide, Provide,"** call into question Frost's conservatism, as do many of Frost's remarks outside of his poetry about his political affiliations. Nevertheless, the propensity of some critics to degrade Frost's poetry based on their sense of his politics is clear, and *A Further Range* cost him the good will of an important part of the literary establishment.

References and further reading: Burnshaw, 38–70; R. Frost, *Collected*, 765; Poirier, *Knowing*, 245–52; reviews are recounted in Wagner, 119, 133–36.

Tyler B. Hoffman

$\mathcal{G}$

"**GATHERING LEAVES**" was first published in *The Measure* in 1923 just before it appeared in *New Hampshire*. Frost seldom read the poem aloud, and few major critical analyses of Frost's poetry discuss it. Those that do tend to focus, as Lawrance Thompson's does in passing, on the poet's effective use of two-stress verse or on his ability to conjure up images of "human transience," as noted in W. W. Robson's essay, reminding some readers of the mutability poems so common in the Renaissance. For others, such as Randall Jarrell, the poem becomes "that saddest, most-carefully-unspecified symbol for our memories." On an initial reading, due in part to the poem's nursery-rhyme sound, one could easily be deceived into thinking that Frost is merely playing. Indeed, he may be, but often his playful tones mask deeper ironies.

Some critics see positive connotations in the fact that "a crop is a crop." While the leaves may be "next to nothing," they remain something, and something positive may come from the act of gathering a "whole shed" full of them. Even if the crop is "Next to nothing for use," the very act of gathering leaves has value, just as the act of creating a poem does. Such an act could represent one of the many "momentary stays against confusion" that Frost believed were the poet's contributions in a chaotic world.

Such positive connotations seem to be present, but so is a tonal shift in the second half of the poem as it changes from a happy-go-lucky frolic in the autumn leaves during the first three stanzas to a reflection about what the leaves represent in the last three. The language shifts from images of fullness and height—"full," "great," "mountains"—to images of little or no substance as the poet repeatedly uses the phrase "next to nothing." At least one critic believes that by ending his poem with a question ("And who's to say where / The harvest shall stop?"), Frost foreshadows all humanity's doom. He may be calling up the image of that great harvester, the Grim Reaper, and relying on a common metaphor for death. In such a context, Frost's "harvests" could take on a very sinister meaning.

By changing the focus from the joy of raking leaves to considerations of what value those leaves have and what they represent, Frost may be positing that the individual and nature are in unison only as they are both caught up in the same inevitable movement toward death. He also raises, implicitly, a difficult and perhaps unanswerable question: Who is in charge of the harvesting?

References and further reading: For an extended discussion of the darker, more ironic nature of the poem, see Dubinsky; Oster, 228–30, highlights the value of the creative act, regardless of the weight of the material; see also Jarrell, "To the Laodiceons"; Perrine, "Frost's 'Gathering Leaves,' " 29; Robson; Thompson, *Fire and Ice*.

James M. Dubinsky

"GENERATIONS OF MEN, THE," first appeared in *North of Boston* **(1914)**. Frost's blank verse narrative replicates a dialogue between two adolescent cousins at the Stark family reunion. The tone of their conversation is at once nostalgic and speculative and, in their allusions to Shakespeare and Homer, indicative of healthy intellectual curiosity and an appreciation of literature. An indication of inventiveness appears in the imaginary characterizing of folksy, slangy Granny Stark. Set in the rain but with the inherent promise of sunshine, the poem celebrates not only the cycle of the "generations" of the title but also birth, death, and rebirth for all humanity.

References and further reading: Poirier, *Knowing*.

Roland H. Lyford

GEORGIAN POETRY. From 1912 to 1922, Georgian poetry, which took its name from the reigning monarch in England, George V, appeared in a series of five anthologies edited by Edward Marsh. A reaction against the ornamental stylistics and overly arcane subject matter of the Aesthetic Movement of the 1890s, Georgian poetry is characterized by its diction, subject matter, and form. In diction, it seeks to replicate actual speech. In subject matter, it depicts the everyday life of common individuals. In form, Georgian poetry is metrical and follows traditional poetic patterns.

Frost arrived in **England** in 1912, the year the first Georgian anthology was published. Only a few months would pass before Frost's connection to the Georgians would be more than coincidental. Once the connection was established, it would run deep. Not long after settling in England, Frost sold his first book, *A Boy's Will* **(1913)**, to the publishing house of **David Nutt**. Frost did not know that the Georgian poet John Drinkwater was the literary adviser to the owner of the press. Drinkwater enthusiastically recommended the book and was, in part, responsible for the press's decision to offer Frost a four-book contract. Nutt would also publish Frost's second book, *North of Boston* **(1914)**. Although the initial connection was virtually anonymous, it indicates that Frost had already met the standards of the new poetic group.

Frost's entrance into these circles occurred on 8 January 1913, when he attended the famous opening of Harold Monro's Poetry Bookshop. There, Frost first met a number of Imagists, Georgians, and other Modernist poets. By the fall, through his friendship with Wilfred Gibson, Frost had been taken up by the Georgian poets in particular; they welcomed him into their circle, and he participated actively in their discussions about poetic form.

Like the Georgians, Frost, especially in his first three collections, insists on a new realism of diction, tone, and subject matter. In particular, when one reads Frost's second and third books, *North of Boston* (1914) and ***Mountain Interval* (1916)**, against the work collected in the Georgian anthologies during those same years, one sees a close aesthetic affinity between Frost and his English friends. Like the poems of his English counterparts, Frost's mostly **pastoral** poems depict the hard reality of contemporary rural life in the early twentieth century; his New England is an American mirror from across the Atlantic. Also, the easy conversational tone of Frost's poems in such volumes belongs to the larger experiments in actual speech rhythms and diction conducted by the Georgians. Frost's close friend, the English poet Edward Thomas, wrote in a review of *North of Boston*, "The result is a unique type of eclogue, homely, racy, and touched by a spirit that might, under other circumstances, have made pure **lyric** on the one hand, or drama on the other" (qtd. in Walsh). Resisting both the overly aestheticized "pure lyric" of the 1890s and the prose requirements of drama, Frost, like his Georgian friends, carved a space for the "racy" and the "homely" in his new pastoral poems.

References and further reading: L. Francis, *Morning Gladness*; Pritchard, *Literary Life*; Myron Simon, *The Georgian Poetic* (Berkeley: University of California Press, 1975), 78; Thompson, *Early Years*; Walsh, 192.

Jonathan N. Barron

"GHOST HOUSE" is the second poem in Frost's first volume, *A Boy's Will* **(1913)**, but it was first published in *The Youth's Companion* (15 Mar. 1906). In a 1912 letter to the magazine's editor, asking for permission to reprint "Ghost House" and others in *A Boy's Will*, Frost described the volume as "a series of lyrics standing in some such loose relation to each other as a ring of children who have just stopped dancing and let go hands" (qtd. in Francis). According to Cramer, Frost recalled that the poem was written in 1901 and was perhaps inspired by a vanished house near his farm in **Derry**. The old Merriam place had burned down in 1867, leaving only a cellar and a chimney.

Appropriately, then, commentators have identified the house as a metaphor of the speaker's childhood. In Dennis Vail's reading, for instance, the house "represents the institutional order of the speaker's early life," whereas other symbols suggest "childhood vitality" and "adult consciousness" and "forgetting."

Other interpretations of the ghost house abound. Sara Lundquist asserts that Frost's houses, especially abandoned houses, are significant as metaphors of the struggle of poetic form trying to assert itself against a chaotic universe.

In the first edition of *A Boy's Will*, a prose gloss appears in the table of contents for all but two of the poems. The gloss of the first poem, **"Into My Own,"** is "The Youth is persuaded that he will be rather more than less himself for having forsworn the world." The gloss of the next poem, "Ghost House," is "He is happy in society of his choosing." Donald T. Haynes notes that this choice "is no society at all." To Haynes, *A Boy's Will* depicts an alienated young man's gradual return to the human community, and so the mowing field of the second stanza of "Ghost House" introduces an image of community that will grow in importance later in the volume, in **"Waiting," "Mowing,"** and **"The Tuft of Flowers."**

References and further reading: Cramer, *Frost among His Poems*; L. Francis, *Morning Gladness*, 27; Haynes, 455; Lundquist; Vail, "Frost's 'Ghost House.' "

Andy Duncan

"GIFT OUTRIGHT, THE," although written, according to Jeffrey S. Cramer, as early as 1936, appeared in print first in the *Virginia Quarterly Review* (Spring 1942) and was collected that same year in *A Witness Tree*, a volume that Frost justifiably believed included some of his best poetry and clarifying wisdom. His wisdom in 1942, however, may be more tragic than in earlier poems because the later poems were written after the death of his wife, **Elinor**, and other personal tragedies. "The Gift Outright" is an anomaly among such poems in that it is ostensibly a public poem, recited first at William and Mary on 5 December 1941 (two days before the bombing of Pearl Harbor), at one of those Phi Beta Kappa ceremonies that Frost said were not the occasions for which good poetry is written. The poem has drawn attention not as much for its merits as a **lyric** or as a public patriotic poem but as the spoken poem with which Frost dramatically saved the day by reciting it very publicly a second time, twenty years later at the Kennedy inauguration, when he could not read his prepared poem because of the blinding reflection of sun on January snow. He faltered momentarily and then from memory said instead "The Gift Outright" with the authority of what William Pritchard called "the old voice." (*See* **"For John F. Kennedy His Inauguration."**) The wisdom imparted is not personal knowledge but a declaration by a collective "we" analogous to the aggregate "we the people" of the Constitution.

If "The Gift Outright" achieved instant fame at the Kennedy inauguration in 1961, in the decade of literary and political deconstruction that characterizes the criticism of the 1990s, it might be viewed as politically incorrect. The traditional *e pluribus unum*, melting-pot version of the American dream implied by the doctrine of "salvation in surrender" has been corrected to a current view that sanctions not a new American identity but resolutely maintained ethnic distinctiveness. Frost's poem seems to invoke the American myth that a virgin and free land fashioned a new identity. Richly delineated for the 1950s by Henry Nash Smith in his influential book *Virgin Land*, the myth had been formulated for historians in the 1890s as the frontier hypothesis of Frederick Jackson Turner. A century later, Turner's thesis has fallen into disrepute as an apology for the doctrine of manifest destiny, a stain on the American conscience in that it provided an ideological justification for many social injustices.

Frost's poem is simplistic neither in thought nor in form. "The Gift Outright" is classified by William Pritchard and other critics as a **sonnet** but not analyzed as such. It deserves note as one of Frost's more radical experiments with that demanding form, a sixteen-line sonnet (similar to the kind George Meredith wrote)—structurally, a fourteen-line sonnet in blank verse continuing the reflection through a final couplet that is complete in thought if not in form.

The time period specified is the colonialism of Massachusetts and Virginia before the Revolutionary War, when the inhabitants were "England's, still colonials." There is some wordplay here with the concept of possession. Before the sacrifices of war, we were "Possessing what we still were unpossessed by." After the deed of war, the perspective is paradoxically reversed; we are from then on "Possessed by what we now no more possessed." The inhabitants, who may have owned their lands, are now the citizens of (belong to) a new nation.

We became Americans by being willing to allow the shape of America to be dictated by a land different here from that in Europe. In making his statement, Frost uses language that is implicitly religious and explicitly legal. Reuben Brower has accurately said that this is a poem about possessing, a concept that has legal ramifications in the sense that possessing is also owning. Legal meanings are further suggested by the contrasting ideas of gift, deed, and finally, surrender. We the citizens must offer a gift to the land, and as it has been since the first war of independence, the gift may be of ourselves. It is also a gift "outright," completely without legal encumbrances. The "gift" is a "deed," a willingness to sacrifice, much as Christian true believers give themselves, surrender their lives to Christ, for salvation in eternal life. The phrase "from our land of living" may have such biblical reference, as in Psalm 116:9: "I will walk before the Lord in the land of the living." The political implication is that through giving of ourselves we the people find a new life, a new identity, in America, "our land of living."

This poem is not flagrantly naive. Frost is fully alert to the political and sociological difficulties in the salvation-through-surrender doctrine. His emphasis is not on the present but on a gift offered during the Revolution that must be renewed, on deed done for the land rather than on any myth justifying expansion or assimilation. President Kennedy showed his understanding of the poem when he requested that if Frost should read "The Gift Outright," he substitute "will become" for "would become," implying a role for his administration toward a goal neither inevitable nor yet achieved. Clearly to Frost there must first be an act, a historical fact as deed, and then there may follow the legends and the creation of myth. Such is the meaning of the puzzling final line. At the grand occasion, when Frost came to recite the last line, he discerningly spoke: "Such as she *would* become, has become—and, for this occasion, let me change that to *will* become." The text of the poem itself, as well as the additions at his readings, make clear that Frost was not politically insensitive, but, like President Kennedy, he saw Americanization as an imperfect but continuing process.

References and further reading: Brower; Bush, "Writing the Myth"; Cramer, *Frost among His Poems*; Parini, *A Life*, 335–37; Pritchard, *Literary Life*; Henry Nash Smith, *Virgin Land: The American West as Symbol and Myth* (New York: Vintage, 1950); Thompson and Winnick.

Richard J. Calhoun

"GIRL'S GARDEN, A," first appeared in *Mountain Interval* **(1916)**. In both 1930 and 1939, it was included in *Collected Poems*, and in 1949, Frost published it in *Complete Poems*. Later, it was incorporated into *Selected Poems* **(1963)**. "A Girl's Garden" is a delightful third-person narrative in which an unidentified speaker relates a neighbor's poignant remembrances about the first garden of her girlhood. The first five stanzas chart the preplanting stages of her garden, from her earliest spark of interest in it to her conversation with her father about it. The poem at first seems to be a casual tale about a girl's yearning for a responsibility solely her own. Now grown, the woman recognizes the merit of her girlhood endeavors. The final stanzas suggest that by cultivating her garden the woman has also managed to gain valuable life experience, and she is now able better to understand the workings of people because of the variety of experiences she gained while farming "A little bit of everything, / a great deal of none."

References and further reading: Brower; Marcus, *Explication*.

Susan M. Stone

"GOING FOR WATER" was first published in *A Boy's Will* **(1913)**. It figured at the end of the first of three sections, and it was only one of two poems (the other being **"Reluctance"**) not to have a gloss. Like many of the poems in the volume, it is set in a natural landscape. Moreover, the images it presents— the brook, the woods, and the hearing of soft music—are typically Frostian, both in their recurrence in Frost's canon and in their symbolic meaning. The situation in the poem is also one of Frost's favorites: The speaker tells of how he and another person were once forced to go in search of a brook because their well was empty. Their quest affords them the opportunity to enter the woods behind their house and to stop there, caught up with a feeling of exhilaration at the sight of a moonlit sylvan scene.

The experience is characterized as ecstatic: The couple join the woods in making the hush, which allows them to hear the soft music coming from the brook. Like **"Directive,"** the poem alludes to the search for a spring, prefiguring the later poem's more explicit reference to the archetype of regeneration through initiatory rites.

In addition, "Going for Water" could be a metaphor for Frost's conception of poetical inspiration as the poet himself derived it from his more complex theory of the sound of sense. The image, then, would be that of a poet whose auditory imagination is triggered by sounds that he later transforms into fully formed images.

References and further reading: Lentricchia, *Modern Poetics*, 40–43, provides an extensive commentary, likening the journey of going for water to the reconstitutive act of imaginative play and referring us to the poem's relation to the work of **Ralph Waldo Emerson**.

Paola Loreto

"GOLD HESPERIDEE, THE," first appeared in *Farm and Fireside* (Sept. 1921) and was later collected in *A Further Range* **(1936)**. The comic poem deserves more attention than it has received. It is a fable about one Square Matthew Hale, who becomes so angry when he discovers the only three apples on a tree are gone that he takes off his hat, stamps it flat, then is relieved to see that he has not been observed.

In a calculated misreading, Frost compares Hale to the wicked King Ahaz, whose "abominations" include human sacrifice, according to 2 Kings 16.3–4. But Hale misses the point:

> This was the sin that Ahaz was forbid
> (The meaning of the passage had been hid):
> To look upon the tree when it was green
> And worship apples. What else could it mean?

The question is disingenuous, suggesting that Frost is either tweaking Hale's religious naïveté or suggesting the errors into which some fall in their insistence on literal interpretations of the Bible.

The title offers another interpretation. The golden apples of Hesperides are, according to Robert Graves, a symbol of immortality. The poem can thus be seen as a comic grafting of Judeo-Christian and Greek mythologies, portraying Hale as a New England Adam who has just discovered he has lost paradise.

References and further reading: Robert Graves, *The White Goddess* (New York: Farrar, Straus, 1948), 256–58; Joyner.

Nancy Carol Joyner

GOLDEN TREASURY OF THE BEST SONGS AND LYRICAL POEMS IN THE ENGLISH LANGUAGE. *See* **Palgrave's** *Golden Treasury*.

"GOOD HOURS"—according to Jeffrey S. Cramer's sources in Angyal, Mertins, and Thompson—was written over the winter of 1911–1912 at Plymouth, New Hampshire, and originally published in italics to highlight its position as the concluding poem of *North of Boston* **(1914)**. The poem is probably meant to be paired with **"The Pasture,"** also italicized as the opening poem of the volume, and with **"The Wood-pile,"** which immediately precedes it and which also describes a solitary walk beyond the reach of human community. Its bleak discovery of guilt in winter isolation looks forward to poems in *Mountain Interval* **(1916)** such as **"An Old Man's Winter Night"** and **"Snow."** Critics often pair it with **"Acquainted with the Night"** in *West-Running Brook* **(1928)**.

Like the latter poem, "Good Hours" relies on anaphora for its primary organization and uses such conspicuous grammatical order and stanzaic structure to underplay the dread that motivates its speaker. Other kinds of expressive repetition of words within the poem reinforce the quaint decorum that defends the speaker and "the folk within" from their fear of the wilderness. The use of "bound" as a verb meaning "going" does not exclude the relevant sense of that word as a noun. What the speaker finds past the boundary of human habitation unsettles his conscience but is left unnamed. His return to the mutuality of the cottages fails to appease him and confirms his offense against the banal imperatives that define the space and rhythms, the "good hours," of social life. "Profanation," like "repented" before it, departs from the poem's unpretentious diction; their meanings, possibly ironic, are dependent in part on the reader's interpretation of the speaker's tone in the last stanza, especially given the disingenuous courtesy of "by your leave." The change in the speaker's understanding of his action is reflected by the difference between "my winter evening walk," a ritualized exploration, and "my creaking feet," an objectified self-accusation. Richard Poirier discusses the poem as an example of Frost's tendency to define wandering as a quest for possibilities, including, of course, poetic possibilities.

References and further reading: Cramer, *Frost among His Poems*; Lentricchia, *Modern Poetics*; Poirier, *Knowing*.

Gary Roberts

"GOOD-BY AND KEEP COLD," first published in *Harper's Magazine* (July 1920) and collected in *New Hampshire* **(1923)**, is a light meditation on an apple orchard facing the imminent dangers of winter. During the cold winter months, the orchard is vulnerable to early thaws that bring the sap to flow and the buds to ripen prematurely, leaving the trees endangered by the next freeze. The speaker is reminded, too, of the resourcefulness of desperate winter animals foraging for food, including deer and rabbits who may strip the bark from the young trees or grouse setting upon the buds. The biggest threat comes from the warmth of the winter sun that might stir the dormant orchard to life too early.

The speaker's quandary over the orchard's winter fate is deepened because he has duty elsewhere, a duty not to care for other trees but to cut them down. Summoning "grouse, rabbit, and deer to the wall" and warning them "away with a stick for a gun" would be useless and "idle" and would not compensate his absence. At least the orchard has been planted on a north-facing slope to secure it against overexposure to the winter sun. "Dread fifty above," he admonishes the trees, "more than fifty below." At the onset of winter and with business elsewhere, Frost closes the poem in the last five lines with an interesting yoking of realism to religious faith.

A biographical anecdote can be used as a template for reading the poem. It concerns a neighbor of Frost's in **Franconia** who often overheard "sharp words" exchanged between Frost and his wife. The morning after one particularly unpleasant exchange, Frost and the neighbor went for a morning walk. Frost gave him a poem—a draft of "Good-by and Keep Cold"—that he said he had written the night before. The last line of the poem concerns a matter of dispute over religious matters: namely, Frost's own religious belief and **Elinor Frost**'s skepticism. The closing line may be seen as Frost's final volley in a quarrel over the issue of God's mercy.

Some critics see too much wit in the closing line for it to bear up under a biographical reading. Keying on the "serio-comic" metrical effect and the "disingenuously adroit" movement and rhymes, Richard Poirier, for example, concludes that "the poem is a jocular and sly insider's view of God's justness."

References and further reading: Poirier, *Knowing,* 194–95; Thompson, *Triumph,* is the source for the story about Frost and his neighbor, Raymond Holden.

David D. Cooper

"GRINDSTONE, THE," is based, according to Cramer, on the young Frost's summer work on Loren Bailey's farm in Salem, New Hampshire. It was first published in *Farm and Fireside* (June 1921) and collected in *New Hampshire* **(1923)**; in the first edition of that volume, Frost appended a footnote to the title poem, lines 238–39, referring the reader to "The Grindstone." The intertextual connection and other remarks suggest that the poem's autobiographical significance lies in the poet's amused chagrin at his impatience and earnest dissatisfaction with notions of perfection in a hopelessly imperfect world.

Marie Borroff discusses "The Grindstone" in the context of other poems about labor, such as **"After Apple-Picking"** and **"Two Tramps in Mud Time,"** in which Frost explores issues of responsibility and "balance between effort and resistance." She also praises the poem as an example of "Frost's greatest gift: his ability to develop meaning with cumulative force, seemingly without art or effort." Here the feel of effortlessness is largely the result of the patternless rhyme scheme that allows the poet to play rhyming couplets against dispersed rhymes in the context of a poem about hard work. Dorothy Judd Hall calls attention to the poem's grammatical arrangement and rhythmic structure; for Hall, the poem's stylistic intricacy, rather than its supposed plainness, carries the structure of an allegorical narrative.

The poem moves from observation to memory, from winter to summer, and from adulthood to youth. Though ostensibly a realistic representation of an actual event, the poem suggests metaphorical possibilities from its beginning. The humorous personification of the grindstone sets up the expectation that things such as the apple tree in the poem are not only themselves but also symbols of human situations. The poem slides toward allegory when, after introducing Frost's honing partner vaguely, it identifies him as "A Father-Time-like man" in the midst of a series of five consecutively rhyming lines. Frost remarked that the grindstone itself was a metaphor for the earth, as is suggested in his description of it as "an oblate / Spheroid." If the grindstone is a metaphor, then so is the blade that is ground; both Borroff and Hall suggest that the blade may stand for poetry.

The conspicuously symbolic language of the first two sections is subdued in the final section, revealing the emotional impetus for the poem. The concluding thirteen lines are a marvel of pacing and proportion. The last couplet is compelling because its strong enjambment follows after three end-stopped lines, and the rhyme hearkens back to the previous enjambments of "tried / The creepy edge" and "decide / It needed." When the poem's last sentence runs over its last line break in this way, the poet gives us "a turn more" to deliver a sense of relieved closure.

References and further reading: Borroff, "Frost: 'To Earthward,' " 29; Cramer, *Frost among His Poems*; Dawes; D. J. Hall, "Old Testament"; Lynen, *Pastoral Art*.

Gary Roberts

GUARDEEN, THE. See **Drama**.

"GUM-GATHERER, THE," first appeared in *The Independent* (9 Oct. 1916) and in *Mountain Interval* the same year. Perhaps one of Frost's less successful poems, "The Gum-Gatherer" is reminiscent of Wordsworth's "Resolution and Independence," in which the speaker uses an interview with a solitary soul as an opportunity for self-evaluation and contemplation of the cosmic meaning of things. We may view the gum-gatherer as an escapist seeking to avoid the pain of living in the world, since he lives away from town and comes to market whenever he pleases. A more Romantic reading would credit the gum-gatherer with eschewing society's restraints in order to make his own meaning of the world—although it is actually the speaker who translates his experience into meaning. In fact, critical comments on the lack of connection between the poem's long first section and its short conclusion may be due to the realization that the speaker's philosophical input goes unanswered—indicating neither assent nor denial—by the poem's subject. Critics disagree about whether gathering gum is actually a metaphor for writing poetry. If so, the pleasantness of writing poetry also is constantly "dim," ironically suggesting the struggle involved in creating what the market may consider "uncut jewels." Frost at one point seemed to view the poem as a less serious work, writing to an editor in a letter of 1919 that it was a favorite if only because it enabled him to treat the subject of chewing gum poetically.

References and further reading: R. Frost, *Selected Letters*, 233; Kemp, 167, examines the validity of gum-gathering as a mechanism for writing poetry and finds the connection weak; Nitchie, 133–34, discusses the gum-gatherer as someone who rejects society in order to make his own meaning; Wilbur suggests the figurative relationship between gathering gum and writing poetry.

L. Tamara Kendig

H

"HAEC FABULA DOCET" first appeared in the *Atlantic Monthly* (Dec. 1946) and was collected in *Steeple Bush* **(1947)**. It is a fable in the tradition of Aesop (ca. 600 B.C.) and Jean de La Fontaine (1621–1695). The Latin title, translated "This Story Teaches," imitates the formulaic conclusions used by Phaedrus, the first-century Roman translator and versifier of Aesop's fables. The use of human instead of animal characters also imitates Phaedrus's harsher tone. In spite of the didactic title, the poem portrays overly independent people as inherently unteachable. The Blindman is able to detect the trench with his own cane but unwilling to take advice from others. Similarly, the moral to the fable is interrupted by the comment "it hardly need be shown," indicating with some exasperation that those who can't see the obvious probably cannot be taught it either. The *Atlantic Monthly* version has an additional quatrain equating "sole alone" with "the independence of Vermont" and generalizing the criticism of unteachableness to a regional group. Nitchie discusses "Haec Fabula Docet" as an example of Frost's view of the individual's social nature, whereas Potter examines indications that the poem mocks both the fable form and the reader.

References and further reading: R. Cook, "Frost as Parablist"; Nitchie; O'Donnell, "Parable in Poetry"; Potter; Vogel, *Frost, Teacher.*

Nanette Cumley Tamer

"HANNIBAL," which first appeared in *West-Running Brook* **(1928)**, is a four-line reflection on poetic interpretations of human endeavors. Hannibal (247–182 B.C.), the last of the great Carthaginian generals who waged war against Rome for commercial and political control of the Mediterranean region, engaged the imaginations of generations of Latin students via the historian Livy's account of Hannibal's daring and nearly successful attempt to lead a massive military force, including teams of elephants, over the snow-covered Alps to attack Rome from the north. Rome's defeat of Hannibal's forces affected the modern world by securing European, instead of African, control over the commerce and culture of the Mediterranean. The poem identifies three aspects of the Hannibal narrative that link it to **lyric** verse: the impossibility of his undertaking, the length of time that has passed, and the persistent human problem that often only the lapse of time shows us which endeavors are possible and which are useless. The poem also links the lyric to youthfulness by attributing emotion and imaginativeness to both.

References and further reading: Frost's use of the narrative mode within the lyric is examined by Richardson, "Motives," 283–85, and Vogt, 530.

Nanette Cumley Tamer

"HAPPINESS MAKES UP IN HEIGHT FOR WHAT IT LACKS IN LENGTH," first published in the *Atlantic Monthly* (Sept. 1938), is a **lyric** written in iambic trimeter. The poem immediately follows **"All Revelation"** in *A Witness Tree* (1942) and is best considered in response to that poem's central theme.

In "All Revelation" the only truth is that created by human vision, a theme that recurs in poems such as **"For Once, Then, Something," "A Passing Glimpse,"** and **"Fragmentary Blue."** In such poems, the inability to know any truth beyond oneself is presented as a limitation to human happiness. In "Happiness Makes Up in Height for What It Lacks in Length," Frost's poetic answer to such uncertainty echoes the Aristotelian maxim, "Good itself will be no more of a good thing by being eternal, for a white thing is no whiter if it lasts a long time than if it lasts a day" (*Nichomachean Ethics*, I.6.1096b).

The poem itself is divided not into stanzas but into three sentences. The first poses the question of happiness; the second suggests an answer; the third declares a final truth about a perfect day. Speaking primarily in the first person, Frost questions the value of momentary joys. In the face of doubt—as in **"Design," "Nothing Gold Can Stay,"** or **"Storm Fear"**—Frost maintains his belief by simply believing in his own experience of one perfect day, using that image to construct a world within which he can reside, one where the promise of warmth and light recurs forever. Notice that the poem ends by shifting from the solitary "I" to the plural "we"—presumably including the poet's wife, **Elinor**—as the couple walks through the "blazing flowers" that suffuse the scene with color, scent, and joy.

The social dimension allows Frost to escape the "solitude" suggested by the solipsistic "All Revelation." Further, Aristotle argued that "we must use what is evident as witness to what is not" (II.2.1104a). Frost's final sentence—grounded in the concrete image of lovers strolling through the sun-dappled meadow—insists that happiness has been evident and therefore must be able to return. As Frank Lentricchia and others have noted, the construction of value is a fundamentally human activity; our striving toward meaning is Frost's fundamental idea of virtue (see, for example, **"Mowing"** or the **prose** piece "Education by Poetry"). Poetic expression itself deals with the concrete, and the poetic utterance is a creation and exploration of possibility. Poetry exists in the present and for the future, like the lingering memory of a perfect day. In a sense, the poem is itself an answer to the very doubts it raises.

References and further reading: Aristotle, *Nichomachean Ethics*, trans. Terence Irwin (Indianapolis: Hackett, 1985); Lentricchia, "Frost and Theory."

Kenneth Rickard

"HARDSHIP OF ACCOUNTING, THE," originally titled "Money," was one of the group of poems called "Ten Mills," first published in the April 1936 issue of *Poetry* magazine. It was later collected in *A Further Range* **(1936)** and has borne its present title in all subsequent book publications.

Frost knew firsthand the hardships of accounting. During Frost's student days at **Dartmouth**, his grandfather, William Prescott Frost, Sr., sent him $5 a week—a respectable sum, since Frost's room, for example, cost only $30 a year. "What made it bad," Frost recalled, "was the fact that he insisted on an itemized account for every penny spent, where it went, and what it was for. I rebelled and wanted to tell him to go to hell. But I didn't, I held" (qtd. in Cramer).

The short verse is vintage Frost. A playful tone is suggested by the five lines of trochaic tetrameter, but the tone of the message is, in fact, sarcastic. Accounting, Frost seems to say, is questionable at best, since there exists a discrepancy between where a spender thinks one's money went and where one actually spent it. He further diminishes the value of keeping accounts when he implies that if one does not remember where the money went, one might just as easily "invent" an accounting. Marcus notes that the "wearily regular meter and continued single rhyme echo the speaker's defensive disgust" at being asked to keep account of his own finances.

References and further reading: Cramer, *Frost among His Poems*, 117–18; Marcus, *Explication*, 158.

Andy Duncan

HARVARD UNIVERSITY. Robert Frost's father, William Prescott Frost, Jr., class of 1872, won distinction at Harvard University: Holder of the Bowditch Scholarship, winner of the Bowdoin Prize for his dissertation on the Hohenstaufens and of a Detur for outstanding academic achievement, he was elected to Phi Beta Kappa and delivered a Commencement oration.

Although Robert took and passed the entrance examinations for Harvard even before his brief stay at **Dartmouth College**, his feelings about his father's alma mater were ambivalent. When, in 1897, he was drawn once again to Harvard— this time by a desire to study the classics and pursue a teaching career—he had already matured in his poetic idiom and published several poems in the *New*

York Independent and elsewhere; he was married, with a growing family, and in need of a steady income to relieve the burden on his ailing mother. With a last-minute letter to Dean LeBaron R. Briggs, the twenty-three-year-old Frost gained admission to the Harvard College Class of 1901. Frost's studies at Harvard were a source of pride and exhilaration, on the one hand, and, on the other, a growing sense of frustration and unease with the intellectual regimentation and drain on his limited energy and financial resources. Although, like his father, he received a small scholarship and won a Detur for his first year's academic record, unlike his father, he had demanding family obligations and was forced to obtain outside employment (which he found as principal of the Shepard Evening School in North Cambridge). He never seemed to find time to mull over the material or to write, and he began to think about writing for keeps. The need to be at home with his wife, **Elinor** (who was expecting their second child), and to assist his mother at the school in Salem combined with a fear of tuberculosis to aggravate his persistent restlessness. Halfway through the spring semester of his second year, Dean Briggs released him from Harvard without prejudice, lamenting the loss of so good a student.

Not many years after the undergraduate experience, upon his return from **England** in 1915 as a recognized poet, Frost was called back to Harvard to deliver the Phi Beta Kappa poem (and receive honorary membership). The delivery of **"The Bonfire"** (later greeted as an antiwar poem) and **"The Ax-Helve"** (which revealed much of the poet's maverick thinking about indoor and outdoor schooling) assured Frost a triumphant return and critical acclaim.

Out of a sense of pride and a certain awe in which he held the institution, Frost hoped for more opportunities to appear at Harvard. In 1935, Professor Robert Hillyer arranged for his friend to read in the Morris Gray series; Hillyer, David McCord, **Bernard DeVoto**, and others soon were urging the selection of Frost for the Charles Eliot Norton Professorship, given to a man of high distinction and international reputation who would deliver six public lectures on poetry. No one at Harvard anticipated the overwhelming reception for Frost on those March and April evenings in 1936. The final lecture had to be moved from the New Lecture Hall to the 1,200-seat-capacity Sanders Theatre. Arranged loosely under the heading of "The Renewal of Words," the titles of the six lectures (which were delivered without notes) convey the sweep of Frost's poetic thinking: "The Old Way to Be New," "Vocal Imagination—the Merger of Form and Content," "Does Wisdom Signify?" "Poetry as Prowess (Feat of Words)," "Before the Beginning of a Poem," and "After the End of a Poem."

But for Frost himself, although he made and kept friends there as elsewhere, the sense of belonging at Harvard was still elusive: "I'm imperfectly academic," he confided to **Louis Untermeyer**, "and no amount of association with the academic will make me perfect. It's too bad, for I like the academic in my way, and up to a certain point the academic likes me." He hated to know he *must* write and lamented that "I made myself wretched and even sick with the dread of what I had let myself in for at Harvard." Only a severe attack of shingles released him from the commitment to present the Phi Beta Kappa poem and Tercentenary ode that fall.

In spite of his antipathy toward the "starchy stiffs" and the pro-English crowd at Harvard, Frost was pleased to accept Harvard's honorary degree of Litt.D. at the 1937 Commencement. President James Bryant Conant cited him as "The poet of New England: his friendship quickens the talent of tomorrow, his art perpetuates the inner spirit of our countryside." Conant and Frost were initially friendly, but the scientist and the poet approached their tasks from opposing vantage points, and the distancing of their views would prove pivotal in shaping the long-term relations of poet and university.

The unexpected and shattering loss of his wife, Elinor, in March 1938 provoked Frost's resignation from **Amherst College**, relieving him, he stated at the time, of "an obscure anxiety to please people I imperfectly understood." Frost would be reconciled with Amherst, but the unexplained rupture prompted an outpouring of sympathy and guidance from his friends, including fellow poets at Harvard—Morrison, McCord, and Hillyer—who were pallbearers at his wife's funeral. At McCord's urging, Frost was nominated and elected to Harvard's Board of Overseers, and the English Department approached President Conant with a proposal to appoint the distraught widower to Harvard's faculty. President Conant resisted the appointment and thought was given to an appointment in the classics department. When an offer was finally made to Frost for the 1938–1939 academic year, it placed him in the English Department. Frost was pleased to accept: "That would be a proud connection. And I think it would be much more sensible for Harvard to have me in the English Department than in the Latin Department. . . . I am in great need of being tied down by my friends to something regular."

President Conant reappointed Frost as **Ralph Waldo Emerson** Fellow in Poetry for the years 1939–1940 and 1940–1941, and for his final year on the Harvard faculty (1941–1942), he was appointed Fellow in American Civilization. Frost could now claim to be a bona fide member of the Harvard faculty, and contacts with students and the larger Boston community were very successful, but the tensions he had experienced at other institutions soon surfaced. In June 1941 Frost broke precedent by delivering a second Harvard Phi Beta Kappa poem. **"The Lesson for Today"** and the anti–New Deal sentiment of another poem, **"Provide, Provide,"** underscored fundamental philosophical differences between Frost and President Conant.

While the ties with his intellectual alma mater soon loosened, they were not entirely severed. Harvard's Signet Society gave him a medal for achievement in the arts in March 1958, and David McCord chaired the committee that established the Emerson-**Thoreau** Medal, bestowed on its first recipient, Robert Frost, by the American Academy of Arts and Sciences in October of that year. McCord played a similar hand in Leverett Saltonstall's action (along with Vermont Senator George Aiken, President Eisenhower, and Sherman Adams) to gain passage of a resolution conferring the Congressional Gold Medal on the eighty-eight-year-old poet in the spring of 1962. President Kennedy presented the medal at the White House, and Frost transferred it to Harvard's Houghton Library with the understanding that "it should be regarded as in memory of my father William Prescott Frost's days as a student at Harvard and my own days later as a student and a **teacher** there."

References and further reading: L. Francis, " 'Imperfectly Academic' "; R. Frost, *Selected Letters* and *Letters to Untermeyer*, 277; Mertins; K. Morrison; Smythe.

Lesley Lee Francis

"HILL WIFE, THE," was first published in the *Yale Review* in April 1916 and was included in the collection *Mountain Interval* that same year. Critically acclaimed, it is among the best known of Frost's poems. The five-poem sequence that makes up "The Hill Wife" is, in **Louis Untermeyer**'s words, "a remarkably rounded portrait of fear and love and loneliness." Philip Gerber notes that the mental instability of Frost's sister Jeanie made the poet familiar with the inconsolable terrors of the mind, enabling Frost to portray the hill wife with "a particular poignancy."

The plot of the poem is simple. A childless husband and wife live together on a farm. She is lonely and often goes out to the fields and woods with him. One day she strays off and doesn't come back, even when he calls her. The poem's recurring motifs—birds and images of imprisonment and escape—foreshadow the wife's leaving, but they don't explain why she leaves. The birds in the first section are objects of mystery to the wife. She sees them as self-absorbed, unconcerned with the husband and wife. By the final section, "The Impulse," the wife herself has become birdlike, "rest[ing] on a log" and singing "a song only to herself." After she has gone and her husband has failed to find her, the broken ties are said to have given way "[s]udden and swift and light as that," again evoking the bird image. The second and fourth sections also contain bird images. In the second section, "House Fear," the husband and wife "rattle the lock and key" when they return to the house at the end of the day so that the unknown, unnamed thing that is inside the house has "Warning and time to be off in flight." In the fourth section, "The Oft-Repeated Dream," the pine tree scratches against the window as "a little bird / Before the mystery of glass!" The first two sections present birds as things that fly away, but in the fourth section the bird is outside the window, fascinated with the idea of getting in. In the final section, "The Impulse," the bird imagery is applied to the wife, and she has become as free and as indifferent to human concerns as the birds of the first section. The center section, "The Smile (*Her Word*)," is the turning point. Before it, the birds, at most, only "seem" to say good-bye; otherwise, they are indifferent to human beings or are going "off in flight" to get away from them. After the center section, the wife is frightened of the birdlike tree that keeps "trying the window-latch" of the bedroom. In the center section, the wife expresses her fear and suspicion of the man who had come to the house, asking for food. Her reaction may mark her fear and suspicion of others; the reader sees the man only as he is filtered through the wife's imagination and can't judge whether his smile is genuine or, as the wife thinks, somehow threatening. She says she thinks the man smiles to mock them for being poor or married or very young. This section can be read as a signal that the wife is losing touch with reality and her mental collapse is imminent, whether brought on by isolation or other factors. It can also be read as an episode of truth-seeing in which the wife sees her life reflected in the man's reaction. He acts as a mirror that shows her the truth of her life: She is poor, married, and she will remain so for the rest of her life.

The wife narrates two sections, "Loneliness (*Her Word*)" and "The Smile (*Her Word*)." The subtitle in each case suggests that another person would call it something else, thereby undermining the credibility of the hill wife as narrator and suggesting there is another version of the events, which remains untold. The other narrator, which Lawrance Thompson characterizes as a "chorus voice," offers no overt judgment of either the husband or the wife. The voice is that of someone from the area who knows the story well and is sure of his information. For instance, in "House Fear" he says, "I tell you this they learned." And it is only through this narrator that the reader knows the husband has "learned of finalities / Besides the grave." The husband himself says nothing until the final section of the poem. When he does speak, it is indirectly, and his speech is ineffective. When the wife strays off, he calls her, but she "didn't answer—didn't speak," although it is clear that she heard, if only "scarcely." The only other time he speaks is to ask her mother if she is there. The portrait of the hill wife's silent husband corroborates the sense of loneliness and isolation she must have felt, underscoring how "The Hill Wife" offers a poignant portrayal of the effects of loneliness and fear.

References and further reading: R. Frost, *Enlarged*, 150; Gerber, *Frost*, 145; Pratt; Thompson, *Fire and Ice*, 118.

Claudia Milstead

"HILLSIDE THAW, A," was written in 1920 and based on experiences shared with Raymond Holden at **Franconia**. First published in the *New Republic* (6 Apr. 1921) and collected in *New Hampshire* (**1923**), it is one of Frost's many spring poems but is also related to his slightly earlier winter **lyric "The Onset,"** collected in the same volume. In a review of *Collected Poems* (**1930**), Isdor Schneider singles out "A Hillside Thaw" as "the most conspicuous example" of Frost's ability to develop a metaphor into a conceit instead of settling for "a mere illuminating flash."

Despite such early praise, the poem has not received much critical notice. It is by far the most playful of his poems on the changing of a season and therefore risks triviality, as if the poet were merely pulling off a stunt on a dare. However, Frost's remark about poetic play at the end of his **prose** piece "Introduction to

E. A. Robinson's *King Jasper*," suggests that such risk-taking is relevant to his ideas on poetic creativity: "Play's the thing. All virtue in 'as if.' " The phrase "as if" licenses the play of imaginative possibilities throughout Frost's poetry and is used to that end in "A Hillside Thaw."

The sense of naive, virtuoso display is produced by the unabashedly childish conceits of the wizard, the witch, and their magic lizards. The unpredictable rhyme scheme, which begins and ends with a triplet but refuses pattern in between, the internal rhyming and consonance, felicitous enjambment ("she makes a gentle cast / And suddenly . . ."), and mimetically arranged syntax (such as the inversion of line 29: "Across each other and side by side they lay") all collude to capture "the excited fun." Understanding the pleasure that the poem takes in its own frivolity depends on one's interpretation of the poetic motive for such a fanciful transformation of a glittering but trivial event. A superficial explanation, which the poem encourages, would rest on the analogy between the vitality of thawing and the release of creativity. However, a too-superficial explanation, which the poem also encourages, though it dissembles by doing so, would stop short of revealing the poem's purpose by trusting the banal if logical conclusion that humans are impotent before the power of nature.

The speaker, disingenuously ignorant of nature's ways, is tempted to choose unity over multiplicity and stasis over flux, though the temptation is futile and absurd. The speaker's desire is twice defeated, since he cannot "hold" the flowing water despite his most desperate attempts, and yet the moon, a synecdoche for the cold night, can do so without effort. The unembarrassed imagination of the lyric "I" and the comic behavior it describes mitigate the self-deprecations concluding each stanza and thereby suggest that the metaphorical conjuration that turns trickles of water into silver lizards serves as compensation for the inadequacy of poetic thinking. Both the offhanded emphasis on "thought" and the use of archaic, vaguely mythological notions of natural causality, such as spells and spontaneous creation, require us to consider the relationships of poetry to language and of language to reality when determining the seriousness of the poem's intent.

References and further reading: Schneider. For R. Frost's comment on Robinson's "King Jasper," see *Collected*, 748.

Gary Roberts

HOLT, HENRY, AND COMPANY. Founded in 1866, the publishing firm of Henry Holt and Company served as Frost's one and only American publisher in his career as a writer. The relationship between the poet and the publishing firm was one of the most significant for each of the parties involved.

As a result of the support of Henry Holt's wife and in spite of obstacles presented by his British publisher, Frost began to publish his work at Henry Holt and Company in 1915. The year before, when Frost was forty years old, living in **England**, and contracted to the English publishing firm of **David Nutt** and Company, Florence Holt, wife of Henry Holt, read *North of Boston* published that year by Nutt. She wrote a letter to Frost expressing her admiration for his poetry and recommended him to her husband's publishing firm. Soon after Frost received Florence Holt's letter, Mrs. Nutt, the head of David Nutt and Company, received an offer from Henry Holt and Company to publish the American edition of Frost's next book. Mrs. Nutt insisted that Holt promote *North of Boston*, arguing that her small publishing firm deserved reward for discovering an American talent, especially considering the war effort occupying England at the time. Holt agreed to these terms but found subsequent demands made by the publisher less easy with which to comply. In fact, the English publishing firm would continue to make claims to rights to Frost's poetry until its bankruptcy in 1921.

Frost's association with David Nutt and Company had been unhappy, for Mrs. Nutt placed limitations on Frost's freedom to offer his poems to magazines for publication. He grew to regret the English publisher's power over him. However, his association with Henry Holt and Company was of a different nature entirely: The firm offered him protection and stability. After 1915 and for the rest of his life, he would turn to friends at Holt for support, encouragement, advice, and assistance (with few exceptions, the head of Holt's trade department served as Frost's primary liaison with the company). Alfred Harcourt, his first editor at Holt, advised him in legal matters involving his association with David Nutt and Company. Lincoln MacVeagh arranged for him a monthly stipend and an appointment as poetry consultant to Holt. Richard Thornton encouraged him to invest in Holt stock. Alfred Edwards, whom Frost named his sole executor and sole trustee of his estate in 1951, particularly attended closely to Frost's concerns. His publishers "had been exemplary toward him," had always been "tenderly solicitous" to him, he told Robert Francis in 1954: "Old Alfred Harcourt had taken that attitude from the first, and the others had followed suit."

The association between Frost and his publisher, however, was not without moments of complication and uncertainty. The first test to the alliance between writer and publisher came in 1919 when Alfred Harcourt left Holt and invited Frost to join his new firm. Frost agreed initially but withdrew his agreement when he began to suspect that Harcourt was being less than forthright with him concerning the future availability of the titles previously published under Holt. Throughout the years, Frost endured the departures of favorite editors from Holt and the arrivals of new editors with whom he would have to learn to work. Frost was tempted during these transitional periods to consider offers from other publishing houses. However, he valued having his work appear under one publisher's name. Also, although he would often comment that his alliance was with a valued Holt editor and not with Henry Holt and Company, he clearly enjoyed the firm's efforts to maintain his favor and to demonstrate its appreciation for him as its premier author. Among the honors bestowed upon Frost by his publisher were the receipt of the first Holt stock certificate, the gift of a bust of Frost sculpted by Araldo du Chene, and the celebration in recognition of Frost's eighty-eighth birthday.

References and further reading: The most complete discussion of the relationship between Frost and Henry Holt and Company can be found in Charles Madison, *The Owl among Colophons*, which is dedicated "[t]o the memory of Robert Frost, who considered himself 'Holt's oldest employee' "; additionally, Ellen D. Gilbert, *The House of Holt 1866–1946: An Editorial History* (Metuchen, NJ: Scarecrow Press, 1993), includes a chapter on poetry published by the firm with a large section devoted to Frost; Alfred Harcourt, *Some Experiences* (Riverside, CT: privately printed, 1951), and Burnshaw reveal insight into Frost from the perspective of his first and his last editor at Holt; the Holt archives deposited at Princeton University's Firestone Library contain much of Frost's business correspondence with the firm (*see* **Collectors and Collections**); see also R. Francis, 26.

Christine Hanks Hait

"HOME BURIAL" was first published in *North of Boston* **(1914)**. The central issue, the lack of understanding between a husband and a wife who grieve the death of their child in two very different ways, is set up as a dialogue. Both characters are partly at fault and partly justified for their attitudes toward each other. The husband is curt but sensible, while the wife is sensitive yet unable to perceive her husband's grief.

Set on a New England farm, the poem opens with Amy, the wife, glancing from a stairway window out to the grave of her child as she moves toward the door to leave her home. Her husband approaches, startling her and asking what she sees. At first unaware of the view from the window, he then glimpses his family burial plot. In the initial action, the wife is descending the stairs, but then she sits while he ascends "mounting until she cowered under him." She shrinks way from her husband, and he pursues her. Her continual withdrawal is matched by his struggle to restrain himself and sit on the stair. The couple maintains a delicate balance. A powerful tension comes from the duality and ambiguity of such work: the opposition between man and woman, the antagonistic communication, the different styles of grief, the will to dominate and the refusal to be dominated, the irreconcilable modes of thinking. Joseph Brodsky puts it best when he suggests that the poem is ballet, a terribly tense dance composed of several *faux pas de deux*.

The husband reflects that his wife goes to others with her grief rather than talking to him. He attempts reconciliation, apologizes, and tries to account for their lack of communication. Trying to explain his difficulty, he observes that "A man must partly give up being a man / With women-folk." Reconciled to death in a way she is not, he communicates differently than she, not in the grief-stricken way the woman reacts. His protest that he should be allowed to speak of his dead child leads her to an attack on what she sees as an unfeeling burial. The physical movement back and forth, up and down the stairs; the subtle pacing

of both narrative and rhythmic structures; the overlays of psychological penetration and dramatic control—all contribute to what Brodsky has identified as
Frost's strong connection to Virgil's **pastoral** "filtered" through Wordsworth
and Browning, especially the latter's perfection of the **dramatic monologue**
form, which Frost borrows and adapts to advantage in "Home Burial."

The poem continues with Amy's memory of her husband's burying their
child, an act that for him enabled him to work out his grief. For Amy, though,
going on with the quotidian is not possible, and his equating the child's body
with rotting fence boards is monstrous. Again communication has failed, for the
reader recognizes the husband's remark about rotting fences as an attempt to
comment on the futility of human actions in the face of nature's destructive
forces; he, too, is devastated by the death of the child and tries to express his
grief through an analogy derived from his personal experience.

In the end, both characters elicit our sympathy: Amy, sometimes seemingly
irrational, is painfully overcome by her genuinely profound grief, and her husband, sometimes self-righteously callous, is sincere, though clumsy and inept,
in wanting to reconcile his own agonies. Whether a state of communion will
ever be reached by this couple is unclear, for, as Randall Jarrell observes, the
poem ends with yet another instance of the wide separation between husband
and wife, the clash between "the will and the imagination" that results in the
husband's turning to raw force, to the brute "inertia of a physical body" in his
final utterance, "I *will!*" Oster similarly deepens our insight into the couple's
differences in her analysis of the poem's brilliant manipulation of "gesture and
action" and its horrible lesson that "when action takes the place of words, it is
as inadequate as the words, and just as misunderstood."

As Pritchard and other biographers have noted, the poem has some relationship to **Elinor** and Frost's loss of their first child, a tragedy that caused a great
deal of "anger, sadness, and recriminations." Another view might be that the
poem shows compassion for two different human types in view of not only their
loss but also their insistence on and exaggeration of their differences.

References and further reading: Brodsky, 20, 23; Jarrell, *Third Book*, 230 and the rest
of the chapter on the poem, offers a detailed, astute analysis of the work's prosody and
other formal elements; Oster, 193 and passim, provides a keen study of the poem's
poignant treatment of the interplay of language and grief and the need for "balance" in
human relationships; Parini, *A Life*, 68–70, points out the fallacy of assuming that this
poem transcribes Frost's relationship with Elinor after the loss of their firstborn child
Elliott; Poirier, *Knowing*; Potter; Pritchard, *Literary Life*; Summerlin.

Dianna Laurent

HOMES OF ROBERT FROST. Although popular perception to this day
places Frost in the fields of some idealized New England farm, gleaning inspiration from the agrarian life, the **teacher**–poet actually lived as a peripatetic,
shifting from one academic community to the next throughout the region. Such
a rootless lifestyle produced a series of "Robert Frost Houses" tucked in different

corners of New England, several of which are proudly claimed and marked by local historical organizations.

After his origins in San Francisco, Frost's early years were spent in the industrial corridor that followed the Merrimack River in northern Massachusetts near the border with New Hampshire. A region of textile-producing factory towns and planned industrial cities, the poet's first landscape was one of mills and boarding houses rather than fields and barns. For the first twenty-five years of his life, Frost moved around in this manufacturing zone, living in and among the "three-decker" houses built for immigrant labor in Lawrence and Methuen, Massachusetts, and Salem, New Hampshire.

In October of 1900 Frost moved to the hinterlands of **Derry**, New Hampshire, to take up farming. With a city-slicker's aplomb, Frost taught his cows to give milk at noon and midnight rather than dawn and dusk to better accommodate his writing schedule. Meeting with mixed success as an agrarian, Frost soon began to teach part-time at **Pinkerton Academy** in Derry and in 1909 gave up farming and moved into town. The Derry farm passed out of the Frost family, fell fallow, and eventually was purchased and restored by the National Park Service to serve as a shrine to the man and the land of which he wrote.

In 1911 Frost shifted to Plymouth, New Hampshire, to teach at the New Hampshire State Normal School, a teacher's college. (See **Plymouth Normal School**.) The move inaugurated the pattern that would come to dominate Frost's life, that of constant movement from one college town to the next. Often living in temporary quarters, Frost lectured throughout the region for the rest of his life.

In 1915 Frost returned from three years in **England** and purchased a forty-five-acre farm in **Franconia, New Hampshire**. "Not Switzerland, but rugged enough," Frost described his new White Mountain retreat, exaggerating on both counts as the White Mountains had been a destination for tourists for almost fifty years. Soon, however, Frost was again lured off the land to teach at **Amherst College** and by 1920 had sold the northern Franconia property in favor of the more hospitable climate of South Shaftsbury, Vermont, near Bennington, a region long favored by writers and artists.

Built in 1779, the South Shaftsbury house had commanding views but was in desperate need of repair. By this point the Frost family had become expert at the art of rusticating in "unimproved" farmhouses and lived the rugged life without running water or indoor plumbing while the house was restored. The poet's son Carol continued to live on the South Shaftsbury farm long after his father had shifted his attentions to other parts of the country.

Unhappy at Amherst, Frost twice traveled to the Midwest to teach at the **University of Michigan**. During his second sojourn in 1925–1926, the poet lived in a striking six-room Greek Revival house on Pontiac Road. Built in 1830 for a local politician named Thompson Sinclair and sporting a pair of grand columns, the impressive façade prompted Frost to describe the house as "poultry architecture" as it had "two legs in front and two wings on the side." Prized for its architectural significance and historical associations, the house was subsequently moved to the open-air museum at Greenfield Village in Dearborn, Michigan, where it remains on display.

In the late 1930s Frost became increasingly involved with the **Bread Loaf Writers' Conference**, and in 1939 he purchased the Homer Noble Farm in Ripton, Vermont, to be near the site of the annual conference. Frost became close to Theodore Morrison and his wife Kay (*see* **Kathleen Morrison**) during this period, sharing quarters and relying on Kay as his personal secretary. The Noble Farm complex consisted of a big house given over to the Morrisons and a three-room cabin where Frost slept and wrote, taking his meals down the hill with his secretary's family and other conference attendees such as **Bernard DeVoto** and **Louis Untermeyer**.

Never enjoying robust health, Frost suffered from bronchial problems and endured bouts of pneumonia throughout his lifetime. To seek relief the Yankee poet purchased land in South Miami and built an estate known as Pencil Pines in 1940. Two prefabricated Hodgson houses were erected on the property and faced with native coral stone. Florida and Pencil Pines became part of Frost's annual schedule when the rigors of the New England winter proved to be too much for the poet's lungs.

In 1938, Frost sold his Amherst home, and in the fall of the year, Kay Morrison secured an apartment for the poet at 88 Mt. Vernon Street in Boston, directly across from the old-money enclave of Louisburg Square. Shifting to more pleasant quarters within the same building failed to solve the poet's need for more space, and his habit of walking his Border collie at all hours in all neighborhoods caused much concern for his safety among friends. Morrison therefore located a house for sale at 35 Brewster Street in Cambridge, and Frost purchased it in 1941.

35 Brewster Street served as Frost's home and headquarters for the final two decades of his life. A public figure of international renown, Frost's later years were spent "barding around the country," in his own words. The Cambridge house served as a way station between summers in the North, winters in the South, and the myriad speaking engagements and academic commitments that filled his schedule. The location of the house provided Frost with convenient access to Harvard Square and the transportation hub of Boston, yet it was also situated in a quiet neighborhood just off exclusive old-guard Brattle Street. Called "Brewster Village" by its inhabitants, Frost's new neighborhood provided a pleasant and safe community for his nocturnal rambles.

The house itself is quite unusual for West Cambridge in that it is the end unit of a row house built in 1883. Designed by John H. Besarick (1844–?) of Boston, an architect better known for his ecclesiastical and commercial architecture, Frost's house shares a theatrical air with Besarick's more public work. Vertically oriented with a prominent gable roof and ornate, perforated bargeboards, the Stick Style house was decidedly "Victorian" in appearance and perhaps reminded the poet of his early years in Lawrence and Methuen.

The homes of Robert Frost were many and surprisingly varied. The popular image of the gray Yankee farmer is, at least partially, grounded in the reality of the plethora of farms owned and improved by the poet in his lifetime. The in-town and urban residences continue to surprise, however, for few of Frost's audience to this day picture the poet among the old-money "Tory Row" mansions of Brattle Street or relaxing in Miami when reading familiar words from his famous volumes.

References and further reading: Cramer, *Frost among His Poems*; K. Morrison; Muir; there are also numerous references to Frost in the *Proceedings of the Cambridge Historical Society*.

Thomas Denenberg

"HOUSEKEEPER, THE," published in *The Egoist* (15 Jan. 1914) and later that same year in *North of Boston*, was one of several dramatic narratives Frost wrote at **Derry** in 1906–1907. **Ezra Pound** arranged for its publication in *The Egoist* a few months before the release of *North of Boston*.

According to **biographer** Lawrance Thompson, the basis of the poem is an acquaintance, John Hall, who is referred to by name. Hall was an expert poultryman who lived near Derry. Like the John of the poem, he had won awards for his exotic birds, which he valued more for their recognized quality than for their monetary value. Also, the actual John Hall lived with a common-law housekeeper–wife and her mother. Apparently Frost appreciated his back-country language and his independent sense of values.

Frost invents the poem's dramatic conflict in the poem, presented in a conversation between the visitor–poet and the mother of Estelle, the housekeeper–wife. Estelle herself has fled the farm to wed someone else, ostensibly because John has declined to make formal their "understood" union of fifteen years. The mother seems to know more than she reveals, but her reticence can be explained by her concern for her own future security; the original refuge-for-labor agreement was for her benefit, and that is surely jeopardized by Estelle's flight. The woman tells of John's odd character, and she thinks it is responsible for her daughter's action and what she believes will be the demise of the house and farm, now that she is gone. She considers John more a dreamer than a practical worker and provider. John returns home at the end of the poem with "some news that maybe isn't news," but the poem, like other Frost dramatic narratives, ends somewhat ambiguously. The poet seems less interested in dramatic resolution than in the regional dialect and personal eccentricity of his rural characters.

References and further reading: Thompson, *Early Years*.

Douglas Watson

"HOW HARD IT IS TO KEEP FROM BEING KING WHEN IT'S IN YOU AND IN THE SITUATION," first published in 1951 in *Proceedings of* *the American Academy of Arts and Letters and the National Institute of Arts and Letters*, is a compendium of Frost's mature religious and philosophical thought. The poem was collected in *In the Clearing* **(1962).** According to Frost in unpublished comments at **Bread Loaf** in 1962, he "lifted the story out of the Arabian Nights." His retelling brings into focus a question that informs both Greek tragedy and Judeo-Christian theology: *Are we masters of our own destiny?* The narrative recounts the futile attempts of the rightful king and prince of Ctesiphon to abandon their royal responsibilities. So that his son, an aspiring poet, may have money to live on, the king permits himself to be sold, anonymously, into slavery—an act by which he unwittingly defies superhuman forces (Fate? Divine Providence?). The outcome—a reversal of the king's scheme—might be summed up by the line "Man proposes; God disposes." But no such formula captures the full meaning of "How Hard," which breaks through rational parameters to disclose the mystery of human freedom. The poem undercuts our autonomy in the practical realm so as to exalt it in the spiritual. The enigma of free will is a recurrent theme in Frost (cf. **"The Road Not Taken," "The Lovely Shall Be Choosers," "Choose Something Like a Star,"** and the **drama** *A Masque of Mercy*). "How Hard" investigates freedom at various levels—aesthetic, moral, spiritual. As an *ars poetica* piece, it explores the tension between verse "running wild" and the constraints of form (cf. "The Constant Symbol" in Frost's **prose** works). As a moral statement it investigates the limits of human choice and the existence of boundaries—indistinct lines separating humanity, the natural world, and divinity (cf. **"There are Roughly Zones," "Two Look at Two"**). As a spiritual venture it reaches beyond irony to celebrate the gift of human creativity—"This perfect moment of bafflement" to which the artist, the poet, dedicates a life: "Our days all pass waiting its return."

References and further reading: D. J. Hall, *Contours*: Kearns offers an alternative reading of the poem in the thematic contexts of fathers and sons, erotics, and issues of freedom; Poirier, *Knowing*.

Dorothy Judd Hall

"HUNDRED COLLARS, A," first appeared in *Poetry and Drama* (Dec. 1913) and was collected in *North of Boston* **(1914).** As do many of his poems, this one relates a brief encounter. Successful and tired, secure yet strangely unsure of himself, isolated by the self-importance of painfully acquired learning, Professor Magoon keeps coming "home" to rural New Hampshire. Asking what kind of man his temporary hotel roommate is, he is compelled to examine what manner of man *he* has become. The roommate, a subscription collector and drunk named Lafayette, seems happier with his unambitious life and easygoing relationship with his mule Jemima than the family man is with his prosperity. He offers the title's hundred collars as a gift, which the overeducated Doctor, unable to understand a simple impulse of generosity, refuses. Frost surely intends for us to see the collars as symbolic: The Professor's life of prim convention, routine, and restriction has confined him in hundreds of tight-fitting collars. Claiming not to be afraid, he audibly is; there are suggestions of male panic and midlife crisis in his hysteria. Beyond the immediate fear of losing his money lies consciousness of inadequacy—the wallet of his personality is also empty. The city slicker clearly envies the yokel who has succeeded in simplifying his life. After the interlude, the drunk goes out drinking, and the Doctor settles down to the sleep for which he came. He has awakened only briefly; the interview leaves him unchanged.

References and further reading: Kearns; Lynen, *Pastoral Art*; Poirier, *Knowing.*

C. P. Seabrook Wilkinson

"HYLA BROOK," first published in **Mountain Interval (1916)**, departs from traditional **sonnet** form in its sententious close—"We love the things we love for what they are"—a pronouncement earned by its unsparing portrait of the **Derry** farm stream, which "always dried up in summer," as Frost wrote to John Haines in 1915 (qtd. in Cramer). Though he adds the "extra," fifteenth line onto what is normally a fourteen-line form, Frost nonetheless makes the line integral to the poem by using it not only to complete the rhyme scheme, as Judith Oster points out, but also to expand the poetic argument. For the principle it states applies to poetry as well as to love, as we see at the poem's climax, where Frost separates Hyla Brook from brooks paid prettier compliments by earlier poets. Like love, Frost implies, poetry wants not sentimental fictions but the effort and caring of true knowledge—what Richard Poirier has called "the work of knowing."

The sonnet's opening line introduces the theme of mutability, or change, along with a Frostian joke that complicates the brook's identity even beyond its alteration with the season. As its name "Hyla Brook" suggests, the "song" it has lost was not wholly or simply its own but belonged largely to the hyla—the tree frogs called "peepers"—whose mating song can be heard in spring around marshes and streams.

In lines 2–7, the poem then takes the brook through a series of tropes that further deconstruct its identity. Subtly and with humor, the speaker entwines his feelings with his story of the brook's decline. "Sought for" hints that the brook is missed as it disappears into summer, and "will be found" lets us feel some disappointment for ourselves, as we find the brook mainly to be "gone"—sent "groping" to an underworld of former brooks. "Either" of line 3 hints at an alternative, but the "flourish[ing]" (when we arrive there three lines later) turns out to be further word play at the brook's expense. There is no mention of jewel-weed's bright flowers, only of the "Weak foliage that is blown upon and bent / Even against the way its waters went." As the narrative nears its climax, what began in song ends in the silence "Of dead leaves stuck together." As if print "faded" from weathered "leaves" of a book, what was loved has vanished to the outer eye. But what is completed here is more than nature's dissolution of the singing brook; it is also the poet's transformation of the natural brook into memory and imagination, where it can remain a brook, no matter what the season.

Through the poem, the poet's manner of telling has made subtle claims on our attention. In the final three lines, it takes the brook's place as the poem's primary subject. With good reason, Frost insists, he will not sentimentalize his stream as other poets (Burns, Tennyson) have theirs: Love, he implies, wants and needs truth. "Anything less than the truth would have seemed too weak," says the speaker of **"Mowing."** In "Hyla Brook" the elision of "song" and "love" claims poetry as a kind of love—a commitment to what we hold dear. But only by shedding illusions, this poem suggests, can poetry do justice to love and withstand nature's worst.

Facing the brook's unsettling, if intriguing, alterations at nature's hands, the poet's song personalizes (and personifies) the brook, making it an intimate partner in the struggle to survive, committing to language and memory each treasured stage of that struggle. No matter, then, if the beloved brook is invisible and silent by July. "Gone underground" is not gone. To the imagination that sees its waters in the jewel-weed, the brook is no more dead than a poem faded from a page or a song not being sung. We "make" the brook "our brook"—and anything in nature ours—through an act of imaginative possession whose other name is love and which the right words will make a poem. Here the poem that registers the brook's annual "death" is an act of imagination that also keeps it alive.

"Hyla Brook" asserts that if it is not to fail, poetry, like love, must know things "as they are." But it also makes clear that, against continual dissolution, no moment will suffice alone and that, in the human imagination, what things "are" is a joint venture of fact, memory, and expectation, a continual compounding of present and future with past. Even the beauty and strength of May are "ghosts" of former winter selves. Here, the last sign of the brook's yearly life reflects the mind's inclination toward the past as it leans against time's invisible current, as if knowing where it leads.

References and further reading: Bagby, *Nature*, places the poem within the larger seasonal drama of time and loss in Frost's verse; Brower, 83, describes a modern, pragmatic Frost "gently mocking" the "Wordsworthian-Tennysonian tradition"; Cramer, *Frost among His Poems*, illuminates the genesis of this poem; in different ways, both Oster and Sanders emphasize the poem's metapoetic dimensions: its self-referential look at the power of imagination in the face of time and change; Poirier, *Knowing*, uses "Hyla Brook" to introduce Frost's complex poetic voice.

David Sanders

I

"I COULD GIVE ALL TO TIME" first appeared in the *Yale Review* in the autumn of 1941 and was subsequently published in *A Witness Tree* **(1942)**. The tangible figure of Time looms large in this decidedly allusive poem. Time is clearly empowered, able to triumph against nature, but Time does not use this power maliciously. Indeed, it is not "overjoyed" at the sheer spectacle of its abilities. Rather, Time is solemn, "contemplative and grave." The true nature of Time's power is the capacity to effect change, an ambivalent and melancholy event in itself. "What now is inland shall be ocean isle," Frost observes. Indeed, he seems to share Time's resignation in the face of change. He gladly offers up to Time his "all," except for "what I myself have held." That which Frost has truly possessed, although "forbidden" in the face of inexorable change, has successfully made it past the metaphorical "Customs" to reach "Safety." Indeed, Frost concludes that he may actually keep that which he holds closest, even in the face of as powerful an adversary as the melancholy Time.

References and further reading: Poirier, *Knowing*.

Craig Monk

"I WILL SING YOU ONE-O" first appeared in the *Yale Review* (Oct. 1923) and in *New Hampshire* that same year. The rhythm is irregular, but the two stressed beats in each line mimic the "tick tock" of a clock. The first section of twenty-two lines finds the speaker lying awake on a cold, snowy night, listening for the tower clock to strike the hours and mark the approach of another day. In the second part, the speaker hears the striking of two clocks, the tower clock and a clock in a steeple, as they strike "One" and speak together of the constellations and the universe. The speaker moves from the particular to the universal as he reminds us that the two chimes speak "for the clock / With whose vast wheels / Theirs interlock."

James Potter writes that the poem examines the relationship between humanity and the universe. If the clock is a metaphor for God, Potter asserts, the poem reflects the individual's intellectual limitations; we can send out speculations only to the farthest constellations, yet God resides beyond these. Lawrance Thompson goes so far as to argue that the poem counters the doubts posited by Frost in other poems concerning the existence of an "all-controlling 'One' of the unknown."

References and further readings: Lynen, "Sing"; Potter; Thompson, *Triumph*, 243.

Chris-Anne Stumpf

ICONOGRAPHY. The images of Robert Frost, from infancy to old age, are well preserved in many art forms, particularly in photographs, but also, after Frost became famous, in oil paintings, busts, etchings, drawings, engravings, woodcuts, and medallions. Frost was probably the most frequently portrayed American poet of his generation, perhaps of all American poets ever. The graphic arts, particularly oil paintings, not only provide the visual image of the poet but implicitly suggest aspects of his character and personality. Frost's pictorial imagination is captured in many visual illustrations. No iconography of Robert Frost exists, and such a project would require a substantial volume for a complete record. The following account provides a bare outline of such a visual record.

Photographs of Frost are included in each of the major research collections of the poet: the Baker Library, **Dartmouth College**; the Robert Frost Library, **Amherst College**; the Jones Library in Amherst, Massachusetts; and the Clifton Waller Barrett collection in the Alderman Library, the University of Virginia. Among the smaller collections, the Louis Mertins materials in the Bancroft Library, in the University of California, Berkeley, contain thirty-seven photographs relating to Frost, all of which are signed or initialed by the poet. The Wales Hawkins collection in the Abernethy Library at Middlebury College contains photographs of Frost, including many of **Bread Loaf**. Photographs of the poet are found in the Tufts University Library; the Trinity College Library (Hartford, Connecticut); The Piskor Collection at Lawrence University; Agnes Scott College in Decatur, Georgia; and other colleges where Frost gave poetry readings. The Library of Congress and the files of the **Holt**, Rinehart and Winston Company also contain photographs of Frost. Among private collections, that of Peter J. Stanlis is probably the largest, with over 260 items on or related to Frost. Individual photographs of Frost are found in business areas such as The Pump Room in the Ambassador East Hotel in Chicago.

Oil paintings of Frost include the following: (1) By Leon A. Makielski, in 1925–1926 at Ann Arbor, Michigan, now in the Rare Book Room at the **University of Michigan** Graduate School Library. This portrait was originally a "Rogues Gallery" portrait of Frost as a member of the University of Michigan faculty. (2) By James Chapin in 1929 at Amherst College, now in the Robert

Frost Library at Amherst College. (3) By Marcella Comes, in 1952 in Vermont. (4) By Gardner Cox, a portrait of Frost in his later years, in the Abernethy Library at Middlebury College.

Busts and sculptured heads of Frost include the following: (1) By Arnoldo Du Chene, a bust of Frost in 1919. A photograph of the bust was used as a frontispiece for an edition of *Mountain Interval* in 1921. (2) By Margaret C. Cassidy, a bronze bust of the poet's head, around 1958. (3) By Walker Hancock, a bust of Frost done in March 1958, now in the Frost Room at Dartmouth College. (4) By Jane B. Armstrong, a head of Frost in marble, done in 1992, now at the Bread Loaf School of English, in Vermont.

Miscellaneous visual records of Frost include the following: in San Francisco, a bronze plaque on Lower Market Street; a stained glass window in Grace Cathedral on Nob Hill; a Congressional Gold Medal voted to Frost by Congress in 1960, with **"The Gift Outright"** engraved on one side and a head of Frost on the other side; a postage stamp of Frost, with his picture above "Robert Frost, American Poet," issued on 26 March 1974 at **Derry**, New Hampshire; Frost on the front cover of *The Atlantic* (June 1951), and the front page of *Life* (30 Mar. 1962); a **film** on Frost, *A Lover's Quarrel with the World* (1963); an interactive reference CD-ROM on the poet titled *Robert Frost: An American Poet*, published by Holtzbrinck Electronic Publishing with Henry Holt and Company and the Frost Estate (1997); **Christmas** cards by Frost, 1929–1962; woodcuts illustrating Frost's poetry, by **Julius John Lankes** and also by Thomas W. Nason, Joseph Low, Leonard Baskin, Fritz Kredel, and Antonio Frasconi. Many books on Frost include photographs, most notable among these is **Kathleen Morrison**'s *Robert Frost: A Pictorial Chronicle* (1974) and Theodore Morrison's *The Bread Loaf Writers' Conference: The First Thirty Years* (1976).

References and further reading: Blumenthal, *Frost and His Printers.*

Peter J. Stanlis

"IMMIGRANTS," a quatrain, oddly enough first appeared in 1921 as the fourth stanza of "The Return of the Pilgrims," a poem presented in George P. Baker's *The Pilgrim Spirit* (Boston: Marshall Jones). Subsequently, "Immigrants" became a part of the "Over Back" section of Frost's *West-Running Brook* **(1928)**. More recently, Helen Plotz included it in *The Gift Outright: America to Her Poets*, her 1977 thematic collection of poems for children. "Immigrants" is a brief but powerful work; in four lines of iambic pentameter, Frost immortalizes the Pilgrims into almost supernatural or mythic voyagers. Indeed, the speaker suggests the arrival of the *Mayflower* in 1620 as a symbolic instant of American epiphany, a momentous occasion marking both the end of a certain nightmare and the beginning of a new and unpredictable dream.

References and further reading: Marcus, *Explication.*

Susan M. Stone

"IMPORTER, AN," was written before 1944 and first published with the title "The Importer" in the *Atlantic Monthly* (Apr. 1947); it was first collected in the fifth section ("Editorials") of *Steeple Bush* **(1947)**. The satire portrays its speaker as much as it does its subject. The sharp wordplay and outrageous rhyming send up "Mrs. Someone's" shopping binge in kitsch-laden Asia and at the same time represent the poet as a cantankerous, skeptical Yankee with an ear for the poetry of Jonathan Swift. Swift's satirical poems used an eight-syllable/four-beat metrical rhythm and specialized in bizarre, multisyllabic rhymes, both of which Frost imports and pays homage to here. The subject of the poem would have seemed highly charged to readers of the late 1940s in light of the complicated political, economic, and cultural relationships among the United States, Japan, and China after World War II. The poem's nimble progress from silliness to nationalist fears to travestied redemption to mild profanity forms the poet's flip personal response to contemporary public uncertainties and prejudices. Accusations concerning the potential racism of this angry editorial poem must be qualified by the poem's ostensible purpose: to attack Americans' complacent pride in their economic system and technological sophistication.

References and further reading: Waggoner, *American Poets*, 211, includes a useful review by George F. Whicher, with specific comments on the poem.

Gary Roberts

"IN A DISUSED GRAVEYARD" first appeared in *The Measure* (Aug. 1923) and was collected later that same year in *New Hampshire*. The poem elaborates on the irony of a place for the dead that is itself defunct. Frost introduces a twist on the traditional epitaph that admonishes, in the voice of the deceased, "As I am, so will you be." On the little hilltop cemetery, the tombstones confidently predict in a quadruple-rhyme monotone that momentary visitors will eventually "come to stay." They are, of course, wrong. Deprived of the universalizing message that everyone must die, the monuments are reduced, on a more local level, to an unwitting falsehood. The personified stones, which have faithfully marked the resting places of the dead, now "can't help marking" that no one is buried here anymore. Frost responds to their naive puzzlement by proposing the "clever" explanation that men hate dying so much that they have ceased to die altogether; and in his memorably sardonic last line, he muses, "I think they would believe the lie." Natural solipsists, the stones cannot venture beyond their grassy world to disprove the fantastic claim. If they could, they might find that the nearby village has begun to fade away, like the ghost town in **"The Census Taker"**; in fact, the stones' question about what men are "shrinking" from echoes the other poem, in which the town's ranks "shrink to none at all."

In a seemingly simple poem of four quatrains, Frost matches a formal restlessness to a series of variations on a theme. The different rhyme scheme of each stanza reflects the changing parts of speech in which life and death appear:

as people (the living and the dead); as adjectival attributes (living and dead); as a state (death); and as verbal action (to die, dying). Though the stones do not offer the biographical certainties of Edgar Lee Masters's epitaphs in the popular *Spoon River Anthology* (published eight years before this poem appeared in *New Hampshire*), they represent a stoicism that aptly registers the thin line between cemetery and village, between inanimate and animate worlds.

References and further reading: Auden, 349, compares the poem with Thomas Gray's "Elegy Written in a Country Churchyard"; Jarrell, *Poetry*, 57, praises the depth of thought and feeling—particularly in the last five lines—beneath what he calls "the slightest and least pretentious of fancies."

Christopher R. Miller

"IN A GLASS OF CIDER" was first published in *In the Clearing* (1962). Frost's speaker acknowledges the repetitious—and largely mundane—nature of human existence. However, he finds happiness in those chance moments that require patience and the desire "to get now and then elated." Mordecai Marcus calls the poem "a parable about ways of knowing" and equates fermentation with the rise of ideas from the imagination. Like a bubble, Marcus asserts, knowledge is tentative and the pleasure derived from pursuing it is ephemeral.

References and further reading: Marcus, *Explication*, 227.

Douglas M. Tedards

"IN A POEM" first appeared in *A Witness Tree* (1942). Philosophically, as well as artistically, attention to process was fundamental for Frost. "In a Poem" is written in a style that is bare of figures but not of argument, depicting not a state but a process. Poetry involves the sequence of words in time, and Frost directs the movement from word to word, line to line, in a way that offers an exposition, however rudimentary, about the act of writing a poem. Through the strategic arrangement and intensification of four iambic-pentameter lines, Frost educates his reader to see through the facts and static appearances to the shaping principles of poetic composition animating them. Salient features of orderliness (meter and rhythm) appear to the empirically and deductively educated imagination not as a collection of discrete particulars shaped by a maker but holistically as a system of interrelated elements in a process that happens casually, blithely, through the very syntax of language. The whole of meaning, arrived at through the process of constraint ("stroke and time"), becomes greater than the sum of its parts or structures. Eventually, as a result of the poem's manner of presentation and arrangement of materials, it is the principle, the "undeviable say," and not the thing that comes into focus. Frost has delineated the sense of complexity and chance within larger systems of regularity that characterize poetic form. *See also* **Poetic Theories**.

References and further reading: Brower; Marcus, *Explication*.

Carol Dietrich

"IN A VALE" is considered one of Frost's apprentice **lyrics**, first appearing in
A Boy's Will **(1913)** with the gloss "Out of old longings he fashions a story."
Thompson indicates that the poem had been originally composed while Frost
was in high school, and the archaic words date the poem near the composition
of **"My Butterfly"** (1894). A fair copy of the poem was sent to **Susan Hayes
Ward** in 1906 signed "RF/**Pinkerton Academy Derry**, N.H." According to
Thompson, the poem is about Frost's "powers of second sight, which helped
him to communicate with the little people [elves and fairies]," and he notes the
influence of Longfellow. Mordecai Marcus describes it as an "allegorical fantasy, reminiscent of poems by Poe." The balladlike poem blends cadence and
rhyme to suggest a desire for youth where flowers metamorphose into fairy
maidens. The magical environment of the poem is created by Frost's use of
hazy-sounding words, including "misty fen," "maidens pale," "gloom," "mist,"
and "heavy with dew," which suggest the inexpressibility of nature. The poem
implies that Frost has some knowledge gained through such encounters with the
fairy people. Thompson notes two related poems in manuscript that deal with
the little people—"Tutelary Elves" and "Spoils of the Dead"—an indication that
Frost was intrigued by the supernatural in his youth.

References and further reading: Marcus, *Explication*, 29; Thompson, *Early Years*, 303–
4, and *Fire and Ice*, 97.

Eric Leuschner

IN AN ART FACTORY. See **Drama**.

"IN DIVÉS' DIVE" is one of the original "Ten Mills" published in the April
1936 issue of *Poetry* magazine. Thanks to a mistranslation of the Latin *homo
quidam erat dives*, meaning "there was a certain rich man," the name "Divés"
is traditionally given to the unnamed rich man in Christ's parable of the rich
man and the beggar Lazarus (Luke 16:19–31). Suffering in the afterlife, the rich
man, who was callous toward the poor in life, begs to be allowed to warn his
family to mend their ways. The poem was collected in *A Further Range* **(1936)**.

In this witty depression-era poem about America, Frost's speaker contemplates his losing streak at a card game. He bases his decision to stay in the game
on the bet that his odds at winning are as great as anyone's because they are
all "equal in number of cards" with which to play. The poem, however, is not
merely about fate and one's unwillingness to give up in the face of loss; written
during a time of great economic hardship in the United States, the poem includes
an ironic reference to the Declaration of Independence and calls into question
the realization of that document's central tenet: that every American has the
right to equal opportunities. The extended metaphor is also ironic in its comparison to America as a kind of gambling hall, a "dive" run by someone other
than the speaker/player/citizen.

References and further reading: Cramer, *Frost among His Poems*; Harvey.

Andy Duncan

"IN HARDWOOD GROVES" was published first as "The Same Leaves" in *The Dearborn Independent* (18 Dec. 1926). The poem appeared with others in *A Boy's Will* (1913), beginning with Frost's *Collected Poems* of 1930. The inclusion may have been thought a substitute for "Spoils of the Dead," a poem that appeared in the 1913 version of *A Boy's Will* but disappeared with the 1930 *Collected Poems*. Both poems take death as the subject and express an ambivalence about the relation of death and life, but in "In Hardwood Groves" Frost shapes the relation as a seasonal cycle in which life is dependent upon death. Such dependence seems to be less a consolation than a necessary recognition of natural order (Frost emphasized the "must" in line 9 when he added the poem to the *Collected Poems*). The "hardwood" in the title may suggest the difficulty of the poet's confession; "groves" may suggest a place of peacefulness or of learning. The leaves pass from "giving shade above" to being plastered on the earth, and then to yet a further going "down past things coming up," a decay that leads to other "mount[ings]"—the coming up of "dancing flowers" through the decayed leaves and the eventual rising up of new leaves (or "The same leaves over and over again!") to the treetops. However consoling the recognition may be, the poet seems to hold out hope in his final lines for an even more optimistic relation of life and death "in some other world." *See* **Nature Poet and Naturalist**.

References and further reading: Bagby, *Nature*.

Douglas Watson

"IN NEGLECT" appeared in *A Boy's Will* (1913). After the Frost family had moved to **England** in 1912 and Frost's reputation was presumptuously being overseen by **Ezra Pound**, Frost told Pound the story, exaggerated beyond truth, of how his grandfather and uncle had left him disinherited. It was a story he was to repeat over twenty years later to his first **biographer**, Robert Newdick. When Pound, however, put the story into a review as the supposed inspiration for the poem "In Neglect," Frost was furious. Sending a copy of the review to his friend Sidney Cox, Frost pointed out the "(very private) [personalities] which are not only in bad taste but also inaccurate."

The inspiration for the poem had instead come from **Elinor Frost**. She, perhaps even more than Frost himself, believed that his poems were good, even if they were not truly the fashion of the moment. She loved the years of neglect and isolation in their "wayside nook" when Frost's poetry was more or less a private matter between the two of them, and she would have been much happier had it remained so. Frost's later reputation was something she was always willing to do without, but not Frost. Although Elinor may have been sincere in her love for their solitude, for Frost the stand he took in the poem was only an attitude. As he later wrote, "A writer can live by writing to himself alone for days and years. Sooner or later to go on he must be read." And again later, "It's an old story. . . . To write is not the horrible thing. The horrible thing is not having anybody want it for a long time." Certainly Elinor's wanting it was never enough, and the years of neglect were a time Frost was willing to put in the past.

References and further reading: Cramer, *Frost among His Poems*, 20–21.

Jeffrey S. Cramer

IN THE CLEARING (1962) was first published in New York by **Holt**, Rinehart and Winston. A limited, signed edition of 1,500 copies was also published. The volume was Frost's first new book of poetry since *Steeple Bush* in 1947, and it was dedicated "Letters in **prose** to **Louis Untermeyer**, Sidney Cox, and **John Bartlett** for them to dispose of as they please; these to you in verse for keeps." The three named dedicatees were close longtime friends of Frost. Frost met Untermeyer in 1915, Cox in 1911, and Bartlett in 1907. The unnamed "you" was **Kathleen Morrison**.

The contents of *In the Clearing* are preceded by an excerpt from what Frost considered one of his most important poems, **"Kitty Hawk"** (1. 219–24, 246–57 with no break between segments and containing one minor textual variant). The excerpt was called **"But God's Own Descent"** in the contents. The volume had two titled sections: **"Cluster of Faith"** ("Accidentally on Purpose" through "Forgive, O Lord") and Quandary (**"Quandary"** through **"[In Winter in the Woods Alone]"**). The second half-title has line 1.3 of **"The Pasture"** printed in italics: *And wait to watch the water clear, I may.* The reference makes a clear tie to Frost's earliest poetry and specifically to the poem he placed as an introduction to his collected poetry. By associating the book with his poems from the **Derry** days, he must have been aware of a sense of closure and completion to what he must have felt would be his final volume.

For years, Frost's intention was to call his last book of poetry *The Great Misgiving*, from line 229 of "Kitty Hawk." He finally determined, upon the urging of friends, to name the volume in a more positive light. The title of the volume was taken from the title of the poem **"A Cabin in the Clearing."**

Publicity made *In the Clearing* one of Frost's best-selling volumes and one of his most widely read. The collection is highly topical, including many references to Cold War themes. Reviews of the elderly poet's final volume were generous in their praise, despite the many slight poems that make up the collection. A poem such as "Kitty Hawk," which is thematically important to the Frost canon, has a meter that pushes it often into the realm of doggerel. Although the volume contained some excellent poems that stand up to the test of time—such as **"Escapist—Never," "Auspex," "The Draft Horse,"** and "[In Winter in the Woods Alone]"—in perspective it would have to stand as Frost's weakest collection.

References and further reading: Typescripts and proofs for the volume, held at **Dartmouth College**, impeccably document the movement from typescript to published volume; Burnshaw, Ch. 3; Thompson and Winnick, Ch. 18.

Jeffrey S. Cramer

"IN THE HOME STRETCH" was written either before 1909 (dated by Lawrance Thompson) or circa 1912–1916 (dated by Frost); it was first published in *Century Magazine* (July 1916) and first collected in *Mountain Interval* **(1916)**. The dramatic dialogue is based on the early **Derry**, New Hampshire, farm experiences of Frost and his wife, **Elinor**, who are recast as an ironic latter-day Adam and Eve; the tired wife at one point remarks, "Dumped down in paradise are we and happy." The poem is one of the less popular of Frost's narratives on the domestic subjects of marriage and home life, usually overshadowed by the grim power of **"Home Burial"** and **"The Death of the Hired Man."** In a letter to Edward Garnett (29 Apr. 1917), Frost anticipated the possibility of a negative reception and offered this response:

I can hear Edward Thomas saying in defense of In the Home Stretch that it would cut just as it is into a dozen or more of your Chinese impressionistic poems and perhaps gain something by the cutting for the reader whose taste had been formed on the kiln-dried tabule poetry of your **Pound**s and Masterses. I look on theirs as synthetical chemical products put together after a formula. It's too long a story to go into with anyone I'm not sure it wouldn't bore. There's something in the living sentence (in the shape of it) that is more important than any phrasing or chosen word. And it's something you can only achieve when going free.

Frost calls attention to the poem's formal characteristics by contrasting his long poem to the short Imagist **lyrics** then in vogue, then referring to a version of his sentence-sound theory of verse ("the living sentence"), which here requires "going free." The freedom of the poet is manifest in the leisurely depiction of the couple's settling in. The dialogue moves from small talk to utilitarian exchanges to quasi-philosophical reflections and mixes humor with seriousness, in order to dramatize the couple's many ways of revealing and evading their emotional states during a time of upheaval and transition. Frost's apparently deliberate attempt to eschew a poetic "formula" of extreme concision is on the whole successful but at times leads him to awkward or contrived combinations of colloquial and pretentious language, as when the wife speaks of the new moon: "A wire she is of silver, as new as we / To everything. Her light won't last us long."

The few critical responses to the poem have tended to focus on the optimism of its narrative. Sidney Cox's appraisal of it in a review of *Mountain Interval* emphasizes the subdued quality of its depiction of mature love, such that "the reader is bound to feel the mysterious oneness of hearts [which] doesn't need to be rhapsodically expressed." The "oneness" of the married couple, however, is more like resigned togetherness than mysterious love. If they are not exactly at odds, neither are they at one about their future of bourgeois retirement from the city to the country. For the wife, who is the more fully realized and therefore sympathetic of the two characters, the "new" home promises no renewal. The poem ends with a lovely and lively image of dancing firelight, and the comic anthropomorphism mitigates the somber tone of the concluding conversation; the poetic imagination secures the possibility of dwelling in familiarity by overcoming strangeness and estrangement.

References and further reading: Cox, in R. Frost, *Selected Letters*, 217; Wagner, 50.

Gary Roberts

"IN THE LONG NIGHT." *See* **"Five Nocturnes."**

"IN TIME OF CLOUDBURST" first appeared in the *Virginia Quarterly* (Apr. 1936) and was included in *A Further Range* later that year. Like other Frost poems that measure human effort against geologic change, it presents a natural world indifferent to human needs. (*See also* **"Our Hold on the Planet," "I Could Give All to Time," "Directive,"** and **"To an Ancient,"** among others.) With a pretense of optimism maintained through six of the poem's seven stanzas, Frost satirizes the widespread, nineteenth-century faith in a beneficent spirit behind nature. The final stanza strips away the protective pose, directly admitting discouragement in the face of nature's tireless repetitions.

Erosion is the starting point of this poetic fable. Just as the poem's farmer–speaker can only watch the "downpour . . . carry [his] garden soil / A little nearer the sea," so is he powerless against the larger attritions of time. He sounds cheerful enough about the whole "world-old way of the rain / When it comes to a mountain farm." But as the weather "exact[s] for a present gain / A little of future harm," we hear something of the devil's bargain offered by nature as a whole, which always, in the end, reclaims what it has given.

When first published in *A Further Range*, "In Time of Cloudburst" was subtitled "The Long View," and in stanzas three through six, Frost's farmer–speaker, ignoring the difference between geologic time and the human life span, pretends that, as nothing is lost to nature, it need not be lost to him. As if trying out **Emerson**'s idea that "we are befriended by the laws of things" ("Politics," qtd. by Brower), he projects eventual restoration of his lost topsoil in a tectonic upheaval that will leave "the bottom of seas raised dry—/ The slope of earth reversed." The poem's final stanza abruptly exposes the hollowness even of such imagined compensation. Not only would the speaker be long under the sod of such a resurrected farm; his fantasized return, if realized, would only tie him endlessly to nature's repeated cycles. Even if he could "Begin all over" on his old "tracts laid new to the sun," it would only be "to hope." His recovered "tool" would be only "as ready to wield as now." Even within the extended life of his fable, the speaker faces the same losses, his relation to nature unchanged.

The disillusioned prayer of the final stanza, asking simply for the strength to endure, is in effect Frost's answer to the wishful faith of his Transcendentalist forebears. In the face of nature's indifference, he implies, what more is there to ask? But, as is often the case in Frost, the compensations unsupplied by nature may be found within the poem. "Some worn old tool of my own"—whether read as the farm implement by which we get our daily bread or even as the phallus that sends our genes into further generations—does nothing to alter the conditions of natural life. But when understood as the pen, implement of his poetic vocation, the "tool" produces fruit and offspring even more his "own," giving more enduring form to one's natural expense of spirit and, ironically, some truth to the poem's fantasy of survival through the ages. Are not the obliterations of time just a little more bearable at the prospect of poems to speak for us when we are dust? As Frost says to the Stone Age ancestor of "To an Ancient," whose meager remains—an eolith and bone—though clearly human, leave him nonetheless unknown, "You make me ask if I would go to time / Would I gain anything by using rhyme?" The question echoes throughout Frost's work and is clearly relevant here. *See also* **Nature Poet and Naturalist**.

References and further reading: Bagby, *Nature*, 15–16, connects this poem to others that explore our relationship to nature's cycles and geologic time; Brower, 116, cites a number of sources in Emerson and **Thoreau** for the nineteenth-century attitudes to which Frost responds.

David Sanders

"[IN WINTER IN THE WOODS ALONE]" first appeared as a holograph facsimile (**Amherst College**, 1962) and was later collected in *In the Clearing* **(1962)**. A copy of *In the Clearing*, given to Edward Hyde Cox by Frost, contains an inscription that briefly explains Frost's thoughts regarding the poem: "written the day the manuscript went in for publication as a book. Last line has come to sound to me like a threat of yet another book." The inscription implies the ease with which Frost created the poem that closes his final collection of poetry. The poem represents what many call Frost's "characteristic" voice—a poem that is well crafted and easily read, portraying the voice of the New Englander struggling with the existing tensions between the individual and the natural world.

On the surface, the poem reads simply as a brief, internal narrative of a speaker who goes to the woods, cuts down a tree, and returns home safe with the knowledge that more trees remain available for cutting if he should choose to return. Both the speaker and the woods benefit from the speaker's actions—the speaker gains his tree for firewood and the knowledge that many more trees remain for his use, while the woods retain most of their own in the face of imminent destruction. However, the individual finds himself trying to maintain a stable position in relation to the natural world while he maintains his self-reliant ways. The woods represent a force over which he has little to no control, yet he continues to make his presence felt and known through his cutting of the tree and the tracks of footsteps in the snow that he leaves behind. While the speaker does not conquer nature, he gains the satisfaction that he has had some impact upon it. At the same time, though, the speaker understands the strength and resilience of the woods and realizes that his ability to fell one tree has had little effect on the overall power and life of the trees.

At the time of publication, Frost was eighty-eight years old. The footsteps, the lingering presence of the individual in the face of the unconquerable force of nature, might very well stand for Frost's poems in the face of literary tradition and how that work would be viewed by future poets and critics.

References and further reading: R. Frost, *100*, 46–48, includes a detailed account of each item present at the *Robert Frost 100* exhibit in 1973; Richardson, "Motives," explores Frost's own thoughts on poetry and the making of a poem and provides useful information about Frost's place in the literary arena of the time.

Jeannette E. Riley

"INGENUITIES OF DEBT," a single-stanza poem consisting of nine heroic couplets in three sentences, was first published in the *Atlantic Monthly* (Dec. 1946) and later in *Steeple Bush* **(1947)**. According to **biographer** Lawrance Thompson, in 1950 Frost told his friend Charles Madison, "I left the Ingenuities of Debt lying round nameless for forty years because I couldn't find a fourth line for it to suit me." The fourth line is a directive—"Take Care to Sell Your Horse before He Dies"—and represents the first half of an inscription left by an ancient Middle East City named Ctesiphon; the second half (line 5 of the poem) is an aphorism, "The Art of Life Is Passing Losses On." Frost's playfulness is evident, for the inscription was not done by human hand but by the words themselves, which were "so deeply meant / They cut themselves in stone for permanent." Sand, the natural enemy of stone-cut words, is likewise personified, becoming "a serpent," the natural enemy of mankind, content to rest "Till it can muster breath inside a hall / To rear against the inscription on the wall." With characteristic irony Frost bears witness both to human failure and to human achievement: The city is gone, and its tangible legacy of wisdom will soon be obliterated, but such "losses" have been passed on by Frost's poem.

References and further reading: Frost lists "Ingenuities" as one of his favorite poems in R. Francis, 97–98; Randall Jarrell, reviewing Frost's eighth volume, claimed, "There is nothing else in *Steeple Bush* like 'Directive'; probably the nearest thing is the dry mercilessness of "The Ingenuities of Debt' " (in Gerber, *Essays*, 113); for Frost's own comments on the poem, see Thompson, *Triumph*, 598.

Jacqueline B. McCurry

"INNATE HELIUM" was first published in *Steeple Bush* **(1947)**. Mordecai Marcus notes that in early editions it was printed on the page facing **"A Steeple on the House,"** as if "placed to balance or complement it." Certainly "Innate Helium" shares the tentative faith of "A Steeple on the House"—the suggestion that faith, however admirable, may spring entirely from us, from human effort, and not from heaven. "Innate Helium" is a vivid metaphor for what Radcliffe Squires calls Frost's repeated "urge toward heaven," though the restrained humorous tone of "most filling vapor," "swirls occluded," "buoyant bird bones," "Some gas like helium must be innate," and the "persistent reiteration" of the theme suggest that Frost's statement of faith is balanced equally, according to Potter, by a tendency to "doubt that belief."

References and further reading: Marcus, *Explication*, 197; Potter, 120–21; Squires, 54.

Andy Duncan

"INTO MY OWN" is a **sonnet** in rhyming couplets, first appearing in *New England Magazine* (May 1909). The poem was subsequently published in *A Boy's Will* (**1913**). In a poem purporting great self-confidence, life is for Frost here still a journey into the unknown. He begins with the wish that the "dark trees" that dominate the horizon in front of him were not simply a surface feature ("the merest mask of gloom") but that they should continue "unto the edge of doom." It is his determination that he should journey fearlessly into the thicket, unconcerned with finding either a clearing or a clear path through them. Indeed, Frost questions why he would ever abandon such an excursion, and he appears to offer a challenge to those "who should miss me here" to undertake the same journey. In their quest to discover "if still I held them dear," Frost claims, they will find the poet unchanged, "Only more sure of all I thought was true."

The noticeably stark opposition between the first two quatrains and the rest of the poem is the source of a great deal of ambiguity. Indeed, the image of the trees that the speaker so admires in the first lines is a source of considerable confusion. Frost seems enthralled by their mystery; they are, after all, "dark trees" that serve as a "mask." But he seems also to hedge on his desires, to not long for the mystery and the promise of change brought by the commencement of his journey. He reckons in the final couplet that experience will not alter him but simply confirm for him a reality and a personality already awaiting realization. Similarly contradictory, the trees are "old and firm," suggesting dependability and security, hardly the qualities sought by a young man who longs to "steal away." More likely, there is a connection here between the forbearance of the old-growth trees and the countenance of Frost's loved ones. Critics have assumed that Frost's challenge to the nameless friends and family members becomes a test for them, reflecting Frost's wish to have them follow him and confirm their lasting qualities. Likewise, the uncertainty and the impermanence of the world revealed in the second quatrain are acceptable to Frost precisely because, after all, he believes that he has other people upon whom to depend.

The ultimate reconciliation of the different tones in each half of the poem helps cast the final two lines in a new light. Life is indeed a journey for Frost, and he may be altered by the experience. The trial presented by the dark wood is not for naught, after all. Rather, the attention of his loved ones is confirmed as that which he "thought was true," that which remains his anchor amidst the turbulence of life.

References and further reading: Oster; Poirier, *Knowing.*

Craig Monk

"INVESTMENT, THE," first published in *West-Running Brook* **(1928)**, portrays a conviction strikingly similar to an old saying that reads, "If thou hast two pennies, spend one for bread. With the other, buy hyacinths for thy soul." Frost surely would have smiled at the sentiment. In a most remote parcel of land where winter meals are grimly counted out potato by potato, where life is called "staying" rather than "living," Frost perceives an "old, old house renewed with paint, / And in it a piano loudly playing." The juxtaposition of the flamboyant paint and strains of piano music against the gray and meager existence captivates his interest: Was it money suddenly bestowed, the extravagance of young lovers, or an expression of older lovers who are certain enough of themselves not to care whether the community disapproves?

As significant as the subject matter of the poem is its crafting, its versification. With its three quatrains and a final couplet, the **sonnet** is closest in structure to the English form, but its rhyme scheme *abba cddc effe gg* combines elements of both Italian and English styles. *West-Running Brook* contains several sonnets, and the volume represents one of the most notable demonstrations of Frost's highest artistry. Yet the conversational irregularity of the lines heightens the reader's awareness that too much conscious crafting—either in the liberal application of paint to a deteriorating house or in the scansion of a sonnet—announces something artificial is at hand. One becomes conscious of the workman's labor rather than of the resourcefulness or integrity of the work itself. "The Investment" thus offers a portrait not only of a couple who treasures color and music balanced against the austerity of real existence but of a poet who does, too.

References and further reading: Poirier, *Knowing.*

Sharon Felton

"IOTA SUBSCRIPT" was first published in *Steeple Bush* **(1947)** but was written prior to 1944 with a manuscript title of "Upsilon Iota Subscript." George F. Whicher, in the 6 July 1947 *New York Herald Tribune Weekly Book Review*, describes "Iota Subscript" as a bit of "sheer cleverness" and a "masterpiece of ingenuity" (qtd. in Wagner). Ward Allen shares Whicher's estimation of the poem, calling Frost's precise yet complex exploration of relationships a tour de force. As Mordecai Marcus observes, Frost's punning on the iota of Greek grammar (which, when placed below a vowel, forms a proper diphthong partaking of each vowel) suggests that the speaker's existence is dependent upon the beloved. Although iota generally acts as subscript to alpha, eta, and omega, the poem positions iota as subscript to upsilon, a rare occurrence in Greek; according to Marcus, an iota will be "completely absorbed" into upsilon, implying that "the speaker's self has its meaning only insofar as it becomes a part of the beloved."

In his explication of the poem, Allen further elaborates the relation between iota and upsilon to argue that Frost makes clear the complicated commingling of lovers. According to Allen, when iota contracts with upsilon, the short "u" is lengthened into a long vowel. Since the lengthening of vowels in Greek means a prolongation of the sound of the short vowel, iota's effect suggests not that the lover takes on the characteristics of the beloved and loses his or her nature but that the lover's being is extended by the prolongation of his or her own nature. Thus, rather than detailing the sacrifice of self, the poem describes the rare mutual edification of a strong relationship. Allen concludes that we might even think of the lover's presence as an "undersong" composed beneath a melody (the beloved): "The undersong does not alter the melody, but it may alter the timing of the melody and enhance the hearer's apprehension of the melody."

Behind all such linguistic complexity and metaphorizing about relationships, however, is Frost's cagey playing with the problem of authorial identity in his work. Frost's expert use of irony and humor often masks not only the multiple nuances of his meanings but the role of his own author's voice in both controlling and misdirecting the reader's understanding. The slippery "I" in Frost is often at the core of his poems' allusive complexities, and "Iota Subscript" calls attention to the importance of reflecting on how we take him.

References and further reading: W. Allen; Crane, *Descriptive Catalogue*, 183, 185; Marcus, *Explication*, 198; Wagner, 211.

Gary Totten

"IRIS BY NIGHT" first appeared in the *Virginia Quarterly Review* (Apr. 1936) and was collected later that same year in *A Further Range*. The poem celebrates the friendship of an Englishman and an American, and the strange setting suggests the birth of the brotherhood between Edward Thomas and Frost. The biographical connection is evident in a line from one of Frost's letters: "Edward Thomas was the only brother I ever had." The poignancy of the comment was deepened when on Easter Monday in 1917 Edward Thomas died, a casualty in World War I.

Perhaps botanizing by the light of the moon, the men in the poem witness a miracle so rare that Frost claims it to be unique in human history. Be that as it may, the mysterious poem presents classical allusions and scientific puzzles. Robert Newdick mentions a connection with Lucretius's *De Rerum Natura*, and Laurence Perrine links the poem with Iris, Isis, and Osiris. The poem seems to owe something to an ancient happening at Memphis, yet Frost cautioned Newdick, an early **biographer**, "Why dont [*sic*] you assume that I may be mistaken about Memphis? . . . Maybe I was thinking of Mt [*sic*] Ida."

In this poem of thirty-one lines, thirty consist of iambic pentameter. After an opening couplet, the poem switches to a pattern in which Frost plays with form and content again: indeed, the very shape of the poem mimics the content inasmuch as the structure itself forms a rainbow that turns into a circle. The rainbow reaches its apogee in line 14, which has eleven syllables. The two lines that lack rhymes (9 and 20) mark, as it were, the point where the rainbow "like a trellis gate" bends into and then back out of the central arch. Five heroic couplets form that arch. One base of the trellis gate is anchored by a quatrain, and just when the reader can expect a second quatrain to anchor the other base, the poet subtly switches the rhyming, choosing to rhyme three lines out of four as he does in **"Stopping by Woods on a Snowy Evening."** When the "pediment" lifts, *found* in line 25 becomes the thread that ties the horseshoe shape into the circle in the "sestet" within the last seven lines of the poem. In mythology, Iris, the messenger of the gods, was "Goddess of the Rainbow," and the word *iris* literally comes from an Indo-European base meaning "to turn, bend." Mysteriously, Frost's double rainbow metamorphoses, that is, bends into a circle, a circle of light—a glory: hence, "Iris by Night."

In the New Testament, miraculously a blind man sees after the application of spittle by Christ (Mark 8: 22–26). Note the possibility of a biblical allusion in the unrhymed lines "Light was a paste of pigment in our eyes" and "And then we were vouchsafed the miracle." The end words in these lines are *eyes* and *miracle*. With the revelation of Frost's poetic form, eyes can see the beauty of the rainbow and circle hidden in the rhyme scheme of this poetic celebration of "elected friends."

References and further reading: R. Frost, *Selected Letters*, 217; Edith Hamilton, *Mythology* (Boston: Little, Brown, 1942), 39; Newdick, *Season*, 62, 154; Perrine, "Frost's 'Iris By Night,' " 39 (he also mentions a "double lunar rainbow"); Thompson, *Triumph*, 93.

Nancy Vogel

"IT BIDS PRETTY FAIR," which first appeared in *Steeple Bush* (1947), suggests uncertainty as it presents a simple parallel between life and a play in four declarative statements. Given its publication date, it may also be read as a wartime poem, a theme suggested in the line "Don't mind a little thing like the actors fighting." According to Robert Pack, Frost believed that a good poem should at first appear deceptively simple. But after further examination, the reader should be somewhat confounded by the mystery of the poem's meaning. Certainly, the analogy between life and a stage performance had been used by writers before Frost, but for Frost the analogy becomes a means of exploring obliquely the notion of a controlling force in the universe.

At the poem's basic level, there are four symbols at work: a play, actors, the sun, and the stage lighting. The first two are fairly simple to grasp: Human beings are the actors in the play of life. In the first line, the speaker states explicitly that the play's run seems infinite, a view that parallels the human tendency to believe that death happens to everyone but oneself. Furthermore, although conflict among humans is a central issue in life, the speaker states that the actors' "fighting" is nothing about which to worry. Instead, in the third and fourth lines, he presents a larger issue about which we should be concerned: the possibility that the sun could malfunction.

Because the first two lines of the poem are clearly symbolic, it seems plausible that the speaker's comments concerning the sun are figurative. In the last two lines of the poem, the speaker's contemplation of a malfunctioning sun could be about the central force of the universe, whether it be God or some other force as central to human life as the sun is to the earth. In the final line of the poem, Frost returns to the imagery of the stage, shifting to the sun's parallel, stage lighting. Just as a lighting system breakdown during a play would be devastating to the performance, so would a failure in the central force of human life prevent us from being "all right," even if all other facets of life's stage are working properly. It seems, therefore, that Frost—who, as Pack points out, always approaches God from a "circle of doubt"—recognizes Him as necessary for human survival; nevertheless, he offsets such serious contemplation with a whimsical title that seems to come straight from a meteorologist's evening forecast but clearly has more serious implications.

References and further reading: Pack; Rosenblatt provides a reader-response analysis of the poem.

Melissa Simpson

"IT IS ALMOST THE YEAR TWO THOUSAND" was first published in *A Witness Tree* (**1942**). The poem draws on biblical speculation about the Second Coming of Christ and the Millennium, the thousand-year reign of Christ on earth following his victory over the Antichrist (see Rev. 6, 19: 11–21). Frost depicts the "final golden glow" of "the true Millennium" as a complement to the Garden of Eden, the original "age of gold / Not labored out of mines."

In contrast to the apocalyptic grandeur that "some say" is approaching, humanity is occupied with "weeding garden beds / And annotating books." There is also an implied contrast between such jobs and the tasks of *planting* gardens and *writing* books that make "weeding" and "annotating" seem insignificant. Frost suggests (by saying, "We well may raise our heads") that people are too caught up in mundane details to notice events of cosmic significance. Yet the import of apocalypse is offset in the poem by Frost's typically wry ironic humor, a defense against the threatening implications of the final Millennium, a tone echoed in poems such as **"Once by the Pacific."**

References and further reading: Readers intrigued by the subject matter may wish to compare this poem with **W. B. Yeats**'s "The Second Coming" or with Frost's more famous poetic commentary on the theme of apocalypse, **"Fire and Ice"** (both published in 1920); Oster shows how portions of the poem grew out of rejected drafts of **"Nothing Gold Can Stay"**; Parini, *A Life*, 341–42.

Christian L. Pyle

"[IT TAKES ALL SORTS OF IN AND OUTDOOR SCHOOLING]" was entitled "The Poet" when Frost first published it in *A Remembrance Collection of New Poems* (1959). The couplet is the penultimate poem in Frost's last book, **In The Clearing (1962)**, and it serves as a teasingly gentle directive. Inner and outer weather, tenderly introduced in **"Tree at My Window"** and frighteningly explored in **"Desert Places,"** is a major idea in Frost's work; thus Frank Lentricchia aptly titled his 1975 study *Robert Frost: Modern Poetics and the Landscape of Self*. The idea of a correspondence between inner and outer weather would undoubtedly occur to someone named "Frost" who sees "frost" outside his window, and the correspondence between "rhyme" and "rime" might easily follow. But lest we should ever be tempted to focus on solemn epistemological questions, Frost reminds us that our challenge will always be to understand what he calls "my kind of fooling." Indoor schooling—formal education, reading, our emotional lives—and outdoor schooling—experience, nature, our physical lives—are both prerequisites to our appreciating Frost's serious play and playful seriousness, his inner and outer "whethers."

References and further reading: Bacon, "Schooling"; Katz, "Humorist"; Slights; W. Sutton, "Some 'Fooling,' " compares Frost to Twain.

Jacqueline B. McCurry

$\mathcal{K}$

"KITCHEN CHIMNEY, THE," was first published in *The Measure* (Aug. 1923) and collected in *New Hampshire* that same year. The poem has an air of maturity, albeit a playful one (especially in the final stanza). Mordecai Marcus goes so far as to claim that it "moves from lightheartedness to pathetic disillusion." Typically, Frost grounds his ideas of value—home, family, stability—in specific objects whose sheer physicality seems reassuring. Consisting of five quatrains, the poem is perhaps best construed as the combination of two dialogues.

The first, obvious dialogue is between the speaker and an unnamed builder hired to build "the little house." The ironic second dialogue is between the speaker and his own past, in which he contrasts the fanciful with the real. The chimney—a sign of stability, home, and family—must not be built upon a shelf above the hearth rather than from the floor up partly for reasons of safety but mainly for the speaker's own peace of mind.

While grounded in practical, physical concerns—where and how to build the chimney—the poem also addresses the habits of mind and memory which objects can evoke. The solid foundation, floor to ceiling, presents a theme of firm commitment that dwarfs the concerns of hazard, stain, or odor. The value placed on the chimney as symbol has remarkable parallels to Nathaniel Hawthorne's short essay "Fire Worship" and with the American nineteenth-century emphasis on the kitchen as the center of home life. Also, Mario D'Avanzo convincingly argues that Frost's inspiration for the poem lies in **Thoreau**'s *Walden*.

References and further reading: D'Avanzo, "Frost Gleans Thoreau"; Marcus, *Explication*, 111.

Kenneth Rickard

"KITTY HAWK" is the centerpiece of Frost's final volume *In the Clearing* **(1962)**. Eighteen lines, beginning "But God's own descent" and including a slight modification, serve as frontispiece to the volume. A long poem that Frost considered to be among the most important of his later works, it unites present and past, personal and public history, the material and the metaphysical, art and technology in a five-part discussion that reviews and affirms the major elements of Frost's life and poetry.

The poem has a complex publication history. **"The Wrights' Biplane"** in *A Further Range* **(1936)** is a vestige of the original inspiration. Frost composed the core of the current poem after visiting Kitty Hawk and Nag's Head with lawyer-friend Huntington Cairns in 1953. As Jeffrey S. Cramer documents, the poem "Kitty Hawk" developed through four versions: a poem of 128 lines as Frost's 1956 **Christmas poem**; a poem of 432 lines published in the *Atlantic Monthly* (Nov. 1957) and reprinted with a few changes in W. S. Braithwaite and Margaret Carpenter's *Anthology of Magazine Verse for 1958* (Schulte's Book Store, 1959); a revision with the added 64 lines titled "The Great Event Is Science. The Great Misgiving, the Fear of God, Is That the Meaning of It Shall Be Lost," published in *Saturday Review* (21 Mar. 1957); and the final version of 471 lines, which appears in *In the Clearing*. At a celebration of his birthday in Washington, D.C., on 26 March 1962, Frost responded to accolades by reading lines 219–24 from the poem, beginning "But God's own descent." Clearly, the poem expresses ideas and experiences central to the poet's personal and creative life.

The poem builds on the geographic coincidence of the Wright brothers' historic 1903 "first" flight at Kitty Hawk and Frost's despondent "flight" to nearby Dismal Swamp in 1894. **Biographers** debate the depth of despair that motivated Frost's journey: He had visited **Elinor White** at her college in Canton, New York, and had received a cool reception. She had taken the gift of *Twilight*, his privately printed collection (two copies only) of four poems and closed the door on him. What drew him to Dismal Swamp has all the biographical attributes of melodrama and the mock-heroic. Remembered in "Kitty Hawk," the experience is treated with playful sympathy as an episode that became a "launching," a risk in flight, a metaphor for the biblical Fall, a transformation of experience into poetry, a reflection of Bergsonian élan vital, the arbitrariness of Fate, and most important, the centrality of risk embodied in each of the contributing elements of the poem, even in God's experiment on earth.

The epigraph playfully characterizes the poem as a "skylark" in "Three-Beat Phrases." The skylark, a bird noted for singing while flying and, eponymously, for boisterous play, is associated with three-beat lines and polysyllabic rhymes (compare Tennyson's "Break, break, break"), affirming the reader's sense of the poem's tone as whimsical in spite of its serious elements.

The poem opens with a review of the poet's own 1894 experience: A successful and reflective persona reminisces about his youthful passions. "Poor-spirited" at the time, he was "blown" by forces and challenged by zodiac signs. He contemplates a launching into the "sublime," and the subsequent reference to Shelley's "Alastor" reminds us that Frost's view of nature was very different from Shelley's, however familiar the landscape might seem. Frost tells us that he once told the story to the "Master" (Orville, the longer-lived of the Wright brothers) and begins the interweaving of themes that govern the remainder of the poem: the "original" flight as material (the Wrights' accomplishment), personal and allegorical significances (the biblical "Fall"), and the transformation of perception into poetry.

Frost's despair is interrupted by hunters (the "committee") whose revels sentimentally parody the emotions Frost was feeling so strongly. He wanders off and meets another interruption, a beach patrolman who tells him of Aaron Burr's daughter Theodosia drowning off the very shore they walked. Here, Frost is told of Burr's "too devoted" attitude toward his daughter and the items of her apparel, like pieces of the true cross, which are treasured by the locals. Even deaths of the famous end up as trinkets of questionable authenticity. The moon reference to Tennyson's "Morte d'Arthur," along with the rhythmic and insistent rhyme, further enlarges the contrast of feeling and fact.

Part Two deals more explicitly with matters spiritual and religious. Here, Frost extends the notion of "risk" even to the divine: "God's own descent / Into flesh was meant / As a demonstration / That the supreme merit / Lay in risking spirit / In substantiation." The divine, the scientific, and the artistic share in that risk, the *supreme* merit. He notes the Westward launching of civilization and its emulation in action by the meditative Orient. It is a celebration of daring, an affirmation of risk, and a reconciliation with his youthful uncertainty and fear. What follows, then, moves the theme to space travel—this was the age of the initial Russo-American space race—and the attempt to "master Nature" by word and deed, from naming (Adam's task) the stars to reaching them, myth and symbol pursued by **science**.

"Talk Aloft," the third section, is a cautionary interruption, the slow movement before the grand finale. What follows in "The Holiness of Wholeness" reads like a credo, a call to dare to risk action on any scale. Emphasize Man, he says, even though we cannot (in Frost's day) create a germ or a lump of coal. But we can by craft (science) or art (poetry) "give the part / Wholeness in a sense." Frost views art and science as symbiotic in quest and in risk, but only art/poetry risks "The becoming fear / That becomes us best," the fear of failure to get thought expressed.

The credo resolves in "The Mixture Mechanic": The individual and machine are joined, giving meaning to a nature that itself is unsure of achievement. Inconsequential though such as Frost, Theodosia Burr, and Darius Green may be, they are one with the Wright brothers, nature, and even the divine.

Readers may find references throughout "Kitty Hawk" to other Frost poems: We recall the opening of the final section of **"Into My Own,"** for example; the lines following "Nothing can go up / But it must come down" toward the end of Part Two link with **"[But Outer Space]"** and **"One More Brevity"**; and the lines "But God's own descent / Into flesh was meant" lead back to **"The Trial by Existence."** *See also* **Religion**.

References and further reading: Abshear-Seale, "What Catullus Means"; Brown; Crane, "Frost's 'Kitty Hawk' "; R. Frost, "Trip to Currituck"; Goldstein; for one account of Frost's Dismal Swamp "flight," see Thompson, *Early Years*.

Stephen D. Warner

L

LANKES, J. J. (1894–1960). Although Robert Frost is known to have admired the paintings of Edward Hopper, Andrew Wyeth, and others, his numerous connections to Julius John Lankes, whose signature medium was the woodcut, may be said to dominate his interests in the pictorial and graphic arts. Between 1923 and 1941 Lankes's designs appeared with the original publication of **"The Star-Splitter"** (*Century Magazine*, Sept. 1923); in *New Hampshire* **(1923)**, *West-Running Brook* **(1928)**, *Collected Poems* **(1930, 1939)**; and with three of the annual **Christmas poems** (1935, 1937, 1941). The presence of Lankes's images in these publications and in other, less prominent, places (such as journalistic and advertising venues) easily qualifies the artist as the primary pictorial interpreter of Frost, who is probably the most frequently illustrated of all twentieth-century American poets.

The pairing of the two was anything but random. Years before they met in 1924, or even began corresponding in 1923, each had discovered mutual affinities between his own work and that of the other. Frost, who characterized these similarities as "a coincidence of taste," first encountered Lankes's work *Winter* on the January 1922 cover of *Liberator*. The first Frost poem that Lankes read was **"After Apple-Picking,"** in *The New Poetry—An Anthology* (1918). Both works concern rural subjects; each speculates upon the significance of human labor within the vastness of the natural order. However, it is the prominence of synecdoche, both verbal and visual, that constitutes the major common denominator. Frost freely declared a penchant for "that figure of speech in which we use a part for the whole," and more than one interpreter has commented upon the "stories" suggested by Lankes's designs. Frost was responsible for the initial combining of talents by designating Lankes to illustrate "The Star-Splitter," but subsequent editors and publishers continued to unite the work of the two men.

The Frost–Lankes connection does not end there, however. The two carried on a correspondence that, at least in the 1920s and early 1930s, constitutes a stimulating artistic dialogue and bears testimony to a meaningful friendship. Lankes visited Frost at least four times in South Shaftsbury, Vermont, and on all of these occasions he sketched profusely. Over time, Lankes converted his various sketches of Frost-related subjects into some 125 woodcut designs, a relatively large number of which remain unpublished.

The relationship was symbiotic on both an artistic and a personal level; however, Frost, for all his praise of Lankes's skills, and for all the pride he took in the joining of their talents, was the greater contributor. For one, his success far outweighed that of Lankes; thus, he frequently assumed the role of counselor and, on occasion, that of promoter. Moreover, Frost's poetry, which Lankes had discovered after only about a year of producing woodcuts, had a transforming effect, whereby mainly representational designs gradually gave way to more thematically suggestive ones. (For example, over a thirty-year period Lankes produced at least five renderings of "After Apple-Picking," attempting each time to achieve the "subjective" quality he admired in the poem.) The relationship, which ended with J. J. Lankes's death in 1960, is as significant for revealing Frost's interactions with an art form other than poetry as for demonstrating his capacity for friendship.

References and further reading: Blumenthal; Nash; Taylor.

Welford Dunaway Taylor

"LAST MOWING, THE," precedes **"The Birthplace"** in *West-Running Brook* (**1928**), where it was first published, and constitutes what might be called a feminine alternative to the more "muscular" implications of "The Birthplace."

Katherine Kearns has suggested that "the iambic foot becomes in Frost's poetry a kind of moral baseline, a strong voice. . . . The anapest and the dactyl become in this context not merely melodic variations but markers of weakness." Additionally, "Feminine rhymes, with their implication of passivity, tend in this iambic context inevitably to designate a departure from seriousness or from control." Such astute remarks help us read "The Last Mowing": Here, instead of the iambic rhythms on which Frost usually depends, we have anapestic triplets lightly supporting three-beat lines—triplets within triplets for a delicately turned **lyric** waltz. We also find, significantly, fourteen feminine endings out of nineteen total lines.

The levity of the meter and of the feminine endings contributes much to the tone of the poem as well as to our feeling about its speaker's identity and gender. We might first suppose that a child speaks and that we are to understand his feeling of solidarity with the flowers—as against the "mowers and plowers"— as one of Youth against Age. However, attending to the language of gender and to the gender of prosody suggests another likelier possibility: that the speaker is marked more by femininity than by youth. We are certainly asked to think of the "mowers" and "plowers" that oppose the speaker as preeminently *masculine*. Such men contend for dominion over the flowering field, as in a battle, with trees that are themselves proprietary martial figures who "March into a shadowy claim." "The Last Mowing" speaks from and to that place in Frost's personality that had been forced into occlusion by what he identified, in a 1913 letter to Sidney Cox, as the "utilitarian" imperatives of American masculinity. Like the "unutilitarian" gardener–poet of Frost's parable in the letter to Cox, the speaker of "The Last Mowing" prefers her flowers wild. So far is the speaker from masculinity, as this poem seems to understand it, that she refuses even the mildly proprietary gesture of *naming* the flowers. Alone in the woods together with her "wasted" flowers, Frost's speaker is released, if only for a moment, from the dominion and oversight of men—and released, it may be said, from the dominion of *masculinity* itself.

The poem suggests that the burly Rooseveltian postures Frost sometimes strikes in his accounts of the poetic vocation—for example, his claim in "Some Definitions" that the poet's words "must be flat and final like the show-down in poker, from which there is no appeal"—are maintained through considerable, or at least noticeable, exertions. "The Last Mowing" registers the relaxation of those exertions and does so with a tact communicated as much in the poem's delicate form as in its theme. And when Frost identifies with "plowers and mowers," he thinks less of the ones figured in "The Last Mowing" than of the one his speaker comes after in **"A Tuft of Flowers"**: This "mower in the dew" loves flowers so much that he *un*utilitarianly leaves a tuft of them behind to "flourish" from "sheer morning gladness at the brim." It is a figure, as Frost liked to point out, for the work of the poet, and there is, within the terms of our culture, nothing particularly "masculine" about it. *See also* **Nature Poet and Naturalist**.

References and further reading: R. Frost's "Some Definitions" can be found in *Collected*, 701; R. Frost, *Selected Letters*, 71; Kearns, 74.

Mark Richardson

"LAST WORD OF A BLUEBIRD, THE," a playful little twenty-two-line poem, shares with **"Locked Out"** both a subtitle—"As told to a child"—and the distinction of having been added to the **Mountain Interval** collection after its initial 1916 publication; they appeared there in the **Collected Poems** of 1930 and irregularly afterward. No certain date of composition for "Bluebird" is known; one may reasonably assume it to be contemporaneous with "Locked Out," which was first published in early 1917, but it seems to have been written some years earlier or is a recollection of past days on the farm at **Derry**, since the poem suggests that daughter Lesley, born in 1899, is of an age to believe in childlike bird conversations.

The poem's gentle whimsy and easy versification tell a simple story—the arrival of winter, the departure of the migrating bluebird, a promise of returning spring. One can easily imagine a parent's fun in passing along the message of the bird to its young human friend. But there is a darker subtext, for the farewell of the colorful bird is sent to the child through the parent by way of the sturdier, darker crow, and it is a story of flight from danger. The same cold wind that cleared the air, made "stars bright," and put "ice on the trough" has caused the bluebird to "Almost . . . cough / His tail feathers off." Nature is not so benign after all, Frost implies, and the return of the bird in spring is both uncertain and conditional upon the child's responsible fulfillment of parental admonitions "to be good / And wear her red hood."

References and further reading: Information on other versions of the poem can be found in Cramer, *Frost among His Poems,* 57.

Douglas Watson

"LATE WALK, A," first printed in *The Pinkerton Critic* (**Pinkerton Academy,** Oct. 1910), was collected in *A Boy's Will* (**1913**). Salska Abnieszka argues that the poem, like so many of Frost's verses, "treats the external scene as but a pretext for examining inner moods." Lawrance Thompson records that, according to Frost, it was originally written as a love poem for **Elinor**.

The first three stanzas of the poem reflect the speaker's mood as autumn comes to the farm. He describes the mowed fields as having a "headless aftermath" and the birds in the garden as sounding sober as they rise from the tangled weeds. From such descriptions, the barrenness of the landscape is clear. When in the third stanza he describes the last leaf falling to the ground as he passes, he completes the picture of a landscape devoid of life.

However, the sadness of the mood created by his vivid description is alleviated in the last stanza. He sees the faded blue of the last aster flower and moves to pluck it to give to another. His address to her and his gift of the flower change the mood of the poem from one of unremitting sadness to one of hope. Through his action we recognize that while autumn will come and will be followed by winter, after winter there will be a spring. For the speaker of the poem there is always a spring—as represented by the flower in the midst of the emptiness—in the love shared between him and the recipient of his gift.

References and further reading: Salska, 191; Thompson, *Early Years,* 360.

Chris-Anne Stumpf

"LEAF TREADER, A," first published in the *American Mercury* (Oct. 1935) and then included in *A Further Range* (1936), is one of Frost's many poems that ponder what we may learn from nature as well as the independence we may exert in deciding how much of the lesson to accept.

The form of the poem helps to establish the mood of the speaker. Frost intends for the interplay of prosody, grammar, and diction to convey the speaker's feelings—even, perhaps, to recreate them in the reader. First, each line contains seven accented beats, usually from fifteen to seventeen syllables. Like most poets writing in English, Frost usually uses either four (tetrameter) or five (pentameter). The result is that "A Leaf Treader" is a very "slow" poem. In his famous "sound of sense" theory, Frost propounded the idea that the very pace of a poem, including its almost imperceptible hesitations and rushes, conveys meaning as surely as and far more forcefully than the literal meaning of the words.

The sense of movement is conveyed by the unusually long lines, all twelve of them end-stopped. The voice rises and falls in long, definite arcs, coming down hard on the concluding words: "tired," "mired," "fear," "year." The movement of the voice is like the speech and stride of a weary man. Not by coincidence, the word to which the first line leads us is "tired." Such slow and downward-arcing lines create a kinesthetic impression of weariness. Each succeeding line, like the heavy footsteps it portrays, is a new effort. Each conclusion is a new resting place. Only one of the twelve lines (the fifth) has a caesura. (The scrupulous reader is directed to R. Frost, *Collected*, which preserves Frost's final versions of his poetry, rather than to *The Poetry of Robert Frost* [1969], which, among Lathem's many changes in Frost's punctuation, includes two commas in the last line that seriously alter the rhythm.)

The paraphrasable meaning of the poem complements its "sound of sense." In the first stanza the poet speculates that perhaps "fear" has caused him to tread down the fallen leaves more energetically than necessary. In the second stanza he says he thought all summer that he "heard them threatening under their breath"—and what he heard, apparently, was the threat of his own death.

In the third, final stanza, however, the leaves seem no longer to have threatened but to have invited. The poet tells us that as they fell he felt they spoke to "the fugitive" in his heart, the desire, perhaps, to flee the burdens and weariness of life. Here appears the ambivalence so characteristic of Frost, the conflicting desires to be a part of nature and to be apart from nature. See, for example, **"In Hardwood Groves,"** in which the falling, decaying leaves are a poignant but necessary part of nature.

In the last two lines the speaker resolves to resist his own desire to succumb, but, of course, the inevitable effects of time and age will eventually do to him just as they have done to the leaves. The speaker turns willfully from the lessons of nature and of his own weariness. Despite the evidence all around him and to which his own line of thought has been directing him, he chooses to reject the obvious conclusion.

Frost shows the influence of the teachings of William James, who declared that we have wide (but not unlimited) latitude in what we choose to believe and that we create truth by proceeding *as if* what we believed were true (compare James's "The Psychology of Belief" with Frost's "Education by Poetry," *Collected*, esp. 726–28). The speaker of "A Leaf Treader" survives the weariness of autumn by proceeding *as if* the correspondence between himself and nature were not binding.

Such very limited optimism, really a variety of stoicism, occurs in many of Frost's poems, including several others in *A Further Range:* **"There Are Roughly Zones," "The Strong Are Saying Nothing," "On the Heart's Be-**

ginning to Cloud the Mind," "On a Bird Singing in Its Sleep." Such poems are balanced by darker ones: **"Desert Places"** and **"Neither Out Far Nor In Deep"**; in these, the speaker chooses not to turn away from the bleakness suggested by his observations.

In **"Not Quite Social,"** also in the same volume, Frost returns explicitly to the theme of nature's final triumph: "And anyone is free to condemn me to death—/ If he leaves it to nature to carry out the sentence." In "A Leaf Treader" it is nature's death sentence with which the speaker is threatened, to which he is attracted, and from which he finally, wearily, turns.

References and further reading: Frost discussed his theories of poetry in various degrees of detail in various places, and they have been widely paraphrased. Among his earliest and clearest statements is his letter to **John Bartlett**, 4 July 1913 (R. Frost, *Selected Letters*, 79–81); see also **Poetic Theories**. Frost's letter to his daughter, in which he criticizes the Imagists (see **Amy Lowell and Imagism**), is included in R. Frost, *Collected*, 734–37. The same volume also includes Frost's "Education by Poetry," in which he talks about the creative power of belief. James discusses the theme in many places but at greatest length in "The Psychology of Belief," *James: Writings, 1878–1899*, (New York: Library of America, 1992).

Richard Wakefield

"LEAVES COMPARED WITH FLOWERS" first appeared in the *Saturday Review of Literature* (2 Feb. 1935) and was subsequently collected in *A Further Range* **(1936)**.

If, as **Emerson** asserted, nature provides a metaphor for the human mind, then trees occupy a central place in Frost's mental landscape. Here, the parts of a tree represent distinct aesthetic ideas: The poet prefers the spare tactile counterpoint of smooth leaves and rough bark over the implicit luxuries of flower and fruit (aroma, sweetness, color). In a witty descent through Linnaean hierarchy, from forest canopy to forest floor, Frost says that "Late in life" he has discovered the still subtler pleasures of ferns and even lichen. This minimalism thus reflects not only a natural inclination but also the simplified needs of an older man.

While Frost considers a cyclical compromise of enjoying flowers in daylight and leaves at night, he remains deeply attracted, in the hypnotic chant of "leaves and bark" in the final stanza, to the nocturnal solace of the latter. Like Keats in his bower in "Ode to a Nightingale," Frost discovers other stimuli in the absence of light: the texture of bark and the sound of leaves in the wind. In his starkest declaration, he says in the final line, "Leaves are all my darker mood." The word *mood* connotes a momentary feeling, but the allegorical life span of human desire implies a more permanent preference. Whereas in such tree poems as **"A Leaf Treader"** Frost considers the symbolically charged fall of autumn foliage, here he resolutely stays this side of winter bareness. If he hints at ultimate things at all, it is in the inclusion of bark—a solid thing to "lean against" after everything else has disappeared.

Critical commentary related to the poem is rich and varied. Richard Foster argues that this poem can be read as a darker study of the ideas expressed in another of Frost's poems, **"Putting in the Seed."** Judith Oster reads the poem as a progression from the detached valuation of natural objects to ultimate identification with them. George Bagby offers an elaboration of the Emersonian correspondence between "natural facts" and "spiritual facts" in Frost's poetry. Frost's admission that he "may have once pursued" flowers might suggest a sexual component to his allegory; and his reference to ferns and lichen, which lack stamen and pistil, might then suggest a sort of hermetic existence. While Katherine Kearns does not specifically address this poem, her discussion of Frost's ambivalence over male desire and consummation might prove helpful in this light.

References and further reading: Bagby, *Nature*; Foster; Kearns; Oster, 147–48.

Christopher R. Miller

"LESSON FOR TODAY, THE," is a verse satire debuted at **Harvard**'s 1941 Phi Beta Kappa anniversary celebration and subsequently collected in *A Witness Tree* **(1942)**. Reflecting the formal tradition of Horace and Pope, the discourse between schoolmen of the twentieth and eighth centuries (Frost and Charlemagne's Alcuin) compares their respective ages in order to counter the tradition of considering contemporary evils as unique and determinant. Central themes in the poem are the presumption and challenge of judgment, *memento mori*, and difficulty as a constant for all ages in matters of the soul and integrity. Particularly on this last issue, the poem can be read as a return to the themes addressed in Frost's famous 1935 "Letter to *The Amherst Student*."

Allusions include the paladins Roland and Oliver (*Song of Roland*), Dione, Horace, Virgil, and the Goliardic song "Levis exsurgit Zephirus." Frost formulated the closing unrhymed epitaph, "I had a lover's quarrel with the world," previously in a letter to **Kathleen Morrison** (1 Nov. 1938). It subsequently became a motto in the Soviet reception of Frost as poet and critic of his age and society.

Contra Lawrance Thompson, Betty S. Sutton explores the function and virtues of the poem's form given the performative context, antecedents, and historical allusions (particularly Alcuin and his epitaph).

References and further reading: Brower; R. Frost, "Letter to *The Amherst Student,"* *Collected*, 39–40; B. Sutton; Zverev.

Kirk C. Allison

"LINE-GANG, THE," first published in *Mountain Interval* **(1916)**, is not as well known as several other poems from that volume, but no poem better serves as a metaphor for the juxtaposition of Frost's rustic environment and the modern world's embrace of his poetry.

A *Boston Post* reporter, visiting Frost at his **Franconia** farm in February

1916, claimed, "This village is forgotten by the whole world." Forgotten or not, Frost and other rural dwellers gather their resources and survive despite their remoteness. In the poem, the "civilized" world encroaches, this time in the guise of workers who arrive to install telephone wires, and Frost captures the ironies of the modern world's intrusion.

The workers transform natural objects—trees—into the unnatural telephone pole, and conversely, they transform inanimate wires into speaking instruments: they "plant dead trees" and string them together with a "living thread." Communication itself suffers a rupture from its natural origins: words normally meant to be spoken and overheard from speaker to listener now travel in hushed impulses through the lines. The workers have made an irrevocable impact on the former silence of the farm. Not only does the activity of putting up the poles and cables create a considerable din, but now that the "telephone and telegraph" technology exists, the farm will never return to its former silence. The wilderness has been enveloped—and altered—by an "oath of towns."

References and further reading: See *Post* article in R. Frost, *Interviews* 9–15; Poirier, *Knowing*; Thompson, *Triumph*; 66–70.

Sharon Felton

"LINES WRITTEN IN DEJECTION ON THE EVE OF GREAT SUCCESS" has appeared in two versions: The first, without the five-stanza "Postscript," was published in *A Remembrance Collection of New Poems* (New York, 1959). Frost added the "Postscript" for publication in *In the Clearing* **(1962)**. Mordecai Marcus considers the poem with two others in this volume, **"The Milky Way Is a Cowpath"** and **"Quandary,"** as reactions to recent developments (and mishaps) in space exploration. Though in "Lines Written" Frost approaches the subject of new technologies in space travel, he does so using contrasting rural motifs from older traditional sources—nursery rhymes and folk stories. The first two stanzas whimsically invoke the Mother Goose nursery rhyme, "Hey, diddle, diddle," and Lawrance Thompson traces the source of the "Postscript" story to Warren R. Brown, Frost's friend in **Amherst**. Brown, a real estate broker and sometime journalist, often relayed stories he had heard about amusing rural characters, like the farmer who appears in the "Postscript." Frost himself cites the first two stanzas as examples of "extravagance" in his poetry in "On Extravagance: A Talk."

References and further reading: R. Frost, "On Extravagance—A Talk," *Collected*, 902–26; Marcus, *Explication*; Thompson, *Triumph*, 112.

Beth L. Diehls

"LINE-STORM SONG, A," was first published in *New England Magazine* (Oct. 1907) and appeared in *A Boy's Will* **(1913)**. It is one of many of Frost's poems in which the weather plays a key part and in which Frost juxtaposes "outer" with "inner weather," as he memorably puts it in **"Tree at My Win-**

dow." The correspondence between outer and inner weather is the driving force in the early poem. Line storms are violent wind and rain storms occurring around the equinoxes. The tempest in the poem is a fall storm, as indicated by some of the poem's natural details and by the gloss Frost attached to the poem: "It is the autumnal mood with a difference." The poem was placed after **"In Hardwood Groves,"** a more philosophical, sober **lyric**, and the "difference" is the high spirits, sense of abandon, and erotic energy of the latter poem. It is, as the title says, a poem that wants to be sung, both in its form and its emotion. It consists of four eight-line stanzas, each a double ballad stanza, with the last two lines of the first, second, and fourth stanza creating a strong sense of refrain, as the speaker calls to his lover to come with him, to rove over hills and through woods and not worry if she gets wet, to "be my love in the rain." As the storm blows across the land, a strong wind of love renewed blows through the poet's heart—such wind and rain brings to the poet's mind a sea inundating the land as in primeval times. Such times of flood are like love when it is overflowing: "And it seems like the time when after doubt / Our love came back amain."

Critics differ on the poem's merit. Lawrance Thompson, for example, expresses admiration for it, while John C. Kemp refers to it as an example of "overwrought romanticism and contrived aestheticism." While it certainly lacks the subtlety and distinctive tone of his mature work, it is at any rate one of the most exuberant poems Frost ever wrote.

References and further reading: Kearns; Kemp, 89; Thompson, *Fire and Ice*, 98.

Howard Nelson

"LITERATE FARMER AND THE PLANET VENUS, THE," was first published in the *Atlantic Monthly* (Mar. 1941), though Frost first read the poem to Louis Mertins in 1932, according to Jeffrey S. Cramer. Later it was included in *A Witness Tree* (**1942**) with the subtitle "A Dated Popular-Science Medley on a Mysterious Light Recently Observed in the Western Sky at Evening." The word "recently" seems purposely ironic in light of the speaker's final comment, which seems to locate the conversation, and perhaps the composition of the poem, in 1926—making the poem "dated" in more than one sense. In manuscript, its subtitle was shorter and more didactic: "A Dated Popular Science Medley on the Bane of War." In a 1940 letter to **Holt**'s William M. Sloane, offering "Literate Farmer" as his annual **Christmas poem**, Frost describes it as "a rather amusing skit in blank verse of one hundred and fifty lines. . . . If length isn't fatal let us know and we'll send it down."

The poem illustrates Frost's use of the "philosophical dialogue," to borrow John F. Lynen's term, to explore what Robert Faggen calls "the interplay of scientific ideas and human drama in Frost's pastorals." As the skeptical vagrant and literate farmer banter about issues of evolution, technology, progress, and faith, we detect not only the impact of Darwin on Frost's thinking but also, as George Monteiro suggests, the influence of **Emerson** and James, Bergson and Fabre. *See also* **Science**.

References and further reading: Cramer, *Frost among His Poems*; Faggen, 102; R. Frost, *Selected Letters*, 490–91; Lynen, *Pastoral Art*, 112; Monteiro, *New England*, 130–37; Perrine, "Frost's 'Literate Farmer' "; Schutz explores Frost's puzzling reference to the year 1926 in the poem's final line.

Andy Duncan

"LOCKED OUT," subtitled "As Told to a Child," appeared first in *The Bouquet* (Sept. 1914), a typewritten magazine produced by the Frost children. It later appeared in *The Forge* (Feb. 1917) and was added to *Mountain Interval* with the 1930 publication of *Collected Poems*. The poem consists of a speaker who comments that in locking up the house each night he "always locked the flowers outside / And cut them off from window light." The flowers were left to contend with the very forces from which the inhabitants of the house were attempting to protect themselves: namely, thieves. Ironically, though, the speaker notes that the flowers, while never having suffered molestation from thieves, have been the victim of his own absent-minded action of picking one and leaving it to wilt and die upon the steps. As in **"Desert Places"** or **"An Old Man's Winter Night,"** Frost suggests that what is inside the house is as much to be feared as that which is locked out each night. Ed Ingebretsen goes so far as to call this poem one of Frost's "narratives of terror."

References and further reading: Cramer, *Frost among His Poems*; Gould; Ingebretsen, *Stone Boat*, 124; Sergeant.

Chris-Anne Stumpf

"LOCKLESS DOOR, THE," first appeared in *A Miscellany of American Poetry 1920* (Harcourt Brace, 1920) and was later collected in *New Hampshire* **(1923)**. The poem is based on an incident during the summer of 1895. According to Lawrance Thompson, Frost, who was so afraid of the dark that he slept on a cot in his mother's bedroom throughout high school and even later, was staying alone on Ossipee Mountain in "a forlorn one-story clapboard cottage with a piece of metal stovepipe sticking through the ridgepole in place of a chimney, with uncurtained windows and a battered, lockless door." One night, Frost was awakened by a knock at the door, and he escaped out a window, stopping to call "Come in" once he was safely outside. As Donald G. Sheehy has shown, Frost returned in his writing again and again to the incident over a twenty-five-year period, from *A Way Out* to *The Guardeen*. The inane "come in," the shortness of the lines, and their Skeltonic or tumbling meter—each of two feet per line composed of one to three syllables, with the last syllable usually stressed—give the poem an ironic, even comic, effect. If so, Frost was in part laughing at himself because the incident truly terrified him. In reprinting "The Lockless Door" in *New Hampshire*, Frost made the threat at the door more abstract, revising the original "whoever" to "whatever," a change more in keeping with the end of the poem than that of the incident itself. In fact, Frost returned at daylight to find a drunken neighbor sleeping peacefully on the cottage floor. But in the poem, the speaker says, "I emptied my cage / To hide in the world / And alter with age"—contrasting a short-term escape with the long-term limitations of the self.

References and further reading: Sheehy, "Frost and 'Lockless Door' "; Thompson, *Early Years*, 204.

David Mesher

"LODGED" was first published in the *New Republic* (6 Feb. 1924) and later in **West-Running Brook** (**1928**). Like so many of Frost's poems, "Lodged" depicts the poet's cautious consideration of nature's powers. Nature is not always beneficent; indeed, "Lodged" posits a malevolent alliance between the rain and wind. Each element, strong enough to destroy on its own, will conjoin forces to pummel the fragile blossoms to the earth: "You push and I'll pelt." The flowers surrender, but importantly, they are "not dead." In his final line, Frost moves from a romantic contemplation to a rustic philosophical reflection: "I know how the flowers felt." The speaker has been similarly battered by vast, impersonal forces; he, too, has endured personally destructive onslaughts. He does not, however, identify the source of his traumas, nor does he articulate their exact nature; such a mystery properly remains implied but unstated.

John F. Lynen chronicles a shift in Frost's subject matter—from his early **pastoral** work "to a more philosophic kind of poetry" in his middle volumes. "Lodged" suggests a provocative balance of both pastoralism and **philosophy**.

References and further reading: Lynen, *Pastoral Art*, 135.

Sharon Felton

"LONE STRIKER, A," included in *A Further Range* (**1936**), was first published in booklet form as *The Lone Striker*, Number Eight of "The Borzoi Chap Books" (Knopf, 1933). As Edward Connery Lathem notes in his editing of the 1969 collection of Frost's work, the subtitle "Without Prejudice to Industry" appeared in the table of contents for *A Further Range* and in four subsequent collections of Frost's work.

"A Lone Striker" explores the plight of a traditional worker faced with an increasingly mechanized workplace. Despite being curious "To see if some forlorn machine / Was standing idle for his sake," the worker decides not to work one day—a strike of sorts but not with any ill will for coworkers or working conditions. Reassuring himself that "Man's ingenuity was good" and that man has a place in the mechanized workplace, he wishes "all the modern speed" to the linen factory and turns to nature to enjoy trees and springs, which "boded action, deed." The worker rationalizes that if the factory workers need him, "they knew where to search." Here, Frost suggests that nature and mechanization must not always be in opposition, though he seems not to advocate coexistence in portraying two very separate worlds.

References and further reading: R. Frost, *Poetry*, 557.

James A. Inman

"LOOKING FOR A SUNSET BIRD IN WINTER" appeared first in *New Hampshire* **(1923)** and involves a speaker who stops just after sunset to look at a tree where, he says, "I thought I saw a bird alight." The same tree, he remembers, held a sweetly singing bird during the summer, but now, in winter, one leaf is all the tree holds. The speaker then turns to other contrasts: "frost to snow," as hard to distinguish between as "gilt to gold"; the more readily distinguished blue of the sky to a white brushstroke of "cloud or smoke"; and finally the appearance of the first "piercing little star" to end a poem that begins when the sun is "getting out of gold."

The regularity of the poem, with its discrete quatrains in iambic tetrameter and full *aabb* rhyme scheme, adds to the commonplace nature of most of the observations and therefore helps to conceal the disconcerting quirk that a poem dependent on observations is based upon a mistaken one. The speaker must be wrong in thinking he sees a bird alight, since upon inspection there is no bird in the tree. Nor did he *see* the bird during summer—the memory is purely aural—and when he lifts his face, it is not to observe but to hear better the "bird with an angelic gift," apparently hidden by the leaves of which only one is left in the winter.

Mordecai Marcus claims that the "longing for something illusive is gently pathetic rather than misleading. . . . The [star] shining through is the only epiphany he can summon, but it seems enough." Such a reading might be easier to accept if the sensory distinction between beauty (aural and immutable) and truth (visual and questionable) were not itself given prominence by the speaker's initial visual error. *See also* **Nature Poet and Naturalist**.

References and further reading: Bagby, *Nature*; Marcus, *Explication*, 111–12.

David Mesher

"LOOSE MOUNTAIN, A," subtitled "(Telescopic)," was first published in *A Witness Tree* **(1942)**. The speaker describes the Leonid meteor shower, always seen in mid-November, and speculates upon the individual's position within the universe. According to Gary Kronk, the Leonid showers, sometimes interpreted by fearful witnesses as an apocalyptic sign, registered unusually extended activity in the years 1933 through 1939, with thirty to forty meteors per hour being common.

Charles Maynard points out that the poem offers a far-seeing view of the universe that a telescope might provide. In contrast, see **"A Considerable Speck (Microscopic),"** which appears only a few poems before "A Loose Mountain (Telescopic)." There, magnification gives a better view of a tiny mite, which the benevolent speaker decides to leave undisturbed. In "A Loose Mountain," however, the speaker feels small and at the mercy of the universe.

The meteors are weapons used in a deliberate attack on humans, who have chosen to rebel by choosing the artificiality of light—perhaps a reference to reason or to optimism—over the natural and "ancient sovereignty" of darkness. Although few meteors ever actually reach earth, the word "Nevertheless" of line 13 turns the poem in a more somber direction as the speaker considers the event a warning, a reminder, "a hint." Humans are in a precarious position within the sphere of the "heartless and enormous Outer Black," personified as a sentient being.

Temporarily undecided about the fate of humanity, the blackness withholds the final firing of the loose mountain (the fragments of meteors) from its "sling." Why the sling is Balearic is somewhat mysterious. As Poirier and Richardson observe in their notes to Frost's *Collected*, the reference to the Balearic Islands off the coast of Spain could refer to the Balearian people's famous slinging expertise, and *belearus* does translate from the Greek as "to throw." Or the word could refer even to the Spanish Civil War of 1936, which presaged the cataclysm of World War II. *See* **Nature Poet and Naturalist.**

References and further reading: R. Frost, *Collected*, 981, n. 328.3; Gerber, *Frost*, 103–4, 167–70, includes the subheading "The Enormous Outer Black," within a chapter on Frost's themes and briefly discusses Frost's use of feminine rhyme in both "A Loose Mountain" and "A Considerable Speck"; Gary Kronk, *Meteor Showers* (Hillside, NJ: Enslow, 1988), 225; Maynard provides information on Frost's lifelong love of astronomy and his use of stars as metaphor.

Linda Lovell

"LOST FOLLOWER, THE," first appeared in the *Boston Herald* (13 Sept. 1936) and was collected in *A Witness Tree* **(1942).** "The Lost Follower" and the two poems that follow it in that volume—**"November"** and **"The Rabbit Hunter"**—make an eloquent argument for a poetics of "grief" and against a poetics of "grievance," to borrow terms Frost uses in his introduction to **E. A. Robinson**'s *King Jasper*. "The Lost Follower" considers the case of one who has left the pure, **"lyric"** poetry of grief for the impure poetry of grievance and social struggle. The form of the poem is very much a part of its meaning. In the first stanza quiet effects of chiasmas (gold-golden-golden-gold), frequent consonance, and tight quartet rhymes enforce a feeling of uncommon sonic unity in the poem. The artificiality—the manifestly designed quality of the poem—is probably very much in point: Part of Frost's argument is that the promise of a "golden age" can exist only in art, never in history. That promise is unreal, and to say so is to argue against utopian reformers such as the "lost follower" Frost has in mind here. The implication seems to be that revolutionary visions of utopia—whether communist ones or otherwise—are generically related to other "literary" visions of it. Frost thus debunks the "scientific" pretensions of Marxist dialectical materialism. The Golden Age can exist only "book-like on a shelf," Frost says, implying that political action and poetry really do not belong together. *See also* **Politics.**

References and further reading: Frost's introduction to Robinson's work can be found in R. Frost, *Collected*, 741–48.

Mark Richardson

"LOST IN HEAVEN," first published in the *Saturday Review of Literature* (30 Nov. 1935), was the lead poem in the "Taken Singly" section of *A Further Range* **(1936)**, which contained mostly personal **lyrics**. Frost's interest in the stars was long-standing, and he had a detailed knowledge of astronomy. Elizabeth Shepley Sergeant reports that in 1925 Frost wrote, "Consumed with stars when I was fifteen, with flowers when I was twenty. Matter of history." In "Lost in Heaven," however, the speaker gazes into the heavens as the clouds part one rainy night and finds himself unable to identify any familiar "skymarks." At first he feels "consternation" but then seemingly accepts his "lostness," inviting a nervous transcendental feeling of surrender to overwhelm him. What Frost recounts here with some ironic reserve is the presumed value of momentarily relinquishing the human drive for orientation and control, accepting and treasuring nature as it is and one's individual insignificance within it, a theme he also sounds with equal diffidence in poems such as **"A Minor Bird," "Acceptance," "In Time of Cloudburst,"** and **"The Need of Being Versed in Country Things."** *See also* **Science**.

References and further reading: Maynard provides information on Frost's lifelong love of astronomy and his use of stars as metaphor; Sergeant, 430.

Todd Lieber

"LOVE AND A QUESTION," first published in *A Boy's Will* **(1913)**, leaves unanswered the difficult question of social responsibility versus personal safety and contentment. The stranger has been read both as a real threat to the couple and as the premonition of future sorrows. The first reading is supported by Lawrance Thompson, who notes that there was an actual stranger whom Frost aided in order to avoid any potential mischief the stranger might perform if denied shelter. The second explanation relies on a more allegorical reading of the poem, inspired, perhaps, by its balladlike rhythm and what Thompson regards as its obvious "borrowing" from an anonymous Scotch ballad in lines 23–24. Mario D'Avanzo compares the poem to Coleridge's "Rime of the Ancient Mariner" not only because of the matrimonial joy the compelling stranger interrupts but also because the dictum of charity threatens personal happiness in both poems. Such a connection is based on the role of the bridegroom, whose situation is similar to that of the Wedding Guest waylaid by the Mariner (or, notes D'Avanzo, the bridegroom could be Frost's projection of the unseen groom in Coleridge's poem). Katherine Kearns relates the poem to Hawthorne's "Young Goodman Brown," suggesting that there is a vital conflict between good and evil in the poem. By choosing to preserve the "innocence" of his bride—

as Goodman Brown does with his dear Faith—the bridegroom inadvertently provides her with a reason for future flight.

References and further reading: See D'Avanzo, *Romantics*, 118–20, for an extensive discussion of Coleridge's influence on Frost; Kearns discusses the stranger as the personification of Sorrow and the poem's relationship to "Young Goodman Brown"; Thompson, *Early Years*, 377–78, provides the story of Frost's encounter with the tramp; Thompson, *Triumph*, 649–50, discusses the Scottish ballad Frost uses in the poem.

L. Tamara Kendig

"LOVELY SHALL BE CHOOSERS, THE," first appeared in booklet form in "The Poetry Quarto" series (Random House, 1929). Each of the twelve brochures in the series featured a poem by a contemporary American poet, and the twelve poems were wrapped in Italian paper inside a black paper-wrapped box. With the publication of Frost's *Collected Poems* in 1930, "Choosers" became part of *West-Running Brook*, appearing as part of that collection in subsequent editions of Frost's selected and collected poems.

The melancholy poem questions whether the stages or "joys" in women's lives may really be nothing more than punishment for loving and serving others. Presented as a dialogue between a singular Voice and a group of attendant Voices, the poem considers the lives of women in general, although, according to Elizabeth Shepley Sergeant, Frost acknowledged that the poem is about one woman in particular, his mother Isabelle Moodie Frost. Lawrance Thompson notes the poem's evocation of "the quiet and uncomplaining tragedy" lived by Frost's parents and the "mute heroism" of his mother in particular.

In an interview with Sergeant, Frost describes "The Lovely Shall Be Choosers" as his "only poem in free verse—with a few iambics thrown in." Sergeant views the poem as "tender ironic," quoting Frost's memory of his mother's life in Lawrence, Massachusetts: "She sank right down, out of sight. And I never even realized that I should have earned more money for her." The poet's regret about his own inability to recompense his mother's sacrifice is clear in the lines "Give her a child at either knee for fourth joy / To tell once and once only, for them never to forget, / How once she walked in brightness, / And make them see it in the winter firelight." While there is pathos in the situation, the mother clearly does not suffer in silence; the children are made aware of her sacrifice.

The poem depicts control of a woman's life by the superior Voice and attendant Voices, who devise a series of seven "joys" that "let her choose" but eventually result in the Voices' triumph at the expense of the woman's self-definition. The seven "joys" coincide roughly with the traditional events in a woman's life. Each "joy" is actually a secret sorrow because the woman must sublimate her desires to fulfill her role as wife and mother. At each stage, the woman "almost speaks," but time and fate prevent communication. The conspiracy between The Voice and The Voices to silence women might be read as any of a variety of forces that affect women. Although the title suggests the possibility that "The Lovely Shall Be Choosers," an inability to choose is what triumphs in the poem. Frost remembers his mother and tries to atone for her sacrifice but finds little comfort in the choices she could not make and those he could.

References and further reading: Brower; Crane, *Descriptive Catalogue*, 40–41; Lentricchia and Lentricchia, 176; Sergeant, 304–5, records Frost's comments and indicates that Frost, after hearing a composer perform at his farm, requested that the young man put the poem to music; Thompson, *Fire and Ice*, 185.

Diane N. Hulett

LOWELL, AMY, AND IMAGISM. In his quest for recognition, Frost came in contact with other poets only after he moved to **England** with his family in 1912. Among those who praised his first two volumes of verse, *A Boy's Will* **(1913)** and *North of Boston* **(1914)**, was a group of poets who became known as Imagists. **Ezra Pound**'s pronouncements on Imagism appeared in the March 1913 issue of *Poetry, A Magazine of Verse*, whose founder and editor, **Harriet Monroe**, had signed him on as foreign correspondent the previous year. Pound's emphasis on the emotional impact of things seen appealed strongly to Amy Lowell, and the following year she traveled to England to meet Pound and the small band of Imagist poets he championed. At The Poetry Bookshop in London she ran across a copy of Frost's recently published *North of Boston*. Years later, she would recall how that night she learned "a lesson I have never forgotten":

For here was our vaunted *mot juste* embedded in a blank verse so fresh, living, and original that nothing on the score of vividness and straightforward presentation—our shibboleths—could be brought up against it. . . . I immediately took off my hat to the unknown poet, and I have been taking it off ever since in a positively wearying repetition. ("Tribute to Frost," 5 Mar. 1925; qtd. in Damon and Gould)

In London, Lowell soon gathered around her a number of writers and artists, some of whom had worked with Pound on his anthology, *Des Imagistes*, and created her own anthology, *Some Imagist Poets*. With the resources of a Bostonian Lowell and a lavishness unheard of among poets, Amy, as Van Wyck Brooks puts it, "handled [poetry] like any other 'big business' "—putting poetry "on the map," so to speak.

The Imagist credo called for the creation of new rhythms and stressed sensuous and emotional immediacy, color and music, qualities of the fine arts rather than verse. Yet Lowell did not insist upon free verse as the only means to that end; her peculiar brand of Imagism was broad enough to embrace most modern American poets, including Frost. From the time of her review of *North of Boston* for the *New Republic* (20 Feb. 1915), she recognized Frost's ability to transform blank verse into a fluid instrument of his own idiomatic speech, although, as Gould records, she never gave up trying to convince him "that cadence was much more effective than meter and that *his* variety of blank verse was merely a step away from cadence and free verse." In her *Tendencies in Modern American Poetry* (1917), she lavishly praised what she called his bucolic realism, his independence as an artist, and his "unerring sense of fitness" in his choice of blank verse.

Frost and Amy Lowell often sparred over their differing uses of humor, dialect, and regional characteristics in their verse, and Frost seemed most comfortable maintaining a certain distance in the mock-serious debate over aesthetic technique. However, their relations gradually became more familiar in tone and substance, reaching out to include members of the Frost family. By the time of her death in 1925, Amy's critical judgment had by now placed Frost high among his contemporaries, and her affection for him and his family never abated.

Although Frost became impatient with Amy as "pyrotechnist," to use Brooks's term, and with her tendency to pervert his work to her theories, he respected her determination to rebel against the trite Romantic attitudes and outworn, false generalities of the previous generation. They shared a love of the dramatic, and they both tried with their students and the larger public to lodge poetry with them to stay. In a letter to Amy (13 Aug. 1915), Frost summed up the feeling of that period: "The great thing is that you and some of the rest of us have landed with both feet on all the little chipping poetry of awhile ago. We have busted 'em up as with cavalry. We have, we have we have."

References and further reading: V. W. Brooks, 532, 534; S. Foster Damon, *Amy Lowell: A Chronicle* (Boston: Houghton Mifflin, 1935), 289; L. Francis, "Decade"; R. Frost, *Selected Letters*, 186; Jean Gould, *Amy* (New York: Dodd, Mead, 1975), 169, 189; Lowell, *Poetry and* Poets and *Tendencies*, 81, 128; Harriet Mc.nroe, *Poets and Their Art* (New York: Macmillan, 1926); **Louis Untermeyer**, "A Memoir by Louis Untermeyer," in *Complete Poetical Works of Amy Lowell*, Cambridge Edition (Boston: Houghton Mifflin, 1955), xxviii.

Lesley Lee Francis

"LUCRETIUS VERSUS THE LAKE POETS," originally published in *Steeple Bush* (1947), is a twelve-line epigram that, according to Lawrance Thompson, continues Frost's 1944 disagreement with Howard Mumford Jones over Walter Savage Landor's four-line poem "The Dying Speech of an Old Philosopher." Frost's poem—with its subtitle "Nature I loved; and next to Nature, Art"—condemns two kinds of presumptuous attitudes. First, the speaker disparages his college dean's interpretation of the line quoted in the epigraph for limiting Landor's use of "nature." The dean's interpretation of "nature" conflicts with his own understanding of "nature" in the works of the Roman Epicurean didactic poet Carus Lucretius (98–55 B.C.), who wrote of nature and perception as mechanical systems of particles in motion, and with his understanding of "nature" in the works of the English Romantic "Lake Poets," including Wordsworth and Landor, who described the natural landscape as living and spiritually communicative. Second, the speaker censures the dean's presumptuous attitude toward educational institutions. He pokes fun at the dean's "college nomenclature," which absurdly constricts the use of a term to "the only meaning possible." In a concluding "sting" typical of an epigram's last line, the speaker wryly defers to the dean's institutionalized interpretive authority. Frost's own predilection at times was for a Darwinian view of nature, as is evident in his occasional depictions of nature as harsh and impersonal yet central to the human experience. Nitchie notes that his rejection of "nature" as "scenery" appears throughout his poetry in the "persistent ethical or metaphysical dimension" of his view of nature.

References and further reading: C. Brooks, "Nature"; Gian Biagio Conte, *Latin Literature: A History*, trans. Joseph B. Solodow (Baltimore: Johns Hopkins University Press, 1994); Faggen; Lea; Lind; Nitchie, 5; Thompson, *Triumph*.

Nanette Cumley Tamer

LYRIC. Etymologically, the word *lyric* comes from *lyre*; ancient Greek lyrics were songs for accompaniment on the lyre. This meaning persists in that the modern lyric is formally songlike, usually having stanzas with patterns of rhyme and a strict underlying rhythm. Lyrics are also often brief: The **sonnet** is typical, though many odes are much longer. Inside such patterns and limits, a lyric deals with emotions in a personal, subjective fashion.

Frost's mother and his high school gave him a good start, but his study of lyric became serious in 1892 when he bought and read the second edition of **Palgrave's** *Golden Treasury of Songs and Lyrics*, the most crucial learning experience he had as a student. In 1894, he published his first lyric, **"My Butterfly,"** concerning which he explained that "in the ten lines there beginning 'The grey grass is scarce dappled with the snow' I found myself." Even when Frost went on to master the narrative form and perfect the art of discussing philosophic issues in simple terms, he did not abandon the lyric. He will suddenly introduce lines of the purest lyricism into narrative and philosophic poems. Frost praised the colloquial-lyrical quality of the writing of William James and **Emerson**: "All writing, I dont care how exalted, how lyrical . . . must be as colloquial as [Emerson's] 'Monadnoc.' . . . The beauty of the high thinking in Emerson . . . is that it is well within the colloquial as I use the word. And so also is all the lyric in *Palgrave's Treasury*." All of Frost's poetry, then, has some lyricism in it: No matter how philosophic it becomes, it keeps the music of personal feeling. The felt lyrics, furthermore, are the building blocks of an epic. Frost praised Walter Savage Landor's project of building an epic by "prolonging the lyric out of all bounds."

Frost himself claimed to have married **drama** and lyric; in his "Preface to *A Way Out*," he wrote, "Everything written is as good as it is dramatic. . . . [I]t is drama or nothing. A least lyric alone may have a hard time, but it can make a beginning, and lyric will be piled on lyric till all are easily heard as sung or spoken by a person in a scene—in character, in a setting."

The formal music of lyric poetry includes rhythmic patterns, metrics, which in Frost are as sophisticated as his rhyme schemes. Reuben Brower has noted that **"For Once, Then, Something"** uses the hendecasyllabic meter of Catullus, eleven-syllable lines with the following rhythm (*x* long, *u* short): *xu* | *xuu* | *xu* | *xu* | *xu*. We find the speaker of the poem scrutinizing the water of a well, trying to see further into reality, and the lyric's rhythm runs impeccably until he begins to see something, possibly Truth, in the depths of the well. This is, of course, bad news philosophically, for in modern **philosophy** Truth is not to be seen with rational clarity. The water has become "too clear," so that Nature responds with a modernist "drop" that falls on the water and shatters the clarity. After ten flawless hendecasyllabic lines, suddenly "too clear" and "One drop" bring in long stresses that shatter the metrical rules, reflecting the shattering of the water's clarity. The hendecasyllabic pattern then stays broken until the end of the poem. This is the sort of philosophic and prosodic finesse we can expect in Frost's lyrics. Such an example, furthermore, may illustrate the radical nature of a man thought to be an old-fashioned imitator of tradition.

Frost's hendecasyllabics gave original response to the great lyricist Catullus: It is clear that Frost suffers no anxiety of influence in his dealings with his forebears. He behaves similarly toward the medieval lyrical poet Alcuin, for instance, in **"The Lesson for Today."** Frost knew many of Shakespeare's sonnets by heart; he alluded with ease to the lyrical poets Donne, Marvell, and Shirley (the meter and some allusions to Shirley's "Death the Leveller" lie as subtext below the iambic tetrameter of **"Provide, Provide,"** bringing the powerful honesty of Shirley's poem into ironic contrast with the sneering surface of Frost's poem, so that the speaker has two conflicting voices).

Frost had high praise for the eighteenth-century lyricist Christopher Smart, and he loved Wordsworth's lyric poetry, much of which he knew by heart and spoke of with discerning praise. In his "Tribute to Wordsworth," he speaks of "essential Wordsworth. That lovely banality and that penetration that . . . goes right down into the soul of man . . . this insipid tone. Sweet, insipid tone. Now that's the Wordsworth I care for." As connoisseur of the tradition, he could compare Wordsworth's lyrics to those of Shelley and Keats—"the tune is so different"—and he knew "The Solitary Reaper" by heart.

He alluded with affection to Bryant, Poe, and particularly to Longfellow, in whose lyrics he had found pockets of brilliance that had not been noticed by Longfellow scholars. Frost was greatly indebted to Emerson's lyric poetry, reflecting on it for years until he penetrated its strong layers. And he had much respect for the lyrics of Dickinson.

Swinburne is often thought of as a great lyric poet, but Frost did not agree. In one interview he spoke of Swinburne's "humming kind of meter . . . conventional poetry without real feeling," and again, of Swinburne, he noted the danger of how "the poet could fall into mere jingles if he made his meter too regular, without the grace and variety of rhythm."

References and further reading: Brower; R. Cook, *Dimensions*; R. Frost, *Family Letters*, and also *Interviews*, 26, *Letters to Untermeyer*, and "A Tribute to Wordsworth," 77–79; Miller, "Design and Drama"; Poirier, *Knowing*; Rood. "Preface to *A Way Out*" can be found in R. Frost, *Collected*, 713. Frost's comment about Emerson is in R. Frost, *Collected*, 693.

Gerard Quinn

"MAPLE" first appeared in the *Yale Review* (Oct. 1921) and was subsequently collected in *New Hampshire* **(1923)**. The poem depicts a woman's speculation on the meaning of her name, Maple, which was given to her by her dying mother. Because her name is unusual, it calls attention to the woman, who struggles to discern exactly "what it asked / In dress or manner" of her. Although she and her husband seek answers to her identity by scouring her birthplace, they find no definitive answers. Her frustration is increased by her inability to ask either her mother or her father what meaning may have been intended by the name. The poem suggests that the analogy of woman and tree may be in the supple strength both exhibit or in the sugar maple's promise of productivity. It ends, however, with the suggestion that while the meaning of the name remains ambiguous, in many ways the name "ruled in her life." Judith Oster points out that "in the *search* for meaning, not in the finding of it, . . . her life became enriched." She goes on to explain how the poem can be read as a commentary on the power and limitations of metaphor.

References and further reading: Kearns, 100–102; Oster, 44–49.

Roland H. Lyford

MASQUE OF MERCY, A. *See* **Drama**.

MASQUE OF REASON, A. *See* **Drama**.

"MASTER SPEED, THE," an epithalamium celebrating the marriage of Frost's daughter Irma and John Cone in 1926, was first published in the *Yale Review* (Winter 1936) and appeared in *A Further Range* later that same year.

Written in **sonnet** form, Frost's poem employs natural images to express the power of both physical and spiritual unity that can come from marriage. The entire poem seems to address the couple, although Mordecai Marcus makes a strong argument that the first nine lines address the "master speed," the metaphysical "essence of the universe" that will carry the couple through life "together wing to wing and oar to oar." As in **"West-Running Brook,"** Frost employs the image of a standing wave, which can appear motionless in a continually rushing stream, as the focal point in his meditation on the efficacy of love in resisting the universal flux. The last few lines suggest that the master speed gives the married couple a supernatural "power of standing still" amidst the "rush of everything to waste." Indeed, love is the abiding force that allows man and woman united as one to transcend nature and time.

Technically, the poem reveals Frost's masterful control of the sonnet. Frost's form parallels the image of a stationary wave, as the rhythm of the poem veers strategically from traditional iambic pentameter. In several lines, the conventional rhythm of the poem slows, mirroring the easing effect of the master speed upon nature, of love upon human life. Such slowed rhythm forces the reader to pause upon words such as *radiance*, *history*, *given*, and *power*, further emphasizing the nature of the master speed and its importance to the couple as a reminder of the vitality of love.

References and further reading: Jackson; Marcus, *Explication*; Parini, *A Life*, Poirier, *Knowing*, and Thompson, *Triumph*, provide useful contexts for understanding the poem's biographical connections and relationship to Frost's thinking on time and evolution.

Lori M. Yates

"MEETING AND PASSING" is based on experiences shared with **Elinor White**; it was first published in *Mountain Interval* **(1916)**. According to Thompson, the **sonnet** commemorates the awkward, random encounters between the poet and his future wife when they were nearby neighbors at Ossipee Mountain in 1895. Like many of Frost's sonnets, "Meeting and Passing" does not conform to either of the basic sonnet patterns but instead combines elements of both: The rhyme scheme (*abba abba cdcd ee*) closely resembles the Petrarchan sonnet (*abbaabba cdecde*), but the poem delays the "turn" of its argument until the final couplet, as in the Shakespearean sonnet.

The rhythmic and grammatical symmetries that the sonnet form encourages are abundant in the poem—appropriately enough, given its subject. For example, the first and fourth lines begin with similar subordinate clauses, each located at opposite ends of the sentence that they initiate and conclude. The parallelism mimetically represents the converging approaches of the speaker and the woman; that the "gate" in line 2 is the contextual subject of the sentence is also important to the scene, since this ritual boundary is literally interposed between the walkers' syntactical positions. After the sinuous unfolding of the poem's first sentence over three-and-one-half lines, the second sentence is extravagantly curt. The contrast introduces the humor of the poem. The second quatrain contains almost all of the third sentence, in which the speaker displaces the sexual tension of the "meeting" onto the mingling of "great and small / Footprints in summer dust," that is, to the transient material record of their confused physical motions. The unusual simile that concludes the third sentence compares the pair's dusty union to a numerical quantity "less than two / But more than one as yet," as if to underscore that at least one implication of this first meeting is that all future meetings will inevitably involve romantic calculation of what remains to be done before unity is achieved. As in its opening, the poem ends with a conspicuous symmetry created by repetitions of words and grammatical orders. Because the final couplet rhymes on the same word ("passed"), the poem's conclusion insists on an understated representation of the scenery, now rendered utterly inconsequential to "you" and "I," who are linked not so much by their inversely related trips as by their implicit memories of "meeting."

References and further reading: Frost dates the poem's composition in 1912 (Angyal, "Checklist," 117), while Thompson argues that it was written in either 1906 or 1907 (*Triumph*, 541); Parini, *A Life*, 53, describes the poem as embodying the "strange mixture of intimacy and emotional distance" between Frost and Elinor early in their relationship; Rood.

Gary Roberts

"MENDING WALL," first published in *North of Boston* **(1914)**, has become more than merely the title of a Frost poem; it is also a now-familiar trope in American culture. Even the Supreme Court invoked this poem when, in 1995, two justices went so far as to cite "Mending Wall" in order to prove their respective views on a point of constitutional law. Perhaps the issue depicted in this poem explains why it continues to have the cultural impact it does. Speaking directly to the American concern with individualism and pragmatism, "Mending Wall" dramatizes, through metaphor and dialogue, a debate central to American culture's core values.

In a **dramatic monologue**, Frost's speaker tells us about a conversation he has with his neighbor. A stone wall separates their properties, and now that it is spring, the two men work together to repair the damage done by what will soon become an important metaphor in the poem: the winter's frost. As they repair the wall, the speaker attempts to engage his neighbor in a debate concerning the merit of walls. Frost's skill with metaphor quickly indicates that the wall itself stands for much more than a mere property marker. In his first words, the speaker suggests that the wall is a vehicle for the lack of imaginative freedom, for a kind of tyranny. The poem begins with the famous first line: "Something there is that doesn't love a wall." By contrast, the neighbor's position that "good fences make good neighbors" indicates that the tenor for this wall is not tyranny but the rule of tradition, the necessity of boundaries, the limits to unbounded individualism. The debate over the meaning of the wall expresses the American debate between two principles, the freedom of the individual imagination to express itself without limitation and the pragmatic need to check a potentially dangerous extension of the rights of some over others. Frost's speaker phrases the issue neatly: "Before I built a wall I'd ask to know / What I was walling in or walling out, / And to whom I was like to give offense." In the famous pun ("offense" for "a fence"), Frost raises his own metaphor to a new pitch. The "fence" now becomes a metaphor not just for specific American political **philosophy** but also for the more universal dilemma of neighborly relations. Is not, asks the speaker, every fence potentially also an "offense" to one's neighbor? In short, the poem speaks to the many aspects, large and small, universal and particular, of the conflict between individualism and pragmatism.

Ironically, this quintessentially American poem was composed and published in Great Britain. According to John Evangelist Walsh, Frost composed "Mending Wall" between August and October 1913. Living in **England** at the time, Frost took a trip to visit friends in Scotland. There, the idea for the poem came to him while on a walk. Apparently, during this walk Frost recalled his own New England and was inspired to write "Mending Wall" about its farms and farmers. Other research into this poem has subsequently discovered that the farmer's claim that "good fences make good neighbors" is itself a motto more common to French-Canadian rural culture than to a specifically American rural culture. On the other hand, this was, according to Lawrance Thompson, most likely the motto of Frost's real neighbor, Napoleon Guay, himself a descendant of French Canadians.

Shortly after composing the poem, Frost published it in England, in his second volume, *North of Boston* (1914). That Frost knew the poem to be significant is indicated by the fact that it was his first principal poem in that collection. It follows an italicized poem, **"The Pasture,"** which introduces the collection as a whole (and which subsequently introduces his collected poems).

Ever since its publication, readers have been struck by the poem's themes as well as by its craft. With regard to its craft, Marie Borroff sees in the poem the specific qualities that make Frost's work unique. She notes, for example, that Frost's poem depends on words derived from Anglo-Saxon and not from Latin or Romance languages. Of the 398 words, only 14 are Romance in origin and only 8 are Latinate. The result is a seemingly "natural" diction that, combined with the straightforward presentation of the facts, allows the issue under scrutiny to be implied rather than stated. Even Frost, in an aside on this poem recounted by **Reginald L. Cook**, emphasized its strategy of implication and the refusal to make a strictly didactic point: "I played exactly fair in it. Twice I say 'Good fences' and twice 'Something there is—' " Nonetheless, uncovering the implications and attempting to determine what side Frost actually did take have led to a wide range of criticism.

A review of just the past thirty years of criticism reveals how many approaches one can take to this poem. Some critics, like Frank Lentricchia, have seen in the poem a philosophical dilemma in the Kantian tradition. Lentricchia argues that the poem is less about "walls" than about consciousness itself. Others, like Edward Jayne, have found in the debate between the neighbors a struggle to suppress the latent homosexual attraction between the two men. More recent criticism, for the most part, has focused on the poem's depiction of neighborly relations as an indication of the tension between freedom and pragmatism. Some critics, such as George Nitchie, argue that in this neighborly conflict Frost sides with the poet and so speaks for imaginative freedom. Those who believe Frost critiques the farmer also believe that Frost means to favor the active imagination; the poem, in other words, is often read as a defense of the utopian dream of a world without boundaries. By contrast, other readers see in Frost's poem a more skeptical view of the freewheeling imagination. Notable among this group are Richard Poirier, George Monteiro, Fritz Oehlschlaeger, and A. R. Coulthard. Such critics insist that the poem ultimately supports the farmer. After all, notes Poirier, the speaker does build the wall (and, in fact, initiates the wall building: "I let my neighbor know"), an act that implies that freedom does need some limitations. And the farmer's view that "good fences make good neighbors" suggests, as George Monteiro explains, that people need clear boundaries. Oehlschlaeger, however, goes so far as to claim that the pragmatic need for walls is less of an issue than the fact that the farmer in the poem, an honest neighbor, needs a wall to separate himself from the selfish narrator. Coulthard agrees with Oehlschlaeger but believes that the poem is actually intended to support the speaker.

Many critics, however, do not believe that the poem ever does take a side. Among these critics are John Lynen, John Kemp, and Patricia Wallace. Lynen argues that Frost, the poet, examines the paradoxes raised by the conflict but takes no stance, an appraisal that has become the dominant critical view of the poem. Most recently, Judith Oster has summarized this view by noting that, in the end, all we are left with is an ambivalent acceptance of the need for walls.

References and further reading: Borroff; *Language and the Poet*; R. Cook, "Frost's Asides," 355; Coulthard; Fleissner, "New Lines"; Jayne; Kemp; Lentricchia, *Modern Poetics*, 105–6; Lynen, *Pastoral Art*, 29; Monteiro, *New England*, 129; Nitchie; Oehlschlaeger, "Fences"; Oster, 179; Parini, *A Life*, 138–39; Poirier, *Knowing*; Thompson, *Early Years*, 313; P. Wallace; Walsh, 132–43. For Supreme Court case, see *Plaut v. Spendthrift Farm, Inc.*, 18 Apr. 1995, 115 S.Ct. 1447 (1995).

Jonathan N. Barron

MICHIGAN AT ANN ARBOR, THE UNIVERSITY OF. Frost's relationship with the University of Michigan at Ann Arbor, a place Frost often referred to as his second home, spanned more than forty years. One might say it began in 1915 when Frost met Morris P. Tilley, a professor of English at Michigan, who was vacationing in **Franconia, New Hampshire**. The two men became friends, and a year later, when Frost's sister Jeanie enrolled at Michigan as a special student, Frost called upon Tilley to look after her. The high points of the relationship were the periods during which Frost served the university as a Fellow in the Creative Arts from 1921 to 1923 and as a Fellow in Letters from 1925 to 1926. Although he never returned to Michigan to teach after 1926, he continued to visit the university, including two visits in 1962 (in April and June), the last full year of his life.

Frost's role as an "Idle Fellow," a term he used wryly to describe the generous conditions of the fellowship, which required virtually no commitment in the way of teaching or public readings, was an important one not only for the university but also for the future of creative writing in this country. Prior to President Burton's appointment of Frost, there had been only one other official poet-in-residence, Percy MacKaye at Miami University (Ohio). It was a fortuitous meeting between MacKaye and Frost at 107 Waverly Place in New York City in December of 1920 that alerted Frost to the possibility of such an appointment, and both MacKaye and Miami's President Hughes played a role in securing the appointment for Frost. Frost's success at Michigan led to other poets' being appointed at Michigan and at other major universities. His appointment and tenure helped shape the notion that there is something to be said for "education by presence," a term he coined to describe his value as an artist-in-residence.

Frost's first year at Michigan was a busy and quite successful one. Despite his relative freedom, Frost worked harder that first year (1921–1922) than he had initially planned. He did some writing, publishing one of his more famous poems, **"The Witch of Coös,"** in the January 1922 issue of *Poetry*. But for the most part, he was too wrapped up in other activities to write. He spent quite a bit of time with a group of young writers who called themselves the *Whimsies*. They met at Professor Roy Cowden's home, where they read their manuscripts with Frost listening and occasionally offering some criticism. More important, he organized five successful readings by well-known poets (Padraic Colum, **Carl Sandburg**, **Louis Untermeyer**, **Amy Lowell**, and Vachel Lindsey) during the spring of 1922. At the end of the first year, Michigan awarded Frost an honorary A.M., an honor over which, Lawrance Thompson records, "he grumbled pleasantly," slightly envious of the honorary doctorate awarded to Secretary of State Hughes.

In June, after his first year, he went home to South Shaftsbury, Vermont, where he plunged into writing. Many of the poems in *New Hampshire*, his fourth volume, were written during that summer. Although Frost returned to Ann Arbor for a second year, it was with an understanding that he would be absent for long periods. He used that time to complete work on *New Hampshire*, a volume he dedicated "To Vermont and Michigan," which was published in 1923. The dedication was somewhat tongue-in-cheek because he didn't write much while in Michigan. However, the $5,000 salary he was paid for that final year contributed to his ability to write the book, and Lawrence Conrad, one of the student members of the *Whimsies* and editor of the student journal of the same name, typed the manuscript for Frost.

At the end of the second year at Michigan, Frost left to return to **Amherst**. For the remainder of his life, he continued to maintain relations with many of the friends he made in Ann Arbor. During his last visit in 1962, he received the honorary doctorate of law, a degree he had long coveted. Frost's connection to Michigan remained strong throughout his life, and it is perhaps expressed best in a letter to his friend George Whicher: "I am not Mr. Frost formerly of Michigan but Mr. Frost formally of Michigan" (qtd. in Sergeant).

References and further reading: Parini, *A Life*, 205–8, 231–38; Sergeant, 254; Thompson, *Triumph*, 184; Tyler provides an insider's view as she recalls Frost's time at Michigan in "Frost's Last Three Visits" and "Frost in Michigan." For a good overview of how Frost's initial appointment was viewed at the time, see Bowen.

James M. Dubinsky

"MIDDLENESS OF THE ROAD, THE," first appeared in the *Virginia Quarterly Review* (Winter 1946) and was collected in **Steeple Bush (1947)**. The poem opens by contemplating the potential of the imagination: A fanciful person might imagine that roads that go uphill and seem to stop at the skyline may continue into the heavens toward infinity. The same imagination could think that a low road, curving suddenly to avoid a wood, in fact ran into the trees and stopped. The narrator rejects these two roads. Then the little two-road drama presented in concrete terms turns out to be a philosophical drama: We are told that these roads lead to absolutes, "absolute flight and rest." The narrator tells us that his own journeys do not deal with absolutes; his own journeys are "limited": He goes to real places, which are "near and far." (Robert Fleissner discusses Frost's golden mean of moderation and his refusal to be romantic in this poem.) Frost's best teachers, William James and Bergson, would have taught him to eschew the absolute.

There seems to be another strand in the poem. Frost once declared, "I am all onion," and it may be that another layer is discovered in the phrase "say what Fancy will." The phrase, of course, rejects a fanciful use of the imagination, but Frost's old-fashioned word with its attention-seeking capital letter is also the word Coleridge used in a similar context, when he claimed that Fancy makes poor metaphors because it is free from time and space. Frost's poem, too, rejects the metaphors made by Fancy because instead of remaining "limited," they deal with "absolute flight and rest."

References and further reading: Samuel Taylor Coleridge, *Biographia Literaria*, ed. George Watson, 2d ed. (London: Dent, 1965), 167; Fleissner, *Road Taken*; Schwartz.

Gerard Quinn

"MILKY WAY IS A COWPATH, THE," can be viewed as another of Frost's contemplations on the relationship between human beings and nature. Originally published in **In the Clearing (1962)**, the poem highlights Frost's interest in **science** and his examination of the scientist and the poet as co-investigators of truth.

The basic image in the poem is the comparison of the stars in the Milky Way to the flowers on a cowpath, but the real subject is an evaluation of the artistic impulse. Poetically, the male is pretentious, whereas the female is more inclined to let a simple nursery rhyme explain the mysteries of space and stars—the cow jumped over the moon.

In the end the poet admits that the strength of his craft is to present metaphor and not truth. Science and poetry compete to explain natural phenomena in much the same way that men and women have differing responses to life. The boy spends his energy pelting and penetrating the heavens; the poet spends his energy creating figurative explanations. Neither gains any more understanding than the woman who is content to let the universe remain a mystery.

References and further reading: For further discussions of Frost and nature, see Bagby, *Nature*; Greiner, *Poet and His Critics*, 207–48.

Belinda D. Bruner

"MINOR BIRD, A," was first published in *Inlander* magazine of the **University of Michigan** in 1926. It is a poem of four couplets, one of a number of short nature **lyrics** in *West-Running Brook* **(1928)**. The myna (or mynah) bird is the name given to Asian birds of the starling family, certain species of which can mimic human speech.

The first two couplets report the speaker's annoyance at having to listen to a bird who sings all day outside his house, apparently in an irritating minor key. In the last two couplets, however, the speaker reprimands himself for wishing to silence or chase away the bird. Two of Frost's characteristic themes emerge here. First, that nature is simply indifferent; the bird does not intend to annoy the speaker but is simply acting on instinct. Second, that "song"—a favorite metaphor of Frost's for any type of creative, free expression—is inherently good, and the desire to stifle it is evil. The revisions Frost made for *West-Running Brook* suggest that he had become more and more confident of his themes and wished to strengthen the poem's expression of them. He changed "may" to "must" in line 5, substituted "of course" for "I own" in line 7, and in the last line emphasized the value of even a "minor" song by changing "ever wanting to silence song" to "wanting to silence *any* song" (emphasis added).

References and further reading: R. Frost, *Poetry*, ed. Lathem, provides detailed accounts of the revisions and emendations made in successive printings of the poems. For an extended discussion of Frost's use of birds, see K. Harris, *Studies*, 143–56.

Todd Lieber

"MISGIVING," published in the *Yale Review* in 1921, was included two years later in *New Hampshire* **(1923)**. The poet's principal misgiving is that nature, a source for emblematic truths, does not provide, in this instance, a usable truth for humankind. Eager from the start to follow the blowing wind, wind-carried leaves end up reversing themselves. In a form of sleep-wish, they finish by preferring a wind that will keep *them* company as they search out a place of rest—a "sheltering wall," a "thicket," a "hollow place." They, who initially flung themselves into existence and who longed to cast themselves on the winds of autumn, now, tiredly, wish to give themselves over to quiet and sleep. The analogy for human beings runs roughly this way: The first burst into life and a subsequent desire for movement and transcendence come down, at the last, to a desire for that stasis that presages the return of the body to its source, to its initial dust. Entropy is not the end for life that this poet would desire. He would prefer to journey forth in search of "knowledge" that transcends the "bounds of life." Neither peace nor rest does he wish for himself—not for a night and not for eternity (as do, one gathers, the personified leaves). The misgiving here is that nature's autumnal emblem of wind and leaves offers a guide to the way human beings should live their lives. Not the leaf's tired wish to rest would the poet choose but to continue his quest beyond the limits of earthly life.

References and further reading: Bagby, *Nature*; Kearns.

George Monteiro

"MISSIVE MISSILE, A," was first published in the *Yale Review* (Autumn 1934) and reappeared as the last poem in *A Further Range* (**1936**), where it was isolated under the rubric "Afterthought." Three years later it concluded the second edition of Frost's *Collected Poems* (**1939**), again appearing under that rubric. The term *afterthought* often connotes a minor or secondary status, and this poem has been little noticed. But Frost's placement of "A Missive Missile" at the close of his books is emphatic, not diffident: An important framing device, it characterizes the experience of reading that the reader of these books has just undergone. Frost deployed this poem as a gloss on the reading of all of his poems.

The speaker, digging with a spade in an unspecified landscape, has unearthed a pebble marked with red, which he identifies as from "Mas d'Azil"—the site, in France, of an archaeological hoard dating from circa 10,000 B.C., discovered near the end of the nineteenth century. Azilian pebbles seem to be decorated according to some symbolic code, but they have never been deciphered. The speaker tries to decipher the apparently encoded pebble in his hand, starting from the vain premise that it is addressed to him, but he fails to construct an adequate interpretation. He blames this failure not only on his own solipsism but also on the extreme temporal distance that separates him from the author of this "missive": Evidently there are temporal limits beyond which inscription and interpretation cannot work. An unstated implication of the poem is that even in the best of circumstances, such as the reading of a contemporary text, interpretation risks solipsism and may falter.

Dramatizing the illusions or frustrations of interpretation, "A Missive Missile" is thematically allied to other poems such as **"A Tuft of Flowers"** and **"For Once, Then, Something."** Stylistically, its easy tetrameter lines, often monosyllabic and rhymed in a casual pattern, belie the difficulties it describes. Nothing in the poem questions the likelihood that one of Frost's pastoral speakers, in **England** or New England, would actually pick up an Azilian pebble; but the possibility that the pebble is marked by nature, not by culture, and carries no code at all will condition some readings of the poem.

References and further reading: Frost may have learned about Azilian pebbles from H. G. Wells's *Outline of History*, 4th ed. (New York: Review of Reviews, 1922), or from the article "Alphabet" in the *Encyclopaedia Britannica*, 11th ed. (1910), which includes some suggestive photographs. Discussions of the poem include Bagby, *Nature*, 133–36; M. Cook, "Dilemmas"; Hancher. Brower mentions it in passing (16), recognizing, in Frost's concluding lines, Virgil's evocation of human longing on the shore of the Styx (*Aeneid* 6.314).

Michael Hancher

MONROE, HARRIET, AND *POETRY*. In 1912, from her home in Chicago, Harriet Monroe founded *Poetry, A Magazine of Verse*. Her magazine would give poets a place of their own where theories of craftsmanship could be discussed and where poems created in the new spirit and the new form could be presented to an ever-increasing public. Monroe would also publish several volumes of her own verse and, with Alice Corbin Henderson, edit *The New Poetry* (1917, 1923, 1932), an anthology of twentieth-century verse that rivaled **Amy Lowell**'s *Some Imagist Poets* and that, over the years, carried a generous selection of Frost's poems.

With the publication in England of Frost's first two books, *A Boy's Will* **(1913)** and *North of Boston* **(1914)**, and through the urgings of **Ezra Pound**, who served as foreign correspondent for the fledgling magazine, Monroe and *Poetry* were enthusiastic about Frost. Besides carrying Pound's favorable reviews in the May 1913 and December 1914 issues, the magazine in its February 1914 issue carried Frost's long blank verse poem, "The Code-Heroics," later titled **"The Code."** Other poems followed: **"Snow"** in the November 1916 issue, **"The Witch of Coös"** in the January 1922 issue on the occasion of the magazine's tenth anniversary, and "Ten Mills" and **"At Woodward's Gardens"** in the April 1936 issue. Frost introduced Monroe to the poems of his close English friend Edward Thomas, and a selection of Thomas's poems was included in the February 1917 issue.

As editor of *Poetry*, Harriet Monroe was eager to embrace vastly differing styles and personalities. As poet, she entered with Frost into the vigorous debate over poetic technique in America. Frost had grown ever more sharply away from Imagist poetry and away from Sidney Lanier's contention in *Science and the English Verse* (1880) that language is a species of music. Conversely, in such essays as "Rhythms of English Verse" and "The Free Verse Movement" (*Poets and Their Art*, 1926), Monroe made clear her predilection for vers libre and the Imagists, especially Richard Aldington. She extended her approach to encourage closer affiliation between poetry and the allied arts of music and **drama**. She approached Frost's poetry (as she did that of his contemporaries) as if it were a form of music, rich in timbres.

The friendship between Frost and Monroe extended to other members of the Frost family, especially during the years Frost was on the faculty at the **University of Michigan at Ann Arbor** (1921–1922, 1922–1923, and 1925–1926). While distancing himself from her form of aesthetic idealism and her championing of Imagism and free verse, Frost admired Monroe as a poet and acknowledged the importance of her contribution to the common cause of poetry through her magazine.

References and further reading: L. Francis, "Between Poets"; Monroe, *A Poet's Life* and *Poets and Their Art*; Wilkinson; Williams. Monroe died in 1936 in Peru (where she is buried in the Pantheon of Arequipa), and *A Poet's Life* was published posthumously; her volumes of verse include *Valeria and Other Poems* (1892); *The Passing Show: Five Modern Plays in Verse* (1903); *You and I* (1914); *The Difference and Other Poems* (1924); *Poems for Every Mood* (1933); *Chosen Poems, A Selection from My Book of Verse* (1935).

Lesley Lee Francis

"MOOD APART, A," was written, according to the date on the manuscript, around 14 June 1943, though Frost may have thought of the poem's theme some twenty-five years earlier. It was first printed, without Frost's permission, in an auction catalog. The first authorized publication was in *Fifty Years of Frost* (1944), a **Dartmouth College** exhibition catalog edited by Ray Nash. The poem appeared without a title. It was collected, with the current title, in *Steeple Bush* **(1947)** as the first poem of seven in the grouping "A Steeple and Belfry."

Like many of the other poems in the same grouping, "A Mood Apart" has religious connotations, relating the thoughts of a man who is disturbed by a group of schoolboys while working in his garden. His kneeling position and chanting suggest that perhaps the man is turning to nature for spiritual comfort. The intrusion, while the boys do not mean any harm, annoys the man. As a result, their disruption of his peace and communion are described as "evil." Such alienation from society, as opposed to a balance between isolation and community, is a theme that appears more often in Frost's later work.

References and further reading: Cramer, *Frost among His Poems*.

Mark Sutton

"MOON COMPASSES" first appeared in the *Yale Review* (Autumn 1934) and was subsequently collected in *A Further Range* **(1936)**. The main point of the poem's conceit is that the mountain, like the beloved, is ameliorated by the moon's evaluation and estimation. The moon's rays provide both tools and light, with the image of not only straight beams of accuracy but also a gentle reflection with which to best show the mountain's qualities. The final line suggests that this same phenomenon occurs when a lover holds the face of the beloved. Metaphor is one of the tools by which the poet becomes something of a scientist. The scientist's job is not to create a phenomenon but to clear the way for it to be viewed in its truest form. The artist, on the other hand, might present a subject in its best light, not necessarily its accurate measure. The poem moves from a metaphor of moonlight as a tool of exact measurement to the idea of love as the ultimate tool, capable of showing a subject in both its true nature and its best light.

Frost does not often use ellipses, and the intention here has been debated in the *Explicator*. Robert Fleissner maintains that the ellipses might have been used to leave the poem open-ended or to refer the reader to Donne's poem "A Valediction: Forbidding Mourning." Roger Slakey, however, argues that more likely the ellipses demonstrate the natural direction of metaphoric thinking, allowing the reader to follow the speaker from one implication to another. *See also* **Science**.

References and further reading: Fleissner, " 'Moon Compasses' "; Slakey.

Belinda D. Bruner

MORRISON, KATHLEEN JOHNSTON "KAY" (1898–1989), was Frost's secretary and confidante from 1938 until 1963. In 1942, Frost dedicated *A Witness Tree* to "K. M. for her part in it." Kay Morrison's part in restoring order to the distraught and despondent poet's life after the death of **Elinor Frost** in 1938 had been substantial. As secretary, she managed Frost's schedule, travel, correspondence, and living arrangements, but her role in his later life far transcended practical concerns. Controversy persists over the nature of the physical relationship between them, but the poetic inspiration that Frost's "passionate preference" for Kay Morrison provided is amply evident in at least one of the lyrical triumphs of *A Witness Tree:* **"Never Again Would Birds' Song Be the Same."** Another **lyric** from that same volume, **"The Silken Tent"** (originally titled "In Praise of Her Poise"), is often tied to Morrison as well, although Frost's daughter Lesley claims to remember typing it in 1938 as a poem for her mother.

The daughter of an affluent Scottish Episcopal minister, Kathleen Florence Johnston was born in Nova Scotia in 1898. The family soon returned to Edinburgh and remained until Robert Johnston took a church in Philadelphia in 1910. Kathleen attended Miss Hill's School, graduated from Bryn Mawr in 1921, and studied English for a year at Oxford. While working at the *Atlantic Monthly*, she met a colleague, Theodore Morrison (1901–1988), who was also a lecturer at **Harvard**. Married in 1927, they settled in Cambridge and had two children, Robert and Anne.

Kay Morrison first met Robert Frost in 1918 while a member of the Bryn Mawr "Reelers and Writhers" literary club, which invited the poet to campus. The acquaintance was renewed and deepened in 1936 when the Morrisons and the **DeVotos** hosted the Frosts during the poet's Norton Lectures at Harvard and in April 1938 when they shared in a memorial service for Elinor Frost. In July 1938, solicitude for the troubled poet led Mrs. Morrison to visit Frost in South Shaftsbury, Vermont, to remind him of a standing invitation to participate in the **Bread Loaf Writers' Conference**, of which Ted had been director since 1932. In the weeks ensuing, a relationship developed that culminated in Frost's proposal of marriage. Despite her repeated refusals to divorce her husband and Frost's frustration with the compromises inherent, Kay Morrison remained the focal figure in the poet's life for his final twenty-five years.

The relationship between Robert Frost and Kathleen Morrison presented difficulties that Lawrance Thompson could resolve neither as friend nor **biographer**, a situation addressed repeatedly and at length in his voluminous and unpublished "Notes from Conversations with Robert Frost." The significance of the relationship to Frost's life and to Thompson's official biography has remained of vital interest to contemporary biographers and critics.

References and further reading: Burnshaw; Meyers; K. Morrison, Parini, *A Life*; Sheehy, "(Re)Figuring"; Thompson, "Notes from Conversations with Robert Frost," are in the Frost–Thompson collection in the University of Virginia Library; Thompson and Winnick.

Donald G. Sheehy

"MOST OF IT, THE," first published in *A Witness Tree* (1942), depicts a universe so empty and vast that the protagonist fails to comprehend the reality of what he sees, even as it moves right past him. His failure is not one of optics but of vision—both moral and scientific. If we train ourselves to see only what we are looking for, we will be satisfied merely by what we find. We will keep "the universe alone." This limiting perspective cannot advance our position in life. We become reduced in size, incapable of seeing that the universe is larger than our own thoughts, incapable of being moved by another response.

For all its pyrotechnics—with words such as "cry," "crashed," "crumpling," and "splashed"—an eerie silence pervades "The Most of It." It is the silence of one. And for all its natural scenery—"cliff," "lake," "beach," and "underbrush"—there is the disquieting notion that such scenes are just figures painted upon a screen. Is what lurks beneath the surface friend or foe? God or not-God? Or is it just a blankness upon which the mind abstractly scribbles its inventions?

If the protagonist seeks to command, if not control, nature's response, expecting a humanlike reply, there seems to be an undercurrent beneath the scenery that is mysteriously, perhaps malevolently, steering the nonhuman world. A stone tossed into a pond produces concentric rings. But has anything really been disturbed? The event is soon lost within the water's mirrorlike calm. Does a powerful buck—or the mirage of a buck—"pushing the crumpled water" vanquish the perceiver's solitude? Has presence conquered emptiness?

Another pair of opposites greets the reader: the natural world versus the abstract world. In the poem, both worlds are neatly folded up inside one another. One grabs the end of one only to pull up the beginning of the other. This dovetailing effect is neatly inscribed in the word "embodiment." The word literally contains the word *body* in its center, but its meaning is of a representation or idea—something standing in place of the real thing. Whatever it is in the poem that seemingly travels across the lake never loses its abstraction, even as the reader tracks this presence as a real animal. Is this magical trick, this illusion, produced by the universe, the perceiver, or Frost?

What further lessens the reader's grasp on meaning is not only how Frost undercuts the real world's image but how his word choices negate action. Look at a few of the potent qualifiers Frost uses: "Some morning" (not this one?), "he would" (but does he?), and "nothing ever came . . . unless" (so is it?). Does anything ever really happen in the poem?

Strangely, all these effects heighten the power of the universe at the man's expense. He appears to shrink before our eyes. His quest (and question) becomes less heroic as the poem evolves. The reader's gaze is drawn to the action of the vanishing buck. Here, a double negative is achieved. Something, an "embodiment" whose essence is unknowable, disappears into the brush, while the visible man remains behind unnoticed. Again, presence and absence are at play.

"The Most of It" seems to finish on a note of finality—"and that was all"—but the expected closure does not really exist; the phrase reverberates almost as a question. To whom or what does the last line refer? Uncertainty abounds. The scene in the poem lacks almost every sign post. We know nothing of its seasons. There is no real sense of touch, human or otherwise. There is no guide—save the ethereal buck. The man has no identity other than his strange cry, which is soundless and offered in the conditional tense. *See also* **Nature Poet and Naturalist**.

References and further reading: Bagby, *Nature*; Brower; R. Frost, "On Extravagance: A Talk," *Collected*, 902–26; Lynen, *Pastoral Art*; Oster; Parini, *A Life*, 260–62; Poirier, *Knowing*.

Robert W. Scott

"MOUNTAIN, THE," published in *North of Boston* (1914), may allude to Mt. Hor, the Old Testament mountain where Aaron is taken to die. But it is also the name of an actual mountain in New England, though not near Lunenberg, Vermont, as this poem implies. In any case, the mountain, as the speaker's interlocutor has come to know it, is as much a fiction—is as much *make-believe*—as it is "real." This is the idea this unprepossessing poem involves: the extent to which we always inhabit a world as much created or imagined as observed. We "enhance" the "storied" land—to borrow Frost's terms in **"The Gift Outright."** "The Mountain" seems to suggest, with "The Gift Outright," that communities—whether national or local—are themselves created through these collective acts of enhancement and storytelling. At the end of the poem, the speaker's interlocutor refers to a time when "Hor was no bigger than a—". He breaks off without completing the thought, but there's truth in his extravagant suggestion that the mountain has grown since he came to know it. The *actual* mountain, of course, has existed as it now exists for countless millennia, but

"Mt. Hor," a named, fabled, even beloved artifact of local lore and legend— *this* mountain—was in fact "created" and built up through the storytelling acts of men like this interlocutor. "Enhancing" the natural world is a theme that very much interests Frost, of course, as in **"Never Again Would Birds' Song Be the Same,"** and "The Gift Outright." Men and women cannot "possess" the land that possesses them until they begin to claim it in their fictions, or as we read in "The Mountain," "All the fun's in how you say a thing."

References and further reading: Brower; Lynen; Marcus, *Explication*; Tharpe, *Centennial* II.

Mark Richardson

MOUNTAIN INTERVAL **(1916),** published in New York by **Henry Holt** on 1 December 1916, was Frost's first volume of poetry published after he had returned to the United States. The book was dedicated, "To you who least need reminding that before this interval of the South Branch under black mountains, there was another interval, the Upper at Plymouth, where we walked in spring beyond the covered bridge; but that the first interval of all was the old farm, our brook interval, so called by the man we had it from in sale." The "you who least need reminding" in the dedication is Frost's wife, **Elinor White**. The "South Branch" interval refers to the Frosts' farm in **Franconia, New Hampshire**, purchased in 1915; the "Upper at Plymouth," their time in Plymouth, New Hampshire (September 1911 to September 1912); the "first interval [. . .] our brook interval," their period on the farm in **Derry**, New Hampshire (1900–1911), the brook being Hyla Brook (cf. **"Hyla Brook"**). The Derry farm was not, however, acquired "in sale" but was bequeathed to Frost by his paternal grandfather.

In the original table of contents, six poems were emphasized by printing them in full capitals rather than small capitals as the other titles had appeared. These were **"Christmas Trees," "In the Home Stretch," "Birches," "The Hill Wife," "The Bonfire,"** and **"Snow."** The opening poem, **"The Road Not Taken,"** and the concluding poem, **"The Sound of the Trees,"** were printed in italic.

In *Collected Poems* (1930 and all subsequent editions), **"The Exposed Nest"** was moved from its original placement between **"A Girl's Garden"** and **" 'Out, Out—' "** to a position immediately following **"An Old Man's Winter Night."** Two poems that were not originally in *Mountain Interval,* **"Locked Out"** and **"The Last Word of a Bluebird,"** were added.

Frost felt that this volume was rushed into print by Alfred Harcourt before the poet had sufficient time to impose on its design a thematic or structural unity equivalent to that of his first two volumes. The sales of *Mountain Interval* were relatively small, particularly in comparison with the best-seller status of *North of Boston*. Following the meteoric rise of his reputation as a "new" poet with his first two books, the decline he met with after his third book was disheartening. Editors, he found, were not knocking down his door looking for poems.

No volume following *North of Boston* could be anything but anticlimactic. **Amy Lowell** in her *Tendencies in Modern American Poetry* (1917) felt that publication of his third volume would add nothing to Frost's achievements, although Clement Wood in his *Poets of America* (1925) claimed that this book lifted Frost's art further. Louise Bogan in *Achievement in American Poetry: 1900–1950*, looking back on Frost's career in 1951, dismisses *Mountain Interval* by not even discussing it. Looking at the order of Frost's book publication in the United States, one can see what could be considered as a decline. *North of Boston* was published first, quickly followed by the earlier and less mature *A Boy's Will* and the next year by *Mountain Interval*.

Despite his disappointment in this volume, it did contain some of Frost's best-known, anthologized and critically examined poems, such as "The Road Not Taken," "An Old Man's Winter Night," "Birches" and " 'Out, Out—'." It also taught Frost the importance of not rushing a book into print simply because his publisher felt the time was ripe for a new volume. With all subsequent volumes, Frost tried, although not always successfully, to impose a structural design similar to that of his first two books.

References and further reading: Louise Bogen, *Achievement in American Poetry: 1900–1950* (Chicago: Regnery, 1951); Amy Lowell, *Tendencies in Modern American Poetry* (New York: Macmillan, 1917); Pritchard, *Literary Life*, Ch. 5; Clement Wood, *Poets of America* (New York: Dutton, 1925).

Jeffrey S. Cramer

"MOWING" was Frost's favorite poem in *A Boy's Will* **(1913)**, one that he often read, mentioned in correspondence, and discussed as a part of his poetic theory. First published in the 1913 volume, the poem was probably written while Frost lived on the **Derry** farm, one of a number of farmwork poems that are central to Frost's philosophical and aesthetic principles. Early critics and friends recognized the accomplishment of the poem, and Frost despaired of equaling its accomplishment. The poem, clearly in the **pastoral** tradition, draws on **Emerson**'s thought but is more indebted, as Coale suggests, to **Thoreau**.

The poem is an irregular **sonnet** with an unusual rhyme scheme and few strictly iambic pentameter lines, most with anapestic substitutions. The effect of the poem is that it sounds like talk, not verse, an accomplishment that Frost continued to practice throughout his career. The anapests and the significant number of *s*, *w*, and *wh* sounds reproduce the whispering sound of a scythe. During the early years of his career, Frost worked on his theory of the "sound of sense" (see **Poetic Theories**) and thought of "Mowing" as a good example of how sound accomplishes the effect of the poem without the poet's having to resort to poetic figures.

"Mowing," a poem of action, depicts a mower alone in a field, using a long-bladed scythe to cut hay, which he leaves in the sun to make. The speaker recalls that there was no sound but his "long scythe whispering to the ground," a phrase repeated with variations throughout the poem and even repeated in **"A Tuft of Flowers"** later in the book. The mower conjectures that the scythe whispered "about the heat of the sun" or the "lack of sound" but does not really know what is whispered. Such speculations are about the observable facts of the physical world, not based on emotions or the imagination, as if he is resisting attributing too much to the sound of the scythe. Still he insists on asserting that the scythe whispered. To emphasize the assertion, he explains that the scythe "whispered and did not speak." Scythes cannot speak, but the explanation that it whispered because of "lack of sound" is only the mower's theory about why. Through the speaker Frost promotes his belief that an unbridgeable gap separates human beings from the world of physical reality. All we ever get from nature are hints and whispers that we have to interpret on our own. Frost makes it clear that the scythe whispered not to the mower but to the ground and that he did not know what was said. The assertion is crucial: Whatever the scythe said, and what is happening in the poem, would be weakened by poetic flights of fancy or thoughts of ambition because the scythe is not human. What follows in the poem are not conjectures about the scythe's words but the mower's own beliefs about truth, facts, and labor. Frost wants to stick only to the truth of the labor that "laid the swale in rows." Thompson records that in an early interview about his poetic theory Frost explained, "Art should follow lines in nature, like the grain of an axehandle. False art puts curves on things that haven't any curve." "Mowing" deliberately avoids metaphor or other poetic devices, but the poem as a whole paradoxically becomes an extended, natural metaphor that the reader has to make, not Frost. This poetic practice grows out of the poet's belief that individuals and nature encounter one another across a gulf in a struggle, an essential encounter or dilemma that defines our being.

The final couplet, unrhymed, represents the key assertions of the mower–poet. The fact is the objective of labor for the worker. But isn't fact itself a creation of the imagination since it becomes fact only by the processes of defining, classifying, and naming? Part of the answer is that as a human being the mower cannot speak without metaphor and that any language that aims at truth is always more than fact. What the final passage suggests without Frost's saying so is that hay making and poem making are comparable. His labor has produced lines of words laid in an order just as the mower "laid the swale in rows." Like the mower, that is all he can do; he must leave the making of the poem in the end to the reader. The poem seems to both encourage this analogy and warn us from falsifying the poem by adding curves of meaning not there. Frost has assiduously avoided and even ridiculed all poetic language ("fay or elf") except for one: By making the scythe whisper he uses personification. The mower insists that for him the scythe's whispering is a fact. If we question his assertion, we can question the very nature of fact, or accept that the scythe's whispering is fact for this person, or accept that the sounds of the scythe are whispering sounds. It is left up to us. Frost has given us the sounds of the lines and left the making of the poem to us. As Judith Oster says, "Perhaps this poem goes about as far as one can go in creating correspondences without recourse to metaphor or any of the tools of analogy, in creating facts by means of sound." *See also* **Nature Poet and Naturalist**.

References and further reading: Borroff, "Frost: 'To Earthward' "; Brower; Coale; Oster, 69; Scott; Thompson, *Triumph*, 77–78.

Newton Smith

"MY BUTTERFLY" is the poet's "discovery" poem and the first to be published professionally. (Some of Frost's poems had been published earlier in his high school newspaper.) It appeared originally in *The Independent* (8 Nov. 1894) and was later collected in *A Boy's Will* (1913). The diction is nineteenth century, punctuated with archaic pronouns and syntax, though at times we hear break through the precious language the unforced, natural rhythms and sounds of speech, which Frost perfected in his theory of the sound of sense: "I found it with the withered leaves / Under the eaves."

The poem is a harbinger of the poet's lifelong concern with mutability, but it is nostalgic as well as prophetic. The beauty of the butterfly's mating in flight and its transitory existence are poignantly evoked. The individual and nature both succumb to the imperious omnipotence of a less-than-benign creator, a "naturalistic note," as George Monteiro observes, that demonstrates several correspondences between Frost's and Emily Dickinson's butterfly poems, particularly "the importance of flight and journey, the butterfly's dalliance with immortality, and the ephemeral nature of the individual's life cycle." George F. Bagby goes so far as to call "My Butterfly" "by far the darkest of all the heuristic emblem poems dealing with the seasonal cycle," though he adds that a glimpse of hope in the elegiac poignancy of recollection serves to "take some of the chill off the autumnal sense of destruction."

As Frost's first published poem, "My Butterfly" carries what Lawrance Thompson calls the "spell of the romantics such as Keats and Shelley," but especially in passages such as the one that pleased Frost most "for purely technical qualities of sound, rhythm, [and] tone" ("The gray grass is scarce dappled with the snow . . ."), the poem reveals much of the talent that would find rich expression later in Frost's work.

References and further reading: Bagby, *Nature*, 141; Kemp; Monteiro, *New England*, 14–15; Sergeant; Thompson, *Early Years*, 163, and *Fire and Ice*, 94.

Roland H. Lyford

"MY NOVEMBER GUEST" was published in *A Boy's Will* (1913). With this lyric, the first suggestion of coupling is made in the volume, or it is if we take into account the gloss Frost attached to the poem in the first edition of the book: "He [the youth of the poems] is in love with being misunderstood." Misunderstood by whom? Obviously by a lover who prefers to believe that she only, and not her partner, knows the melancholy pleasure of getting good and lost in the romantic November weather. (He refers to her, agreeably enough, with an epithet: "My Sorrow.") The relation between speaker and lover is a little uncertain; they are less than two but more than one, to borrow a phrase from **"Meeting and Passing."** But really, who could withstand the charm of getting himself "misunderstood" in precisely this way? No wonder the poet—he is describing his moody lover to a friend, or anyway to a third party—is so much in love.

"My November Guest" is a technical tour de force. Frost nicely varies the caesurae, which fall now toward the beginning, now in the middle, now toward the end, of the lines. He modulates, quite deftly, the relation of sentence to line, shifting in and out of run-on and end-stopped lines. He perfectly plays the tendency of the rhymed iambic tetrameter lines to want closure against the tendency of the sentences themselves to wander beyond the fixed, eight-syllable boundary of the line. The remarkable music of the poem engages effects of consonance, assonance, and internal rhyme so pronounced as nearly to make a "tongue twister" of such lines as the following: "The beauties she so truly sees, / She thinks I have no eye for these." It is easy enough to stumble when reading the poem aloud; its elastic sounds are in certain respects not typical of Frost's better-known work—a point worth dwelling on here.

In a 1913 letter to **John Bartlett**, Frost writes: "You see the great successes in recent poetry have been made on the assumption that the music of words was a matter of harmonized vowels and consonants. Both Swinburne and Tennyson arrived largely at effects in assonation. But they were on the wrong track or at any rate on a short track." Of course, "My November Guest" is a success in exactly this assonant vein. And yet, even as it depends upon music associated with the "short track" laid out by Swinburne and Tennyson, "My November Guest" also depends on what, by 1913, Frost was calling "sentence sounds"— even in the tongue-twisting lines just quoted. As it happens, Frost cites "My November Guest" in another letter on sentence sounds in which he attempts to distance himself from the Tennysonian-Swinburnian mode. "Take My November Guest," he writes, again to Bartlett. "Did you know at once how we say such sentences as these when we talk? She thinks I have no eye for these. / Not yesterday I learned etc / But it were vain to tell her so." The sounds Frost points to here are strictly conversational (*"when we talk,"* he says); they have nothing to do with "harmonized vowels and consonants." Frost fastens three distinct "sentence sounds" to the page in the last stanza alone: The first three lines of the stanza register a tone of finger-wagging, mock exasperation; the fourth registers another tone altogether, with its concessive, yielding mood; the last line catches another still, with its air of admiration (and, it must be said, of utter capitulation). So, in illustrating his theory of sentence sounds in the letter to Bartlett, Frost directs attention to a poem that unforgettably performs the old nineteenth-century music of Tennyson—which only suggests how comfortable Frost already was in working his own voice in among the voices of his English and American precursors. Literary-historical considerations should not make us forget, however, that "My November Guest" is, in the first place, among the most ingratiating poems of courtship Robert Frost ever wrote.

References and further reading: R. Frost, *Collected*, 664, 676.

Mark Richardson

$\mathcal{X}$

"NATURE NOTE, A," a sixteen-line poem first published as "A Nature Note on Whippoorwills" in the *Coolidge Hill Gazette* (Dec. 1938) and later in *A Witness Tree* (**1942**), consists of four quatrains rhyming *abba* and relies on puns, chiasmus, and renovated cliché. The "note" of the title refers both to the musical sound made by a family of whippoorwills (whose name is echoic, from the bird's note) and to the speaker's taking notice of the birds' out-of-season song. Such crisscrossing of a nature note and a human note is rhetorically enacted in Frost's use of chiasmus in the final stanza: "The twenty-third of September, / / September the twenty-third." What is remarkable to the speaker is the arrival of the birds so late in the season; they are "All out of time pell-mell!" But the remark, juxtaposed with the repetition of a precise date, also calls attention to the arbitrary specificity of human time and so further differentiates a nature note from a human note. Place as well as time is important to the speaker, who begins the poem by noting that the whippoorwills have left their "native ledge" for "the open country edge." Combining the human penchants for personification, cliché, and logic, the speaker asserts that the birds have come "To give us a piece of their bills." The poem combines humor, wordplay, and precise crafting ("September" and "twenty-third," human notes, echo in their three syllables the nature note, "whippoorwill").

References and further reading: Bagby, *Nature*, on nature in Frost generally; Harris, "Lyric Impulse."

Jacqueline B. McCurry

NATURE POET AND NATURALIST, ROBERT FROST AS. "Simply put," writes Cheryll Glotfelty, "ecocriticism is the study of the relationship between literature and the physical environment." Make that the relationship between the poet and the natural world, and we have in brief one of Frost's grand themes.

When we read Frost's poetry broadly as a record of the impact of the natural world upon the poet, we can see how powerfully indeed Frost lived in the physical world and how sensitive he was to its influences. This is not to deny his conscious and intelligent participation in the poetic tradition, nor to deny his philosophical and epistemological complexity; Poirier and Bagby have written two of the seminal books on Frost, and readers and critics of Frost would be impoverished without them. But in our need to understand Frost as a thinker and craftsman, we often forget that he was a man who spent time outdoors, carefully observing natural phenomena and recording them as accurately as he could. The insights that arise from some of his most celebrated poems, we sometimes neglect to remember, came to him as a result of his having observed the world of nature with care and caution. Indeed, as Frost himself says in **"To the Thawing Wind,"** it was necessary at times to escape from his "narrow stall," with "poems on the floor," and be blown "out of door," driven by natural forces themselves to leave the hermitlike obsession with verse and the mind and come into the natural world of spring, where, clearly, the poet, finding "the brown beneath the white," will be renewed as is the landscape.

In his detailed responses to the natural world, he is a realist, however much, in his philosophical poems, he questions common sense and our grasp on a common reality. Careful observation informs poems such as **"Birches"** that seem to be about something besides nature but that begin with a scrupulous detailing of what the world in certain circumstances looks like. In "Birches," for example, the poet and the reader are situated directly in the closely observed New England landscape in passages about limbs "Loaded with ice a sunny winter morning / After a rain" and "click[ing] upon themselves / As the breeze rises" and the "sun's warmth makes them shed crystal shells / Shattering and avalanching on the snow-crust." When in **"Stopping by Woods"** the poet tells us that "the only other sound's the sweep of easy wind and downy flake," we trust that he has been in the woods during snowstorms and that his deepest perceptions about the meaning of experience are shaped by and negotiated in the actual.

Few poets have been more influenced by, more obsessed by, the turning of the seasons than Frost, and to be aware of the seasons is to be obsessed by the natural world and its disinterestedness, yet always alert to its influence upon human life and culture. "Outer weather" impinges upon "inner weather" and implies a world beyond human culture, beyond human understanding. There are poems for each season, as a partial listing reveals: for winter, **"An Old Man's Winter Night,"** "Stopping by Woods," **"Dust of Snow,"** "Snow," **"Looking for a Sunset Bird in Winter,"** **"Desert Places."** For spring, **"Two Tramps in Mud Time,"** **"Spring Pools,"** **"Blue-Butterfly Day,"** **"Our Singing Strength,"** "To the Thawing Wind." For summer, **"The Valley's Singing Day,"** **"The Oven Bird,"** **"Mowing,"** **"The Tuft of Flowers,"** **"The Silken Tent."** For fall, **"October,"** **"Unharvested,"** **"After Apple-Picking,"** **"November,"** **"My November Guest,"** **"The Road Not Taken,"** **"Wild Grapes."** While the uses to which Frost puts the seasons are often either symbolic or synecdochic, each poem gives evidence of the care with which Frost has been absorbed into the accurate and necessary perceptions of the natural realities out of which such poems arise. The ruefulness and quiet sadness of "My November Guest," for instance, is at least as much about the psychological state of a mind losing something important as it is about the fall itself. Frost's imagery ("these dark days of autumn rain," "the desolate, deserted trees, / The faded earth, the heavy sky"), however, is not freighted only with "poetic" meaning; it is also a photographic rendering of New England weather in the fall.

But as alert and apparently comfortable as Frost is in his environment, he is seldom a relaxed presence in it, for he is never certain that the environment is either dependable or meaningful in any fixed way. Such a wrought poem as **"Design"** poses the question to himself and the reader starkly. If there is a design behind the comings-together of the environment, it is the "design of darkness to appall"; if there is no design, appalling things happen by accident. That is not much of a comfort, not much of a choice. And the rhetoric of the final line is puzzling as well: "If design govern in a thing so small." As we have been talking of things, what is the thing so small? The little white design that Frost has stumbled across? or the mind itself that questions and attempts to understand the (apparent) pattern? Again, for Frost, no easy comfort is available. "Design" is perhaps the bleakest of the poems of doubt and discomfort, but the others test and probe meaning in similar ways.

"The Most of It" begins, "He thought he kept the universe alone," and it ends, "—and that was all"; but it is never clear that the buck, whose beauty and virility surprise the speaker so much, is his companion in the universe or that it helps him avoid his aloneness. In **"For Once, Then, Something,"** Frost thinks he sees "beyond the picture, / Through the picture . . . Something more," but a "drop . . . / / Blurred it." "What was that whiteness?" he wants to know: "Truth? A pebble of quartz?" The poet sees his reflection in the well water as "godlike," but the allusion to Narcissus is also useful here, for Frost is underlining the terrible problem his mind has in escaping from itself and seeing some certainty in the natural world beyond what his own mind might have placed there.

Frost is not simply a poet trying to figure out the meaning of his own experience and the meaning of the phenomena his mental brilliance and alertness have allowed him to observe. His mind from the beginning was shaped by the **science** of the day, the great scientific discoveries and the questions to which they led. He was an avid student of botany and as a young man made trips with his colleague and friend Carl Burell to collect specimens. He studied geology at **Harvard** under Nathan Shaler. He studied the writings of Charles Darwin and argued Darwin's theories with his mother. As both the published and unpublished versions of his essay "The Future of Man" (1959) make clear, he remained until the end of his life a student of the new scientific knowledge. This detailed and intellectually responsible knowledge lies behind all his poems but occasionally makes an appearance in poems as subject matter. **"In Time of Cloudburst," "On Looking Up by Chance at the Constellations,"** and **"Why Wait for Science"** deal with the implications of those inconceivably long stretches of years that contrast so sharply with the apparent circularity and repetitiveness of events in the natural world. However chilly and distant the implied "desert places" seem to be, however accidental and chancy is our existence within a system that huge and impersonal, "calm seems certainly safe to last tonight," Frost reminds us in "On Looking Up by Chance."

Some evidence suggests that Frost's scientific intelligence was such that he would have been a brilliant theoretical scientist, had he given himself the chance. He could speculate about the implications of various theories and, by following them to their logical conclusions, make startling claims about the universe. In the poem **"A Loose Mountain,"** written long before the general acceptance of the theory that the extinction of the dinosaurs was caused by the explosion of a meteor striking the planet at the boundary of the Cretaceous and Tertiary Eras, Frost was imagining what might be the effect of such an event. "The heartless and enormous Outer Black" is ready to hurl that mountain at us with its "Balearic sling"; it is simply waiting until it will make the most impact upon us. But as always, scientific knowledge of the natural world yields to and enhances the philosophic existential difficulty: The universe is not only limitless but heartless.

As Frost's intelligence allowed him to anticipate later radical scientific theories, his understanding of the New England landscape and farming culture forced him to be an environmental critic before there was any such thing and before the word *ecology* entered our popular language. **"The Black Cottage,"** for example, anticipates the scourge of absentee landlords, and **"The Last Mowing"** acknowledges that by allowing farming activities to stop, the world of nature will reassert itself: "The meadow is done with the tame." As the meadow reverts to nature, the flowers will "go to waste and go wild." The implicit tragedy of the dying human culture is offset by the tendency inherent in the natural world to restore itself, to survive the human, and having survived it, to obliterate it.

The ecological vision is darker in **"A Brook in the City."** The brook is in a "dungeon under stone / / . . . being kept forever under." But since the city is built over the still-running brook, Frost "wonder[s]" how the people in it can "work and sleep." The cost of the city to the natural world is high, "all for nothing it had ever done." The poet has known the brook before it was buried, when it "held the house as in an elbow-crook," and because he could make it "leap," has known that it was alive, though now it is forced to live in "fetid darkness."

So the natural world influences Frost and his poetry from the beginnings of his career to the end. He is aware that humans including himself may be some grim Darwinian mistake, in that they seem not to fit into the natural world even while being "natural." Things seem to run down, as "dawn goes down to day," and all we can do is resist. We resist by knowing, by noticing, by being as fully in the natural world as we can. Living gives us what Frost calls in **"A Question"** "soul-and-body scars," but still, as he points out in **"Our Hold on the Planet,"** nature "must be a little more in favor of man" or "Our hold on the planet wouldn't have so increased." Or, as he says in "Birches" in a different context, "Earth's the right place for love: / I don't know where it's likely to go better."

References and further reading: Bagby, *Nature*; Baym; C. Brooks, "Nature"; Faggen; Cheryll Glotfelty and Harold Fromm, eds., *The Ecocriticism Reader: Landmarks in Literary Ecology* (Athens: University of Georgia Press, 1996), xviii; Harris, "Early Education"; Hiers; Lynen, *Pastoral Art*; Parini, "Frost"; Poirier, *Knowing*; Squires.

Thomas C. Bailey

"NEED OF BEING VERSED IN COUNTRY THINGS, THE," published originally in *Harper's Magazine* (Dec. 1920), is the final poem in *New Hampshire* **(1923)**. By placing this poem as the end piece and setting it in italics, Frost clearly intended the poem in part to carry on the message begun in the title poem **"New Hampshire."**

Probably inspired primarily by Frost's belief that nature is disinterested in human affairs, the poem opens with a somewhat nostalgic scene of a burned-out house with only its chimney standing, "Like a pistil after the petals go." We are told with a surprising detachment that the fire had brought to "the midnight sky a sunset glow." The next stanza reports that the barn "across the way" might have burned too if it had been "the will of the wind," but now it is all that is left. Here, Frost allows the speaker of the poem to slip into a sentimental mood as if lamenting the loss of human habitation in the landscape. The comment about the forsaken name of the farm recalls **Emerson**'s "Hamatreya," suggesting that our names, titles, and deeds will be long forgotten while the land will continue. In the third stanza the observer contrasts the abandoned barn with the bustle when the farm had people and horses carrying loads in and out during summer harvests.

The fourth stanza focuses on the barn where birds fly "out and in" through broken windows instead of horses coming and going from the road. The phoebes' murmur is "more like the sigh we sigh / From too much dwelling on what has been," words that take us to the edge of pathetic fallacy. The nostalgia is natural—for a human. Frost, himself, was all too aware that the way of life represented by the New England farm was disappearing and that all over the region farms were being abandoned, and meadows and fields were being left for the woods to take over. Frost considers the theme repeatedly in poems such as **"Directive"** or **"The Last Mowing."**

The temptation Frost resists, however, is to believe that nature, too, mourns the loss. In stanza five, Frost tells us in effect that the birds feel no loss; they cherish no memories, no nostalgia. The leaves come out, the pump and the fence provide perches, and humans are not missed. George Bagby notes that the personification of the landscape makes the point that any "feelings" that the birds have, if at all, are not for us but for themselves, a reading emphasized in stanza six.

The last two lines deserve considerable attention. The temptation is to believe that there is a sympathetic union with nature and that, as Emerson or Wordsworth would have it, nature feels for humankind. Frost allows such sentiment to be voiced through the speaker as if to say that he, too, wishes it were true. In the end, though, Frost rejects the romantic view with skepticism and irony. Only humans have long memories of what has been. The house will not regenerate itself despite the fertile imagery of the flower's pistil as the chimney. Nature's only need of a pump or wire is as a perch. The significance of human artifacts and meaning is lost on the birds. The lesson to be learned here from nature is differentiation, not unity, as is evidenced by Frost's use of similes, not metaphors, in the passage. The natural world is impersonal, unfeeling, and occasionally threatening. The significance of the scene depends upon who observes it, but to read it correctly, Frost warns, "One had to be versed in country things."

References and further reading: Bagby, *Nature*; Brower; Hays, "Two Landscapes"; Ingebretsen, *Stone Boat*; Lentricchia, *Modern Poetics*; Thompson, *Triumph*.

Newton Smith

"NEITHER OUT FAR NOR IN DEEP" first appeared in the *Yale Review* in 1934 and was included in *A Further Range* **(1936)**. According to Frost, the poem was written in California at the time of the 1932 Olympic Games.

Randall Jarrell asserts that the poem's strength lies in its subtleties. According to Jarrell, the poem presents a notion common to Frost's poetry: a "recognition of the essential limitations of man, without denial or protest or rhetoric or palliation." Indeed, despite its deceptively simple veneer, the poem alludes to complex issues. Though the juxtaposition of land and sea is reminiscent of Matthew Arnold's treatment of the subject in "The Forsaken Merman," for example, Frost upsets Arnold's convenient dichotomy between land and sea and overturns the notion of the land's constancy versus the seductively dangerous allure of the sea through his coupling of the land with the notion of variance and the sea with an expression of constancy and hope. The speaker of Frost's poem implies that though locating truth is impossible, the people continue to "turn their back on the land" and "look at the sea all day." Despite their inability to locate truth, or even to acknowledge its existence, the people of the poem look with a kind of hope—or expectancy, at least—toward the sea.

The speaker also seems to imply that standing "along the sand," at that boundary where land touches sea, affords one the best vantage point. The speaker's interest in the ambiguity and fluidity of the shifting line of demarcation between water and sand suggests the dynamism and efficacy of such a position. Accepting such ambiguity and its simultaneous danger and promise contrasts with the imagery of another Arnold poem, "Dover Beach," for Frost's shoreline represents not only a tenuous negotiation of the land and sea but also a much less foreboding image than Arnold's "drear" and "darkling plain." Although Frost's watchers on the beach have a restricted access to the truth or insight they seek and "cannot look out far" nor "in deep" when they gaze at the sea, they still keep the watch. The people on Frost's beach, having relinquished a desire for transcendent truth, the loss of which Arnold's speaker mourns in "Dover Beach," find purpose in the activity of simply watching; despite their lack of access to truth, they experience life most fully by straddling that border between land and sea, not allowing their inability to see far and deep to "bar" them from "any watch they keep."

As William Pritchard recounts, in a speech delivered at Frost's eighty-fifth birthday party in 1959, Lionel Trilling characterized Frost as a "tragic poet" whose work reflected a "terrifying universe," using the poems **"Design"** and "Neither Out Far" as examples of Frost's dark side. In a letter to Trilling after the incident, Frost reveals that he was not displeased with Trilling's remarks but was in fact pleased that Trilling "depart[ed] from the Rotarian norm in a Rotarian situation." However, as Pritchard continues, Trilling does seem to miss Frost's "irony" and "playfulness" and certainly ignores the fact that "Neither Out Far" may not be so much about the despair of humankind in the face of the loss of truth but rather more about a recognition and affirmation of life's ambiguities.

References and further reading: Frost, *Selected Letters*, 500; Jarrell, "Laodiceans," 39; Pritchard, *Literary Life*, 252–53; Wagner, 114, for critical reception of *A Further Range* generally and "Neither Out Far" specifically.

Gary Totten

"NEVER AGAIN WOULD BIRDS' SONG BE THE SAME," first published in *A Witness Tree* **(1942)**, takes a traditional form—the Shakespearean **sonnet**— and through it gives us an unconventional version of a well-known biblical tale. The poem is in effect a poetic rewriting of one aspect of the Garden of Eden story. Frost brings the character of Eve from out of the Old Testament into his verse in order to show how the human and natural worlds are intricately and permanently fused. Eve in the poem is not the evil temptress whose proffering of the apple led to the Fall and an expulsion from paradise. Her role here is rather more positive, and it calls to mind somehow the poet's own purpose. The delicate sound of Eve's voice in the garden, the speaker tell us, has had a lasting influence on the song of birds. From repeatedly hearing her voice, the birds "added to their own an oversound, / Her tone of meaning but without the words." Eve's verbal presence was so effective that we continue even today to hear the sounds of the natural world altogether differently. Like a good poem, Eve's voice has forever altered, indeed enhanced, what we "hear" or discern in our environment.

"Never Again" is perhaps also directly about Frost's adaptation of formal

poetic conventions. Evans Lansing Smith notes that although the sonnet closely
keeps the traditional Shakespearean rhyme scheme, Frost avoids ending each
quatrain with a conventional full stop. The sentences of the poem are not contained within the standard form, suggesting that "sentence sounds and structure
are 'crossed' over the metrical and formal structures of the sonnet."

With a knowledge of some of the significant details of Frost's life, we can
also read the poem as a tribute to two women who greatly influenced the poet:
his wife, **Elinor**, who died just a few years before the composition of the poem,
and **Kathleen Morrison**, Frost's secretary and confidante from 1938 until 1963
and the woman to whom Frost dedicated *A Witness Tree*. In an intriguing close
reading of the poem, Matthew A. Fike presents evidence to show that the sonnet
is a subtle meditation on the Fall, in which Frost complements affectionate
portrayal with sadness—his love for Kay and for his wife is tempered by feelings of failure and loss related to his marriage. By undercutting the joy of
paradisal love and the sense that Eve's unfallen voice will never be completely
lost, the poem conveys the lamentation to which all fallen love is heir.

Fike's argument assumes that in Frost's poetry transformation is a less-than-
positive phenomenon; however, most of Frost's verse generally depends upon
the desirability of change. The poet, like Eve before him, has come to combine
his voice with the sounds of nature and so transform it. If poetry is to have
lasting value, it must be able to initiate change, to "add" something to the world
on a subtle level. Importantly, Eve does not "inflict injury or pain" as Fike
suggests the poem's words "to do that to" indicate. Indeed, it is Eve's "laughter"
and "eloquence" that stay in the birds' song. The fact that the birds' song will
never be the same is thus not so much a lament as a commemoration of those
whose soft eloquence has an enduring influence on the way we interpret our
world.

References and further reading: Fike, 111; Kearns; E. Smith, 36.

Sabine Sautter-Leger

"NEW HAMPSHIRE" is the eponymous poem of Frost's 1923 volume, his
first book of new verse since *Mountain Interval* (**1916**) and one for which Frost
received, in 1924, his first Pulitzer Prize. It had not been previously published
before its inclusion in *New Hampshire*.

The poem, as Richard Poirier indicates, includes quotations from Matthew
Arnold's "In Harmony with Nature," "Sohrab and Rustrum," and "The Scholar
Gipsy"; it begins with a series of casual meetings and conversations with people
from across America, illustrating New Hampshire's lack: The state has had one
president, one "real reformer," "Just enough gold" for "engagement rings," and
one witch. While the rest of America may have things in quantity enough to
sell, New Hampshire has but a "specimen of everything." Despite such lack,
Frost praises the states of New Hampshire and Vermont as "the two best states
in the Union" because they offer things more important. Though he says, "New

Hampshire offered / The nearest boundary to escape across," it is easy to see, in tone and mood, how much he admires the state and its people. Poirier notes, however, that "[s]ometimes Frost so wants to be old New England, poor boy from California that he is, that . . . he can surrender himself . . . to the delusion that to have lived in New Hampshire or Vermont is to have become philosophically enabled."

Responding to the claim that his work is marked by its provincialism, Frost writes in the poem, "Because I wrote my novels in New Hampshire / Is no proof that I aimed them at New Hampshire." In so doing Frost asserts that his work is directed at universality of place, idea, and character rather than mere locality and idiosyncrasy. A second criticism is based upon Frost's explicit reverence of nature. Yet while Frost has always insisted upon the educational function of nature, he draws a line in this poem at true pantheism. Out for a walk in the woods, the speaker comes across the remnants of a campfire in a clearing, the ashes of which seem to purport that "the groves were God's first temples," an echo of William Cullen Bryant's "Forest Hymn." But Frost concludes that "Nothing not built with hands of course is sacred," refusing to deny the authority of man.

More than a place for philosophic contemplations, the New Hampshire of the poem offers a refuge to the speaker: It enables him to escape from, among other things, the objections of literary critics: "How are we to write / The Russian novel in America / As long as life goes so unterribly?" Some critics, such as Jean Gould, see the statement ironically: There is no real reason to think that America is anything but ruled by the same global forces that have generated the "Russian novel." But others, such as George W. Nitchie, see the comment as typical of Frost's withdrawal from asking the hard questions of existence. When Frost is asked whether he would rather be a "prude or a puke," he never really answers the question. When pressed, he chooses to be a farmer: "I choose to be a plain New Hampshire farmer / With an income in cash of say a thousand." Frost's New England does not automatically answer hard questions nor does it solve problems; rather, it takes situations involving ethically complicated choices and reduces them to their fundamental components. Frost's point is that only when we disregard side issues can we consciously choose. The choices we face are morally difficult, and neither Frost nor New England provides any easy solution. While the New Hampshire of the poem seems to offer the philosopher a great deal, Frost states that he is, at the time of the poem's writing, "living in Vermont."

References and further reading: Gould; Nitchie; Oster; Poirier, *Knowing*, 46–48, 111; Sergeant.

Derrick Stone

NEW HAMPSHIRE (1923). When Frost's fourth volume of poetry, *New Hampshire: A Poem with Notes and Grace Notes*, appeared in November 1923 with woodcut illustrations by the artist **J. J. Lankes**, it won unanimous praise and earned the Pulitzer Prize. Critics hailed the book for its depictions of rural New England life and noted that in it Frost was at the top of his form; as John Farrar put it: "Perhaps this is the perfection of Frost's singing. Perhaps this is the fruit of his ripest powers." Reviewers typically took note of the poet's masterful use of the colloquial (one remarked that "Mr. Frost's lines sound as if they had been overheard in a telephone booth"), the regional focus of his work, and the interesting mixture of narrative and lyric poems that comprise the volume (reviews qtd. in Van Egmond).

The formatting of the book parodies **T. S. Eliot**'s *The Waste Land* (published for the first time in book form in Dec. 1922), which included Eliot's copious and sometimes misleading footnotes. The title page of *New Hampshire* carries the mock-scholarly subtitle "A Poem with Notes and Grace Notes," indicating its tripartite division: the title poem, a section of "Notes" (including fourteen poems, mostly **dramatic monologues** and dialogues), and a final section of "Grace Notes" (featuring thirty shorter **lyrics**). Many items in the title poem are footnoted, and the reader is led to other poems in the "Notes" section that "gloss" these items. For instance, when the title poem mentions "a man who failing as a farmer / Burned down his farmhouse for the fire insurance," we are directed by a footnote to **"The Star-Splitter"** in "Notes," a poem that tells the story of that farmer in greater detail. Unlike Eliot's footnotes, which refer readers to a list of scholarly citations meant to elucidate symbols within the poem but which often obscure them further, Frost's footnotes lead the reader to other poems in the same book, as if to insist that outside knowledge is not necessary to interpret and appreciate the figures that he imagines. Frost thereby announces his text as a self-enclosed intellectual system and invites a wider range of readers than Eliot does.

Frost credits the inception of the long title poem **"New Hampshire,"** which runs to 413 lines, to a series of articles by well-known writers who appeared in 1922 in *The Nation* under the banner "These United States." As Lawrance Thompson reports, Frost believed the articles were primarily fault-finding, explaining what was wrong with commercial enterprise in the states featured, and most likely were written by anticapitalist radicals. Frost declined the invitation of *The Nation* to contribute to the series but began to think about the possibility of a poem that would present a positive image of the (economic) state of New Hampshire. Speaking to a Rotary Club in Ann Arbor, Michigan, in the spring of 1922, Frost first developed the satirical ideas that structure the poem. Using Horace's satirical discourses, the *Sermones*, as a model, Frost composed a long poem that, according to Thompson, "scatter[s] friendly banter through a rhapsody of anecdotes, exempla, dialogue, self-appraisal, self-disparagements, epigrams, and proverbs." By way of such diverse poetic modes he praises the economic self-sufficiency of New Hampshire.

Citing statements by **Emerson** and the Imagist poet **Amy Lowell** (both Massachusetts poets) that call into question the greatness and prosperity of the people of New Hampshire, Frost counters by saying that things could not be better, that, indeed, we could wish the people of New Hampshire worse. Ultimately, he takes aim at the academic elite, offering up a sarcastic characterization of intellectual fads, particularly Freudian psychology. In the title poem, the speaker's discussion with a "New York alec / About the new school of the pseudo-phallic" provokes the retort, "Me for the hills where I don't have to choose." As Frost later explained in a letter, "[T]he crude importunacy of those who would have you a prude or a puke" (and, if not a puke, "disowned by the [politically liberal] intelligentsia") mirrored "the disgusting alternatives" of "collectivist or rugged individualist" in the 1930s. Clearly, the speaker's prejudices and beliefs in "New Hampshire" are Frost's own.

Frost said that he wrote "New Hampshire" in one night, working from dusk until dawn. Instead of going immediately to bed when he had completed the poem, however, Frost was inspired to write another poem, and he claimed to have sat down and composed it in a matter of a few minutes. The second poem, which he included in *New Hampshire*, was **"Stopping by Woods on a Snowy Evening."** In it Frost's speaker meditates on the dangerous allure of the woods at a pause in his commute; rather than succumb to the call, however, he reminds himself of his human obligations and his need to continue home. The poem ends with an incantatory repetition that signifies the struggle of the speaker and the trancelike state into which he falls.

In the "Notes" to "New Hampshire" Frost sets an array of dramatic monologues and dialogues that gloss the contents of the title poem. **"The Census-Taker"** reports his melancholy mood upon confronting a landscape devoid of human activity (a wasteland comparable to Eliot's). Other dramatic monologues include **"Maple,"** a poem about a girl given the name "Maple" by her mother and her attempts to figure out and live up to the significance of that name, and **"Wild Grapes,"** a meditation on the relationship between knowledge and feeling (the head and the heart) by a tomboy pitched into the air by a birch. Frost's dramatic dialogue **"The Ax-Helve"** explores the nature of knowledge and, more surreptitiously, the art of poetry. In the poem, a man and his neighbor, a French Canadian woodchopper, exchange their "doubts / Of laid-on education," and yet any connection between that and the curves of an ax-helve is disclaimed. But Frost is only playing, since he believed that the one has everything to do with the other and with the craft of poetry; as he told a reporter, poetry is "in the ax-handle of a French Canadian woodchopper. . . . You know the Canadian woodchoppers . . . [make their own] axe-handles, following the curve of the grain, and they're strong and beautiful. Art should follow lines in nature, like the grain of an axe-handle. False art puts curves on things that haven't any curves" (qtd. in Thompson).

The section "Grace Notes," a musical term that means notes in a composition that are purely ornamental and do not further the exposition of a theme, features a range of poems that do not bear directly on the contents of *New Hampshire* but fill out the volume with a diversity of forms and themes. In addition to

"Stopping by Woods on a Snowy Evening," several of Frost's most famous poems appear here, including his apocalyptic (and playful) **"Fire and Ice"** and another short lyric (a mere eight lines long), **"Nothing Gold Can Stay,"** about mutability as figured in the change of seasons. **"For Once, Then, Something,"** a rare experiment in "quantitative" meter (each line is eleven syllables long), questions the limits of human knowledge and the possibility of knowing Truth. In **"The Need of Being Versed in Country Things,"** the last poem of the book, Frost represents a scene of desolation similar to the one in "The Census-Taker," this time in order to expose the fiction of the pathetic fallacy, the idea that nature is in sympathy with human loss. As the poem reveals, only humans mourn when a house burns to the ground; the natural world goes on, unmoved by such catastrophe. Working with various poetic meters and tropes, Frost's final grouping of poems "graces" his book in impressively inventive ways.

References and further reading: R. Frost, *Selected Letters*, 466; Thompson, *Triumph*, 77, 230–31, 236–37; Van Egmond, *Reception*, 6; Wagner, 58–59.

Tyler B. Hoffman

NEW HAMPSHIRE STATE NORMAL SCHOOL. *See* **Plymouth Normal School**.

"NIGHT LIGHT, THE." *See* **"Five Nocturnes."**

"NO HOLY WARS FOR THEM," first published in the *Atlantic Monthly* (Apr. 1947), is a political **sonnet** from *Steeple Bush* **(1947),** Frost's first collection of poetry after World War II. Frost utilizes the basic English form and in the first two quatrains outlines the problem: Small nations are incapable of participating in global wars; for them "being good" means "standing by / to watch a war in nominal alliance" and looking on as the larger "winning giants" divide the spoils. In an apostrophe, the speaker asks if God has an opinion about such an inequitable situation. In true modernist form, though, Frost's sonnet offers no answer to its questions but only resignation that "the most the small / Can ever give us is a nuisance brawl."

References and further reading: Barry, 79–98; Rood.

Belinda D. Bruner

NORTH OF BOSTON **(1914),** Frost's second book of verse, is arguably his most significant. Published in London in 1914, barely a year after *A Boy's Will* **(1913),** and appearing in the United States first before the 1913 collection, it brought Frost suddenly into literary prominence, revealing the poetic voice, seemingly so simple and direct, for which he became widely known. Though it contains fewer poems than any other Frost collection, *North of Boston* remains unsurpassed in its overall quality and intensity, including five of the poems widely considered Frost's best—**"Mending Wall," "After Apple-Picking,"**

"The Wood-pile," "Home Burial," and **"The Death of the Hired Man"**—
along with others of genuine depth and subtlety, including **"The Black Cottage," "A Hundred Collars,"** and **"A Servant to Servants."**

Deliberately experimental, *North of Boston* represents, both in substance and style, a clear departure from *A Boy's Will*, with its traditional **lyric** subjectivity, its self-conscious melancholy and wistful longing, and its touches of archaic diction. Most *North of Boston* poems direct us away from the "self" of the poet and into the lives of ordinary working people in Frost's turn-of-the-century New England. Even its more personal lyrics retain the unadorned quality of the narratives, helping to shape the characteristic Frostian voice: unpretentious and shrewd; understated, seemingly objective, but often elusive in tone; in all, apparently simple but in truth quite tricky and complex. In its idiomatic vigor, bringing everyday language with real speaking tones and rhythms into metrical verse, *North of Boston* establishes Frost—along with **T. S. Eliot, Ezra Pound**, and **Wallace Stevens**—as one of the founders of Modernism.

Like *A Boy's Will*, *North of Boston* was published during the three-year sojourn in **England** that Frost saw as his last chance to gain the literary recognition he had not found at home, where magazine editors had accepted only a few of his poems over the preceding decade. He arrived on English soil in September 1912. Within half a year, in March 1913, the London firm of **David Nutt** had brought out *A Boy's Will*; and in May 1914—the year Frost turned forty—Nutt published *North of Boston* (the original edition of which did not include the poem **"Good Hours"**). Through the summer and fall of 1914, the volume was well reviewed, thanks largely to the literary friends Frost had cultivated in England, who were ready to recognize both the importance of his work and the subtleties of his apparently artless style. By the end of 1914, the poems had attracted the attention of the New York publisher **Henry Holt**, who bought the American rights to both Frost volumes. Their publication shortly after Frost's return to the United States in 1915 effectively announced his "arrival" as an American poet.

While *A Boy's Will* was assembled almost wholly of poems that Frost had brought from home, most of the sixteen poems that comprise *North of Boston* were completed in England, many of them in a burst of creative activity during the winter of 1913, when the Frosts occupied a rented cottage called the Bungalow in the London suburb of Beaconsfield. Yet the creative sources for the poems and their "conversational" style can be traced back to the years (1900–1909) when Frost and his growing family occupied a small poultry farm in **Derry**, New Hampshire. While never quite making Frost a farmer, the experience shaped the poet he was determined to become. By involving him deeply in rural life, it immersed him in the cycles of nature and the "country things" that characterize his verse; it lodged in his imagination the New England vernacular that sounds through his mature poetic voice; and it made vivid and real the lives of the women and men who, in wresting a living from the hard climate and poor soil, would find their way into *North of Boston*. Frost's early, tentative

title for the volume was, in fact, *Farm Servants and Other People*. By his own
report he was, as poet, first drawn to "their tones of speech," as Frost wrote in
March 1915. Yet Frost was equally moved by their efforts to preserve life and
dignity against the pressures of geography, poverty, and personal tragedy—
struggles that, in "A Servant to Servants," "The Death of the Hired Man," and
"Home Burial," among other *North of Boston* poems, etch their humanity in the
starkest, most revealing terms.

Drama is the volume's mark of distinction, and *North of Boston* offers drama
in many forms. Most obviously dramatic, perhaps, are the long passages of
dialogue almost unbroken by narration in, for example, **"The Mountain"** and
"A Hundred Collars" or in "Home Burial" and "The Death of the Hired Man,"
both of which have enjoyed success on stage or **film**. Others, such as "A Servant
to Servants" and "The Black Cottage," develop **dramatic monologues** in the
manner of Robert Browning, in which the storyteller implicitly reacts and responds to a silent listener. Essential to drama, of course, is the writer's capacity
to *establish* character through speech, and in the volume Frost's language creates
a series of characters who speak in voices that are no less varied and distinctive
for being consistently real and down-to-earth.

North of Boston develops another form of drama that is philosophically central
to Frost's outlook: the drama of the individual in nature. This is the drama of
mortality: the human confrontation with time and change that reveals that what
we have is passing, that all growth is a movement toward death, and that the
passage of time that brings the spring and harvest must also, finally, bring the
end of life or love. "Nature," Frost has said, "is always more or less cruel" in
its equal readiness to sustain or threaten life, its indifference to human concerns.
And while such "cruelty" is most obvious where husband and wife grieve over
their dead infant in "Home Burial," Frost suggests that such ultimate threats to
life and happiness are subtly present in the most ordinary attritions of time: in
the fog and rain that "rot the best birch fence a man can build" ("Home Burial"),
in the "frozen ground swell" that tumbles down stone walls ("Mending Wall"),
and in the slow decay that returns a cord of maple to the soil from which it
grew ("The Wood-pile"). Such moments, where the fact of mortality is felt in
the most innocent of changes, occur throughout *North of Boston* and show how
the human struggle with nature becomes internalized. This is a central feature
of the lyric poems where Frost's speakers betray some discomfort at nature's
tendency to ignore or even erase the human presence. The internal drama is
perhaps most complex in "After Apple-Picking," where the first frost has ended
the bountiful harvest, where a sense of celebration is mixed with a powerful
fatigue, and where anxiety about survival precludes the dreamless, perfect rest
of hibernation.

The verse form of *North of Boston* confirms its dramatic character, for, excepting **"Blueberries,"** "After Apple-Picking," and "Good Hours," which closes
the volume with tetrameter couplets, it is written in blank verse, the classic
medium of poetic drama. Adopted by Elizabethan playwrights expressly for the

stage and perfected by William Shakespeare, blank verse—iambic pentameter without rhyme—offers the poet a flexible instrument for dramatic purposes, allowing room for the natural rhythms of impassioned speech within the elevation of poetic meter. In writing to Sidney Cox in January 1914, Frost even defined his principle of versification in dramatic terms—as "*breaking* the sounds of sense [the intonations of living speech] with all their irregularity of accent *across* the regular beat of the meter" (emphasis added). Frost's originality in describing what happens in much great poetry is matched by the deliberate way in which he attempted—as he said to **John Bartlett** in July 1913—"to make music out of . . . the sound of sense." (*See* **Poetic Theories.**)

Though blank verse remained a staple of Frost's poetry throughout his long career, its nearly exclusive use in *North of Boston* coincides with his conscious effort to break from the norms for lyric verse that prevailed at the turn of the century. Dominated by the smooth, regular harmonies of nineteenth-century English poets such as Tennyson and Swinburne, these were norms to which *A Boy's Will* largely adheres. As an American, Frost wished to divorce poetry from an aestheticism largely English and upper class, to write a poetry that spoke for Americans in the language that Americans spoke. (One of the fascinating ironies of literary history is that three of the most influential modern efforts to bring the vernacular back into verse—those of Frost, T. S. Eliot, and Ezra Pound—were being carried out almost simultaneously, between 1910 and 1915, by Americans who had transplanted themselves to London.)

Between June 1913 and March 1914, the period when Frost was putting *North of Boston* in final form, he undertook—in conversations with English poets Frank S. Flint and T. E. Hulme and in letters to his American friends, Cox and Bartlett—to define the poetic principles on which the poems were based. Frost's explanatory efforts were in part a dry run for a contemplated preface to his forthcoming book along the lines of Wordsworth's Preface to the *Lyrical Ballads* of 1800. In the end Frost, who disliked writing **prose**, did not write an essay to accompany the poems. But the effort to articulate their underlying principles probably bolstered his own confidence in the verse experiments, seen at this point by few persons outside his immediate circle in England. Such private discussions of poetic theory may also have aided the favorable reception of the book so crucial to Frost's career by supplying a few of its future reviewers with the principles by which they might appreciate his accomplishment. Certainly Frost, who by 1913 considered himself "one of the most notable craftsmen of my time," had reasons to fear that his artistry and achievement might be overlooked. Responses to *A Boy's Will* had already shown him how easy it was for cultivated readers to see little more than the natural utterance of an untutored primitive in his down-to-earth literary style.

The precise role of ordinary speech in *North of Boston*—and in Frost's style generally—remains hard to define because even where the vocabulary is commonplace, Frost combines the most direct, colloquial phrasing with word order that bears the mark of conscious craft. Frost believed that the power of all good writing depended on the writer's ear for "sentence-sounds," patterns of vocal intonation that can determine or even change the meaning of the words themselves. (Irony is but one familiar example.) "No writer invents" such patterns, Frost wrote in 1914 to Cox and Bartlett; they must be caught "fresh from talk" and "entangled somehow in the syntax idiom and meaning of a sentence." But as we can see in "Mending Wall," for example, phrases that carry such sentence-sounds need not follow conversational word order. "Good fences make good neighbors" could pass as real speech; so too: "I could say 'Elves' to him, / But it's not elves exactly, and I'd rather / He said it for himself." But the poem's opening line, repeated later—"*Something there is* that doesn't love a wall"— and the comment about hunters who "have left *not one stone on a stone*" (emphasis added)—capture the force of living language within elegant inversions of syntax rarely found in speech. Whether intuitively or deliberately or both, Frost seemed to know that his poetry drew power precisely from the interaction of low and high, the natural and the contrived.

In Frost's long career, *North of Boston* holds a unique position, defining the moment when the unknown Frost becomes the known and the place where an earlier poetic voice is left behind for the more rigorous lyricism that incorporates drama at almost every level. The volume announces a Frost who would be a force in American poetry, an icon in American culture, for almost five decades. But in its concentration on a disappearing rural New England to which our culture would never return, and in its celebration of ordinary folk in all their extraordinary humanity, it offers a social and moral vision that nothing else in Frost's career would ever quite surpass.

References and further reading: For more about *North of Boston* in relation to Frost's life, see Pritchard, *Literary Life*, and Walsh; both expand and sometimes comment upon Thompson's treatment of the subject in *Early Years*; much is revealed by Frost's correspondence from the period (1912–1915), included in *Selected Letters*, 79, 107, 111, 159; all such works are augmented by Cramer, *Frost among His Poems*; for full-length critical studies, see Poirier, *Knowing*, and Brower; for a view of Frost and *North of Boston* in the context of modern American poetry, see the chapter on Frost in Lentricchia's *Modernist Quartet*; Frost, *Collected*, 970, notes that the early editions of the book carried a note on the page preceding "Mending Wall": "*Mending Wall* takes up the theme where *A Tuft of Flowers* in *A Boy's Will* laid it down."

David Sanders

"NOT ALL THERE" is one of the original "Ten Mills" first published in the April 1936 issue of *Poetry* magazine. In manuscript it bore the title "Don't Anybody Laugh." It was collected in *A Further Range* **(1936)**.

Lawrance Thompson sees "Not All There" as typical of Frost's rhetorical tendency to assume the guise of a strong viewpoint—in this case, atheism— only to subvert and, ultimately, ridicule it. The title's double meaning reinforces the tone of ridicule, Thompson argues, calling this a "bitter and sarcastic" poem equal to **"Provide, Provide."** Robert F. Fleissner, however, likens the shift between stanzas to the **sonnet**'s traditional argumentative shift from octave to sestet. Frost's shift is from "description to explanation, or from implication to explication." The first stanza, Fleissner argues, presents a God distant and unknowable; the second, a God personal and immediate. Richard Eberhart believes "Not All There" "allows the reader to have it both ways, an atheistical negation balanced by a dualistic system which can be read either in terms of God or man." Eberhart adds that in this poem, as in other poems, "the trouble is that Frost does not give God credit for making him what he is."

References and further reading: Cramer, *Frost among His Poems*; Eberhart, "Personality," 780; Fleissner, "Frost's 'Not All There' "; see Thompson in R. Frost, *Selected Letters*, xvi.

Andy Duncan

"NOT OF SCHOOL AGE," originally titled "An Admirer of the Flag" in manuscript, first appeared in the 1942 collection *A Witness Tree*, though it carried a composition date of 1932.

In addition to its patriotic strain, the poem bears witness to Frost's thematic interest in the topic of childhood generally. One has only to think of Frost's first volume *A Boy's Will* (**1913**), the well-known poem **"Birches,"** or the less-well-known **"What Fifty Said"** or **"Questioning Faces"** to realize the persistence of the theme in Frost's poetry. Also, in 1959 Frost published a collection of his poems primarily for young readers—*You Come Too*. It includes "Birches" and "Not of School Age" as well as forty-six other poems he deemed appropriate for young readers—not, however, to the exclusion of adults. The volume is dedicated to his mother with the words: "To Belle Moodie Frost. Who knew as a teacher that no poetry was good for children that wasn't equally good for their elders."

The seven quatrains, rhyming *aaba*, address the disappointment of a preschool boy encountered on the road by a lone traveler, the speaker of the poem, who remarks, "I came to but one house / I made but the one friend." The boy's sadness and the man's loneliness intersect on this especially windy day as they try to communicate, and their mutual condition of poignant expectancy is crystalized by the nearby school's "big flag, the red—white— / And blue flag, the great sight" which the boy cannot go see like the other kids who are of school age.

References and further reading: R. Frost, *You Come Too*.

Douglas M. Tedards

"NOT QUITE SOCIAL," first published in *Saturday Review of Literature* (30 Mar. 1935) and included the next year in *A Further Range* (**1936**), is a somewhat obscure poem, referring to something the speaker has done that "though not forbid / Yet wasn't enjoined and wasn't expected." Mordecai Marcus assumes the reference is to Frost's "flight from society to rural life," but since in 1935 that particular flight was a good many years in the past, it seems safer to read the poem as a description of the speaker's general attitude than to try to identify its relation to some specific act.

The "not quite social" speaker is not quite antisocial either. The poem formulates a middle ground between isolation and community, freedom and commitment, which is one of Frost's characteristic aspirations. The poem describes an individualism that stops short of rebellion, something akin, perhaps, to the "lover's quarrel with the world" that Frost suggests for his epitaph in **"The Lesson for Today."** The speaker breaks the "city's hold" but remains connected to earth and to the people he is addressing, though loosely. The speaker says he willingly accepts the taunts and negative judgments of those who disapprove of his actions (whatever they might be) but insists that he be left alone to live out the consequences. Others may condemn him so long as they leave "it to nature to carry out the sentence."

References and further reading: Marcus, *Explication.*

Todd Lieber

"NOT TO KEEP," a blank verse poem that appears in the collection *New Hampshire* (**1923**), was first published in the *Yale Review* for January 1917. It recounts the high cost of war from the perspective of one left behind, a woman whose sacrifice seems as great as that of the soldier she loves. Understated but ultimately moving, the poem touches on the emotions that accompany a wounded soldier's arrival home: first worry, then relief and even joy, then resignation, the grim knowledge that they will both have it all to do over again. For the irony of the homecoming is that it cannot last; the moment is ephemeral. She has not been rewarded with her lover but asked to give of herself and him once more; as soon as he heals from one bullet he will be free to go take another. The ominous title closes the poem and hints at the finality of the couple's next parting. Elizabeth Shepley Sergeant has written how the verb "to keep" is one Frost "has used with special pathos and poignancy" in his work. Certainly the pathos is effective here.

There is abundant evidence that the poem is one of the earliest to have been inspired by Frost's dear friend and fellow poet Edward Thomas, who fell in World War I. As such, "Not to Keep" can be read productively beside **"To E. T.,"** **"The Road Not Taken,"** **"Iris by Night,"** **"A Soldier,"** and others.

References and further reading: Lehmann; Sergeant, 207; Thompson, *Triumph.*

Scott Earle

"NOTHING GOLD CAN STAY" first appeared in the *Yale Review* (Oct. 1923) and was collected in *New Hampshire* that same year. Though placed in a section titled "Grace Notes," "Nothing Gold" is no mere ornament but a **lyric** of surprising reach and power, displaying, in its eight short lines, Frost's genius for revealing the largest of issues in the smallest of events. Contemplating "Nature's first green," it celebrates the magic of spring's freshness, expressing our longing for perfection in a world of transience. A lament for mutability, "Nothing Gold" becomes a poem about poetry as it invites us to notice the effort and power of language to arrest the changes it records—to hold what in nature is always slipping away.

Beginning with the most subtle of changes in early spring, Frost shows how the exquisite yields to the ordinary, the infinite promise of beginnings giving way to the attritions of time. Not only does Frost connect such changes to Eden, the golden age from which our culture traces its descent; he reenacts that mythic fall from grace by dramatizing, within four rhymed couplets, the coming of change to a world of momentary perfection.

The first two couplets create that world of poised beauty with two metaphoric equations, each followed by a brief qualification. The opening lines create a space that is intimate and stilled, almost paradisal by virtue of what it excludes. For the duration of this extended moment, aided by verbs of being rather than action, things do not happen but simply *are*. And while lines 2 and 4 warn of change to come, they remain grammatically subordinate, for the moment leaving green as *gold* and the leaf *a flower*, holding change at bay.

In lines 5–8, time enters with active verbs. In four swift lines, each with a new image, the world of the poem is set in motion. With "Then" and "So" reinforcing the logic of time, the leaf "subsides," Eden sinks again, and dawn "goes down." Gone suddenly is the special state in which "green" was "gold" and the "leaf" a "flower," and the recognition leads in two swift analogies to "Nothing gold can stay," as if a single alteration has told the story of a world— as of course it does. And as such losses mount, the poem contemplates what is left behind. Looking back to the "gold" of the opening, "Nothing . . . can stay" gives decisive, summary form to those early notes of warning. The discouragement is final: Humanity has lost immortality, and the "grace note" records the fall from grace. James L. Potter finds it "hard to say whether the desire for Eden or the sense that it has gone is stronger." We are homeless, and we long for home.

The expansion in the second two couplets is dramatic. From the world of a single leaf, we enter a world inclusive and vast, reaching beyond the visible horizon and back to the start of history. And with such expansion comes a sense of loss. Though "grief" is mentioned only once, it is reinforced by the verbs of descent and by the final line, the poem's only one-line sentence, which speaks of what cannot be.

The desire to "hold" something back from time, even as one knows it to be impossible, is a central feature of Frost's nature lyrics from *A Boy's Will* (1913) to *Steeple Bush* (1947). Repeatedly, such poems dramatize the difficulty of giving up what is loved and the knowledge that, for all creatures, time and change mean death. To one who knows where time leads, death is present in the most innocent of changes—and present from the start, so that "Nature's first green" is "gold" not only by being treasured and brief but by having autumn within it. To know the meaning of time is not, however, to welcome it, and in Frost such knowledge is often met by reluctance and something of resistance.

"Nothing Gold" expresses this resistance not only in its mention of "grief" and its pervasive elegiac tone but in the drama enacted by the rhythm and sound of each line. The poem's trimeter line is uncommonly short in English verse, and against such brevity, Frost has amassed long vowels and a density of consonants that actually lengthen the time of utterance. For example, in the first line, the massing of "r," "s," and "t" sounds (especially with the double-stress in "first green") combines with the long vowels in "green" and "gold" to slow a line that, like the experience it describes, will end all too soon. In the second line, the alliterative "h's" retard the expelled breath to slow the advancing line and reproduce in the throat the holding effort of heart and mind. Even as change speeds forward in the poem's second half, the series of long vowels in each line not only voices a lament for what passes but holds the note as long as it can.

It is always hard to know how consciously a poet designs such effects when sound is so intuitive a matter, especially for one with an ear as fine as Frost's. More clearly deliberate is Frost's brand of "outdoor fooling," which here combines the poet's metaphoric license with a naturalist's adherence to fact. As it happens, the "gold" of "Nature's first green" is more than an omen of fall or a measure of value. This green is gold not only because it is transitory and precious or even because in trees such as birch it will turn an autumn gold. Frost the botanist would also know that the yellow blossoms of forsythia (sometimes called "the golden bell") emerge well before its tender, chartreuse leaves, which darken into truer green only as spring turns into summer. The figure turns equally literal in the sugar maples native to Frost's New England, whose soft yellow flowers also anticipate their leaves and can cover whole hillsides with their greenish gold. (*See* **Nature Poet and Naturalist**.)

Equally dramatic is the way that even a late draft brings home the artistry of Frost's completed poem. The plurals in the draft—"Her early leaves are flowers; / But only so for hours"—are more botanical and less philosophical than the singular "leaf" and "flower" of the published version, just as they lack the poignancy of that single "hour," with its understated hyperbole. The draft version also makes autumn explicit and climactic:

> Then leaves subside to leaves.
> In autumn she achieves
> A still more gold blaze.
> But nothing golden stays.

Here, fall's "blaze" is offered as something "more" than spring's gold, though doomed to fade. In a way that is subtler and more profound, the revision turns the plot of repeated disappointment into a longer season of disillusion and discontent, transforming Frost's nature poem into one of human nature and time itself. *See also* **"It Is Almost the Year Two Thousand."**

References and further reading: Bagby, *Nature*, 47, discusses "Nothing Gold" as "the structural prototype for Frost's nature lyrics," placing Frost's synechdochic strategy within the American tradition of emblematic nature writing; Mertins, 218, places two drafts of the poem side-by-side; Monteiro, *New England*, 121–22, traces the poem to an imaginative and possibly textual source in **Thoreau**'s *Walden*; Oster, 224–28, offers a revealing look at the poem against its earlier manuscript drafts; Potter, 81; Sanders looks at "Nothing Gold" in the context of Frost's metapoetic lyrics—poems that comment on the poetic act itself.

David Sanders and Nancy Vogel

"NOVEMBER," a poem collected first in *A Witness Tree* **(1942)**, suggests in its last eleven lines that nothing we "keep" is ever really preserved, no matter what our efforts, from the inexorable tendency toward decay symbolized by the season of fall. Ours is a fallen world not subject to any but a "divine" redemption—and that, one gathers, is not forthcoming. "The world's defeat," as Frost puts it in **"The Lost Follower,"** is simply irrevocable. And yet it is somehow "treason" to the "heart of man," this poem maintains with **"Reluctance,"** meekly to give in to dissolution. In fact, poetry is itself a response to decay, however imperfect a stay against confusion it may be. Poetry is where we may find if not the Golden Age then at least something like it. The only grace sustaining this world is the grace of **lyrics** such as "November": One way to "ignore" all the "waste" and "warring," one way strategically to endure it, is to tell ourselves beautiful lies about the keeping of time in poetry. And the last lines of "November" open up still further implications. In **"A Prayer in Spring"** and **"Putting in the Seed,"** human procreative energies are allied with the larger, natural creative energies of spring. "November" completes the idea by associating our destructive energies—"the waste of nations warring"—with the destructive energies of fall and winter. Human "nature" forms a part of such larger natural processes of desolation. There is a little winter, a little of the killing season, in all of us—that is what these poems suggest. Suffering—even when *socially* derived as in war—is simply intractable. Our woes are "immedicable," as Frost puts it in the introduction to **E. A. Robinson**'s *King Jasper. See also* **Nature Poet and Naturalist**.

References and further reading: Bagby, *Nature*; Frost's piece on Robinson's work can be found in R. Frost, *Collected*, 741–48.

Mark Richardson

"NOW CLOSE THE WINDOWS," first published in *A Boy's Will* **(1913)**, begins with a directive aimed at silencing both the wind and the trees. There might possibly be loss of a bird's song, but it seems a necessary price to pay, and anyway, this late in the season the speaker hears no birds and assumes that "It will be long ere the earliest bird." In place of *hearing* the wind, the speaker will see all wind-stirred, thus not closing off his perception of the windy day, merely the sound and the feel of it. More important, he is putting a solid, if transparent, barrier between himself and what is going on outside.

The human-made barrier—the window and the human action of shutting it—
is what not only protects the people inside but allows the speaker to feel in
control of the situation, in this case, nature, autumn, wind, the sound of trees.
Of course, in actuality such elements are totally beyond his control; he cannot
"hush all the fields." The best he can do is shut himself inside where he will
not hear them, where he may thus give himself the illusion of control. What he
can control is what he will allow himself to perceive: the visual effect of the
wind on trees and fields, the picture with the sound turned off.

In this short **lyric**, Frost introduces issues that will surface in several other
tree poems. In **"The Sound of the Trees,"** Frost speaks of bearing and suffering
their noise, ultimately listening to them, being tempted, prodded to "make the
reckless choice" to be gone. Even where he finds affinity between himself and
the tree at his window (*see* **"Tree at My Window"**), where he declares "let
there never be curtain drawn / Between you and me," he has lowered the sash,
kept the tree and its sounds outside but in full view. But regardless of the
presence or absence of trees, it is still the wind he wants to silence and shut
out. Katherine Kearns finds that Frost equates the wind with passion and thus
"a force productive of ambivalence and confusion." Related to this poem, she
finds the wind "brings subversion of control and may awaken the passion that
bruits down the sound of sense."

One answer, then, to fearing loss of control (or fearing an uncontrollable
nature) is to assert control in the best way we can: to close the window, or to
harness the sound to sense, to exert the control of form over chaos, be it by
means of verse or windowpane. We can build houses with walls and doors to
shut ourselves up completely from what threatens to disrupt our equilibrium.
But we can also arrange our perceptions, put in windows, so that we can enjoy
the view without the sound and the cold; or we can decide to open them to
winds that are not threatening, not hostile and cold. "Now Close" is a fall poem,
placed in the "autumnal" section of *A Boy's Will* with such poems as **"Reluctance"** and **"October,"** which point toward our mortality. In the same volume
there is a "spring wind" poem, **"To the Thawing Wind,"** where the speaker
opens the window to creative disruption. Frost often wrote and spoke of the
tension between "wildness" and control, both necessary in creativity. In **"The
Aim Was Song,"** control and measure turn wind into song. In this poem, closing
the window but looking out of it resolves the tension. In other poems too, **"The
Freedom of the Moon"** or **"The Vantage Point,"** for example, the creative act
lies in arranging the way an object can be seen, with the perceiver doing the
moving or turning in order to see different "pictures." The observed object never
changes; what changes the picture is the way the observer deliberately tries out
different stances or angles of vision. In "Now Close," he can decide to use his
sense of sight but not hearing or touch. In this respect, the poem is also about
art: its freedoms, its controls, and the ways it allows us to exert the controlling,
forming principles that not only create beauty but save our sanity, as Frost

implies: "When in doubt there is always form for us to go on with. . . . It is really everybody's sanity to feel it and live by it." The form of the poem, incidentally, bears out its action: In both of the four-line stanzas, three lines of tetrameter are followed by a shorter line, those abrupt closing lines appropriate to the abrupt, probably forceful, closing of the windows.

The draft of the poem was originally titled "In November," appropriate to its autumnal place in the book; the change to "Now Close the Windows" shifts the emphasis from the traditions associated with autumn (with its too-easy set of associations the reader would bring) to other possibilities—richer, more varied, and more original. It is not "a time to cease speaking"—the original gloss—but a time to shut what is not wanted out of hearing, a time, rather, for the artist to speak instead of the wind.

An amusing biographical note is supplied by Thompson: Apparently this was one of the poems Frost submitted in English A at **Harvard** (where he received a B- from Sheffield in English composition), but as it was a lyric he had previously written, it was unacceptable to the instructor. He had written it at **Dartmouth** in the fall of 1892.

References and further reading: R. Frost, "Letter to *The Amherst Student*," *Collected*, 739–40; Kearns, 167; Oster; Thompson, *Early Years*.

Judith Oster

NUTT, DAVID B., was the founder of a small London publishing house that still bore his name when Frost approached it in the fall of 1912 with the manuscript of *A Boy's Will* in hand. Within a year and a half, Nutt had brought out Frost's first two books of poems—*A Boy's Will* in March 1913 and in May 1914 the more ambitious and experimental *North of Boston*, which quickly earned attention on both sides of the Atlantic, including interest from the New York publisher **Henry Holt**. In the fall of 1914, shortly before Frost returned to the United States, Nutt sold Holt the American rights to these and the future volumes held under contract with Frost.

For just such literary recognition, Frost had worked long and hard. Having despaired of finding a publisher at home, he had moved with his family to **England** in the fall of 1912. In publishing Frost's work, Nutt not only ended a decade of frustration and doubt but set in motion a series of events that would soon make Frost the most celebrated poet in America and perhaps worldwide. In more immediate terms, it fed Frost's hope of making his way, and living his life, as a man of letters rather than as a schoolteacher.

Frost had approached the firm of David Nutt at the suggestion of a friend at *T. P.'s Weekly*, a London literary journal. Attracted by Nutt's reputation for literary quality, he soon found that becoming one of their "few but select authors," as Frost put it years later (qtd. by Walsh), entailed some unpleasant surprises. Upon entering their offices, Frost found himself dealing not with David Nutt or his son, M. L. Nutt, who had died two years earlier, but with Mrs. Nutt, the son's widow, who now headed the firm. Responsible for supporting herself and two young children, she turned out to be a demanding negotiator.

Because verse by unknown poets rarely made money, publishers often asked poets to defray the costs of a first book, and Mrs. Nutt may well have done so, for Frost found reason to insist that he "had never stooped to paying to have [his] poems published, and . . . would never do it" (qtd. by Mertins). Although the contract she finally offered Frost asked no advance payment, it proposed to withhold royalties on the first 250 copies sold. Such an arrangement was also common and could be mutually beneficial; for by applying future earnings to the costs of publication, the writer compensated the publisher's risk without paying cash or compromising his integrity. What was unusual and unfair about the contract with Nutt was that it tied Frost to the Nutt firm on the very same terms for his next four books. That he agreed to such extreme conditions is a sign of Frost's eagerness to see his poems in print.

In the end, unforeseen events cut short such unpromising arrangements. Appearing in the spring of 1914; *North of Boston* attracted favorable reviews and, by summer's end, Henry Holt had offered to pay Nutt for the exclusive American rights to Frost's future volumes. In characteristic style, Mrs. Nutt asked payment for the first two volumes as well, writing to Holt in September 1914 that "American publishers ought to . . . help English publishers who have had sufficient daring and intelligence to recognize the talent of one of their countrymen." With something of a name at home, and with World War I threatening to keep him in England with little chance of further publication there, Frost and his family sailed for New York in February 1915, with German submarines prowling the Atlantic. By the end of the war and perhaps as a result, the firm of David Nutt had gone bankrupt and ceased operations.

References and further reading: A discriminating account of Frost's dealings with Nutt is found in Walsh, 38; for a transcription of Frost's account of these events, see Mertins, *Life,* 105–15, 140–43; Thompson, *Early Years,* also describes how Frost's dealings with the American publisher Thomas Mosher were frustrated by his contract with Nutt; R. Frost, *Selected Letters,* 133–34, includes the letters between Mrs. Nutt and Henry Holt.

David Sanders

O

"OBJECTION TO BEING STEPPED ON, THE," first appeared in 1957 as one of Frost's **Christmas poems** with the title "My Objection to Being Stepped On" and was collected in *In the Clearing* **(1962)**. The poem was possibly based on an experience in the life of **Elinor Frost**, who broke her nose by stepping on a rake in 1927. Frost's interest in the dangers of tool use is also present in earlier poems such as **" 'Out, Out—,' " "The Grindstone,"** and **"At Woodward's Gardens,"** as well as in several recorded remarks noting that tools of labor and peace—such as the scythe, ax, and pitchfork—also have been used as weapons of war. Such predilections are recorded by Jeffrey Cramer, but Helen Bacon has also plausibly claimed that one poetic source for Frost's subject is Virgil's *Georgics*, which invests bucolic materials with political significance.

"The Objection to Being Stepped On" is Frost's later revision of this poem, pushing its wit to a more comic end. It aims at the straightforward commonness of its subject by restricting the meter to a choppy, erratic arrangement of five- or six-syllable lines with either two or three accentual stresses. The mixtures of iambs and singsong anapests, along with deliberately clumsy enjambment such as "And I must say it dealt / Me a blow," roughen the poem's metrical sound. The supposedly forgotten "rule" to which the poet alludes is actually a prophesy from Isaiah 2:4: "And he shall judge among the nations, and shall rebuke many people: and they shall beat their swords into plowshares, and their spears into pruninghooks: nation shall not lift up sword against nation, neither shall they learn war anymore." But Frost's rebuttal to any optimism about the benefits of technology is deftly delivered by the slapstick humor of the final couplet. Its slightly slant rhyme is especially effective because the use of two syllables allows the phrase "step on" to itself literally "turn into" a single new word made by a poetic device. For related uses of "weapon," see **"The Bonfire," "The Star-Splitter," "The Flood,"** and **"From Iron"** (subtitled "Tools and Weapons").

References and further reading: Bacon, "Schooling"; Cramer, *Frost among His Poems*; Katz, *Elinor Frost*, 123.

Gary Roberts

"OCTOBER" first appeared in *The Youth's Companion* (3 Oct. 1912) and was later collected in *A Boy's Will* **(1913)**. A reverential poem to a mild October morning, it is written with respect for the month's potential destructive power, although the speaker's tone demonstrates a reluctance to accept the inevitable death of Nature for another season. Reginald Cook points out that Frost admitted to giving the poem consciously a reverential sound by adding the word "mild" to the first line and juxtaposing it with the word "morning," setting up the use of alliteration that complements the prayerlike repetition and parallel structure.

In "October" the speaker prays for the morning's mildness to continue to deceive "Hearts not averse to being beguiled." This willingness to be deceived demonstrates what Roberts French sees as the speaker's yearning to escape the darkness of nature by permitting himself to be deluded by the ephemeral mildness of the season. The plea is for the season to slow the passage of time. In lines 8–13, the repetition of the words "day" and "leaf" shows a desire to retard the repetitive cycle of the seasons that results in the intermittent death of nature.

Frost's use of the conditional also demonstrates nature's potential "dark side." *If* tomorrow's wind is wild, the speaker points out, all the trees will be left bare and the beautiful autumn colors wasted. When his attention shifts from self-concern to "the grapes' sake," we sense an attempt to reason with nature—to make a pragmatic appeal to nature's instinctual sense of self-preservation. However, the pragmatic appeal ultimately proves futile within the context of the poem. Nature is not ruled by reason, for the grapes' leaves are already "burnt with frost," emphasizing the hopelessness inherent in the narrator's prayer. *See also* **Nature Poet and Naturalist**.

References and further reading: C. Brooks, "Nature"; R. Cook, *Living Voice*, 248; R. French, 155.

Alex Ambrozic

"OF THE STONES OF THE PLACE" was first published as "Rich in Stones" in *The Old Farmer's Almanac* in 1942. It was later collected in *A Witness Tree* **(1942)**. The poem embodies Frost's belief in the individual's inherent connection to place. It is addressed to someone, presumably a grandchild, who has moved from an ancestral home and now lives on a farm that is vastly more fertile. Despite the richness of the younger person's new land, the older speaker wants to send a large boulder from his farm to be set up like an "eolith palladium." For Frost the new farm is necessarily incomplete without a reminder of the owner's past, a token of one's history. The stone can, if necessary, be designated by the youth as "The portrait of the soul of my gransir Ira." The boulder is a concrete expression of the addressee's history, for it came from the place from which his family, in particular his grandfather, originated.

References and further reading: Bieganowski, "Sense of Place"; R. Cook, *Dimensions*; Kemp; Lynen, *Pastoral Art*, 86, notes that the use of "Ira" to rhyme with "inquiry" is one of Frost's rare uses of dialect pronunciation.

Derrick Stone

"OLD BARN AT THE BOTTOM OF THE FOGS, THE," first appeared in *A Further Range* (1936) with the subtitle "Class Prejudice Afoot." The theme of this meandering poem in loose iambic pentameter is best described as homelessness. The barn, briefly personified as a lonely child bereft of playmates, functions as a storage outpost for hunters, but as the poem begins, a caretaker is closing it up for the season by placing "prop-locks" (heavy wooden shafts) against the large double doors, which can be secured only from the outside. If a drifter wishes to sleep within, he must betray his presence by leaving the doors open.

The speaker recalls meeting a nameless wanderer who had stayed in the barn and remembered the strange locks. The man delivers a diatribe (mediated in the poem by the speaker's playfully ironic third-person account) against his securely housed "unacquaintances," the rich, who are too culturally myopic to see the old prop-locks as precious artifacts of a disappearing way of life. Punning on the Latin etymon *servare* (to keep or preserve), he laments that the rich may be "conservatives" but "don't know what to save."

In an archaeological fantasia similar to that in **"A Missive Missile,"** the man imagines the locks as honored specimens in some future museum, their wood the last remains of a "vanished race" of New England chestnuts. But the stranger, stubbornly unaware that he is a tramp himself, breaks off the wistful reverie to express a more immediate, mundane concern—namely, that "the cheapest tramp" could devilishly lock him in while he slept.

Despite the wry portrayal of the stranger and his "bitter politics," Frost shares his elegiac regret of the obsolescence that prop-locks represent. By assuming the voice of a laconic New Englander who provides a deadpan empirical coda to the man's rant ("Yes, right I was the locks were props outside"), the poet playfully undercuts the potential pathos of a decaying barn. The poem thus lacks the sad solemnity of **"Directive,"** in which the speaker laments the ruins of "a house that is no more a house."

References and further reading: Cramer, *Frost among His Poems*; on the significance of home and homelessness in Frost's poetry, see Ekins; Kemp, 192–96; Lentricchia, *Modern Poetics*, 59–86, explores Frost's use of enclosures.

Christopher R. Miller

"OLD MAN'S WINTER NIGHT, AN," originally from *Mountain Interval* **(1916)**, concerns senility and incompetence, but it is carried off with virtuoso ease and grace, despite its demanding Miltonic qualities. Drafted in 1906–1907 during the **Derry** years and often regarded by Frost himself as the best piece in the 1916 collection, the poem predates **Eliot**'s masterpiece "Gerontion" by more than a decade, revealing Frost's complete engagement in the philosophical and aesthetic concerns of modern poetry with the tension between the dark outer world and the staying power, if momentary, of imagination and artistic form.

Such tension, fully modernist in character, is disclosed at the poem's end, where the old man's "incompetence" is made general: the implication is that *no man*, not just the old one described here, can "keep" a house, a farm, or a countryside. After all, the outer night "shades off into black and utter chaos," to borrow Frost's words in the "Letter to *The Amherst Student*." Similarly, the human presence within the house is as disconcerting and given to empty solitude, "like beating in a box." The shifting log and the sleeping man are disturbingly analogous. At best, Frost suggests, we can hope only for some small "man-made" concentration of order to set against inner and outer dark as a "stay": This is what keeps us, what holds us, however temporarily.

And the *form* of "An Old Man's Winter Night" is exactly such a man-made concentration of order. One response to "the outer night," the poem implies, is simply to make *form*—the only kind of form we really can manage or "keep": art. And any "keeping" done here is the "keeping" of poetry—the "keeping" of a beautifully managed lyric. Our attentions are directed away from the befuddled old man and toward the shape Frost gives to the poem that describes the aged, sleeping man: a graceful, perfectly managed stretch of blank verse. The poem's artfulness absorbs our attentions as much as the incapacities of the man. We hear Frost's quiet, deft metrics working within and across the iambic pentameter lines, not the clumsy "clomping" of the old man. In lines 18–23, metrical variations lend lightness of movement to lines whose grammatical and syntactical complexity might otherwise embarrass us. Frost manages the suspended grammar delicately and with a colloquial indirection that sorts well, though unusually, with the Miltonic subtleties. *See also* **Nature Poet and Naturalist**.

References and further reading: Greiner, "Factual Men"; Lynen, *Pastoral Art*; Oster; Pritchard, *Literary Life*.

Mark Richardson

"ON A BIRD SINGING IN ITS SLEEP," from *A Further Range* (1936), was first printed in *Scribner's Magazine* (Dec. 1934). The **sonnet** is ostensibly a conventional expression of the sovereignty of nature, but instead of using standard sonnet structures, Frost employs couplets successively throughout the poem.

Echoing Wordsworth's "devotion to the intimacies of earth," as **Louis Untermeyer** points out generally about Frost's trust in the arrangements of nature, the speaker at first sees the night singing as an aberration, even a danger to the bird, but later concedes that nature's parameters are wide in scope and capable of containing many behaviors without being overset.

A darker subtext emerges, however, when the poem is scrutinized more closely. Irving Howe observes that beneath Frost's obvious concern with nature is an awareness of the "hardness and recalcitrance of the natural world" (qtd. in Waggoner). The uneasy undertone of the final six lines sounds less like an accolade to nature's attention to detail and more like a covert plea for mercy from an insensate universe. *See also* **Nature Poet and Naturalist.**

References and further reading: Untermeyer, 181; Waggoner, *American Poets*, 294.

Lynn Barrett

"ON A TREE FALLEN ACROSS THE ROAD" was first published in *Farm and Fireside* (Oct. 1921) and included in *New Hampshire* **(1923)** with the subtitle "To hear us talk." The fallen tree is a barrier that causes reflection, much like the obstacles in **"Mending Wall"** and **"Two Look at Two."** The road suggests life's journey, as it does in **"The Road Not Taken."** Even the final image of grasping the earth anticipates **"Our Hold on the Planet."** The **sonnet** is a good example of Frost's intertextuality, of his tendency to evoke and play off his other works. Eben Bass says that the poem's optimistic vision ends with "determination, even certainty, that man will meet and overcome obstacles." He notes, however, that the poem's subtitle undercuts some of this confidence. George Nitchie faults Frost for failing to clarify the final goal and for concluding with an equivocal affirmation. Frost himself valued the poem enough to use it as his 1949 **Christmas poem** to friends and associates.

References and further reading: Bass, 83; Nitchie, 149–50; Sergeant, xv–xvi.

Christopher Krentz

"ON BEING CHOSEN POET OF VERMONT" is an occasional poem that first appeared without a title in news releases announcing Frost's selection as Poet Laureate of Vermont on 22 July 1961. Collected in *In the Clearing* **(1962),** the poem—a one-sentence question in four lines—is a parody of the situation of the prophet without honor in his own country. Understated, but not without pride, the implicit gratitude of the honoree is whispered rather than shouted, the exclamation point eschewed for the rhetorical question. Mordecai Marcus notes the parody of Sir Walter Scott's "Lay of the Last Minstrel," specifically the lines "Breathes there a man with soul so dead / who never to himself has said: This is my own my native land."

References and further reading: Marcus, *Explication*, 228; Pritchard, *Literary Life*, 251–52.

Roland H. Lyford

"ON BEING IDOLIZED," first published in *Steeple Bush* **(1947),** follows another small poem describing a single discrete incident, **"A Rogers Group,"** the title referring to the work of popular American sculptor John Rogers, who often constructed statues of family groupings. "On Being Idolized" invites us, likewise, to imagine the speaker in a statuesque pose on the beach, standing motionless, perhaps to be admired or simply in egotistical self-satisfaction, until a retreating wave tosses debris (seaweed) around his legs and sucks the sand from underneath his feet, forcing him to totter. He must give up his statuesque pose, or he will suffer the fate of all "idols" and be "tipped over / Like the ideal of some mistaken lover."

Demonstrating Frost's talent at managing sounds and rhythm, the poem consists of a quatrain followed by a couplet, but grammatically it is a single sentence that turns or changes direction in the third line. Rhythmically, through irregular iambic lines and unaccented leftover syllables, Frost makes the poem reflect the power and speed of the wave upsetting his balance. Likewise, the dominant sounds are the alliterative *w* and *s* sounds that culminate in the "swift rush."

References and further reading: Two early studies of Frost's prosody are Newdick, "Frost and Sound of Sense," and Willige.

Todd Lieber

"ON GOING UNNOTICED" first appeared as "Unnoticed" in the *Saturday Review of Literature* (28 Mar. 1925) and was subsequently collected in *West-Running Brook* (1928). An author's note places its composition in 1901, but Frost had written an earlier version of parts of the poem, entitled "Nature's Neglect," as early as 1895. It is a sixteen-line poem consisting of four quatrains, each made up of a pair of rhyming couplets. **Louis Untermeyer** uses the poem as an example of the intuitive genius of a young Frost. The poem itself places humankind in the realm of nature, where nature finds for a human being some place of relative standing. Staring at the seemingly unattainable leaves of a tall tree, the figure in the poem seeks a tenuous hold. "You grasp the bark by a rugged pleat," Frost wryly observes. Indeed, the weight of the poem emphasizes the dominance of the natural world. After all, humankind can depend upon little more than the ability to "look up small from the forest's feet." The distant leaves remain unattainable, save for a single specimen discarded by the tree itself. Tellingly, the leaf falls away; humanity will not be master here. The implied lesson is that because of our apparent dissatisfaction, we have less standing than the seemingly content coral-root, an orchid with flowers but no leaves. The woods do not miss the flower subsequently taken by the human intruder. But the suggestion is that the keepsake of the orchid should encourage us to be content with a more modest lot within the natural world.

References and further reading: Bagby, *Nature*; Cramer, *Frost among His Poems*, 88–89; Untermeyer, 181.

Craig Monk

"ON LOOKING UP BY CHANCE AT THE CONSTELLATIONS" is a sixteen-line poem first published in *West-Running Brook* (1928). Frost uses his preoccupation with stargazing and speculating about stars as the occasion for asserting a patient stoicism toward nature and even human society. Life is dynamic, the speaker realizes, but the pace of change—both in the heavens and on earth—is so slow as to be of little consequence to the individual. Dramatic change is certain for eternity but improbable in "particular time and personal sight." Individuals can observe the clouds floating in the sky and the "tingling" of Northern Lights, but they should not expect important events such as crashing intersections of sun and moon or stars to occur while they are watching. Therefore, "We may as well go patiently on with our life." Life's "shocks and changes" must be found elsewhere.

For all the reasoned stoicism of the poem, the title suggests a "chance" observation, and its reference to "constellations" recalls a dynamic, mythopoetic view of the heavens that conflicts with the "nothing ever happens" perspective argued by the poet. The rhyme scheme of the poem is similarly conflicting. It evolves gradually from the *abcabc* of the first lines to *dedffe* of the center to a pair of couplets at the end. Perhaps the safer couplet rhymes reflect the narrowed expectations of the stoic vision.

Some critics regard Frost's shift from the beauty of the constellations to the futility of looking to the heavens as indicative of Frost's growing sense of doom and loneliness, but an alternate view would appreciate Frost's unflinching acceptance of universal design, whatever that design, so hinted at in constellations of stars, might be. *See also* **Nature Poet and Naturalist**.

References and further reading: Nitchie; Potter.

Douglas Watson and Chris-Anne Stumpf

"ON MAKING CERTAIN ANYTHING HAS HAPPENED." *See* **"Five Nocturnes."**

"ON OUR SYMPATHY WITH THE UNDER DOG," only four lines long, first appeared in *A Witness Tree* (1942). Jeffrey S. Cramer records that it was originally entitled "On the Difficulty of Keeping Up in Sympathy." Frost plays on the term *under dog* and its opposite, *top dog*, by depicting life as "a circus of revolving dogs," an emblem of changing positions in the "dog-eat-dog" world. We sympathize with the under dog, Frost implies, because the dog that is down today may be up tomorrow. Politicians (symbolized as a Roman senator) remain inactive because they fear offending and being "bitten" by such a change in the balance of power.

References and further reading: Cramer, *Frost among His Poems*, 140; Marcus, *Explication*, 182, reads the poem as a gentle satire on politicians.

Christian L. Pyle

"ON TAKING FROM THE TOP TO BROADEN THE BASE" appeared originally in *A Further Range* (1936), a book that is, as James L. Potter suggests, full of social and political significances. "On Taking from the Top" can be read as a depression-era comment on the destructiveness of any kind of social engineering that uses artificial means to bring about social leveling. The poem may also be read as a satire of those who underestimate the power of nature. In the poem, an avalanche of mud buries a family who thinks the particular old mountain mentioned in the poem has exhausted its destructive potential. Since Frost viewed social engineering, in some sense, as man's presumption to control essentially natural processes, the two readings of the poem are complementary. George Bagby places this poem in the context of "Frost's quasi-geological poems" in which the poet laughs ominously at the "complacently anthropocentric perspective" of human efforts to defy nature. *See also* **Politics**.

References and further reading: Bagby, *Nature*, 16; Potter.

Todd Lieber

"ON THE HEART'S BEGINNING TO CLOUD THE MIND" was first published in *Scribner's Magazine* (Apr. 1934) with the subtitle "From Sight to Insight," and it was later collected in *A Further Range* **(1936)**. In the poem, Frost explores one of his dominant concerns—the literal and figurative distances that exist among people. As in the earlier, related poem **"The Vantage Point,"** "On the Heart's Beginning" derives much of its context and tension from the location in which the poet situates himself. The speaker's vantage is a berth on a train, which effectively distances him from the world outside and demands an act of imagination to bridge the gap that his isolation creates. The process combines, for Frank Lentricchia, the two dominant theoretical strains—romanticism and realism—of Frost's aesthetic vision.

The tenuous nature of the imaginative relationship to the outside world, however, is immediately revealed through the initial qualification of the speaker's observations. As in many of Frost's poems, the equivocation is central to his vision of an intrinsically mutable world. As Lewis Miller notes, Frost assumes a shifting truth; to remain fixed in a perpetually changing universe is to "hibernate." The latter notion serves, in part, to explain the pessimism of the speaker's first interpretation of the flickering light. He envisions people huddled about a light in a "pathetic" effort to stave off their despair, yet the despair is predicated upon the mute acceptance of their situation as final. The speaker senses his heart's response to such an imagined vision and reacts by rejecting its closure, literally choosing an alternative and more hopeful explanation for the flickering of the light.

Frost's epistemological rejection of stasis, dramatized in this poem, forces an active role upon readers: Once the apparent meaning of the poem has shifted and redefined itself, readers are consequently forced to interpret and judge the speaker's interpretive acts, thereby taking part in the speaker's rejection of closure. The tactic is central to Frost's aesthetic design, which is, according to Rexford Stamper, akin to imagist or symbolist aims. The reader, upon judging the speaker's imaginative recreations of the external world, must simultaneously interpret the same scene, a process that mediates among the various possibilities of meaning. Through such a process, the reader ideally uncovers the imbedded idea of the poem. Thus, "On the Heart's Beginning" offers insight into the functioning of the interpretive, metaphor-making imagination and links Frost's achievement to contemporary theories about language development and the role of tropes in thought.

References and further reading: R. Cook, *Living Voice*, 279; Lentricchia, "Frost and Theory"; Miller, "William James"; Parini, *A Life*, 273–75; Stamper.

Gavin Schulz

"ONCE BY THE PACIFIC" appeared originally in the *New Republic* (29 Dec. 1926) and later in *West-Running Brook* **(1928)**. An underrated, darkly toned **sonnet**, "Once by the Pacific" deserves a place among Frost's "terrifying" poems along with **"Desert Places"** and the two poems that Lionel Trilling—and before him, Randall Jarrell—had singled out as representative of the darker Frost: **"Design"** and **"Neither Out Far Nor in Deep."**

"Once by the Pacific" should also be known as one of the most serious of his personal poems, based on an early, genuinely traumatic event that could unnerve him even years afterwards, leaving a permanent imprint of storm fear. Every so often at his readings of this poem, Frost would discuss his recurring fear of being alone on the beach when his father would leave him there while taking his long-distance swims out into the ocean, disappearing in the waves and then, to his small son's relief, reappearing and returning safely to shore. The climax of his fear of abandonment to the terrors of the sea occurred at the Cliff House, a popular dining spot above a San Francisco ocean beach when, while on a beach walk with his father and mother, he was left behind and found himself alone to face a sudden and terrible storm coming toward land from the darkening sea. It was years later that he wrote this poem about an event that still could "terrorize" him.

Frost clearly intends to depersonalize his angst by universalizing his fear into a destructive threat against anything and everything human or natural that water could threaten. To his imagination the terrifying rush of water not only could be destructive but, perhaps, could even destroy the continent and terminate life itself. When divulging the origins of the poem, Frost, with assumed modesty, was inclined to tease that "Once by the Pacific" seemed to some readers prophetic of later, massive twentieth-century destruction, though actually it was based on a private incident "before both wars." William Pritchard is probably right: In this and in other dark lyrics in *West-Running Brook*, Frost tries not just to face but to transform personal fears into more permanent "states of the soul" rather than leave them as "the gloomy musings of an aging man." It is not just Frost who should feel storm fear but anyone and everyone who might happen to be in its path. His warning is generic rather than personal: "Someone had better be prepared for rage."

Frost achieves his transformation of a personal fear, primarily by doing something rare for him, employing personification, injecting malevolent qualities into the natural world and altering nature's characteristic indifference by suggesting that such show of destructive power may signify malevolence. There is even a kind of dark humor to the poem. For example, there is the setting: The terror occurs just "once" by the ocean that is ironically named the "Pacific." "Once" is often used as an introduction of something fictional, purely imaginative, a child's fairy tale beginning "Once upon a time." "Once" can also suggest an event so cataclysmic that it need strike only once. The tone suggests warnings given as if pronouncements to frighten children. If this poem is a prophecy of doomsday, it is not announced in the voice of Jehovah speaking loftily; instead the growing force of the storm is expressed almost conversationally, even in the vernacular with the outcome a matter of "luck" rather than destiny.

The destruction is expressed in terms of shattering, breaking. The terror emanates not just from the destructive force of the sea's assault, its shattering of things in its path, but from the thought that it may be premeditated. It is the word *thought* that invokes the terror, and the thought is not just of intent but of something so destructive that it is far beyond normal thought.

The speaker also does not know exactly to what or to whom the destruction may be done. It is "something" to be done to "someone" or "something." In the poem, "it looked as if / . . . a night of dark intent / Was coming," and it may be on a spatial and temporal scale almost beyond human belief. The intensity of the threat increases as Frost alludes to the titanic metaphysical question of God's responsibility for evil: Is the creator who commanded "Let there be light" also the destroyer? Frost can provide only a human analogy, Othello's fateful command with its terrible double entendre: Othello will put out the light and then, in the darkness, put out the light of his life by murdering Desdemona. The threat of what might happen in the dark is inferred. A personal fear has become a more universal human fear. Frost always gave this poem one of his dramatic readings. It seemed to have a cathartic effect; on some occasions he was so pleased he would repeat his reading, say it twice, as one would to exorcise a spell.

References and further reading: R. Cook, *Living Voice*; Mertins, *Life*; Poirier, *Knowing*; Pritchard, *Literary Life*, 190; Thompson, *Early Years* and *Triumph*.

Richard J. Calhoun

"ONE GUESS" first appeared in *A Further Range* (1936) as part of a collection of poems entitled "Ten Mills," although it was not one of the original "Ten Mills" that appeared in *Poetry* (Apr. 1936). Jeffrey S. Cramer notes that the poem was probably written around 1911 as "A Riddle—Who Is Intended." Mordecai Marcus asserts that the answer to the riddle in this three-line playful verse is the grasshopper, but if we hear sarcasm in the phrase "one guess"—as if to suggest that the answer to the riddle is very obvious—and if there is any significance in the "who" in the aborted title, Frost might also be describing, in comic terms, the poet. The "dust in his eyes" would then suggest the poet's vision, perhaps clouded by romantic delusions or limited simply by the dust of his mortality. The poet may wish to fly but, like the grasshopper, is instead reduced largely to hopping in mock flight. That poetry offers but a "momentary stay against confusion" is underscored humorously by the comparison of the poet to the grasshopper who has no stinger but who has, instead, a "mouthful of dye stuff."

References and further reading: Cramer, *Frost among His Poems*; Marcus, *Explication.*

Nancy Lewis Tuten

"ONE MORE BREVITY," written in couplets of somewhat irregular four-stress lines, was first published in booklet form as Frost's 1953 **Christmas poem** and later became part of *In the Clearing* **(1962)**. It tells of a brief encounter with a dog and of the poet's reflection on the experience. Typically, Frost moves from lighthearted description of the event to more serious reflection on its possible meaning.

Preparing for sleep, the poet opens his door, ostensibly to look out at Sirius, the dog-star. A strange "earthly dog" enters and settles itself on the floor. The poet, "so dog-preferred," offers water and food to his visitor, but when the dog responds indifferently, the poet excuses it and goes to sleep. In the morning, when the dog is let out, it goes quietly on its way, leaving the poet to wonder about the meaning or even the reality of the visitation. He supposes that the event may have been a dream or that the dog may have been Sirius himself, "an avatar / Who had made an overnight descent."

The visitation and the poet's puzzlement present a simple device for confessing the ambiguity of experience in general, but the Christmas occasion of the poem's first publication adds a religious dimension to the "brevity" of the encounter. Such a heavenly visitation as the poet supposes remains beyond explanation or interpretation, perhaps due to insufficiency of language, perhaps due to an indisposition to speech, just as when the first star-associated visitation marked the first Christmas event.

Though the contrast of Sirius (dog-star) and "earthly dog" may offer a natural occasion for a star-obsessed poet like Frost to philosophize, it seems reasonable to suppose that the poem owes something to the memory of the poet's own beloved border collie, Gillie, who, as Thompson and Winnick record, was with Frost from 1940 to 1949.

References and further reading: Poirier, *Knowing*, 312; Thompson and Winnick, 204.

Douglas Watson

"ONE STEP BACKWARD TAKEN," first published in *The Book Collector's Packet* (Jan. 1946) and later included in *Steeple Bush* **(1947)**, describes a speaker's reaction to the immediate threat of a "universal crisis," a torrent of mud, dirt, and water washing down a gully and threatening the speaker's "stand-point" so much that he is forced to take a step backward in order to avoid being swept away. What is threatened is not just the physical ground but also his psychological stability. After stepping back the speaker watches while a "world torn loose went by." Stepping back allows the speaker to feel safe again, but the critical question of the poem is whether stepping back signifies a more deep-seated fear.

Elizabeth Shepley Sergeant relates Frost's account of the origins of the poem in an episode in which Frost witnessed a near catastrophe when a car crossing a bridge in Arizona was nearly swept away by flooding waters; the event af-fected Frost personally. Before finally titling "One Step," Frost considered call-ing it "I Felt My Standpoint Shaken." The intrusion and emphasis of the "I" into what seems mostly a descriptive piece reveal that the "crisis" from which the speaker steps back is at least as personal as it is physical.

The speaker's resistance to the threat of chaos is not unexpected; it is almost requisite in the twentieth century. But the person who resists impulsively will end up resisting everything and will never develop. Also, Frost knows that any such acts of order against confusion are momentary at best. Perhaps such am-biguity is what fuels the subtle ironic humor of the poem captured by the whim-sical rhymes and meter, comic imagery, and overly sunny ending.

References and further reading: Nitchie; Parini, *A Life*, 360–61; Sergeant, 381; Wake-field, *Opposing Lights*, 212–13.

Derrick Stone

"ONSET, THE," which first appeared in the *Yale Review* (Jan. 1921) and was collected in **New Hampshire (1923)**, elicits two different but popular readings. Both views recognize the narrator's fear of the darkness of the wood and the evil hiss of snow as it enshrouds the forest in its white winter mantle; both see his terror as he almost stumbles "As one who overtaken by the end / Gives up his errand, and lets death descend / Upon him where he is," looking furtively here and there, fearing perhaps a confrontation with the author of evil against whom he has been unable to win any significant battles.

The difference in the two interpretations lies in the second half of the poem. Lentricchia and Pritchard acknowledge the dark opening of the poem but see the hiss of evil melt away with the onset of spring. They see it as a positive stanza, spoken almost in relief. Line 12, "Yet all the precedent is on my side," is seen as a sudden retreat away from the fear generated by the first stanza toward the life-giving cycle of the seasons. The hiss of winter snow is trans-formed into gentle spring rivulets of water. The "clump of houses with a church" at the end of the poem is safe and comfortable.

Variations of the second interpretation, expressed by such critics as Carmi-chael and Marcus, hear sound overwhelming meaning. Snow and whiteness contain within them both the eventuality of death and innocence. In this interpretation, the sudden repetition of the "s" following "the peeper's silver croak" becomes almost deafening in lines 18–21. Here the hissing is merely transformed, but it is nevertheless winding its serpentine way "all . . . down hill" toward an unsuspecting "clump of houses with a church." Lines 12–16 become a kind of whistling in the dark, soon confirmed by the reality that evil is with us all year around.

References and further reading: Carmichael, 156; Lentricchia, *Modern Poetics*, 94; Marcus, *Explication*; Pritchard, *Knowing*, 162.

Wm. Thomas Hill

"OUR DOOM TO BLOOM" first appeared as "Doom to Bloom" and was Frost's 1950 **Christmas poem**. Three months earlier, entitled "Doomed to Bloom," it was sent by Frost with a letter to friends Louis Henry and Marguerite Cohn. It was collected in Frost's last book *In the Clearing* (1962) with an epigraph by Robinson Jeffers: "Shine, perishing republic." Thompson and Winnick write that the poem's "title referred to the inevitable proliferation of the welfare state."

The poem surely takes its impetus from Wordsworth's profoundly hopeful description of pre-Revolutionary France as "promise—that which sets . . . The budding rose above the rose full blown" (Prelude XI, ll. 118–21). In Frost's poem we as a country are well past the revolutionary phase and "doomed" to fade: "The bud must bloom till blowsy blown." Frost's epigraph by Jeffers, who saw man as a mere doomed animal, adds to the disillusioned perspective. Yet the poem is not without humor, as its two puns indicate: "trade on" in line 3 means both "barter" and "believe"; and the key line of the poem, "The state's one function is to give," plays with "give" as "dole out," "yield," and "undergo change." The poem was written by a master rhetorician. It is a single stanza comprised of eight iambic tetrameter couplets in which Frost relies on classical allusion for authority, apostrophe and a question-and-answer format for dramatic effect, puns and internal rhyme ("coats, oats, votes") for self-deflating humor. The poem begins as its speaker addresses the Cumaean Sibyl (a prophetess consulted by Aeneas before his descent into Hades), asking her, "What are the simple facts of Progress?" The remaining twelve lines consist of the speaker's quoting the Sibyl's response to his question.

References and further reading: Cramer, *Frost among His Poems*, 173, records that the epigraph is the title and twelfth line of a Jeffers poem published in the *Roan Stallion, Tamar, and Other Poems* (New York: Boni and Liveright, 1925); R. Frost, *Collected*, 578, and *Selected Letters*, 421, 546; Thompson and Winnick, 204.

Jacqueline B. McCurry

"OUR HOLD ON THE PLANET" originally appeared in booklet form as Frost's **Christmas poem** in 1940. It later appeared in the *Virginia Quarterly Review* (Spring 1942) and was collected in *A Witness Tree* (1942). Jeffrey S.

Cramer notes that the title of the manuscript version was "A Fraction of One Percent." The poem concerns nature's apparent frequent opposition to humankind and is a cautious but positive reply to the question of the preponderance of evil in the world. Thompson strongly suggests the influence of John Burroughs's *Accepting the Universe* (1920) on the theme of the poem: "Some power other than ourselves . . . is more positive than negative, more for us than against us, else we should not be here." At the groundbreaking ceremony of the Robert Frost Library at **Amherst College** on 26 October 1963, President Kennedy concluded his speech with lines from the poem: "Because of Mr. Frost's life and work . . . our hold on this planet has increased." *See also* **Nature Poet and Naturalist**.

References and further reading: Cramer, *Frost among His Poems*, 133; Thompson, *Triumph*, 679; Thompson and Winnick, 350.

Eric Leuschner

"OUR SINGING STRENGTH" first appeared in the *New Republic* (2 May 1923) and was placed near the end of *New Hampshire* **(1923)**. "Our Singing Strength" displays a delightfully observant description of a late spring snow, wisdom in the lessons the individual may gain from some humble birds, and a solitary moment of contemplation amidst nature's unpredictable demands.

In iambic pentameter, featuring primarily couplets, these lines exhibit Frost's desire to capture authentic conversational tones in verse. Important for their naturalness and their authenticity, as well, are the images. The late snow is at first too light to cover the ground, but as the earth cools overnight, the land, except for the warmer road, turns white. The birds, exhausted from their migrations northward and confused by the late snow, rest in the path. So numerous are the birds gathered there that as the speaker walks through, they tiredly flutter out of his way: "The road became a channel running flocks / Of glossy birds like ripples over rocks." Despite this setback, however, the birds resolutely wait for spring's wildflowers.

Frost tells an interviewer that the late spring, as the "backbone of winter breaks," especially appeals to him. "Our Singing Strength" nicely articulates this fragile transition, confirming nature's command and her ultimate wisdom. *See also* **Conversationalist** and **Nature Poet and Naturalist**.

References and further reading: Bagby, *Nature*; R. Frost, "The Figure a Poem Makes," in *Collected*, and *Interviews*, 33.

Sharon Felton

" 'OUT, OUT—' " was first published in *McClure's Magazine* (July 1916) and collected in *Mountain Interval* **(1916)**. A poem Robert Frost refused to read aloud in public because of its brutal rendering of a young boy mutilated by a chain saw, " 'Out, Out—' " is based on an actual incident that occurred in

Bethlehem, New Hampshire, in March 1910. Frost did not write the poem until 1915. It concerns a sixteen-year-old boy, Raymond Fitzgerald, whom Frost and his children had met during summer visits to Bethlehem and whose hand was nearly severed by a power saw while he was cutting up stove wood in the door yard of his farmhouse. Fitzgerald died quickly from the effects of shock. The poem's title, borrowed from Macbeth's anguished soliloquy over the death of his wife, keys the tragedy of the boy's life snuffed out so early and so senselessly to Macbeth's pained realization that life is like a candle flame—"Out, out, brief candle!"—and can be extinguished in an instant. The entire thrust of " 'Out, Out—' " seeks ways to mitigate such a tragedy. The poem exhausts itself, ambiguously and almost too callously, without arriving at a satisfactory answer.

" 'Out, Out—' " is written in blank verse, in an almost journalistic narrative style. Dorothy Judd Hall suggests that terrible tragedy depicted in Frost's poetry "is held in check by the discipline of artistic form." The only first-person intrusion into the matter-of-fact chronicle of the events of that tragic day occurs in the tenth line, before the boy "must have given the hand" to the saw, as Frost later puts it. A wish or a plea to replay or reimagine events in a different way—if only the boy had been given permission to knock off work earlier—injects a typically human response to a senseless tragedy into the otherwise inexorable and strangely understated march of events leading to the boy's death. Nonetheless, no matter how much the speaker empathizes with the boy's desire for a precious half hour, the saw snarls its ominous threat and, in a touch of cruel irony, leaps to take the boy's hand at the moment his sister yells, "Supper." "The animation of the saw," notes Mordecai Marcus, "is strangely blended with the human desire for supper, and its seeming leap implies a vicious motivation." Frost writes, however, that neither the saw nor the boy's hand "refused the meeting." The boy's first reaction is to utter "a rueful laugh." Could it be that Frost's diction and tone serve to paint a softer and gentler scene than that rendered by any reader's imagination at this crucial point in the poem?

Whatever Frost's intention, the boy quickly comes to a fateful and fatal consciousness of his dreadful predicament: "He saw all spoiled." The boy realizes that without a hand he cannot have a manhood, live as a complete man, or live a complete life in the masculine ethos of New England farm life. The doctor arrives and puts the young man into "the dark of ether." Soon, as onlookers watch helplessly and incredulously, the boy's breathing becomes labored. His pulse weakens. "They listened at his heart. / Little—and less—nothing!—and that ended it." The poem ends with a pair of lines that intrigue and infuriate: "No more to build on there. And they, since they / Were not the one dead, turned to their affairs."

Marie Borroff allows the subtle ironies that play throughout the poem—the sweet scent of the sawdust, for example, juxtaposed against the anxious and sinister snarling of the saw—to carry through to the end. In a world dominated by adults who hold to such a rigid, even fanatical, work ethic, refusing the boy that spare half hour that would have meant so much, the speaker, "far from indicating approval of 'their' stoical acceptance of bereavement, dismisses them with contempt as they turn to their 'affairs' " at the close of the poem.

James Potter contends with the "severely understated ending" by accepting it exactly on its own terms without recasting the lines into an ironic editorial on Frost's part. "[O]ne point of this conclusion," he states, "is that it tries to mitigate the tragedy . . . by accepting its inevitability and underplaying it." The last two lines, Potter maintains, "sound cold-blooded and antipoetic, yet acknowledge the pathos indirectly." Like Potter, Philip Gerber comes down on the side of the "gathered witnesses" who "have already mastered the difficult art of allowing what will be to be." The stoic acceptance of the survivors may be, then, a higher moral response to the senseless accident than a paralytic grief, although one may find too little consolation or compassion in either reaction. "If accused of cruelty," Gerber reminds us, "the survivors might answer with the old woman in [Frost's poem] **'A Servant to Servants'**: 'By good rights I ought not to have so much / Put on me, but there seems no other way.' "

In any event, " 'Out, Out—' " is a poem about human vulnerability and the resources one must muster to manage misfortune. Like Silas in Frost's **"The Death of the Hired Man"** or the aged farmer in **"An Old Man's Winter Night,"** the young boy in the poem and on the farm in Bethlehem occasion for Frost a familiar meditation on what it takes to endure in the face of suffering. *See also* **Nature Poet and Naturalist** and **Pastoral Poetry**.

References and further reading: Borroff "Simplicity," 76; Gerber, *Frost*, 142; D. J. Hall, *Contours*, 7; Marcus, *Explication*, 79; Potter, 60, 76; Thompson, *Early Years*, 567, relates the story of Raymond Fitzgerald.

David D. Cooper

"OVEN BIRD, THE," first published in *Mountain Interval* (1916), exemplifies Frost's adaptations of traditional **sonnet** form and his figurative use of natural fact. The poem takes its title from a warbler found in mature American woodlands where, in the sparse undergrowth, it can build its unusual ground-nest resembling a "miniature Dutch oven." More central to the poem, however, is the ovenbird's primary "song," which it broadcasts late into summer from high in the trees, making it more often heard than seen.

Wryly, Frost acknowledges that the bird's cry is hard *not* to hear, especially as it continues long after other birds have fallen silent for the season. The poem will develop the irony of this insistent and persistent crier who "knows in singing not to sing" yet "says" and "says," exposing painful truths and posing the hard question. The bird's vocal force is conveyed by the alliteration of iambs and spondees that, in line 3, "makes the solid tree trunks sound again." Further suggesting its unprettiness is the series of final "d" sounds in line 2, starting with "heard, / Loud," which interrupts the iambic beat, and ending with the triply stressed "mid-wood bird."

Like other natural creatures in Frost's verse, the ovenbird occupies a middle ground between nature itself, always destroying the beauty it makes, and our human awareness, which mourns what is passing and tries to hold what it loves. Here, the bird, speaking unseen within nature, announces its changes with apparent authority. But in its refusal to follow other birds into midsummer silence, the ovenbird parallels the poet, who knows the mortal implications of spring's passing. The blunt and unsparing announcement "leaves are old," like the ratio "one to ten," suggests an unwillingness to disguise the painful truth: Spring's wealth of blossom—and birdsong, as this survivor reminds us—is gone, and the loss hurts. That leaves develop at the expense of flowers, and summer at expense of spring—an idea found also in **"Spring Pools," "Hyla Brook,"** and **"Nothing Gold Can Stay"**—is part of the larger idea, seen throughout Frost, that every season is sacrificed to the next. (*See*, for example, **"In Hardwood Groves," "The Leaf Treader,"** and **"The Onset."**)

In "The Oven Bird," such "falling off" is made quite literal in the poem's most arresting visual image of "early petal-fall." The cloud of petals naturally precipitates further announcements by poet and bird, to which the rhyme calls particular attention. The wordplay moves among "falls" literal and figurative, visual, seasonal, and mythic. The "petal-fall" suggests not only the coming "fall" of autumn leaves and the snowfalls beyond that but also the Fall from grace in Eden from which descend all pain and death.

In terms of poetic convention, it is fitting that this line should enlarge the frame of reference, for it initiates the sonnet's sestet, which often introduces a turn or shift in argument. In keeping with its thematic expansion, the poem now hints at the difference between its human speaker and the bird he has made his crier of mutability—a distinction toward which the poem now builds. In line 9, the speaker addresses us directly, his use of "we" acknowledging our shared humanity, just as his reference to naming and his play on "fall" reveal a human mind that uses language and moves, inevitably, between past and future, figure and fact. In line 10 the bird who "says the highway dust is over all" can "speak," however eloquently, only of present fact. Here, as from the start, the bird "knows" what to call to our attention, but it is we who must grasp its meaning: in this case, that the "highway dust" is the dust of transit, of passing, of earth, to which all mortal things must return.

While the final question, then, reflects our bafflement in the face of loss, we know all too well the death toward which time moves us, and that knowledge is a threshold that the bird cannot cross. What diminished things signify is a question that his undiminished voice "frames," but it is not one that his wordless tongue can answer or even quite ask. And meanwhile, the most literal sense of "make"—the meaning of the Greek verb from which the word *poet* is derived— reminds us that what poets "make" of diminished things are poems such as this.

We understand, in the end, that it is the poet's voice that questions change, protesting the dying flowers as it will the falling leaves and melting snow. It is the poet's voice that sings its sadness in the midst of current joy, as the bird seems to do, and the poet's voice that preserves our vanishing protests, taking us beyond the bird's inarticulate cry. Yet there is also the poet's need to work by implication and suggestion, his need to "frame" in expressive fact what cannot be said (or said as well) directly: These are features of the poet's art that bring us, and the poet, back to the bird. In "Education by Poetry" Frost says, "People say, 'Why don't you say what you mean?' We never do that, do we, being all of us too much poets. We like to speak in parables and hints and indirections." Perhaps that as much as anything is the lesson of Frost's teaching bird.

References and further reading: Regarding the ovenbird itself, *The Audubon Society Field Guide to North American Birds (Eastern Region)* (New York: Knopf, 1977) mentions a "bubbling" and "exuberant" flight song, often uttered at night, in addition to the bird's regular, "loud, staccato" song (667)—illustrating the poet's selective use of fact in constructing his poem; Bagby, *Nature*, Ch. 5, takes its title from this poem and illuminates it indirectly through its discussion of Frost's "emblematic" nature lyrics; Brower concisely analyzes Frost's prosody and poetic tact, touching on the poem's metapoetics— its statement about poetry itself, a theme more directly addressed by two others: Borroff, "Language and the Poem," and Sanders; Cramer, *Frost among His Poems*, illuminates a strand of biographical reference running through the poem; Monteiro, *New England*, points out a number of literary texts to which Frost may have been responding in "The Oven Bird" (93–98); Rotella, "Metaphor"; see also R. Frost *Collected*, 719–20 and *Selected Letters*, 79.

David Sanders

$\mathcal{P}$

PALGRAVE'S *GOLDEN TREASURY.* British critic and poet Francis Turner Palgrave (1824–1897) is best known as the editor of the highly influential anthology *The Golden Treasury of the Best Songs and Lyrical Poems in the English Language*, a volume that, although frequently emended by later editors, has never been out of print since its first publication in 1861. In making his selections, Palgrave excluded "narrative, descriptive, or didactic poems" in favor of **lyric** poetry, which "turn[s] on some single thought, feeling, or situation." Such poetry offers "a storehouse of delight to Labour and to Poverty" and "gives treasure 'more golden than gold,' leading us in higher and healthier ways than those of the world, and interpreting to us the lessons of Nature." This highly specific notion of what poetry is, and clear agenda for what it should do, sent a powerful message to succeeding generations of poets. As Frank Lentricchia has noted, Palgrave's *Golden Treasury* established a canonical norm for poetry whose "unprecedented dominance . . . had the effect of equating poetry in [the] period of the earliest stirrings of modernist literary activity with lyric itself."

Frost first discovered the volume while a student at **Dartmouth**; when he left school, according to Jean Gould, "in one hand he held his grandfather's satchel, and in the other he carried the cherished copy of *The Golden Treasury*." Palgrave's definition of lyric poetry, notes William H. Pritchard, markedly influenced *A Boy's Will*; in turn, Frost appealed to Palgrave's authority when he claimed that "all the lyric" in *The Golden Treasury* "is well within the colloquial as I use the word." When teaching at **Pinkerton Academy**, Frost gave Palgrave's book a central place on his syllabus for English I, which called for students to memorize "Twenty poems from the Golden Treasury" as the "basis of subsequent study of the history of English literature." And when he finally traveled to **England**, Frost felt that he had come to "the land of *The Golden Treasury*." In short, *The Golden Treasury* was, in Pritchard's words, "to figure for Frost throughout his life as something magically synonymous with the very idea of Poetry." Clearly, for Frost, Palgrave's anthology was one thing gold that stayed.

References and further reading: Gould, 49, 101; Lentricchia, *Modernist Quartet*; Megan Nelson, "Francis Turner Palgrave," *Dictionary of Literary Biography*, vol. 35: *Victorian Poets after 1850*, ed. William E. Fredeman and Ira B. Nadel (Detroit: Gale Research, 1985), 174–80; Francis Turner Palgrave, *The Golden Treasury of the Best Songs and Lyrical Poems in the English Language*, 5th ed., ed. John Press (New York: Oxford University Press, 1986); Poirier, *Knowing*; Pritchard, *Literary Life*, 43; Thompson, *Early Years*, 347; R. Frost, *Selected Letters*, 228.

F. Brett Cox

"PAN WITH US" first appeared in *A Boy's Will* **(1913)**. The woodland god who plays the primary part in this poem, once a deity who induced "panic" in bucolic flocks, is a less obstreperous being in Frost's hand. With echoes of Wordsworth's sonnet "The World Is Too Much with Us," the poem ends, rare in Frost, with a rhetorical interrogation: "What should he play?" However, the figure of mossy-gray Pan stamping a hoof on a zephyrous, hillside pasture is at first untroubled. "His heart knew peace," the speaker relates, and Pan casts his pipes aside to better absorb the sylvan songs of hawks and jays. The poem nowhere suggests an encroachment upon such scenes—"In all the country he did command / He saw no smoke and he saw no roof." Rather than settling on the simple dichotomy of nature and civilization, Frost entertains here the notion that the fabric of the whole pagan world has unraveled. The meadow flowers and pine trees have drifted as far from Pan's sphere as the homes where children bring their "clicking pails." Even the steer are only "half-wild." The lines possess a lyricism appropriate to a poem so concerned with song, but the music itself is often subdued, matching the pipes of Pan with "less of power to stir / . . . Than the merest aimless breath of air." The final question both disturbs and enchants: One wonders whether Pan is at a loss because he has nothing to sing or too much.

"Pan with Us" has drawn a fair amount of critical attention. Margaret Edwards responds to its concluding line by supposing that the "entire body of Frost's work in his long and prolific life is his truest answer to this question." Without addressing the particularities of the piece, Bruce Fogelman contextualizes it by tracing the tradition of eclogues to which he feels it belongs. Jean Gould calls the poem "a rather skeptical evaluation by the new-world poet of his own art." Bluntly, Lawrance Thompson states that "the poet *is* Pan and Pan *is* the poet" and notices the importance of an audience to any poet's craft, often compromised by "the poet's shyness which makes him love the solitude which is his." *See also* **Pastoral Poetry**.

References and further reading: Edwards, "Pan's Song," 114; Fogelman; Gould, 102; Thompson, *Fire and Ice*, 130.

Eric C. Brown

"PASSING GLIMPSE, A," originally published as "The Passing Glimpse" in the *New Republic* (21 Apr. 1926), was better received than other **lyric** poems in *West-Running Brook* **(1928). Harriet Monroe** thought it "a poem delicate and beautiful but also . . . a swift and true characterization of his friend's exquisite book." Dedicated to midwestern poet Ridgely Torrence's *Hesperides* (1925), it responds to the idea, dramatized in the volume's title poem, **"West-Running Brook,"** that the poet could experience direct, visionary knowledge of the ideal and use that knowledge to renovate people's perception of the world. Frost uses flowers glimpsed from a moving train as his metaphor for an ideal we can see only briefly and indirectly. His question "Was something brushed across my mind / That no one on earth will ever find?" uses a passive construction to wonder if he, like the young man in Torrence's poem, has been given a transcendent insight. Frost's response, "Heaven gives its glimpses only to those / Not in position to look too close," suggests little confidence in our ability to see beyond appearances, despite our desire to stop the world and go back to see such glimpsed ideals clearly. Frost's artistry is apparent in the way his word choices and syntax complement the theme. The word "brushed" likens the impression he gets from the flowers to the blurred brush stroke of an impressionistic painting, which, by emphasizing the apparent and momentary, accentuates our focus on appearances. Similarly, the poet's attempt to identify the flowers by listing what they are not illustrates the indirect reasoning we must use to understand a secretive universe. *See also* **"For Once, Then, Something."**

References and further reading: Bagby, *Nature*, uses the poem to show Frost's awareness of current scientific ideas, particularly the Heisenberg uncertainty principle; R. Cook, *Living Voice*, 88–105, includes Frost's comments on the poem; Monroe, "Frugal," 78; for a classic study of Frost's treatment of humans and nature, see Montgomery; Torrence.

Michael Berndt

PASTORAL POETRY. The pastoral genre depends on a tension between the political reality and the philosophical ideal of its subject matter. As William Empson has explained, the genre manifests such a dichotomy through an implicit tension between the city and the country. Typically, pastoral poetry, even in its most idyllic mode, suggests the contrast by arguing through analogy that nature, unlike the city, offers solace for one's pain. Such tension so fundamental to the genre is also part of Frost's pastoral poetry—most famously in **"Build Soil— A Political Pastoral,"** which refers directly back to Virgil's First Eclogue. In Frost's pastoral work, however, nature is not seen as a refuge in contrast to the city. John F. Lynen, the first critic to give serious attention to Frost's role in the development of the genre, explains that the rural landscape of Frost's New England pastorals cannot be read as idyllic because the poems come "from the point of view of an actual New England farmer." In *North of Boston* **(1914),** for example, Frost implicitly contrasts a specific rural area with a specific city. As is typical of pastoral poetry, the contrast does not favor the city. When the city's machines enter the rural landscape, they cause destruction and despair ("**The Self-Seeker,**" " **'Out, Out—'** "). But at the same time, nature's influence in such rural landscapes rarely offers the antidote one would expect from pastoral poetry.

Frost's poems suggest that in the country, unlike in the city, people do attempt to find solace in a spirituality larger than themselves. But Frost differs from other pastoral poets such as Wordsworth because often his people fail to find such comfort even in nature. Although Frost's characters have both the desire to see beyond themselves and a landscape that will facilitate their desire, nature does not always respond favorably. When it does, the solace is all too brief, fleeting, tenuous—as is the case in **"Nothing Gold Can Stay"** and **"For Once, Then, Something."**

Even more common in Frost's poems than nature's silence or the mystery of its temporary solace is nature's suggestion that things are even worse than we imagine them to be; nature's "design" "appalls," Frost tells us in **"Design."** In other poems, such as **"The Census-Taker"** and **"The Black Cottage,"** nature transforms seemingly secure houses, even whole communities of houses, into ruins. And even when the houses stand, the ideal of home they represent, when nature asserts itself, is often destroyed, as in **"Home Burial."** Left alone outside of one's four walls and the social world those walls imply, Frost's characters either submit to a radical skepticism or attempt, however, futilely, to build their own faith. As the speaker in **"Desert Places"** says, neither the city nor the country necessarily comforts him: "I have it in me so much nearer home / To scare myself with my own desert places."

In Frost's New England, those who look to nature for solace may well be dreamers. But one could, as Frost writes in **"Birches,"** do much worse. In short, Frost creates a wry version of the pastoral poem. Even if his characters know that nature may well make their pain worse, they nonetheless persist in the desire to "get away from earth awhile." That desire, uttered by the speaker of "Birches," also explains that pastoral poem's famous last line. In such a world, nature may not always offer solace, but at least those who live there, unlike those who live in the city, have the hope that it might. In **"The Pasture,"** the introductory poem to his collected work, Frost invites us into his world: "I shan't be gone long.—You come too." Although the gesture is wry, given the world we enter, it is, nonetheless, a genuine invitation to possibility. *See also* **Nature Poet and Naturalist**.

References and further reading: Brower; Empson, William, *Some Versions of Pastoral* (New York: New Directions, 1974); Greiner, "Robert Frost as Nature Poet," in *Poet and His Critics*; Lentricchia, *Modern Poetics*; Lerner; Lynen, *Pastoral Art*, 19; Parini, *A Life*, 208–12; Patterson; Poirier, *Knowing*, Ch. 3, explores the role of houses in Frost's poetry; Theodore Ziolkowski, *Virgil and the Moderns* (Princeton, NJ: Princeton University Press, 1993).

Jonathan N. Barron

"PASTURE, THE," was first published as a prefatory to *North of Boston* **(1914)**. Frost later selected it to introduce his 1930 edition of *Collected Poems* and insisted that the piece introduce further collections. Such prominence indicates Frost's own sense of the poem's merit, and he considered its effect to be wholly original in English poetry. In terms of the poem's place in Frost's works, William Freedman rightly compares "The Pasture" to Whitman's "One's-Self I Sing" from the Inscriptions to *Leaves of Grass*, for both poems invoke the distinct persona and thematic center of their respective author's work. As Frost noted to Elizabeth Shepley Sergeant, "The Pasture" is a transitional poem between the boyish dreaming of *A Boy's Will* (1913) and the mature themes of *North of Boston*. Composed for his wife **Elinor** as a form of apology or as an expression of devotion, the poem invites comparison with **"Hyla Brook"** and **"Going for Water"**—related poems about love also set on the Frosts' **Derry** farm in New Hampshire. The symbolic richness of the scene, Lawrance Thompson adds, allows the reader to extend such personal meaning toward a vision of rebirth and renewal.

A **lyric** invocation in the Greek **pastoral** tradition, the poem inaugurates a specific way of reading that is essential to Frost's poetry. John F. Lynen provides the classic commentary on the poem, noting that the presentation of the scene depends upon a specific type of vision that sets the natural world in opposition to the social. Nature evokes new ways of perceiving, and the clearing of the spring suggests new clarity of vision and reflection. Water as symbol foregrounds the role of perception in the making of meaning, and Frank Lentricchia argues that such an image forces the reader to recognize how experience is mediated by perception and how poetic creation can lead both author and reader to new insight. The personal dimension of the poem suggests the necessity of love and the need for Frost to include his companion, Elinor, in his excursions and visions, and the symbol of the young calf reinforces the rebirth of life. Through the intimacy of the scene and the recurring invocation "You come too," the poem evokes a knowing sensuality that underscores the themes of love, birth, renewal, and return.

Yet such themes are set in counterpoint to the uncertainties that continually appear in Frost's poetic voice. John C. Kemp argues that the speaker's evasiveness and hesitancy are incongruent with the pastoral tradition, forcing the reader to accept the invitation on Frost's terms. The invitation "You come too" is withheld until the fourth line, and its utterance mars the flow of the preceding iambic lines. The line seems both an afterthought and a command, but its force is muted by the apologetic "I shan't be gone long." Indeed, the speaker seems unsure of exactly what he will find on his journey but fully aware of what awaits upon his return. Such sense of obligation recurs in **"Stopping by Woods on a Snowy Evening"** and indicates Frost's acceptance of his responsibilities. The theme is underscored by the fact that the pasture itself is not aboriginal nature: It is a cultivated tract designed for human use. The journey of the poem is that of a task—to fetch the calf so that the mother may be milked—supplemented by the joy of clearing and contemplating the spring. Frost seems aware that he might lose himself in the latter joy rather than immerse himself in the task at hand; thus he gives his repeated promises not to be gone too long, lines that reinforce the sense of duty and obligation.

But such a sense of duty is one born of love. Fritz Oehlschlaeger compares the attitude of the poetic voice here to the pastoral tradition of Marlowe's "The Passionate Shepherd to His Love" and Raleigh's rejoinder "The Nymph's Reply to the Shepherd." Frost mediates between the two poems, sharing the passionate desire of Marlowe's speaker and the blunt factuality of Raleigh's. The balance allows Frost to offer an invitation that is true to his own feeling and that demonstrates love and respect for his intended. The poem shows a similar balance between the natural world of disorder and growth and the human world of order and containment. As such, the poem has counterparts in **"Putting in the Seed,"** **"To Earthward,"** and **"Mowing."** As in these three poems, the world expressed in "The Pasture" is not a wholly idyllic one. Aware of such a reality, Frost artfully balances his commitments to love and duty, beauty and utility, setting forth a unique vision of a world in which harmony is possible. *See also* **Nature Poet and Naturalist**.

References and further reading: Freedman; Ingebretsen, "Figures of Love"; Kemp; Lentricchia, *Modern Poetics*; Lynen, *Pastoral Art*; Oehlschlaeger, "Frost's 'Pasture' "; Sergeant, 126; Thompson, *Early Years*, 311–12.

Kenneth Rickard

"PATCH OF OLD SNOW, A," which first appeared in *Mountain Interval* **(1916)**, is an eight-line poem written in 1914 while Frost was in **England**. In a letter to **John Bartlett**, Frost uses the poem to illustrate his theory of sentence sounds, but it has received little critical attention. The poem is a brief perception similar to "In a Station of the Metro" by **Ezra Pound**. Frost had met Pound shortly after moving to England and was pressured to accept but mostly refused Pound's poetic dictums. At one point Frost wrote, "I must write something much more like *vers libre* or [Pound] will let me perish of neglect."

In the first stanza, the speaker notices a patch of old snow that at first leads him to guess it was a newspaper blown there and soaked by rain. In the second stanza, the speaker notes that the specks of grime in the snow resemble the small print of a newspaper, but the news of that day is now forgotten if indeed the speaker ever noticed it. According to Mordecai Marcus, Frost juggles two ideas: that yesterday's news is not much use and that "once the beauty of winter is gone, one forgets it, only later . . . to realize that one hadn't appreciated it enough." The verb "should" in line 2 implies that the speaker regrets forgetting the message of the snowy day, but the offhand cadence in the last two lines, as Marcus notes, justifies his totally ignoring it. *See also* **"Dust of Snow."**

References and further reading: R. Frost, *Selected Letters*, 84, 111; Greiner, "Dark Woods," 375; Marcus, *Explication*, 67; Thompson, *Fire and Ice*, 121–22.

Newton Smith

"PAUL'S WIFE" first appeared in *The Century Magazine* (Nov. 1921) and was collected in *New Hampshire* (**1923**). According to Jeffrey S. Cramer, Frost singled out the poem as "one of the important ones" in the volume. Cramer further cites Frost's comment that the poem "is merely about the kind of person who refuses to share socially in his spiritual possessions."

Frost adds his own touch to the legend of Paul Bunyan, the gigantic lumber-jack whose strength allows him to defy the laws of nature. Frost cites two instances of the Bunyan tall-tale tradition and then adds his own, as his Paul extracts a beautiful wife from a log.

Critics debate the effect of Frost's addition. For some, the poem diminishes Bunyan's stature. Katherine Kearns characterizes Frost's Paul as obsessed, driven by his fairy wife about a poetic landscape in which women have extraor-dinary power. Others argue that Paul's role in his wife's birth elevates him to the status of artist–creator.

For many critics, the decisive moment of the poem comes at the end, as Paul physically hides his wife from a world that cannot adequately speak of her. Herbert Marks explains that given the metaphorical nature of language, which either hides or disguises its subject, any attempt to describe or name Paul's wife would be slanderous. Thus, the poem considers the challenge facing any artist whose medium is language, particularly poetic language, which, for Frost, was essentially metaphorical.

References and further reading: Benoit; Cramer, *Frost among His Poems*, 69; Kearns, 2, 104; Marks, 128.

Jason Pearce

"PAUPER WITCH OF GRAFTON, THE." *See* **"Two Witches."**

"PEA BRUSH" first appeared as "Pea-sticks"in *The Bouquet*, a small, typed collection compiled by Frost's children in July 1914. It was later collected in *Mountain Interval* (**1916**). The poem's original title reflects the intended use of the birch trees: The speaker can recycle limbs from the recently cut trees to provide support for his garden peas. Both the traditional *abab* rhyme and a stanzaic form indented at alternating lines help to convey the image of a trellis-like supporting structure for both the peas and the poem. In stanza two, the speaker recognizes the sacrificial nature of the birches, and stanza three brings a turning point as the speaker enters the territory of the "thousand shrill" frogs, who, interrupted by his alien presence, suddenly cease their peeping and become curious witnesses.

The double meaning of line 16 conveys both the physical and colloquial notion of getting the birch limbs "off the wildflowers' backs," for the speaker now sets in opposition two kinds of flora: the "garden things," or cultivated peas, and the trillium, or "anything growing wild." The birches are available for an individual's artificial training of the tendrils or "fingers" of the peas, which hold on to the birch boughs to "lift themselves up off the ground" and into thriving bushes. The cat's cradle is a children's puzzle made by looping string around the fingers and pulling to form different shapes, looking just as a staked garden might look.

The poem begins with the peas but ends with the trillium, placing final emphasis upon the inevitability of natural growth, the organic, and upon the already budded trillium, flowers with erect stems, which can rise and stand alone without assistance or human intervention and which are disturbed by the "crooking" or bending, and thus corruption, of artificial methods. The poem appears in *Mountain Interval* immediately after **"Birches,"** but while there may be a temptation to read it in the light of "Birches," "Pea Brush," like the trillium, can stand on its own.

References and further reading: Lentricchia, "Redemptive," 29, offers relevant comments in the context of his discussion of "Birches"; Thompson, *Triumph*, 541, 560 n.8, includes background information about *The Bouquet*.

Linda Lovell

"PEACEFUL SHEPHERD, THE," collected in *West-Running Brook* **(1928)**, first appeared in the *New York Herald Tribune* Books Section (22 Mar. 1925). It is one of several poems in which Frost uses constellations as the central metaphor. The poem's speaker is presumably a shepherd, who is leaning on a pasture fence and imagining how he might reorder the universe. Connecting the stars with the lines traditionally used to group clusters of stars into recognizable constellations, the speaker declares that the "Crown of Rule" (or Pleidaes), the "Scales of Trade," and the "Cross of Faith"—representing government, commerce, and **religion**—do not deserve a place in the heavenly order since they have been responsible for as much damage as war itself (represented by the sword of Orion's belt). However, the language of the poem suggests that the speaker's words are idle, even hesitant, musings since all four constellations will continue to govern.

Additionally, some questions arise concerning the speaker's identity. One view of the speaker suggests that he is an ordinary person lamenting the current state of affairs. Such lamentation prompts Dennis Vail to suggest that the shepherd is not really at peace, as the title suggests, because he is not reconciled to the world. Upon close consideration, the speaker appears not so much peaceful as peace-loving. Interestingly, according to Jeffrey S. Cramer, Frost claimed that the poem "was about World War I."

References and further reading: Cramer, *Frost among His Poems*, 93; Marcus, *Explication*, 123; Vail, "Point of View."

George S. Scouten

"PECK OF GOLD, A," written in 1924, was first published as "The Common Fate" in the *Yale Review* (July 1927) and was included in **West-Running Brook (1928)**. Frost claimed the poem was about his youth in California and noted that it rewrites the New England saying "We all must eat our peck of dirt." While Frost frequently uses gold in his poems to signify the desirable ideal, the reference is usually qualified by the inevitable presence of the real. For example, in **"The Vindictives,"** gold is depicted as a serpentlike chain coiled under dust and ash, taunting humans with an "unsatisfied love of the high" and forcing them "down to the real." The speaker in "A Peck of Gold" complains of being told as a child that "Some of the dust was really gold" because the comment reinforced the palpability of the ideal for him. The phrase "a peck of gold" gives allusive depth to the poem because a peck, as a common measurement for apples, connects the poem to another exploration of the real and ideal, **"The Gold Hesperidee,"** and to the biblical Fall. In Eden, associated in "A Peck of Gold" with the "Golden Gate" of Frost's youth, Adam and Eve eat the fruit in order to approach the godlike ideal; consequently, they are cursed like the serpent to eat dust. The struggle to transcend the real, seen as part of Frost's and humanity's heritage, helps to explain the poem's original title.

References and further reading: R. Cook, *Living Voice*, includes two transcribed readings where Frost briefly discusses the poems of his California youth; R. Frost, *Selected Letters*, 500.

Michael Berndt

"PERIL OF HOPE" first appeared in *The Agnes Scott News* (Agnes Scott College, Decatur, Georgia) on 8 February 1961 and later in *In the Clearing* **(1962)**. With its romantic description of orchard scenery and with its otherwise classically correctly rhymed lines, the poem deals with the shift from warm to cold scenery and its effect upon the white buds on the trees in spring. The ironic point is that although we long for springtime and its flowery effects, such aspiration can be perilous if wintry frost still intercedes. Yet the value of the **lyric** appears to be likewise in its being a transformation of Edith Thomas's poem "Frost Tonight"—and not merely in terms of the phrase from Frost's own last line. Thus even the pun on Frost's last name in his last line (leading to such performances based on it as *An Evening's Frost*—see Burnshaw) had a certain precedent in Thomas's own conclusion.

The poems are similar structurally in their horticultural imagery (both thereby derivative, to some extent, of Wordsworth) and in their temporal references

(Thomas's "late" / "hours" anticipating Frost's "time"). Most fascinating verbally is Thomas's line "Apple-green west and an orchard bar" and Frost's "The orchard bar[e] / And the orchard green." Onomastics enters the picture too: Even as Thomas capitalized the word *Frost* thrice in her poem, so Frost admitted to being inspired by E. Thomas—though, in most cases, Edward Thomas would have come to his fertile mind first. His friend **Louis Untermeyer** then incidentally incorporated both Frost's and Edward Thomas's poetry in his celebrated anthology *Modern American Poetry, Modern British Poetry.*

References and further reading: Burnshaw, 202; Fleissner, *Road Taken*, 45, 115–19; Untermeyer.

Robert F. Fleissner

"PERTINAX" appeared initially in *Poetry* (Apr. 1936) and was subsequently collected in *A Further Range* (**1936**). Reminiscent of a haiku, the three-line verse provides simple formal rhyme in spite of its seeming at first to go beyond normal poetic bounds with unconventional use of exclamation points. Suggestive of Frost's familiar penchant for not "playing tennis with the net down," the **lyric** best expresses the overall notion of order created out of a chaotic situation. Although such a thematic description is reminiscent of great art in general (and, of course, of the biblical story of Creation), it most probably is meant to hint also at the basic influence of the Romantics on the New Englander. The point is that the skies often portend the coming of what appears to be total disorder (most obviously symbolized in an encroaching thunderstorm) but which the controller of natural forces, the poet, is supposed then to reconstruct in his own creative way. The apt title derives from the Latin for *stubborn* or *persevering*.

References and further reading: J. Cox, "Clearing"; D'Avanzo, *Romantics*; Fleissner, *Road Taken*, 20; for Frost on order and chaos, see R. Frost, "Letter to *The Amherst Student*," *Collected*, 739–40.

Robert F. Fleissner

PHILOSOPHY. Frost's richness and depth of thought, manifested not only in his poetry but in his **prose** writings and letters, is carried in a current of deep speculation about the nature of humanity, the presence or absence of any guiding principles for humanity's interactions, and the relationship of that humanity with a transcendent other. Eddies in that current lead him to question, in very informal ways, the nature of art and the place of logic in the human condition.

Early critics of Frost attempted to show an affinity between his thought and that of the New England Transcendentalists. They fell prey to Frost's trappings but never really penetrated to the thought below his surface, the systemic reasoning that informed his poetry. Yvor Winters, for example, connects Frost and **Emerson**, noting especially a distrust of reason in Frost and the Transcendentalists and making this connection to Frost's detriment, claiming that Frost believes "that impulse is trustworthy and reason contemptible." Winters argues,

"The principles which have hampered Frost's development, the principles of Emersonian and Thoreauistic Romanticism [see **Thoreau**], are the principles which he has openly espoused."

Later critics, such as Alvan S. Ryan and W. W. Robson, take a dimmer view of Frost's connection to the Transcendentalists and carve out a niche, both positive and negative, for Frost's unique philosophical speculations. Ryan notes the differing views toward that most important of Transcendentalist subjects, Nature, in Frost's and Emerson's works. Robson condemns the critics who borrow weight from Emerson because they cannot divine the weight in Frost's own words. Both give Frost a philosophical space of his own, created through eclectic reading and a firm sense of the paradoxes of the human condition.

An informed discussion of Frost's philosophy, both in its influences and its method, must hold with the latter-day view. Frost had much personal energy invested in his public persona as a rural New England farmer, close to the earth and following in the philosophical tradition of the New England Transcendentalists, especially Emerson and Thoreau. To take him at his public face, however, would be misleading, for his current of thought runs much deeper, and in a much more systematic vein, than American Transcendentalism would allow.

Frost's philosophical influences are many and are not solely American. In describing one of his earliest published poems, **"The Trial by Existence,"** he alludes to the influence of Schopenhauer on his own thought. Thompson writes that Frost eliminated all traces of the philosopher, but even a cursory glance at Schopenhauer's system and Frost's poem shows that he imbued the poem with much that was digested from the classical and continental philosophical traditions. Indeed, the very conceit of the poem, that after death souls willingly choose to be reincarnated even though this means giving up not only a paradisal existence but also all memories of a previous earthly existence, is a Platonic notion coupled with elements of both Western and Eastern philosophy and mysticism.

In both Schopenhauer and Frost there is a reaction against Kantian epistemology, where Kant claimed that an individual could know the appearance of a thing but never the thing in itself. Schopenhauer, looking at the Self, disagreed. He knew himself both as noumenon (a thing in itself) and phenomenon (a collection of accidents). As noumenon, he was self-moved, an active being possessing overt behavior that directly expressed his Will. As phenomenon, he was an object among objects. Denying the Cartesian mind/body dualism, he claimed that he was aware of his body and his Will, but both are subsumed in the lived experience of the Self. The body is the manifestation of the Will, its objectification as it appears under the conditions of external perception. So what is willed and what is done are in reality the same thing viewed from two different loci. At the bottom of all behavior, of all embodiment of willing, is the Will to Live. This grounding principle of Schopenhauer's thought motivates the souls in "The Trial by Existence" who wish to return to earth.

Frost's thoughts on Nature may be seen as an exploration of such a reaction to rational imposition upon the external world. Nature exists outside the Self, is formed there, and has existence beyond the idealistic notion that thought determines reality. This is not to say that Frost eschews rationality but that it is not sufficient for a total understanding of Nature and the human experience. Poems such as **"Fire and Ice,"** ending in a paradox that cannot be rationally resolved, or **"The Witch of Coös,"** where extrarationality is an essential part of life, show Frost's insistence of the existence of something else, neither more nor less but parallel to rational thought. Frost recognizes the equality of both rational and extrarational processes and situationally gives prominence to one or the other. Richard Poirier's chapter on Frost's epistemology and especially his thoughts on Frost's ideas on love demonstrate the juxtaposition throughout Frost's corpus.

Frost's method of arriving at the "truth" of a poem is obviously indebted to the Hegelian notion of thesis and antithesis in conflict, which produces a synthesis. This is particularly clear in the dialogue poems, especially **"Home Burial"** and **"The Death of the Hired Man."** In both poems, Frost sets up a dialogic conflict, and resolution of the conflict is the business of the poem. Rationality and extrarationality combine to create a synthesis, something different than either one alone. The movement toward such synthetic truth, something that combines the conflicts of human existence, is the philosophical work of such dialogue poems.

Perhaps Frost's strongest philosophical connection was with William James, the American pragmatist. Poirier cites James's *Pragmatism* as a source of many of Frost's metaphors and of his "general disposition." The final lines of **"The Road Not Taken"** owe much to the final paragraph of James's essay "The Will to Believe," and James's lecture "Some Metaphysical Problems Metaphysically Considered" is certainly a primary source for Frost's **"Design."** Pragmatism as a philosophical movement was concerned with the connection in humanity between thinking and acting. The pragmatist philosophers found little value in modes of thought that did not have some value in daily existence, and yet they placed the foundation of all action in thought itself. Pragmatism attempted to unite the disparate fields of empiricism and idealism, acknowledging a pluralistic approach to knowledge that would also include the extrarational, especially **religion** and morality. The pragmatic "method" of consideration for any theory was to ask what difference in daily existence the acceptance or rejection of that set of ideas and facts would make. Such concern for the outward manifestation of thought and feeling can be seen as the work of Frost's poetry. He does not reconcile opposing forces, nor does he side with one end of the spectrum or another. Rather, he acknowledges the tension between opposing ideas such as emotion and rationality, the individual and the community, morality and immorality, home and the outside world, existence and nonbeing, and he situates himself in the midst of the creative tension that the often paradoxical alternatives create.

References and further reading: Parini, *A Life*, 61–63, discusses William James's influence on Frost; for a study of Frost and Schopenhauer, see Pellegrino; Poirier, *Knowing*, is an essential tool for the study of Frost's philosophy; also helpful are Monteiro, *New*

England and "Redemption"; Robson, 750; Ryan; Wakefield, *Opposing Lights*; Winters, 75, 82.

Joe Pellegrino

PINKERTON ACADEMY. In 1906 when income from his farm could not sustain his family, Frost obtained a part-time teaching job at Pinkerton Academy, a small private boys' school in **Derry**, New Hampshire. Pinkerton Academy, was founded by two Scottish merchantmen in 1815. The Reverend George Washington Bingham was the principal of the school when Frost began his five-year term there. Prior to that time, he had teaching experience helping his mother in her district school. His poem **"The Tuft of Flowers,"** read at a Men's League Banquet by Charles L. Merriam, a minister and trustee of Pinkerton, secured him the job. Frost's teaching was unconventional, characterized by informal but demanding originality and thoughtful effort. His job included coaching debaters, organizing and directing plays, and reorganizing the English curriculum. While Frost was teaching at Pinkerton, the state superintendent of public instruction observed his classes and "called him the best teacher in New Hampshire." When Frost was offered the principalship of Pinkerton Academy, he turned it down, citing his lack of a college degree to the trustees, but privately he knew he was about to declare himself a full-time poet. Frost left Pinkerton to teach at **Plymouth Normal School** in 1911. *See also* **Teacher**.

References and further reading: Potter; Thompson, *Early Years*; to explore Frost's teaching career further, see Vogel, *Frost, Teacher*.

Dianna Laurent

"PLACE FOR A THIRD," called by Frost "one of my less amiable poems," was first published in *Harper's Magazine* (July 1920) and was later collected in *New Hampshire* (1923). It evokes bitter comic echoes of **"Home Burial"** in its depiction of romantic relationships. Laban, a man already twice predeceased by wives and confronting the death of a third, Eliza, is asked by her not to be buried alongside the other two. Catching a "glimpse of lingering person in Eliza," triggering "something he remembered in himself," Laban feels a strong sense of marital duty and embarks on a quest to find his wife an alternative burial site. He travels to Eliza's first husband's sister to ask if she may be buried next to the one "Who married her for playmate more than helpmate." However, his sense of duty only mocks any romantic feelings traditionally associated with marriage. Katherine Kearns sees in this poem a "pattern of imagery" established in "Home Burial": "committing to earth the proof of a couple's sexual love." With each fragment of Laban's and Eliza's pasts (both together and apart from each other) rising to the surface, there also emerges an equal number of calculated survival strategies enacted by each partner. Not only has Eliza been a practical "helpmate" for Laban; she also has interpreted her role in marriage as "Housekeeping" for her last two husbands and another man she never married. Now, even in death, her plight depends on the value Laban determines for her: "He'd sell a yoke of steers to pay for" an appropriate stone. In short, when

Eliza's first husband, John, is buried, so too is any sense of love; even John's sister equates Eliza's "too many other men" with a cheapened status by punning on the word "sense": "There wouldn't be no sense" in Eliza's resting place beside John. In place of love exists prudence, responsibility, and the coldly self-determined "lot" in one's life that Frost symbolizes by way of a cemetery plot.

References and further reading: R. Frost, *Selected Letters*, 243; Kearns, 91, 210, n.8.

Dana E. Aspinall

"PLANNERS, THE," first appeared in the *Atlantic Monthly* (Dec. 1946) and was subsequently included in **Steeple Bush (1947)**. The poem investigates humanity's response to a possible nuclear disaster, beginning with three iambic pentameter tercets, one for each of the contenders in the chance to protest nuclear destruction: the unborn, the dead, and the few. The last five lines describe the few as merely a social group rallying for change with no insight into the seriousness of the issue; the speaker refers to them as "social planners" who might find the course of history "important." The end of the world would merely interfere with their agenda to "change our manners."

In his political **sonnets**, Frost typically states a problem or makes an observation about a social situation and then employs a sestet or a couplet to present a response. The brevity and limitation of the form serve to suggest that political problems cannot be easily resolved, even though "social planners" may think it possible. By ending the poem with a sarcastic couplet, Frost points out one of the most dangerous aspects of social movements and **politics**: that well-intended ideas are often reduced to superficial banter.

References and further reading: Barry, 79–98; for further studies of Frost's use of the sonnet form, see O. Evans; Rood.

Belinda D. Bruner

"PLOWMEN" was first published in *A Miscellany of American Poetry 1920* (New York: Harcourt Brace, 1920) and later revised for inclusion in *New Hampshire* **(1923)**. Perhaps because of its size, it has received little critical attention. "Plowmen" addresses the irony of the snowplow's name, since, unlike the traditional plow, it is not used for growing things—a productive task—but rather for uncovering the rocklike roads that only will need plowing again. The speaker pointedly distinguishes himself from both those who have named the machine and those who use it; by making such a distinction and by aligning the snowplow with the barrenness of winter, the speaker suggests that the pastoral is superior to the industrial.

Lawrance Thompson has suggested that the terseness of the four-stress verse accentuates the poem's irony. The earlier version of the poem is also available in a letter from Frost to his daughter Lesley.

References and further reading: R. Frost, *Family Letters*, 75; Thompson, *Fire and Ice.*

George S. Scouten

PLYMOUTH NORMAL SCHOOL, a teacher's college for about 100 women in Plymouth, New Hampshire, hired Robert Frost to teach psychology and the history of education in 1911. James Potter reveals that there Frost developed his emphasis on "voice," particularly on natural speech as the poetic medium. Frost spent only one year at the school, but his tenure served to increase his confidence and skill at public speaking. *See also* **Teacher.**

References and further reading: L. Francis, *Morning Gladness*, 12–15; Potter; Thompson, *Early Years*; Vogel, *Frost, Teacher.*

Dianna Laurent

"POD OF THE MILKWEED" first appeared as "From a Milkweed Pod" when Frost, as Jeffrey S. Cramer informs us, used it in 1954 as his **Christmas poem.** The note with asterisk was added for publication in *In the Clearing* **(1962)** in which it serves as the opening poem. It is another Frost poem using a detail of rural life to address a cosmic issue—in this case, waste and prodigality (cf. **"November," "Away," "Carpe Diem,"** and **"In Hardwood Groves,"** among others; Frost told George Nitchie of "November," "You wouldn't know that here I was praising waste"). The specific occasion is the attention paid by butterflies to the sweet syrup of the blossoming milkweed pod. Unlike bees, the homeless/hiveless butterflies do not cache their find for the good of community, thus stirring a selfish frenzy; the scene brings home to the persona "The theme of wanton waste in peace and war / As it has never been to me before." The couplet draws our attention to the poem's contrast of the significant and mundane, the general and specific, the physical and metaphysical, the utilitarian and useless, the drab and colorful.

The speaker's language suggests a range of literary and mythic referents: "milk and honey," "slumber," the contrast of the "sober" weed and the intemperate butterflies. The persona describes the activity, noting its every detail, thinking of the butterflies' "having beaten all day long in vain / Against the wrong side of a window pane." The word "wrong" is the destabilizing element that characterizes a Frost poem, a precision leading to ambiguity. The contribution of all the activity is to "leave as their posterity one pod / With an inheritance of restless dream." Here are Frost's familiar themes of restlessness, uncertainty, and risk in pursuit of the elusive, problems "fairly faced" at a playful, inquisitive distance.

"But waste was of the essence of the scheme." That much is clear. The final lines are a pessimistic affirmation. The butterfly reminds us of a principle in Nature that **science** (is the butterfly a scientist manqué?) must confront, and time will inevitably reveal, the dim secret of the good of waste. The poem suggests the inevitability of such waste: We are in the nuclear age, and the prospect of our self-destruction is in the additional line with asterisk, an addendum by the poet behind the persona. Is there hidden in the example some potential principle of good? In a letter to **Louis Untermeyer** on 9 July 1931, Frost wrote, "We were brought up on principles of saving everything, ourselves included. The war taught us a new gospel. My next book is to be called The Right to Waste. The Right? The duty, the obligation, to waste everything, time, material, *and* the man."

References and further reading: Cramer, *Frost among His Poems*; R. Frost, *Letters to Untermeyer*, 209; Perrine, "Frost's 'Pod.' "

Stephen D. Warner

POETIC THEORIES. In 1894 Frost wrote a letter to **Susan Hayes Ward**, literary editor of *The Independent*, in which he recorded his early interest in the element of sound in poetry, "one," he said, "but for which imagination would become reason." As yet only a figurative consideration, this auditory property would be developed some twenty years later into Frost's predominant prosodic theory. During his stay in **England** (1912–1915), Frost, in a letter quoted in Lawrance Thompson's biography, (*see* **Biographers**), signaled his understanding of the need to declare his aesthetic to the Imagist poet Frank S. Flint, one of his first British acquaintances: "I don't know what theory you may be committed or dedicated to as an affiliated poet of Devonshire St., but for my part give me an out-and-out metaphor." Frost knew, though, that he could not rely on such a simple formulation of his poetics, that his interest in metaphor alone would fall flat in the polemical wars of modernist London. He recognized that he would need to appear more sophisticated and scientific in order to keep from being lumped together with a poet like W. H. Davies, whom Frost himself accused of being "absolutely uncritical untechnical untheoretical." Here Frost's elitist rhetoric resembles that of other modernist poets and is designed to defuse critics who would dismiss him as a parochial American.

In consultation with Flint and the poet–philosopher T. E. Hulme, one of the principal theoreticians of Imagism (*see* **Lowell, Amy, and Imagism**), Frost formulated his principle of versification in notebooks and letters to friends, many of whom were would-be reviewers. In 1913, Frost embarked on an ambitious campaign, working through such friends to promulgate his deeply held formalist views. In large part, he decided to step up his promotional efforts after reading reviews of his first books of poetry, *A Boy's Will* (**1913**) and *North of Boston* (**1914**). Although critical reaction to the books was mostly positive, Frost was disturbed by the not-infrequent charge of metrical disinterest or, worse, incompetence. In self-defense, Frost sought to clarify his poetic method and establish the terms by which his poetry would be judged. At the same time, he made an effort to distinguish himself from the crowd. On the Fourth of July 1913, Frost declared his artistic independence in a letter to his friend **John Bartlett**: "To be perfectly frank with you I am one of the most notable craftsmen of my time.

... I am possibly the only person going who works on any but a worn out theory (principle I had better say) of versification." Despite his boastful claim to originality, Frost's advertisement of himself as a poetic innovator is perfectly consistent with claims made by other modernist poets, who were calling attention to their position in the vanguard of literary reform. Rebelling against the consonance and assonance of Victorian verse (the "harmonized vowels and consonants" of Tennyson and Swinburne), Frost echoes other modernist poets who demoted such segmental sound effects in favor of speech rhythms, most notably **Ezra Pound**.

However, in his attempt to call attention to his exceptionality, he keeps Pound and other high-profile modernists at arm's length, insisting that "I alone of English writers have consciously set myself to make music out of what I may call the sound of sense." As he explains, "the sound of sense" is intonation—the rhythm of speech that communicates sense without regard to the meanings of the words of a sentence: "The best place to get the abstract sound of sense is from voices behind a door that cuts off the words." To illustrate his point, Frost set down in his letter to Bartlett several sentences that embody striking tones of voice: "I said no such thing"; "You're not my teacher"; "Oh, say!" Frost insists that such speech rhythms must be brought into poetry so that the sounds of poetry are no different from the sounds we hear every day in talk.

Although Frost discounts the importance of words in his poetry (he went so far as to say in a 1915 interview, "Words in themselves do not convey meaning"), he suggests in letters and critical **prose** the importance of using colloquial language. As he proudly announced to Thomas Bird Mosher about *North of Boston*: "I dropped to an everyday level of diction that even Wordsworth kept above." Taking to heart Wordsworth's dictum in his Preface to *Lyrical Ballads* (1800), Frost pledged to represent in poetry the language of common people. But it was "the sound of sense," not diction, that mattered most, or so Frost claimed, and he attributed that priority to **Emerson**. In "On Emerson" (1959), an address to the American Academy of Arts and Sciences, he says that it was Emerson who turned him into "an anti-vocabularian," pointing out lines in Emerson's self-descriptive poem "Monadnoc" that exhibit expressive intonation contours and plain speech. Despite his rhetoric, Frost (and Emerson) cared a great deal about language and prosodic forms unrelated to intonation, and one must be careful to note discrepancies between the hyperbole surrounding Frost's theory and the actual performance of his poetry.

However, "the sound of sense" is not the sole constituent of his theory; such speech rhythms, Frost asserted, must be set to work within a metrical grid: "[I]f one is to be a poet he must learn to get cadences by skillfully breaking the sounds of sense with all their irregularity of accent across the regular beat of the metre." Significantly, Frost champions the use of meter at a time when many other modernist poets were choosing to write unmetered (or "free") verse; his impatience with the rejection of meter by many of his contemporaries stands behind one of his most famous quips (and playful metaphors): "For my pleasure

I had as soon write free verse as play tennis with the net down." But he also promotes rhythmic variation, which allows a poet to escape the singsong of meter. Despite his early insistence on the originality of his theory, what he proposes is nothing other than the art of metrical substitution—an art as old as poetry. However, it was not until 1915—after the rhetoric of early Modernism had begun to reflect an interest in literary history—that Frost conceded the ancestry of his theory, noting that the best poetry in English (including that of Shakespeare, Shelley, Wordsworth, and Emerson) projects "sounds of sense" onto a regular meter.

Frost continued to come back to the terms of his theory throughout his career. In "The Poetry of Amy Lowell" (1925), originally published in the *Christian Science Monitor*, Frost hails that free verse poet for her daring reform of poetry: "Her Imagism lay chiefly in images to the eye. . . . Her poetry was forever a clear resonant calling off of things seen." Here he moderates his position regarding the superiority of the auditory imagination, dropping his insistence that the poet who writes for the eye is a "barbarian," as he elsewhere maintained. His description of Lowell, though, implicitly contrasts his method to hers; as Frost recorded in an early notebook entry: "We value poetry too much as it makes pictures. The imagination of the ear is more peculiarly poetical than the imaginative eye, since it deals with sound[,] which is what poetry is before it is sight. Write with the ear to the speaking voice. Seek first in poetry images of sound—concrete tone images." In his Preface to his play *A Way Out* (1929), Frost again asserts the importance of expressive tones of voice in poetry, charging that all writing, including **lyric** poetry, "is as good as it is dramatic"; he reiterates his concept of "the sound of sense" as it enables writing to achieve this ideal: "Sentences are not different enough to hold the attention unless they are dramatic. No ingenuity of varying structure will do. All that can save them is the speaking tone of voice somehow entangled in the words and fastened to the page for the ear of the imagination."

During the 1930s, Frost continued to emphasize the interaction between a regular meter and the rhythms of speech, constructing metaphorically rich prose that describes his prosodic theory in figurative, rather than strictly technical, terms. In "The Figure a Poem Makes" (1939), first published as the introduction to his expanded *Collected Poems*, he reminds readers that "[t]he possibilities for tune from the dramatic tones of meaning struck across the rigidity of a limited meter are endless" and constructs an oxymoronic figure for such a crossing—"the straight crookedness of a good walking stick." Further insisting on the figurative dimension of his poetics, Frost asserts that his commitment to form amounts to a commitment to a principle of order: A poem, he says, should end "in a clarification of life—not necessarily a great clarification of life, such as sects and cults are founded on, but in a momentary stay against confusion." Frost's claim that poetry should not attempt to reflect the confusion and indeterminacy of the world around it, but instead should provide a point of rest in contrast to it, sets him apart from some other modernist poets who believed that poetry should not be orderly (i.e., written in traditional poetic forms) because the world in which it exists is not. In his letter to *The Amherst Student* (1935), an undergraduate newspaper at **Amherst College**, he sounds a similar note, remarking on the comfort that any imposition of form provides at least temporarily—whether it be the form of a letter, a garden, a picture, or a poem. Again, Frost expresses his view that art should make life more manageable and intelligible, not compound our isolation and bewilderment: "The background is hugeness and confusion shading away from where we stand into black and utter chaos; and against the background any small man-made figure of order and concentration. What pleasanter than that this should be so?" According to Frost, metrical verse has "salutary" effects for poet and reader, and his epigrammatic statement in *Atlantic Monthly* (1951) registers his understanding of its use to poets: "There is nothing more composing than composition."

In his introduction to **E. A. Robinson**'s poem *King Jasper* (1935), Frost rails against what he calls "new ways to be new," radical experiments that stripped poetry of punctuation, meter, dramatic tones of voice, and other conventions of versification. Resurrecting his interest in "the sound of sense," Frost singles out for praise Robinson's ability to imagine speech and to do so within the limits of traditional meters; as he judges, Robinson "stayed content with the old-fashioned way to be new." What Frost says about Robinson applies equally well to himself, and Frost used the Introduction to clarify his own poetry and vent his own prejudices to the public. Robinson, like Frost, attempted to steer a middle course between two extremes—modernist formal experimentation, on the one hand, and slavish adoption of traditional poetic forms, on the other. Rejecting such poles, both poets take liberties with the forms that they inherit.

In "Education by Poetry" (1931) Frost returns to his early belief that metaphor is the most important part of poetry and asserts the centrality of trope to poetry and life. Alleging that nearly all thinking is metaphorical, he suggests that one's ability to evaluate the world is compromised without a thorough understanding of the ways in which figures of speech, which represent that world to us, work. If we cannot see that "[a]ll metaphor breaks down somewhere," Frost maintains, we cannot know what to believe or how far to believe in anything. In a later essay, "The Constant Symbol" (1946), Frost restates his view of metaphor, that is, "saying one thing and meaning another, saying one thing in terms of another." He also restates the importance of meter to poetry and mythologizes it. As Frost says, he has written his verse "regular" his entire life "from fascination with this constant symbol I celebrate," namely, that "[e]very single poem written regular is a symbol small or great of the way the will has to pitch into commitments deeper and deeper to a rounded conclusion and then be judged for whether any original intention it had has been strongly spent or weakly lost; be it in art, **politics**, school, church, business, love, or marriage—in a piece of work or in a career." In other words, he claims that the discipline required to write, say, a **sonnet**, is analogous to the discipline required to participate fully in any one of a number of institutions; each pursuit demands faithful adherence to a set of rules and a steadfastness to see it through.

Ultimately, then, Frost's theory of poetic form grows from prosody into personal mythology. Through an expressive theory of poetic form—one that resembles Wordsworth's and Coleridge's—Frost insists on the need for meter as a check on our emotions, a way of taming the passionate "sounds of sense." His poetic theory stands as a figure for the contradictory impulses he works to resolve within himself and in the world around him.

References and further reading: R. Frost, *Prose Jottings*, 119; *Collected*, 712, 713, 721, 723, 740, 741, 746, 776–77, 786, 808–9, 861; and *Selected Letters*, 25, 79–80, 83–84; Thompson, *Early Years*, 409.

Tyler B. Hoffman

POETRY, A MAGAZINE OF VERSE. See **Monroe, Harriet, and** *Poetry*.

POETRY OF ROBERT FROST, THE **(1969).** This collection of Frost's poetry, edited by Edward Connery Lathem and published by **Holt**, Rinehart and Winston, includes the works in *The Complete Poems of Robert Frost 1949*, to which Lathem adds *The Masque of Reason*, *The Masque of Mercy*, and the poems published in Frost's final volume, *In the Clearing* **(1962)**. It has been the source of significant controversy centering primarily on the substantial differences between it and the collection published in 1949. The introductory essay to the earlier edition—written by the poet himself—is removed by Lathem, and in its place is a brief "Publisher's Note" defining the philosophy upon which the 1969 collection is based. It states that the book "contains those poems which . . . it is believed Robert Frost himself would have chosen to represent his poetic achievement had he lived to supervise a comprehensive edition of his work." The irony, of course, is that Frost himself oversaw the 1949 collection, while Lathem's emendations rest on several assumptions about the author's intentions.

Just before the index, Lathem includes a lengthy section entitled "Bibliographical and Textual Notes." In the editor's statement preceding the Notes, Lathem claims that he has used the text of the 1949 collection, except where changes were necessary for "greater textual clarity." Spelling has been normalized for consistency, and quotation and double quotation marks have been standardized, but capitalization remains unaltered throughout.

In a detailed essay published in 1982, Donald Hall clearly explains what he and other Frost scholars find objectionable in Lathem's collection: Of the more than 1,300 emendations made by Lathem—including deletions and additions of punctuation and the compounding of words—only 247 can be even remotely justified by reference to an earlier printing of the poem. Even those changes, Hall argues, are inconsistent with versions published and read aloud numerously during Frost's lifetime. Hall offers many examples of poems in which Lathem's changes substantively alter not only the literal readings of Frost's lines but also the cadences, which are vitally important for a poet who believed that the "sound of sense" often conveys more than the words themselves. (*See* **Poetic Theories.**)

In addition to those substantive changes, there are other less controversial differences. The 1969 edition begins, as does the 1949 edition, with the poem **"The Pasture."** However, where the *Complete Poems* offers a close-up of Frost indoors in what could be interpreted as a sad, if not troubled, mood, the photograph incorporated into the later edition shows a mildly meditative Frost in a pleasant outdoor setting. (Both photographs are the work of Clara Sipprell.) The appearance of the poems on the page is unique in the 1969 edition; the distinctive font is Fairchild, while the titles are set in Fairfield Medium, Linotype faces. Unlike the 1949 edition, the later collection runs poems together on the page and numbers lines. The sections following the poetry also differ. The index of first lines and index of titles in the earlier collection are collapsed into one index of first lines and titles in the latter.

Despite scholarly objection, Lathem's edition has seen wide circulation and has been, in many reputable circles, considered the text of choice. *Benet's Reader's Encyclopedia of American Literature* and the *Norton Anthology of Modern Poetry*, for example, have treated the Lathem edition as the definitive collection of Frost's work. However, in the 1995 Library of America edition, the 1969 edition is not used (*see* R. Frost, *Collected*). Editors Poirier and Richardson remark, "The core of the [Library of America] collection is the 1949 *Complete Poems of Robert Frost*, the last edition supervised by the poet himself." They imply further condemnation of Lathem's work in their statement that only the 1949 edition is "free of the unauthorized editorial changes introduced into subsequent editions." In a 1977 study, Poirier repeatedly undermines the authority of Lathem's edition, remarking, for example, that Lathem's emendations to **"Home Burial"** rob the poem of "poignant delicacy." He implies as well that Lathem's editorial judgment is arbitrary and unilateral. In addition, Poirier, as Hall before him, denounces Lathem's addition of a comma after "dark" in the famous line "lovely, dark and deep" (from **"Stopping by Woods"**), pointing out that Frost intended "dark and deep" to explain in what way the speaker finds the woods "lovely," not as two additional adjectives describing the woods. While the Lathem edition has been used widely until the appearance of Poirier and Richardson's collection, the 1995 volume promises to supplant the Lathem edition as the definitive collection of Frost's work.

References and further reading: R. Frost, *Collected*, 126; D. Hall; Poirier, *Knowing*, 126, 181.

Kelly Cannon

POLITICS. In both poetry and **prose**, Frost variously expressed his views on politics, on his relationship with political leaders (especially John F. Kennedy), on his interest and participation in U.S. and even world political government, and on his enduring resonance as a symbol of certain political ideologies. Frost often wrote glibly on political issues, masking his true allegiances with a jocular manner, as in his brief poem **"Precaution"**: "I never dared be radical when young / For fear it would make me conservative when old."

However, despite such an occasional whimsical tone concerning politics and politicians, Frost's personal letters reveal that his view of human political systems and institutions was informed by the same profound sense of fallenness that can be seen in much of his most famous poetical works. Frost, that is, held little or no faith in the works of humankind's political systems to assuage the suffering of fellow humans or to erase the deep-seated guilt, sorrow, and grief that he believed were the very basis of human life. Politics cannot change the tragic essence of the individual's daily existence, according to Frost. Such an outlook is depicted especially well in his epistolary exchanges with his good friend, the well-known poet and avowed socialist **Louis Untermeyer**, who later collected, edited, and published a volume of letters he received from Frost. He candidly wrote, for example, "I consider politics settled . . . no change of system could possibly make me a bit better or abler, the only two things of importance to me personally." Despite such cynicism, the letters show that Frost always considered democracy the best form of government and individual freedom its most valuable political virtue. More concretely, Frost maintained a lifelong loyalty to the Democratic Party, even when he perceived it to be departing from its traditional doctrines under the influence of Roosevelt and other New Deal politicians. Untermeyer's collection now serves as perhaps the best source of Frost's philosophical views concerning politics and human governments; it also contains caustic criticism of contemporary New Dealers, especially Franklin D. Roosevelt.

There are, to be sure, poems by Frost that directly or indirectly take up political government as their topic or theme. For example, **"A Case for Jefferson"** betrays a searing disdain for a particular Marxist ideologue: "He's Freudian Viennese by night. / By day he's Marxian Muscovite." The long poem **"Build Soil,"** subtitled "A Political Pastoral," remarks on topics such as socialism and ultimately argues for a sort of individualized ethical system of politics, including the memorable lines, "You see the beauty of my proposal is / It needn't wait on general revolution. / I bid you to a one-man revolution—/ The only revolution that is coming." The poem **"To a Thinker"** can be understood largely as criticism directed at the New Deal and particularly at President Roosevelt: Frost goes so far as to charge that Roosevelt's doctrines are "leaning on dictatorship." Similarly, much of *A Masque of Mercy* discusses issues of political import and includes a character called "Keeper" who may be read as a thinly veiled New Dealer (again, perhaps, as Roosevelt himself). Despite his frequently voiced animosity toward socialistic practices, Frost demonstrates an awareness of the problems caused by class difference in a poem such as **"An Equalizer."** Another poem is entitled **"On Taking from the Top to Broaden the Base."**

"The Vanishing Red" demonstrates a sympathy for the historic abuse of Native Americans even as it foregrounds Frost's characteristic ambivalence.

If we expand our concept of politics to include the fostering of political consensus and the articulation of national myth and ideology, we could argue that one of Frost's truly great poems deals directly with politics. Furthermore, the powerful meditation on the purpose and meaning of America, entitled **"The Gift Outright,"** marked the occasion of Frost's most visible moment as a political figure: the inaugural festivities of John F. Kennedy on 20 January 1961. Given his prominent public exposure at the beginning of what was at least symbolically one of America's most idealistic presidential administrations, we would do well to consider what Frost, near the end of his lifetime, had come to represent politically.

By that time, Frost had been associated with American mythic ideologies for most of his public life and so represented a ruling consensus. Thus, for example, when literary critic Lionel Trilling spoke of the "terrifying" side of Frost's poetry in a famous celebratory speech in 1959, he was perceived in many quarters as critiquing the popular national mythos that had come to be represented by the aging poet. Careful analysis of the public rhetoric that ensued from Trilling's comments suggests that Trilling's analysis was interpreted by many as a subversive attack on the conservative ideologies of the Eisenhower era with which Frost had come to be associated.

Stanley Burnshaw records that in an interview in conjunction with the eighty-fifth birthday celebration, one writer asked if New England had lost its vitality. Frost responded with the prediction that the next president would be from Boston: "He's a Puritan named Kennedy. The only Puritans left these days are the Roman Catholics. There! I guess I wear my politics on my sleeve." The remark gained widespread attention at the time, with headlines appearing all over the country proclaiming Frost's enthusiasm for the emergence of John F. Kennedy. Kennedy acknowledged the apparent endorsement with some satisfaction in a note to Frost dated 11 April 1959, and he later met briefly with Frost at the Library of Congress. According to Frost's friend, Arizona congressman Stewart Udall, Frost and Kennedy hit it off well in their initial meeting, and as the 1960 campaign progressed, "Kennedy [often] used [a] familiar Frost quotation as a late evening farewell to his followers": "But I have promises to keep / And miles to go before I sleep / And miles to go before I sleep." In the constant implementation of some of Frost's most resonant verses, according to Udall, Kennedy enlisted Frost as one of his "quiet collaborators in the 1960 campaign"; it was a collaboration of which Frost apparently approved. When Udall suggested that the poet be invited to participate in Kennedy's inauguration, Kennedy liked the idea and asked Udall to contact Frost and determine if he was interested. Later, according to Frost's official **biographers**, when Frost accepted the invitation, Kennedy himself chose the poem to be read; of course, it was "The Gift Outright." Udall's version differs in claiming that Frost suggested "The Gift

Outright," which he called his "most national" poem; Thomas G. Smith has recently argued that Frost's longtime assistant **Kay Morrison** suggested that specific poem. In any event, the politician and the poet reached consensus, and "The Gift Outright" stands uniquely in American history as the first poem to be recited in full at a presidential inauguration. (*See also* **"For John F. Kennedy His Inauguration,"** the preface Frost wrote for "The Gift Outright" but was unable to read because of the sun's glare.)

Any presidential inauguration, and certainly that of Kennedy at the outset of what many anticipated as one of America's most youthful and idealistic administrations, is in large part a ritual that fosters and confirms the regnant American ideologies. In such a context, we might ask, With what precisely is the poet aligning himself by the appearance? What "idea" of America did Frost wish to evoke with his appearance? We must remember that Frost was well into his eighties by this time and that the prestige of participating in the event cannot be discounted. It is certainly worth noting Frost's later attempts to influence the politics of the nation, especially his gaffes during and following his visit to the Soviet Union, including the controversy that arose as a result of his meeting with Soviet Premier Nikita Khrushchev. Again, however, our interest might focus more on the cultural phenomenon of his political appearances and less on the poet's motives. For example, why did the political movers consider Frost's appearance to be an asset, and why did Kennedy request the specific poem? The simplest answer is that, by then, Frost had become a symbolic manifestation of many of America's most enduring virtues: hardworking farmer, pastoral visionary, New England stoic, fiery and loyal patriot, and cracker-barrel philosopher.

Such qualities are reflected, more or less, in "The Gift Outright." The poem opens with one of Frost's more memorable lines—"The land was ours before we were the land's"—immediately foregrounding one of the key themes, that of possession. The overall effect of the poem's focus on possession, however, is to emphasize the contradictions inherent in the "American state of mind," and Frost's own comments on his poem support the recognition of such tension. Perhaps this is why Kennedy asked Frost to alter the ending lines to assert a more positive and optimistic tone. At the inauguration, Frost ended the poem this way: "such as she *would* become, *has* become, and I—and for this occasion let me change that to—what she *will* become."

Still, it seems ironic that the poem read by Frost takes a rather hard look at American ideological belief. In short, "The Gift Outright," while appearing to represent patriotism at its best, does hint at another, darker version of the American myth, a version that Frost makes explicit in several other poems in his final volume, *In the Clearing*, issued in March of 1962, some fourteen months after his reading at the inauguration. The reinsertion of the poem in this volume is significant for two reasons. First, it is preceded in the text by Frost's long occasional poem written especially for the inaugural, called "For John F. Kennedy His Inauguration." Second, and more important, several of the poems leading up to these two in the volume—especially **"Pod of the Milkweed,"**

"Away!", **"A Cabin in the Clearing,"** and **"America Is Hard to See"**—deal explicitly with the issue of the meaning of the myth of America. When read as a sequence, the opening poems, followed abruptly by the two inaugural poems, create a tension typical of much of Frost's greatest work and assert his paradoxical sense of America's prevalent myth. The irony of the opening poems of the volume is advanced in what may be Frost's most skeptical poem concerning American myth, "America Is Hard to See." Thus, the opening section of *In the Clearing* juxtaposes ironic analyses of America's myths, mission, meaning, and politics, as depicted in the first seven poems, with the more conservative versions presented in the eighth and ninth poems (the Kennedy inaugural poem and "The Gift Outright"). It certainly is odd to hear the poet condemning "literary chatter" in "America Is Hard to See," only to find a few pages later lines from Frost's verses for the inauguration. One wonders about Frost's authentic view: Are we to understand the meaning of America as merely another form of communal "doom" covered up by "literary chatter" or as a heroic "venture" that is repeatedly "justified" in "glory upon glory"?

Any critic attempting to pigeonhole Frost's politics or concept of America and its myth of origin and purpose must somehow reckon with the mixed signals presented by the poet. One might well argue that, in the opening pages of *In the Clearing*, Frost's poetical consideration of political governments and the myths and ideologies that undergird them is given its greatest and most enduring expression; further, "The Gift Outright" stands as one of the most important artistically successful of Frost's "political" poems.

References and further reading: Burnshaw, 102; Bush, "Writing the Myth"; R. Frost, *Letters to Untermeyer*; Parini, *A Life*, 264, 278–82; T. Smith; Stanlis, *Individual* and "Politics"; Udall.

Harold K. Bush, Jr.

POUND, EZRA (1885–1972), a poet who progressed through numerous movements such as Imagism (*see* **Lowell, Amy, and Imagism**) and vorticism, helped to establish the careers of other poets, including Robert Frost. As the foreign editor for **Harriet Monroe**'s *Poetry*, Pound published reviews of Frost's first two volumes of poetry. In the May 1913 issue he wrote in reference to *A Boy's Will* that Frost was yet another American poet who had been scorned by American publishers and who had to seek support in **England**. Prior to the review, Pound had written to Alice Corbin Henderson, Monroe's assistant, that he had "just discovered another Amur'kn. VURRY Amur'k'n, with, I think, the seeds of grace." While Frost appreciated the attention, he feared being identified as another Pound satellite, especially since Pound's abrasiveness chafed American publishers. In a letter to Thomas Mosher in October 1913, Frost wrote, "I am out with Pound pretty much altogether. . . . Pound is an incredible ass and he hurts more than he helps the person he praises." Of his friend Sidney Cox, Frost asked in January 1915 that he discreetly let it be known that he was not an

American exile relying on Pound: "He made up his mind in the short time I was friends with him (we quarreled in six weeks) to add me to his party of American literary refugees in London. Nothing could be more unfair, nothing better calculated to make me an exile for life. Another such review as the one in Poetry and I shan't be admitted at Ellis Island."

In later speeches reminiscing about his early publications, Frost would say that it was F. S. Flint, not Pound, who had discovered him. Frost had met Flint at the opening of Harold Monro's bookshop, and it was Flint who had told Pound of his fellow American writer. Although Flint published a review of *A Boy's Will* in England, Pound's review had more influence in establishing Frost in America.

After Frost returned to the United States in 1915, he did not have much contact with Pound. Frost fully supported Pound's arrest and incarceration in 1946 for broadcasting, from Italy, propaganda treasonous to the United States during World War II. Frost told Lawrance Thompson that his attitude toward Pound softened after reading Horace Gregory's 1954 review of *The Literary Essays of Ezra Pound* in which Gregory quoted part of Pound's review of *North of Boston*. Frost realized that Pound was one of his best critics after reading that Pound regarded him as "an honest writer, writing from himself, from his knowledge and emotion; not simply picking up the manner which magazines are accepting at the moment, and applying it to topics in vogue" (qtd. in Thompson). However, it was not until 1957, when Archibald MacLeish moved to have Pound released from St. Elizabeth's Hospital in Washington, on the grounds that Pound was too mentally ill to stand trial, that Frost agreed to sign a letter of petition—along with **T. S. Eliot** and Ernest Hemingway—because he felt that Pound had been punished enough. According to Thompson, Frost tried to claim sole credit for freeing Pound. **Reginald L. Cook** records that although Frost had helped by meeting with the attorney general, Archibald MacLeish was the primary instigator. On his release in 1958, when he was informed of Frost's help on the matter, Pound replied, "[H]e ain't been in much of a hurry."

Although Frost distanced himself from Pound, he still appreciated his contribution to twentieth-century literature. In a 1934 letter to his daughter Lesley, who was preparing to deliver a talk on poetry, Frost wrote, "Ezra Pound was the Prime Mover in the Movement and must always have the credit for whats [sic] in it. . . . Pound began to talk very early about rhythm alone without meter. . . . [W]hatever you do, do Pound justice as the great original."

References and further reading: R. Cook, "Context," 123–73, includes a discussion of Frost and Pound, especially Pound's release from St. Elizabeth's Hospital; R. Frost, *Collected*, 734, *Family Letters*, 160–61, and *Selected Letters*, 96, 147–48; Grieder; Pound, *Letters*, 14, and Rev.; Thompson's three-volume biography recounts Frost's relationship with Pound in great detail: see especially *Early Years*, 472–73, and Thompson and Winnick, 248, 258; for further information on Frost's experience in England, see L. Francis, *Morning Gladness*, and Walsh.

John P. Samonds

"PRAYER IN SPRING, A," was originally published, Jeffrey S. Cramer tells us, in the first edition of *A Boy's Will* (**1913**) but was written, according to Frost, in 1903. A poem of four quatrains, each consisting of two pairs of iambic pentameter lines coupled in rhyme but not in syntax, "A Prayer in Spring" is primarily a formal, collective supplication to seize the joy of the moment, realized in nature's springtime reverie of bees and blossoms. Frost's gloss of the poem in the table of contents for *A Boy's Will* states, "He discovers that the greatness of love lies not in forward-looking thoughts." Like other Frost prayer poems, it has little of the rural or boyish diction one might expect in *A Boy's Will*, and its use of the collective first person lends a formality fitting to its religious tone. The poet as priest prays twice "Oh, give us pleasure," and it is pleasure of the present, not the future, that is begged, pleasure in the sensuous, even sensual activity of bees and birds seen pollinating the flowers. But in the final stanza, the poet seems to speak with an assuredness beyond even that of priest, pronouncing that such utter love of pleasure links the individual with "God above" in fulfillment of what He sanctifies here on earth. Such untempered reverie is rare in Frost's poetry, but "A Prayer in Spring" fits into the progression of *A Boy's Will* from the bleak autumn landscapes of the early poems to the "thawing wind" of spring in the poem preceding it.

References and further reading: Cramer, *Frost among His Poems*, 11, 18; Poirier, *Knowing*.

Douglas Watson

"PRECAUTION," one of the "Ten Mills" in *A Further Range* (**1936**), first appeared as part of that grouping of poems in *Poetry* (Apr. 1936). Frost began reciting the unrhymed couplet—"a couplet that isn't a couplet," he called it—at his readings in the early 1930s. Although he sometimes indicated that he wrote it spontaneously during a conversation, it may have been a salvaged couplet from an earlier, nonextant poem. The poem became a standard answer for those questioning his political views in regard to whether he considered himself a conservative or a radical. *See also* **Politics**.

References and further reading: R. Cook, *Living Voice*, 145; R. Frost, *Interviews*, 85; Mertins, 338.

Jeffrey S. Cramer

PROSE. Frost's reluctance to publish and collect his prose became a matter of some notoriety among the few scholars and editors who expressed interest in undertaking editions of his work. They found Frost singularly uncooperative. Robert S. Newdick, an early **biographer**, organized a manuscript of the prose in the late 1930s titled "Prefaces and Parleyings." He was in earnest correspondence with **Henry Holt and Company** (Frost's American publisher) before Frost caused the edition to be held back. At about the same time, Lawrance Thompson, later the author of a three-volume biography of the poet, was also working on a collection of Frost's prose. In those years, too, **Harvard University** Press still entertained hopes that Frost would prepare his 1936 Charles Eliot Norton Lectures for publication. None of the projects was ever advanced, and the transcript of the Norton Lectures that Harvard prepared for Frost disappeared while in his possession. He explained in a February 1938 letter to R.P.T. Coffin, "I thought I was about ready to let [the lectures] set when I accepted the Harvard invitation to deliver them in writing after delivering them by word of mouth. Something in me still fights off the written prose."

Frost did, however, produce an uncommonly engaging body of prose, ranging from short stories, to essays, to prefaces and introductions, and to lectures. His first "professional" prose writings were a handful of potboiler stories and articles published between 1903 and 1905 in two New England poultry-farming magazines. In regard to these, it must be acknowledged first that they are surely the best "poultry stories" written by a modern American poet. They are in fact quite good. In "The Original and Only," Frost works in the monologue form that he would realize fully in *North of Boston* **(1914)**, his second book of poetry: " 'You want to hear about our hen,' said the practical poultryman," this story begins, and the rest of the piece is entirely in the poultryman's voice. In such stories we can see Frost's increasingly sure efforts to "fix" the tones of his characters' speech to the page, to use a term he later favored in discussions of *North of Boston*. Several of the comical sketches are worthy of Mark Twain. But the communities in such stories show little of the pettiness and meanness described in much of Twain's small-town fiction. There are no Hadleyburgs here. Quite the contrary: In stories such as "A Just Judge" and "The Question of a Feather" there is comedy but little satire—and no invective. Frost's writing for the poultry journals shows how sympathetic his ear was for the voices of the rural people about whom he wrote. In his work they are given a subtlety of speech and humor not found, for example, in the New England stories of Edith Wharton, *Ethan Frome* (1911) and *Summer* (1917), both set in the time and place of *North of Boston*.

In 1906 Frost took a position at **Pinkerton Academy** in **Derry**, New Hampshire, which he would hold through June 1911. The association produced two items that bear looking into here, both written for the Pinkerton Academy *Catalogue*: a general article about the Academy and a description of its English curriculum. The documents tell us much about Frost as a **teacher**, much that was borne out by the course of his remarkably long and varied career in education. In the general article he explains that the Academy

undertakes to teach with sense and thoroughness the subjects proper to its curriculum. For the rest, its concern is to aim high enough. Work is methodical without subservience to methods. It is held that, for the instructor, "no method nor discipline can supersede the necessity of being forever on the alert." Much must be left to the inspiration of the classroom and the exigency of the case. The constant appeal is to honor, reason and native energy. Government is less by rule than by suggestion. Pupils are taught to think for themselves, and to do things by having to do them for themselves.

Frost's conversational manner is refreshing in so stuffy a forum as the catalog of a proper late-Victorian boys' academy, and it gives some intimation of what his classroom demeanor was like. Clearly he favors an improvisational mode. And we know from the curriculum Frost subsequently wrote for the *Catalogue* that he stressed the oral performance of poetry and prose. He wanted to teach students "the *satisfaction* of superior speech," as he characteristically put it. To this end, "expression in oral reading rather than intelligent comment [was] made the test of appreciation." Frost sought unstructured class meetings, meetings that approached the condition of conversation: "Discussion proceeds more and more without the goad of the direct question." He wanted to relax the regimentation of the schoolroom, giving it over to the libertarian "satisfactions" of conversation, where personality is best unfolded and understood.

After leaving Pinkerton, Frost taught for a year at **Plymouth Normal School** in Plymouth, New Hampshire, before departing for **England** with his family in 1912. Returning to America three years later, he had published two books of poetry and won a reputation. At this point the contours of his career assume recognizable dimensions, and the pattern of his published prose reflects such contours: There are lectures, largely before academic audiences; prefaces to poetry anthologies, two of them of student verse; prefaces to his own works or works by other poets; "tributes" to contemporaries in the literary and academic worlds. Much of Frost's prose investigates what it means to the artist to "go to college." In a 1919 speech at **Amherst College** he said, "I have been a great deal worried about an ancient institution, namely, poverty. . . . Let poverty be abolished and where will the young poet, the young scholar, the young painter go then? I only see one place left for him to go and that is to college." By 1919 Frost had himself settled into what would become a lifelong affiliation with colleges as a lecturer and teacher. It was one means to abolish his own "poverty." This was not necessarily a satisfactory arrangement, as the diffident tone of the 1919 speech just quoted implies. The college, at least in thought, would remain for him something of a last resort or "refuge." Early on, Frost came to doubt whether refuge from "poverty" and from the main currents and abrasions of American life was something an artist really ought to endure. To his way of thinking, in fact, shelter from the "crudity" and "rawness" of our "national life" (as he sometimes put it) was at best enervating for the poet and quite possibly worse.

We must read his relatively unknown 1925 tribute to the poet and dramatist Percy MacKaye in light of such concerns. MacKaye had been instrumental in securing Frost's own refuge as poet-in-residence at the **University of Michigan** in 1921, and in a tribute prepared for a banquet celebrating MacKaye's fiftieth birthday Frost remarked, "Percy MacKaye has spent precious time trying to make the world an easier place to write poetry in. Everybody knows how he has spread himself over the country, as with two very large wings, to get his fellow poets all fellowships at the universities. That is but an incident in the general campaign he is forever on, to hasten the day when our national life, the raw material of poetry, having become less and less raw, shall at last cease to be raw at all, and poetry shall almost write itself without the intervention of the artist." The subtler implications of such remarks are interesting. Frost obliquely criticizes the institutional supports for poets and writers that were then beginning to assume the form they have today, even though these were institutions of which Frost was himself something of an architect. It is as if Frost's position *felt* powerful and vital to him only insofar as it remained precarious. In any event, that is the mythology he developed. His idea is that the poet *must* suffer resistance to his aspirations: linguistic and formal "resistance" *in* his poems— as Frost's essay "The Constant Symbol" shows—but also *social* resistance *outside* of them. That is why he was troubled by efforts to circumscribe or protect the society of poets and writers, whether in academia or in writers' colonies. Something must work against the poet, who comes to know his own "will," to feel its power and direction, only as he "braves alien entanglements" and the "harsher discipline from without," as Frost puts it in "The Constant Symbol," perhaps his greatest essay on poetics. (*See* **Poetic Theories**.) If MacKaye wished poets "a beauty of life that shall be poetry without being worked up into poetry," Frost's hard reply to him is this: Too ready a system of "fellowship" (both social and monetary) actually diminishes the power and beauty of the poet's performance.

One might conclude, then, that Frost's defense of poetry written in form— his defense of the discipline of art—is associated with arguments he made about the place of the poet in academia and in society as a whole. Importantly, his ideas about how poems work have larger social implications. "Education by Poetry" (1931), for example, is a meditation on the nature of metaphor in poetry but also on the role of metaphor in nearly every department of our lives: Frost is interested in the metaphors *we live by*. "The Figure a Poem Makes" (1939), and Frost's well-known 1913 and 1914 letters elaborating his theory of "the sound of sense," astutely considers the relation of sound to meaning in poetry and in writing more generally. Frost tries to account for what he calls "the *abstract* vitality of our speech." His "Letter to *The Amherst Student*" (1935) and preface to **E. A. Robinson**'s *King Jasper* (1935) consider exercises in poetic form as small, local ways to establish some manner of control over potentially disruptive emotional and social forces that might otherwise prove overwhelming. "It is really everybody's sanity," he says in the "Letter," to live by exercises in form. Such exercises have a *therapeutic* value, as Frost's 1958 tribute to his friend Merrill Moore, the psychiatrist and poet, suggests. In other words, form in poetry, and in art more generally, has a *sanitary* quality: It keeps us sound and sane.

The prose Frost published after 1950 demonstrates his appeal well beyond the confines of the literary establishment and the academy. He hoped to establish poetry's claims on endeavors ranging from **sports** (as in his 1956 essay on baseball for *Sports Illustrated*) to **politics** to **science**. In 1959, for example, Frost appeared on a panel to discuss "The Future of Man." The occasion was the dedication of the Joseph E. Seagram & Sons Building in New York City. Other panelists included Bertrand Russell, biologist and Nobel laureate Hermann Muller, anthropologist and social biologist Ashley Montagu, and biologist Sir Julian Huxley. By this late date Frost's presence in the company of scientists and philosophers to discuss a topic such as "The Future of Man" seemed natural. Frost mounted an eloquent defense of the humanities against the disturbing scientism represented, for him, by the eugenic evolutionary theories of his fellow "Future of Man" panelist Muller, who advocated "genetic selection and manipulation, unhampered by ancient taboos and superstitions." Later in the session, the newspaper columnist Inez Robb remarked, "I think what we wanted to ask you especially, Mr. Frost, was whether your testament to man was an affirmation that he will need love in the future as he has in the past and in the present." The remarkable assumptions underlying the query agitated Frost, and one senses that his reply is as much directed to Muller as to Robb: "Look! Look! Man has come this way. Shakespeare himself says the best children are love children. . . . That sinful enough for you?" "Love children" are the best: Man has come and will proceed by way of passionate spontaneity, not by way of the rational "selection and manipulation" of the eugenicist. Frost writes in a longer version of his essay on "The Future of Man":

Science seems about to ask us what we are going to do about taking in hand our own further evolution. . . . We have the laboratorians ready and willing to tend to this. We can commission them any day to go ahead messing around with rays on genes for mutations or with sperm on ovules for eugenics till they get us somewhere, make something of us for a board or foundation to approve of. But . . . I foresee no society where artificial insemination won't be in bad taste.

It is a chilling thought—and Frost means it to be chilling—that we should "take in hand our further evolution" in order to meet the requirements of "a board or foundation." Frost adopts, here, a somewhat proprietary attitude toward the biological sciences. He remarks in the discussion session to "The Future of Man" panel:

Who are we? Science can't describe us; it contributes very little to our description, a very little bit in all this newness wonder of science that they talk about—it's very slight. The wonderful description of us is the humanities, the book of the worthies and unworthies through the ages, and anything you talk about in the future must be a projection from that.

Notwithstanding the blandishments of the eugenicists, Frost argues, science will never be able adequately to describe—let alone properly to *value*—the men and women who make it. Frost delicately but firmly marks the outer limits of scientific inquiry, an enterprise on behalf of poetry in which he had been engaged, in his prose writings, since publishing "Education by Poetry" in 1931.

References and further reading: Quotations from Frost's prose cited above are from R.

Frost, *Collected*, 644, 662, 698, 711, 786–91, 867–72; see also R. Frost, *Poetry and Prose* and *Writing*; Richardson, "Prose."

Mark Richardson

"PROVIDE, PROVIDE" was first published in *The New Frontier* (Sept. 1934) and was subsequently included in *A Further Range* (**1936**). The poem seems to be about a fallen star of Hollywood, the once beautiful Abishag, who has now turned into a withered hag and a cleaning woman. The speaker—or storyteller—comments on the common destiny of the fall from riches and the loss of status, and he advises his audience to provide for their approaching old age and possibly sadder times by buying themselves a safe position. His wisdom, though, is soon perceived as dubious. The use of overstatement in his impractical suggestions ("Make the whole stock exchange your own!" or "occupy a throne") and the overemphasized warning and moralizing tone of the ending ("Provide, provide!") reveal the poem's ironic tone. The childish lullaby lilt and the slightly comic effect of the triple end rhymes increase the ironic distance, especially where rhyming words provide grotesque contrasts ("throne/crone").

"Provide, Provide" has elicited a controversial critical reaction, due especially to the ambiguity of its tone. As **Reginald L. Cook** notes, Frost himself said that the poem was full of "tune" and—probably in jest—that it was "horrible." According to Lawrance Thompson, it was occasioned by Frost's reaction to a charwomen's strike that had been supported by some **Harvard** reformers. The students were inspired by a sentimental humanitarianism that had recently been brought into fashion by the New Deal. Thus, Thompson sees the poem as a *"laissez-faire* declaration against the 'providers-for-others.' " Richard Poirier seems to be of the same opinion and is even more radical in his reading of "Provide, Provide" as an *"ad-hoc* political aside to Frost's left-liberal friend Henry Wallace." He quotes the comment Frost liked to add to his public reading of the poem: "Provide, provide! . . . Or somebody else'll provide *for* ya." (*See also* **Politics**.)

Another comment by Frost, though, seems to corroborate Dorothy Judd Hall's interpretation of the poem as a stoic and religious statement. Hall reports that at **Bread Loaf**, on 26 August 1961, after reading the poem aloud, Frost said, "The worst part of life is the end. You can't keep the end from being hard, not the state—nobody but God." On the side of a noncynical interpretation, Laurence Perrine suggests that Frost's real choice is that of being true to oneself, and David Perkins believes that faced with nihilistic alternatives the poet recommends the "diminished" choice of a common, human compromise. Randall Jarrell also thinks that the ambiguity of Frost's tone in "Provide, Provide" helps him to conceal a serious attitude under an apparently light verse and that lines 14–17 present a sample of nonworldly wisdom of moving restraint. William Pritchard, though, finds the poem's "pleasures and satisfactions . . . more theatrical, less humanly and morally profound" than Jarrell claims.

The poem is characterized as a ballad by means of its rhythm and register.

A heavy cadence is established from the beginning through the iambic tetrameters and simple rhyme scheme of seven tercets. The register reminds the reader of oral narratives of exemplary episodes culminating in a moral lesson.

References and further reading: R. Cook, *Living Voice*, 135, 151; D. J. Hall, *Contours*, 134; Jarrell, "Laodiceans"; Parini, *A Life*, 286–87; Perkins, "Frost"; Perrine, "Frost's 'Provide, Provide' " and "Provide, Provide"; Poirier, *Knowing*, 258; Pritchard, *Literary Life*, 209; Thompson, *Triumph*, 437–38.

Paola Loreto

PULITZER PRIZE, THE. *See* **Awards, Honors, and Prizes**.

"PUTTING IN THE SEED," a **sonnet** from *Mountain Interval* **(1916)**, first appeared in *Poetry and Drama* (Dec. 1914). It combines features of Petrarchan and Shakespearean forms. More exactly, Frost retains the strong two-part development of the Italian form but structures the rhymes of the octave in *abab* quatrains more closely approximating the English form. "Putting in the Seed" belongs to a tradition of poetry likening human procreation to "husbandry" and tillage: Man is to woman as farmer is to land. Frost's idea seems to be that in making love we place ourselves in alignment with larger seasonal rhythms. The octave of the sonnet lays out the situation: The husband is out planting; the wife is in cooking. The sestet then explores the symbolic reaches of that situation. At the "turn" in the sonnet, the speaking voice rises up out of the colloquial patterns of the first eight lines to assume a much deeper resonance. The sonnet transcends the rhetorical and argumentative limits it seemed to set for itself in the octave, "shouldering its way" up out of the medium in which it was at first grounded, as Richard Poirier has suggested. And Frost's phrasing is indeed arresting: "How Love burns through the Putting in the Seed." Whether in agricultural or in marital situations, the act of *putting in*, as imagined here, is quite deliberate: The "seed" spoken of in the sonnet is a human (and male) imposition, not anything wild or uncultivated. "Putting in the Seed" is a poem of sexuality *acculturated*, though not, of course, brought entirely out of the realm of Nature: It is, in short, a poem of marriage—a poem of sexuality made social and sanctified (as it is in **"A Prayer in Spring"**).

References and further reading: For a discussion of **"Leaves Compared with Flowers"** as a dark companion poem to "Putting in the Seed," see Foster; Poirier, *Knowing*.

Mark Richardson

"QUANDARY" was first published as "Somewhat Dietary" in the *Massachusetts Review* (Fall 1959). Lines 5–6 later appeared as "The Old Pair" in the *New England Galaxy* (Summer 1960). **Reginald L. Cook** recalls Frost's assertion that the couplet was inspired by his reading of **Emerson**, and Jeffrey S. Cramer suggests that Frost was alluding to lines in "Uriel" in which Emerson says, "Evil will bless," and in which he writes "of the good of evil born." Indeed, as Lawrance Thompson points out, the poem can be read as an expansion of the theme in *A Masque of Reason* (*see* **Drama**) that "bad was essential to good in the divine scheme of things." It was collected in *In the Clearing* **(1962)**.

The poem begins with the speaker's argument that evil must exist for good to be meaningful and that knowledge is needed to discriminate between the two; the observation develops into a discussion of the importance of varying types of knowledge. The poem pivots on the quandary that the tension between reason and emotion underlies human understanding and moral enlightenment.

Thomas K. Hearn sees "Quandary" as one of Frost's poems on moral discernment and on the idea that there are no infallible guides, whereas Mordecai Marcus calls it a lighthearted look at evil, criticizing "liberals who find evil intolerable and who refuse to make various kinds of discriminations." Marcus points out that the reference to sweetbreads alludes to "the similarity in appearance between sweetbread (the pancreas or thymus of animals) and brains."

References and further reading: R. Cook, *Living Voice*, 145; Cramer, *Frost among His Poems*, 177; Hearn; Marcus, *Explication*, 227; Thompson, *Triumph*, 400 n.15.

Belinda D. Bruner

"QUEST OF THE PURPLE-FRINGED, THE," first appeared as "The Quest of the Orchis" in *The Independent* (27 June 1901). It was reprinted under its original title in *Three Poems* (1935) and as "The Quest of the Purple-Fringed" in *A Witness Tree* **(1942)**. The explanation for Frost's delay in collecting the poem seems to be that the poem slipped his mind. Frost made this notation next to the poem in Louis Mertins's copy of *The Independent*: "I had almost forgotten this when I came on it a few years back and put it into one of my later books. This R. L. Frost [his name as it appeared in 1901] seems like a stranger to me." George Monteiro has explained the change of title by noting that Frost may have mistaken the gentian (which blooms earlier in the year) for the orchis and that Frost, discovering his error, may have deleted the name of the flower to cover the mistake.

Regardless of which flower Frost actually saw, the poem describes the poet's search for a rare and delicate purple-fringed flower that blooms only briefly. He follows "the slender fox" to find the "far-sought flower" in a tranquil spot beneath an alder tree where the orchis is undisturbed by breeze or by bee. The poet takes the flower as a sign of the coming autumn (symbolically, of death).

According to Lawrance Thompson, the writing of the poem stems from Frost's belated honeymoon with **Elinor** in 1896 in Allenstown, New Hampshire. There his friend **Carl Burell** introduced Frost to the hobby of botany. Burell lent Frost a copy of a botanical guidebook, *How to Know the Wild Flowers* (1893), by Mrs. William Starr Dana (Francis Theodora Parsons).

The poem is typically connected to the nature writings of **Henry David Thoreau.** *How to Know the Wild Flowers* includes excerpts from Thoreau's *Journal*, and Dana uses material from Thoreau's journal entry for 9 June 1854 in her description of the large purple-fringed orchis: "Find the great fringed-orchis out apparently two or three days, two are almost fully out, two or three already budded; a large spike of peculiarly delicate, pale-purple flowers growing in the luxuriant and shady swamp. . . . The village belle never sees this more delicate belle of the swamp. . . . A beauty reared in the shade of a convent, who has never strayed beyond the convent-bell. Only the skunk or owl, or other inhabitant of the swamp, beholds it" (qtd. in West 41).

References and further reading: Mertins, 16–18, 22, 39; Monteiro, *New England* and "Frost's 'Quest' "; Parini, *A Life*, 57–58; Thomas; Thompson, *Early Years*, 216–23, 270; West, 41 (West's essay responds to Monteiro's).

Christian L. Pyle

"QUESTION, A," is one of several epigrammatic pieces that make up the "Quantula" section of *A Witness Tree* **(1942)**, where it first appeared. Thematically, Frost's poem allows for certain autobiographical readings; he admitted as much years later in a 1956 interview, when he characterized "A Question" as a "mood, when you sometimes wonder if it is worth it, all the pain" (qtd. in Gerber). The recent and unexpected deaths of his wife and son and his complex relationship with **Kay Morrison** may have precipitated a personal crisis of sorts during the writing of *A Witness Tree*. That Frost himself was able to universalize his pain, render it comically (*see* **"An Answer"**), and generate a Pulitzer Prize–

winning collection during such a time leads potentially to a more positive reading. The "voice" in the poem seems to hint that its own "scars" are indeed "too much," although the request to "look into my stars" suggests that the voice might even be that of God.

References and further reading: Gerber, *Essays*, 123.

George Lopez

"QUESTIONING FACES" first appeared in the *Saturday Review* as "Of a Winter Evening" (12 Apr. 1958), later published under its current title in Frost's last volume, *In The Clearing*, on his eighty-eighth birthday (26 Mar. 1962). Frost presented the little poem at two important public readings during the last months of his life. In July 1962, four months after publication of *In The Clearing*, Frost read his poetry at the **Bread Loaf School of English** at Middlebury College, Vermont. As we learn in **Reginald L. Cook**'s account, Frost introduced "Questioning Faces" fondly, read the poem, commented on its importance for him, and then recited it a second time. Later, just two months prior to his death, Frost gave a final public reading at Jordan Hall in Boston on 2 December 1962; Stanley Burnshaw's work reveals that the very first poem Frost selected from *In the Clearing* was "Questioning Faces."

"Questioning Faces" serves as a good example of Frost's reimagining an earlier autobiographical incident from a different perspective. According to Dorothy Judd Hall's discussion of the poem's origins, Frost saw the owl referred to in the poem at sunset outside his window in **Franconia, New Hampshire**, sometime prior to 1920. When the poem came to be written much later, he shifted the point of view to that of "glassed-in children at the window sill." Frost, of course, is not the first poet to reshape first-person experiences into third-person poems, nor is his adoption of a child's point of view so extraordinary either. Yet, given the continuous appearance of children or at least a childlike naïveté and innocence about the world and nature throughout his poetry, readers should not be surprised that such a little-known poem reappeared as one of Frost's favorites late in life.

References and further reading: Burnshaw, 188; R. Cook, *Living Voice*, 192; D. J. Hall, *Contours*, 28.

Douglas M. Tedards

R

"RABBIT HUNTER, THE," first published in *A Witness Tree* (1942), establishes winter as a part of the hunter's mood. Or perhaps it is more accurate to say that the hunter's mood forms a part of winter. The phrase "Ghastly snow-white" attaches equally to the hunter and to the bleak swamps, grimly merging them into a single thought, into a unit. The hound works, we are told, as "one possessed"; it is subject to a greater will. But the hunter is no better off than his hound: He lacks wit to "comprehend" his own actions and from the outset is "careless." The latter word, as used here, does not mean "clumsy" or "imprudent"; it means "bereft of deliberation." It is as if the hunter merely has executed some larger, more "comprehensive" will that things should die; like his hound, he is agency—not agent—making it seem as if even *human* violence were beyond our management, as if our destructions were subsidiary functions of some larger natural force. All of these suggestions give the funereal theme of **"November"**—which precedes "The Rabbit Hunter" in *A Witness Tree*—a still more sinister twist, as if finally to put to rest the hopes of dreamers like the young poet spoken of in **"The Lost Follower."** In the final lines of "The Rabbit Hunter," the speaker/poet is *himself* no better able than the hunter or the hound to "comprehend" what happens here and no better able to manage it— at least not *outside* the **lyric** line of poetry. It is worth noting that the only two unrhymed words in the poem are "death" and "still": Every other word has a rhyming partner. Perhaps "still" and "death" may be said to rhyme conceptually rather than sonically.

References and further reading: Greiner, "Factual Men."

Mark Richardson

"RANGE-FINDING," a **sonnet** originally titled "The Little Things of War," presents a scene in which nothing, not even the smallest flower, is exempt from war. Frost claimed he wrote the poem as early as 1902 "in a time of profound peace," but it sat for years before he sent it, along with sixteen other poems, to **Susan Hayes Ward** at Christmastime in 1911. According to Elizabeth Shepley Sergeant, he finally published it in *Mountain Interval* **(1916)** at the urgings of Edward Thomas, who, in a letter from the trenches in France, told Frost that the poem was a "surprisingly exact description of no man's land."

The title of the poem is a technical term used by riflemen and artillerymen to describe the process of zeroing in on the target. By analyzing the results of each round, the marksman can adjust his sights and "find the range." The act of finding the range, heightened by the poet's introduction of a spider seeking prey, creates a little drama, similar to the one in **"Design,"** centering on the knowledge that the death of one thing in nature is often essential for another to live. The drama turns what might have been a sentimental poem about the disturbance of the "innocent" natural world by war into a sinister and ironic statement about the nature of humanity. Both the spider and humans are predators, and the war is simply another example of the predation that occurs regularly in nature.

References and further reading: Abel, "Frost's 'Range-Finding' "; Cramer, *Frost among His Poems*, 54, 223; R. Frost, *Selected Letters*, 220; for a good discussion of the poet's use of irony and form, see Moore; Sergeant, 189.

James M. Dubinsky

"RECORD STRIDE, A," was first published in the *Atlantic Monthly* (May 1936) and later included in *A Further Range* **(1936)** with the subtitle "The United States Stated." Lawrance Thompson records that Frost wrote the poem, originally entitled "My Olympic Record Stride," several months after a visit to his birthplace, San Francisco, in the summer of 1931, but Frost claimed in 1942 that he had written the poem "in California at the time of the Olympic Games" in 1932.

In a December 1932 letter to **Louis Untermeyer**, Frost recounts a humorous tale surrounding the poem. In the fall of 1932 at a banquet in honor of **T. S. Eliot**, Frost was disgusted by the Eliot sycophants and insulted by Eliot's British snobbery concerning Scottish poets. When Eliot agreed to read a poem aloud on the condition that Frost would read one of his, Frost saw an opportunity for jest and claimed that he would actually *write* a new poem while Eliot read. When Eliot finished, Frost announced his "new" poem, "My Olympic Record Stride," and read eight stanzas, pretending to write the ninth as he recited. His audience, however, unaware that the poem was months old, failed to see the humor and instead applauded Frost's feat. Frost writes to Untermeyer, "All were so solemn I hadn't the courage to tell them that of course I was lying! . . . I'm much to blame, but I just couldn't be serious when Eliot was taking himself so seriously."

Lawrance Thompson claims that Frost wrote the verses of the poem "to please his children and grandchildren," Carol's son Prescott, who lived in California, and Lesley's daughter Elinor, who lived on Long Island. In the playful poem, Frost boasts that a pair of old shoes in his Vermont closet harbors salt from the water of oceans on both sides of the country, one shoe having been wet in the Atlantic and the other in the Pacific: "One foot in each great ocean / Is a record stride," he claims in the poem, and he quips that the "thick-skins needn't act thin-skinned" about no longer being taken on walks because they are now devoted to Frost's "museum and muse."

Jeffrey S. Cramer notes that Frost may have hyphenated "extra-vagant" in the fourth stanza either "to control the rhythm of the line" or to allude to **Thoreau**, who hyphenated the word in *Walden*.

References and further reading: Cramer, *Frost among His Poems*; R. Frost, *Selected Letters*, 390, 500; Thompson, *Triumph*, 392–98, 402–3.

Nancy Lewis Tuten

"REFLEX, A," first appeared in Frost's final volume, *In the Clearing* (1962). The poem crowds six sentences into eleven short lines, which Frost aptly terms "my rigmarole," signifying both a complex, ritualistic procedure and a meaningless talk. Personifying **Science** as an obtrusive male whose prodding and poking into nature meet with aggressive opposition, the poem's skepticism culminates in the questions "what / ARE we to believe? / That there is an It?" Frost chooses a provocative title, since "a reflex" has several meanings. It is an automatic response to a stimulus as well as the act of bending or turning the mind back upon a subject (the poem is a reflection on how and what we think we know). A reflex also refers to a linguistic element or system derived from an older element or system (the written poem is itself a reflex of speech, another "science"). The poem is complex, funny, and unique. Its rhyme scheme combines the three basic rhyming units (couplet, triplet, and quatrain) into one remarkable stanza whose sound adds to both the complexity and the humor of its sense.

"A Reflex" was one of twenty-five poems performed by The Open Eye, a company of actors and musicians led by choreographer Jean Erdman in *"Robert Frost, with Rhyme and Reason,"* done in a centennial celebration.

References and further reading: For more on Frost's relationship with science, see Faggen; Harris, "Early Education"; Hiers; Yogi; see also Library of Congress.

Jacqueline B. McCurry

RELIGION. Robert Frost's family background provided him with his early experience of religious faith. His mother was originally a Scotch covenanter and Presbyterian. After reading the essays of **Ralph Waldo Emerson**, she converted briefly to Unitarianism but finally adopted the highly mystical faith of Emanuel Swedenborg. Like his mother, Frost came to believe that no humanly rational explanation of humanity's nature and destiny would suffice: Something must always be left to God. Frost was baptized and married in the Swedenborgian Church, and although he retained some important aspects of that religion into maturity, such as its doctrine of "correspondences," by the early 1920s he stated that he was no longer a Swedenborgian. On his father's side the poet's New England ancestors had a long tradition as Congregationalists, but while a student at **Harvard**, Frost's father became a freethinking agnostic. Frost himself stated that he never had any doubts about God's existence, and his theism led him to reject atheism and especially agnosticism, which he regarded as a cowardly evasion or failure to make a courageous commitment about the meaning of life.

Frost once defined religion as "a straining of the spirit forward to a wisdom beyond wisdom." Whereas **science** deals with matter, the visible physical reality in the universe, religion is concerned with the invisible world of the human's spirit. As the source of consciousness, memory, and original creativity, the spirit of the individual permeates all things but especially poetry and all of the arts, which provide humanity with the power and means to mediate between matter and spirit. Frost was a philosophical dualist, so that matter alone or spirit alone never satisfied him. He defined poetry as the only way humanity has of saying spirit in terms of matter, or matter in terms of spirit, to seek the final unity between them. Religion, science, and poetry were to Frost three different metaphorical ways of perceiving reality, and he believed there was no necessary conflict among them. In the pursuit of truth through science, religion, and poetry, Frost always adhered to his philosophical dualism regarding spirit and matter and rejected all ideological thinkers who imposed prefabricated monistic systems upon reality.

In his essay "Education by Poetry" Frost identified the basic beliefs of humanity as "the self-belief, the love-belief, and the art-belief" and noted that they "are all closely related to the God-belief." He underscored religion as the capstone of all beliefs by saying that the belief in God is a "relationship we enter into with God to believe the future in." Through religion, humanity does not believe in the future but believes the future in. The close connection between Frost's poetry and his religion is most evident not in any doctrines or ideas but in how emotionally charged his poems are with piety and reverence toward external nature and human nature. Contrary to the assertions of some literary critics, Frost never made poetry a substitute for religion: They remained intimate yet wholly distinct, two independent forms of revelation. The precise nature of how the basic human beliefs are related was never spelled out by Frost because the core that surrounds human existence on earth remains an unsolved mystery. Frost was convinced that neither science, religion, nor poetry provides final, indisputable answers to the great questions regarding humanity: Who are we? Where did we come from? Whither are we going?

Whereas most of humanity has pursued things of the spirit through institutional religion—in church, temple, synagogue, or mosque—and accepted their theological doctrines and articles of faith, Frost believed that the process of seeking spiritual truth should remain personal, open-ended, and constant throughout his life. His view of institutional religion was of a piece with his conception of institutional education: He respected both church and school but wished to transcend their limitations. Yet Frost was highly critical of college **teachers** who thought it their right or duty to destroy the religious faith of their students and to replace it with faith in science or some form of humanism. Respect for traditional Christianity was a part of Frost's religion. He held that whereas other poets, such as **T. S. Eliot**, were "more churchy," he was "more religious." Frost enjoyed talking theology with those whose religious views differed from his own, such as Irish Jesuits and his friend Rabbi Victor Reichert, because he was always open-minded about what he could learn about things of the spirit. But whatever insights he received from others, he always turned them into his own metaphorical ways of thinking. Thus his religious beliefs were at once highly eclectic yet individualistic.

Frost's religion is the most complex and difficult subject in his total **philosophy** of life, partly because he always resisted any attempt to categorize his religious beliefs. Only when pushed hard enough did he refer to himself as "an Old Testament Christian." This meant that in the conflict between justice and mercy he preferred the justice of the Old Testament as prior to the mercy of the New Testament. Frost disliked what he called "New Testament sapheads," who sentimentalized Christ out of the gospels of Christianity. The range of his religious views on the Old and New Testaments is dramatized in *A Masque of Reason* and *A Masque of Mercy* (*see* **Drama**).

Frost's religious faith was saturated with a profound knowledge of the Bible and the history of Christianity, but his lifelong habit of personal enquiry, his nonmembership in any church, his resistance to being categorized, and his love of banter even about religion have led some critics to claim, as has Yvor Winters, that he was "a spiritual drifter" or even an atheist who lacked piety and was sacrilegious. Members of Frost's family, his closest friends, and the poet himself insisted that he was highly religious. In January 1942, in a letter to **Louis Untermeyer**, Frost sent a poem not included in his published poems, "[To prayer I think I go]," a work filled with religious implications. For insights into Frost's religious thought the following poems should be read: **"The Trial by Existence," "A Prayer in Spring," "Revelation," "All Revelation," "A Steeple on the House," "West-Running Brook," "After Apple-Picking," "Directive," "The Lesson for Today,"** *A Masque of Reason, A Masque of Mercy*, and **"Kitty Hawk."**

References and further reading: Clark; Dougherty; Doyle, "Reading"; L. Frost, "Aladdin's"; R. Frost, "Education by Poetry," *Collected*, 726, and "[To prayer I think I go]," *Collected*, 550; Greenleaf; D. J. Hall, *Contours*; Juhnke; Parini, *A Life*, 266; Reichert; Winters.

Peter J. Stanlis

"RELUCTANCE," rejected by the *Atlantic Monthly*, first appeared in *The Youth's Companion* (7 Nov. 1912) and then as the last poem of *A Boy's Will*

(1913) with the gloss, "There are things that can never be the same." Frost was particularly fond of the poem and referred to it often throughout his life, describing it as an "unforced expression of a life I was forced to live." Thomas Mosher wanted to purchase the poem and later used it as a prelude to a small book-size "Catalogue" of Mosher imprints (1913). Frost wrote to Mosher that although neither "Reluctance" nor **"My November Guest"** "heralds a new force in literature," he believed they were "a beginning."

The poem addresses the continual theme of the conflict between Reason's acceptance of "the drift of things" and the heart's resistance. The poem begins with the persona in the ranging landscape typical of Frost but quickly turns to a recognition of a darker side where dead leaves and ominous sounds prevail. The final rhetorical question is a return to the opening poem of *A Boy's Will,* **"Into My Own."** Lawrance Thompson suggests that the poem is about the apparent loss of **Elinor White**'s love in 1894, but the poem handles melancholia without morbidity.

References and further reading: R. Frost, *Selected Letters*, 47, 73; Thompson, *Early Years*, 188–89.

Eric Leuschner

"REVELATION" first appeared in *A Boy's Will* **(1913)**, although Frost himself claimed to have written the poem at least fifteen years earlier. In the original table of contents for that collection, Frost glosses "Revelation" (which appears in Part II of the book) as the youth's resolve "to become intelligible, at least to himself, since there is no help else." William H. Pritchard notices that "Revelation" reveals Frost's reluctance to categorize. Indeed, Pritchard suggests, though the final lines of the poem admit that eventually "all who hide too well away / Must speak and tell us where they are," the poem also mourns that we must often "speak the literal to inspire / The understanding of a friend." Dorothy Judd Hall finds the "hide-and-seek metaphor" in the poem "an image which becomes a key to interpreting all of Robert Frost" as critics and readers strive to find coherent systems of belief in a poet and poetry marked by incongruities and ambiguity. While Hall calls "Revelation" "a light-hearted trifle," she finds it meaningful when read beside the later **"All Revelation."**

References and further reading: D. J. Hall, *Contours*, 10, 73; Pritchard, *Literary Life*, 143.

Gary Totten

"RIDERS" was first published in *West-Running Brook* **(1928)**. A three-quatrain poem written in couplets, it presents one of Frost's strongest affirmations of humanity, directly addressing the question of human agency in a chaotic world. Inspired by the marvels of contemporary aviation, Frost lauds the human will through the symbolism of the rider. Newborn babes come into the world like naked riders astride a wild horse, fiercely clinging to the beast in hopes of steering its course. Yet the world is likened to a headless horse that is heedless of danger or intent, challenging its riders to hold fast. While it may seem sometimes as if the world defies human will, the human capacity to adapt and to survive ensures that we also have the strength to thrive.

The poem thus counterpoints the twin themes of fear and faith. Lawrance Thompson traces the first of these themes to Job 37:23 and notes that Frost believes that humanity's ignorance about the nature of life makes us treasure life all the more—an idea developed in Frost's 1936 **Harvard** speech "Does Wisdom Signify?" and in the aphoristic poem **"The Secret Sits."** Elizabeth Shepley Sergeant finds the conviction of the second theme resonant with the cosmic optimism of **"I Will Sing You One-O."** The same two themes recur in **"At Woodward's Gardens"** and **"Our Hold on the Planet,"** but "Riders" most closely resembles the fierce optimism of **"The Trial by Existence."** Like the latter poem, "Riders" asserts that human beings choose their own fate by the very act of accepting the challenge of life. As such, the poem contrasts with the more dour Frost of **"Design"** and **"Bereft"**—two poems in which nature's indifference overwhelms the poet's faith in humanity. In affirming the power of the rider, Sergeant notes, the poem celebrates "cosmic courage."

References and further reading: Sergeant, 421; Thompson, *Triumph*, 446–47, 672–73.

Kenneth Rickard

"ROAD NOT TAKEN, THE," was first published in the *Atlantic Monthly* (Aug. 1915) and collected as the opening poem in *Mountain Interval* **(1916)**. As he had done in his previous volume, *North of Boston* **(1914)**, Frost set the opening and concluding poems of his third collection in italic type.

After selling his farm in **Derry**, New Hampshire, Frost moved in 1912 with **Elinor** and their children to **England**. There, two of the most important events of his life occurred: the publication of his first volume of poetry, *A Boy's Will* **(1913)**, and his deep friendship with English poet Edward Thomas. The friendship would be all too brief. Thomas died in 1917 in World War I, but the friendship left a profound and lasting impact upon Frost. According to Lawrance Thompson, "The Road Not Taken" was originally written in a piece of correspondence to Thomas, and, Thompson speculates, it was intended to satirize the indecisive Thomas. Indeed, one detects a tone of jesting but friendly conversation in the poem.

In his essay "The Constant Symbol," first published in the *Atlantic Monthly* (Oct. 1946), Frost declared that the "mind is a baby giant," hurling its toys ahead of itself. So too it is with the poet, flinging out words, prosody, and other playthings of the craft ahead of him. But they land in zigzag paths—thus, the "straight crookedness" of the poem. We should not misunderstand Frost as abdicating method and design but rather using them seductively to bring the reader into the poem and thereby unveiling shades of meaning to the reader.

The point is important to "The Road Not Taken," for it is indeed one of

Frost's superb poems, perfectly capturing as if by camera one momentary scene in nature. A wistful tone is evoked by the autumn setting, nearly always a nostalgic and sometimes melancholy season in Frost's poetry. Nature's life is passing; if, as Frost tells us in **"Nothing Gold Can Stay,"** "Nature's first green is gold," its last green is yellow. But nature in this poem has not merely evoked wistfulness in the speaker; it has also acted upon him, presenting him, at one unexpected point, with two leaf-fallen paths—divergent, branching off into the unseen distance. So it is with human nature: One reaches such a point, one makes a decision, one travels on. But the poem itself branches off into complexities as we observe the speaker's reaction to the choices that nature presents him.

After the objective description in stanza one—what in fact lay before him—the speaker engages in an explanation of his choices. The evidence in stanzas two and three is inconclusive. Yet in the third stanza the imposition of the context of time on the poem again subtly shifts the meaning. At the present moment, the yellow leaves have not been "trodden black." Something of the narrator's passage will indelibly change that fact, but so too will he be changed. Although he claims to keep the first for another day, he knows full well that with one step the other path disappears forever into the past. The "sigh" of the fourth stanza is anticipated in the third as the speaker makes his choice, "Oh, I kept the first for another day!" But there will be no other day, no other precise moment such as this.

Even as he stands in the present, then, at a seemingly harmless juncture in the woods, the poet feels the dramatic moment of the future. The fourth stanza shifts to the future, which, of course, he cannot know. All he has is the present moment in which he fully acknowledges that at some time in the future he will look back on this moment and regard his present decision to have made a significant difference. Finally he steps out on one path, which he chooses to call "less traveled," but it is, in fact, his *choosing* to regard it so that will make all the difference for the future, for the paths, in truth, "equally lay."

The poem, then, does indeed follow several zigzag contours. It may be an ironic jest with the poet's friend Thomas; it may reveal the complexity of making choices between two seemingly similar options. Finally, it is a poem of tension—unresolved, surely, in spite of the last line—between the present moment and the way the speaker will regard the impact of his decision in the future. *See also* **Nature Poet and Naturalist**.

References and further reading: Fleissner, "A Road Taken"; George; Kjørven focuses upon the I-narrator of the poem, 56–59, 108–9; Thompson, *Triumph*, 88–89, 544–48.

                                                                                              John H. Timmerman

"ROADSIDE STAND, A," originally appeared in the *Atlantic Monthly* (June 1936) and was included in *A Further Range* **(1936)** with the subtitle "On Being Put Out of Our Misery." Both Jeffrey S. Cramer and Lawrance Thompson record that Frost considered the title "Euthanasia." It is a poem **Reginald L. Cook** calls "a downright failure in human effort." Though the speaker seems to intend a cataloguing of the attributes of rural life compared to the ills of urban sprawl, the poem's sense of self-righteousness overburdens its imagery and degenerates into a maudlin betrayal of its own supposed loyalty in lines 47 and 48.

The reader is left with the impression of a speaker and poet who places no great faith in the instincts and choices of individuals whether they be good country people or city dwellers. Using Frost's own criterion that a poem "begins in delight and ends in wisdom" (from his essay "The Figure a Poem Makes"), "A Roadside Stand" must be judged as a bitter reflection of how far modern society has strayed from the possibility of poetic redemption. Perhaps the real essence of the poem is as a metaphor of the "failed human effort" that plagues the consciousness of twentieth-century culture.

References and further reading: R. Cook, *Dimensions*, 86; Cramer, *Frost among His Poems*; R. Frost, "The Figure a Poem Makes," *Collected*; Thompson, *Triumph*.

Lynn Barrett

ROBERT FROST: COLLECTED POEMS, PROSE, & PLAYS (1995). Edited by Richard Poirier and Mark Richardson, this Library of America edition of Frost's collected writings is the most comprehensive to date. The book uses as its source Frost's poetry as it appeared in *The Complete Poems of Robert Frost 1949*, the last edition supervised by the poet himself, and *In the Clearing* (1962), Frost's final volume. In addition, the book includes Frost's *A Masque of Reason*, *A Masque of Mercy*, and three unpublished plays (*see* **Drama**), previously **uncollected poetry**, and a significant body of critical **prose**, much of which had been either out of print or difficult to locate.

The need for a new edition of Frost's verse has long been expressed by critics unhappy with the editorial procedures of Edward Connery Lathem, who was commissioned by the Frost estate to prepare an edition of Frost's poetry for general readers and scholars. Critics' objections are directed at Lathem's "corrections" of the punctuation in many of the poems in *The Poetry of Robert Frost* (1969); he adds and deletes commas, colons, and hyphens without citing textual sources to justify many of his emendations. As critics such as William H. Pritchard have charged, such editorial license frequently disrupts the cadences that Frost intended to embody in his poems and that Frost claimed to be central to his poetics (*see* **Poetic Theories**).

The publisher of Lathem's edition of the poems noted in 1969 that "[t]he time will come for a variorum or definitive edition in which it will be appropriate to print every scrap of verse that can be attributed to Frost, but the materials are not yet adequately in hand." In addition to restoring the punctuation of the poems as they appear in *Complete Poems*, Poirier and Richardson's edition includes just about "every scrap of verse" not collected previously. Especially interesting are poems dating from the turn of the century (before Frost had published his first book of poetry) that express a sympathy with the plight of the working class. While some of these poems were available in print before, they were not easily accessible (some of them buried in letters and partially reproduced in biographies). "The Mill City," written in 1905, represents life for industrial laborers in all its grim reality. The poem functions as a sharp corrective to the idealized portrait of factory life in **"A Lone Striker,"** published in *A Further Range* **(1936)**, and provides a new perspective on Frost's early class identification when read in the company of poems such as "When the Speed Comes," written in 1906, and "The Parlor Joke," written in 1910, neither of which was published during Frost's lifetime. A major resource for the volume's section on uncollected poetry was Jeffrey S. Cramer's two-part series on Frost's unpublished poetry, "Forgotten Frost: A Study of the Uncollected and Unpublished Poetry of Robert Frost," which first appeared in the *Robert Frost Review*.

Also important are the many prose pieces that have been tracked down and gathered together in the edition. Some of the items express important ideas not found in Frost's major critical prose and were available before only in *Selected Prose of Robert Frost* **(1966)** or Elaine Barry's anthology *Robert Frost on Writing* (1973), neither of which remains in print. Others provide for the first time a complete text of previously published material. Then there are book prefaces and magazine and newspaper articles that had not been collected before, offering insights into Frost's ideas about his own poetry, other writers, and the American political scene.

Frost may not have appreciated the notes that are included in the volume; he expressed his disdain of supplemental materials in a short essay "The Prerequisites," first published in the *New York Times Book Review* (21 Mar. 1954): "The heart sinks when robbed of the chance to see for itself what a poem is all about. . . . Any footnote while the poem is going is too late. Any subsequent explanation is as dispiriting as the explanation of a joke. Being taught poems reduces them to the rank of mere information." However, the glosses that Poirier and Richardson provide are unobtrusive (coming not at the bottom of pages but at the end of the book) and do not seek to explicate the poems so much as to clarify allusions in the work.

The Library of America collection is an important contribution to Frost studies because it resolves a long-standing controversy over the proper form that Frost's poetry should take, represents Frost as a more wide-ranging thinker than he usually is thought to be, and brings under one cover a vast number of his writings.

References and further reading: Cramer, "Forgotten Frost"; R. Frost, *Poetry*, iv, and *Collected*, 815; Pritchard, *Playing*, 23–26.

Tyler B. Hoffman

ROBERT FROST: POETRY AND PROSE **(1972)** appeared first as No. 154 of **Holt**, Rinehart and Winston's Rinehart Editions, a paperback series of standard authors; the front cover carried a predictable photograph of a less-traveled-by-dirt road in New England. The publication was unusual since the Rinehart Editions already included *Selected Poems of Robert-Frost* (**1963**)—chosen by the poet and introduced by Robert Graves—but only two other volumes of twentieth-century American poetry. *Poetry and Prose* was reissued once in hardcover by the same publisher in 1973 and, after that issue had lapsed out of print, once again in a new paperback series, Owl Book Editions, in 1984, with text unchanged and still in print. The selections were made jointly by Edward Connery Lathem, editor of *The Poetry of Robert Frost* (**1969**), and Lawrance Thompson, whose first two volumes of the authorized biography had appeared in 1966 and 1970. The editors introduced the book as containing "some of [Frost's] best and best-known poems against a background of his other writings, many of them little known and some, indeed, heretofore unpublished." The choice of poems in the new book partially overlapped but did not replicate that in the earlier Rinehart *Selected Poems*, and since all the poems in Part I, taken from Frost's nine books of poetry and the two *Masques*, were readily available in *The Poetry*, the unfamiliar work lay in Part II, where varied "samplings" of Frost's **prose** and verse were arranged in roughly chronological order, starting with four love letters from the twelve-year-old Rob and closing with the last letter dictated by "America's favorite poet" at eighty-nine, two weeks before his death. The contents pages are awkwardly crammed, making it difficult to find particular items, but a complete index compensates for the flaw. The works published for the first time, besides a couple of rhymed letters and a bawdy limerick, include letters to Sidney Cox and his wife (subsequently issued in the context of their larger correspondence edited by William R. Evans) and eleven letters to Charles H. Foster from 1931 to 1950, titled by Lathem and Thompson "Coaching a Younger Writer"—a persuasive demonstration of the depth and endurance of Frost's capacity for friendship and of his acuity as a writing **teacher**. The Foster letters remain the only portion of the entire book not yet printed elsewhere and thus its sole original contribution to the Frost canon.

In Part II, the editors provide headnotes to every selection, identifying and dating its source and usually sketching the circumstances under which it was written. Taken with a four-page chronology, the notes present an outlined sketch of Frost's career and life, far less thoroughly than that in the Library of America Frost volume (*see Robert Frost: Collected Poems, Prose, & Plays*) but less loaded with the critical interpretations that Thompson's decades of research had put on the facts of Frost's life in his annotations to the *Selected Letters* of 1964 and later in his **biography**. The fullest notes in *Poetry and Prose* accompany the previously unpublished letters to Cox and Foster. Probably the most important letters in the book, however, are the six written from **England** in 1913–1914 to Frost's former student **John Bartlett**, headed by the editors as the "beginning of a book's career." These letters about the publication of *A Boy's Will* and about writing in general had been published in the *Selected Letters* and before that, in 1963, in *Robert Frost and John Bartlett* by Margaret Bartlett

Anderson, the recipient's daughter. The Bartlett letters lay out more comprehensively and vigorously than anywhere else Frost's now-famous **poetic theories** of the "sound of sense" and its importance to all vital writing.

In general, the volume showed new students of Frost that the strength of his prose equaled that of his best poems, while sounding more definitively "modern" or even "Modernist" than the strict and loose iambics of his verse. Such qualities are displayed in a broad variety of genres, through examples previously scattered in more or less inaccessible publications: stories for his children; anecdotal stories for a poultry farming magazine; a one-act play performed at **Amherst College** in 1917; interviews from Lathem's *Interviews with Robert Frost* (1966); prefaces and introductions, some published earlier in *Selected Prose* (ed. Hyde Cox and E. C. Lathem, 1966); notebook entries such as those on "Poetry and School"; and several "talks" transcribed from recordings. In addition to providing a major source of income, such platform performances had been a major outlet for Frost's creative imagination from the time he returned from England until two months before his death (*see* **Addresses**).

In addition to the prose pieces, Part II contains five groups of "Poems He Left Behind Him." Since all twenty-eight of these uncollected poems, along with some seventy others, have now been gathered into the Library of America volume, a reader no longer needs to seek them out in *Poetry and Prose*, where they originally made a surprising and refreshing counterpoint to the prose. The promise apparent in some very early poems such as "Clear and Colder—Boston Common," the witty rhymed letters, and such unexpected pieces as the raunchy, rough-hewn broadside ballad "The Middletown Murder" enlarged most readers' sense of Frost's poetic scope. That, in fact, was the effect of the volume as a whole, thanks to Part II. Up to the publication in 1995 of the much larger Library of America volume, *Poetry and Prose* was a student's best introduction to the "many different sides of the poet-as-literary-artist" promised by its editors.

References and further reading: For complete transcriptions of a dozen of Frost's "talks," see R. Cook, *Living Voice*. A number of important letters and talks on writing included in neither *Poetry and Prose* nor the Library of America are found in R. Frost, *Writing*. For further analysis of *Poetry and Prose*, see Ridland.

John Ridland

ROBERT FROST REVIEW evolved from two previous newsletters of the Robert Frost Society. The first newsletter of the society was edited by Peter Van Egmond, the society's first director. When organization headquarters moved to Winthrop University and Earl J. Wilcox became director, he began publishing the newsletter in the annual Frost issue of the *South Carolina Review*, published at Clemson University. In 1991 Wilcox founded the *Robert Frost Review*, and newsletter items thereafter appeared in the journal. Beginning with the first issue of the *Review*, dues became $15 annually for membership in the society, and all members receive a copy of the annual journal. Individuals and institutions may also subscribe to the journal without society affiliation. Beginning with the second issue and continuing to the present, the journal has received a subsidy from the Winthrop University Foundation.

From its outset, the journal has focused on explication of Frost's poems, including items such as newly discovered Frost letters and printed reviews of new books on the poet. A major contribution of the journal to Frost studies was the publication of the two-part series by Jeffrey S. Cramer, "Forgotten Frost: A Study of the Uncollected and Unpublished Poetry of Robert Frost." Cramer's compilation and commentary were basic resources for the inclusion of **uncollected poetry** in the publication of the Library of America's volume *Robert Frost: Collected Poems, Prose, & Plays*, edited by Richard Poirier and Mark Richardson. In its first seven issues the journal published essays by almost every major Frost scholar in the United States and, beginning in 1993, has included a current bibliography of Frost studies. Essays by Laurence Perrine, Dorothy Judd Hall, Nancy L. Tuten, Robert F. Fleissner, Edward Ingebretsen, John Zubizarreta, Lesley Lee Francis, George Monteiro, Mark Richardson. Donald Sheehy, Peter J. Stanlis, and many others have appeared in the journal. Jeffrey C. Glasgow was associate and managing editor for the first three years, with Rebecca Weaver and Julie Townsend serving as managing editors between 1994 and 1997. Joe Walters designed the cover for the journal that won a regional graphics award in 1992. Jonathan Barron and Debra Boyd are associate and assistant editors, respectively, and Evelyne Weeks is the journal's illustrator.

Earl J. Wilcox

ROBERT FROST SOCIETY. Academic interest in Robert Frost was increased significantly when, in the late 1970s, Jac L. Tharpe edited three volumes of critical essays celebrating the centennial of the poet's birth. Volumes appeared in 1974, 1976, and 1978. The success and wide notice of the collections undoubtedly had a marked influence on efforts to form an organization solely for the purpose of fostering the study of Robert Frost. Special sessions on Frost's poetry were organized in the late 1970s. One outcome of such national meetings was the eventual formation of the Robert Frost Society (RFS) in 1984 as an Allied Organization of the Modern Language Association (MLA). A constitution was presented prior to the business meeting of the society at the 1983 MLA Special Session. (The RFS also became an affiliate member of the American Literature Association in 1993.) By becoming an Allied Organization of MLA, the members were not required to resubmit program justification each year.

The founder of the society was Kathryn Beatrice Gibbs Harris. The first director of the society was Peter Van Egmond, who was also the editor of the *RFS Newsletter*. Members of the first Executive Committee and Editorial Advisory Board were Marjorie Cook, Nancy Joyner, Ron Bieganowski, Mordecai Marcus, Robert Fleissner, Philip Gerber, and Peter Van Egmond. Ron Bieganowski was named secretary. The first seat of the society was the University of Maryland. A section of the constitution indicates the structure of the organization: "The Robert Frost Society is run by its Executive Committee. This Committee consists of the Director, the Secretary, the Chairman of the Executive Committee (elected by the Committee), and five other members." Others were brought into the Executive Committee of the society through elections, and by 1986 scholars such as William R. Evans, Craig Challender, and Earl J. Wilcox were members. The Executive Committee during the first fifteen years also has included Lesley Lee Francis, Sandra Katz, Edward Ingebretsen, George Monteiro, George Bagby, Katherine Kearns, John Zubizarreta, Richard Calhoun, and Donald Sheehy, among others. At its origin, society dues were $10 and included a subscription to the newsletter. Peter Van Egmond relinquished his role as director in 1987, and in 1988 Earl J. Wilcox was named director with the headquarters of the Robert Frost Society moving to Winthrop University.

Beginning in 1987 and for four years, the *South Carolina Review* (*SCR*) published a special Frost issue each summer. In that same year, the *Newsletter of the Robert Frost Society* began appearing in the *SCR* in this annual Frost issue. The arrangement was maintained until 1991 when the first issue of the **Robert Frost Review** appeared.

Earl J. Wilcox

ROBINSON, EDWIN ARLINGTON (1869–1935). Proximities of age, locale, and writing style have encouraged comparisons between the poetry of Frost and Edwin Arlington Robinson. Born five years apart and strongly associated with New England, they are the two major American poets of the twentieth century who wrote exclusively in metered verse. Both are considered transitional figures, adhering to conventional form while providing innovations in subject matter, tone, and philosophic stance.

Early reviews of Frost's work frequently note the similarities between Frost's poetry and that of Robinson, who, having published first seventeen years before Frost, was arguably the most prominent American poet writing in the second decade of the century. Later critics, such as John C. Kemp, have found useful distinctions between the two. At this writing Frost has far exceeded Robinson in reputation.

From the time the two poets met in 1915 until Robinson's death in 1935, they maintained an occasional correspondence that reveals a cordial but distant relationship. Although each claimed to admire the other's work, Frost saw Robinson as his worthiest rival. Frost wrote in a 1942 letter, "I admired Robinson most of my contemporaries and he knew it," but in an earlier letter to **Louis Untermeyer**, he called him an "enervated old soak." The ambiguous relationship between the two is mentioned by **biographers** of both poets, most elaborately in Frost studies by Lawrance Thompson.

Frost's introduction to Robinson's posthumously published volume *King Jasper* (1935) is similarly ambiguous. While it makes no mention of the poem it purports to introduce, it characterizes Robinson as a poet "content with the old-fashioned way to be new" and someone who preferred "griefs" to "grievances."

After he makes comments on several of Robinson's early poems, he writes, "His theme was unhappiness itself, but his skill was as happy as it was playful." Donald J. Greiner is among the many critics who have noted that such characteristics manifest themselves in Frost's poetry and who rank the essay among the major statements relating to Frost's **poetic theory**.

References and further reading: R. Frost, "Introduction to E. A. Robinson's *King Jasper,"* *Collected,* 741–48, *Selected Letters,* 496, and *Letters to Untermeyer,* 200; Greiner, *Poet and His Critics,* 186–90; Kemp, 157–62; Thompson, *Triumph.*

Nancy Carol Joyner

"ROGERS GROUP, A," first appeared in the *Atlantic Monthly* (Dec. 1946) and was collected in *Steeple Bush* **(1947)**. A gem of social criticism, the poem consists of three declarative sentences, each formed into a ballad stanza (*abcb*) of iambic trimeter lines. The poem is "dated" in the sense that its meaning depends on the reader's knowing that John Rogers (1829–1904) was an American sculptor known for realistic figural groups such as *The Slave Auction* and that his extremely popular works were often mass-produced. Frost depicts a group of travelers lost in a big city. Carrying babies and baggage, they wait on the wrong street corner and so miss their trolley car. But they must find their own way, since no one stops to help them or give directions. Why? The speaker explains in the poem's final lines that none of the passersby recognized the "young and unassuming" strangers as people in need of assistance because they saw no resemblance between this actual group and those memorialized by Rogers. Frost seems to assert something about art's inability to affect human behavior. The poem is musical, poignant, and disturbing. Through sound, Frost emphasizes that something is wrong with this city scene: Full rhymes ("street / feet," "aid / made") in the first and third stanzas surround the not-quite-right eye rhyme ("gong / wrong") at the poem's center.

References and further reading: Marcus, *Explication.*

Jacqueline B. McCurry

"ROSE FAMILY, THE," originally published in the *Yale Review* and the *London Mercury* in July 1927 and later in *West-Running Brook* **(1928)**, was singled out by Babette Deutsch as "unworthy of inclusion," the kind of poem "that might have been written by Austin Dobson in his sleep." The poet voices his impatience with botanists who would classify the rose with apples and plums, detracting from its privileged status as a poetic metaphor. Echoing the line "Rose is a rose is a rose is a rose" from Gertrude Stein's 1913 poem "Sacred Emily," the poet denies the flower's denotation in the Rosaceae family and reaffirms its membership in the family of poetic tradition, using it to substantiate the shared qualities of flower and lover. Having read Mrs. William Starr Dana's *How to Know the Wild Flowers* (1893) while studying botany with **Carl Burell**, Frost must have recognized that taxonomic and poetic descriptions were not mutually exclusive. Rather, the poem justifies its inclusion in the collection by affirming the power of creative acts to resist a reductive materialism. His declaration, "You, of course, are a rose," rejects an exclusionary scientific schema. It also expresses Frost's delight, as he once told **Louis Untermeyer**, of "seeing our theories knocked into cocked hats."

References and further reading: Deutsch; R. Frost, *Letters to Untermeyer*, 47; Oster, 69–70; Thompson, *Triumph*.

Michael Berndt

"ROSE POGONIAS," a poem that first appeared in *A Boy's Will*, is about *sanctuary*: The speaker and his companion happen upon an almost magical preserve, or clearing, in the midst of the woods. But the preserve is fragile, as all sanctuaries are in Frost's work. The little meadow, "Sun-shaped and jewel-small," is hermetic, almost cloying. It *seems* queerly to exist out of time—though the poem acknowledges this to be an illusion—and its timeless quality lends the meadow its unreal aspect of sanctity. The balance achieved against disorder and destruction in the meadow is beautiful but also precarious and doomed, as the speaker well knows. He *willfully* prays that the meadow be spared "the general mowing"—the "mowing" Time does with his scythe, one suspects. The petition recalls the Elizabethan idea that poetry can preserve a moment of experience or a particular aspect of fragile beauty from the depredations of Time. But as always in such situations, Frost's speaker knows that what he asks (as also in **"October"**) cannot be granted and that there probably is no Being to apply to anyway. Experience can be kept from Time only in the fiction of poetry, never in fact or in life. The admission probably accounts, as Richard Poirier suggests, for the self-conscious eloquence and formality of Frost's diction in "Rose Pogonias": It is noticeably poetic, noticeably an *artifice*. "Rose Pogonias" inasmuch as says, as Frost later puts it, "Nothing gold can stay."

References and further reading: Poirier, *Knowing*.

Mark Richardson

"RUNAWAY, THE," was written in 1916 and first published in *The Amherst Monthly* (June 1918). It later was included in *New Hampshire* **(1923)**. Many critics link "The Runaway" to Frost's **"The Cow in Apple Time."** Both poems are seen as rural vignettes, capturing country life with prudent use of physical detail, while each considers, in an anthropomorphic manner, the theme of human rebellion. A textual approach to the poem may reveal the certainty of the young to rebel and the need to control and tame such wildness for the sake of their preservation. From such a perspective, the responsibility of control falls on the colt's guardians, who "Ought to be told to come and take him in." An alternate reading, however, may be constructed from a biographical reference. The inspiration for the poem seems to have been a group of students at **Amherst**

College, where Frost held a teaching post. At Amherst, Frost had difficulty dealing with rebellious students of a different sort, students who ironically rebelled on the side of conformity. Frost's desire to guide his students was tempered with his recognition of their need to think for themselves. The ambiguity surrounding any attempt to conclude from the poem Frost's attitude toward rebellion emphasizes the difficulty involved in the maturation process, where all of us must "run away," at some point, into the adult world.

References and further reading: D'Avanzo, *Romantics*, focuses his reading on the need for humans to control animal desires; Doyle, *Poetry*, discusses Frost's use of physical material; Edwards, "Play," explains Frost's dilemma during his tenure at Amherst College.

John R. Woznicki

S

"SAND DUNES" appeared in the *New Republic: A Journal of Opinion* (15 Dec. 1926) prior to its inclusion in **West-Running Brook (1928)**. Elemental opposites unite (ocean waves and sand), effacing human traces (ships and abandoned huts); however, the mind can, in the face of sublimity, comprehend and ultimately form *something* (see Frost's "Letter to *The Amherst Student*"). The poem's tone leans toward the sardonic while celebrating the supremacy of the mind (in contrast to the later **"Etherealizing"**), unvanquished by the mutable forces in nature. A less triumphant response is found in **"Once by the Pacific."**

Scholarship differs considerably: Mario D'Avanzo explores parallels to **Thoreau**'s *Cape Cod*. Joseph Brogunier advances Emily Dickinson's "I started early—Took my Dog—" as impetus, establishing gender inversions concerning the sea and culmination in Emersonian freedom. Hyatt Waggoner's exegesis compares the poem to **Emerson**'s "Fate." Laurence Perrine focuses on the mind, pointing out that Frost judges nature to be less benevolent than does Emerson. Finally, Lawrance Thompson hears echoes of Oliver Wendell Holmes's "The Chambered Nautilus."

References and further reading: Brogunier; D'Avanzo, " 'Sand Dunes' "; R. Frost, "Letter to *The Amherst Student*," *Collected*, 739–40; Perrine, " 'Sand Dunes' "; Thompson, *Triumph*, 627; Waggoner, "Humanistic Idealism."

Kirk C. Allison

SANDBURG, CARL (1878–1967). Born in Galesburg, Illinois, of Swedish immigrant parents, Charles A. (Carl) Sandburg dropped out of school after the eighth grade. After working at several jobs over a brief period, he made his first move to Chicago in 1894. Still unable to remain at a single job for any length of time, he hopped trains and lived with hobos while working at several jobs across Iowa, Nebraska, Kansas, and Colorado. In 1898 he served briefly in the military in Puerto Rico in the war with Spain. During this time he worked also as a correspondent for the *Evening Mail* in Galesburg. Upon his release from the military, he entered Lombard College as a special student; however, shortly before he would have graduated, he dropped out without explanation and took to the road, traveling extensively throughout the country. Over the next several years, Sandburg became increasingly attracted to populism and the political causes of the "working man," working for the Social Democrats in Wisconsin and writing articles for various newspapers. He also published some exploratory verse on the private press of his friend Professor Philip Green Wright of Lombard College.

More settled by his marriage in 1908 to the far more practical Lillian (Paula) Steichen, Sandburg began to take his writing more seriously as a career. He grew to prominence in 1916 through the publication of his *Chicago Poems*, nine of which had been published by **Harriet Monroe** in *Poetry, A Magazine of Verse* in 1914. The shocking boldness of the opening poem "Chicago" created controversy immediately:

> Hog Butcher for the World,
> Tool Maker, Stacker of Wheat,
> Player with Railroads and the Nation's Freight Handler;
> Stormy, husky, brawling,
> City of the Big Shoulders.

The Dial and other publications attacked him openly as crude and unrefined.

Characterized by sweeping generalizations about life in America and often tiresome sentimentality and optimistic idealism, Sandburg's poetry is largely ignored by critics today. His casual free verse style—portraying the common worker, vigorous and violent and loving every minute of it—is often portrayed as a paltry copy of Whitman's. He did, however, experiment with other styles as in "Fog," which resembles the style of the Imagists (*see* **Lowell, Amy, and Imagism**) in its sharp careful outlines. He also wrote numerous poems that amount to little more than heavy-handed American propaganda. But Sandburg remained largely Whitmanesque throughout his lifetime.

Later important collections of his work include *Cornhuskers* (1918), *Smoke and Steel* (1920), *Slabs of the Sunburnt West* (1922), and *The People, Yes* (1936). Beyond his poetry, he also wrote children's stories, a novel, historical commentary, and a biography of his hero, Abraham Lincoln, which won him the Pulitzer Prize for history in 1940. His *Complete Poetry* was to win him the Pulitzer Prize once again in 1950.

As Lawrance Thompson points out, with wild prematurely gray hair, and often in a blue shirt with an open collar, Sandburg affected the image and manner of the people's poet. He often seemed more the stage performer than the poet with his guitar, singing folk ballads on the stage. In fact, he helped to popularize the folk ballad, clearing the way for many folk artists who would follow him on the radio over the years to come.

Thompson records that when Frost and Sandburg first met in Chicago in 1917, Frost took an instant dislike to Sandburg. The latter had no idea that he was disliked and wrote in a letter to Alfred Harcourt, "Met Frost; about the strongest, loneliest, friendliest personality among the poets today; I'm going to write him once a year; and feel the love of him everyday" (qtd. in Thompson). Eventually, Sandburg's practiced folksiness annoyed Frost beyond polite tolerance, and the two grew to avoid one another. It was toward Sandburg that Frost targeted his famous line comparing free verse to playing tennis without a net. Sandburg's less known reply to Frost's comment can be found in the March 1942 issue of the *Atlantic Monthly*. Sandburg argues in part, "The poet that without imagination or folly enough to play tennis by serving and returning the ball over an invisible net may see himself as highly disciplined. There have been poets who could and did play more than one game of tennis with unseen rackets, volleying airy and fantastic balls over an insubstantial net, on a frail moonlit fabric of a court."

Lawrance Thompson's biography of Frost attributes his enmity toward Sandburg to jealousy; however, it is equally possible that Frost's awareness of his physical resemblance to Sandburg with their white tousled hair and their folksy ways and the media's tendency to compare the two uncritically (or with a modicum of ill-informed criticism) was simply more than Frost could bear.

References and further reading: Penelope Niven, *Carl Sandburg: A Biography* (New York: Scribner's, 1991); Carl Sandburg, *The Complete Poems of Carl Sandburg* (New York: Harcourt Brace Jovanovich, 1970); Thompson, *Triumph,* 180–81, 577; Gladys Zehnpfennig, *Carl Sandburg: Poet and Patriot* (Minneapolis: T. S. Denison, 1963). On Frost and Sandburg, see Sutton, "Rivalry."

Wm. Thomas Hill

SCIENCE. Robert Frost was profoundly influenced by the British astronomer Richard Anthony Proctor, who stated that it was impossible to get any clear ideas of God through science; by William James, who was critical of a pursuit of scientific knowledge on purely empirical terms; and by Henri Bergson, who was critical of the attempt to over-rationalize life at the expense of intuition.

Proctor, James, and Bergson reinforced Frost's aversion to rigid systems of thought (e.g., **"Reluctance"**) and posited open-ended epistemologies that ultimately resisted human understanding. Insofar as scientific "theories" were concerned, Frost was intrigued by science's metaphorical possibilities, but he otherwise regarded it as a sterile attempt to explain the unexplainable. His philosophy about science was well developed, and a careful reader of his poetry will find that his poems about science fall roughly into three categories: (1) science as technology, (2) science as abstract theory, and (3) science as metaphysics. While the poems in these categories differ in their emphases, they always value the spiritual or the ethereal over the plain material aspect of life.

The first of these subdivisions occupied his attention the least and is represented by his amused response to new inventions, as, for instance, in **"The Line-Gang," "An Encounter,"** and **"An Importer."** The most significant invention of his time was the atomic bomb whose implementation he satirizes as a catastrophic toy played with by boys (**"U.S. 1946 King's X"**) and as a "ministry of fear" (**"Why Wait for Science"**) which "Sarcastic Science" has introduced, placing the human race in the untenable position of having to leave earth or be "wiped out." (See also **"Bursting Rapture"**).

Poems about theoretical science are primarily concerned with the dominant intellectual discoveries of his era, Einsteinian physics (**"Skeptic," "Any Size We Please"**), and Darwinian evolution (**"The White-tailed Hornet," "At Woodward's Gardens," "The Literate Farmer and the Planet Venus," "Design," "Etherealizing"**). In **"Accidentally on Purpose,"** he clearly expresses his deepest conviction when he writes, "[I]ntention, purpose, and design— / That's near enough for me to the Divine," and in **"Desert Places"** the persona's psychological struggle is more frightening than the science that grandly diminishes the essence of human existence but is of no help in enabling us to navigate our internal spaces.

Finally, in his poems of metaphysical science (**"The Bear," "A Star in a Stone Boat," "All Revelation," "Astrometaphysical," "Lost in Heaven"**), Frost articulates his deepest-held beliefs. In **"The Lesson for Today,"** he writes that "space ails us moderns: we are sick with space," but concludes that "science and religion really meet." The poem **"Kitty Hawk"** is the defining statement of his life in which the plane ("God of the machine") is a metaphor for the "flight" of poetry. In this poem Frost confronts the "great misgiving" that science represents to people of faith and reconciles both science and poetry as creative endeavors that constitute acts of worship.

Frost, in his poetry and prose, always affirmed the practical value of science but objected to its "Downward comparisons" ("The White-tailed Hornet") and never made the mistake of allowing it to become "gospel" (**"Some Science Fiction"**). While recognizing its limitations, he also considered it a great enterprise and characterized it as the "mighty charge . . . Of the . . . ethereal / Into the material" ("Kitty Hawk").

References and further reading: Abel; Bagby; Faggen; Harris, "Education in Science"; Hiers; Rotella, "Comparing Conceptions"; Thompson, *Early Years, Years of Triumph*, Thompson and Winnick.

Michael Karounos

"SECRET SITS, THE," was collected in *A Witness Tree* (1942) but first appeared as "Ring Around" in *Poetry* (Apr. 1936). The two-line poem conjures up the Kantian notion that the individual is incapable of discerning the true *Ding-an-sich* (or escapist "thing-in-itself"). Thus he can talk only "around" subjects without getting to their heart (which only God can ascertain). Because Immanuel Kant (and, with him, Western Idealism in general) had such an enormous impact on subsequent modern thought, the correlation is by no means unusual or unexpected. Like **"Boeotian,"** the couplet steers away from the more standard Aristotelian tradition (concerned, for one thing, with *physical* reality) and rather toward a form of Platonism. The idea is that the "Secret" (as its capital clearly indicates) must be an inner reality, divine in nature. One Puritan reason for accepting such a verdict would be the effects of Original Sin, the encroachment of which prevents humanity from coming into direct contact often enough with the mainstream of a realistic issue—prime reality being something left for the next world.

References and further reading: Cramer, *Frost among His Poems*; Fleissner, *Road Taken*, 107–9; Parini, *A Life*, 342.

Robert F. Fleissner

SELECTED POEMS **(1923, 1928, 1934, 1963).** The first edition was published by **Henry Holt and Company** on 15 March 1923, exactly eight months before the publication of *New Hampshire* **(1923).** (An English edition of this volume was published in London by William Heinemann.) Frost was originally against the idea of a volume of selected poems; he wanted his new books of poetry to have priority, and he believed reviewers would see such a collection only as a plea for attention. In contrast, reviews primarily praised *Selected Poems* and found the volume important as the first selection of his published work. Frost played a significant role in the publication of the volume by selecting forty-three poems from *A Boy's Will* **(1913),** *North of Boston* **(1914),** and *Mountain Interval* **(1916)** and creatively arranging them into groups. (The poem **"The Runaway"** is the only exception; it later appeared in *New Hampshire*.) The volume also contains a dedication: "To Helen Thomas in Memory of Edward Thomas."

Selected Poems (revised edition) was published by Holt on 19 November 1928, the same day that Holt published *West-Running Brook* **(1928).** The simultaneous publication was part of a promise Frost had received from Richard H. Thornton at Holt during the contract negotiations for *West-Running Brook*. Holt was determined to offer Frost an attractive and lucrative contract in exchange for Frost's allegiance to the company. The volume contains fifty-seven poems, selected from *A Boy's Will, North of Boston, Mountain Interval,* and *New Hampshire* and arranged by Frost himself. Frost was too late in requesting the removal of the dedication to Helen Thomas; he wanted it removed once he and **Elinor** met Helen Thomas in **England** after Edward's death and realized the once-warm friendship was over.

Selected Poems (third edition) was published by Holt in 1934. The volume contains seventy-three poems, selected from *A Boy's Will, North of Boston, Mountain Interval, New Hampshire,* and *West-Running Brook* and arranged by Frost himself. Frost was able to have the dedication to Helen Thomas removed from all but 300 copies of this edition.

Selected Poems of Robert Frost (1963) was published by Holt, Rinehart and Winston as a paperback in the "Rinehart Editions" series. The volume contains an introduction by Robert Graves, Frost's essay "The Figure a Poem Makes," and selected poems from *A Boy's Will, North of Boston, Mountain Interval, New Hampshire, West-Running Brook, A **Further Range** (1936), A **Witness Tree** (1942), Steeple Bush (1947)*, and *In the Clearing* (1962); it also contains *A Masque of Reason* (*see* **Drama**).

References and further reading: Lentricchia and Lentricchia provide a list of specific poems included in each of the above entries for *Selected Poems*; Van Egmond, *Reception*, contains excerpts of reviews of *Selected Poems* (1923) and *Selected Poems* (1928).

Scott Robert Stankey

SELECTED PROSE OF ROBERT FROST (1966). First published in July 1966 by **Holt**, Rinehart and Winston, the volume was edited by Hyde Cox and Edward Connery Lathem, both intimate friends of Frost. On several different occasions during his later life, Frost intimated that he was planning a volume of prose that would be a selection of his previously published essays, talks, and prefaces. However, due to other commitments—to his poetry, to his teaching, and to his "barding" around the country—Frost never found time to gather and publish his **prose** or to ask someone else to do it. The volume contains fifteen selections of Frost's prose—four prefaces to his own work, four essays, four prefaces to the works of other authors, and three essays that began as talks but were later edited and approved by Frost–and range in date from 1924 to 1959. The selections cover such different topics as poetry, **religion**, and **sports**. The volume does not claim to be the "complete" prose of Robert Frost, and the editors avoided Frost's personal letters and transcripts of recorded talks. The collection contains several textual errors that have been corrected in *Robert Frost: Collected Poems, Prose, & Plays* (1995).

References and further reading: Greiner, *Poet and His Critics*.

Scott Robert Stankey

"SELF-SEEKER, THE," a blank verse dramatic dialogue composed in 1913 in **England**, was conspicuously placed as the last and longest (228 lines) of the twelve long poems in the interlocked structure of *North of Boston* **(1914)**, where it first appeared.

According to Lawrance Thompson, the story is based on a near-fatal accident involving **Carl Burell** and witnessed by Frost in 1895, while he and **Elinor** were enjoying an "almost idyllic honeymoon-vacation" in Allenstown, New Hampshire. Their cottage had been procured by Burell, a friend from Lawrence High School, where Burell had been a returning student ten years older than Frost. Starting in 1889, Burell's personal library had opened three extracurricular fields of lifelong fascination to Frost: astronomy (through Richard A. Proctor's *Our Place among Infinities*), American humor, and the conflict between **science** and **religion** raised by Darwin's theories of evolution. Burell also encouraged Frost to join the debating club, and most important, as a writer of verses published in the Lawrence High School *Bulletin*, he set an example that Frost began to emulate in that first year of their friendship. In the summer of 1895, Burell inducted Frost into another lifelong interest, botanizing, as a theatrically effective guide and mentor. Burell was friendly with Frost's grandfather, and when the latter set his grandson up on the farm at **Derry**, he arranged for Carl and Carl's grandfather to live in and help with the farm. They did from 1900 to 1902, leaving under strained circumstances. The extent to which his injury hampered his botanizing is unclear, but Newdick writes that Burell later became "state president of the Maine–New Hampshire–Vermont branch of the Shut-in Society."

In the poem, the unnamed central character, based on Burell, is referred to as "The Broken One," having suffered a crippling injury in a box factory. His feet may have to be amputated, and he is about to agree to an insurance compensation for which no one who was truly "self-seeking" would settle. His friend Willis is outraged and tries to intervene when the insurance company's Boston lawyer arrives with the unfair agreement, but the bed-ridden man won't let him, holding off his "savage" expressions of concern by making light of his own situation with puns and quips ("I'm going to sell my soul, or, rather, feet"). Before the business is transacted, a young girl, Anne, brings in two rare wild-flowers, Ram's Horn Orchids. The Broken One, an avid, conservation-minded botanist, has taught Anne not to pick large bouquets, so that the flowers won't die out, and to identify and appreciate the uncommon species. If, as he fears, he can no longer tramp the countryside himself, Anne may do it for him. The poem's title comes closest to being borne out when he remarks ironically, "You see / I have to keep on the good side of Anne. / I'm a great boy to think of number one." Since "Looking out for number one" as a synonym for "self-seeking" applies usually to acquisitive enterprises, the irony of the poem's title is self-evident. His flowers "never earned me so much as one cent," the crippled man explains, and so "Money can't pay me for the loss of them." This ideal of unself-seeking devotion to something you love, set against the need to make a living, is a frequent theme in Frost (cf. the poultryman John's raising of exotic hens for their beauty, not their commercial value, in **"The Housekeeper,"** the talk about taking one's work to market in **"New Hampshire,"** and the desire to blend vocation and avocation in **"Two Tramps in Mud Time"**).

In terms of the distinction Frost drew frequently between public "grievances" and deeply personal "griefs" (see Frost's "Introduction to *King Jasper*"), the lawyer represents those who comprehend only the former. The poem's hero is in a state of grief for the loss of what he has loved the most—seeking out flowers, to understand their lives, appreciate their beauty, and share them with others (his discovery of one orchid in the region has already been noticed by the great naturalist writer John Burroughs). He has intended to write "a flora of the valley"—a guide to all the plants of the area—over "the next forty summers," an ambition curtailed by his injury. But his feelings, in keeping with Frost's customary public reticence about the deepest griefs of his own life, are not expressed directly until the despairing gesture of the poem's last line, when, after everyone else has left the room, "He flung his arms around his face."

To what extent an actual incident was fictionalized in the poem is unknown. No original for Anne has been suggested, and her part in the scene may have been invented; the Boston lawyer is a mercenary melodrama villain unusual in the *North of Boston* world of equal standoffs (as in **"Mending Wall"**); and Willis, although displaying the hotheadedness Frost showed in his run-ins with the law as a young man, is not the author; he expresses no special involvement in botanizing and speaks at times ungrammatically ("the lawyer don't know"). Nevertheless, although The Broken One should not be read as an unretouched portrait of Carl Burell, his tenderness, good humor and gentleness, and his courage in the face of a devastating loss can fairly be said to stand as a sympathetic memorial to one of the formative influences on Frost's intellectual and imaginative development. *See also* **Pastoral Poetry**.

References and further reading: R. Frost, "Introduction to **E. A. Robinson**'s *King Jasper*," *Collected*, 741–48; the fullest study is Marcus, *Explication*, 59–60; Newdick, *Season*; for the biographical background, see Thompson, *Early Years*, 220–24.

John Ridland

"SEMI-REVOLUTION, A," first appeared as part of the aphoristic "Quantula" section of *A Witness Tree* **(1942)**. Though some have criticized the poem as an example of Frost's political and artistic conservatism (e.g., one reviewer dubbed Frost a "semi-poet"), most commentators have voiced an appreciation for its playful yet biting irony. Echoing two of its neighboring poems, **"On Our Sympathy with the Underdog"** and **"An Equalizer,"** "A Semi-Revolution" works the definitions of "revolution" against each other. The speaker deflates the notion of revolution as progressive social change, primarily by reminding us that "revolution" also denotes cyclical movement, which is, from one point of view, no movement at all. The speaker further satirizes romantic notions of revolution by invoking the Rosicrucian Order, perhaps because this mystical/philosophical organization endorses, among other things, a belief in reincarnation; it is unlikely that Frost would have offered a similar endorsement. The poem's mock-serious tone perfectly matches its absurd proposals; Frost employs the rhetoric of the logician ("therefore") against itself. The rhyme scheme of the poem complements the tone. The first two lines do not so much rhyme as repeat their end words; the speaker uses a "total" rhyme, so to speak, in order to "advocate a semi-revolution." Depending upon how one pronounces "salves," the final two lines offer either a full rhyme or an eye rhyme. Either way, the poem closes as it begins, criticizing political revolutions while at the same time mocking those "Executives" and thinkers who purport to have a viable alternative to such revolutions.

References and further reading: Thompson and Winnick.

George Lopez

"SERIOUS STEP LIGHTLY TAKEN, A," first appeared in *A Witness Tree* **(1942)**. Land and farming were always important to Frost as symbols of stability and values. The poem has autobiographical overtones. In 1934, after the death of their daughter, the Frosts could not face another summer in **Franconia** in the place Marjorie had loved so well. Moving to another location, they bought a group of old farms north of St. Johnsbury, Vermont—"between two burrs on the map."

Frost tells the story of a family settling in a town because their car has broken down. The "burrs," "snake," "hollowhead," and "dot" refer figuratively to the hills, stream, lake, and town on the map. Frost's family had been on this side of the Atlantic for 300 years, and he proudly anticipates 300 more years (a hundred thousand days) of his family's dedication to farming and to the land.

References and further reading: Gould; Winslow.

Sarah R. Jackson

"SERVANT TO SERVANTS, A," appeared first in *North of Boston* **(1914)**. Frost wrote in Edward Connery Lathem's copy of that volume that the woman in the poem is "a composite of at least three farm wives" (qtd. in Cramer), but the poem is generally thought to be a portrait of a Vermont woman on Willoughby Lake. The source of the title and, arguably, much of the poem's meaning is Genesis 9:20–25, in which Noah curses Ham's son Canaan because Ham has seen his nakedness. The text explains how children take on the guilt and shame of their parents. "A Servant to Servants" is a confession, a complaint, and like the catalog of the generations of Noah, a myth of origins.

Like Frost's other **dramatic monologues** spoken by women, "A Servant to Servants" uses blank verse to create a psychology and a voice for a woman trapped in a daily cycle of drudgery and a family cycle of madness and sexual trauma. The poet exploits the tension between the blank verse line and conversational rhythm to create this psychology: "And you like it here? / I can see how you might. But I don't know! / . . . As it is, / The cottages Len built, sometimes we rent them, / Sometimes we don't." We are compelled to try to know the speaking self of the poem, but since the narrator is clearly unreliable, such knowledge is difficult.

The monologue is delivered by an overworked woman to a man, perhaps a naturalist, camping on her husband's property. As the title suggests, she "serves" both her husband and his hired men and seems exhausted by sheer repetition, "doing / Things over and over that just won't stay done." We are quickly made aware of her odd detachment from the world around her and from her own feelings:

> It's got so I don't even know for sure
> Whether I *am* glad, sorry, or anything.
> There's nothing but a voice-like left inside
> That seems to tell me how I ought to feel.

Even the beautiful vista outside is associated with entrapment: She measures five miles from the lake to her dishwater.

The apparent cause of the narrator's dislocation is a family secret—an uncle who was locked away in a cage in the attic, an uncle she seems to have reconstructed rather than remembered. Like Noah's, the uncle's seems to have been a sexual crime, a sin of exposure: "Anyway all he talked about was love. . . . They tried to keep him clothed, but he paraded / With his clothes on his arm— all his clothes." Like Canaan, the narrator has inherited the guilt of witnessing from her mother; she explains, "That was what marrying father meant to her. / She had to lie and hear love things made dreadful / By his shouts in the night," and like the generations of the Canaanites (Gen. 10:18), she goes abroad. But the land of the Canaanites bordered Sodom and Gomorrah, the cities of sin; clearly the narrator embodies the very "curse" from which she runs, a trauma that contaminates her life and her marriage.

Several critics see "A Servant to Servants" as a poem about a psychosis stemming from sexual abuse. Some assert that the narrator seeks healing contact with the natural scenes around her. But as in many of Frost's poems, nature seems more malevolent than soothing. "I see it's a fair, pretty sheet of water," repeats the narrator about the lake, but to her it is associated with threatening storms and chills, and it feels trapped and cut off "[l]ike a deep piece of some old running river / Cut short off at both ends." Likewise, the longing to live out in the freedom of tents soon gives way to a fear of exposure. In fact, the narrator wants enclosures: the asylum, "a good roof overhead," locks on the doors, and her uncle's cage, "a room within a room" in which she has wished herself. She seems simultaneously to need and to loath the enclosures that oppress her, telling the poem's listener, "you're keeping me from work, / But the thing of it is, I need to *be* kept."

Perhaps Noah's curse, like these enclosures, is yet less terrifying than self-determination. Walter Benn Michaels makes a compelling reading of "A Servant to Servants" based on the phenomenological writings of William James, who isolated the individual's experience of self in the activity between the head and glottis. Michaels quotes Frost, an avid student of James, as saying, "The brute tones of our human throat . . . may once have been all our meaning." Michaels explores how the narrator's search for self begins in a problem of articulation, as she struggles from fragments ("but I don't know!" ". . . I guess you'd find. . . . It seems to me / I can't express my feelings any more") to the problem of meaning ("It's got so I don't know for sure / Whether I *am* glad, sorry") to identity ("or [whether I am] anything. There's nothing but a voice-like left inside"). The problem, according to this view, is epistemological. The narrator locates a version of herself in a family myth of origins by imagining, as Michaels asserts, the moment of her own generation, a moment punctuated by her uncle's "shouts in the night." The narrative itself *creates* an objectified version of self, particularly if, as Richard Poirier has argued, the uncle is himself a psychotic figure of the speaker's own imagining; the dramatic monologue is, then, the very locus of the speaker's self-creation. By such logic, her fear of external spaces can be read as a fear of losing the tangible, knowable self, and her need for enclosures is a nostalgia for coherent signs. Understood this way, the speaker's "madness" is the modern predicament posed by the loss of what empiricists call the fiction of self.

A problem for critics is how to read the unreliability of the narrator as well as her relationship to the speaker. Poirier even asserts that the speaker "indulge[s] in lying" or at least exaggeration and that her imagination feeds on her travels, her stories, and her conversations, distorting and coloring them at will. If she lies, we might ask ourselves to what purpose; if she is delusional, we can look for the kernel of truth in her delusions. The monologue, suspiciously like a soliloquy, gives us few clues to the auditor's possible reaction until the end of the poem, when the speaker's words "I need to *be* kept. . . . I'd *rather* you'd not go unless you must" suggest she is frightening him away. Hearing her candid talk of madness, the listener might easily be alarmed that she has "lain awake thinking of [him]" and more frightened by her veiled threat: "The wonder was the tents weren't snatched away / From over you as you lay in your beds."

References and further reading: Cramer, *Frost among His Poems*, 38, Kearns; Michaels; Poirier, *Knowing*, 114, 117.

Mary Adams

"SILKEN TENT, THE," first appeared in the *Virginia Quarterly Review* (Winter 1939) and was collected in *A Witness Tree* **(1942)**. The poem begins with a graceful metaphor, which Frost extends into a lovely paean to a woman close to the poet's heart. Speculation about the identity of that woman continues. As William Pritchard notes, "Lesley Frost remembers typing out this poem for her father while **Elinor** was still alive, so although **Kathleen Morrison** was eventually its recipent [*sic*] and was celebrated in its original title, there is no reason to think of her as the unique inspiration for 'The Silken Tent.' "

Heretofore overshadowed by the success of other classic Frost poems, "The Silken Tent" stands as a profound metaphor about women. Frost's tent, unlike a military tent, has fabric of silk, and the omnipresent sibilant sounds in the **sonnet** suggest the rustle of silk. The breezy airyness of silk belies the poem's weighty topic: balance. Frost's only sibling, Jeanie, had to be institutionalized; so did one of his daughters, Irma. Thus, the human challenge to remain centered and stable never was far from the poet's mind, a theme evident, for instance, in **"Choose Something Like a Star."**

The tent's support comes from two dimensions: horizontal and vertical. Both are essential, for without the "countless silken ties of love and thought," the tent would surely be blown about by the winds. Moreover, without the "central cedar pole," the tent would collapse upon itself. In addition, no one tie is pulled tighter than another. The poem, then, seems to say that for women to lack a multiplicity of horizontal ties is to risk destruction. Likewise, to rely on only one tie among many is to invite calamity if that one tie should pull loose. The implication is that woman, if she is to remain strong and poised, must be firmly anchored, even tied down. To Frost's way of thinking, *bonding* does not equal *bondage*. In an interview of 26 March 1954, he defined freedom as "feeling easy in your harness." The statement that Frost makes through the tent metaphor is that woman finds freedom (i.e., "gently sways at ease") through 360 degrees of horizontal bonding: It is the nature of the well-balanced woman to be bound "the compass round." The poet leaves it up to the reader to imagine the ties.

Turning now to the vertical dimension, the reader can see that Frost's diction suggests something religious. The tent, conceivably a circular house, has a "pinnacle to heavenward." The word *cedar* brings to mind those ancient trees of Lebanon. Cedar trees stay green the year around; traditionally, Christmas trees are green, symbolizing life. The pole of cedar "signifies the sureness of the soul." With the *central* "cedar pole," the poet clearly suggests a spiritual inner life. Such strength resides in the heart, mind, and soul of the woman, just as the cedar pole belongs at the core of the tent. In his " 'Sermon' at Rockdale Avenue Temple," Frost commented, "Religion always seems to me to come round to something beyond wisdom. It's a straining of the spirit forward to a wisdom beyond wisdom." (*See also* **Religion**.)

Frost's tent is responsive to outside forces, but it is responsive within a limited range of movement, a movement anchored in part by the steadiness of the inner pillar, outwardly unseen. Frost's tent is synergistic: All parts, visible and invisible, collaborate; the ties and the guys, the silk, and the cedar pole create an image that is simultaneously mysterious and serene.

Interestingly enough, the poet, too, is "tied down." He is tied to the **sonnet** form, fourteen times of iambic pentameter, an *ababcdcdefefgg* rhyme scheme, and in the case of a Shakespearean sonnet, three quatrains and a couplet. Tied down to such prerequisites, how can a poet compose a masterpiece? Such is the challenge. Not only does Frost succeed in meeting the challenge, but he also adds one more limitation: He writes the poem in just one sentence. Allowing himself to be disciplined to the sonnet form, he finds the freedom to articulate his thoughts about balance in a woman's life, a beautiful life. For Frost, such consummate skill constitutes prowess, a golden triumph.

When in a woman's life does such balance occur? By positioning the sun "at midday" on a summer day, Frost suggests that the time is after youth, the springtime of life. No longer a maiden and certainly no crone, the woman is somewhere in maturity, heading for the early autumn side of midsummer.

With its elaborate metaphor, Frost's sonnet is in the metaphysical tradition, and "The Silken Tent" has much to say about the wholesomeness of life lived in equilibrium with "symmetry of selfhood" in the midst of tension. The sonnet suggests that life is best lived by fulfilling responsibilities, not by evading them. Staked down firmly, the tent points to an existence above and beyond earth.

References and further reading: Brower; R. Frost, *Interviews*, 135, and " 'Sermon' at Rockdale Avenue Temple," *Collected*, 792; Oster, 297–98, for discussion of Old Testament references to cedar; Parini, *A Life*, 320–22; Poirier, *Knowing*; Pritchard, *Literary Life*, 229; Rood.

Nancy Vogel

"SITTING BY A BUSH IN BROAD SUNLIGHT" originally appeared in *West-Running Brook* **(1928).** The poem significantly recasts the ideas of spontaneous generation, long since debunked, which are reflected in Shakespeare's *Antony and Cleopatra* when the Roman leader Lepidus relates to Antony, "Your serpent of Egypt is bred now of your mud by the operation of your sun: so is your crocodile" (II.vii.25–6). "There was one time and only the one," remarks the speaker, "When dust really took in the sun." Since that moment of genesis, none has ever witnessed "sun-smitten slime/ Again come to life and crawl off." The sun, now, seems to lack creative power; the "lasting effect" has diminished to a playful ray or two, only enough to toast gently the palm of a hand. And no one expects crocodiles or any other form of life to be birthed from a marriage of sun and muck. Still, Frost uses the analogy of the sun's primordial potency to link the natural and spiritual worlds. Mingling pseudo-zoological creation theories with biblical history, the poem hinges on the conjunction of sun and God. For despite the cooling ardor of the once generative sun, its initial flame was sufficient to maintain what Frost calls "our breath," our sustaining life force. So, too, God—who once addressed his followers by name, as with Moses and the burning bush alluded to in the title—still "persists as our faith." The sentiment resembles a popular Christian hymn, asserting belief in the sun even when it isn't shining. Faith (in a God who has withdrawn from everyday appearance) and breath (the only residue of that first inspiration of sun-fire) sustain themselves in the same way.

Lawrance Thompson feels that the poem is Frost's attempt at "reconciling the scientific hypothesis with a Christian axiom." Others are less convinced. Arguing rather for a religious agnosticism, H. M. Campbell sees God portrayed as both "whimsical and arbitrary." When Frost writes that God "took the veil and withdrew," Campbell sees an allusion to "a nun retiring into a convent" and questions whether both origin theories—creation by sun or God—are not equally dubious. Campbell's relatively early analysis filters into later readings, as well. One of the most insightful treatments of the poem is by Charles Berger, who rightly contends that otherwise it "has drawn surprisingly little comment from the critics." He finds the tone "balanced between scoffing . . . and . . . awe" and believes Frost to be "interested primarily in what he calls our persistence." In a similar vein, George Bagby feels that the poem achieves "at best a precarious kind of faith." Truly, the faith of which Frost writes is a difficult one to sort out.

In a poem so concerned with beginnings, Frost curiously chooses to reflect upon a biblical paradigm not from Genesis but from Exodus. The speaker of the poem assumes the role of Moses, not speaking with but simply sitting by a bush. Moses, troubled by his ineffective speech and inability to communicate, felt quite inadequate as a divine mouthpiece; he proclaimed his own desire to withdraw but ended up leading his people to the Promised Land. So, too, Frost's speaker begins with only a placid motion, a cradling of sunlight "between thumb and fingers." By the conclusion, however, he is virtually sermonizing. To the degree that the poem is about evolution and transformation, it is also about conversion from one state to another and the power of poetic inspiration to effect such changes.

References and further reading: Bagby, *Nature*, 56; Berger, 152–53; Campbell; Thompson, *Triumph*, 629.

Eric C. Brown

"SKEPTIC," first published in *Steeple Bush* **(1947)**, is clearly informed by early twentieth-century astronomical discoveries. In 1912, the work of V. M. Slipher demonstrated that objects not only resided outside our galaxy but in fact resided great distances from it. Basing his measurements of stellar distance upon what later came to be known as the "red shift," Slipher noticed that light emitted from distant stars and galaxies always shifted toward the red spectrum. In 1929, Edwin Hubble concluded that the red shift is proportional to a stellar object's distance from our galaxy and that the greater the distance between any two galaxies, the greater the speed at which they separate. His observations, later called Hubble's Law, were seen by many as confirmation of Georges Lemaître's Big Bang theory (1927), as the universe seemed to be expanding uniformly toward higher states of entropy.

As in **"Any Size We Please,"** the speaker in the rarely discussed poem "Skeptic" tries to contain the immense size of the universe by challenging the epistemological status of the poem's informing concepts. The idiomatic expression "I don't believe I believe" reveals the poet's vacillation between belief and doubt—an epistemological position that emanates from his knowledge that light exhibits the characteristics of both particles and waves. He can put "no faith in the seeming facts of light" because we do not yet fully understand light's true nature. In the second stanza the poet vacillates even further. While he seems able to accept the idea that the far star is not the "last" or the only galaxy in space, he appears reluctant to accept the fact that the universe is continually expanding in the "after explosion" of the Big Bang. The final stanza calls all prior evidence into doubt and suggests that the only way to measure the true size of the universe is to measure it by its responsiveness to individual need. Although scientific evidence may inform us that the universe is expanding, imaginative reverie and common sense become the "matters of fact" most relevant to immediate experience.

References and further reading: Abel, "Instinct"; Jeremy Bernstein, *Einstein* (New York: Viking, 1973), 147–59; Rotella, "Comparing."

Robert Bernard Hass

"SNOW" first appeared in *Poetry* magazine (Feb. 1916), the same year it was collected in *Mountain Interval*. The protagonist, Meserve, in many ways represents the poet as "player"—playing on his audience's curiosity and willingness to be beguiled for the sake of entertainment. Meserve, as his name suggests, serves himself but needs an audience in order to achieve self-gratification. His "play" with the Coles's commonsense approach to life grants him the chance to make light of an otherwise strenuous situation. That it takes Meserve four hours to travel three miles to the Coles's farm—the half-point of his trip where he decides to rest his horses—emphasizes the severity of the storm with which he must contend, should he continue his six-mile journey home. Thus, the most evident conflict in the poem is Meserve's obstinacy with regard to continuing his trip despite the severity of the storm outside and the protests of Fred and Helen Cole. However, as John Sears points out, the most obvious conflict in the poem is not necessarily the most important. Sears notes a more significant conflict with regard to Meserve's challenging the rigid borderline that Fred and Helen seem to have drawn between themselves and the storm. By not being able to see their human affinity with the storm outside, Fred and Helen neglect to cultivate a side to their nature that the poet figure, Meserve, brings out in them. In this way, nature's beauty with regard to its challenging changes and physical possibilities becomes an important idea in "Snow." The opposition between nature and order, for example, is displayed in the metaphorical drama played out between the Coles and Meserve.

Meserve (the poet figure), like nature, changes on a whim. By virtue of his prolific ability "for seeing likeness," Meserve is able to render new shape to the landscape outside. About the snow, Meserve says to the Coles, "You can just see it glancing off the roof / Making a great scroll upward toward the sky, / Long enough for recording all our names on." Demonstrating an ability to view natural phenomena in different ways, Meserve creatively changes the snow outside from a menacing evil of nature to something poetic. In this way, Meserve points out the intricacies of snow itself. It, too, takes on different shapes and creates alternate landscapes—physically challenging our need to impose rigid meanings and patterns to things.

The play in the title of the poem itself suggests that Meserve is merely "snowing" his audience. Seeming to pay little or no attention to the Coles's protests, Meserve diverts their attention from their concern for his safety to a leaf in their open book that has stood erect ever since he came into their home. His commenting on its indecision to fall backwards or forwards reflects Meserve's own situation. He must decide either to listen to the Coles's sense of reason or, by going, to respond to nature's challenge. As John F. Sears notes, by diverting their attention, Meserve purposely tests the Coles's patience, knowing that they are concerned for his safety but also curious to see how the drama will end. The Coles's mixed feelings manifest themselves at the end of the poem after they are assured of Meserve's safety, and their frustration with having been overly concerned for their playful neighbor is diminished somewhat by their sense of having been entertained. Subsequent to pointing out to each other that their concern was "just [Meserve's] fun," Fred Cole asks Helen to forgive him. "We've had a share in one night of his life," he says. "What'll you bet he ever calls again?"

References and further reading: Bell; Sears, 85.

Alex Ambrozic

"SOLDIER, A," is one of four poems Frost wrote for his friend and fellow poet Edward Thomas, who was killed by an artillery shell in France on Easter Monday in 1917. The **sonnet** was first published as "The Soldier" in *McCall's* (May 1927) and was included in *West-Running Brook* **(1928). Reginald Cook** notes that during poetry readings, he often paired "A Soldier" and **"Design,"** claiming they made "a pairing in form but not in content."

Frost characterizes the soldier as a lance, an instrument of war hurled by society. The metaphor transports us back in time to the age of great heroes, freeing us from temporal restrictions and setting up the metaphysical imagery of the poem. But there are no great heroic actions here, just the act of a lance being hurled through space and landing in the dust. One can almost hear the impact and feel the metallic, violent force that is combat.

The soldier, as he charges into action, is like a steel-headed spear destructively winging its way through the air; there is little meaning behind the action. The act of hurling belongs to someone else; the soldier is, simply put, part of the process. There are, in a sense, two very different lance-throwers here: the society and a much greater force that ultimately propels the spirit into the cosmos. The first one is destructive and terrifying; the second, positive and redemptive.

References and further reading: Bagby, *Nature*; R. Cook, *Living Voice*, 216; for a link between **Emerson**'s "The Concord Hymn" and "A Soldier," see Monteiro, *New England*, 142–43.

James M. Dubinsky

"SOME SCIENCE FICTION," one of the outer-space meditations of Frost's final volume, *In the Clearing* **(1962),** was first published, without the "Envoi," in a 1955 chapbook as Frost's **Christmas poem.** As we learn from Jeffrey S. Cramer, the "Envoi" dedicates the poem to his friend Edward Hyde Cox, who lived on Crow Island, Massachusetts. The two men had met in Key West, Florida, in 1940.

Mordecai Marcus believes the poem was written before the other outer-space poems in the volume, such as "[**But Outer Space**]." Frost was friends with at least one science-fiction writer, Philip Wylie, but the poems do not reveal an enthusiast's knowledge of science-fiction literature. They suggest, instead, the musings of an intelligent newspaper reader at a time when space exploration was the stuff of daily headlines. Clearly, Frost is questioning society's "bigoted . . . reliance / On the gospel of modern science."

References and further reading: Cramer, *Frost among His Poems*, 176; Marcus, *Explication.*

Andy Duncan

"SOMETHING FOR HOPE," first published in the *Atlantic Monthly* (Dec. 1946), is the second poem in *Steeple Bush* **(1947)**. In George Bagby's words, the poem is a statement of Frost's "faith in natural process." The steeple bush is considered a weed because it is unpalatable and because it crowds out useful pasture grasses. The poem celebrates the slow cycle of natural succession— grass to weeds to trees and back to grass again—and suggests that, rather than fighting the cycle, the individual might patiently work with it, waiting for the mature trees to yield lumber, then after harvesting them, use the field once again for pasture. The poem thus calls on us to adapt life to nature and take advantage of the particular sort of nourishment it may offer at any given time. James L. Potter sees the poem as evidence that Frost "believed at times, or with part of his mind, that the world and man's position in it are fundamentally satisfactory, even pleasant. It may not be the best of all possible worlds, but it seems, on balance, to be manageable."

References and further reading: Bagby, *Nature*, 85; Potter, 85.

Todd Lieber

SONNETS. Frost wrote more than forty sonnets during his career. An accurate count of Frost's sonnets may not be entirely possible, though, since categorizing his medium-length **lyrics** would test almost any definition of the sonnet: He has four "sonnets" in couplets and roughly a dozen in irregular stanzas, including one terza rima sonnet (**"Acquainted with the Night"**); and among the remaining twenty-nine sonnets, which negotiate variously between the traditional Petrarchan and Shakespearean forms, seven were not collected during Frost's life. But among this idiosyncratic group of lyrics stand some of the finest sonnets in our language, remarkable both for their variation against the form and their artful play within it.

One of Frost's achievements is in a form he seems to have invented as he went along, which we can call the "nonce-sonnet": a poem, generally of fourteen lines, rhyming by no set pattern, which suggests the sonnet form by its rhetorical unity and closure and by the intricacy of its construction. Frost's **"Mowing,"** for example, rhymes *abc abd ec dfeg fg*, allowing one and only one rhyme for each end word, and never rhyming within a small syntactical unit, repeating a rhyme pattern, or placing a rhyme within two lines of its partner until the final line. Such distant, almost inaudible rhyme seems to reinforce the message of "Mowing," in which the speaker listens to the real, wordless whisper of a scythe rather than any fantasy of speech: In a poem in part about "the lack of sound," overly lyrical rhyming would seem dubious and out of place. Other nonce-sonnets include **"Hyla Brook"** (which rhymes *abb acc add eef gfg*) and **"The Oven Bird"** (which rhymes *aab cb dcd ee fgfg*), both of which treat the question of what happens to the songs of nature in summertime, when water, flowers, and birds seem less plentiful. The ovenbird's solution, "in singing not to sing," seems to be part of what motivates such lovely but irregular nonce-sonnets. Frost's more traditional sonnets, in Petrarchan or Shakespearean forms, tend to place a slightly different emphasis on the ovenbird's injunction, incorporating some devices and elements of "not singing" into a form that inherently sings. *"Never Again Would Birds' Song Be the Same,"* another sonnet that deals with the dynamics of nature's songs, rhymes as a perfectly regular Shakespearean sonnet; but Frost varies his sentence syntax against the traditional three quatrains and a couplet, so that the poem rhymes, effectively, *ababc dcd e fef g g*. When it is read aloud, the poem almost doesn't sound like a sonnet because Frost's sentences break up his rhyme pattern. In effect, within the line groupings of the traditional sonnet, Frost plays his "sentence sounds" against a structure larger than the iambic pentameter of a single line—and the question of sound structure, in the "oversound" of meaning that Eve's voice seems to have imposed on the music of birds, is after all this poem's central preoccupation.

"The Silken Tent," which could be taken as a metaphorical ars poetica for sonnet writing, likewise treats the themes of perceived order or perceived freedom. Frost's ambiguous "she" is compared to a silken tent gently swaying in its guy ropes, bound by "countless ties" but, apparently, "strictly held by none." And in just this way Frost's sonnets, while bound by their forms (although sometimes these forms are invented, not traditional) *seem* to operate freely, writing themselves into sonnets almost by accident. At times the rigors of sonnet form are more apparent, as in the slightly constrained *moth-cloth-broth-froth* rhyme of the Petrarchan sonnet **"Design,"** but such threadbare versification is often deliberate: In "Design," for example, the speaker is preoccupied with perceived excesses of form (the "design of darkness to appall" he finds in his moth-and-spider apparition). Generally, Frost's sonnets seem to generate their form rather than being generated by it.

In a late letter to **Louis Untermeyer**, Frost wrote, "The sonnet is the strictest form I have behaved in, and that mainly by pretending it wasn't a sonnet." Although it is difficult to say precisely *how* one "pretends" not to have set out to write a sonnet, Frost gives clues about *why* one would make such pretense in "The Constant Symbol," where he claims that because the sonnet became a habitual form for so many poets—his example is Shakespeare's Sonnet XXIX— and because poems were often written as sonnets for the form's own sake (so that "any worry" on the part of the reader "is as to whether [the poet] will outlast or last out the fourteen lines"), our century has become distrustful of the sonnet. Frost argues that the preeminence of form over content "has driven so many [readers and poets] to free verse and even to the novel." What is crucial for Frost, clearly, is that a poem should suggest its own form, as it gets written— or, in the case of his sonnets, that the poem should at least *pretend* to be inventing its form, should *seem* to sway freely despite the guy ropes that may have always bound it in place.

References and further reading: O. Evans argues for a number of what he calls Frost's "longer sonnets," up to and including the twenty-one-line blank verse poem "Not to Keep," and summarizes previous articles about Frost's sonnets; R. Frost, *Letters to Untermeyer*, 381, and "The Constant Symbol," *Collected*, 786–91; Paul Fussell, in *Poetic Meter and Poetic Form* (New York: Random House, 1979), has a thorough and crucial chapter on the sonnet as a form and discusses Frost's fine Petrarchan sonnet **"The Vantage Point"**; Maxson provides a book-length discussion of Frost's sonnets; Rood.

Isaac Cates

"SOUND OF THE TREES, THE," was first published in *Poetry and Drama* (Dec. 1914), then in *The Atlantic* (Aug. 1915), with the title "The Sound of Trees." Later, it appeared as the closing poem in *Mountain Interval* **(1916)** under the title "The Sound of the Trees." Little critical notice has been given to the change in title, although the former title draws attention to trees in general rather than to a particular stand of trees, a distinction that may be of interest since it emphasizes Frost's growing identification with the importance of the particularity of place or region. Rather more attention has been given to issues of publication than to the actual meaning of the poem, though it has been considered both Emersonian (*see* **Emerson**) and Coleridgean. Frost's connection to nature and its human qualities is a source of discussion, especially as the role of nature as mirror is explored in many of Frost's other poems, including **"Tree at My Window."** Passing notice has also been given to the ambiguity of the trees as a threat not only to "clouds" but to humans as well. The poem also meditates playfully on the condition of being rooted to "dwelling place" as set against the desire to make "the reckless choice" and "be gone."

References and further reading: Bagby, *Nature*, explores the poem's link to Emerson; Cramer, *Frost among His Poems*, 60, quotes John W. Haines on the subject of which trees provided the inspiration for the poem; R. Frost, *Selected Letters*, 169, gives background information on the poem's selection for publication in the two journals as well as a reference to the poem in a letter Frost wrote to **Amy Lowell**; Hadas, 106–9, discusses at length the mirroring of nature in the poem.

L. Tamara Kendig

"SPAN OF LIFE, THE," was first published as "The Old Dog" in **Louis Untermeyer**'s 1935 anthology *Rainbow in the Sky*. As "The Span of Life," it was published as one of the original "Ten Mills" in the April 1936 issue of

Poetry magazine, and it retained that title and that company when it was included in *A Further Range* (1936).

Richard Eberhart uses the poem to demonstrate that Frost's couplets are "concentrated essences of meaning and suggestion." At first glance the couplet seems "entirely unpoetical, two barefaced prosaic statements," but then the reader makes the connections and feels the impact of such a "life-inclusive poem."

Eberhart's attempt to paraphrase the situation depicted in the couplet has been challenged, demonstrating that the poem is indeed subject to more varied interpretation than at first seems possible. Laurence Perrine, for instance, counters Eberhart's interpretation: "The old dog's bark is friendly, not hostile: it is a greeting, not a challenge." Barking can be friendly or unfriendly, Perrine argues, and Frost's choice of a neutral verb for the dog's action lends great weight to the final word, "pup," which has unmistakable connotations of friendliness.

References and further reading: Eberhart, "Personality," 777–79; Perrine, "Span."

Andy Duncan

SPORTS. As a senior, Frost was recruited for the Lawrence High School football team. Robert Newdick records that Frost was, in the words of the team's captain, "like some wild animal let loose. He charged, tackled and played like a fighting bull. He had no fear. Right then and there he became one of us." Yet Newdick also reports that "after every game their quick-charging, fast-running, hard-hitting right end had gone home dizzy and ill." Conquering fear remained a lifelong challenge for Frost, who tended toward solitariness, even to the point of being end on a football team. Moreover, as in **"Birches,"** he admired a swinger of birches, a boy too far from town to play team sports, a boy able to make his own play.

Nonetheless, as Leonard Lyons notes, sports captivated the sensitive youth, whose ambition was to be a pitcher and a poet. Once a poet, as a 1939 interview indicates, Frost often spoke about the affinity between the arts and sports: "It's live or die in a football game . . . and that's the way it should be with writing. . . . One should write only when he has something to say, and then it should be live or die, as in the football game."

Sports demand rules and boundaries, a playing field for the game. So does the kind of poetry that Frost preferred: blank verse over free verse. A member of a victorious Lawrence High football team, Frost admired the spirit of discipline and competitiveness. In "The Poet's Next of Kin in a College," he writes, "I wish that some of my boys in writing would do . . . well in athletics. . . . sight and insight. You must have form—performance. The thing itself is indescribable, but it is felt like athletic form."

In his essay "A Perfect Day—A Day of Prowess," originally published in *Sports Illustrated* in 1956, Frost notes the importance of action: "Prowess of course comes first, the ability to perform with success in games, in the arts and, come right down to it, in battle. The nearest of kin to the artists in college where we all become bachelors of arts are their fellow performers in baseball, football and tennis." Ever the competitor, Frost played baseball, softball, and tennis. Wilbert Snow, a former governor of Connecticut, recalled Frost's saying that "[i]n verse as on the trapeze and tennis court performance is all. And that's why nothing around college absolutely nothing is as near poetry and the arts in general as the sports of the stadium." Points win ballgames, and Frost wanted to win; moreover, he sought to play the game of poetry like an Olympic champion.

References and further reading: R. Frost, *Interviews*, 103, "A Perfect Day—A Day of Prowess," *Collected*, 835, and "The Poet's Next of Kin," *Collected*, 768–72; L. Lyons; Newdick, *Season*, 27–28; Snow, 29; for the joyous feeling of "athletic form," see the sixth stanza of **"Two Tramps in Mud Time."**

Nancy Vogel

"SPRING POOLS" first appeared in *The Dearborn Independent* (23 Apr. 1927) and later as the first poem in **West-Running Brook (1928)**. As Richard Poirier has pointed out, the poem is not about a man standing in a forest somewhere looking at spring pools. The only pools here are the ones in his mind. And the trees are the overpowering forces of life that overshadow and threaten to pull the foundation of his being out from under him.

At first glance the narrator seems to be concerned with the summer maturation of trees and the observation that such a maturation process will involve the overshadowing and eventual death of youthful spring flowers and the pools that reflect them. The fear expressed is that the roots of the trees will suck up all of the spring pools underneath "From snow that melted only yesterday," drying up and withering the flowery undergrowth.

We find in "The Oft-Repeated Dream" of **The Hill Wife** and in **"Come In"** that trees are seen as fearsome, overshadowing forces, trying the bedroom window latch or inviting the narrator in among the trees toward death. The trees in "Spring Pools" appear to have the human capacity to think twice. According to the narrator, they have no concern for the beauty beneath them. Here they are willful, prepared to soak up the life-giving pools that give freshness to spring flowers and undergrowth that would otherwise give hope and pleasure to the narrator if not for their inevitable demise.

The narrator points out that in the spring the pools are capable of clear reflection, even under the overshadowing and constantly draining presence of the trees. They, like the flowers beside them, are conscious of and feel the chill of impending death and shiver in the increasing darkness beneath the trees. Line 5 begins with "And yet . . . ," signaling a change in direction toward not simply the natural change of seasons but the violence of the powerful and fittest over the fragile and more transient. The spring pools will disappear "not out by any brook or river, / But up by roots to bring dark foliage on."

In the second stanza, the narrator refers to "The trees that have it in their pent-up buds / To darken nature and be summer woods—." The buds are pent-up, filled with youthful enthusiasm, ready to burst forth at the first opportunity as summer blossoms, without reflection, even though like the spring pools, they are fully capable of "think[ing] twice."

Line 10 is a powerful, emotion-filled accusation against the powers of the overshadowing, threatening forces. The poem then speaks of the delicate balance in the relationship between the flowers and their watery foundation, arguing that they are essentially one and the same; thus, the water cannot be consumed without losing the flowers. The final line of the poem serves a double purpose: first, as a reminder that the spring pools have only just arrived, and second, that they, like the winter snow and pent-up buds of the trees, signal the inevitable destruction of the beauty that grows out of every season. See also **Nature Poet and Naturalist**.

References and further reading: Lentricchia, *Modern Poetics*; discusses the poem in terms of its "vision of violence"; Oster; Parini, *A Life*, 233–35; Poirier, *Knowing*.

Wm. Thomas Hill

"STAR IN A STONEBOAT, A," subtitled "For Lincoln MacVeagh," first appeared without its dedication in the *Yale Review* (Jan. 1921) and later in *New Hampshire* **(1923)**. It is the first poem of the "Notes" section of that volume. Lincoln MacVeagh, the object of the poem's dedication, met Frost as a representative of **Henry Holt and Company** in 1919. The two became good friends, and later in 1920, when Frost was having some financial difficulties, MacVeagh arranged for Frost's post as consulting editor for the company, putting him on the monthly payroll of Henry Holt.

The ironic opening line of the poem sets the tone, at once playfully argumentative and defensive, identifying the posture of the narrator as one ready to stand for his position against all others. The narrator, disputing any opinion the listener might have to the contrary, argues that at least one meteorite has been used for the mundane purpose of merely filling in a space in a stone fence. The poem can be read, then, as a complaint against the misappropriation of creative inspiration.

Some farmer, he argues, "not used to handling stars" has no doubt at one time or another plucked from its resting place a meteorite that has fallen from its course in the heavens. The farmer does not realize the damage he has done. In language filled with irony, the narrator charges that such an act has been performed by one with no understanding of the human soul or imagination, by one who does not see the potential for creative growth inherent in the star, by one who does not realize that left free from the restraints of the wall, the meteorite would have been free to increase to seemingly endless proportions like ant eggs.

The seventh and eighth stanzas make a point that is touched upon repeatedly in Frost's poetry: that, when allowed to, creative inspiration has the power to transform. The farmer, he insists, acts not as he or his listener might have acted under similar circumstances by using "a flying car"—and thus uniting creative inspiration with imagination. Rather, the farmer in an insensitive, almost bestial, act of labor rips the meteorite out of the ground with an iron bar, places it in an old stoneboat (a sled used in New England for carrying stones), and hauls it off to be used like any other stone to build a fence.

The narrator points out that the farmer's behavior is "faintly reminiscent" of all humans who, as he has already stated, are unused to handling stars. It is thus left to him "as though / Commanded in a dream" to find the misplaced element or meteorite; nevertheless, even if he does, there is a strong sense that once the meteorite has been moved and used inappropriately, he will be unable to set it upon its proper course. In fact, in lines 37–38, he admits that he may not have been able to find a better place for the star himself, had he discovered it first.

Lines 34–42 recall **"Bond and Free."** The narrator keeps his eyes firmly fixed upon stone fences, the real or practical constructions of human endeavor, during the day, no matter how imperfect they may be, lifting his eyes to the heavens only at night "Where showers of charted meteors let fly" and where his thoughts are free to sit "in Sirius' disc all night."

The fifteenth stanza emphasizes the point made in "Bond and Free" that the practical world—not school or church—is the place for living. The narrator/ poet must keep his eyes on the practical world, hopping along like a bird from stone to stone "perch on perch," keeping uppermost in his mind the measure of the stone fences before him.

The final stanza is an appeal to leave meteorites as they are. They are complete in themselves in whatever size and shape they appear. The line "That I am like to compass, fool or wise" speaks of the narrator's awareness of his own limitations, his own inability to improve upon the completeness of the meteorite as it is.

References and further reading: Fleissner, *Road Taken*; Poirier, *Knowing*; Thompson, *Triumph*.

Wm. Thomas Hill

"STARS," which first appeared in *A Boy's Will* (1913) with the gloss "There is no oversight of human affairs," is a poem in which Frost explores one of his central themes, what Frank Lentricchia describes as "those moments of perception when we objectivize our humanness." Stars symbolize both humanity's humble place in the universe and the possibilities latent within the human imagination. **Reginald Cook** notes that conjoined to this symbol is the expanse of unbroken snow, which stands for the empty places within and without while simultaneously representing a tabula rasa upon which the individual inscribes "the metaphors by which he identifies his relationship to things." According to Lawrance Thompson, "Stars" is thus constructed upon a duality that expresses both "outer mood and inner mood" and that is further emphasized by the disjunction between the apparent interest the stars show for humanity's fate—which Victor Reichert calls the "starlight of affirmation, aspiration and dedication"—and the figurative distance through which they gaze silently down upon humanity's struggle with that fate. Finally, Frost's use of Minerva—the Roman goddess of wisdom, art, and war—to express the thoughts latent within the images of the stars and the snowscape supports Cook's assertion that Frost's is "[m]ore of a speculative imagination than a figurative one."

References and further reading: R. Cook, *Living Voice*, 79, 235; Lentricchia, *Modern Poetics*, 29; Reichert, 425; Thompson, *Fire and Ice*, 100.

Gavin Schulz

"STAR-SPLITTER, THE," was published first in *The Century Magazine* (Sept. 1923) and collected in *New Hampshire* **(1923)**. The narrator of the poem tells the story of Brad McLaughlin, a New England farmer who burns his house for the insurance money and buys a telescope so he can look at the stars. Like many of Frost's other poems, this one questions the place of human beings in the universe and implies that they seem insignificant when compared to the stars. In the face of such insignificance, the poem suggests that a sense of community among humans is essential.

The physical environment of the community is rugged, a place where farm soil is full of rocks and "Few farms changed hands." It is a place where economic difficulties result in farms being auctioned off in a sort of "new-fashioned" sacrifice. In such a place, human companionship is important, and each person has a place in the community. A thief is referred to not as *a* thief, or *the* thief, but rather "Our thief, the one who does our stealing from us," suggesting that stealing is as necessary to the community as any other service. The townspeople, because they are social, are forgiving: "For to be social is to be forgiving."

Brad McLaughlin is presented as a flawed person in the narrator's judgment, a "hugger-mugger," or incompetent, farmer. That he can mix "reckless talk / Of heavenly stars with hugger-mugger farming" seems odd and noteworthy to the narrator, as odd as McLaughlin's desire to own a telescope. McLaughlin's greatest flaw is his burning down his house for the insurance money. Even this act, however, the townspeople forgive after thinking about it overnight. After all, they reason, "If one by one we counted people out / For the least sin, it wouldn't take us long / To get so we had no one left to live with." In this statement, the townspeople are presented as an inclusive, forgiving group.

Significantly, they clearly recognize McLaughlin's sin, just as they see the sin of "our thief," and still accept both, for ultimately the poem is about "seeing." It begins with McLaughlin telling about Orion's (in the constellation Orion) watching him while he catches up with work he should already have done. When asked why he wants a telescope, McLaughlin says he believes that sight is the greatest gift that humankind has been given, and a telescope is "the strongest thing that's given us" with which to see. The telescope, then, amplifies the best feature of humanity, the ability to see, and McLaughlin uses the telescope to look back at the stars. The narrator often comes along with him, and the two of them spend the nights looking at the stars and thinking about them, saying "some of the best things we ever said." Here again, as in lines about seeing the sin of the thief and forgiving him, the sense of social bonding is combined with the act of seeing clearly. Frost seems to say that social bonding is a conscious act that people want to perform, knowing that they are all imperfect.

In contrast to the images of social bonding, the telescope is identified as a "Star-splitter" because it appears to split stars into two or three images through its lens. The narrator considers whether splitting stars can be compared to splitting wood and concludes that if it can, then it is of some use. But the message is not that the telescope has split stars but rather that the activity of using the telescope has bonded the narrator and McLaughlin. In the final stanza the narrator asks whether "we know any better where we are" and whether things are any "different from the way [they] ever stood." The answer is that things are no different, but by looking clearly back at the stars, humanity knows where it stands.

References and further reading: Waddell, "By Precept."

Claudia Milstead

STEEPLE BUSH (1947), Frost's penultimate volume of poems, was received with mixed reviews. While many critics were pleased by individual poems such as **"Directive"** and **"One Step Backward Taken,"** many others were displeased by how greatly the book differs in tone and subject matter from Frost's earlier works. In a famous review, Randall Jarrell wrote that "the poems merely remind you, by their persistence in the mannerisms of what was genius, that they are productions of somebody who once, and somewhere else, was a great poet." A more moderate appraisal was that of George F. Whicher, who wrote that Frost "does not write in his seventies imitations of what he was writing in his forties. Where there is likeness there is increase of skill. The present gathering of poems mainly written during the last three years is more topical, more sharply intellectual, and more given to teasing than any of its predecessors."

Steeple Bush treats contemporary issues of the middle to late 1940s, though on a broader scale it deals with Frost's concern with how to think originally in the midst of historical and public turmoil and conflict. Several of the poems in the book make direct mention of the atomic bomb and of the hopes for a lasting peace being discussed in the public press in 1946. (One of the poems was even originally published with the title "1946.") A common assumption of the time was that the world was now, or was soon to be, permanently at peace, united by the victory of the Allies in World War II but more so by the threat of instant annihilation by the atomic bomb (dropped twice on Japan a year and nine months before *Steeple Bush* was published). The *Atlantic Monthly* in 1946, in which twelve of the poems in *Steeple Bush* first appeared, contains repeated references to such a view. In addition to the twelve poems, three of the poems in *Steeple Bush* first appeared in the Autumn 1946 *Yale Review*, and three more in the Winter 1946 *Virginia Quarterly Review*. Sixteen of the poems first appeared in the volume itself, and three others appeared as Frost's 1944, 1945, and 1946 **Christmas poems**. (Four made less splashy, more incidental appearances: one as a Christmas poem put out by a major collector of Frost manuscripts; one in a 1943 **Dartmouth College** calendar; one in a Dartmouth College Library retrospective of Frost; and one as a broadside distributed at dedicatory ceremonies of a Ripton, Vermont, park.)

The poems in *Steeple Bush* are arranged in five groups, the last four of which are named **"Five Nocturnes,"** "A Spire and Belfry," "Out and Away," and "Editorials." The first group, untitled and made up of seven poems, is by far the strongest. Its subject, it may be argued, is thinking; the other groups, sometimes directly and sometimes more subtly, support this subject. Poems in "Five Nocturnes" focus on fears that can undermine original thinking; poems in "A Spire and Belfry" consider, among other topics, how religious belief and love can serve as correctives to self-importance; while two poems in "Out and Away" and all in "Editorials" offer examples of contemporary problems, such as nuclear war, which need to be thought about originally.

The last poem of the volume, **"To the Right Person,"** echoes an essay Frost wrote for the October 1946 issue of the *Atlantic Monthly* entitled "The Constant Symbol." In the essay Frost discusses the relationship between originality, poetic conventions (such as stanzaic forms and meter), and language, saying, "To the right person it must seem naive to distrust form as such. The very words of a dictionary are a restriction to make the best of or stay out of and be silent. . . . Form in language is such a disjected lot of old broken pieces it seems almost nonexistent as the spirit until the two embrace in the sky. They are not to be thought of as encountering in rivalry but in creation." In "To the Right Person," Frost's narrator describes a disused schoolhouse, ascribing its being closed to someone's determination that "mere learning" would no longer be the school's mission and that the schoolhouse would remain shut to all except those who wished to "make up for a lack of meditation." Frost's emphasis in "The Constant Symbol," "To the Right Person," and the other poems in *Steeple Bush* on the need for truly original thinking, for meditation about life, is characteristic. The poet cared deeply about education and shaping individual minds with a measure of independence that would make possible some degree of originality. (*See also* **Teacher**.)

The experience of thinking originally is compared in "The Constant Symbol" to form and spirit embracing in the sky. In one of the poems found in the first group of *Steeple Bush*, **"An Unstamped Letter in Our Rural Letter Box,"** Frost uses a similar figure. The poem depicts the experience of a tramp who, sleeping overnight on a farmer's land, happens to see two falling stars that join and fall together. The sight causes him to make an unexpected connection between two memories of his own, so that "for a moment all was plain / That men have thought about in vain." The falling stars signify how original thought is often an unexpected, fiery connection between two previously unrelated thoughts or memories, one of the ways in which Frost depicts the subject of thinking in the first group of poems.

Frost argues for certain prerequisites to original thought. One is perspective about one's own life and times. In "Directive," the major poem of the volume, Frost's speaker takes his reader on a mock journey through two abandoned New England villages and fields to a brook that can somehow restore one to wholeness. As in **"Choose Something Like a Star,"** the theme is rediscovery of some idea or person whose example is enduring, to which or to whom one can return imaginatively for example and refreshment. In a talk at the **Bread Loaf School of English**, Frost gave the Latin poet Catullus as an example of a writer Frost himself read when he wanted to restore his sense of balance in life. Developing mental freedom so that one can think clearly is a thematic thread throughout Frost's poetry. In *Steeple Bush* the theme receives some of its fullest treatment.

Of the four named groups of poems in *Steeple Bush*, only "Five Nocturnes" works as a thematic whole. They depict various strategies for surviving the night and for dealing with various kinds of fear: with a night light, with walks, with observing and counting the stars, with drink and company. The first two poems of the group acknowledge the potency of irrational personal fears, while the last three scoff at what the speakers consider a less imminent threat: the world's end. The last three poems together offer a playful and sarcastic but also serious response to prophecies about the future of the world or the human race in the face of nuclear threats. Frost's sarcasm rests on his long-held view that there is nothing novel about the prospect of the human race disappearing from the earth. Hence, the nervous sense of inevitable apocalyptic annihilation is tempered in Frost by humor and irony.

The "Five Nocturnes" group lacks the dramatic, convincing depiction of personally threatening physical and emotional forces found in an earlier group of Frost's night poems, "Fiat Nox." There is nothing like **"Once by the Pacific"** in the later group, certainly. But if we accept Frost's notion that the conditions of life—especially the fact that it may end at any time—make everyone gamblers, the speakers' various stratagems and gambling tactics, including bravado and humor, used as lines of defense against a fear for the world's future, are not bad approaches. They might carry anyone through, say, one night. This group of poems, together with the first, is one of the more compelling of the book because the type of thinking it advocates is centered on the good of preserving a stable self in the face of a variety of threatening fears.

The least successful group of poems in the book is "A Spire and Belfry." The collective theme of the group—maintaining one's reserve, protecting one's privacy, respecting one's own integrity (best expressed in **"The Fear of God"**)—collapses in **"A Steeple on the House"** and **"Innate Helium"** into a religiously heightened justification of self-importance. The latter two poems also seem to reflect Frost's self-satisfaction in his position as the type of "somebody" against whom "The Fear of God" warns so cheerfully. Such religious justification of the need to protect one's privacy may show that Frost is serious in his religious beliefs, but allowing such beliefs to suggest that his own personal integrity is above reproach discourages serious attention to the finer poems in the group.

The section titled "Out and Away," which follows "A Spire and Belfry," provides a respite from the political and religious stances in the previous groups. The group works by way of mildly surprising and amusing juxtapositions in theme, stanza forms, meter, and tone. For example, in **"Astrometaphysical"** and the poem that follows it, **"Skeptic,"** the speakers have very different dispositions, with the first laughing at his own ambitions for fame and the second feeling seriously his organic and even moral connection with the entire universe. The last two poems in the group branch out into the political and academic worlds and lead the way to the last group, "Editorials."

The virtue of the last section is that it does not pretend to contain much more than opinionated verse letters on the **politics** of the day. The major flaw of the group is that the ideas in the editorials themselves are often dull. Frost's critics have, for the most part, been irritated or disappointed by these poems. Randall Jarrell nearly despaired of the "Yankee Editorialist side of Frost [which] gets in the way of *everything*—of us, of the real Frost, of the real poems and their real subject-matter. And a poet so magically good at making the subtlest of points surely shouldn't evolve into one who regularly comes out and tells you the point after it's made." James M. Cox remarks of Frost, "If there are times when his poetry fails, as in the editorializing poems which have been increasing in ratio until they fairly dot 'Steeple Bush,' he fails because he is remembering something he knew all the time, and his poetry hardens into provincial cynicism." This kind of response is understandable; what remains to be noted is that the derisive, sarcastic or knowing tones employed in these poems are as much the focus as the more topical or occasional subject each develops. Such tones, clearly, are anything but lyrical, quietly reflective, respectful, or conventionally aware of the existence of legitimate opinions other than the speaker's own. Early in his career Frost articulated his ideas about "sentence sounds." We commonly read Frost's earlier poems with his injunctions about the "sound of sense" and voice tones in mind, but perhaps critics have neglected to do the same as objectively with his "Editorials." Reuben Brower makes a similar point: "Nothing shows more surely the persistence of the Romantic definition of true poetry than the shock of critics who have discovered that Frost is the poet not only of **'Spring Pools'** and **'Design,'** but also of **'Departmental'** and **'The Lesson for Today.'** Like Pope and Swift, he shares with his reader his fun and jokes in the form of verse letters and fables, epigrams and inscriptions." This assessment seems very fair, though it should also be noted that Frost is capable, too, of mean-spiritedness on occasion, the equal of the eighteenth-century English poet

Alexander Pope. Admittedly, Frost loses his playfulness in some of the "Editorials" and is swept away by enthusiasm for his own political thinking, but his experiment of adopting the conventionally self-righteous, self-convinced tone of a newspaper editorial should rescue the better poems in the group from oblivion.

In *Steeple Bush*, living among the array of weaker poems, "Directive" is a reminder that being able to think originally sometimes requires a careful withdrawal from the ordinary affairs of the world that threaten one's stability or capacity to think clearly. Such a withdrawal means going beyond self-isolation, into thinking playfully, inventively, and luckily, like the tramp in "An Unstamped Letter in Our Rural Letter Box." And it means taking the self with a degree of objectivity that, if Frost the poet is unable to practice consistently in the volume, the speakers of his poems can nevertheless describe playfully and cheerfully, as in "The Fear of God" and **"To an Ancient."** As a whole, *Steeple Bush* contains enough fine thinking to justify its being read carefully and seriously.

References and further reading: Brower, 200; R. Cook, *Living Voice*, 183; J. Cox, "Clearing," 152; R. Frost, "The Constant Symbol," *Collected*, 790; Jarrell, "Laodiceans," 37; Wagner, 209–10.

Lisa Seale

"STEEPLE ON THE HOUSE, A," first appeared in *Steeple Bush* (1947). The poem postulates that nothing firm is known about eternity and the soul; all that has been offered regarding eternity is conjectural ("what if"). Frost, in questioning the notion of eternity—an existence without beginning or end, without "flesh"—assigns it to some place, a house of worship, and some thing, a steeple. Such metaphors of locality—of time and space—are curiously related: A steeple has a definite connection to the physical structure, the roof; yet the steeple also points to the eternal, rising above the earthly to the ethereal. But because the poet can form no conclusive idea of the soul, he hazards the belief that the soul is nothing else than a vital something, an extraneous fixture, which is seemingly unnecessary ("Nor need we ever go up there to live"), for when the body dies eternity is dissipated.

In this poem, Frost plays with the idea that the soul is the inmost and highest part of humanity that lives after death. Rather, he ventures, the soul is the extension of life itself whose form is flesh, whose existence relies upon adoring the sacredness of the secular. The implied relation of the soul to flesh, "our house of life," is echoed by Lesley Frost, who cites the poem in pointing out her father's "passionate preferences" for "emotions," for "love . . . the original source, the instinctual way, through nature, of being in touch with Divinity." Frost's stance in the poem, as Reuben Brower suggests, "may seem to favor the pursuit of metaphysical truth" and "imply a thoroughly conventional view" of Christianity, but "the equation comes in a not too serious question," demonstrating the poet's characteristic grounding in the natural and human world and his hedging in his "commerce with Ultimate Truth."

References and further reading: Brower, 145–46; L. Frost, "Aladdin's," 314; Juhnke.

                                                                 Carol Dietrich

STEVENS, WALLACE (1879–1955), born in Reading, Pennsylvania, attended **Harvard** as a special student for three years from 1897 to 1900. After failing an attempted journalism career in New York, Stevens entered law school, graduating in 1903. He began working as an insurance lawyer and eventually became vice-president of the Hartford Accident and Indemnity Company in Hartford, Connecticut. Stevens continued writing poetry (which he had done since childhood) as his career in law grew, publishing his first book, *Harmonium*, in 1923. Stevens kept his poetry distinctly separate from his business to the point that his coworkers were often unaware he was a poet. While not popularly recognized, he received several prizes, including the Bollingen Prize in Poetry, two National Book Awards, and the Pulitzer Prize. His more well-known poems include "Anecdote of the Jar," "The Snowman," "Thirteen Ways of Looking at a Blackbird," "Emperor of Ice Cream," "Sunday Morning," "The Idea of Order at Key West," and "Notes toward a Supreme Fiction." Stevens's poetry, characterized by the struggle to reconcile reality and the imagination, is filled with delightfully aural images, often bordering on nonsense, which hide the deep philosophical basis of the poems.

Contemporaries, Frost and Stevens are considered quite similar yet strikingly different. Both influenced by William James while at Harvard (*see also* **Philosophy**), they are at times described as Nature poets, post-Emersonian poets, poets of the Real, or poets of the Imagination, but each defies simple classification. Marie Boroff notes that, generally, Frost's verse and diction are characterized as pastoral and simple, whereas Stevens's are varied and unpredictable. Both appear to be concerned with their image: Frost creates the persona of the rustic New England farmer, while Stevens maintains the image of an aloof aesthete, neither of which is completely accurate. A marked competition, almost hostile, existed between the two men; each attempted to belittle the other or reject any knowledge of the other. Harold Bloom believes that Frost—not **Eliot, Pound**, or Williams—was Stevens's "true twentieth-century rival."

Frost first met Stevens while visiting Key West, Florida. While there, they had pleasant meetings, attended the same cocktail parties, and dined together several times. There was nothing remarkable in their encounters, which were more casual and accidental than anything else. Such an image, however, is shattered by Brendan Gill in an anecdote of an incident that occurred at Key West. The story begins with the two poets drinking at a bar somewhere on the island: "Tipsily, in perfect contentment, they are making their way back to the hotel on a boardwalk that runs a foot or so above the sand. They are holding fast to each other, and each is sure that it is he who is supporting his companion. Frost staggers, catches his heel on the edge of the boardwalk, and starts to fall. Stevens strengthens his hold on him, but in vain—over Frost goes, with Stevens on top of him. The two bulky old poets fall in a single knot onto the sand and start rolling over and over in the moonlight down the long slope of the beach to the edge of the sea."

Stevens and Frost met again in Key West during the winter of 1940. Lawrance Thompson records that at one of their meetings that winter they participated in an often-quoted exchange of poetic judgment. After another night of excessive drinking, the two began to criticize each other: " 'The trouble with you, Robert, is that you're too academic,' said Stevens. 'The trouble with you, Wallace, is that you're too executive,' retorted Frost. 'The trouble with you, Robert, is that you write about—subjects.' 'The trouble with you, Wallace, is that you write about—bric-a-brac.' "

In 1942, Stevens invited Frost to his home in Hartford, and Frost accepted. This visit and the Florida encounters are the only documented cases of the two poets meeting in person. Although they met only a few times, Stevens and Frost's relationship existed before their first meeting and continued after their final meeting in 1942. Remarks made in passing by Stevens and Frost to other acquaintances and in correspondence tell a great deal about the feelings they had for each other and the masks they attempted to make for themselves.

Even before Frost and Stevens met in Key West, Frost apparently held a negative view of his contemporary. Thompson reports that Frost was annoyed that the critic William Stanley Braithwaite would choose as one of the five best poems of 1915 Stevens's "Peter Quince at the Clavier" (Frost's **"The Road Not Taken"** was also on the list). Writing to **Louis Untermeyer**, Frost critiques each of the poems, including Stevens's: "Susanner . . . simply bothers me. A priori I ought to like any latter-day poem that uses the word 'bawdy.' I don't know why I don't like this one unless it is because it purports to make me think. A bawdy poem should go as easy as a song: 'In Amsterdam there lived a maid,' frinstance" (qtd. in Thompson).

Stevens's attitude toward Frost as recorded in his letters and remarks to others is equally puzzling. Two letters, written in the 1950s, contain lines that are critical of Frost. In a letter to Genevieve F. Pratt, registrar at Mt. Holyoke College, in 1952 on the occasion of his receiving an honorary degree, Stevens expresses amazement at their asking for information on previous degrees: "This is the first time that anyone has asked me for this information and I am rather surprised that one diploma should refer to the degrees of other colleges. I should just as lief you left out any reference to any degree. After all, I am not Robert Frost who has about 25 or 30." Richard Eberhart discusses the competition he sees between Frost and Stevens, noting that "Stevens would never have demeaned himself to want to go to a presidential inauguration and read a poem. . . . He had a much more private idea of what art was" (qtd. in Brazeau). An even more curious statement appears in a letter Stevens wrote to Barbara Church. Following a celebration of Frost's eightieth birthday, which Stevens declined to attend, Stevens stated in a letter, "Frost is greatly admired by many people. I do not know his work well enough to be either impressed or unimpressed. . . . When I visited the rare book library at Harvard some years ago the first thing I saw was [Frost's] bust. His work is full (or said to be full) of humanity. I suppose I shall never be eighty no matter how old I become."

References and further reading: Harold Bloom, *Wallace Stevens: Poems of Our Climate* (Ithaca, NY: Cornell University Press, 1977), 68; Brendan Gill, *Here at the New Yorker* (New York: Random, 1975), 58. Biographical information regarding Frost and Stevens is scattered throughout various sources, including Peter Brazeau's *Parts of a World: Wallace Stevens Remembered: An Oral Biography* (New York: Random, 1983), 68, 130, 181; Stevens's *Letters* (New York: Knopf, 1966), 748, 825; Thompson, *Triumph*, 63; Thompson and Winnick, 61. Four studies of the poetic connections between the poets are Borroff, *Language and the Poet*; Greiner, "Factual Men"; Lentricchia, *Modernist Quartet*; Lieber.

Eric Leuschner

"STOPPING BY WOODS ON A SNOWY EVENING" was first published in the *New Republic* (7 Mar. 1923) and was later collected in *New Hampshire* **(1923)**. In a letter to **Louis Untermeyer**, Frost called the poem "my best bid for remembrance." Today, no American poem is better known or more widely read, yet many recent critical studies treat it only in passing. Frost himself once said of "Stopping by Woods" that he was bothered by those "pressing it for more than it should be pressed for. It means enough without its being pressed. . . . I don't say that somebody shouldn't press it, but I don't want to be there" (qtd. in **R. Cook,** *Living Voice*).

Perhaps because of Frost's preference for the poem, he spoke often of its composition—though, as Lawrance Thompson has shown, Frost's repeated claim that the poem almost wrote itself is at some variance with the truth. Frost liked to relate that he had been working all night on **"New Hampshire,"** the long poem that would become the title work of Frost's 1923 Pulitzer Prize–winning volume. Then, as Frost would have us believe, "tired as he was, he sat down, and heard the old sound of the voice speaking words clearly. Half asleep, and without any consciousness of ever having thought of the idea before, he continued to write steadily until the short poem was done." According to Thompson, however, Frost had a tendency to mythicize some of his acts of poetic creation, subscribing as he sometimes did to the notion that poetry is "divinely inspired." In fact, as the published facsimile of the last three stanzas shows, the original draft of "Stopping by Woods" had false starts in the second and fourth stanzas, and small revisions in the second and third. Thompson, however, may have overstated the "worrying" of this poem, to use Frost's own term: Charles Cooper points out that the major changes appear to have been made during the draft's transcription, which occurred so rapidly in places that articles were omitted before "harness" and "sweep." One of Frost's own comments on the poem is in "The Constant Symbol," where he refers to the "recklessness" of the first line in the second stanza, adding that "I was riding too high to care what trouble I incurred. And it was all right so long as I didn't suffer deflection." If not entirely written "with one stroke of the pen," the first draft of "Stopping by Woods" seems to have been achieved with a comparative ease of composition.

The autobiographical basis for the poem, according to N. Arthur Bleau's account and confirmed by Frost's daughter Lesley, can be traced to a December evening during the decade (1900–1910) the Frosts lived on a farm near West **Derry**, New Hampshire. Frost described to Bleau a particularly difficult winter, "bleak . . . both weatherwise and financially." Returning home from an unsuccessful trip to market, Frost realized there would be no Christmas presents for his children, and as they approached a "bend in the road, near the woods," where the house would come into sight, "[t]he horse slowed down and then stopped. It knew what he had to do. He had to cry, and he did." Bleau recalls "the very words he spoke. 'I just sat there and bawled like a baby'—until there were no more tears." Then the bells on the horse's harness helped revive the poet's spirits, and they continued home. Lesley Frost adds her own memory of her father, saying, in explanation, "A man has as much right as a woman to a good cry now and again. The snow gave me its shelter; the horse understood and gave me the time" (qtd. in Bleau).

A large part of the achievement of the poem is its use of simple but evocative images: On the "darkest evening of the year," the speaker has stopped his horse-drawn wagon by a woods while snow is falling. He first thinks of the woods' owner; then about his horse's reaction to stopping "without a farmhouse near"; then about ambient sounds, "the sweep / Of easy wind and downy flake." Finally, and despite the attraction of the woods, he rouses himself to continue on his way. Readers have tended to be most interested in the apparent opposition at the end of the poem between the woods and the speaker's reason for continuing. "The woods are lovely, dark and deep," but the speaker decides to forgo their attraction because, he says, "I have promises to keep / And miles to go before I sleep."

The interest in the final stanza is heightened by Frost's use of the repetend, or doubled last line. Soon after publishing the poem, Frost asserted that the usage fit the form as well as the content, in part because of the poem's unusual rhyme scheme, with the third line of each stanza anticipating the rhyme of the following stanza. In a letter to Sylvester Baxter, Frost claimed that leaving the third line unrhymed "in the last stanza alone would have been a flaw. I considered for a moment four of a kind in the last stanza but that would have made five including the third in the stanza before it. I considered for a moment winding up with a three line stanza. The repetend was the only logical way to end such a poem" (qtd. in Townsend). The form of the final stanza further fits the content: As the speaker moves toward the conclusion that he must meet his obligations, the poem becomes more tightly structured; the form of the poem in effect helps him rein in his impulse to escape. The haunting repetition, along with the anticipatory rhyme scheme and the regularity of the iambic tetrameter lines, helps give "Stopping by Woods" its distinctive quality.

Early interpretations of the poem tend to understand those "promises" as an affirmation of the traditional American—and especially New England—value of duty. The woods, an image of indulgence and corruption since the days of the Puritans, are seductive but eventually rejected by a speaker mindful of his obligations; that indulgence has also been viewed as aesthetic rather than spiritual, and the obligations moral rather than social. More romantic readings have retained the same opposition but reversed its poles: In forgoing the transcendent experience of nature, as represented by the woods, the speaker is perceived as less dutiful than harried; and in the ambivalence of his decision to continue, he can be seen as resigned to remaining alienated from the natural world and, by implication, from himself. In all these cases, the "sleep" with which the poem ends can refer either to the night's rest at the end of the speaker's journey— well earned or troubled, depending on the interpretation—or to the more final rest at the end of the speaker's life. But not all critics agree that the speaker eventually turns from the woods. Richard Poirier, for example, has suggested that the "the somnolent repetition of the last two lines" indicates that the speaker is "ready to drop off" and is able to keep his promises "thanks mostly to his little horse," and Samuel Coale sees the repetend as "a sleepy, final attempt to deny what in fact is already happening."

The theme of death receives its most controversial treatment in John Ciardi's "Robert Frost: The Way to the Poem," where "the dark and the snowfall symbolize a death-wish, however momentary"—an interpretation that caused a public uproar. Critics have pointed out, perhaps unnecessarily, that at most the poem might express a death-wish rejected, since the speaker turns away from the woods; others have taken Ciardi to task over factual errors in the essay, and an offending passage was omitted when Ciardi reprinted the essay in a later collection. But the autobiographical story of depression and poverty underlying "Stopping by Woods," which was published a full two decades after Ciardi's essay, lends support to his reading.

Recent critical theory has not yet deconstructed "Stopping by Woods" in ways significantly different from more traditional readings, but some new insights emerge from renewed interest in the poem's self-conscious play with both the freedom and limitations of language. For example, Katherine Kearns's comment on the poem in a book-length study of the poet is that "to stop and feel a closed space filling up, as does the watcher in 'Stopping by Woods,' is to resist the road, to acknowledge the opacities and layerings within the words themselves." Yet Frost's speaker turns away from this acknowledgment, toward experience itself, as if the poet were rejecting the power of his own words.

Fascination with the last stanza of the poem seems to have left little room for critical consideration of other elements, especially the "owner" of the woods in the first stanza and the anthropomorphism of the horse in the middle two, both of which reveal much about the speaker. Margaret Edwards, one of the few to tackle the latter subject, seems to claim too much for the "comic anthropomorphism" of the speaker's little horse, when she describes it as reinforcing "the narrator's isolation" while playfully "saving him from freezing." As Frost's only extended use of the technique, the horse and the speaker's projection of his thoughts on it deserve more attention than they have received. Similarly, the speaker's mention of an owner is often attributed to his sense of apprehension about trespassing. But he is not trespassing: He has only stopped *by* the woods, not *in* them. Further, the man in question may not be the owner at all—the speaker only *thinks* he knows who it is. This ill-defined, shadowy figure has an overwhelming presence in the speaker's consciousness—as shown by the first stanza, where he is mentioned in every line and leads off three of them—yet has attracted minimal critical comment.

In a 1948 essay, **Reginald L. Cook** recalls Frost's having said that the poem contains "all I ever knew." In its elusive coding of experience and compelling incantation of image and rhythm, "Stopping by Woods" may well contain the essence of all we will ever know of him. *See also* **Nature Poet and Naturalist**.

References and further reading: Bleau, 175–77; Ciardi, 13–15, 65; Coale, 103; R. Cook, "Frost's Asides" and *Living Voice*, 52; Charles W. Cooper and John Holmes, eds., *Preface to Poetry* (New York: Harcourt, Brace, 1946), 604; Cowley; Edwards, "Play"; R. Frost, "The Constant Symbol," *Collected*, 788, and *Letters to Untermeyer*, 163; D. Hall; D. J. Hall, *"Figura"*; Kearns, 80; Parini, *A Life*, 213; Poirier, *Knowing*, 183; Thompson, *Early Years*, 597; Townsend.

David Mesher

"STORM FEAR" complicates the theme introduced in **"Stars,"** which precedes it in *A Boy's Will* (1913), where it first appeared. "Stars" suggests that "there is no oversight of human affairs," as Frost writes in his gloss on the poem in the first edition of A *Boy's Will*; "Storm Fear" goes much further to suggest that there may in fact be malign natural forces "working against" us "in the dark." A rigid structure would not do for "Storm Fear," given the "subdued," dissipating energies of its speaker and given also that, here, natural forces are imagined as threatening the stability and integrity—even the very existence— of human impositions on the land. Frost works in lines of varying length and rhythm and with a series of rhymes that never shapes up into a pattern. The threat implied is that this house should become like the one in **"Ghost House,"** where natural forces have reclaimed what once a family carved out of the woods. "Storm Fear" personifies, even demonizes, the storm. But Frost recognizes also that this is an impertinence—even a kind of arrogance: Why *should* the natural world bother itself with a single family or with the entire human race, for that matter? Read together with "Stars," "Storm Fear" looks forward to **"The Need of Being Versed in Country Things"** and **"Design,"** two poems that consider the idea, familiar from literary naturalism, that Nature does not concern itself with us and indeed does not have the *capacity* to be "concerned" at all. In "Storm Fear," Frost is with **Emerson**, who writes in "Fate," "The cold, inconsiderate of persons, tingles your blood, benumbs your feet, freezes a man like an apple."

References and further reading: Pritchard, *Literary Life*.

Mark Richardson

"STRONG ARE SAYING NOTHING, THE," first appeared in the *American Mercury* (May 1936) and was included in *A Further Range* **(1936). Reginald L. Cook** reports that Frost attributed the origin of this poem to "the look in the face of an old man with a fine head whom the poet had known—whose expression seemed to say, 'Well, I'll wait and *see* what is to be *seen*.' " Mordecai Marcus compares the poem's themes of "human isolation, frailty, and persistence" to the themes of Thomas Hardy. The poem describes farmers doing their spring planting, with no guarantee that the work will lead to a fruitful harvest, and the last stanza compares their situation to that of all people, who live with no certainty about what comes after death. Anna Juhnke and Todd Lieber have read the poem more optimistically. Juhnke points out the farmers' "tremendous investment of faith in the future," and Lieber notes that Frost uses the same language as the last line of the poem in his essay "Education by Poetry" to describe the tacit belief and quiet self-confidence one must have in order to accomplish anything, a belief "that you don't want to tell other people about because you cannot prove that you know. You are saying nothing about it till you see."

References and further reading: R. Cook, "Frost on Frost," 43; R. Frost, "Education by Poetry," *Collected*, 727; Juhnke, 64; Lieber, 116; Marcus, *Explication*, 150.

Todd Lieber

"SUBVERTED FLOWER, THE," published first in *A Witness Tree* **(1942),** is an overtly sexual poem. According to Lawrance Thompson, Frost had delayed its publication until after **Elinor**'s death in 1938 and claimed a version had existed that could have been printed in *A Boy's Will* **(1913).** Frost feared the poem was "too daring and too revealingly autobiographical." Thompson maintains that Elinor Frost "would never have given" permission to print the poem and says that no early version of the poem has been discovered, adding that the published version is obviously written in the manner of Frost's later style.

Because the poem is uncharacteristically explicit in its sexuality, much of the criticism has been biographical and psychological. The biographical criticism is further confused by Frost's relationship with **Kathleen Morrison**, to whom *A Witness Tree* is dedicated. According to Lawrance Thompson, though, Frost claimed that the poem is based on an incident early in his courtship of Elinor that led to a crisis because his passionate advances were met by her rejection. Judith Oster, relying on Thompson, notes that Frost often felt guilty because of his sex drive, believing his passionate demands on Elinor had produced six children from a woman who was reluctant and whose heart was weak. Elinor often used silence and reticence to punish Frost. Frost said his poems were mostly about her but added that "they were as much about her as she liked and

permitted them to be. Without ever saying a word she set limits I must continue
to observe" (qtd. in Oster, her emphasis).

The poem can be read as a powerful drama of a young man who makes
sexual advances upon a young woman who rejects his lovemaking in horror,
sees him as bestial, and is changed into an animal-like creature herself as she
is drawn away from the scene by her mother. The poem begins in the middle
of the action and is reported by a third-person narrator who is detached from
the scene and able to pass judgment on the pair. The trimeter pattern and the
rhyme scheme are irregular, illustrating a hesitancy in the dialogue and in ap-
prehending or reporting what is happening.

The stage is set with the first four lines, where the girl pulls away from
whatever the male figure is saying even though he is calm as he tries to make
his point. The flower is clearly the focus of the poem, and, as he says, it has
power, emphasizing his point by lashing the flower against his palm. Even
though the verb "lashing" exhibits the strong emotions that the young man feels,
Sidney Cox says, "He has just made a loving gesture toward her, impelled by
a wildness akin, he feels, to the lovely wildness of the flower in his hand. . . .
The actual flower becomes the emblem of his wild attraction" (qtd. in Morse).

Frost generally uses flowers in his poems as emblems of beauty, femininity,
fragility, wonder, or wildness but never as a representative of anything harsh.
Some critics suggest that the flower in this poem represents the phallus, but such
a reading denies the flower's female sexual nature. The power of the flower as
a symbol resides in its attraction, its beauty, and its ability to excite our admiration.

The young man's point, made with an expectant smile, is rejected by the
young woman. Apparently, he tries to persuade her that it is her sexual attractiveness that has aroused him and that such enticement is as natural as flowers
attracting bees. The speaker observes that the woman is "either blind / Or willfully unkind," while the man, puzzled by her failure to return his desire, waits
for her to respond momentarily. The wait is too long, and he "flicked and flung
the flower," angered at her rejection. Not understanding what she is experiencing, the young man takes her reticence cynically, seeing it as a deliberate rejection. The flower symbol he uses has been subverted, overturned, and perverted
by her rejection and his anger, which contorts his natural passion. His smile
changes and becomes artificial like one made by using one's fingers. To the
woman, his face now appears to be transformed into a "ragged muzzle."

The observer then focuses on the woman, describing her as a flower in a field
of flowers. She seems in this picture to be wildly attractive and has come willingly to the field, where she has been agreeable to the young man's lovemaking
up to this point, as her displaced hair shows. The male figure continues his
importuning, stretching out "either arm / As if she made it ache / To clasp her—
not to harm." He seems to be pleading for an embrace, not threatening. He
wants her to respond in kind and to know that she, too, shares the erotic attraction. She thinks she hears him ask, " 'If this has come to *us* / And not to me

alone' " (my emphasis). But his words are unsettling to her, and he seems to choke on them, breathing unnaturally, "Like a tiger at a bone." She stiffens, frightened, afraid that any movement will set off "The demon of pursuit / That slumbers in a brute."

The energy in the scene comes from more than just the lad's thwarted sexual passion. Even though we understand that the woman is denying her own sexuality and its attraction, Frost understands the culturally based fears a young woman has in such a circumstance. Her fear is real. She is afraid that when she hears her mother call he will "pounce to end it all." Even though she sees his shame, her fear—"Circe-like," as Oster puts it—transforms her apprehension of him into a series of animals: His hand becomes "a paw," his "ingratiating laugh" turns his face into a "snout," and his "eye become[s] evasive." His arm, moving "like a saw" to be more persuasive, is seen as an obscene gesture by some critics.

In the next lines—expressed from the perspective of a girl, not a mature woman—it is the flower, or sexuality, that has marred her companion. She sees no beauty in it. She cannot see that her inability to accept and respond to her own sexual nature and his actually completes the terrible transformation. She sees only the worst in him, changing him into a dog "Obeying bestial laws" or a coward who "Turned from the place and ran." The metamorphosis is so complete that she hears him bark as he stumbles away.

She, too, has been metamorphosed into an animal, spitting out words like a horse trying to rid itself of a "tenacious bit." The word choice is appropriate for a girl who thinks of sex as subduing, as a horse is given the bit before being ridden. Even as she is drawn away by her mother, she is foaming at the mouth, as horses or other animals do. The "horror clung" to her, but she stares back at the man as her mother takes her home. Denying her natural sexuality, she subverts her own flower.

References and further reading: Katz, *Elinor Frost*; Morse, 171; Oster, 200, 301–2; Parini, *A Life*, 334; Thompson, *Early Years*, 512.

Newton Smith

"SYCAMORE" appears as the second poem in *A Witness Tree* (1942) and is the only poem in the Frost canon that is not written by Frost. It is a direct quotation from the rhymed alphabet pages of *The New England Primer*, a textbook first published circa 1690 and used in New England and other English settlements in North America. It contained alphabet rhymes, the catechism, and Calvinistic religious injunctions. The paradigm is based on Luke 19:1–4, although the type of tree appears to be Frost's invention, being mentioned neither in *The New England Primer* nor in the New Testament.

References and further reading: Cramer, *Frost among His Poems*; Lynen, *Pastoral*; Marcus, *Explication*.

Jeffrey S. Cramer

T

TEACHER. For most of his adult life, Robert Frost was a teacher. As a young boy, he did not attend school, and he never earned enough credits for a college diploma (although he collected dozens of honorary degrees). Nevertheless, he taught in a district school, a private academy, a normal school, and in colleges and universities, both public and private. His longest tenure was at **Amherst College**.

In a letter to **Louis Untermeyer**, Frost wrote, "I began to read to myself at thirteen. . . . I read my first poem at 15, wrote my first poem at 16, wrote **My Butterfly** at eighteen." At **Dartmouth**, he withdrew suddenly to assist his mother in her district school; shortly thereafter, he taught the first six grades in Salem. Always somewhat unorthodox, Frost aimed in his early experiences to fulfill the necessary tasks of meeting classes, marking papers, and even disciplining students. In 1906, a reading of **"The Tuft of Flowers"** won him a position at **Pinkerton Academy** in **Derry**, although someone else read the poem because Frost was too frightened to read it himself.

Sidney Cox records that at Pinkerton Frost advised his pupils to find something " 'common to experience but uncommon to expression.' Could one of them, for instance, make him see pigeons on the street: their primly placed lavender feet, their iridescent necks, the way they poked their heads in walking, and the dainty way they picked out a grain of oats?" Another Pinkerton story, recorded by Louis Mertins, followed him all his life: Frost asked a class if they wanted their papers back; when no one answered in the affirmative, he threw the papers, ungraded, into the wastebasket. Firm of purpose, he announced, "I don't intend to become a reader perfunctory of perfunctory writing."

Teaching at Pinkerton and at **Plymouth Normal School** bolstered Frost's shaky self-confidence, and ultimately the family man found the boldness he needed to declare himself wholly for poetry. In 1912, the six Frosts sailed to

England. In 1913 *A Boy's Will* was published, and *North of Boston* appeared in 1914. Thereafter, Frost would be known as a poet who also taught, instead of as a teacher who sometimes wrote poetry.

In retrospect, Frost observed to Roger Kahn, "Writing, teaching and farming. The three strands of my life." In fact, as Mildred R. Larson records, "The rural school which Frost attended in Salem gave him an enjoyment of books and convinced him that a rural school's technique of giving a student time to study by himself and then to come before the teacher for help, should be widely used." In spite of many classical beliefs, Frost came close to the cutting edge in the twentieth century: He was one of the first artists-in-residence on a campus (**University of Michigan**). He urged that American literature be included in the curriculum (Amherst). He advocated endowed chairs for high schools, and Amherst Regional High School named two for him. As young parents, he and Elinor even did some home schooling. An international troubadour, he disliked snobbery and pretension; he favored freedom, enthusiasm, and, of course, books. In Lawrence, Massachusetts, an elementary school is named Robert Lee Frost School. When he left Dartmouth College without a diploma, Robert Frost could not have foreseen that the school would eventually grant him two honorary degrees. The citation for his Doctor of Laws reads in part, "You have done more good teaching than any other man we know, teaching us to like and know that which we do not know we know . . . a teacher who has always sort of known that the hardest part of getting wise is being always just a little otherwise."

References and further reading: S. Cox, "Educational Beliefs," 420; R. Frost, *Letters to Untermeyer*, 61; "Honorary Degrees Awarded to Eleven"; Kahn; Larson, 155; Mertins, 93; Pack; Parini, *A Life*, 92–114, 173, 183–85, 193, 222–23; Vogel, " 'Earner, Learner, Yearner' " and *Frost, Teacher*.

Nancy Vogel

"TELEPHONE, THE," first appeared in *The Independent* (9 Oct. 1916) but was probably written on the **Derry** farm sometime before 1910. It was collected in *Mountain Interval* **(1916)**. The poem shows Frost in one of his most endearing, open, and redemptive guises. The poem takes the form of a dialogue between two lovers who are, in the words of Laurence Perrine, "dramatically differentiated—the male ardent, fanciful, playful, but also diffident; the female more down to earth, but open and responsive." The dialogue is intricately rhymed; what he says whimsically rhymes with what she says.

The communion between the couple is made possible because, as Judith Oster points out, "the flowers act as telephone: love of flowers is another common bond between the couple. . . . This flower is *not* subverted, not denied, but accepted for the lovely thing in nature that it is." (*See also* **"The Subverted Flower."**) There is a sense of integration not only between the two lovers but between humans and nature. While "The Telephone" is one of Frost's many flower poems, it is also, as Frank Lentricchia notes, "a 'we' poem consistent

with other 'we' poems" such as **"Two Look at Two"** and **"Rose Pogonias."**
It presents a harmonious unity possible in love and marriage rather than the
isolation and subjectivity so often evident in his poetry.

References and further reading: Lentricchia, *Modern Poetics*, 184; Oster, 210; Perrine,
"Frost's 'Telephone,' " 12.

Newton Smith

"THATCH, THE," which first appeared in *West-Running Brook* **(1928)**, bears
the note "As of 1914." Despite the actual date of composition, therefore, which
was probably shortly before publication, the poem seems to be about events of
many years before.

In 1914 the Frosts lived in **England** as guests in a very old house with a
thatched roof. Although Frost's first two books, *A Boy's Will* **(1913)** and *North
of Boston* **(1914)**, had been published to surprising success, Frost was still far
from earning a living from his poetry. Very possibly the mixed emotions of
artistic success coupled with continued poverty exacerbated the strains between
Robert and his wife **Elinor**. The tensions that Lawrance Thompson, among other
biographers, claims were endemic in the Frost marriage apparently frequently
resulted in the kind of struggle of wills depicted in the poem.

In the poem a man has left his house and is walking in the dark in the winter
rain. He keeps the light from the upstairs bedroom window in sight, as he and
his wife seem to have almost a code or agreement: If she shuts out the light,
she signals that she concedes the dispute to him; if he returns before she shuts
out the light, he concedes.

However, as he passes along the low-hanging eaves of the thatched roof he
frightens nesting birds into flight. He knows they will not be able to find their
way back in the dark and that they may well end up exposed to the cold and
wet. He says that contemplating the birds' plight has caused his own "grief . . .
to melt." Yet this hint of willingness to reconcile never becomes explicit. The
poem closes with the image of the house in ruins, the roof left unmended and
rain water seeping into the very room from which the light has shone. The
implication is that the marriage, like the house, has died for lack of day-to-day
caretaking. However, the suggestion is contradicted by the narrator's preceding
statement that his mood has undergone a change when he realizes the distress
he has caused the frightened birds. Such lack of clear resolution occurs frequently in Frost's poetry, especially in those poems depicting marital conflict.
(*See*, for example, **"Home Burial"** and **"The Fear."**)

References and further reading: The marriage of Robert and Elinor Frost is painted as
a dark and tumultuous one in Lawrance Thompson's three-volume biography; most relevant to the discord depicted in "The Thatch" is *Early Years*, especially chapters 16–21.
A more sympathetic, balanced portrayal of the Frosts's marriage and of their years in
England appears in Burnshaw; L. Francis, *Morning Gladness*; Walsh.

Richard Wakefield

"THERE ARE ROUGHLY ZONES" is a twenty-one-line poem first published in *A Further Range* (1936). In this piece, unnamed individuals safely indoors worry about the effects of a storm raging outside. Apparently from the beginning their concern is really about the safety of the house and hence their own continued safety. But the rugged structure has proven itself; it "has long been tried," and so the attention quickly turns to the plight of a less rugged, seemingly fragile peach tree that has been removed from its usual environment and is obviously under real threat. The plight of the tree becomes the vehicle by which Frost discusses the hubris of humankind, a self-importance that drives us to defy what is most natural and to put forward a scheme of our own.

Frost observes that the ambition to transplant the tree further north is a foolhardy but representative act of our apparent need to impinge upon the natural domain, "to extend the reach" of humanity to measure the very extremes of the natural world. But through such ambition, the true essence of humanity remains unknowable: What is the character of that which leads us to overstep our bounds? The lesson to be learned, ultimately, is that while "there is no fixed line between wrong and right," there are approximate limits that provide boundaries that can be identified and realities that must be obeyed. Such observation explains the title. Through the poet, humanity does accept responsibility for the peril that the tree confronts. "But if it is destined never again to grow," he admits, "It can blame this limitless trait in the hearts of men." However, there is considerable irony in Frost's use of the word "destined," for destiny, in its truest sense, is not what relocates the peach tree in a northern winter storm but rather humanity's unkind encroachment upon the natural world in an attempt to redirect destiny.

In spite of such mounting testimony, the poet is still indignant enough to claim that "we can't help feeling more than a little betrayed" by the poor fortune connected with the weather. It is, after all, the combination of high winds and cold that poses the threat to the tree, a cruel turn of events that Frost almost characterizes as a conspiracy of nature. Yet this is perhaps simply one more reflection of humanity's insensitivity, for when left alone, nature can adequately regulate itself; it is only when people interfere that nature is turned against itself. The poem, then, dramatizes the uneasy truce between humanity and the natural world that the poet wishes to broker.

References and further reading: Bagby, *Nature*; Doyle, *Poetry*.

Craig Monk

"THEY WERE WELCOME TO THEIR BELIEF" first appeared in *Scribner's Magazine* in August 1936 and was collected in *A Further Range* that same year. It is another of the poet's perspectives on mutability, dismissing two personified scapegoats, Grief and Care, as agents of aging and instead focusing on erosive time, winters, and snowfalls for the snow-white hair of age. The acceptance of the inevitable is implicit in the denial of emotion in the inexorable progression of time.

References and further reading: Cramer, *Frost among His Poems*; Marcus, *Explication.*

Roland H. Lyford

THOREAU, HENRY DAVID (1817–1862). American nature writer, journal keeper, poet, thinker, and protégé of **Ralph Waldo Emerson**, Thoreau is best known as the author of *Walden* (1854) and *Resistance to Civil Government* (1849), sometimes known as *Civil Disobedience.*

Parts of *Walden*, Frost wrote in 1915, "must have had a good deal to do with the making of me." His imaginative kinship with Thoreau is exceeded by that with no other writer with the possible exception of Emerson. Frost follows Thoreau (following Emerson) in characteristically viewing the natural world as "a text albeit done in plant" (**"Time Out"**). The two share not only an abiding interest in the details of the trees, flowers, birds, and bodies of water around them but a deep-seated sense of kinship between the natural and the human— of analogies or correspondences between "outer" and "inner weather." As a result of such analogies, natural phenomena for Frost as for Thoreau are often hieroglyphics that—despite the greater complications for the twentieth-century writer—may be deciphered by and thus offer wisdom to the observer who is properly versed in country things. The basic structure of Frost's emblem poems, like that of many emblem passages in *Walden*, reflects this view of nature as text: description of natural phenomena (e.g., the tableau of white flower, spider, and moth in the octave of **"Design"**) followed by a "reading" of its human significance (the sestet of that **sonnet**).

Frost likewise follows Thoreau in dramatizing the imaginative states that the observer must nurture if he is to receive such natural wisdom: isolation from others, "extra-vagance" or wandering beyond the limits of normal human activity into the expanses of the natural world, and ultimately, getting lost in that world—achieving "heavenly lostness," in Frost's words, in order to find the self more truly.

Beyond this fundamental approach to making literature out of natural experience, Frost shares with Thoreau an extraordinary familiarity with Greek and Latin literature and a preoccupation with certain images. Cellars or other remains of dwellings slowly being reclaimed by nature are for both reminders of the ultimate tenuousness of human presence in the natural world and, especially for Frost in a poem like **"The Census-Taker,"** causes of powerful nostalgia for such presence. Both are unfailingly absorbed by changes of seasons, though Thoreau tends to focus chiefly on the renewal that he associates with spring, whereas Frost dwells on the threat implicit in the onset of winter. Both recurrently find the source of imaginative power in bodies of water—Walden Pond in Thoreau; wells, springs, and brooks in Frost.

Thoreau sees in *Walden* a model for the depth that we ought to cultivate in our spirits, and Frost certainly seeks at least imaginative depth in poems such as **"For Once, Then, Something."** But while Frost may share Thoreau's sense that sources of water are strikingly pure, he does not seek to cultivate such purity in his own life; the asceticism of "Higher Laws" finds no equivalent in Frost's vision. Likewise, Thoreau's conservative religious views—of the glory of God and the immortality of the soul—are not echoed by the insistently agnostic modern poet. The celebration of newness and renewal in *Walden* reappears at moments in Frost, as in the last stanza of **"Sand Dunes,"** but like so many other Thoreauvian elements may be qualified by twentieth-century complications, as it is by the idea of entropy in **"The Wood-pile."**

References and further reading: Bagby, *Nature*; R. Frost, *Selected Letters*, 182; Monteiro, *New England*.

George F. Bagby

"TIME OUT" appeared in *A Witness Tree* **(1942)**, where the poem's title is also used for the section of the book in which the poem appears. It first appeared in the *Virginia Quarterly Review* (Spring 1942). Frost showed the **sonnet** to Lawrance Thompson in 1939, at which time it bore the title "On the Ascent."

The other seven poems included in the section headed by "Time Out" are unified, more or less, by the theme of trying to read and understand nature and of the need for repose (time out, so to speak) in which our reading and understanding can take place (although it should be noted that many, perhaps most, of Frost's poems could fit neatly under that heading).

Critics agree that Frost here draws on a long tradition of "reading" nature, although they diverge slightly on his conclusions. George F. Bagby links the poem with a tradition that became prominent in the seventeenth century of seeing nature as God's coded gospel, seen sometimes as a complement to the written gospels, sometimes as a substitute for them. He claims, as well, that Frost picks up the tradition as carried forward by **Henry David Thoreau**.

Judith Oster sees a more modern Frost in the poem. The poem, as she points out, draws no overt lesson from nature. It is instead about our self-consciousness in pondering whether we can learn from nature: "The lesson of life learned from flowers is subordinated to the lessons he learns about how we learn."

References and further reading: Bagby, "Synecdochism"; Oster, 49; Wakefield, "Making Snug," offers an extended treatment of the poem, discussing its relationship to the work of **Emerson** and William James as well as to Frost's other poetry.

Richard Wakefield

"TIME TO TALK, A," first appeared in *The Prospect* **(Plymouth Normal School)** in June 1916 and was collected in *Mountain Interval* **(1916)**. In the context of *Mountain Interval*, with its studied reflections on human relationships and nature, it is, perhaps, more important than its lack of scholarly attention might imply.

Only ten lines, the poem captures in one photographic frame a rural event. One friend passing by on horseback calls to another working in the field, and the photographic event turns epiphanic as Frost brings us inside the mind of the speaker working in the field. The narrator loves the work he is doing some distance from the wall where the friend calls. The ground, he says, is "mellow." It is a good day for hoeing.

If he enjoys the work, the speaker is nonetheless fully aware that there is work to be done. As his friend hails him, there *are* hills to be hoed, yet the speaker insists that he will not "stand still and look around" upon them, an affront to his friend. In his insistence, of course, lies the clear fact that he is mindful of that work.

Then why does he turn? We notice that in line 2 the friend slows his horse "to a meaning walk." The phrase is ambiguous. What differentiates this walk from any other? What does the walk mean? Or is the walk simply meaningful because the friend hails him and slows down to chat? The speaker, thinking perhaps of the work that he will not let hinder him, posits a possible response. Somewhat like the crotchety neighbor of **"Mending Wall,"** he could stand where he is and shout, "What is it?"—employing an irritated, not-to-be-bothered voice. Instead, he tells us, "No, not as there is a time to talk." If we construe *as* here as the more common *since*, it clearly suggests that for the speaker human contact and conversation are more important than the work that can get done later.

Possibly, of course, we may view all such interior protestations of the speaker as actual complaints, as fundamentally unfriendly, even resentful protests of the neighbor's intrusion. The concluding actions, however, suggest a different picture. The narrator thrusts his hoe, blade end up, into the ground. It is a significant gesture. A busy worker would leave the hoe blade down in his row, ready to be picked up again. But in this picture, the human end of the hoe, the handle, is rooted in the earth, suggesting that even though the work has been momentarily broken by the conversation, the contact remains. And then perhaps the most significant words in the poem follow: "I . . . plod." His walk to the stone wall nicely matches the slowed "meaning walk" of the horse as the two friends meet to visit.

It is not a meeting of huge consequence—simply a visit, after all. But in the poem, Frost demonstrates that friends need to set aside their labor for "A Time to Talk."

References and further reading: Brower; Cramer, *Frost among His Poems*; Marcus, *Explication.*

John H. Timmerman

"TIMES TABLE, THE," was published originally in the *New Republic* (9 Feb. 1927) and later became part of *West-Running Brook* **(1928)**. The poem expresses the importance of hope in humanity's resistance to the disintegrating forces of nature. The farmer's times table would view life as a multiplication of woes: For so much living, we can expect so much trouble; for so much trouble, we can expect so many deaths. Yet, as the narrator warns, whether the adage is true or not, its effect is harmful: "I know of no better way / To close a road, abandon a farm, / Reduce the births of the human race." Such pernicious effects seem already at work in the farmer's life. The spring along the road has a "broken drinking glass," the farm horse is "straining her ribs for a monster sigh," and the farmer's wife is the regular audience of his unprofitable saying. Ironically, Frost uses the natural metaphor of the spring to symbolize the rest and refreshment necessary for maintaining hope and perpetuating civilization against nature. Nature gains on the farmer because he has failed to heed another adage that Frost himself presents in **"Directive,"** a poem that explores a similar collection of themes: "Here are your waters and your watering place. / Drink and be whole again beyond confusion."

References and further reading: O'Donnell, "New England," discusses the poem in the context of Frost's New England heritage.

Michael Berndt

"TO A MOTH SEEN IN WINTER" first appeared in the *Virginia Quarterly Review* (Spring 1942) and was collected that same year in *A Witness Tree*. Frost's ode, composed originally around the turn of the century, joins a tradition of such poems that includes "Ode to Psyche" by John Keats and two poems by William Wordsworth, both entitled "To a Butterfly." The Greek word *psyche* was used to describe both the butterfly and the soul, and the Psyche of myth, beloved of Cupid, draws on both ideas; so too does Frost's moth. Indeed, Frost seems to be answering in this poem a line from another Keats ode, "On Melancholy," which implores the reader not to let "the death-moth be / Your mournful Psyche." For the ill-fated moth of Frost's poem is that mournful Psyche, never to join its Cupid: "Nor will you find love either nor love you." The moth has unfortunately appeared in the barren months of winter, and the pocket-warmed hand offered by the narrator as a perch appears to be the only sign of affection for which the silvery creature can hope. The poem soon artfully connects the moth's tragedy with the human condition, until the moth becomes an emblem of the soul or, more properly, an extension of "something human, / The old incurable untimeliness." When the moth finally flutters from the narrator's hand, it pursues a fate with which the narrator finds further empathy. His own life, ultimately as frail and inwardly as stark as the moth's, requires all his attention. Both man and moth share a frustrated inability to affect the destiny of others.

Many readers see this early poem as bearing the seeds of much later writing. "It is in passages like these," remarks John Lynen of the concluding lines, "that Frost's mature art first begins to emerge." George Bagby, who treats the poem at some length, believes it describes "chiefly the wintry state of the imagination's life, with its sense of isolation and of the fragility, even futility, of human desire and effort in the face of external forces." Reuben Brower finds the poem full of irony and "joking," although he suggests that the last line is "Romantically serious." In addition to the poem's Romantic predecessors, one might profitably compare it with Frost's own **"My Butterfly."**

References and further reading: Bagby, *Nature*, 105; Brower, 88; Lynen, *Pastoral Art*, 173; Nitchie.

Eric C. Brown

"TO A THINKER" first appeared as "To a Thinker in Office" in the *Saturday Review of Literature* (11 Jan. 1936) and was later collected in *A Further Range* **(1936)**. In the poem, Frost accuses the thinker of being only a rocker, straddling the fence and swaying with every new idea. In lines 8–12, Frost's back-and-forth pattern imitates the philosopher's mindless shifting with the current trends indicated. Frost alludes to his own innovation of the "sound of sense," the balance of the sound of form with the sense of the sentence (*See* **Poetic Theories.**) The entire poem is in rhymed couplets, an exploration of pairs and polarities.

Mordecai Marcus explains that although Frost claimed to have written the poem well before President Franklin D. Roosevelt took office, it is most likely about Frost's criticism of Roosevelt's changing social programs. Marcus provides an informative reading of the poem as a direct response to Roosevelt's plan to help the nation recover from the Great Depression. (*See* **Politics.**)

References and further reading: Marcus, *Explication*; Newdick, Frost and "Sound of Sense."

Belinda D. Bruner

"TO A YOUNG WRETCH" was first published in booklet form as Frost's 1937 **Christmas poem** and in the *Saturday Review of Literature* (25 Dec. 1937). It later appeared as part of *A Witness Tree* **(1942)**. In its first edition, *A Witness Tree* was divided into five sections; the placement of "To a Young Wretch" in the second section, entitled "Two or More," suggests a grouping of poems concerning the self and society, in contrast to the volume's first section, called "One or Two." If we look at major poems in both sections, we see the difference in orientation immediately. In "One or Two" such poems as **"The Most of It"** and **"The Subverted Flower"** are concerned with the individual's relationship to an animal in the first case and to a woman in the second. In each there is a sense of disappointment caused by unclear or failed communication. In the section "Two or More," such poems as **"The Gift Outright"** and "To a Young Wretch" concern larger societal issues; in the former, Frost addresses the nature of the American people and their relationship to one another, and in the latter, the conflict between a culture's interests and those of an individual.

"To a Young Wretch" consists of four stanzas of six lines each in flexible iambic pentameter. Its subtitle, "Boethian," refers to the Roman philosopher Boethius, who held that humans fail to see evil as part of the divine whole, whose purpose we cannot understand due to our limited perspective. The speaker attempts to reconcile two conflicting views, seeing evil as a young thief's chopping down a tree from his woods but also sensing the larger good that the tree will serve as a symbol of the Christmas spirit. Several factors worth noting in the poem are the way that Frost personifies the tree by attributing to it human characteristics and the way that he calls to mind his persistent theme of the value of getting something by virtue of one's own work. We might do well to recall his earlier poem **"Two Tramps in Mud Time,"** where the speaker reaps the rewards of chopping his wood by himself rather than paying itinerant workers to do it for him.

The seriousness of the speaker's feeling for his stolen tree is evidenced by his characterization of the youth who takes it. He equates the young man's actions with **sport** by referring to the way the thief uses his father's ax in the same way that he would his gun or rod to hunt or fish. The verb "nick" also enforces the speaker's belittlement of the thief; to nick the tree is to chip away at it in a childlike or weak manner instead of felling it in one stroke, but "nick" also is slang for stealing, implying a childlike theft as that of candy from a store. For the speaker, the tree is worthy of more than such juvenile theft and the trivial, artificial "tinsel chain and popcorn rope" that will decorate it. In the last stanza, the speaker hopes to accept its loss—not only his loss of property but the tree's loss of freedom and connection to the mountainside earth. The poem, therefore, becomes an occasion to consider the benefits of human appropriation of nature, while not diminishing the loss. We can see in this poem why some critics have referred to *A Witness Tree* as being more about "mental discoveries" rather than "rural incident."

References and further reading: For a discussion of classical influences (such as the ode form) in Frost's poetry, see Lind; Munson, "Classicism"; for a discussion of Frost's discovery of the "witness" tree, used by surveyors to mark property boundaries, see Winslow.

Susan Burns

"TO AN ANCIENT," collected in *Steeple Bush* (**1947**), first appeared in the *Atlantic Monthly* (Dec. 1946). Like astronomy and botany, archaeology appealed to Frost because of the concrete knowledge it could provide about our world, knowledge that, in Frost's hands, often became a source of metaphor. "To an Ancient," written in iambic pentameter triplets, refers to an archaeological find— a bone and an eolith (a primitive stone tool)—which becomes the occasion for a meditation on time, immortality, and human nature.

In a whimsical tone, Frost addresses the ancient, whose anonymity seems emblematic of the fate that awaits us all in the course of time. However, in the third and fourth stanzas, the very act of searching for such remains, dating them, and speculating about them is said to be "expressive of the human race," reflecting our desire to overcome anonymity and obliteration. We endow the ancient remains with an importance that produces for the ancient a kind of immortality. The presence of the two objects, bone and tool, leads Frost to distinguish between an importance that is intrinsic simply to being who we are, the significance (one might say, sacredness) of the individual life, and an importance derived from what we produce, our useful and artistic creations. Frost thinks the bone is "likely to have been enough" to assure the ancient's immortality, and in the last stanza he wonders if his own chances of immortality will be any greater as a result of the poetry he leaves behind. The suggestion seems to be that leaving our bones should be enough, and the poem takes a slightly satirical tone toward those people, including Frost himself, who aspire to some special and greater immortality.

References and further reading: For a discussion of Frost's interests in archaeology, see L. Francis, "Majesty of Stones."

Todd Lieber

"TO E. T." first appeared in the *Yale Review* (Apr. 1920) and was included in *New Hampshire* **(1923)**. It is a tribute to Edward Thomas, Frost's "brother," a British casualty of World War I. Despite the ultimate Allied victory, lingering grief blocks closure for the survivor. The early transcendent atmosphere is dreamlike, concluding in the implicit promise of reunification and communication in the brotherhood of poets. Here the unspoken may be voiced in tacit acceptance of casualties and conquests.

References and further reading: Lehmann, 135–65; Parini, *A Life*, 179–81; Pritchard, *Literary Life*; Thompson, *Triumph*.

Roland H. Lyford

"TO EARTHWARD" was first published in the *Yale Review* (Oct. 1923) and is one of thirty poems that comprised the "Grace Notes" section of the Pulitzer Prize–winning *New Hampshire* **(1923)**. In it, Frost addresses living out the balance of his life—amid the struggles between youth and age, heart and mind, foolishness and wisdom, life and death—alone and on his own terms. It acts as a fulcrum upon which he can weigh and measure such opposing forces. By such a process, he can test the internal strength of who he is against the forces of nature that so sweetly and bitterly war upon his character.

Like the earlier **"After Apple-Picking"** and **"Birches,"** "To Earthward" is a poem about rising and lowering, yielding and resisting. Unlike the earlier pieces, it takes a more difficult, less confident approach to human solutions. It is also a countermove to such later poems as **"Away!"** in which the tension and pressure come from the human desire to escape from the bonds of earth, to fly heavenward (either through love or after death). Outside the limits of love and death, such quixotic desire for flight, waged against the bonds of earth in both physical and metaphysical terms, is also staged in the late poem **"Kitty Hawk."** In that poem, Frost comes down on this side of the belief that, however resisted, "Earth is still our fate."

From the vantage point of midlife, the poet in "To Earthward" seeks to bridge both his past and his future. He realizes that when in his youthful past he used to rise up intoxicated with life and love, he was also simultaneously lowering himself to a grounded position that linked him to death. When he was young, he could not feel real contact with the earth; his mind was too much in the clouds. Only later in life does he sense and long for a downward pull. Death takes on the role of lover; the heart's desire is now tempered by the mind's wisdom. Grief acts as a necessary counterweight to joy.

In the poem's expression of a mature attitude toward life and love, it is not just sweets that are asked for, but bitterness coupled with sweets. The poet's craving (a word he uses twice in the poem) takes on an added dimension. What was once a youthful pursuit of no real substance has now gravitated into the wish "for weight and strength," for corporeality and earthly contact.

As in **"Wild Grapes,"** the contest in "To Earthward" is between desire and will: the youthful thrill of escaping the earth through sexual abandon coupled with an adult's reasoned fear that wisdom is attained only by maintaining enough contact with the rough ground. Again, it is a question of striking a balance. Emotion must be weighed and held in check; the heart should not cloud the mind. The goal is not only to let go (as the boy advised the girl in "Wild Grapes"), so much as it is to come back—return earthward. It is a return both in the present and future tense. (Note, too, that in "To Earthward" it is the scent of wild grapes that interrupts the flow of the speaker's words and propels him forward and backwards into his narrative and literally brings him back down to earth.) Frost's meaning is elucidated by a 1938 letter to **Bernard DeVoto**, saying that "To Earthward" marked a revolutionary development in his thinking and admitting that "I began life wanting perfection and determined to have it. I got so I ceased to expect it and could do without it. Now I find I actually crave the flaws of human handiwork. I gloat over imperfection."

References and further reading: R. Frost, *Selected Letters*, 482; Parini, *A Life*, 224–26; Poirier, *Knowing*, 186–87, makes a compelling comparison between Frost and **Emerson**; Pritchard, *Literary Life*.

Robert W. Scott

"TO THE RIGHT PERSON," the final poem in *Steeple Bush* (1947), is a **sonnet** that first appeared at the end of Frost's essay "The Constant Symbol," with the subtitle "Fourteen Lines," in the *Atlantic Monthly* (Oct. 1946). The uninviting aura of the schoolhouse described in the poem and the speaker's observations of the school's "tight shut look" may suggest Frost's discontent with formal education, for Frost long held the belief that conventional, ordinary formal education largely serves only to help one compensate for the lack of a pure and meditative mind and spirit. (*See* **Teacher**.)

References and further reading: Barry; O. Evans; Rood.

Belinda D. Bruner

"TO THE THAWING WIND," glossed "He calls on change through the violence of the elements" in the table of contents to *A Boy's Will* **(1913)**, was first known as "To the Loud Southwester" in a letter to **Susan Hayes Ward** (Christmas 1911). This invocatory prayer to spring is in the mode of the anonymous sixteenth-century lyric "Western Wind" and Shelley's "Ode to the West Wind" (compare "Scatter, as from an unextinguished hearth / Ashes and sparks, my word among mankind!" to "Scatter poems on the floor"). The poem is also an early example of the cluster of modernist interests in abrupt change, tumultuous movement, and unmediated experience, all inherited from Romantic poetry.

Frost's "call on change" is made up of a string of imperatives that form a single sentence. With an exception near the poem's center, each imperative is given one end-stopped trochaic line of seven to eight syllables, a form intended to match the presumed loudness and strength of the titular subject, as is the insistent triple rhyme at the end. The most characteristic moment is the injunction to "Find the brown beneath the white": Frost's creative thawing requires exposing the ground of life obscured by the forms of austere denial. Frost in a letter to G. R. Elliott (27 Apr. 1920) cites "To the Thawing Wind" as one of "the few **lyrics** I ever really liked in my first book."

Wind from the Sea, a tempera by Andrew Wyeth, is cited in a *Time* magazine article as "Robert Frost's favorite painting." As the tattered curtains of lace billow in the gusty fresh air, the viewer senses a burst of primordial energy: earth, air, fire (sunlight), and water. The affinity between Frost's poem and Wyeth's painting is strong. The two artists, mutual admirers of the other's work, met once in New York. On behalf of friends, E. Hyde Cox presented *Winter Sunlight* to Frost at the poet's birthday party in Amherst in 1954: Wyeth had selected the painting. Charles Hill Morgan once lent the poet *Wind from the Sea*. Frost never sat for a Wyeth portrait, but Wyeth has indicated that portraits of Frost do exist in *Christina's World, Wind from the Sea*, and other works. In uncanny coincidence, at the time of Frost's memorial services at **Harvard**, Fogg Art Museum was holding a Wyeth exhibit. *See also* **Nature Poet and Naturalist**.

References and further reading: R. Frost, *Selected Letters*, 248; Stillians; "Andy's World," *Time*, 27 Dec. 1963: 46; Vogel, "Frost and Wyeth," 23–24.

Gary Roberts and Nancy Vogel

"TOO ANXIOUS FOR RIVERS" first appeared in *Steeple Bush* **(1947)**. It challenges materialist assumptions that all natural phenomena can be reduced to matter and the dynamic interrelationships among material events. As the title implies, Frost is "anxious" about rivers because he believes that scientists have confined knowledge only to what can be known by empirical observation and have therefore forsaken metaphysical inquiry. Following Bergson, however, Frost asserts that the river—a metaphor for a dynamic, spiritual reality—expresses itself through matter and beyond, despite our inability to see where it will eventually "pour itself into and empty." To the poet, reality does not end at the mountain; rather, the mountain serves as the epistemological limit beyond which scientific inquiry cannot proceed. As the reference to the Hindu creation story suggests, scientific explanation must eventually take on the characteristics of myth. The idea is further underscored by Frost's allusion to Lucretius's *De Rerum Natura:* "Ergo vivida vis animi pervicit, et extra / Processit longe flammantia moenia mundi / Atque omne immensum peragravit, mente animoque" (i.72) ("So the vital strength of his spirit won through, and he made his way far outside the flaming walls of the world and ranged over the measureless whole, both in mind and spirit"). Responding to Epicurus's account of matter, Frost offers his own creation myth, which is indebted not only to the Lucretian belief that Venus is the author of the physical world but also to the Book of Genesis. Reality is not merely a collection of atoms falling continually through infinite space, as Epicurus thought, but rather the physical expression—"the essay"—of divine love. *See also* **Science**.

References and further reading: Abel, "Instinct"; Henri Bergson, *Creative Evolution*, trans. by Arthur Mitchell (New York: Henry Holt, 1911), 26.

Robert Bernard Hass

TRAVELS ABROAD. New England—especially New Hampshire and Vermont—lays justifiable claim to Robert Frost as a favorite son. Four of his children were born in **Derry**, New Hampshire, and Frost himself remarked that "the core of all my writing was probably the five free years (1900–1905) I had there on the farm." We need look no further for evidence than such frequently quoted verses as **"Mending Wall," "Birches,"** and **"The Road Not Taken."** Yet "Mending Wall" was first published in **England**, "Birches" was written in England, and "The Road Not Taken" was inspired by walks with the English poet Edward Thomas. Frost found that being in England with his family (1912–1915) helped him to love New England with greater passion and clarity. He and his wife, **Elinor**, accompanied by their youngest daughter, Marjorie, would return to England for a brief visit in 1928.

Many of Frost's poems reach beyond the parochial or provincial, reflecting sources foreign to his New England heritage and enriched by his role as cultural ambassador. Since his high school days in Lawrence, Massachusetts, he was fascinated with Indian civilizations in precolonial times, part of a lifelong exploration of humanity's shadowy origins. Late in life he had a number of official honors bestowed on him outside the country. In August 1954, he attended as U.S. delegate (with William Faulkner) the World Congress of Writers in São Paulo, Brazil, with a brief stopover in Peru; in May 1957, he traveled to England

(and Ireland) to receive honorary degrees at a number of universities, including Oxford and Cambridge; in March 1961, he traveled to Jerusalem as the first Samuel Paley Lecturer at the Hebrew University (followed by brief stopovers in Athens and London); in August 1962, in his final journey abroad, he traveled to Russia, where he met with Premier Nikita Khrushchev.

As the four-time Pulitzer Prize winner reached the pinnacle of success and public recognition, having celebrated his eightieth birthday, Frost was receptive to invitations from Washington to undertake a series of intercultural missions on behalf of the United States. Although he hated to fly—he had been on an airplane only once, in 1939—he agreed to attend the World Congress of Writers in São Paulo at the importuning of the State Department and his daughter Lesley, who would accompany him. When Henry F. Holland, assistant secretary of state, wrote Frost on 26 July 1954 to acknowledge his acceptance of the invitation, he stressed the mission's importance:

Your eminence as a poet, the admiration and affection with which your work is regarded abroad as well as at home, will make your participation in this meeting a memorable contribution toward intensifying the good will and friendship which have long united Brazil and the United States, and which is one of the bulwarks of hemisphere solidarity.

In voicing American faith and American aspirations, your poetry has not only regional but hemispheric significance. It is a service to your country for you to undertake this mission as a cultural ambassador.

It would be through Sherman Adams, former governor of New Hampshire and by then assistant to President Eisenhower, that Frost received another invitation, this time in 1957, to represent his government on a mission of Anglo-American fellowship. Accompanied by his "official" **biographer**, Lawrance Thompson, and by his granddaughter Lesley Lee Francis while in England, Frost would receive many accolades, including honorary degrees from Oxford and Cambridge Universities, the first American since Henry Wadsworth Longfellow in 1868 and James Russell Lowell in 1873 to be so honored. Harold E. Howland, then Chief, Special Cultural Programs Branch, International Educational Exchange Service, Department of State, later explained the circumstances of the mission:

When we in the State Department discussed our desire to invite Mr. Frost to take on this cultural "mission" we debated in our minds whether we should ask this distinguished and venerable man to undertake the arduous task of lecturing and traveling throughout England. Our experience with much younger men on these cultural lecturing tours had provided us with ample evidence that these assignments could be taxing ones, indeed. The "stakes were high," however. . . .

It was our belief that we needed someone, not in **politics**, not in government, but rather from "our people" who was loved and respected by both England and America, to remind the British people of our mutual aspirations and hopes. Mr. Frost's greatness as a poet was discovered in England even before our country recognized his abilities. . . .

So we called on Mr. Frost and discussed with him our desire for him to go, but also our especial concern over his age and his well-being. I shall never forget his words: "I was re-reading recently the life of Voltaire. You will recall that Voltaire, in 1778, left the serenity of his village residence in Ferney, Switzerland, to again appear with the crowds of Paris. It was a stren[u]ous visit and he died on that trip. His age then was, as is mine now, 82. Nevertheless, if my country believes I can be of any use in reminding the British people of our own warm affection and strong friendship, why, of course, I'll go. I don't want to be an unguided missile, however; don't spare me. Tell me where you want me to go and when. I'll be ready."

Despite a very tight schedule of public functions and press conferences, Frost was able to find the time to drive into the Gloucestershire/Herefordshire countryside and visit Little Iddens, the laborer's cottage he and his family had rented in 1914.

The trip to Israel in 1961 was inspired by a meeting in 1949 in the Morgan Library, where its librarian, Frederick B. Adams, Jr., introduced him to the Israeli archeologist Dr. Eleazar Sukenik. Frost and Sukenik shared their excitement over the Dead Sea Scrolls; Frost told Sukenik about his archaeology poem—**"Closed for Good"** (the original six-stanza version)—and promised to come to Israel, which he did a dozen years later. As the first Samuel Paley Lecturer at the Hebrew University, Frost attended innumerable public receptions and news conferences: He noted that the " 'endless chain' dramatically connecting the ancient past with the present was best seen here" and that "[p]erhaps nothing in his long life had more vividly linked his entire career with the beginning of history than this visit." He was moved by the stony majesty of Jerusalem: "You have rocks piled on rocks. One civilization built another," he said. Indeed, the Old Testament Christian felt at home in the land of the exiled David, in the storied city of Ashkelon, and on the Hill of Healing, overlooking Judaea. He was reminded of the *Lawrence High School Bulletin* essay on Petra when he crossed over into the Jordanian sector of Jerusalem and stayed at the Petra Hotel. Above all, he was moved by the innumerable traces—stones like in Vermont, the vaulted Ain Feshka scrolls, a broken Corinthian column, the Sanhedria Tombs, and walls upon walls—of an ancient, biblical past.

Having taken part in John F. Kennedy's inaugural ceremonies in January 1961 (*See* **For John F. Kennedy His Inauguration**) and barely surviving a bout with pneumonia and his eighty-eighth birthday, Frost would live long enough to accept President Kennedy's invitation to go to Russia. Lawrance Thompson had accompanied Frost on his 1957 trip to England and his 1961 trip to Israel. Others—Frederick B. Adams, Jr., Franklin D. Reeve, and Stewart Udall—were to be his companions on this final mission. Having met and read to many of the contemporary Russian poets and their public in Moscow and Petrograd, and fighting fatigue, Frost accepted a last-minute invitation to fly to Gagra on the Black Sea to meet with Premier Nikita Khrushchev. Franklin Reeve, who served as translator, provides us a detailed report of this dramatic encounter. Frost asked that the relations of the two nations should be based on rivalry carried out on the highest possible plane. In their conversation that had lasted more than ninety minutes, Khrushchev credited Frost with having "the soul of a poet."

References and further reading: Adams; L. Francis, "Majesty of Stones," "Robert Frost and Helen Thomas," 84–85; K. Morrison; Reeve.

Lesley Lee Francis

"TREE AT MY WINDOW," first published in the *Yale Review* in 1927, was included in *West-Running Brook* **(1928)**, where it appeared as the fifth of ten poems under the heading "Fiat Nox." While this organization was not carried over when Frost's books were subsumed into his *Complete Poems of Robert Frost 1949* and *Collected Poems, Prose, & Plays* **(1995)**, the context gives us a clue to how Frost saw the poem.

"Fiat Nox," Latin for "Let there be darkness," is a sinister turn on Genesis 1:3, "Let there be light." More immediately, the phrase alludes to the last line of **"Once by the Pacific,"** the poem that opens the "Fiat Nox" section. That poem, about the apocalyptic violence of a storm Frost witnessed as a boy on a beach near San Francisco, ends, "There would be more than ocean water broken / Before God's *Put out the Light* was spoken" (Frost's italics). The words also quote Othello as he prepares to murder Desdemona.

The form of the four stanzas is slightly unusual for Frost. It is a modified ballad form, with three lines of four beats each and a final line of two beats, rhymed *abba*. As in many of his poems, however, each stanza is one complete sentence and can stand more or less alone, just as the separate verses of a sung ballad usually do.

In a 1931 letter to **Louis Untermeyer**, who had proposed including "Tree at My Window" in an anthology, Frost expressed some uncertainty about the poem. He suggested deleting the second stanza, saying he had doubts about whether it contributed to what he called "the poetic logic." Indeed, the stanza is a bit obscure. It seems to say that the tree, even when its leaves rustle in the wind, expresses nothing "profound," but the point of the poem seems to be quite the opposite. The second stanza, especially in its last two lines, seems like an intrusion of objective fact into a poem that is about subjective experience.

Yet Frost often interrupts or qualifies a poem with objectivity, as if to acknowledge the world of verifiable facts without submitting to it. In the conclusion of **"The Need of Being Versed in Country Things,"** for example, after the speaker has described a burned-out farmhouse, he says that one who truly knows the ways of nature would understand that the birds' song was not sad. In **"Birches,"** the narrator admits that the trees he contemplates have been doubled over by ice storms, not by a boy swinging on them. In such poems, the poet acknowledges the difference between objective and subjective truths but doesn't give any higher value to one over the other.

The slight shift in perspective in the second stanza of "Tree at My Window" makes the same point and doesn't confuse most readers, Frost's concerns notwithstanding. And as Frost pointed out in the same letter, the stanza uses the word "head" ("dream-head," actually), which sets up a resonance with the same word in the final stanza, where the tree's "head" and the poet's are made explicitly analogous.

In another comment on the poem, recorded by **Reginald L. Cook**, Frost confessed to being "infatuated" with the rhymes of the last stanza. We can only guess what so pleased him. No doubt the natural sound of the rhymes is one thing he liked, but unobtrusive, unstrained rhyme is so typical of Frost that it hardly seems a reason to single out this particular stanza of this particular poem. One possible reason for his comment is the aural linking that results from the heavy assonance between the *a*-rhymes ("together"/"weather") and the *b*-rhymes ("about her"/"outer"). The repetition of the "er" sound at the ends of all four lines creates an especially emphatic sense of closure or completeness. The poem seems to come together, so to speak, in a stanza that is about things being "put . . . together."

Although written nearly twenty years after the family moved away, "Tree at My Window" is one of Frost's many poems that hark back to the decade they lived on a thirty-acre farm near **Derry**, New Hampshire, 1900–1910. Lawrance Thompson claims that the actual tree was a birch that scraped and scratched against the window of the room where Robert and **Elinor** slept. During these years Frost was afflicted with insomnia and nightmares. The period followed closely on the deaths of his son Elliot, his mother, and his grandfather, who had bought the farm and bequeathed it to Robert. It was also a period during which Frost felt himself aging out of his role as a promising young poet: His late twenties and most of his thirties failed to fulfill the hopes raised when, at the age of only twenty, he saw his first published poem bring him the tidy sum of $15 (a good week's wages in 1894).

In **"New Hampshire"** Frost satirizes a man who went single-handedly to cut down a grove of trees but then fled in fear. The man's act was an expression, Frost writes, of "dendrophobia" (fear of trees). "Tree at My Window" is more nearly about a man's brotherhood with a tree, but the kinship is between troubled spirits. Indeed, "Tree at My Window" fits into a long Western tradition of nature poetry. The Romantics, especially Shelley in "Hymn to Intellectual Beauty" and "Ode to the West Wind," frequently used wind as a metaphor for spirit (*spirit* being, in fact, Latin for "breath"). In their search for correspondences between the inner world of the emotions and the outer world of nature, they often represented the wind as the unseen agent that moves all things, that causes our emotions to vibrate in harmony with nature.

Frost knew his Romantic poets, but he eschewed the sublimity that makes much Romantic poetry seem overwrought today. In "Tree at My Window" we are assured by homey details and plain speech that this is the voice of an ordinary man describing a real experience. We cannot doubt that he has really seen some parallel between his own restiveness and the tree's. But we also sense that he feels self-conscious about claiming too much for the correspondence.

References and further reading: R. Cook, *Living Voice*, 124; R. Frost, *Letters to Untermeyer*, 208; Parini, *A Life*, 237; Thompson, *Early Years*, 309.

Richard Wakefield

"TRESPASS," first published in *American Prefaces* (University Press of Iowa, Apr. 1939) and later in *A Witness Tree* (1942), defines "trespass" as both passing over another's boundary and committing an offense that injures or annoys another. "I was being trespassed on and against," insists the poet, suggesting that such trespass is both a legal matter and a personal injury. The culprit has taken a "surly freedom" with his property, he complains, employing an adjective that is more appropriate to himself as the injured party than it is to the transgressor he has not yet seen. However, what bothers him most is that he continues to be totally in the dark about what has happened, his mind running wild, as he speculates that the interloper might have been reading "leaves of stone" or surveying the "specimen crab in specimen rock." Yet if, strictly speaking, there are no property rights at stake in the actions of such Thoreauvian observers (*see* **Thoreau**), there is nevertheless transgression in that "what was whose" has obviously been ignored. But there is a turn in the proprietor's mood that comes when the culprit comes to the kitchen door to ask for a drink. The act of supplication might be an invented "errand," he considers, but no matter, for in it he chooses to see an implicit recognition of his own proprietary rights. The gesture has "made my property mine once more," exults the poet, for it has reaffirmed the principle of ownership even in property that is unsigned, unmarked, or "hardly fenced." (*See* **"Mending Wall."**)

References and further reading: M. Cook, "Complexity."

George Monteiro

"TRIAL BY EXISTENCE, THE," first published in 1906 in *The New York Independent* and later in *A Boy's Will* (1913), is a young man's paradoxical statement of belief, his credo. Lawrance Thompson's biography, which details the gestation of the poem, tells of a mystical experience the eighteen-year-old Frost had in the spring of 1892, a sudden understanding that personal sorrow is part of a grander design. Perhaps girded by his reading of William James, the persona affirms a complex and occasionally contradictory set of attitudes that Frost would revisit for the rest of his career.

Richard Poirier has judged "Trial by Existence" a "magnificent Dante-esque poem," "mysterious and wonderful." But to most readers it seems an act of faith in the absence of faith, a celebration of abstract certainty, a youthful application of William James's testimony that the effort the hero "is able to put forth to hold himself erect and keep his heart unshaken is the direct measure of his worth." Simply stated, the trial by existence of which the poem speaks is the choice each of us has made, in an unremembered heavenly preexistence, to confront the trials and uncertainties of life. Frost had frequently contemplated suicide, but, as he wrote to **Louis Untermeyer** (4 May 1916),

The day I did The Trial by Existence (*Boy's Will*) says I to myself, this is the way of all flesh. I was not much over twenty, but I was wise for my years. I knew then that it was a race between me the poet and that in me that would be flirting with the entelechies or the coming on of [running to philosophy] in me. I must get as much done as possible before thirty.

Having felt and done so, the forty-year-old poet playfully continues that "my time is now my own." His confidence is the "great effect of strength and mastery!"

The tone of the letter is tongue in cheek and yet serious: self-consciousness moderating declaration. But the poem itself is the earliest declaration Frost made on what Thompson calls "the salvation of the soul." It opens with the discovery, in death, that valor reigns in paradise as on earth. The asphodel, a flower associated with death and Elysium, perfumes the key line in an otherwise murky clause, "the utmost reward / Of daring should be still to dare." The oracular voice carries a rhetorical certainty not clarified in the language. The nut of the message is that the brave, the daring, voluntarily give up paradise—and the memory of the choice—for the trial by existence on earth. It is such "devoted souls" for whom God "makes his especial care." But for whom does the poet speak? Are all of us on earth heroic spirits who stood simply forth? Are we all daring ones who dared existence " 'neath the sun" where "earth's unhonored things" pale in the light of reality? Lest the woe of existence not seem woeful, the consolation of remembering our choice is denied us. We asked for what we get, but the poem has already noted that what we ask for seems "nobler" before the choice than " 'neath the sun." But apparently we weren't duped. There are notes of desperate confusion here. Randall Jarrell considers Frost "one of the subtlest and saddest of poets." The final lines seem to have germinated in a sadness that is sometimes despair.

Frost overcame the tendency to vague generality in his better poems by relating specific objects and events to his abstract ideas, but he seldom deviated from the faith of this poem. The superior works have more to do with **religion** than faith, a religion defined by Frost in his 'Sermon' at the Rockdale Avenue Temple as a "straining of the spirit forward to a wisdom beyond wisdom." The ambiguities of seeking fit Frost better than the occasional certainties he attained.

References and further reading: Frost's "Sermon" is reprinted in R. Frost, *Collected*; R. Frost, *Selected Letters*, 202; William James, *Psychology: Briefer Course* (New York: Collier Books, 1962), 455; Jarrell, "Tenderness"; Poirier, *Knowing*, 50, 263; Sergeant views Frost's career through the poem's testament, but readers might check Greiner's *Poet and His Critics*, especially 21–25, for details of Sergeant's shortcomings; Thompson, *Early Years*, 120–21, 554, and Pritchard, *Literary Life*, both give clear and positive readings of the poem.

Stephen D. Warner

"TRIAL RUN, A," an example of Frost's flexible use of the **sonnet**, first appeared in the *Atlantic Monthly* (June 1936) and was included in *A Further*

Range that same year. In the poem, the speaker must stand firm in spite of his apprehension of the machine he calls "It." The title suggests the speaker has never before operated such a device. The dangerous rotation and tremendous sound are expressed by the phrase "homicidal roar"; such impressions, combined with the image of battle, invoke the killing potential of the machine.

The ultimate issue of "A Trial Run" is control. The only comfort the speaker receives is from his own control over the subject. Neither hesitation nor a prayerful attitude offers reassurance in the face of the machine. This is a human-made threat, but in that fact lies a potential solace as well, that the individual might impose order and thereby maintain some control over the form and function of the human invention.

References and further reading: Barry, 79–98; W. Evans; Rood.

Belinda D. Bruner

"TRIPLE BRONZE" first appeared in booklet form with the title *Triple Plate* as Frost's 1939 **Christmas poem** and was later collected in *A Witness Tree* **(1942)**. It recalls the curt, epigrammatic style of many poems in *West-Running Brook* **(1928)**. With its three-stress lines and full rhyme scheme, the poem's self-contained form places Frost himself deep into the background. Lawrance Thompson suggests that the poet assumes a mask of impartiality, speaking epigrammatically in a tone that follows more from the rational mind than from the heart.

The detachment on Frost's part is more than appropriate, considering the poem's underlying meaning. By "bronzing," Frost means the securing of an object against harmful outside elements, and he outlines three levels of such bronzing. The most immediate of these is his "hide," the shell by which the self is contained. The second is a wall, a synecdoche for the homes we build to separate our various families. Finally, there is the "national boundary," an arbitrary but nonetheless useful measure of isolating nations amidst the vastness of the human race.

Indeed, it is such vastness that troubles Frost, who, like other writers of the modern period, craves escape from an increasingly complex world. Mario L. D'Avanzo explains "Triple Bronze" as a direct refutation of the Romantic notion that the individual soul can expand to absorb the whole of the universe. Instead, Frost shows the positive implications of detachment from the "too much" of the universe, as all levels of identification require a manageable scope.

References and further reading: D'Avanzo, *Romantics*, 113–14; Thompson, *Fire and Ice*, 172.

Jason Pearce

"TUFT OF FLOWERS, THE," is one of Frost's most frequently anthologized poems. First published in 1906 in a local newspaper, *The Derry Enterprise*, it was included in his first volume, *A Boy's Will* **(1913)**. Although John Kemp considers the poem inferior to much of Frost's other earlier work (e.g., **"Mowing"**), he and others still consider it to be one of Frost's most distinctive poems of the New England region. Some, including George Bagby, respond to it by claiming that Frost achieves a "mutual fellowship with nature" by discovering the wisdom in the natural world and carefully crafting an appropriate literary fiction, much like poets such as Keats. Others, such as Robert Fleissner, see him as less reverential, transforming Wordsworth's poetry as only a *"New* Englander" could do, or, as William Waddell argues, adding an edge of contrariety to the nineteenth-century tradition of wonder toward nature as expressed by poets such as Longfellow, **Emerson**, and **Thoreau**.

Frost wrote the poem as a response to an assignment for his English A class at **Harvard** in 1897, a class that was less than an ideal experience for him. Pleased that his **teacher** permitted him to write poems (or use ones he had written previously) as responses to the assignments, he quickly became displeased when the poems, at least two of which were later published (including "The Tuft of Flowers"), were not sufficiently impressive to earn him an "A." Robert Newdick records that Frost earned a "B" from his teacher, Alfred Dwight Sheffield, a first-year teaching assistant who found Frost "taking his own line as a writer [who] could give any young teacher as good as he got."

Frost's "line" was his belief in recreating the sounds of speech, the language of the everyday. The emphasis on speech and sentence sounds was one of the points on which Frost and Sheffield disagreed. In reminiscences to Newdick, Sheffield recalls the events: "I remember very congenial talks with [Frost] in which he effectively contrasted the potent element of 'sentence-tone' with the syntactic mechanisms in terms of which I tended to work for sentence-sense in the freshman group."

While the contrast between a focus on syntax and on sentence tone may explain why Sheffield awarded only a "B" for "The Tuft of Flowers," it may also explain why the poem went over so well in the spring of 1906 when Frost chose it as the example of his poetry to read to a meeting of the Men's League of the Congregational Church in **Derry**, New Hampshire. He trusted that these men would be more impressed by someone speaking to them about life as they knew it in a language they used, even if it did include a few archaisms, than by someone writing academic poetry of the kind Sheffield admired. The meeting was critical for Frost; he needed paying work, for he and his family were struggling financially. Thus, Frost went in search of what Elizabeth Sergeant quotes Frost as calling his first "real job," a position teaching English at **Pinkerton Academy**, and the men were going to decide whether or not he was hired.

To convince his fellow citizens that he could both write well and teach writing, Frost chose his poem deliberately, a poem that he later glossed in *A Boy's Will* as one "about fellowship." Interestingly enough, Frost did not read the poem himself. Claiming to be shy, he convinced his advocate, Charles Merriam, to read the poem for him. The move probably helped his cause. Not only were his words coming from an established member of the community but also, by virtue of someone else's reading it, one of the poem's themes was enacted: a second party celebrating and sharing an object—a poem or "tuft of flowers"—written or left by a first party. The result was the re-creation during the meeting of the kind of fellowship Frost celebrated in the poem.

The poem and its author immediately found favor with the citizens, and Frost earned a job at Pinkerton Academy, where he remained from 1906 to 1911. Frost later claimed that the poem not only helped him get his first job but also helped him return to life. According to Sergeant, he explained the importance of "The Tuft of Flowers" when he said, "*A Boy's Will* told how I was scared away from life and crept back to it through this poem."

The poem was well received by the members of the Men's League because it spoke about something they knew—hand mowing—in a familiar, yet fresh way. They were aware that mowers were often followed later by someone who would "turn" the grass to dry. **Reginald L. Cook** records Frost himself saying, "Now let me just say to those that don't know me: that was my job when I was young, to turn the grass after the mower. We called it 'just turning it.' It scattered it a little in the sun."

The idea of someone coming after and "turning" the already mown grass emphasizes an important aspect of the craft of poetry, one linked to the idea of community: the poet "turning" the material of those who have come before him and recognizing his fellow artists as "kindred spirits," an association made by Bagby. The kind of poetic fellowship described metaphorically in "The Tuft of Flowers" is suggested in an essay entitled "The Prerequisites," where Frost says, "A poem is best read in the light of all the other poems ever written. We read A the better to read B (we have to start somewhere; we may get very little out of A). We read B the better to read C, C the better to read D, D the better to go back and get something more out of A. Progress is not the aim, but circulation."

In "The Tuft of Flowers," Frost also celebrates the act of creation for creation's sake and lays the groundwork for other poems such as **"The Wood-pile."** A poet writes or leaves a poem, much as the mower leaves the tuft of flowers, because he is someone who "lived in turning to fresh tasks." According to Cook, Frost commented on "The Tuft of Flowers," saying that "the heart of it lies right in the middle: 'The mower in the dew had loved them thus.' That's the poem you write. To leave them to flourish but not for us, 'Nor yet to draw one thought of ours to him, / But from sheer morning gladness at the brim.' " Frost believed artists often create from a "gladness" and from a desire to leave something orderly in the midst of a wilderness, something that later might be found, shared, circulated, and enjoyed.

In "The Tuft of Flowers," by using a familiar event and speech capable of evoking unique, powerful feelings in his listeners, Frost enacted one of his primary principles about writing: He believed, as **John Bartlett** reports in a letter quoted by Gorham B. Munson, too much writing done in English classes was "common in experience—common in writing." He wanted something else;

he wanted writing that was "common in experience—uncommon in writing." He wanted writing like "The Tuft of Flowers." *See also* **Nature Poet and Naturalist**.

References and further reading: Bagby *Nature*, 163; R. Cook, *Living Voice*, 179, 189; Fleissner, "Tufting"; R. Frost, "The Prerequisites," *Collected*, 815; Kemp, 69–72; Monteiro, "Linked Analogies"; Munson, *Study in Sensibility*, 48; Newdick, *Season*, 381–82; Pritchard, *Literary Life*; Sergeant, 67; Thompson, *Early Years*; Waddell, "Aphorism in 'The Tuft of Flowers.' "

James M. Dubinsky

TWILIGHT (1894). In the fall of 1894, the twenty-year-old Frost took five of his poems to a job printer in Lawrence, Massachusetts. The result, *Twilight*, was printed in an edition of two copies, on antique paper, and bound in brown pebbled leather with the title stamped in gold. One copy was given to **Elinor White** with an inscription by Frost (this leaf was later excised); the second copy, kept for himself, was later destroyed.

Frost made a special trip to visit Elinor, who was attending St. Lawrence University in Canton, New York, to present her with this token of his love. He hoped his very personal gift would put him in the lead of another suitor. Because of both the unexpectedness of Frost's arrival and the university's rules of propriety, which did not allow for a man to visit a young woman except during certain prescribed hours, he was not as warmly received as he had hoped. Elinor took the book from him, instructing him to take the next train home. He never had the chance to show her his own copy of *Twilight*, which he felt created an indelible link between them. Feeling deeply rejected, he destroyed his copy of *Twilight* and returned home.

In 1939 Frost was approached by an avid collector, Earle J. Bernheimer, who coveted the unique Frost volume. He asked Frost if there was any way he would be able to acquire it. At first, Frost declined, claiming it truly belonged to Elinor, who had died the previous year, but considering the unpleasant associations of its history, he eventually agreed to discuss the idea with Bernheimer. Frost felt that if it were financially helpful to each of his four surviving children, he would sell, and so he named a starting price of $4,000—$1,000 for each child—a price much higher than the lowest he would accept. Bernheimer agreed on the price, which was far less than he knew he would be willing to go. The unique volume is now housed in the Barrett Collection at the University of Virginia.

The slender volume contained five poems: the title poem, "Twilight"; **"My Butterfly,"** which was soon to be published in the November 8 issue of *The Independent*; "Summering"; "The Falls"; and "An Unhistoric Spot." At the end of *Twilight* is a couplet in Frost's hand apparently excerpted from a poem that is no longer extant; when the couplet was written out by Frost is unknown.

Of the five poems, only "My Butterfly" was later collected by Frost in *A Boy's Will* **(1913)**, although he did allow "The Falls" to be reprinted by Earle

Bernheimer in 1947 in an edition of sixty numbered copies. "My Butterfly" was always considered by the poet his first real poem. He particularly liked the eight lines beginning, "The gray grass . . ." in which he felt he had found his poetic voice.

References and further reading: The four previously uncollected poems appear in R. Frost, *Collected*; see also Barrett; Crane, "Printing History of *Twilight*"; Thompson, *Early Years*.

Jeffrey S. Cramer

"TWO LEADING LIGHTS," from the 1947 *Steeple Bush* collection, first appeared in **collector** Earle J. Bernheimer's 1944 **Christmas** booklet. It explores two of the most common symbols in poetry, the sun and the moon. Clare Gibson notes that following historical precedent the speaker has personified each of the "celestial cast" with gender—maleness for the sun, femaleness for the moon.

Though the speaker's tone is light and playful, a discerning critic might find reason to protest the underlying antifeminist sentiment expressed in the poem. The sun, the masculine character, is described with adjectives calculated to reinforce the notion of masculine supremacy. He is "satisfied with days"; they are his "eminent domain." He is totally predictable and steady, like a benevolent father. Though he "could in one burst overwhelm" the night sky, or the planet earth for that matter, "He has the greatness to refrain." The language is designed to engender confidence in the ability and willingness of the sun/father to take care of the business of the day. The pun in line 9 on the word "dayify" with its obvious links to the power to immortalize (deify) also underscores the sun's authority. The moon, on the other hand, is characterized as a stereotypical giddy female. She is prey to "some lunatic or lunar whim." She is an "irresponsible divinity" who "Has never learned to know her place." Her power is derived in its entirety from the sun, yet she does not show proper respect for his position.

In the poem's governing metaphor of "stardom," we might also read an oblique reference to Hollywood; the moon's behavior reminds us of a spoiled and impulsive starlet or sex symbol, and the phrases "leading lights" and "celestial cast" call to mind the notion of a leading man and woman in a Hollywood production.

References and further reading: Bagby, *Nature*, 54, includes this poem in a list of those he finds "closer to true fables than to emblem poems"; Gibson, 90–91.

Lynn Barrett

"TWO LOOK AT TWO," first printed in *New Hampshire* (1923), begins with the journey of an unidentified couple up a mountain, suggestive of struggle and peril as well as incremental progress toward vision and enlightenment. The reader assumes that the two people have ventured out in search of something, but what they actually find and the subtle questioning of the value of the discovery are slowly revealed throughout the poem. The connotative value of

"Love and forgetting" remains unclear, though there could be some suggestion that both properties together point to forgiveness, an amnesty mutually agreed that might allow any couple to move forward without fear of the impediments of the past. However, it is equally clear that uninhibited progress is not valued in the poem, as it serves also to obliterate the legacy and the lessons of the past. The two people must stop in any case, conscious of their "thoughts of the path back," which is "unsafe in darkness." Because nightfall is in itself a natural and wholly predictable occurrence, to be neither feared nor lamented, one has the sense that the apparent lovers have actually journeyed as far as they ought while still tending a shared past, represented by the darkening path that has brought them forward to their present position. Ironically, perhaps, neither the night nor the peril of their path ultimately stops the couple at the particular moment captured by the poem; rather, Frost tells us that they are "halted by a tumbled wall / With barbed-wire binding," a formidable, man-made impediment that marks the furthest physical boundary of their journey, holding off "the failing path" beyond which is "the way they must not go." Indeed, confronting the barrier drains from the couple their "onward impulse."

In the face of the closure threatened by the crumbled wall, the natural world in which the two find themselves holds further surprises: A doe confronts the humans from the far side of the wall. The continued reference to the barrier at this point, along with the line "She saw them in their field, they her in hers," underlines the separation of human and natural worlds. Picking up on their apparent serenity, the doe is also content, and in her, the couple sees "no fear." For their part, the humans seem content because they have found a communion with nature. The earlier "This is all" is echoed and amplified by *"This*, then, is all. What more is there to ask?" after they encounter the animal.

But, on one final occasion, nature provides the couple with an additional surprise. A buck, presumably the mate of the earlier animal, appears in virtually the same manner as did the doe, and the buck, too, stares at the couple. The new confrontation is significantly different from the former. The buck's "jerks of head," for example, reveal a certain aggression. The active masculine posture of the animal effectively dares the humans to move, to challenge him. Frost represents the confrontation in the buck's imagined claim, "I doubt if you're as living as you look." The movement of the couple would affirm for the animal not only the reality of their being but also the reality of their relationship in terms the buck could comprehend. The exchange highlights once again the difference between the animals and the people. The couple continues to stand still and allow the animal to pass along quietly, as did its mate. That the buck, too, is "unscared" is noteworthy, but it must be attributed to something different than is the ease of the doe. The more aggressive animal recognizes the humans but appears indifferent to them in his own self-assuredness. Finally satisfied that the breadth of the experience has passed them, the couple exclaims, "This *must* be all." Frost immediately confirms, "It was all."

In the case of "Two Look at Two," what separates, then, unifies. The wall stands between human and animal as they stand in their distinct worlds. Lest too much be made of the tempting romantic interpretation, powerful as it is, of parallel or reciprocal worlds, the distinctions also need emphasis. Too easily one might see an identification between the male and female humans and the male and female deer. But the narrator avoids the suggestions of romantic mysticism by being carefully objective in his telling, reporting words and events as they occur. Even the twofold seeing beginning in line 17 is kept in perfect journalistic order. Very possibly the most crucial phrase in the poem is "as if," used in lines 22, 32, 41, and an inversion in line 34. The objective rendering precludes the temptation to see a romantic interpretation of reciprocity between the two couples. They inhabit separate worlds. What is significant is that the deer move "unscared" along the wall and that is all.

References and further reading: Bagby, *Nature*, examines the poem as an egregious fiction about fellowship between man and woman; Brower; M. Cook, "Serious Play," examines the role of irony in interpretation; D. J. Hall, *Contours*, examines the relationships between human and divine love, tying them to Frost's own beliefs; Lentricchia, *Modern Poetics*; Oster; Parini, *A Life*, 202–3.

Craig Monk and John H. Timmerman

"TWO TRAMPS IN MUD TIME" was first published in the *Saturday Review of Literature* (Oct. 1934) and later became part of *A Further Range* **(1936)**. According to George Monteiro, who cites Louis Mertins, Frost claimed that the poem had been written "against having hobbies." Hobbies, as an expression of selfish desire, function contrary to the conclusion of the poem, which endorses a unification of work and love as the prime motivation for human action. As Frost concludes, "My object in living is to unite / My avocation and my vocation." In a very similar manner, **Thoreau**, in "Life without Principles," writes what could be the epigram for Frost's poem: "Do not hire a man who does your work for money, but him who does it for the love of it." Frost understands that in a world of social obligations, economic pressures, and conflicting desires, to unite vocation and avocation in one act is difficult if not impossible. His awareness of such difficulty stops the poem from declaring any outright conclusions. Rather, the poem ends with one of Frost's most conspicuously didactic, yet ambiguous statements: "Only where love and need are one / . . . Is the deed ever really done / For Heaven and the future's sakes."

The first stanza introduces the problem: The speaker is chopping wood when he is interrupted by two tramps who see the speaker's action as impinging upon their "right": What he does for pleasure, they would do for work. The two claims for the job, pleasure and need, are not equable, but they are both valid. While the speaker is not indifferent to the tramps' need for food and shelter, he is, much like **Emerson**, too self-reliant wholly to attribute priority to satisfying only basic human needs. Frost maintains that individuals have immaterial needs that are clearly as important as the physical ones. Such nonphysical needs are illustrated by the speaker who finds chopping wood an expression of joy, a way of loosening his soul. The reverse is demonstrated by the tramps who are able to evaluate human beings only by the way "a fellow handled an ax."

Frost, of course, grieves at the predicament of the tramps, whose circumstances force them into a situation whereby they are unable to desire anything other than the basic human needs of food and shelter. The tramps have completely estranged what Frost insists upon being united: need and love, vocation and avocation, work and play. While Frost does not deny that poverty is deplorable, he does demonstrate that if a person must devote the majority of one's time and effort to mere monetary reward, one will eventually lose a sense of human values, self, and spirit.

Having framed the problem, Frost spends the next four stanzas in a protracted discussion of the ambiguous transformation from winter to spring. The stanzas are warnings that the world is not compartmentalized in strictly binary modes. Spring and winter converge in a continuum, and understanding the continuum forms a greater perspective on a single truth. Such sense of unity and the necessity of understanding its constitution give a more "natural" weight to the final stanza and its proposition of unification. The discussion helps to reinforce the idea that the decision the speaker makes in the last stanza must be in accord with what is "right" in nature.

The problem depicted in the poem is characteristic of Frost: One can see the first stanza as typical of his affection for situations in which the dilemma of personal choice is reduced to a simple but ultimate either/or. **"The Road Not Taken"** is probably the most famous of the Frostian ur-dilemmas, but the motif also occurs in **"A Servant to Servants," "The Self-Seeker,"** and others. Such ur-dilemmas result in the speaker's taking what George W. Nitchie calls "gambler's gestures": The narrator takes a step and makes a decision based not upon weighted consideration but upon caprice, desire, or providence.

Stanza nine, in effect, offers a new model of separating without dividing, which applies equally to the job of woodcutting and to writing poetry. Some critics, such as Judith Oster, see the final stanza as ambiguous, claiming that it is unclear whether the speaker finally gives the job to the woodcutters. The last stanza—which declares the necessity for uniting vocation and avocation, need and love, work and play as the ideal way of doing a deed—does not explicitly state who should be chopping the wood. As Oster states, "The resolution of the poem will depend on whether feeling wins out over logic, and then the question is *which* feeling—sympathetic feeling for another or feeling about the task that unites work and play, love and need."

If the ending of the poem is read such that the speaker gives the work to the tramps, Frost in effect concedes that while values do often exist "in twain," they also exist in a continuum. The tramps are in no position to philosophize over uniting need and love, work and play. Thus, the giving of the work would signal Frost's admission that the tramps' perspective is valid; their needs are validated without being simply negated. What Frost has done, then, is to give us an experience that demonstrates how to discover, through creative thinking, a workable solution to a moral problem.

Read in this way, the poem explores the necessity of relinquishing one's personal desires and thus becomes relevant to the situation of the artist, for if such thinking is applied to poetry, then the unification of need and love, work and play, becomes Frost's credo for the "philosophic poet": one who unites thought and action into art. The poet as philosopher is the one seeking to inspire investigation, to create new perceptions of the self, and to alter our understanding of the world. For Nitchie, the poem is based upon the idea that "personal tragedy is not so much a matter of choosing wrongly or failing to unite vocation and avocation but rather being denied the chance to choose, or of failing to choose and going with the drift of things." The real emphasis for Frost—as is evident in "The Road Not Taken," "A Servant to Servants," and "Two Tramps in Mud Time"—is on the act of choosing rather than on the consequences of action.

References and further reading: Jost; Monteiro, *New England*, 76; Nitchie, 154; Oster, 182; Parini, *A Life*, 288–89; Henry David Thoreau, "Life without Principle," *The Writings of Henry David Thoreau* (Boston: Houghton Mifflin, 1906), 455–82.

Derrick Stone

"TWO WITCHES" is actually two poems first published under the collective title in Frost's fourth volume, *New Hampshire* (**1923**). The first of the two poems, "The Pauper Witch of Grafton," was originally published in *The Nation* (13 Apr. 1921), and the other, "The Witch of Coös," appeared in *Poetry* (Jan. 1922). Collections subsequent to *New Hampshire* place them together as "Two Witches." Both the tables of contents and the running titles suggest Frost wanted "Two Witches" to be read as a single work in two parts. Each is a dramatic poem telling a rich and compressed narrative that works largely by hints and indirections, but the witches themselves are a study in contrasts. The story told by the witch of Coös concerns the skeleton (literally) in her family closet: She tells how the bones of her lover—whom her husband had murdered, she says, "instead of me"—once escaped from the cellar and climbed to the attic, where they remain trapped. But the poem strongly suggests that the whole episode is only a figment of her imagination, a symptom of repressed guilt. The Grafton witch, on the other hand, sustains a defiant personal and sexual energy, cherishing memories of an eccentric but satisfying sexual and emotional life. Together, as Mordecai Marcus has suggested, the poems compose a diptych portrait of the repressed and expressed unconscious.

Neither witch is involved in sorcery or magic in the ordinary sense; instead, each has responded in her own way to the demands of her unconscious mind, and "witchcraft" proves to be more a spell that each woman is under than a supernatural power she commands. In the case of the poem placed first, "The Witch of Coös," the drama is framed by brief observations on the part of a narrator; otherwise, the voices of "Mother" and "Son" relate the entire tale. "Mother," the Coös witch, hints in several ways that her marriage was sexless, her emotional life frozen by her inability to put the past to rest. Moreover, the fact that the witch awakened from sleep to see and hear fleeting signs of the skeleton, but could see nothing of it in the light, hints that the pilgrimage of the bones from the cellar to the attic was all a morbid hallucination produced by inner torment. Her husband, Toffile, she admits, heard and saw nothing, and it is fitting that the skeleton should have disinterred itself to end up trapped behind the headboard of the marriage bed, as though it stood for her own restless conscience. At the end of the poem, the narrator remarks that the witch had been unable to find the finger-bone she had been looking for, and next morning he "verified" the name on the letter box, "Toffile Lajway." The anglicization of "Théophile Lajoie" appears, as Marcus observes, to pun on the phrase "to file away," which of course is what the couple has tried to do with both her affair and her lover's corpse.

The Grafton witch is a mirror image of the Coös witch: While her neighbors are superstitious and repressive, she remains self-possessed and defiant. Although she is pained by the indignity of her circumstances in old age, she revels in her old vitality and her unconventional but deeply satisfying life with her husband. Loosely based on an episode related in *The History of Warren* by William Little (see Thompson), the poem is one of Frost's few pure **dramatic monologues**. The speaker playfully boasts of a reputation for witchcraft that at the same time she reveals to be specious. The New Hampshire towns of Wentworth and Warren have each sued to oblige the other to support the impoverished witch in her old age, but she insists that the judgment in favor of Wentworth is based on a confusion of her husband with her husband's father, for both men bore the name Arthur Amy, and she relishes the opportunity to bring her own suit against Wentworth and create "double trouble." In the middle portion of the poem, the pauper witch replies to old accusations brought against her by one Mallice Huse and indirectly reveals much about both herself and her husband. Huse, in the days when the witch had been "a strapping girl of twenty," accused her of putting him under a spell and riding him like a horse throughout the county, leaving him "hitched unblanketed" in front of the Town Hall. But a skeptical stranger (a "smarty someone" who will prove to be Arthur Amy) intervenes and instructs Huse to gnaw the posts in order to leave a "trade mark" as proof. Of course, "Not a post / That they could hear tell of was scarified." Amy then suggests that in reality Huse had been gnawing on the posts of his own bed, and again he is proven right. Evidently, Huse's allegations reveal only his own frustrated sexual fantasies, gnawing away inside of him and indeed outside of him. The speaker, however, professes irritation with Amy, for she had taken some pleasure in being thought to possess special powers for bewitching the opposite sex. Soon Amy himself falls under her "spell," and after they marry, he begins to submit willingly to her and even finds it convenient to uphold her reputation for flying through the night on a broomstick. For the couple keep to themselves, enjoying a rich sexual and emotional life that would have horrified their puritanical neighbors. The poem ends with a highly charged passage that works by indirection but is no less powerfully erotic for the fact that the imagery and the inflections of the speaker's "sentence sounds" leave almost everything to the imagination. Far from the house, she showed him "woman signs to man, / Only bewitched so I would last him longer. / Up where the trees grow short, the mosses tall, / I made him gather me wet snow berries / On slippery rocks beside a waterfall. / I made him do it for me in the dark. / And he liked everything I made him do." Randall Jarrell has remarked that "there is more sexuality there than in several hothouses full of Dylan Thomas; and, of course, there is love there." The *hortus conclusus* ("garden enclosed") tradition allows the reader to identify the mountaintop garden with the female body, and Frost's language obliquely but effectively suggests sexual organs and acts. Her powers of bewitchment have passed away with the years, but she remains plucky and defiant even if she has "come down from everything to nothing." Among Frost's female characters, she is unusually life affirming, liberated and strong, in stark contrast to the grim, death-obsessed witch of Coös.

"The Witch of Coös" has received far more praise and critical attention than "The Pauper Witch of Grafton," and the poems have rarely been discussed as a pair. Yet the fine mixture of comedy, pathos, and psychological insight that sustains each poem separately is even richer when the poems are read as companion pieces.

References and further reading: Briggs; Brower; Jarrell, "Laodiceans"; Kearns, for decidedly feminist readings of the poems; Lynen, *Pastoral Art*; Marcus, *Explication* and "Whole Pattern"; Thompson, *Triumph*, 563, n.16.

Matthew Parfitt

U

UNCOLLECTED POETRY. When the posthumously collected volume *The Poetry of Robert Frost* was published in 1969, it was the intention of the publisher, **Holt**, Rinehart and Winston, to publish only those poems that Frost had included in his previous volumes. It was not their intention, as is made clear in the "publisher's note," to include any of the poems Frost had left either uncollected or unpublished at the time of his death, believing that Frost would not have wanted such poems to represent his "poetic achievement."

Yet beyond the 345 poems in the collected edition, there is a corpus of over 100 poems—one quarter of Frost's entire poetic output—most of which, until the recent publication of *Collected Poems, Prose, & Plays* **(1995)**, had remained inaccessible to readers of Frost. Many of these poems deserve close study as they are either thematically or stylistically related to Frost's published oeuvre.

"The Black Cottage," familiar to readers of *North of Boston* **(1914)**, was originally a quite different poem written first in a rhymed version of five octets around 1905, which Frost, mistaken, claims to have lost on purpose. The final four lines of the unpublished "New Grief" from 1911 were resurrected in 1962 as the quatrain **"[We vainly wrestle with the blind belief]"** in *In the Clearing*. The 32-line "The Return of the Pilgrims" from 1920 had lines 17–20 excerpted as **"Immigrants"** in *West-Running Brook* **(1928)**. Some poems, such as "[To prayer I think I go . . .]," were worked on over a period of twenty years before being ultimately abandoned. Although the 1891 poem "Clear and Colder—Boston Common" was not published by Frost, he reused the title as simply **"Clear and Colder"** in 1934. Images in "A Winter's Night" reemerge in **"An Old Man's Winter Night."** Three poems—"Asking for Roses," "In Equal Sacrifice," and "Spoils of the Dead"—were dropped from *A Boy's Will* **(1913)**. Three of eight poems—"The Prophet," "The Philosopher," and "Marx and Engels"—from his 1959 booklet *A Remembrance Collection of New Poems* were not recollected, as were the other five, in *In the Clearing*.

The 1906 **sonnet** "When the Speed Comes" recalls Frost's days in the mills of Lawrence. There he would have been witness to the machinery that turns people into slavish automatons unable to vary from the exacting "music of the iron." The inhumanity found in the mills haunted Frost for over ten years before he found an outlet in this early but mature poem.

Although it was not always popular to admit being an admirer of Longfellow's poetry, Frost never denied or hid his debt to Longfellow. The title of Frost's first book, *A Boy's Will*, was taken from Longfellow's poem "My Lost Youth." While teaching at **Pinkerton Academy** in 1907, the centennial of Longfellow's birth, Frost wrote "The Later Minstrel," which was printed as a broadside for the centennial celebration Pinkerton was having. In total admiration, Frost refers to Longfellow's "perfect songs to sing." A poet's fame comes and goes with time, his reputation a slave to current taste. Frost reminds us that a poem's "times and seasons are its own, / Its ways past finding out," but despite our doubts over Longfellow's worth, his song "fills the earth / And triumphs over doubt."

"My Giving" was finished shortly before Christmas 1911. In it the poet asks for no merrier a Christmas than that which "the hungry bereft and cold shall know." The true Christian spirit of Christmas is shown if he can be "thirsty with them that thirst, / Hungry with them that hunger and are accurst." The truest gift is compassion. He cannot ask of the poor that they be glad with him and share his gladness. It is more fitting that he should be sad with them.

The Frosts sold their farm in **Derry**, New Hampshire, in November 1911, closing an important period in their life together. Soon, although unknown to them at the time, their family life would be irrevocably changed by Frost's fame as a poet. Inspired by such closure, Frost wrote "On the Sale of My Farm" to his wife **Elinor**. He describes how cheerfully he yields to the new owners of the orchard, field, house, barn, and shed, which he can "unlearn to love," provided it is understood that it will not be considered a trespass if, one day, he were to come back again "seeking ache of memory here."

In early 1922 the now-famous Robert Frost sent "The Nose Ring" to **Louis Untermeyer**, explaining that the poem "is for you, not particularly for anyone else." The subject matter of the poem was of a private nature for this public man. Finding himself a successful poet, he felt occasional indignation and dismay with the honors with which the poet is led, making his "sensitive nose more sensitive." He certainly did not want to make public a feeling that might make him seem ungrateful or unappreciative of the acceptance and honors he had received. Tethered to the nose ring of popularity and thinking too much of the reception of a poem rather than its subject, the poet winces when he tries to use his nose as a plow to go "below the surface." In the closing couplet, he expresses his willingness to forgo honor and fame if he could simply regain his ability to "get down again to the root of things."

The unpublished "Gone Astray" is thematically linked with "The Nose Ring." It is a first-person lament, in language similar to **"Directive,"** of a man who feels lost in a place not his own. He is weary of having to say who he is, to make a badge of his fame, to be treated well. He concludes by realizing that he should have kept some place where he could have found rest for more than just his body.

"The Offer" was one of Frost's poems originally intended for inclusion in a volume—in this case, *A Further Range* **(1936)**—but left out. The narrator is out in a snowstorm where he must "narrow eyes and double night" in order to avoid the hard and dry flakes that "smite" him. What more, he wonders, do the flakes want of him; are he and the flakes comparable because they might both be considered "hard and dry"? Should he or the flakes or both melt? He ends by asking, in words reminiscent of **"The Wind and the Rain,"** "If I supply the sorrow felt, / Will they supply the tears?"

In the last decade of his life, Frost occasionally attempted to write narrative poems similar to those in *North of Boston*. Although he had completed and published one in 1949, **"From Plane to Plane,"** and another in 1950, **"How Hard It Is to Keep from Being King When It's in You and in the Situation,"** there are extant two others that were never completed. "Cocktail Bar in 45th Street" finds the narrator sitting alone in a dark corner of a bar, sipping, like Frost, his ginger-ale. He listens to the babble of the people around him who "sound as if they had the authority / To send one down to hell for being wrong." The narrator knows there are many things for which he can be sent to hell but for which in this secular world he cannot be sent to jail. If the people in the bar are going to judge and punish him for his heresies, whatever they might be, they should do it now while there is still flesh on his bones to burn. How, he wonders, could these people know so much about him and his wrongs? In a dismissing comment on current theater, he answers, "They'd just been to a play / About it all." The people he listens to talk about sin: One says that one should sin more to have more for which to repent; another that one should sin fast and get it over with; a third that one could sin until the age of forty before really needing to bother about repentance. The narrator decides not to add anything to their conversation but concludes to the bartender that sin is not anything one commits but comes of being born when our first outcry calls out selfishly for attention someone else might better deserve.

The other unfinished narrative poem, "Old Gold for Christmas," exists in three versions, each more or less in the same state of incompleteness. "Old Gold for Christmas," alternatively titled "Gold for Christmas," tells the story of a man named Rice whom the narrator meets on the street one winter night. Rice has just slipped on the ice and asks for permission to lean on the narrator until he can get his thoughts straight. Rice explains that he needs to get home but that he needs help. Rice needs to think of what he will tell his daughter-in-law who will have been waiting up for him; the narrator needs to think of what he will do with the man. They go to a friend of Rice, where Rice's son is called to bring him home. Rice's story, pieced together through the poem, is that he was known as the Gold for Christmas Man because the company for which he had stoked the furnace for forty years paid him in gold the week of Christmas. His wife wanted him to demand more than the $20 he made a week, bringing up their children to the idea that their father robbed them of what he did not earn. Rice could not ask for more. He felt that there is one art to work, another to getting compensated for it. He would not ask for a raise because it involved self-praise, which is a poor substitute for the praise of others, a concept brought out in Frost's earlier uncollected "A Bed in the Barn."

"Homology" was originally planned for *In the Clearing* but was never completed. It is an important poem, despite its unfinished state, in that it is thematically tied to two Frost works from the 1930s: his poem **"All Revelation"** and his **prose** introduction to **E. A. Robinson**'s *King Jasper*. The poem discusses the homological relationship between infants and adults. The relationship is shown in human nonverbal communication in which eye corresponds to eye, smile to smile, indicating that it is not so much what we say as how we say it that is most significant.

The draft manuscript for the unpublished "[Up here where late I face the end ...]" is written below a prose variant of Frost's dedication to *In the Clearing* and may have been intended as an introductory poem to his final volume. It carries the feeling of a summary, written from the vantage point of the end of a long life. The narrator is no longer a farmer or breeder of dairy cows—one who represses nature into controlled forms. Now he tends a wild garden. Although there are some who want to have their own individual say, make their mark in the world's outcome by controlling nature, the poet admonishes us to "respect the variant / And let the force of nature vary." The poem is a sympathetic philosophical outlook toward **poetic theory** from a poet who, as Frost said of Robinson, found the "old-fashioned way to be new."

To know Frost one must know not only those poems that he finally collected but those that he did not. The poems he did not collect or publish tell us much about Frost. Only by examining his total poetic output can one fully evaluate his work.

References and further reading: Many of these and other observations about Frost's uncollected poems appear in Cramer, *Frost among His Poems*; R. Frost, *Collected* and *Letters to Untermeyer*, 143.

Jeffrey S. Cramer

"UNHARVESTED" first appeared in the *Saturday Review of Literature* on 10 November 1934 under the title of "Ungathered Apples." Upon revision, Frost added the second, third, and fifth lines; changed a few other words; and changed the title to "Unharvested." It was collected in *A Further Range* **(1936)**.

The speaker—a philosophical, pastoral farmer/poet—leaves the "routine road" and invites the reader as he follows his nose over the wall to find an apple tree that is encircled by its fallen ripe apples. Frost muses that some treasures are simply to be appreciated freely, naturally, not circumscribed or predetermined by "routine" or "stated plan." There is something quintessentially American in this poem, a feeling of plenty, a sense of freedom, a Thoreauvian and Emersonian (*see* **Thoreau** and **Emerson**) celebration of essences, a predilection for "extra-vagance," as suggested by Richard Poirier, who additionally reads political implications in the poem's circumspect tension between freedom and confinement in the context of the 1930s. The "scent of ripeness" and "sweetness" of apples also recall biblical connections and refer us to the intoxicating undertones of **"After Apple-Picking"** and **"The Cow in Apple Time."** *See also* **Nature Poet and Naturalist**.

References and further reading: Bagby, *Nature*; Poirier, *Knowing*.

Judy Richter

"UNSTAMPED LETTER IN OUR RURAL LETTER BOX, AN," first appeared in pamphlet form as Frost's **Christmas poem** in 1944; it was subsequently published in *Steeple Bush* **(1947)**. The poem is written as a letter to a farmer from the vagrant who spent the night in the pasture outside his home. Intended as an apology—the "watchdog barked all night" and roused the farmer from his bed, after all—the poem actually chronicles the tramp's night outdoors. He maintains that in the dark the field takes on the appearance of a city park, presumably a surrounding with which the tramp is familiar. The irony, of course, is that the urban park seeks only to simulate the pastoral setting by providing a rustic refuge for city dwellers. The tramp experiences the country idyll and is well rewarded in his odyssey. Careful not to shift in the night and lose heat, he wakes when a rock on which he rests disturbs him. In the dark, the "tramp astrologer" notes "the largest firedrop ever formed" from the union of two stars. Where these two worlds come together, the tramp finds enlightenment. He refuses to reveal the nature of his illumination to his host, for the sake of real or feigned modesty. He prefers to entertain the possibility that the farmer saw the same sight and perhaps had the same revelation, albeit from some distance behind the "rusty screen" of his door. Alternatively, the tramp accepts that his host may have experienced a similar realization while at work in his field. The overall impression is that there is great power in experience, and the tramp contends that different life paths hold equally valuable experiences. *See also* *Steeple Bush* for a discussion of the theme of metaphor in this poem.

References and further reading: Cramer, *Frost among His Poems*; Marcus, *Explication*.

Craig Monk

UNTERMEYER, LOUIS (1885–1977). If the number of letters one writes to another reveals the depth of a friendship, then Louis Untermeyer was clearly one of Frost's dearest friends, though Untermeyer was the complete antithesis of Frost in everything except their common love of poetry and good talk. This link was enough to enable them to overcome their many important differences in family origins, cultural background, religious and philosophical convictions, and economic and political commitments. Untermeyer was "[t]he friend I have written more letters to than anyone else," as Frost words it in an unusually lengthy letter to Untermeyer in 1947. For his part, Untermeyer was more than willing to listen to the poet he believed to be the "most penetrating" and "more profound" of the twentieth century.

The depth of the friendship—one of the most personal, devoted, complex, and contradictory ones in American literature—emerges in Untermeyer's finest gift to Frost studies: *The Letters of Robert Frost to Louis Untermeyer* (1963). Frost wrote over 200 letters to Untermeyer. The correspondence between them began in earnest in 1915, just after Untermeyer had favorably reviewed Frost's *North of Boston* **(1914)** for the *Chicago Evening Post*. The two men had met just that same year, during Frost's first public reading of his poetry at Tufts College. Frost, while in **England**, had earlier heard about Untermeyer from his friend Lascelles Abercrombie, and in 1913 Untermeyer had read Frost's poems **"The Fear"** and **"A Hundred Collars"** in the British journal *Poetry and Drama* and had sensed that the author was an unknown American. Untermeyer would sense much more about Frost as the letters reveal, exposing as they do a friendship that ran the whole gamut of emotions from tenderness to blitzkrieg, including the entire range of personal comedy and tragedy, and that endured all obstacles for almost forty-eight years, until Frost's death in January 1963.

The letters had opened lightly enough with Frost's suggesting that the two men be "generous to each other as fellow artists." Generous they were, with Frost kindly encouraging his friend's literary pursuits and Untermeyer tirelessly promoting the poet, writing "admittedly partisan" reviews, publishing favorable articles, placing Frost's work with fellow editors, and in 1943, securing for Frost an unprecedented fourth Pulitzer Prize for *A Witness Tree* **(1942)**. The letters point as well to the tragic ties between the men, Frost's playful bantering often giving way to more serious and painful matters. Both Untermeyer and Frost were well acquainted with the darker side of life, as when their sons committed suicide, when Untermeyer's several marriages failed, or when Frost's wife **Elinor** and several children died or family members lost their sanity. As the letters show, they sustained each other through each of their many personal tragedies.

World War II precipitated a crisis in their friendship, however, when Frost refused Untermeyer's request to join him in the Office of War Information to write anti-Nazi propaganda. As early as 27 October 1917, he had written to Untermeyer: "There's one thing I shan't write in the past, present, or future, and that is glad mad stuff or mad glad stuff." To Frost, propaganda was the corruption of art, and he was determined not to sacrifice his poetry for propaganda, no matter how noble the cause. But on 12 August 1944 he felt compelled to justify himself to Untermeyer and sent him a long personal poem reviewing their long friendship. The poem captures the essence of their friendship, from Frost's viewpoint. He acknowledges that Untermeyer knew him better than anyone, and he notes "How many kinds of friend I[']ve had in you." Their friendship survived this crisis, and in a letter to Untermeyer on 14 April 1962, Frost wrote, "We've been through a lot together and both know how to make allowances." They had been through much together by 1962, and much of Frost's public success can be attributed to his friend's devotion, shrewd business mind, and astute understanding of the literary profession.

Untermeyer had begun his own literary career writing poems and occasional critical reviews after marrying the poet Jean Starr in 1907. He published several books of verse, literary biographies, and his autobiography, *From Another World*, published in 1939 and in revised form in 1965 as *Bygones*. His numerous introductory texts include *The Road Not Taken: An Introduction to Robert Frost* (1962), a book that still serves as a useful primer for understanding Frost's work. Untermeyer edited and provided commentary for dozens of anthologies of British and American poetry as well, many of which nurtured Frost's reputation, as the volumes increasingly featured the poet's work. And in 1943, he edited and introduced a generous selection of Frost's poems, published as *Come In and Other Poems*, which went through several printings and became a popular pocketbook edition of Frost's best-known poems. As Frost acknowledged in a letter on 16 April 1957, with Untermeyer's help, he became "an almost national American poet."

Nowhere is the deepening relationship between Frost and Untermeyer more evident than in their time together at **Bread Loaf**. In 1939 Frost bought the Homer Noble Farm, near Bread Loaf, and spent every summer there until 1962; Untermeyer lived just fifty miles away across Lake Champlain, and he visited Frost frequently and spent the last ten days of August with him during the Bread Loaf Writers' Conference. At Bread Loaf, Frost and Untermeyer shared in a wide range of literary and social activities, and when Theodore Morrison, the director of the Writers' Conference, asked Frost to conduct the "poetry clinics," Frost agreed on condition that Untermeyer would read and comment upon the poems submitted for criticism by conference members. For several summers they formed a close-knit team and ran poetry clinics four or five times each week during the Writers' Conference. Frost soon became a key figure at Bread Loaf, where he would deliver some of his more lively talks and powerful poetry; and when someone complained about his dominating presence, Untermeyer, ever "the punning pundit of Bread Loaf," retorted: "Bread Loaf is the most Frostbitten place in America."

Late in life, Frost was fond of claiming that Untermeyer gave him his "critical start" as a poet and that for the most part he was his friend's creation. Untermeyer saw himself more modestly as only one of Frost's early admirers. Both men were good for one another, to be sure, their friendship mutually rewarding. Given the wealth of words that passed between them, Frost and Untermeyer evidently created a bit of each other.

References and further reading: R. Frost, *Letters to Untermeyer*, 4, 59, 339, 342, 369,

384; Stanlis, "Acceptable," 268; Untermeyer, ed., *Come In and Other Poems* (New York: Holt, 1943), and *The Road Not Taken: An Introduction to Robert Frost* (New York: 1951).

Jason G. Horn

"U.S. 1946 KING'S X" is one of six Frost poems preceding Massachusetts Institute of Technology (MIT) physicist–president Karl T. Compton's polemic "If the Atomic Bomb Had Not Been Used" in the *Atlantic Monthly* (Dec. 1946). It was subsequently collected in *Steeple Bush* **(1947)**. This chiastic quatrain is an early example of a new topos—nuclear literature.

"King's X!"—a truce term called with fingers crossed—invokes "time out" during tag. Etymologies vary, but most likely the term is an echo of royal clemency or excuse ("double crossing," of later origin, indicates reneging on commitments).

In July 1946, a month after introducing a United Nations plan for establishing international controls over nuclear activities, the United States detonated two atomic tests in the Pacific. Children's idioms embodying hypocrisy carry the satire. Frost also notably capitalizes "Holocaust," a wholly burnt offering (*Septuagint*), referring to nuclear destruction. Frost's note, "—Recent Riptonian," refers to one of his **homes**, Ripton, Vermont.

Steeple Bush (1947) contains eleven "Editorials" addressing folly, **politics, science**, and things nuclear—all elements of the poem. **"The Planners," "Bursting Rapture,"** and obliquely **"Why Wait for Science"** also include nuclear allusions. Thompson and Winnick note nuclear prescience already in **"It Is Almost the Year Two Thousand" (A Witness Tree, [1942])**.

References and further reading: Hadley Hamilton, *The United States: Guardian of Atomic Weapons* (New York. B. H. Tyrrel, 1947); Thompson and Winnick.

Kirk C. Allison

v

"VALLEY'S SINGING DAY, THE," was first published in *Harper's* (Dec. 1920) and later included in *New Hampshire* **(1923)** as one of the volume's "Grace Notes." The poem's ten couplets are written in relatively long lines—ten to twelve syllables—in a combination of anapestic and iambic feet not unusual in Frost's poetry. The "you" to whom the poem is addressed (often understood to be Frost's wife **Elinor**) has risen before dawn and slipped quietly out of the house and thus claims, for once, to have awakened the first songbird "that awakened all the rest." The speaker, although he reports that he was asleep while all this happened, nevertheless states that he believes and will confirm her claim.

This is a poem whose language is full of love and sensual delight: from sleeping under a dripping roof to walking on wet grass, from watching the first slender rays of morning sun cross a cloud to watching the "pearls" of rain turn "to diamonds in the sun." It is a poem in which the individual and nature together celebrate being alive by "loosing the pent-up music of over-night." Kathryn Gibbs Harris reads it as a tribute to Elinor for inspiring Frost's own work. Readers less inclined to such symbolic interpretation may see the tribute to the woman in the poem as simply an extension of the happiness that the speaker feels in the sheer delight of morning.

James L. Potter points out that the poem may also be about the creation of poetry. He writes, "Frost suggests that song—that is, poetry—is potential in nature, but that it needs man to bring it out, to shape it." In the poem, Frost inverts the common idea that nature inspires human song by suggesting that, at least this once, nature's song was not "self-begun." Additionally, the poem speaks to the power of language to shape an experience and give it meaning for the individual. That the early riser in the poem actually "opened the valley's singing day" becomes truth through the speaker's telling of it, which is itself an imaginative reconstruction since he was asleep at the time. Frost would argue some years later that "Nature reaches its height of form and through us exceeds itself." The woman's predawn walk—like the speaker's confirmation and the poet's poem—is a "small man-made figure of order and concentration." In his "Letter to *The Amherst Student*," Frost continues, "To me, any form I assert upon [chaos] is velvet, as the saying is, and to be considered for how much more it is than nothing." *See also* **Nature Poet and Naturalist**.

References and further reading: R. Frost, "Letter to *The Amherst Student*," *Collected*, 740; Harris, "Lyric Impulse"; Potter, 94.

Todd Lieber

"VANISHING RED, THE," was first published in *The Craftsman* (July 1916) and included in *Mountain Interval* that same year. Lawrance Thompson places "The Vanishing Red" as having been written in 1915 or 1916 at Frost's farm in **Franconia, New Hampshire**.

The poem, set around the turn of the nineteenth century, tells the story of a miller who deliberately pushes an American Indian man into the machinery of the wheel pit, thus killing "the last Red Man / In Acton." Not only is there no sign of hesitation or remorse on the murderer's part, but there is no indication of moral repugnance on the poet's part, either. The poet says, in fact, "You can't get back and see it as he [the miller] saw it. / It's too long a story to go into now."

The poem suggests that John (the Indian) and the mill simply could not co-exist. The miller had found himself "disgusted" by John's amazement at the mill's workings: John had unintentionally made it clear that he doesn't belong in the world of industry. The miller simply decides that the long history of the destruction of American Indians might as well be concluded at this moment. As the miller says, "I hold with getting a thing done with"—"thing" meaning, apparently, the extermination of the American Indians.

Jean Gould notes briefly that the sober, nonjudgmental depiction of murder has been compared to the account of the homicides that conclude Frost's one-act play *A Way Out*. The unagitated tone might be compared with other poems about death as well, such as "The Witch of Coös" and " **'Out, Out—.'** "

Although, as Robert Newdick reports, Frost complained that his publisher had hurried him in getting *Mountain Interval* into print and that he therefore hadn't been able to arrange the poems to his liking, the sequence of poems does cast some light on "The Vanishing Red." It appears immediately after **"The Line-Gang,"** which presents the heedless destruction of nature in order to make way for telephone and telegraph lines. The forest that the line-gang destroys is left "less cut than broken," as is John. The pairing of the poems suggests that the forest primeval and its inhabitants are sacrifices to the march of Progress.

References and further reading: Gould; Mertins, 151; Newdick, *Season*, 272; Thompson, *Triumph*.

Richard Wakefield

"VANTAGE POINT, THE," was first collected in *A Boy's Will* (1913), although according to Jeffrey Cramer, **Susan Hayes Ward** received an earlier draft of the poem in August 1907, then entitled "Choice of Society." "The Vantage Point" suggests how skillfully Frost handles the **sonnet** form; it is a Petrarchan sonnet, with a slight variation in rhyme scheme (the octave rhymes *abbaacca* instead of *abbaabba*). A "vantage point," of course, is a fixed position of control—a place from which to command something. It affords one a way to throw things into order, the better to manage and contain them. "Vantage" also has a specifically military meaning: It is high ground used for attack or reconnaissance. The various definitions explain why the matter of form is so important in this sonnet, which is itself humorously aggressive, even a little imperial and proprietary in its bearing. Frost manages the Petrarchan form tightly, as is perfectly appropriate in a poem that considers one way to handle, by a kind of leveraging perspective, our experience. The "vantage" in the sonnet is telescopic in the octave, where the speaker, himself "unseen," sees "in white defined / Far off the homes of men, and farther still, / The graves of men . . . / Living or dead," jauntily adding, "whichever are to mind." By contrast, the "vantage" is microscopic in the sestet, where the speaker, himself much magnified, takes a Thoreauvian (*see* **Thoreau**) look down into "the crater of the ant": his breathing, Gulliver-like, "shakes the bluet like a breeze." The joint linking the two vantages is the "turn" in the sonnet, and Paul Fussell has called attention to the wit with which Frost aligns the turn with the *physical* turn that the speaker himself executes: "I have but to turn on my arm," he says, and glides into the sestet. (The turn, it should be added, is delayed in fine Miltonic fashion.) The performance, in a word, is bravura: Frost, self-possessed as ever in the sonnet form, and every bit as secure as his speaker, is simply showing off. The cocky manner of the poem, its mood of ease and surplus power, sorts well with one theme that the title of the volume in which it first appeared suggests: the intransigent, gratifying willfullness and self-assurance of a certain kind of American boy. Frost's gloss on the poem in the first edition of *A Boy's Will* suggests that, in it, the speaker is "again scornful, but there is no one hurt." The mood of the poem is perhaps best characterized by a phrase from **Emerson**'s "Uriel," one of Frost's favorite poems: "cherub scorn." It is one of the more engaging moods of *A Boy's Will*, though not by any means the mood most often engaged.

References and further reading: Cramer, *Frost among His Poems*; Paul Fussell, *Poetic Meter and Poetic Form* (New York: Random House, 1979), 101–3, 109–26; Poirier, *Knowing*.

Mark Richardson

"VINDICTIVES, THE," first appeared in *A Further Range* (1936), where it was grouped under the title "The Outlands" along with **"The Bearer of Evil Tidings"** and **"Iris by Night."** The poem is somewhat unusual for Frost in its setting of ancient South American history as opposed to a traditional New England rural setting. J. M. Linebarger argues that Frost conflated and changed the details he found in William H. Prescott's *The Conquest of Peru* and *The Conquest of Mexico* as the basis for the poem. The titular subjects are the Inca people who hide their gold from the conquering Spanish led by Francisco Pizarro. A harsh, moralistic tone is evident, beginning with the accusatory "You like to hear about gold." The contrast is clear between the native Inca Indians, who see gold in quotidian terms, and the Spanish conquistadores, who see it in terms of wealth and power.

References and further reading: L. Francis, "Majesty of Stones"; Linebarger.

Eric Leuschner

"VOICE WAYS," first published in the *Yale Review* (Winter 1936) and collected that same year in *A Further Range*, is an eight-line poem in which Frost's speaker imagines a brief, playful exchange between himself and an unnamed person. The setting of the poem, a clear night when the stars and mountains are visible, inspires the speaker to compare the apparent clarity of the physical world to the mystery of things that can never be known. Playing on the various meanings of the word "clear" used throughout the poem, the speaker's cynical interlocutor quips that some things can be "clear" but implies that clarity is only superficial. Thus, through an intimate, lighthearted moment of human interaction, the poem ultimately affirms a skeptical vision of people's inability to comprehend the world.

Although "Voice Ways" has received little critical attention, it briefly explores a number of Frost's recurrent themes, including the connections between the human mind and the natural world and the questioning of our ability to understand ourselves and the universe.

References and further reading: Cramer, *Frost among His Poems*; Marcus, *Explication*; Poirier, *Knowing*.

Audra Rouse

W

"WAITING," when it appeared first in **A Boy's Will (1913)**, was glossed in the contents with its subtitle, "Afield at Dusk," and the statement, "He arrives at the turn of the year." Both suggest a poem concerned with margins—between day and evening and between years—but the reader is likely to find only obscure connections to such thematic concerns, which are more obvious in other poems. The speaker, presumably the youth of *A Boy's Will*, enters a "stubble field" in which numerous haycocks stand beneath a "rising full moon." He sits down, leaning against a haycock in the moonlight, with a "worn book" (perhaps **Palgrave's *Golden Treasury***) in hand, and "dream[s] upon" the flying antics of several birds (nighthawks, bats, and swallows), upon the "worn book" (which he does not read here but seems to know well), and upon, most of all, "the memory of one absent" for whom the poem itself is said to be composed as an offering. By such progression of dreams, Frost links nature's sounds to human emotions. The rural, moonlit field, deserted by its day laborers, is well fitted for a young poet's dreaming, and nature offers him a range of voices for response. He hears the nighthawk's "vague unearthly cry," senses the bat's "mute antics," and listens to a grating "rasp" (of a cricket?)—an "antiphony of afterglow." For a poet hoping to find his own voice, such calls of nature's singers and those of already published human voices of "old-golden song" invite a responding song, and the poem itself is that response—not a strong, dramatic assertion of his own voice but simple testimony to his "waiting" and listening, to his desire to "freshen" the old songs in service of remembering his absent beloved.

References and further reading: Poirier, *Knowing*.

Douglas Watson

WARD, SUSAN HAYES. The Frost and Ward Papers, the latter housed in the Huntington Library, reveal an empathic correspondence between the two families that began with the acceptance of **"My Butterfly"** for publication on the front page of the 8 November 1894 issue of *The New York Independent*, of which Susan Hayes Ward served as literary editor and her brother, Dr. William Hayes Ward, as editor. Up until shortly before Frost's departure for **England** and public recognition, other of his poems would appear in the pages of *The Independent*: "The Birds Do Thus," "Caesar's Lost Transport Ships," "Warning," "The Quest of the Orchis," **"The Trial by Existence,"** and "Across the Atlantic."

Frost's lifelong friendship with Susan Hayes Ward was unusual in the depth of reciprocal caring. The timing of their initial encounter—Ward an accomplished editor and author of books, Frost the sensitive youth of nineteen, ready to assume his identity as poet—shaped their relations. Frost doubtless stood in awe of the illustrious Ward family, but he instinctively trusted Ward's spiritual strength and intelligence, receiving from her the praise for which he yearned.

The Reverend Ward, however, was more severe in his assessment of the young poet. A missionary and scholar in the classics and archaeology, he also wrote religious poetry and literary criticism, including a lengthy memorial to Sidney Lanier; he urged Frost to improve both his theoretical base and sense of moral purpose by studying Lanier's verses and his recently published treatise *The Science of English Verse*. He considered sterling attributes Lanier's passion for music and search for moral beauty and truth. He denounced as atheistic Henri Bergson's work *Creative Evolution*, whose dualistic approach to **science** and **religion** appealed to Frost, and he criticized what he viewed as ridicule of the Christian ideals in Frost's early uncollected poem "My Giving." The aspiring youth should not have been surprised when other poems were viewed as inferior for their proximity to talk. In discussions with the Wards, Frost was just beginning to formulate his peculiar approach to the "sound of sense"; he only vaguely sensed that the musicality his would-be benefactors were urging upon him was almost diametrically opposed to a sought-for diction, rooted in experience and reflecting the vernacular. While "My Butterfly" had catered to the late Victorian fashion of the day, Frost soon recognized in certain of its lines the suggestion of his emerging idiom.

Frost had first met Susan Hayes Ward in Boston's North Station to receive the $15 payment for "My Butterfly." Putting the timid poet at ease, Ward opened the way for a friendship spanning almost four decades that included **Elinor** and the children. In 1911, Frost wrote Ward requesting an invitation to visit her at her home in Newark; with his request, he forwarded a Christmas packet of seventeen of his unpublished poems: "It represents, needless to tell *you*, not the long deferred forward movement you are living in wait for, but only the grim stand it was necessary for me to make until I should gather myself together. The forward movement is to begin next year," he announced prophetically.

Since the appearance of "My Butterfly" in *The Independent*, only a smattering of Frost's poems had been printed in U.S. magazines and periodicals. He was understandably elated when *A Boy's Will* was accepted for publication shortly after his arrival in England, and he quickly sent a copy to Ward, whose belief in his poetic talents had sustained him. Following his return to America in 1915 to enthusiastic reviews of his first two books, Frost on occasion would visit Ward in South Berwick, Maine, where she and her brother and sister were living out their days in the family homestead. During one such visit, shortly before her death in 1916, Ward importuned Frost to compose a poem based on some childhood memory of hers about a "little boyish girl" who could not let go of the birch tree while trying to reach the fox grapes growing there. The result was **"Wild Grapes,"** acknowledged by Frost as having been

written by request of Susan Hayes Ward as a companion piece of mine called **Birches**. She said Birches was for boys and she wanted me to do another like it on nearly the same subject for girls. For all we so seldom saw each other we were great friends. My wife and I both cared for her more than I can tell. (Frost to Herbert Ward, 27 Dec. 1923, **Amherst College** Library)

References and further reading: R. Frost, *Selected Letters*, 43; Pritchard, *Literary Life*; Thompson, *Early Years*; The Ward Papers, Huntington Library, San Marino, CA.

Lesley Lee Francis

"WASPISH" was collected in *A Further Range* (**1936**). It was titled "Name Untried" when Frost sent Louis Mertins a copy on 10 September 1935 and "Untried" when it was first published as one of the original "Ten Mills" in the April 1936 issue of *Poetry* magazine. It has been titled "Waspish" in all its subsequent book publications, perhaps to avoid two riddle poems in a row, as the next "Mill" is the riddle poem **"One Guess."**

A playful poem, it nonetheless alludes to one of Frost's more serious themes: that of the individual's powerlessness in the face of nature. Just as it is fallacious for the relatively small wasp to consider himself "as good as anybody going" simply because he possesses an annoying weapon, so are we humans often mistaken regarding our ability to control the forces of nature. Given the political nature of the volume in which the poem appeared, it can be read as a warning against nationalistic pride. (*See* **Politics**.)

When Frost's friend Leonidas W. Payne, Jr., of the University of Texas, surprised him with a list of stylistic "errors" in the **Collected Poems**, Frost bridled. He responded particularly waspishly to Payne's "correction" of "Waspish": "Substituting *but that* for *but* in 'Waspish' would show school girl timidity and spoil my metrics. *But* alone will be found all the way down our literature. I noticed it tonight in Robinson Crusoe."

References and further reading: Cramer, *Frost among His Poems*; R. Frost, *Selected Letters*, 370.

Andy Duncan

WAY OUT, A. See Drama.

"[WE VAINLY WRESTLE WITH THE BLIND BELIEF]," published in Frost's final volume of poetry, *In the Clearing* **(1962)**, actually predates his first published volume, *A Boy's Will* **(1913)**. The poem is the final quatrain of his unpublished 1911 poem "New Grief." Frost would often salvage a good couplet or quatrain from an unsuccessful **sonnet** or longer poem.

"New Grief" describes a broken-hearted lover wandering alone "like a holy nun" where two had walked before. The lover, a woman, cannot indicate when love may return or when it had departed. The poem explains that love does not die easily since it is difficult to believe that anything one cherished "Can ever quite pass into utter grief, / Or wholly perish."

Removed from the context of the longer love poem, the quatrain takes on a more universal significance regarding belief. Looking back over his life and career—his placing this poem so near the end of what he knew was his final volume gives the poem an ultimate sense of summing up—the poet realizes that although it is a "blind belief," nonetheless it is difficult truly to believe that those things that are of great importance to a person could ever quite pass into complete oblivion. That Frost includes poetry among those things of importance is confirmed in the phrase "utter grief," for in his introduction to **E. A. Robinson**'s *King Jasper*, he asserts his preference for poetry made not of "grievances" but of "griefs."

References and further reading: Cramer, *Frost among His Poems*; R. Frost, "Introduction to E. A. Robinson's 'King Jasper,' " *Collected*, 743.

Jeffrey S. Cramer

"WERE I IN TROUBLE." *See* **"Five Nocturnes."**

"WEST-RUNNING BROOK," first published in *West-Running Brook* **(1928)**, is a dialogue with a few very brief narrative intrusions. Although the poem is set near the Frost farm in **Derry**, New Hampshire, by 1926, when Frost wrote the poem (although some sources cite an unfinished version as early as 1920), he and his family had been away from Derry for fifteen years. The poem is not nostalgic, nor does it convey the immediate, felt experience of many of his other poems set in the area. In this case Frost seems to have deliberately chosen a natural phenomenon, a brook that runs west in a region where most brooks run east, for its metaphorical uses rather than for its acquired meaning for him personally.

In particular, Frost sees the brook's perversity as a metaphor for what he believes is an essential human impulse to move against the grain. He suggests that we become aware of ourselves as individuals when we resist natural or social forces. In the very early poem **"Reluctance,"** for example, he asks when it is "ever less than a treason / To go with the drift of things." A well-known example is **"The Road Not Taken,"** where, whatever the reality of the evidence on which the speaker has made his choice, he at least has desired to take the road that he believes may have seen less traffic.

In "West-Running Brook" the thought runs a course from playful to profound. The dialogue begins in facts, moves to banter, and flows into profundity. As the couple talk about the brook, they talk about themselves as well. They find themselves (and their relationship) represented in the brook.

They begin with the simple fact of orientation. The woman asks which way north lies, and the man answers, adding that the brook runs west. The woman responds that its name should therefore be "West-running Brook." In a parenthetical aside a narrative voice interrupts to tell us, "West-running Brook men call it to this day." The implication is that the dialogue will have influence beyond these two people and beyond this moment; the parenthetical comment suggests that some little current of history will flow from their conversation.

A metaphor springs from the facts as the woman claims that she can "go by contraries" with her husband just as the brook goes by contraries—that is, against what is expected or demanded. The woman is so taken with the comparison that she declares the brook a third partner in their marriage; she adds that the bridge they build across the brook will be "Our arm thrown over it asleep beside it." She points to a waving ripple in the water as evidence that the brook hears and understands her.

The man good-naturedly brings in more fact to counterbalance his wife's fanciful ideas. He tells her the wave has always been there, caused by a rock below the surface. But he slyly allows some truth to his wife's metaphor by making a play on words. He tells her the wave has been there "Ever since rivers . . . / Were made in heaven," a twist on the old saying that marriages are made in heaven. The woman concedes that he is correct, but she maintains that she is, too. In saying that they are both right, she claims in effect that subjective truth can complement rather than contradict objective truth.

After some more teasing, the man launches into a philosophical treatise on the brook as a metaphor for human origins, human ontology, human consummations. To him the brook's wave, its gesture, so to speak, reflects the deep human tendency to resist flowing into "The universal cataract of death." He says, "It is this backward motion toward the source, / Against the stream, that most we see ourselves in."

For some critics "West-Running Brook" is one of Frost's more unfortunate lapses into didacticism. Indeed, it lacks the small but telling details that create vivid scenes and characters in Frost's other dialogue poems, including such lighthearted ones as **"A Hundred Collars"** and **"The Housekeeper."** Almost half the poem is made up of the man's somber, rather pompous disquisition on the brook's symbolism of metaphysical truths. The man alludes to the first-century B.C. Roman philosopher Lucretius and to the nineteenth-century physician and philosopher Havelock Ellis. Neither possibility is far-fetched. Frost's knowledge of classical poetry and philosophy matched his knowledge of the great thinkers of his own day. And certainly such allusions occur all through his work, sometimes even at the level of the prosody itself, as in **"For Once, Then, Something,"** in which he uses lines based on the Latin form of hendecasyllables and then weaves in allusions to classical **philosophy** and mythology.

Here, however, the allusions are part of a set-piece speech, already rather abstract despite its ostensible inspiration in nature. In, say, **"The Tuft of Flowers"** the subtle allusions to the Ninetieth Psalm and to Isaiah 40:6–8 (where the individual's life is compared to that of the flowers and grass of the field) work because it is a deep part of the speaker's way of looking at the world. On the other hand, in "West-Running Brook" the allusions tell us only that the man has perhaps read more than he has digested.

However, if we read the man's long speech as if it were itself a stream, we can see Lucretius and Ellis (and any other undetected influences) as the course his consciousness must run. They are the obstacles that would turn him if he allowed them to, but in each instance, he resists. Viewed in this way, the poem becomes an expression of ideas Frost derived from William James. Once we see James's influence we recognize that the poem is truly "made of metaphor" as Frost said a poem should be in his essay "The Constant Symbol."

The entire poem can be read as an extension of William James's famous metaphor "the stream of consciousness." James used the phrase as the title for a chapter of *Psychology: Briefer Course* (1892), which Frost studied as a student at **Harvard** and which he assigned his own students when he taught at the **Plymouth Normal School**, New Hampshire. Then, in "Will," a subsequent chapter of the same book, James proposes that we can define an "ideal" or "moral" action (or thought) as one that is undertaken against resistance, as the wave of the stream in "West-Running Brook" is an action against resistance. Although such actions make up only a small portion of our lives, James says, the rest being habit, they are nevertheless when we are most aware of ourselves, most alive. In James, then, Frost found his metaphors: the stream of consciousness, the backward gesture of resistance.

In "Education by Poetry" (1930) Frost wrote, "Poetry begins in trivial metaphors, pretty metaphors, 'grace' metaphors, and goes on to the profoundest thinking that we have." The sequence, from trivial to profound, describes the "flow" of "West-Running Brook." In the same essay he wrote, "Greatest of all attempts to say one thing in terms of another is the philosophical attempt to say matter in terms of spirit, or spirit in terms of matter, to make the final unity." In the country brook near his farm Frost found a way to say spirit in terms of matter. He found the stream that flowed and paused in its own characteristic way, the perfect natural metaphor for William James's theory of psychology.

Frost uses some of the same themes and imagery to more lyrical effect in the **sonnet "The Master Speed,"** written as a gift upon his daughter's wedding.

References and further reading: R. Frost, "The Constant Symbol," *Collected*, 786, and "Education by Poetry," *Collected*, 719, 723; William James, *Writings: 1878–1899* (New York: Library of America, 1992); Parini, *A Life*, 240–43.

Richard Wakefield

WEST-RUNNING BROOK **(1928)** was Frost's fifth collection of poetry. The initial critical response was somewhat less enthusiastic than that which had greeted its predecessors; reviewers were disappointed, for example, by the fact that Frost seemed to be turning away from his innovative narrative poetry. In general, the volume betrays an enhanced appetite for overt philosophical reflection and public pronouncement of the sort in which Frost would increasingly indulge in later work. The volume has never been regarded as among Frost's strongest; nonetheless, it does contain a number of poems that have come to be widely admired, including the long title poem, as well as **"Spring Pools," "Acceptance," "Once by the Pacific," "Bereft," "Tree at My Window,"** and **"Acquainted with the Night."**

The book was initially divided into six sections, some with epigraphs: I, entitled "Spring Pools" (with the epigraph, "From snow that melted only yesterday"), from the poem of that title to "Acceptance"; II, "Fiat Nox" (epigraph, "Let the night be too dark for me to see / Into the future. Let what will be, be."), from "Once by the Pacific" to "Acquainted with the Night"; III, **"West-Running Brook"**; IV, "Sand Dunes," from **"Sand Dunes"** to **"The Flower Boat"**; V, "Over Back," from **"The Times Table"** to **"The Birthplace"**; and VI, "My Native Simile" (epigraph, "The sevenfold sophie of Minerve"), from **"The Door in the Dark"** to **"The Bear."** When the poems were republished in *Collected Poems* in 1930, the divisions were omitted and three more pieces— **"The Lovely Shall be Choosers," "What Fifty Said,"** and **"The Egg and the Machine"**—were included. The division into sections loosely reflects what may be said to be the overriding theme of the volume—a conflict between natural forces of destruction and decline and those of resistance and recovery—a theme most completely developed in the poem from which the volume took its title.

The best-known poem in section I, "Spring Pools," establishes the opposition between the fragile space of beauty, represented by the bright puddles left by recently melted snow, and the ominous indifference of "The trees that have it in their pent-up buds / To darken nature" and "blot out and drink up and sweep away" the delicate pools. Nature, in *West-Running Brook*, appears as often as not in a "darkened" form, and John Lynen has, not without reason, called the poem "sinister." Nature threatens not just its own transiently beautiful phenomena but, more profoundly, the possibility of any meaningful relation with the human. The spring pools may also stand for the reflective power of poetic response, which creates significant patterns just as the pools do when they reflect the flowers around them, as is suggested by the emphatic symmetry of the line, "These flowery waters and these watery flowers." Nature thus has the power to "blot out" poetry as well, in its indifference to human attempts to find meaning in it.

The other poems in the first section take up, in various ways, the question of whether there is any correspondence between the human and the natural. Some seem to allow for a relaxed exchange. In **"The Freedom of the Moon,"** the speaker playfully imagines himself placing the moon at will, "As you might try a jewel in your hair" or pulling it "from a crate of crooked trees." **"The Rose Family"** juxtaposes the shifting botanical definitions of "rose" and its endurance as metaphor. The eternal rhythm of the sea seems to serve in **"Devotion"** as the perfect metaphor for the human aspiration to deathless fidelity. But in other pieces, the relation is more troubled. In **"Fireflies in the Garden,"** the earthly fireflies seem to achieve a momentary correspondence with "real stars" but "can't sustain the part"; **"Atmosphere"** opposes an enclosed garden to the world outside, where "Winds blow the open grassy places bleak"; and in **"On Going Unnoticed,"** the speaker looks up at the indifferent towering forest above him. **"The Cocoon"** is somewhat ambiguous: The "cocoon" of smoke that surrounds the lonely cottage, on the one hand, anchors it to earth and moon but, on the other, only enhances its isolation. **"A Passing Glimpse"** suggests that whatever meaning we see in nature is given only on the condition that we do not look too directly or closely. The section closes with "Acceptance," which depicts the coming on of a somewhat ominous night and so leads into the next section, "Fiat Nox."

This segment opens with the well-known "Once by the Pacific," a portentous vision of an imminent apocalypse. A similarly dark vision of nature persists in **"Lodged,"** "Bereft," "Tree at My Window," and **"The Peaceful Shepherd."** Even in **"A Winter Eden,"** which depicts a snow-bound "paradise," the emphasis is on the fragility and brevity of the interlude. Another poem that finds a positive power in nature is **"The Thatch,"** where the speaker is moved beyond what is probably spite toward his wife by the sight of birds patiently suffering through a winter night; but here again, the piece ends with a coda that suggests that the interval of domestic harmony was at best temporary.

Most of the poems, however, have an edge of irony, which makes it clear that the poet is inventing nature in the image of his own mood. In "Bereft" he imagines wind-blown leaves striking at his leg like a snake, but in "The Peaceful Shepherd," the speaker acknowledges he is reading a meaning into nature. Perhaps the bleakest piece is the last one, "Acquainted with the Night," in which the speaker can find no connection at all with the world around him, human or natural. One of Frost's rare poems with an urban setting, it has often been read as his gloomiest reflection on the alienated condition of the individual in the twentieth century. By inserting "The Lovely Shall Be Choosers" in the 1930 *Collected Poems*, Frost ends on a more affirmative note. The poem is a veiled tribute to his beloved mother, hurled down by choosing to "refuse love safe with wealth and honor"; in spite of her afflictions, she is redeemed by endurance and recognition of "some *one* with eyes to see," one who will one day write this poem.

"West-Running Brook" occupies a central position in the collection and may be said to mark the shift from a tone of despair to something more hopeful. It is the only example in the book of the dialogue form that Frost had handled so brilliantly in previous volumes. Although it bears some similarity to his earlier husband-wife scripts, "West-Running Brook" is really more interested in the contest of philosophical ideas than in the dramatic confrontation of individuals and is closer to dialectic than dialogue. The themes of the poem are the recurrent themes of the book: the conflict between the forces of decline and the sources of recovery, and the possibility of finding human significance in the natural world.

The section entitled "Sand Dunes" opens with the piece of that name. As in "Spring Pools" and "Once by the Pacific," nature's designs with regard to the individual seem mostly malevolent. But, in contrast to the earlier poems, the conclusion is hopeful, for men can abandon their buried structures and be "but more free to think." The other poems are equally affirmative. Some celebrate heroism in adversity, like **"Hannibal"** or **"A Soldier."** Some commemorate more homely examples of fortitude, like **"Canis Major,"** in which the speaker finds in the constellations of the "great Overdog" an inspiration for the underdog, or "The Flower Boat," an amiable portrait of a retired fisherman who has planted his dory with flowers, while he waits for a death confidently imagined as a journey to "the Happy Isles."

As the title "Over Back" implies, the four poems in the next section have rustic settings and characters. All, in one way or another, deal with the constant struggle to make a space for human habitation in the wild and the rapidity with which the wild takes back that space. The lugubrious fatalism of the farmer in "The Times Table," for whom every sigh is one more step in the direction of death, represents for the speaker a surrender that threatens to "bring back nature in people's place." The inhabitants of the freshly painted house with its jangling piano in **"The Investment,"** on the other hand, represent a more positive response, a decision "Not to sink under being man and wife, / But get some color and music out of life." In **"The Last Mowing,"** an abandoned field has been ceded to nature, and only for an interval will there be a "chance for the flowers" before the trees, like those in "Spring Pools," "March into a shadowy claim" and take away their light. **"The Birthplace"** depicts a more benign Wordsworthian nature, in the form of a motherly mountain, but one that is quickly done with humans: "The mountain pushed us off her knees. / And now her lap is full of trees."

The final segment, "My Native Simile," is a miscellaneous collection of poetical reflections, many highly self-conscious in their use of whimsical correspondences and conceits. "The Door in the Dark" appears to be preparing the reader for some of the imaginative exercises that will follow. Walking into the door, the speaker has his "native simile jarred. / So people and things don't pair any more / With what they used to pair with before." The next poem, **"Dust in the Eyes,"** proposes to seek out the cognitive disorientation that arrived unexpectedly in "The Door in the Dark," even if it should "blind me to a standstill if it must." **"Sitting by a Bush in Broad Sunlight"** is the only overtly religious poem in the volume and one of Frost's most direct statements of faith. The wit in **"The Armful"** lies in its allegorical depiction of the speaker, trying to hold together a lifetime's accumulation of diverse and contradictory convictions and ideas, as a slapstick acrobat struggling to balance a heap of awkward parcels. "What Fifty Said," written in Housman-like meters, is a gently ironic reflection on the vicissitudes of fashion—perhaps specifically, it has been suggested, poetic fashion, which underwent such dramatic shifts in Frost's lifetime as a poet. The remaining poems are dedicated to broader philosophical questions, what Frost elsewhere calls the "larger excruciations." **"Riders"** takes up a favored metaphor in his critical writings, suggesting that the individual's relation to the world is that of rider to his mount; it ends on a hopeful note, concluding that although the latter may be running "unbridled off its course," nonetheless "We have ideas yet that we haven't tried." In another night sky poem, **"On Looking Up by Chance at the Constellations,"** the speaker deflates the human ambition to find disastrous signs in the vast spectacle of the universe. "The Bear" continues this ironic vein, contrasting the unconscious liberty of a roaming bear with the restless mind of the individual, caged by his own scientific theories and philosophical systems, who "all day fights a nervous inward rage, / His mood rejecting all his mind suggests." *West-Running Brook* concluded with "The Bear," but in *Collected Poems* (1930) Frost added "The Egg and the Machine," which carries the strain of discontent with civilization to the borders of self-parody: So enraged is the man in the poem by the noisy intrusion of a railroad engine into his pastoral that he digs up a nest of turtle eggs and declares himself "armed for war" against "the gods in the machine."

References and further reading: Brower; Lentricchia, *Modern Poetics*; Lynen, *Pastoral Art*, 149; Poirier, *Knowing*; Thompson, *Triumph*.

David Evans

"WHAT FIFTY SAID," added to *West-Running Brook* (1928) in the 1930 *Collected Poems*, examines Frost's attitudes at age fifty toward education, schooling, and creativity. The two stanzas contrast his experiences as a student and as a **teacher**, rejecting the conformity required by traditional schooling. The first stanza suggests that teachers' attempts to mold students' minds according to ideas of the past are ineffectual, an idea confirmed by the second stanza in the phrase "what can't be molded." The poem also examines the contrasts between youth and age, concluding optimistically that one generation can learn from the next. Frost discusses his ideas about the appropriate content of schooling in "Poetry and School." Joan Peters reviews Frost's promotion of the poet's role as teacher. Richard Poirier and Kyle Norwood explore Frost's attitudes toward the poetic creation of order, identified in the poem's contrast between "fire" and "form."

References and further reading: R. Frost, "Poetry and School," *Collected*; Norwood; Peters; Poirier, *Knowing*.

Nanette Cumley Tamer

WHITE, ELINOR MIRIAM. *See* **Frost, Elinor Miriam White**.

"WHITE-TAILED HORNET, THE," subtitled "The Revision of Theories" in the "Taken Doubly" section of *A Further Range* (**1936**), appeared earlier in spring of that same year in the *Yale Review* with the subtitle "Or Doubts about an Instinct." The poem, a satiric fable, questions the idea that animal instinct is infallible, or in Frost's words, the theory that "to err is human, not to, animal."

Frost's topic at a 1953 talk at **Bread Loaf School of English** was "On Being Let in on Symbols." While Frost didn't want people to be "straining too much" to understand symbols, he said that any story that has value must have "intimations of something more than itself." He added that "the first surface meaning, the anecdote, the parable . . . has got to be good and got to be sufficient in itself. If you don't want any more you can leave it at that." He then read "The White-Tailed Hornet" as an example of a story whose surface meaning is sufficient in itself.

The poem begins with the narrator's observation of a white-tailed hornet. The narrator notes that a hornet emerging from its nest is "more unerring than a bullet" because it can "change his aim in flight." Yet the hornet is an "execrable judge of motives" because it cannot see the narrator as the exception to the usual run of humanity who would hang an empty hornet's nest in the house as a trophy. After the hornet stings the narrator, the narrator goes to the hornet's nest to observe him. The hornet is going after flies to feed "his thumping grubs as big as he is," but he mistakenly gets a nailhead instead, not just once but twice. Next the hornet goes after a huckleberry. Finally, he goes after a fly, but misses. Here the narrator compares the erring hornet to a poet working with metaphor.

The hornet's poor performance raises the narrator's skepticism about the whole idea of the difference between human beings and animals. As long as the comparisons are upwards, comparing human beings with "gods and angels," he argues, "we were men at least." But when we begin to compare ourselves with the so-called lower animals, he argues, we find that only our fallibility separates us from the animals. And now the narrator observes that even an insect, thought to be driven by pure instinct, is fallible, suggesting that we are no different from the lower animals after all. Evidently, as George Monteiro and Robert Faggen demonstrate, Frost is playing with his own profound understanding of not only Darwinian evolutionary theory but the general view of both human and natural value and place in philosophical and scientific terms as described by **Emerson**, J. Henri Fabre, Henri Bergson, and others whose work fascinated Frost.

A note of explanation about the hornet's nest is in order since it has become the object of critical attention. Richard Poirier explains that the "balloon" where the hornet lives in the first line is actually a "Japanese crepe-paper globe" mentioned in line 18. Laurence Perrine objects, saying that both phrases are metaphors for the hornet's nest. The hornet's nest is shaped somewhat like a balloon, and it is made of a paperlike substance that the hornet produces by chewing wood and spitting it up. The hornet builds its nest on a tree limb. As the narrator mentions, some people take down an empty hornet's nest and display it as a home decoration.

B. J. Sokol raises a question about the type of hornet used in the poem. There is no white-tailed *hornet* in North America, but there is a white-tailed *hawk* and a white-*headed* hornet. Sokol argues that Frost is being deliberately confusing in combining the two terms, pointing out Frost's use of the term "hawking for flies."

The poem is, in fact, a study of metaphor, continually combining two seemingly unlike objects in a search for their similarities. The larger metaphor is that of human beings and the so-called lower animals; both, it seems, are alike in their fallibility. As Sokol points out, the hornet is like a hawk. The hornet's nest is like a balloon, which is like a Japanese crepe-paper globe. The hornet is like a poet making metaphors, seeing similarities between a fly and a nailhead, a fly and a huckleberry. The hole from which the hornet emerges from his nest is compared to "the pupil of a pointed gun," and the hornet coming out of the hole is compared to a bullet. In the third stanza, the narrator questions the value of making comparisons—or at least ones that compare humankind to anything lower. Finding the similarities between people and animals makes us "see our images / Reflected in the mud and even dust." On one level, the narrator is arguing against the use of poetry by saying that the use of metaphor denigrates humankind. But on another level, he is arguing that poetic metaphor is so powerful that it constructs reality.

References and further reading: **R. Cook**, "On Being Let in on Symbols: June 25, 1953," *Living Voice*, 36–44; Faggen; Monteiro, *New England*; Perrine, "House"; Poirier, *Knowing*; 270; Sokol.

Claudia Milstead

"WHY WAIT FOR SCIENCE" was first published as "Our Getaway" in *The New Hampshire Troubadour* (Nov. 1946) and appeared later in **Steeple Bush (1947)**, a volume that featured a triumphal return to the **sonnet** form. It is one of Frost's humorous sonnets on a subject about which he could also be serious. **Science** is unexpectedly characterized as feminine, perhaps suggesting its fatal attractions.

The questions Frost raises about the legacy of science were timely for the commencement of the nuclear age. Why should we trust science when she has made atomic weapons that could threaten our planet to the extent that we may need to flee to another world, to "some star off there say a half light-year / Through temperature of absolute zero"?

Against science, the speaker, as mere "amateur" (with its implications of "lover" and, thereby, poet), can only suggest that we can go "the same / As fifty million years ago we came." The problem with that solution, Frost seems to assert, is that there is no historical record and science cannot agree on that "way," whether with a "big bang" or not. What the poet has to offer is dependent first on human memory—and there is none—and then on the imagination. Having revealed the shortcomings of science, he can conclude only with ironic modesty: "I have a theory, but it hardly does." *See also* **Nature Poet and Naturalist**.

References and further reading: Comments on science in D. J. Hall, *Contours*; Thompson and Winnick.

Richard J. Calhoun

"WILD GRAPES," a 104-line poem published in *Harpers Magazine* (Dec. 1920) and later in *A Witness Tree* **(1942)**, counters a better-known birch swinger in trajectory and gender (*see* **"Birches"**). The inspiration behind the blank verse narrative is **Susan Hayes Ward**, Frost's discoverer and poetry editor of *The Independent* (published by her brother William). Frost's essay "The Way There" (1958) relates the request for a "Birches" for girls and cites an inner logic between the two birch-swinging poems for the progression of an unpublished collection. This birch is entwined by the tendrils of wild grapes, siblings, and gender tensions. Central are considerations of letting go with either hand, mind, or heart (for which Laurence Perrine finds parallels in **"Devotion"** and **"Reluctance"**) and the motion of translation and return.

Classical and historical allusions include "Leif the Lucky's German," either Tyrker, who discovered and returned with grape-laden vines, described by Helen Bacon as a New World Dionysus, or, in the view of Richard Poirier and Mark Richardson, Adam of Bremen, the eleventh-century chronicler who recounts Ericson's return from "Vinland" in *Gesta Hammaburgenis Ecclesiae Pontificum*, 1595.

George Bagby finds intertextual parallels in two works of Wordsworth, first in the poem "Nutting" (published 1800), where a young boy encounters a hazel tree that is laden with tempting clusters of fruit. (The boughs in "Nutting," however, are left broken and ravished, whereas those of "Wild Grapes" rebuff the human intruder.) A parallel in structure and lesson is drawn from the Simplon Pass episode of *The Prelude* (Book 6, 1790). Finally, Bagby emphasizes the Promethean elements of the poem in its dramatized opposition between "the power of the heart" and "prudential wisdom" or intellect.

Bacon uncovers connections to the ascending and descending Eurydice and to other pagan representations of emancipation of the feminine from traditional cultural regimes of domestication, and Katherine Kearns finds correspondences in Frost's **"Maple,"** interpreting the theme of return and rebirth as co-optation into a masculine order. *See also* **Nature Poet and Naturalist** and **"To Earthward."**

References and further reading: Bacon, "For Girls"; Bagby, *Nature*, 117–18; R. Frost, "The Way There," *Collected*, 847–48; Kearns; Perrine, "Letting Go."

Kirk C. Allison

"WILLFUL HOMING" first appeared in the *Saturday Review of Literature* (with **Louis Untermeyer**'s "Play in Poetry," Feb. 1938) and was collected in

A Witness Tree (1942), Frost's seventh volume of poetry. According to Jean Gould, the poem was written "just in his head, for he had no paper and pencil at hand," while Frost lay sick in bed with a fever. The cause of his illness, a long and cold journey home after dinner with **T. S. Eliot** and other poets at the St. Botolph Club, Boston, on 16 November 1932, may inform partially the poem's tone. Frost left the dinner gleeful over cleverly upbraiding his supposed rival Eliot for remarks concerning Robert Burns's poetic talents. Upon his arrival home, however, the illness set in, tempering the personally rewarding victory. In much the same way, "Willful Homing" at first seems to evoke a momentary triumph over the harsh forces of nature. Lost in a blizzard, a man finds himself forced to "sit astride a drift, / Imprint a saddle and calmly consider a course." After his brief rumination, the man finds his way back to a door and to a belated welcome.

Many critics, among them Marjorie Cook and **Reginald L. Cook**, see in the movement from suffering detachment to warm reunification a belief that, in the words of Marjorie Cook, "man can accomplish much of what doesn't seem possible." Reginald Cook concurs, stating that Frost sees the individual as not "wholly at the mercy of a mechanistic process." However, the poem also reverberates with Frost's more lingering fear: While verse serves as a "momentary stay against confusion" (from Frost's "The Figure a Poem Makes") and, as stated in "Willful Homing's" most powerful line, "Since he means to come to a door he will come to a door," humanity nevertheless finds itself "compromised" in its striving toward resolution. Although humanity ultimately arrives somewhere, its destination nearly always is "compromised of aim and rate" and "late," thus deserving of a somewhat muted welcome. Independence reluctantly is exchanged for a tepid welcome—oftentimes to a home one has not sought intentionally.

References and further reading: M. Cook, "Acceptance," 227; R. Cook, *Living Voice*, 279; R. Frost, "The Figure a Poem Makes," *Collected*, 777; Gould, 266; Lentricchia, *Modern Poetics*.

Dana E. Aspinall

"WIND AND THE RAIN, THE," first published in *A Witness Tree* (1942), is a poem about the disillusion that results from a life of suffering and loss. The poem is divided into two sections, in which nature imagery represents the speaker's various emotional states. In the first section, the speaker reflects on the naïveté of his youth from his present perspective of desolation and despair. He remembers walking through the woods in stormy autumn weather and embracing the season's signs of death with a sweet melancholy, untainted by the pain of actual death. Yet such pleasurable sadness of youth, the speaker suggests, foretells the real pain he will suffer as he experiences death repeatedly through the loss of others.

The second section of the poem begins with the image of a flower struggling to grow in an arid climate. The speaker wishes that he could flood the flower with oceans of water and symbolically regain the passion of his youth. Numbed by the losses he has suffered, he seeks out falling rain to replace the tears he can cry no longer. Unlike Shakespeare's Feste, whose final song in *Twelfth Night* is the source for the poem's title, the speaker is not content with singing about life's absurdities but seeks renewal in nature.

References and further reading: Cramer, *Frost among His Poems*; Parini, *A Life*, 317–19.

Audra Rouse

"WIND AND WINDOW FLOWER," first published in *A Boy's Will* (1913), has received little critical attention. Frost said in his preface to poems in *This Is My Best* that in compiling the book he "took thirty poems . . . to plot a curved line of flight away from people and so back to people." Notes in the table of contents of *A Boy's Will* explained each poem's place on the "curved line" that Frost ascribed to an alter ego he called "the youth," and of "Wind and Window Flower" he said, "Out of the winter things he fashions a story of modern love."

The "story" is about a flower that is safe in a warm house and the winter wind that would seduce it. Failing to win the flower from its secure dwelling, the wind moves on, seemingly unaffected. We can only guess how Frost intended the poem to comment on "modern love." Perhaps he saw the modern world as stimulating attractions between incompatible temperaments: The wind cannot be still and the flower cannot move. Frost saw such disharmony in his own parents' relationship, as various **biographers** have shown, and Lawrance Thompson, among others, claims that Frost's own marriage to **Elinor White** was equally ill-suited at times.

The poem is also a very early example of Frost's uses of wind and windows. See, for example, **"Storm Fear," "Tree at My Window,"** and "The Oft-Repeated Dream" from the sequence titled **"The Hill Wife."**

References and further reading: Burnshaw gives a sunny picture of Robert and Elinor's relationship but does not speculate on Frost's parents' marriage; the preface to poems in *This Is My Best* can be found in R. Frost, *Collected*, 783–84; Poirier, *Knowing*, mentions this poem briefly in his discussion of the psychological continuity among the poems in *A Boy's Will*; Thompson, *Early Years*, gives a detailed and dark view of the marriage of Frost's parents and of the marriage of Robert and Elinor.

Richard Wakefield

"WINTER EDEN, A," written in 1925, was first published in the *New Republic* (12 Jan. 1927) before being included in **West-Running Brook** (1928). Some critics read the poem as a suggestion for how to make the best of situations under less-than-favorable conditions. Most readers find the Eden of the poem to be postlapsarian. (For a prelapsarian reading, *see* **Reginald L. Cook.**) One critic has argued that all of Frost's forests are feminine temptations that call the innocent male Adam to sin and death; in this poem, the sexual corruption is evinced by the gaunt deer's reaching up to strip a bare apple tree. The animals in the poem are natural representations of the human condition; thus, the poem works as metaphor on several levels. There has even been the suggestion that line 13 is a reference to a poem by Andrew Marvell that remarks slyly that paradise is doubled if one does not have to share it with a lover—a notion apparently upheld by the unpaired birds. The poem is ironic, but not bitter, and the final question leaves us wondering if Frost is actually encouraging an ethic of "romping" rather than a doctrine of hard labor typically expected of New Englanders. On the other hand, the poem may be read as the work of a skeptic who sees only a harsh deity—or none at all—behind the unlikely Eden of near-starvation he describes.

References and further reading: R. Cook, *Living Voice*, provides a detailed reading of the poem and shows why the poem does not work as a fable; Kearns provides an innovative approach to the poem as representation of the Fall; Marcus, *Explication*, suggests the connection to Marvell; Potter discusses Eden as it is represented in a variety of Frost's poems.

L. Tamara Kendig

"WISH TO COMPLY, A," first appeared in *Steeple Bush* **(1947)**, where it is one of many poems dealing with Frost's thinking on **science** and **philosophy**. It cleverly intertwines his respect for scientific progress and his belief that such progress would never eliminate the difference that human belief makes in the world. The poem is made up of thirteen lines, two accented beats each, with many anapestic feet. The result is very singsong, with the rhymes coming so close together that the poem sounds like a nursery rhyme.

The poem describes the re-creation of a famous experiment first performed by the physicist Robert Millikan (1868–1953; Nobel Prize in 1923 for this experiment). By bombarding oil droplets with electrons and then suspending them in a weak electric field, Millikan was the first to measure the charge of the electron. The apparatus involved requires extended, patient observation by the experimenter, however, as the tiny droplets drift almost invisibly across a faint measuring scale.

Frost's uncertainty about whether he truly observed the oil droplet ("that Millikan mote") reflects his familiarity with the work of another physicist, Werner Heisenberg (1901–1976; Nobel Prize in 1932). Heisenberg was one of the pioneers of quantum theory, which includes, among other counterintuitive ideas, the principles that there are inherent limits to our knowledge of the physical world and that our expectations about an experiment influence the results we perceive.

The latter point underpins Frost's belief that most of our thinking is metaphorical and that in choosing our metaphors we give shape to the future. Frost's thinking along these lines was greatly influenced by William James, with whom Frost had once hoped to study at **Harvard**.

References and further reading: Any encyclopedia will explain the rudiments of Millikan's and Heisenberg's works; Faggen offers valuable insights into Frost's views on Darwinism and science; Frost explicitly discusses his beliefs about metaphor and science in "Education by Poetry," an **address** given to the **Amherst** alumni in 1930 and reprinted in R. Frost, *Collected*, 717–28; the two essays by William James that are most pertinent are "The Will to Believe," in *William James: Writings, 1878–1899* (New York: Library of America, 1992), and "Pragmatism," in *William James: Writings, 1902–1910* (New York: Library of America, 1987); an important study of Frost's thinking on science is Rotella, "Comparing"; Thompson and Winnick cite many of Frost's comments on the limits of scientific thought.

Richard Wakefield

"WITCH OF COÖS, THE." *See* **"Two Witches."**

WITNESS TREE, A **(1942).** Frost's seventh book of poetry was published on 23 April 1942, when the poet was sixty-seven. The book's jacket design showed a beech tree in which a blaze is cut to make it witness to a territorial claim. The book sold well, 10,000 copies within six weeks. The first poem in the book—**"Beech"**—is a sort of epigraph about a 'beech' that gives provisional security in the chaos of the forest. Then follows a section called "One or Two," consisting of fourteen poems, several of which are poems of such passion and lyricism that they astonished the poetry-reading public. There follows a section called "Two or More," which turns largely to social questions. Next is a set of eight poems with the title "Time Out," followed by nine tiny verses called "Quantula." The final section is called "Over Back" and contains six poems on rustic themes.

A *Witness Tree* earned Frost his fourth Pulitzer Prize and a plethora of reviews. **Louis Untermeyer** reviewed it as "one of Frost's richest collections in wit, ripest in **philosophy**, and youngest in spirit." Stephen Vincent Benét said it was "work that is both firmer in texture and fresher in impact than that of so many of [Frost's] juniors." Wilbert Snow said that there were "enough first-rate poems here to satisfy the most exacting critic." The *Time* magazine reviewer would admit only that "the plus outweighs the minus" in the book: *Time* resented Frost's role as national institution: "When he goes limpingly, as he does on many pages of his book, it is less because of his age than because he has come more and more to favor his worst poetical fault—his ... preternatural self-esteem. When full of this ... Frost writes like a wise man ensconced in a pickle jar." Another reviewer said that Frost's "writing is clearer, more pointed, simpler, and richer than it ever has been [but] in his homespun optimism, his somewhat self-conscious love of the more barren aspects of New England, his intellectual's anti-intellectualism, there is something pedestrian and prosy"; he accused Frost of writing "doggerel," reaching the level of "Ogden Nash's nonsense." A critic in *Poetry* dismissed one-third of the book as "moralistic, flat and smug" but called the rest "an often astonishingly able continuance of Frost's most characteristic triumphs" and contended that "several of the lyrics should stand with his best." This critic praised "the Frost genius for raising perfectly common, seemingly simple, speech to a moving and memorable experience." George F. Whicher wrote in the *Yale Review*, "The new poems are the Frost we have always known, yet with a plenitude never before realized." Whicher was impressed by the "profound" narrative **"The Discovery of the Madeiras,"** and he claimed that no dialogue Frost had ever written was "gayer or more surprising" than **"The Literate Farmer and the Planet Venus."** He called **"The Silken Tent"** and **"Never Again Would Birds' Song Be the Same"** "two magnificent compliments to women," and he deemed **"The Lesson for Today"** "one of the greatest poems that Frost has ever written." The *Times Literary Supplement*, on the other hand, found "The Literate Farmer" to be "rather laboured," and William Donaghy faulted the historical sense in "The Lesson for Today."

Clearly the early reception of *A Witness Tree*, like that afforded Frost's *A Further Range* (1936), was mixed. Donald Greiner's book includes an important study of Frost's negative critics in a chapter that opens ironically with a caption from Randall Jarrell: "No poet has had . . . his work more unforgiveably underestimated by the influential critics of our time." Greiner cites Louise Bogan, among others, as accusing Frost of adopting a role of "country philosopher." He also quotes Harold Watts, who found Frost skeptical and tentative: It seems Watts did not expect modernist qualities in Frost.

Biographers have claimed that Frost's private life had a strong influence on the poems of *A Witness Tree*. It is well known that his personal life included many tragedies, but one of the greatest was the loss of his wife, **Elinor**, in March 1938, an event that left him with little will to live. **Kay Morrison**, who served as Frost's secretary–manager for the last twenty-five years of his life and to whom Frost once proposed marriage, certainly had some effect on his poetry, as is tersely acknowledged in the dedication to *A Witness Tree*: "To K. M. for her part in it." Yet even this claim must be without prejudice to Frost's wife, Elinor, about whom Frost said in 1938, "Pretty nearly every one of my poems will be found to be about her if rightly read."

The book's opening section is titled "One or Two," a celebration of love that is both sensuous and spiritual. Elizabeth Shepley Sergeant says of it, "RF returned to lyricism. *A Witness Tree* . . . suggests a break-through of heart, mind, senses from some cold prison." William Pritchard calls the sequence "the most impressive one found anywhere in the *Complete Poems* . . . [It is] suffused with [feelings] not hitherto achieved in such depth." And elsewhere Pritchard speaks of "the depth of the note these poems cumulatively strike . . . they ache with the tears of things."

The section "Two or More" marks a change in the book. In Sergeant's view, "*A Witness Tree* forgets women as it proceeds, and leads on into the mind of the man constantly aware of the age in which he lives." **"Triple Bronze"** treats our efforts to keep at bay the chaos of the outer world, whereas, **"Our Hold**

on the Planet" claims that humanity is marginally favored by nature. **"To a Young Wretch"** explores the philosophy of property rights in society. The section ends with "The Lesson for Today," which is about society's judgment on the work of poets condemned to die minor, incomplete, their "fame . . . denied." The poem ends with Frost's auto-epitaph, the usual reading of which Poirier calls self-conscious and eccentric.

The next section, "Time Out," develops the "Lesson for Today's" meditation on death. The section deals with reading nature and its many threats to our fragile life. The penultimate section, called "Quantula," consists of nine tiny fragments. The final section is titled "Over Back," a group of poems set in rustic locations where humanity tries to establish security. The final poem of the section and of the book is "The Literate Farmer and the Planet Venus," in which the two characters are subtly drawn—if we read slowly and thoughtfully enough to hear them. We must distinguish clearly between an apparently half-educated farmer and a traveler–poet who is trying subtly to poke fun at him. The poem is an intellectual challenge for any reader; those with competence in philosophy will recognize that a fuller understanding of the ideas of this and other Frost poems will require a grasp of pointed allusions to all the work of William James, **Emerson**, and Bergson. George Monteiro has noted the relevance of Bergson to "The Literate Farmer," and he makes a valuable cross-reference to **"The White-tailed Hornet"** where the theme of evolution is also under scrutiny. Familiarity with such philosophers is prerequisite for a fuller understanding of Frost's ideas in the achievement of *A Witness Tree*.

References and further reading: R. Frost, *Selected Letters*, 471; Greiner, *Poet and His Critics*, 109, 123–24; Monteiro, *New England*, 134–35; Poirier, *Knowing*, 236; Pritchard, "Bearing Witness" and *Literary Life*, 228; Sergeant, 375, 388; Thompson and Winnick, 395; Wagner, for reviews, 169–82.

Gerard Quinn

"WOOD-PILE, THE," probably written while Frost was living in **Derry**, New Hampshire, was first published in *North of Boston* **(1914)**. Along with several other poems from that volume, "The Wood-pile" established Frost's reputation as a master of blank verse.

The poem's situation—walking alone in the woods—is reminiscent of English Romantic poetry and especially of the work of William Wordsworth. The ostensible purposelessness of the walk is conveyed by the grammar of the opening line (a subordinate participial phrase), which tells us that the action is already in progress without telling us why. The mundane diction deflects questions of motivation: the chilly breeziness of "Out walking in the frozen swamp one gray day" assumes the validity of this action without inviting its justification. The poet thereby tacitly assumes the literary history of this kind of walking. The Romantic context is also alluded to in the third line: "No, I will go on farther— and we shall see." The colloquial idiom "we shall see" seems at first like the trivial dilation of a plain-speaking ethos, but the subtle emphasis on vision places the poem squarely in the tradition of Romantic quests for transcendence.

Richard Poirier points out the predominance of "elaborate forms of denial" that shape such quest-narratives "in which the reader is deceived into visions." Frost's deceptive revision of the Romantic approach to sublime knowledge therefore requires us to think about the significance of realistic details that seem only descriptive. For example, Poirier claims that the sentence running over the fourth and fifth lines ("The hard snow held me, save where now and then / One foot went through") suggests "the kind of paranoia that goes with any feeling of being lost and of losing thereby a confident sense of self." We should add that it also conveys the kind of gratification that goes with puncturing a resistant surface and thereby leaving one's mark; there is a thrilling combination of anxiety, pleasure, and defiance in this walk, since what jeopardizes the speaker's progress—that is, his own weight—is also what asserts his presence in an inhuman setting.

The short sentence in lines 4 and 5 also alludes to the poem's interest in poetry itself, since the pun on "foot" in the context of a blank verse line that ends with the word "lines" is too conspicuous to be ignored. As in many of Frost's poems, there is tension between an implied metaphor about poetic production and quotidian literalness. Ultimately, however, the poet's claim to be lost in the middle of nowhere is disingenuous, since, as his puns indicate, he knows at least that he is in the middle of a Romantic poem.

If "The Wood-pile" takes as its point of departure Frost's need "to mark or name a place" (line 7) in the tradition of Romantic poetry, then the bird of the poem must inevitably take on the poetic significance of Wordsworth's cuckoo or John Keats's nightingale. Frost's anonymous bird, however, fails to live up to this expectation. The twentieth-century American poet provokes the bird's defensive reaction to him, whereas the English Romantic poet would have sought his own defensive stance to the bird's elusiveness. Frost's speaker goes out of his way to condescend to the bird by being amused at its chance appearance and fearful instinct of self-preservation, made comically "foolish" by the meaningless coincidence of its path of retreat and his forward motion; the bird is only accidentally the harbinger or portent that it promised to be when it "flew before" him.

The witty simile comparing the bird to "one who takes / Everything said as personal to himself" is gratuitous and reveals more about the poet than the bird. Here a new personality is introduced with grammar that is later repeated in the famous speculation about the wood-pile's maker, "Someone who lived in turning to fresh tasks." The repetition of "thought" ("He thought," line 14; "I thought," line 35) draws together for comparison these personalities, which seem to represent two potential but not wholly acceptable identities for the aspiring Romantic poet. The first is the less favorable because it is self-deceived and overvalues its importance. The value of the second is ambiguous because "turning to fresh tasks" connotes autonomy but also requires disregarding commitments to the moral and aesthetic order of a self-reliant life in the wilderness. Elizabeth Shepley Sergeant reports that Frost wrote "What I have most aspired to be" next to line 36 in her copy of *North of Boston*. We should be careful not to accept Frost's marginal comment at face value: Both personalities have too much regard for messages from the world, or more precisely, they lack an ability to ignore whatever might lead them away from a reliable sense of place and self. Because the decaying wood-pile connotes a kind of failure, the poem leaves us to make our own difficult conclusion about the meaning that it reveals to the poet in search of models of creative fulfillment.

Although the poem is in important ways about poetic making, it cannot be reduced to this subject. The mystery of the wood-pile also lies in its power "to mark . . . a place," that is, to clear a space for dwelling, much like the power of **Wallace Stevens**'s jar "placed" in the Tennessee wilderness and thereby taking "dominion everywhere" (see "Anecdote of the Jar"). The wood-pile, a carefully constructed thing, is perhaps worth considering in terms of the philosopher Martin Heidegger's essay "Building Dwelling Thinking" in which "things" are defined by their ability to open up room for settlement and thereby allow a gathering together of mortals, divinities, and the natural elements. In Frost's poem, however, such a gathering is only a forgotten promise nullified by the reclamation of nature, which itself has no use for human promises. The abandoned wood-pile is caught halfway between one state of existence and another: It belongs where it is found because it was made there and never moved; but it does not belong because it has not fulfilled its human purpose. Instead, it disintegrates slowly in the same way as the trees around it. Frost stakes a claim in the tradition of Romantic poetry by admiring the vitality of the maker who can "forget his handiwork" (which is not quite the same as "labor"), but the poet also subordinates this vitality to the pathos of a humble, pragmatic (and modernist) attempt to do without a sublime view of nature.

References and further reading: Bagby, *Nature*; Martin Heidegger, *Poetry, Language, Thought* (New York: Harper and Row, 1971), 145–61; Lynen, *Pastoral Art*; Monteiro, *New England*, 67–70; Poirier, *Knowing*, 82; Christopher Ricks, "Wordsworth I: 'A pure organic pleasure from the lines,' " *The Force of Poetry* (Oxford: Oxford University Press, 1984), 89–116; Sergeant, 117–19.

Gary Roberts

"WRIGHTS' BIPLANE, THE," was titled "The Biplane of Wilbur and Orville Wright" when Frost mailed it to **Louis Untermeyer** in August 1932, along with another poem about the Wrights, "Let Congress See to It." It was not one of the original "Ten Mills" published in *Poetry* magazine, but, as "The Wrights' Biplane," it was added to the group for *A Further Range* **(1936)** and has been printed with the others ever since.

Frost greatly admired the Wrights and was indignant in the early 1930s when other claimants to the world's first airplane flight were publicized. Louis Mertins recalled that Frost didn't think the Wrights had been sufficiently honored in their own country. "Orville is eating his heart out over in Dayton because of what's being done and not being done," Frost said. "Shabby treatment. . . . I wanted to do all I could to help establish them in their rights" (qtd. in Cramer 116).

The culmination of Frost's fascination with the Wrights is **"Kitty Hawk,"** which he considered one of his most important poems.

References and further reading: Cramer, *Frost among His Poems.*

Andy Duncan

y

YEATS, WILLIAM BUTLER (1865–1939), is sometimes considered the greatest poet of the twentieth century. Certainly no other modern poet wrote as many different kinds of poems—songs, ballads, elegies, verse dramas—using such a variety of themes—personal, political, mythological, doctrinal—for as long a period of time—over fifty years—as did Yeats. Frost was a great admirer of Yeats the artist, if not Yeats the man.

Yeats first came to prominence as a driving force behind the Celtic Renaissance, a movement aimed at reintroducing Gaelic myths from the past and reinvigorating a distinctly Irish spirit in the arts. Yeats participated in the movement as a poet (e.g, his first book of poems, *The Wanderings of Oisin)*, but his greatest contribution was as cofounder, comanager, and in-house dramatist for the Abbey Theatre, a playhouse in Dublin dedicated to producing plays with a decidedly Irish emphasis (such as Yeats's own *The Countess Cathleen* and *Cathleen ni Houlihan*). His efforts to reclaim Ireland's past soon led him to assume an active role in the tumultuous political climate of contemporary Ireland. Some of his most moving work dramatizes the Irish struggle for independence from British rule, as in "Easter 1916," a poem dedicated to comrades executed by the British for leading an uprising on Easter of 1916. Yeats's political activism also brought him into contact with Maud Gonne, a captivating Irish nationalist for whom he would carry a torch of unrequited love for the rest of his life. A number of his most memorable poems were inspired by Maud Gonne, including "Adams's Curse," "No Second Troy," and "Among School Children."

In 1923 Yeats was awarded the Nobel Prize in Literature. This prestigious honor is usually bestowed upon an artist at the end of an extraordinarily successful career, but some of Yeats's greatest work still lay ahead of him. Much of his later work revolves around his mystical manifesto *A Vision* (published first in 1926 and significantly revised in 1937), a prose work in which Yeats systematically lays out his world philosophy. It should be noted, however, that, though familiarity with Yeats's eccentric philosophy adds a useful extra dimension of understanding to these later poems, one need not believe or even fully understand this world vision to appreciate the frightening power of poems like "The Second Coming" and "A Prayer for My Daughter." And one need know nothing at all of *A Vision* to appreciate the sensual, colloquial humor of the Crazy Jane poems or the painfully honest self-reflection of "The Circus Animals' Desertion." In other words, despite his personal and philosophical eccentricities, most of Yeats's later poetry remains as vital and accessible as any of his earlier masterpieces. By the time he died in 1939, he was already generally acknowledged by his contemporaries as one of the most accomplished poets of the century, and if anything, his reputation has only grown since then.

Early on in his own career, Frost acknowledged Yeats as one of his favorite living poets. He knew him as the chief spokesperson for the Celtic Renaissance, promoting the common Irish folk as worthy subjects for art and insisting that the lyricism of everyday Irish speech made it the perfect vehicle for such artistic expression. This emphasis on common subjects and colloquial speech was very much in keeping with Frost's own efforts to render the "sentence sounds" of his native New Englanders into original verse. In 1910, when Frost produced a series of five plays for **Pinkerton Academy**, he chose two plays by Yeats (*Cathleen ni Houlihan* and *The Land of Heart's Desire*) as representative of the best the twentieth century had to offer. Yeats, for his part, also admired Frost's work. According to **Ezra Pound**, Yeats declared Frost's first collection, *A Boy's Will* **(1913)**, "the best poetry written in America for a long time." Frost and Yeats finally met one another (via Pound) on Frost's excursion to **England** in 1913. Frost's letters to Sydney Cox indicate, however, that the meeting was less than successful. Frost found Yeats wildly eccentric and totally absorbed in his own thoughts and actions. The two met a couple of times afterward, but, as Lawrance Thompson reports, "The hoped-for friendship was never established."

Frost's disappointment with Yeats the man may have soured him somewhat to Yeats the poet. Though he rarely alluded to the elder bard directly, those few allusions were generally unflattering. In *A Masque of Reason*, Thyatira makes mocking reference to the "gold enameled artificial birds" from Yeats's "Sailing to Byzantium." Later, in *A Masque of Mercy*, Paul plays upon the absurdity of Yeats's elaborate cyclical world philosophy. Such references are more droll than malicious, however, and should not diminish the affinities the two men shared as poets. Both produced their best poetry using colloquial, accessible, lyrical language—eschewing the intentional obscurity employed by most of their modernist contemporaries. Both chose to work within the medium of metered verse, a decision that, again, went against the general trend of modernist prosody. Both were adept at donning various poetic "masks," creating personae that were alternately scornful, cryptic, sarcastic, and profound. Finally, both enjoyed unusually long and extraordinarily successful careers, establishing popular and critical reputations that place them among the most highly regarded of twentieth-century poets.

References and further reading: Richard Ellman, *Yeats: The Man and the Masks* (New York: Norton, 1978); Richard J. Finneran, ed., *Critical Essays on W. B. Yeats* (Boston: G. K. Hall, 1986); A. Norman Jeffares, *A New Commentary on the Poems of W. B. Yeats* (London: Macmillan, 1984); A. Norman Jeffares and A. S. Knowland, *Commentary on the Collected Plays of W. B. Yeats* (Stanford: Stanford University Press, 1975); Nitchie; Thompson, *Early Years*, 414.

Graley V. Herren

"YOUNG BIRCH, A," was originally published in booklet form as Frost's 1946 **Christmas poem** but was later included as the first poem in *Steeple Bush* **(1947)**. While many critics praised the book, Randall Jarrell expressed disappointment, saying that most of its poems "are productions of somebody who once, and somewhere else, was a great poet." In some respects the remark characterizes "A Young Birch." Like **"The Tuft of Flowers,"** the poem describes a fragile part of nature that is too beautiful to cut down, and its subject almost inevitably reminds one of **"Birches."** Yet the poem is not as developed as the great early works. "The Tuft of Flowers" and "Birches" generally comply with Frost's formula of beginning in delight and ending in wisdom, but "A Young Birch" never moves far beyond delight. The speaker considers the tree's beauty, offers insight into the trusting nature of "the fair," and concludes that the birch exists mainly "as an ornament." Like its subject, the poem seems slight but pleasing. As **Reginald L. Cook** points out, it succeeds in conveying "delight in the attractiveness of nature." Frost himself had special affection for this poem and enjoyed reading it to audiences at the **Bread Loaf School** in the 1950s.

References and further reading: R. Cook, *Living Voice*, 133, 145, 308; D'Avanzo, " 'Young Birch' "; Jarrell, "Tenderness."

Christopher Krentz

Bibliography

The following works have been cited throughout this volume in a truncated form:

Abel, Darrel. "The Instinct of a Bard, Robert Frost on Science, Logic, and Poetic Truth." *Essays in Arts and Sciences* 9.1 (May 1980): 59–75.

———. "Robert Frost's 'Range-Finding.' " *Colby Library Quarterly* 22 (1986): 225–37.

Abercrombie, Lascelles. "A New Voice." [Rev. of *A Boy's Will*] *The Nation* 13 June 1914: 423–24.

Abshear-Seale, Lisa. "The Play of Thought: The Later Books of Robert Frost." Diss., University of Michigan, 1992.

———. "What Catullus Means by *Mens Animi*: Robert Frost's 'Kitty Hawk.' " *Robert Frost Review* (Fall 1993): 37–46.

Adams, Frederick B., Jr. *To Russia with Frost*. Boston: Club of Odd Volumes, 1963.

Allen, Margaret V. " 'The Black Cottage': Robert Frost and the Jeffersonian Ideal of Equality." Tharpe, *Centennial*, 221–29.

Allen, Ward. "Robert Frost's 'Iota Subscript,' " *English Language Notes* 6.4 (June 1969): 285–87.

Anderson, Charles R. "Robert Frost, 1874–1963." *Saturday Review of Literature* 23 Feb. 1963:20.

Anderson, George K. *Bread Loaf School of English: The First Fifty Years*. Middlebury, VT: Middlebury College, 1969.

Anderson, Margaret Bartlett. *Robert Frost and John Bartlett: The Record of a Friendship*. New York: Holt, 1963.

Angyal, Andrew J. "From Swedenborg to William James: The Shaping of Frost's Religious Beliefs." *Robert Frost Review* (Fall 1994): 69–81.

———. "Robert Frost's Poetry before 1913, a Checklist." *Proof 5: The Yearbook of American Bibliographical and Textual Studies*. Ed. Joseph Katz. Columbia, SC: J. Faust, 1978. 67–125.

Auden, W. H. *The Dyer's Hand and Other Essays*. New York: Random House, 1962.

Bacon, Helen. "For Girls: From 'Birches' to 'Wild Grapes.' " *Yale Review* 67 (1977): 13–29.

————. "In- and Outdoor Schooling: Robert Frost and the Classics." *American Scholar* 43 (1974): 640–49.

Bagby, George F. *Frost and the Book of Nature.* Knoxville: University of Tennessee Press, 1993.

————. "Frost's Synecdochism." Cady and Budd, 133–46.

————. "The Promethean Frost." *Twentieth Century Literature* 38 (1992): 1–19.

Bain, David H., and Mary S. Duffy, eds. *Whose Woods These Are: A History of the Bread Loaf Writers' Conference, 1926–1992.* Hopewell, NJ: Ecco, 1993.

Baker, David, ed. *Meter in English: A Critical Engagement.* Fayetteville: University Press of Arkansas, 1996.

Barrett, Clifton Waller. "*Twilight*: Robert Frost's First Book." *Proof 4: The Yearbook of American Bibliographical and Textual Studies.* Ed. Joseph Katz. Columbia, SC: J. Faust, 1975. 3–5.

Barry, Elaine. *Robert Frost.* New York: Frederick Ungar, 1973.

Bass, Eben. "Frost's Poetry of Fear." Cady and Budd, 83–84.

Baym, Nina. "An Approach to Robert Frost's Nature Poetry." *American Quarterly* 17 (1965): 713–23.

Beacham, Walton. "Technique and the Sense of Play in the Poetry of Robert Frost." Tharpe, *Centennial II*, 246–61.

Bell, Barbara Currier. "Frost on Humanity in Nature." *Arizona Quarterly* 42.3 (1986): 223–38.

Benoit, Raymond. "Folklore by Frost: 'Paul's Wife.' " *Notes on Modern American Literature* 5.4 (1981): Item 22.

Berger, Charles. "Echoing Eden: Frost and Origins." Bloom, 147–65.

Bieganowski, Ronald. "Robert Frost's *A Boy's Will* and Henri Bergson's *Creative Evolution.*" *South Carolina Review* 21.1 (1988): 9–16.

————. "Robert Frost's 'An Encounter.' " *Notes on Contemporary Literature* 10.2 (1980): 4–5.

————. "Sense of Place and Religious Consciousness." Harris, *Studies*, 29–49.

Bleau, N. Arthur. "Robert Frost's Favorite Poem." Tharpe, *Centennial III*, 174–77.

Bloom, Harold. ed. *Robert Frost.* Modern Critical Views. New York: Chelsea House, 1986.

Blumenthal, Joseph. *Robert Frost and His Printers.* Austin, TX: W. Thomas Taylor, 1985.

————. *Robert Frost and the Spiral Press.* New York: Spiral Press, 1963.

Bly, Robert. "Search for a Vision." *Modern Maturity* Oct.–Nov. 1985: 72–78.

Bober, Natalie S. *A Restless Spirit: The Story of Robert Frost.* New York: Holt, 1991.

Borroff, Marie. *Language and the Poet: Verbal Artistry in Frost, Stevens, and Moore.* Chicago: Chicago University Press, 1979.

————. "Robert Frost: 'To Earthward.' " Tharpe, *Centennial II*, 21–39.

————. "Robert Frost's New Testament: Language and the Poem." *Modern Philology* 69 (1971): 36–54.

————. "Robert Frost's New Testament: The Uses of Simplicity." Bloom, 63–83.

Bowen, Stirling. "A Poet on the Campus of the University of Michigan." *Detroit Free Press* 27 Nov. 1921: Pt. 7, 1.

Briggs, Christine. "The Dramatic Monologue in Robert Frost's 'The Pauper Witch of Grafton.' " *Ball State University Forum* 21.2 (1980): 48–53.

Brock, Heyward. "Robert Frost's Masques Reconsidered." *Renascence* 30 (1978): 137–51.

Brodsky, Joseph. "On Grief and Reason." *Homage to Robert Frost*. By Joseph Brodsky, Seamus Heaney, and Derek Walcott. New York: Farrar Straus Giroux, 1996.

Brogunier, Joseph. "Walking My Dog in Frost's 'Sand Dunes.'" *Journal of Modern Literature* 16.4 (Spring 1990): 648–50.

Brooks, Cleanth. "Frost and Nature." Wilcox, *The Man*, 1–18.

Brooks, Cleanth, and Robert Penn Warren. *Understanding Poetry*. New York: Henry Holt, 1938.

Brooks, Van Wyck. *New England: Indian Summer, 1865–1915*. New York: Dutton, 1940.

Brower, Reuben. *The Poetry of Robert Frost: Constellations of Intention*. New York: Oxford University Press, 1963.

Brown, Terrence. "Robert Frost's *In the Clearing*: An Attempt to Reestablish the Persona of the 'Kindly Grey Poet.'" *Papers on Language and Literature* 5 (Summer Supp. 1969): 110–18.

Burnshaw, Stanley. *Robert Frost Himself*. New York: George Braziller, 1986.

Burrell, Paul. "Frost's 'The Draft Horse.'" *Explicator* 25 (1967): Item 60.

Bush, Harold Karl, Jr. "Endicott's Ghost: The Rhetoric of American Myth." *DAI* 56 (1995): 549A. Indiana University.

———. "Robert Frost Writing the Myth of America: Rereading 'The Gift Outright.'" *Robert Frost Review* (Fall 1995): 45–55.

Byers, Edna Hanley, comp. *Robert Frost at Agnes Scott College*. Decatur, GA: McCain Library, 1963.

Cady, Edwin H., and Louis J. Budd, eds. *On Frost: The Best from American Literature*. Durham: Duke University Press, 1991.

Campbell, Harry M. "Frost's 'Sitting by a Bush in Broad Sunlight.'" *Explicator* 5 (Dec. 1946): Item 18.

Carmichael, Charles. "Frost as a Romantic." Tharpe, *Centennial*, 147–65.

Ciardi, John. "Robert Frost: The Way to the Poem." *Saturday Review of Literature* 41 (12 Apr. 1958): 13–15, 65.

Clark, David R. "An Excursion upon the Criticism of Robert Frost's 'Directive.'" *Costerus Essays in English and American Language and Literature* 8 (1973): 37–56.

Clarke, Marian G. M., comp. *The Robert Frost Collection in the Watkinson Library*. Hartford, CT: Trinity College, 1974.

Coale, Samuel. "The Emblematic Encounter of Robert Frost." Tharpe, *Centennial*, 89–107.

Condor, John. "'After Apple-Picking': Frost's Troubled Sleep." Tharpe, *Centennial*, 171–81.

Cook, Marjorie E. "Acceptance in Frost's Poetry: Conflict as Play." Tharpe, *Centennial II*, 223–35.

———. "The Complexity of Boundaries: 'Trespass' by Robert Frost." *Notes on Contemporary Literature* 5 (Fall 1975): 2–5.

———. "Dilemmas of Interpretation: Ambiguities and Practicalities." Wilcox, *The Man*, 125–41.

———. "The Serious Play of Interpretation." *South Carolina Review* (Spring 1983): 77–87.

Cook, Reginald Lansing. *The Dimensions of Robert Frost*. New York: Rinehart, 1958. Rpt. Barnes & Noble, 1968.

———. "Frost as Parablist." *Accent* 10 (Fall 1949): 33–41.

———. "Frost on Frost: The Making of Poems." Cady and Budd, 39–49.

———. *Robert Frost: A Living Voice*. Amherst: University of Massachusetts Press, 1974.

———. "Robert Frost and the Edge of the Clearing." Gerber, *Essays*, 144–54.

———. "Robert Frost in Context." Tharpe, *Centennial III*, 123–73.

———. "Robert Frost's Asides on His Poetry." *American Literature* 19 (1948): 351–59. Rpt. in Cady and Budd, 30–38.

Coulthard, A. R. "Frost's 'Mending Wall.' " *Explicator* 45.2 (1987): 40–42.

Cowley, Malcolm. "Frost: A Dissenting Opinion." *New Republic* 111 (11 Sept. 1944): 312–13.

Cox, James M. "Robert Frost and the Edge of the Clearing." Gerber, *Essays*, 144–54.

———, ed. *Robert Frost: A Collection of Critical Essays*. Englewood Cliffs, NJ: Prentice-Hall, 1962.

Cox, Sidney. *Robert Frost: Original "Ordinary Man."* New York: Holt, 1929.

———. "Some Educational Beliefs and Practices of Robert Frost." *Educational Record* 29 (Oct. 1948): 410–22.

———. *A Swinger of Birches: A Portrait of Robert Frost*. New York: New York University Press, 1957.

Cramer, Jeffrey S. "Forgotten Frost: A Study of the Uncollected and Unpublished Poetry of Robert Frost." *The Robert Frost Review*. Pt. 1 (Fall 1992): 1–27; Pt. 2 (Fall 1993): 1–23.

———. *Robert Frost Among His Poems: A Literary Companion to the Poet's Own Biographical Contexts and Associations*. Jefferson, NC: McFarland, 1996.

Crane, Joan St. C. "The Printing History of *Twilight*." *Proof 4: The Yearbook of American Bibliographical and Textual Studies*. Ed. Joseph Katz. Columbia, SC: J. Faust, 1975. 1–30.

———. "Robert Frost's 'Kitty Hawk.' " *Studies in Bibliography: Papers of the Bibliographical Society of the University of Virginia* 30 (1977): 241–49.

———, comp. *Robert Frost: A Descriptive Catalogue of Books and Manuscripts in the Clifton Waller Barrett Library, University of Virginia*. Charlottesville: University Press of Virginia, 1974.

Daiches, David. "Enduring Wisdom from a Poet-Sage." *New York Times Book Review* 29 May 1949: 1, 13.

D'Avanzo, Mario L. *A Cloud of Other Poets: Robert Frost and the Romantics*. Lanham, MD: University Press of America, 1991.

———. "Frost's 'A Young Birch': A Thing of Beauty." *Concerning Poetry* 3.2 (Fall 1970): 69–70.

———. "Frost's 'Departmental' and Emerson: A Further Range of Satire." *Concerning Poetry* 10.2 (1977): 67–69.

———. "Frost's 'Sand Dunes' and Thoreau's *Cape Cod*." *Notes on Contemporary Literature* 10.5 (1980): 2–4.

———. "How to Build a Chimney: Frost Gleans Thoreau." *Thoreau Journal Quarterly* 9 (Oct. 1977): 24–26.

Dawes, James R. "Masculinity and Transgression in Robert Frost." *American Literature* 65 (June 1993): 297–312.

Deutsch, Babette. "Poets and Poetasters." *The Bookman* 68 (Dec. 1928): 471–73. Rpt. in Wagner, 69–79.

DeVoto, Bernard. "The Critics and Robert Frost." *Saturday Review of Literature* 17 (1 Jan. 1938): 3–4, 14–15.

Dolbier, Maurice. "Frost Predicts Kennedy Will Be President." R. Frost, *Interviews*, 195–98.

Doreski, William. "Robert Frost's 'The Census-Taker' and the Problem of Wilderness." *Twentieth-Century Literature: A Scholarly and Critical Journal* 34. 1 (Spring 1988): 30–39.

Dougherty, James P. "Robert Frost's 'Directive' to the Wilderness." *American Quarterly* 18 (Summer 1966): 208–19.

Doyle, John Robert, Jr. *The Poetry of Robert Frost: An Analysis*. New York: Hafner; Johannesburg: Witwatersrand University Press, 1962.

———. "A Reading of Robert Frost's 'Directive.' " *Georgia Review* 22 (Winter 1968): 501–8.

Dubinsky, James. "War and Rumors of War in Frost." *Robert Frost Review* (1995): 1–22.

Duvall, S.P.C. "Robert Frost's 'Directive' Out of *Walden*." *American Literature* 31 (1960): 480–88.

Eberhart, Richard. "Robert Frost: His Personality." *Southern Review* n.s. 2 (1966): 762–88.

———. "Robert Frost in the Clearing." *Southern Review* 11 (1975): 260–68.

Edwards, Margaret. "Pan's Song Revised." Tharpe, *Centennial*, 108–20.

———. "The Play of 'Downward Comparisons': Animal Anthropomorphism in the Poems of Robert Frost." Tharpe, *Centennial II*, 236–45.

Ekins, Roger. " 'At Home' with Robert Frost." Tharpe, *Centennial*, 191–200.

Ellis, James. "Frost's 'Desert Places' and Hawthorne." *English Record* 15 (Apr. 1965): 15–17.

———. "Robert Frost's Four Types of Belief in 'Birches.' " *Robert Frost Review* (Fall 1993): 70–74.

Evans, Oliver H. " 'Deeds That Count': Robert Frost's Sonnets." *Texas Studies in Literature and Language* 23 (1981): 123–37.

Evans, William R., ed. *Robert Frost and Sidney Cox: Forty Years of Friendship*. Hanover, NH: University Press of New England, 1981.

Faggen, Robert. *Robert Frost and the Challenge of Darwin*. Ann Arbor: University of Michigan Press, 1997.

Feaster, John. "Robert Frost's 'The Code': Context and Commentary." *Cresset* 55 (1992): 6–10.

Ferguson, A. R. "Frost, Sill, and 'A-Wishing Well.' " *American Literature* (Nov. 1961): 370–73.

Ferguson, Joe. "Frost's 'After Apple-Picking.' " *Explicator* 22 (1964): Item 53.

Fike, Matthew A. "Frost's 'Never Again Would Birds' Song Be the Same.' " *Explicator* 49 (1991): 108–11.

Fitts, Dudley. *Poems from the Greek Anthology*. New York: New Directions, 1956.

Fleissner, Robert F. "Frost as Ironist: 'After Apple-Picking' and the Pre-Autumnal Fall." *South Carolina Review* 21 (1988): 50–57.

———. "Frost's Fireflies in the Garden." *Explicator* 39.4 (1981): 26–28.

———. "Frost's 'Not All There.' " *Explicator* 31 (1973): Item 33.

———. "Moon Compasses." *Explicator* 32 (1974): Item 66.

———. "New Lines by Robert Frost: His 'Addendum' to 'Mending Wall.' " *English Language Notes* 25.3 (1988): 63–66.

———. "A Road Taken: The Romantically Different *Ruelle*." Harris, *Studies*, 117–31.

———. *Robert Frost's Road Taken*. New York: Peter Lang, 1996.

———. "A Title and the Contents: Correlating Frost's Poem for JFK with the STC Reverie-Lyric." *Robert Frost Society Newsletter* (Summer 1998): 1, 3.

———. "Tufting the Host: Frost's Further Use of Wordsworth." *Notes on Contemporary Literature* 12 (1982): 6–8.

Flint, F. S. [Rev. of *A Boy's Will*] *Poetry and Drama* 1 (June 1913): 250.

Fogelman, Bruce. " 'Pan with Us': The Continuity of the Eclogue in Twentieth-Century Poetry," *Classical and Modern Literature* 6.2 (1986): 109–25.

Foster, Richard. " 'Leaves Compared with Flowers': A Reading in Robert Frost's Poems." *New England Quarterly* 46 (Sept. 1973): 403–23.

Francis, Lesley Lee. "Between Poets: Robert Frost and Harriet Monroe." *South Carolina Review* 19 (Special Issue, Summer 1987): 2–15.

———. "A Decade of 'Stirring Times': Robert Frost and Amy Lowell." *New England Quarterly* 59 (Dec. 1986): 508–22.

———. *The Frost Family's Adventure in Poetry: Sheer Morning Gladness at the Brim.* Columbia: University of Missouri Press, 1994.

———. " 'Imperfectly Academic': Robert Frost and Harvard." *Harvard Magazine* (Mar.–Apr. 1984): 51–56.

———. "Robert Frost and Helen Thomas Revisited." *Robert Frost Review* (Fall 1993): 77–85.

———. "Robert Frost and the Majesty of Stones upon Stones." *Journal of Modern Literature* 9.1 (1981–1982): 3–26.

Francis, Robert. *Robert Frost: A Time to Talk* Amherst: University of Massachusetts Press, 1972.

Freedman, William. "Frost's 'The Pasture.' " *Explicator* 29 (1971): Item 80.

French, Roberts W. "Robert Frost and the Darkness of Nature." Gerber, *Essays*, 155–62.

French, Warren. " 'The Death of the Hired Man': Modernism and Transcendence." Tharpe, *Centennial III*, 394.

Frost, Lesley. "In Aladdin's Lamp Light." Tharpe, *Centennial III*, 313–15.

———. *New Hampshire's Child: The Derry Journals of Lesley Frost*. Ed. Arnold Grade and Lawrance Thompson. Albany: State University of New York Press, 1969.

Frost, Robert. *Christmas Trees*. Illust. Ted Rand. New York: Holt, 1916, 1990.

———. *The Family Letters of Robert and Elinor Frost*. Ed. Arnold Grade. Albany: State University of New York Press, 1972.

———. *Interviews with Robert Frost*. Ed. Edward Connery Lathem. New York: Holt, 1966.

———. *The Letters of Robert Frost to Louis Untermeyer*. Ed. Louis Untermeyer. New York: Holt, 1963.

———. *New Enlarged Anthology of Robert Frost's Poems*. Ed. Louis Untermeyer. New York: Washington Square, 1971.

———. *The Poetry of Robert Frost*. Ed. Edward Connery Lathem. New York: Holt, 1969.

———. *Prose Jottings of Robert Frost: Selections from His Notebooks and Miscellaneous Manuscripts*. Lunenburg, VT: Northeast-Kingdom, 1982.

———. *Robert Frost at 100*. Ed. Edward Connery Lathem. Boston: David R. Godine, 1974.

———. *Robert Frost: Collected Poems, Prose, & Plays*. Ed. Richard Poirier and Mark Richardson. New York: Library of America, 1995.

———. *Robert Frost on Writing*. Ed. Elaine Barry. New Brunswick, NJ: Rutgers University Press, 1973.

———. *Robert Frost: Poetry and Prose*. Ed. Edward Connery Lathem and Lawrance Thompson. New York: Holt, 1972.

———. *Selected Letters of Robert Frost*. Ed. Lawrance Thompson. New York: Holt, 1964.

———. *Selected Prose*. Ed. Hyde Cox and Edward Connery Lathem. New York: Holt, 1966.

———. *Stories for Lesley*. Ed. Roger D. Sell. Charlottesville: University Press of Virginia, 1984.

———. "A Tribute to Wordsworth." *Cornell Library Journal* 11 (Spring 1970): 77–79.

———. "A Trip to Currituck, Elizabeth City, and Kitty Hawk (1894)." *North Carolina Folklore Journal* 16 (1968): 3–8.

———. *You Come Too: Favorite Poems for Young Readers*. New York: Henry Holt, 1959.

George, William. "Frost's 'The Road Not Taken.' " *Explicator* 49 (Summer 1991): 230–32.

Gerber, Philip L., ed. *Critical Essays on Robert Frost*. Boston: G. K. Hall, 1982.

———. *Robert Frost*. Rev. ed. Boston: Twayne, 1982.

Gibson, Clare. *Signs and Symbols*. New York: Barnes and Noble, 1996.

Gierasch, Walter. "Frost's 'Devotion. ' "*Explicator* 10 (1952): Item 50.

Goede, William. "The 'Code Hero' in Frost's 'Blueberries.' " *Discourse* 11 (Winter 1968): 26–31.

Goldstein, Laurence. " 'Kitty Hawk' and the Question of American Destiny." *Iowa Review* 9.1 (1978): 41–49.

Gould, Jean. *Robert Frost: The Aim Was Song*. New York: Dodd, Mead, 1964.

Greenleaf, Robert K. *Robert Frost's "Directive" and the Spiritual Journey*. Boston: Nimrod, 1963.

Greider, Josephine. "Robert Frost on Ezra Pound, 1913: Manuscript Corrections of 'Portrait D'une Femme.' " *New England Quarterly* 44 (1971): 301–5.

Greiner, Donald J. "Factual Men and Imagining Rabbits: Robert Frost and Wallace Stevens." Wilcox, *The Man*, 61–67.

———. *Robert Frost: The Poet and His Critics*. Chicago: American Library Association, 1974.

———. "Robert Frost's Dark Woods and the Function of Metaphor." Tharpe, *Centennial*, 373–98.

Gwynn, Frederick L. "Analysis and Synthesis of Frost's 'The Draft Horse.' " *College English* 26 (1964): 223–25.

Hadas, Rachel. *Form, Cycle, Infinity: Landscape Imagery in the Poetry of Robert Frost*. Lewisburg, PA: Bucknell University Press, 1985.

Hall, Donald. "Robert Frost Corrupted." *Atlantic Monthly* Mar. 1982: 60–64.

Hall, Dorothy Judd. "The Height of Feeling Free: Frost and Bergson." *Texas Quarterly* 19 (Spring 1976): 128–43.

————. "The Mystic Lens of Robert Frost: Bent Rays from Swedenborg." *Studia Swedenborgiana* 9 (Oct. 1994): 1–26.

————. "An Old Testament Christian." Tharpe, *Centennial III*, 316–49.

————. "Reserve in the Art of Robert Frost." *Texas Quarterly* 6 (Summer 1963): 60–67 [published under the name Dorothy Judd].

————. *Robert Frost: Contours of Belief.* Athens: Ohio University Press, 1984.

————. "Robert Frost's Hidden *Figura.*" *Robert Frost Review* (Fall 1992): 29–32.

Hancher, Michael. "Sermons in Stones." *Centrum* 2 (1974): 79–86.

Harris, Kathryn Gibbs. "Lyric Impulse: Birds and Other Voices." Harris, *Studies*, 143–56.

————. "Robert Frost's Early Education in Science." *South Carolina Review* 7.1 (1974): 13–33.

————, ed. *Robert Frost: Studies of the Poetry.* Boston: G. K. Hall, 1979.

Harvey, Bonnie Carman. "A Movement toward the Integrated Self: Antinomianism Reflected in the Poetry of Taylor, Emerson, Dickinson, and Frost." *DAI* 51 (1990): 2018A. Georgia State University.

Haynes, Donald T. "The Narrative Unity of *A Boy's Will.*" *PMLA* 87 (1972): 452–64.

Hays, Peter L. "Frost and the Critics: More Revelation on 'All Revelation.' " *English Language Notes* 18 (June 1981): 283–90.

————. "Two Landscapes: Frost's and Eliot's." Tharpe, *Centennial*, 256–64.

Heaney, Seamus. "Above the Brim." *Homage to Robert Frost.* By Joseph Brodsky, Seamus Heaney, and Derek Walcott. New York: Farrar Straus & Giroux, 1996. 61–88.

Hearn, Thomas K., Jr. "Making Sweetbreads Do: Robert Frost and Moral Empiricism." *New England Quarterly* 49 (1976): 65–81.

Hiatt, David. "Frost's 'In White' and 'Design.' " *Explicator* 28 (1970): Item 41.

Hiers, John T. "Robert Frost's Quarrel with Science and Technology." *Georgia Review* 25 (1971): 182–205.

Holland, Norman N. *The Brain of Robert Frost: A Cognitive Approach to Literature.* New York: Routledge, 1988.

"Honorary Degrees Awarded to Eleven." *Dartmouth Alumni Magazine* 47 (July 1955): 18.

Hopkins, Vivian C. "The Houses of Robert Frost." Tharpe, *Centennial*, 182–90.

Humphries, Rolfe. "Verse Chronicle." *The Nation*, 23 July 1949: 92–93.

Ingebretsen, Ed., S. J., "Robert Frost's 'The Pasture' and Wendell Berry's 'Stay Home': Figures of Love and the Figure the Poem Makes." Wilcox, *Essays*, 81–88.

————, ed. *Robert Frost's Star in a Stone Boat: A Grammar of Belief.* San Francisco: Catholic Scholars Press, 1994.

"Intolerable Touch, The." *Time* 27 June 1949: 94–100.

Jackson, Sarah R. "Frost's 'The Master Speed.' " *Explicator* 51 (Fall 1992): 33–35.

Jarrell, Randall. *Poetry and the Age.* New York: Vintage, 1955.

————. "Tenderness and Passive Sadness." Rev. of *Steeple Bush*, by Robert Frost. *New York Times Book Review* 1 June 1947: 4.

————. *The Third Book of Criticism.* New York: Farrar Straus & Giroux, 1965.

————. "To the Laodiceans." Chapter in *Poetry and the Age.* 34–62. Rpt. in J. Cox, *Collection*, 83–104.

Jayne, Edward. "Up against the 'Mending Wall': The Psycho-Analysis of a Poem by Frost." *College English* 34 (1973): 934–51.

Jost, Walter. " 'The Lurking Frost': Poetic and Rhetoric in 'Two Tramps in Mud Time.' " Cady and Budd, 207–21.

Joyner, Nancy Carol. "Comic Exegete." Harris, *Studies*, 143–56.

Juhnke, Anna K. "Religion in Robert Frost's Poetry: The Play for Self-Possession." Cady and Budd, 61–72.

Kahn, Roger. "A Visit with Robert Frost." *Saturday Evening Post* 19 Nov. 1960: 26+.

Katz, Sandra L. *Elinor Frost: A Poet's Wife*. Westfield: Institute for Massachusetts Studies, 1988.

———. "Robert Frost, Humorist." *Robert Frost Review* (Fall 1991): 24–29.

Kau, Joseph. "Frost's 'Away!': Illusions and Allusions." *Notes on Modern American Literature* 7.3 (1983): Item 17.

Kearns, Katherine. *Robert Frost and a Poetics of Appetite*. Cambridge: Cambridge University Press, 1994.

Kemp, John C. *Robert Frost and New England: The Poet as Regionalist*. Princeton, NJ: Princeton University Press, 1979.

Killingsworth, Paula. "Four Dimensions of the Isolation Theme in Frost's Poetry." *Publications of the Mississippi Philological Association* 3 (Summer 1984): 1–13.

Kjørven, Johannes. *Robert Frost's Emergent Design: The Truth of the Self In-between Belief and Unbelief*. Atlantic Highlands, NJ: Humanities Press International, 1987.

Kuzma, Greg, ed. *Gone Into If Not Explained: Essays on Poems by Robert Frost*. Crete, NE: Best Cellar, 1976.

Lancaster, John. "A Descriptive Catalogue of the Robert Frost Collection." 87 pp. In *The Parkman Dexter Howe Library, Part VII*. Ed. Sidney Ives. Gainesville: University of Florida Press, 1990.

Langbaum, Robert. *The Poetry of Experience: The Dramatic Monologue in Modern Literary Tradition*. London: Chatto and Windus, 1957.

Larson, Mildred R. "Robert Frost as a Teacher." Diss., New York University, 1949.

Lathem, Edward Connery, ed. *The Poetry of Robert Frost*. New York: Henry Holt, 1969.

Lea, Sydney. "From Sublime to Rigamarole: Relations of Frost to Wordsworth." *Studies in Romanticism* 19 (Spring 1980): 83–108.

Lehmann, John. *Three Literary Friendships*. New York: Holt, 1983.

Lentricchia, Frank. *Modernist Quartet*. New York: Cambridge University Press, 1994.

———. "The Redemptive Imagination." Bloom, 23–41.

———. "Robert Frost and Modern Literary Theory." Tharpe, *Centennial*, 315–32.

———. *Robert Frost: Modern Poetics and the Landscapes of Self*. Durham, NC: Duke University Press, 1975.

Lentricchia, Frank, and Melissa Christensen Lentricchia, comps. *Robert Frost: A Bibliography, 1913–1974*. Scarecrow Author Bibliographies No. 25. Metuchen, NJ: Scarecrow, 1976.

Lerner, Laurence. "An Essay on Pastoral." *Essays in Criticism* 20 (1970): 275–97.

Library of Congress. *Robert Frost: Lectures on the Centennial of His Birth*. Washington, DC: Library of Congress, 1975.

Lieber, Todd. "Robert Frost and Wallace Stevens: What to Make of a Diminished Thing." Cady and Budd, 100–119.

Lind, L. R. "Robert Frost, Classicist." *Classical and Modern Literature* 1 (Fall 1980): 7–23.

Linebarger, J. M. "Sources of Frost's 'The Vindictives.' " *American Notes and Queries* 12 (1974): 150–54.

Lowell, Amy. *Poetry and Poets*. Boston: Houghton Mifflin, 1930.

———. *Tendencies in Modern American Poetry*. New York: Haskell House Publishers, Ltd., 1970.

Lundquist, Sara. "Local Habitations: Poetic Dwelling in the Work of Robert Frost and James Merrill." *DAI* 54 (1994): 3032A. Boston College.

Lynen, John F. "Du Cote de Chez Frost." Tharpe, *Centennial*, 562–94.

———. "I Will Sing You One-O." Kuzma, 163–70.

———. *The Pastoral Art of Robert Frost*. New Haven, CT: Yale University Press, 1960.

Lyons, Clifford. "Not Unbounded." Harris, *Studies*, 77–87.

Lyons, Leonard. "Frost Wanted to Be Ballplayer But Chose Insight over Sight." *Lawrence Daily Journal-World* 4 Feb. 1963: 4.

Madison, Charles. *The Owl Among Colophons: Henry Holt as Publisher and Editor*. New York: Holt, 1966.

Magill, Frank N., ed. *Masterpieces of World Philosophy*. New York: HarperCollins, 1990.

Marcus, Mordecai. *The Poems of Robert Frost: An Explication*. Boston: G. K. Hall, 1991.

———. "Robert Frost's 'Bond and Free': Structure and Meaning." *Concerning Poetry* (Spring 1975): 61–64.

———. "The Whole Pattern of Robert Frost's 'Two Witches': Contrasting Psycho-Sexual Modes." *Literature and Psychology* 26 (1976): 69–78.

Marks, Herbert. "The Counter-Intelligence of Robert Frost." Bloom, 125–46.

Martin, Wallace. "Frost's 'Acquainted with the Night.' " *Explicator* 26 (1968): Item 64.

Mason, Julian. "Frost's Conscious Accommodation of Contraries." *CEA Critic* 38 (Mar. 1976): 26–31.

Maxson, H. A. *On the Sonnets of Robert Frost: A Critical Examination of the 37 Poems*. Jefferson, NC: McFarland, 1997.

Maynard, Charles. "Robert Frost: Poet of the Night." *Sky & Telescope* (June 1992): 692–93.

McAuley, James. *Versification: A Short Introduction*. Lansing: Michigan State University Press, 1966.

McGavran, Dorothy. "The Building Community: Houses and Other Structures in the Poetry of Robert Frost." *Robert Frost Review* (Fall 1994): 1–12.

Mertins, Louis. *Robert Frost: Life and Talks-Walking*. Norman: University of Oklahoma Press, 1965.

Mertins, Louis, and Esther Mertins. *The Intervals of Robert Frost: A Critical Bibliography*. Berkeley: University Press of California, 1947.

Meyers, Jeffrey. *Robert Frost: A Biography*. New York: Houghton, 1996.

Michaels, Walter Benn. "Getting Physical." *Raritan Quarterly Review* (Fall 1982): 103–13.

Miller, Lewis H., Jr. "Design and Drama in *A Boy's Will*." Tharpe, *Centennial*, 351–68.

———. "William James, Robert Frost, and 'The Black Cottage.' " Tharpe, *Centennial III*, 368–81.

Monroe, Harriet. "A Frugal Master." Wagner, 78–79.

———. *Poets and Their Art*. New York: Macmillan, 1926.

———. *A Poet's Life: Seventy Years in a Changing World*. New York: Macmillan, 1938.

Monteiro, George. "Frost's 'After Apple-Picking.' " *Explicator* 30 (1972): Item 62.

————. "Frost's Hired Hand." *College Literature* 14 (1987): 128–35.

————. "Frost's 'Quest for the Purple-Fringed.' " *English Language Notes* 13 (1976): 204–6.

————. "Redemption through Nature: A Recurring Theme in Thoreau, Frost, and Richard Wilbur." *American Quarterly* 20 (Winter 1968): 795–809.

————. *Robert Frost and the New England Renaissance.* Lexington: University Press of Kentucky, 1988.

————. "Robert Frost's Linked Analogies." *New England Quarterly* 46 (1973): 463–68.

Montgomery, Marion. "Robert Frost and His Use of Barriers: Man vs. Nature toward God." *South Atlantic Quarterly* 57 (Summer 1958): 339–53.

Moore, Richard. "Of Form, Closed and Open: With Glances at Frost and Williams." *Iowa Review* 17 (1987): 86–103.

Morrison, Kathleen. *Robert Frost: A Pictorial Chronicle.* New York: Holt, 1974.

Morrison, Theodore. "The Agitated Heart." *Atlantic Monthly* (July 1967): 72–79.

————. *The Bread Loaf Writers' Conference: The First Thirty Years.* Middlebury, VT: Middlebury College, 1976.

Morse, Stearns. " 'The Subverted Flower': An Exercise in Triangulation." Tharpe, *Centennial II*, 170–76.

Muir, Helen. *Frost in Florida: A Memoir.* Miami, FL: Valient, 1995.

Munson, Gorham. "The Classicism of Robert Frost." *Modern Age* 8 (1964): 291–305.

————. *Robert Frost: A Study in Sensibility and Good Sense.* New York: Dorham, 1927.

Nash, Ray. "Meeting of Mounted Men." *Print* 3.1 (Spring 1942): 63–64.

Newdick, Robert S. *Newdick's Season of Frost: An Interrupted Biography.* Ed. William A. Sutton. Albany: State University of New York Press, 1976.

————. "Robert Frost and the Sound of Sense." *American Literature* 9 (1937): 289–300. Rpt. in Cady and Budd, 1–12.

Nitchie, George W. *Human Values in the Poetry of Robert Frost: A Study of a Poet's Convictions.* Durham, NC: Duke University Press, 1960.

Norwood, Kyle. "The Work of Not Knowing: Robert Frost and the Abject." *Southwest Review* 78 (1993): 57–72.

O'Donnell, William G. "Parable in Poetry." *Virginia Quarterly Review* 25 (1949): 269–82.

————. "Robert Frost and New England: A Revaluation." *Yale Review* (Summer 1948): 698–712.

————. "Robert Frost at Eighty-eight." Gerber, *Essays*, 163–68.

Oehlschlaeger, Fritz. "Fences Make Neighbors: Process, Identity, and Ego in Robert Frost's 'Mending Wall.' " *Arizona Quarterly* 40.3 (1984): 242–54.

————. "Robert Frost's 'The Pasture': A Reconsideration." *Concerning Poetry* 16.2 (1983): 1–9.

————. "Two Woodchucks, or Frost and Thoreau on the Art of the Burrow." *Colby Library Quarterly* 18.4 (1982): 214–19.

"The Old Masters." *Times Literary Supplement* 21 Dec. 1962: 987.

Orlov, Paul A. "The World's Disorder and the Word's Design in Two Poems by Frost." *Journal of the Midwest Modern Language Association* 19.2 (1986): 30–38.

Oster, Judith. *Toward Robert Frost: The Reader and the Poet.* Athens: University of Georgia Press, 1991.

Pack, Robert. "Frost's Enigmatical Reserve: The Poet as Teacher and Preacher." In Bloom, 9–21.

Parini, Jay. "Emerson and Frost: The Present Act of Vision." *Sewanee Review* 89.2 (Spring 1981): 206–27.

———. "Robert Frost." *The Columbia Literary History of the United States*. Ed. Emory Elliott et al. New York: Columbia University Press, 1988. 937–46.

———. *Robert Frost: A Life*. London: Heinemann, 1998; New York: Holt, 1999.

Patterson, Annabel. "Hard Pastoral: Frost, Wordsworth, and Modernist Poetics." *Criticism* 29.1 (1987): 67–87.

Pellegrino, Joe. "Frost, Schopenhauer, and 'The Trial by Existence.' " *Robert Frost Review* (Fall 1993): 93–100.

Perkins, David. "Robert Frost." *A History of Modern Poetry*. 2 vols. Cambridge, MA: Belknap Press of Harvard University Press, 1976. 1: 227–51.

Perrine, Laurence. "Frost's 'Acquainted with the Night.' " *Explicator* 25 (1967): Item 50.

———. "Frost's 'An Empty Threat.' " *Explicator* 30.8 (Apr. 1972): Item 63.

———. "Frost's 'Dust of Snow.' " *Explicator* 29 (Mar. 1971): Item 61.

———. "Frost's 'Gathering Leaves.' " *CEA Critic* 34 (1971): 29.

———. "Frost's 'Iris by Night.' " *Concerning Poetry* 12.1 (Spring 1979): 34–43.

———. "Frost's 'Pod of the Milkweed.' " *Notes on Modern American Literature* 5 (1980): Item 5.

———. "Frost's 'Sand Dunes.' " *Explicator* 14.6 (Mar. 1956): Item 38.

———. "Frost's 'The Span of Life.' " *Explicator* 37.4 (1979): 4.

———. "Frost's 'The Telephone.' " *Notes on Contemporary Literature* 10.3 (1980): 11–12.

———. "A House for Frost's 'White-Tailed Hornet.' " *Notes on Contemporary Literature* 10.1 (Jan. 1980): 3.

———. "Letting Go with the Heart: Frost's 'Wild Grapes.' " *Notes on Modern American Literature* 2.3 (Summer 1978): Item 20.

———. "Provide, Provide." *Robert Frost Review* (Fall 1992): 33–39.

———. "Robert Frost's 'Provide, Provide.' " *Notes on Modern American Literature* 8.1 (Spring 1984): Item 5.

———. "The Tone of Frost's 'The Literate Farmer and the Planet Venus.' " *Notes on Contemporary Literature* 5.2 (1975): 10–13.

Peters, Joan D. "Education by Poetry: Robert Frost's Departure from the Modern Critical Tradition." *South Carolina Review* 21.1 (1988): 27–37.

Poirier, Richard. "The Art of Poetry II: Robert Frost." *Paris Review* 24 (1960): 88–120.

———. "Choices." Bloom, 43–61. Rpt. from Poirier, *Knowing*, 50–75.

———. *Robert Frost: The Work of Knowing*. New York: Oxford University Press, 1977.

Poole, Robert. "Robert Frost, William Carlos Williams, and Wallace Stevens: Reality and Poetic Vitality." *CLA Journal* 26 (1992): 12–23.

Potter, James L. *The Robert Frost Handbook*. University Park: Pennsylvania State University Press, 1980.

Pound, Ezra. *The Letters of Ezra Pound*. Ed. D. D. Paige. New York: Harcourt, Brace, 1950.

———. "Modern Georgics." *Poetry* 5 (Dec. 1914): 127–30.

———. Rev. of *A Boy's Will*, by Robert Frost. *Poetry: A Magazine of Verse* 2.2 (May 1913): 72–74.

Pratt, Linda Ray. "Prosody as Meaning in Frost's 'The Hill Wife.' " Kuzma, 97–109.

Pritchard, William H. "Bearing Witness: 'The Wind and the Rain' " Kuzma, 129–34.

———. *Frost: A Literary Life Reconsidered*. New York: Oxford University Press, 1984.

————. *Playing It by Ear: Literary Essays and Reviews*. Amherst: University Press of Massachusetts, 1994.

Reed, Richard. "The Animal World in Robert Frost's Poetry." Tharpe, *Centennial II*, 159–69.

Reeve, Franklin D. *Robert Frost in Russia*. Boston: Atlantic–Little, Brown, 1963.

Reichert, Victor. "The Faith of Robert Frost." Tharpe, *Centennial*, 415–26.

Richardson, Mark. "Frost's 'Closed for Good': Editorial and Interpretive Problems." *Robert Frost Review* (Fall 1996): 22–35.

————. *The Ordeal of Robert Frost: The Poet and His Poetics*. Urbana: University of Illinois Press, 1997.

————. "Robert Frost and the Motives of Poetry." *Essays in Literature* 20.2 (1993): 273–91.

————. "Robert Frost's Prose Writings: A Comprehensive Annotated Checklist and Introductory Essay." *Resources for American Literary Study* 22.1 (1996): 37–78.

Ricks, Christopher. *The Force of Poetry*. Oxford: Oxford University Press, 1984.

Ridland, John. "Fourteen Ways of Looking at a Bad Man." *Southwest Review* 71.2 (Spring 1986): 222–42.

Robson, W. W. "The Achievement of Robert Frost." *Southern Review* ns 2 (Oct. 1966): 735–61.

Rodman, Selden. *Tongues of Fallen Angels*. New York: New Directions, 1972.

Rodman, Tom. "Robert Frost at Amherst." *Touchstone* 4 (Feb. 1939): 7–8.

Rood, Karen Lane. "Robert Frost's 'Sentence Sounds': Wildness Opposing the Sonnet Form." Tharpe, *Centennial II*, 196–210.

Rosenblatt, Louise M. *The Reader, the Text, the Poem: The Transactional Theory of the Literary Work*. Carbondale: Southern Illinois University Press, 1978.

Rotella, Guy. "Comparing Conceptions: Frost and Eddington, Heisenberg, and Bohr." *American Literature* 59.2 (1987): 167–89.

————. "Metaphor in Frost's 'Oven Bird.' " Wilcox, *The Man and the Poet*, 19–30.

Ryan, Alvan S. "Frost and Emerson: Voice and Vision." *Massachusetts Review* 1 (Oct. 1959): 5–23.

Salska, Agnieszka. "Knowledge and Experience in the Early Frost." *American Poetry between Tradition and Modernism 1865–1914*. Ed. Roland Hagenbüchle. Regensburg: Pustet, 1984. 191–96.

Sanders, David A. "Words in the Rush of Everything to Waste." *South Carolina Review* 7.1 (1974): 34–47.

Scheele, Roy. "The Laborious Dream: Frost's 'After Apple-Picking.' " Kuzma, 147–53.

Schneider, Isdor. [Rev. of *Collected Poems 1930*] *The Nation* 28 Jan. 1931: 101–2.

Schutz, Fred C. "Frost's 'The Literate Farmer and the Planet Venus': Why 1926?" *Notes on Contemporary Literature* 4.5 (1974): 8–11.

Schwartz, Sanford. *The Matrix of Modernism*. Princeton, NJ: Princeton University Press, 1985.

Scott, Mark. "Andrew Lang's 'Scythe Song' Becomes Robert Frost's 'Mowing.' " *Robert Frost Review* (Fall 1991): 30–38.

Sears, John F. "The Subversive Performer in Frost's 'Snow' and 'Out, Out—.' " *The Motive for Metaphor: Essays on Modern Poetry in Honor of Samuel French Morse*. Ed. Francis C. Blessington and Guy Rotella. Boston: Northeastern University Press, 1983. 82–92.

Sell, Roger D. "Robert Frost: Two Unpublished Plays: *In an Art Factory* and *The Guardeen*," with an introduction. *Massachusetts Review* 26 (1985): 265–340.

Sergeant, Elizabeth Shepley. *Robert Frost: The Trial by Existence*. New York: Holt, 1960.

Sessions, Ina B. "The Dramatic Monologue." *PMLA* 62 (1947): 503–16.

Sheehy, Donald G. "The Poet as Neurotic: The Official Biography of Robert Frost." *American Literature* 58 (1986): 393–410.

———. "(Re)Figuring Love: Robert Frost in Crisis." *New England Quarterly* 63 (June 1990): 179–231.

———. "Robert Frost and 'The Lockless Door.' " *New England Quarterly* 56 (Mar. 1983): 39–59.

———. " 'To Otto as of Old': The Letters of Robert Frost and Otto Manthey-Zorn, Part 1." *New England Quarterly* 67 (Sep. 1994): 355–402.

Slakey, Roger L. "Moon Compasses." *Explicator* 37 (1978): 22–23.

Slights, William. "The Sense of Frost's Humor." *Concerning Poetry* 16.1 (Spring 1983): 29–42.

Smith, Evans Lansing. "Frost's 'On a Bird Singing in Its Sleep,' 'Never Again Would Birds' Song Be the Same,' and 'The Silken Tent.' " *Explicator* 50 (1991): 35–37.

Smith, Thomas G. "Robert Frost, Stewart Udall, and the 'Last Go-Down.' " *New England Quarterly* 70.1 (Mar. 1997): 3–32.

Smythe, Daniel. *Robert Frost Speaks*. New York: Twayne, 1964.

Snow, Wilbert. "The Robert Frost I Knew." *Texas Quarterly* 11 (Autumn 1968): 6–48.

Sokol, B. J. "Bergson, Instinct, and Frost's 'The White-Tailed Hornet.' " *American Literature: A Journal of Literary History, Criticism, and Bibliography* 62.1 (1990): 45–55.

Squires, Radcliffe. *The Major Themes of Robert Frost*. Ann Arbor: University of Michigan Press, 1963.

Stamper, Rexford. "An Assessment of Criticism, Realism, and Modernity." Tharpe, *Centennial*, 60–86.

Stanlis, Peter J. "Acceptable in Heaven's Sight: Frost at Bread Loaf: 1939–1941." Tharpe, *Centennial III*, 179–311.

———. *Robert Frost at Bread Loaf*. Middlebury, VT: Middlebury College, 1964. A pamphlet.

———. "Robert Frost: Politics in Theory and Practice." Tharpe, *Centennial II*, 48–82.

———. *Robert Frost: The Individual and Society*. Rockford, IL: Rockford College, 1973.

———. "Robert Frost's *Masques* and the Classic American Tradition." Tharpe, *Centennial*, 441–68.

Stegner, Wallace. *Robert Frost & Bernard DeVoto*. Palo Alto, CA: Associates of the Stanford University Libraries, 1974.

Stein, William B. " 'After Apple-Picking': Echoic Parody." *University Review* 35 (1969): 301–5.

Stiller, Walter N. "The Measure of Meaning: The Concept of Order in the Poetry of Robert Frost." *DAI* 47 (1986): 1327A. City University of New York.

Stillians, Bruce. "Frost's 'To the Thawing Wind.' " *Explicator* 31 (1972): Item 31.

Stone, Edward. "Other 'Desert Places': Frost and Hawthorne." Tharpe, *Centennial*, 275–88.

Stott, Jon C. *An Outline of the Poetry of Robert Frost*. Toronto: Forum House, 1971.

Sullivan, Bradley. " 'Education by Poetry' in Robert Frost's Masques." *Papers on Language and Literature* 22 (1986): 312–21.

Summerlin, Charles Timothy. "The Romantic Absolute in Frost's 'Home Burial.' " *Robert Frost Review* (Fall 1994): 53–57.

Sutton, Betty S. "Form as Argument: Frost's 'Lesson for Today.' " *Fu Jen Studies* 18 (1985): 81–96.

Sutton, William A. "A Frost–Sandburg Rivalry?" *Ball State University Forum* 11 (Winter 1970): 58–61.

———. "Problems of Biography," Harris, *Studies*, 89–93.

———. "Some Robert Frost 'Fooling.' " *Mark Twain Journal* 21.3 (Spring 1983): 61–62.

Taylor, Welford Dunaway. *Robert Frost and J. J. Lankes: Riders on Pegasus*. Hanover, NH: Dartmouth College Library, 1996.

Tharpe, Jac L., ed. *Frost: Centennial Essays*. Jackson: University Press of Mississippi, 1974.

———. *Frost: Centennial Essays II*. Jackson: University Press of Mississippi, 1976.

———. *Frost: Centennial Essays III*. Jackson: University Press of Mississippi, 1978.

Thomas, Ron. "Thoreau, William James, and Frost's 'Quest of the Purple-Fringed': A Contextual Reading." *American Literature* 60 (1988): 433–50.

Thompson, Lawrance. *Fire and Ice: The Art and Thought of Robert Frost*. New York: Russel, 1961.

———. *Robert Frost: The Early Years: 1874–1915*. New York: Holt, 1966.

———. *The Years of Triumph*. New York: Holt, 1970.

Thompson, Lawrance, and R. H. Winnick. *The Later Years: 1938–63*. New York: Holt, 1976.

———. *Robert Frost, A Biography*. Ed. Edward Connery Lathem. New York: Holt, 1981.

Tomlinson, Sandra W. "Frost's 'The Draft Horse.' " *Explicator* 42 (1984): 28–29.

Torrence, Ridgely. *Hesperides*. New York: Macmillan, 1925.

Townsend, R. C. "In Defense of Form: A Letter from Robert Frost to Sylvester Baxter, 1923." *New England Quarterly* 36.2 (1963): 241–49.

Tyler, Dorothy. "Frost's Last Three Visits to Michigan." Tharpe, *Centennial*, 518–34.

———. "Robert Frost in Michigan." Tharpe, *Centennial III*, 7–69.

Udall, Stewart L. "Robert Frost, Kennedy and Khrushchev: A Memoir of Poetry and Power." *Shenandoah* 26 (Winter 1975): 52–68.

Untermeyer, Louis, ed. *Modern American Poetry, Modern British Poetry*. Combined Mid-Century Edition. New York: Harcourt, Brace, 1950.

Vail, Dennis. "Frost's 'Ghost House.' " *Explicator* 30 (1971): 11.

———. "Point of View in Frost's 'The Peaceful Shepherd.' " *Notes on Contemporary Literature* 4.5 (1974): 2–4.

Van Egmond, Peter. *The Critical Reception of Robert Frost*. Boston: G. K. Hall, 1974.

———. *Robert Frost: A Reference Guide, 1974–1990*. Boston: G. K. Hall, 1991.

Virgil. *Virgil: The Eclogues*. London: Penguin, 1984.

Vogel, Nancy. "Robert Frost and Andrew Wyeth: Closeness to the Swaying Line." Master's thesis, University of Kansas, 1965.

———. *Robert Frost, Teacher*. Bloomington, IN: Phi Delta Kappa, 1974.

———. "Robert Frost—Teacher: 'Earner, Learner, Yearner.' " Diss., University of Kansas, 1971.

Vogt, Victor E. "Narrative and Drama in the Lyric: Robert Frost's Strategic Withdrawal." *Critical Inquiry* 5 (1979): 529–51.

Waddell, William S., Jr. "Aphorism in Frost's 'The Tuft of Flowers': The Sound of Certainty." *Concerning Poetry* 13 (1980): 41–44.

———. "By Precept and Example: Aphorism in 'The Star-Splitter.' " Wilcox, *The Man*, 99–107.

Waggoner, Hyatt Howe. *American Poets, from the Puritans to the Present*. Rev. ed. Baton Rouge: Louisiana State University Press, 1984.

———. "The Humanistic Idealism of Robert Frost." *American Literature* 12 (1941): 207–23. Rpt. in Cady and Budd, 13–29.

Wagner, Linda W., ed. *Robert Frost: The Critical Reception*. New York: Burt Franklin, 1977.

Wakefield, Richard. "Making Snug in the Limitless: Frost's 'Time Out.' " *Robert Frost Review* (Fall 1995): 56–61.

———. *Robert Frost and the Opposing Lights of the Hour*. New York: Peter Lang, 1985.

Wallace, Anne Denice. "Walking Where the Sower Dwelt: Origins and Uses of Peripatetic in the Nineteenth Century." *DAI* 50 (1990): 349A. University of Texas.

Wallace, Patricia. "Separateness and Solitude in Frost." *Kenyon Review* 6.1 (1984): 1–12.

Walsh, John Evangelist. *Into My Own: The English Years of Robert Frost, 1912–1915*. New York: Grove, 1988.

West, Michael. "Versifying Thoreau: Frost's 'The Quest of the Purple-Fringed' and 'Fire and Ice.' " *English Language Notes* 16 (1978): 40–47.

Wilbur, Richard. "On Robert Frost's 'The Gum-Gatherer.' " Kuzma, 141–43.

Wilcox, Earl J., ed. *His Incalculable Influence on Others: Essays on Robert Frost in Our Time*. ELS No. 63. Victoria, British Columbia: University of Victoria, 1994.

———. *Robert Frost: The Man and the Poet*. Rock Hill, SC: Winthrop College, 1981.

Wilkinson, Marguerite. *New Voices. An Introduction to Contemporary Poetry*. New York: Macmillan, 1919.

Williams, Ellen. *Harriet Monroe and the Poetry Renaissance: The First Ten Years of Poetry, 1912–1922*. Urbana: University of Illinois Press, 1977.

Willige, Eckart. "Formal Devices in Robert Frost's Short Poems." *Georgia Review* 15 (Fall 1961): 324–30.

Winslow, Donald. "The Origin of Robert Frost's 'Witness Tree.' " *American Notes and Queries* 13 (June 1975): 153–54.

Winters, Yvor. "Robert Frost: Or, The Spiritual Drifter as Poet." *Sewanee Review* 56 (1948): 564–96. Rpt. in J. Cox, *Collection*, 58–82.

Yogi, L. L. "The Scientist in Robert Frost's Poetry." *Rajasthan University Studies in English* 10 (1977): 27–37.

Zubizarreta, John. "Eliot's 'Gerontion' and Frost's 'An Old Man's Winter Night': Counterparts of Modernism." *Robert Frost Review* (Fall 1993): 62–69.

Zverev, A. "A Lover's Quarrel with the World: Robert Frost." *20th Century American Literature: A Soviet View*. Trans. Ronald Vroon. Moscow: Progress Publishers, 1976. 241–60.

OTHER MEDIA

Frostiana: Seven Country Songs for Men's, Women's and Mixed Voices with Piano Accompaniment. Words by Robert Frost. Music by Randall Thompson. E. C. Schirmer Music, 1959.

Robert Frost in Recital. New York: Caedmon, HarperCollins, 1976 (1922). Audio-recording.

Robert Frost Reads His Poetry. Rec. 9 Dec. 1953, University of California–Berkeley. Audio Forum cassette 23066.

Index

Note: **Bold** page numbers designate main entries in the volume.

About the Editors and Contributors

MARY ADAMS is Assistant Professor of English at Western Carolina University, Cullowhee, North Carolina. She is the author of a book of poems, *Epistles from the Planet Photosynthesis*, as well as articles on Milton and on Modernism.

KIRK C. ALLISON, a University of Minnesota doctoral candidate in German and comparative literature, has served as guest lector at the University of Salzburg Department of English and American Studies. His publications include poetry and translations of Georg Trakl in *The Poet's Voice*; articles on twentieth-century German ideology and cartography; articles on the confluence of politics, pilgrimage, and folk literary tradition; and, forthcoming, an article on immersion, second-language acquisition, and social context. His dissertation concerns Gottfried Benn and exoticism.

ALEX AMBROZIC is a graduate student at Memorial University of Newfoundland.

DANA E. ASPINALL is Assistant Professor of English at Assumption College. His research interests include drama of the English Renaissance and travel narratives from the sixteenth to the nineteenth centuries.

GEORGE F. BAGBY teaches at Hampden-Sydney College in Virginia and has published on Frost—especially *Frost and the Book of Nature*—and Cooper. He has delivered papers on American nature writing and on various African American writers, including Claude McKay and Richard Wright. He is currently working on a biography of Hollis F. Price (1904–1982), an Afro-American educator.

THOMAS C. BAILEY is Ombudsman at Western Michigan University and a member of Western's English Department. His interests are modern and contemporary American poetry and nature writing.

LYNN BARRETT is Education Director at Herzing College in New Orleans, Louisiana.

JONATHAN N. BARRON, Associate Professor of English at the University of Southern Mississippi, is Associate Editor of the *Robert Frost Review* and has published articles on Robert Frost, William Wordsworth, and Jewish American poetry.

MICHAEL BERNDT is a Teaching Specialist at the University of Minnesota. He is a Ph.D. candidate in American literature at Southern Illinois University at Carbondale and is currently writing a dissertation on promotional literature.

JOHN C. BRADLEY, JR. is a full-time trial attorney and incurable bibliophile. He lives, works, and reads in Columbia, South Carolina, with his wife, Roxane, and daughters, Rebecca and Rachel.

ERIC C. BROWN is Assistant Professor of English at the University of Southwestern Louisiana. He has previously published on modern poetry in the *Yeats-Eliot Review*.

BELINDA D. BRUNER is currently completing her dissertation on student/teacher relationships in Sherwood Anderson's *Winesburg, Ohio*. Her areas of specialty include Modernism, American Studies, Cultural Studies, and critical theory.

SUSAN BURNS is a doctoral candidate in English and American literature at New York University, where she has taught modern and contemporary American poetry.

HAROLD K. BUSH, JR. is Assistant Professor of English at Saint Louis University. His book on American literary and cultural history, *American Declarations: Rebellion and Repentance in American Cultural History*, contains a chapter on Frost's participation in presidential politics during the Kennedy era.

RICHARD J. CALHOUN is Alumni Distinguished Professor, Emeritus, Clemson University. For twenty-six years he edited the *South Carolina Review*, which published much on Frost. He edited the contemporary poetry section of *American Literary Scholarship* for six years and published books on James Dickey and Galway Kinnell and articles on many modern poets including Lowell, Wilbur, Jarrell, and Frost. He is a past president of The Robert Frost Society.

KELLY CANNON is Humanities Reference Librarian at Muhlenberg College in Allentown, Pennsylvania. He teaches American literature at the Muhlenberg Evening College and is engaged in a second critical work on the fiction of Henry James.

ISAAC CATES is a Ph.D. student in English at Yale University, where he writes both on the sonnet and on nature writing. His dissertation, entitled "Nature Poetry after Darwin," includes a chapter on Robert Frost.

DAVID D. COOPER, Director of the American Studies Program at Michigan State University, is Professor of American Thought & Language.

F. BRETT COX is Assistant Professor of English at Gordon College in Barnesville, Georgia. His essays, reviews, notes, and fiction have appeared or are forthcoming in the *New England Quarterly, Dictionary of Literary Biography, St. James Guide to Science Fiction Writers*, the *New York Review of Science Fiction, Century*, the Baltimore *Sun*, and elsewhere.

JEFFREY S. CRAMER is the author of *Robert Frost Among His Poems: A Literary Companion to the Poet's Own Biographical Contexts and Associations*. His work has also appeared in various journals, including the *Robert Frost Society Review*, the *Thomas Hardy Yearbook*, and the *Christian Science Monitor*.

THOMAS DENENBERG is Richard Koopman Curator of American Decorative Arts at the Wadsworth Atheneum in Hartford, Connecticut. He is also a doctoral candidate in American and New England Studies at Boston University.

BETH L. DIEHLS is a graduate student at the University of South Carolina, where she studies early American literature and women's studies.

CAROL DIETRICH is Professor of General Education at DeVry Institute of Technology, where she teaches composition and literature. A published poet, she is currently pursuing a degree in theology.

JAMES M. DUBINSKY taught for four years at the United States Military Academy and is now an Assistant Professor in the English Department at Virginia Tech. He wrote his master's thesis at the University of California at Berkeley on Robert Frost and has published in the *Robert Frost Review* and elsewhere.

ANDY DUNCAN teaches undergraduate composition, creative writing, and literature at the University of Alabama, where he is an M.F.A. student in Program in Creative Writing. He has published fiction and poetry in *Asimov's Science Fiction* and in anthologies from Tor and HarperPrism and critical articles in *Tangent*, the *New York Review of Science Fiction*, and the *North Carolina Literary Review*.

SCOTT EARLE is writing a dissertation on John Steinbeck at the University of Arkansas.

DAVID EVANS teaches at State University of New Jersey–Rutgers and has written on a number of American authors, including Robert Frost, William Faulkner, and Herman Melville.

SHARON FELTON received her Ph.D. from Purdue University. She is currently teaching English in middle Tennessee.

ROBERT F. FLEISSNER is author of several books relating in part to Frost, namely, *The Prince and the Professor: The Wittenberg Connection to Marlowe, Shakespeare, Goethe, and Frost* (one-third of which deals with the Job relation in the Faustian elements in *A Masque of Reason*) and *A Rose by Another Name*; recently he has published *Frost's Road Taken*. He directed the 1982 three-day Frost conference in Ohio. He has also published over forty articles, notes, and reviews on Frost in academic journals.

LESLEY LEE FRANCIS is the granddaughter of Robert Frost. She recently retired from the professional staff of the American Association of University Professors (AAUP). Dr. Francis received her A.B. degree from Radcliffe College and her Ph.D. in Romance Languages from Duke University. She taught Spanish language and literature at Sweet Briar College and St. Edward's University before moving with her three daughters to Arlington, Virginia. For many years she owned and operated a summer school in La Granja (Segovia), Spain. She has lectured and published extensively on her grandfather; in 1994, she published a biographical study of the Derry and English years entitled *The Frost Family's Adventure in Poetry: Sheer Morning Gladness at the Brim*.

DONALD J. GREINER holds the chair of Carolina Distinguished Professor of English at the University of South Carolina, where he is also Associate Provost and Dean of Undergraduate Affairs. He is executive editor of *Critique: Studies in Contemporary Fiction*. Among his many books and articles is *Robert Frost: The Poet and His Critics*.

CHRISTINE HANKS HAIT is Associate Professor of English at Columbia College in Columbia, South Carolina. Her research interests include literary modernism, southern literature, autobiography, and film. She completed her dissertation on issues of creativity and gender in the work of Katherine Anne Porter. She recently published an essay on innovations in autobiography in Kay Boyle's *Being Geniuses Together*.

DOROTHY JUDD HALL teaches religion and literature at Boston University, where she received her doctorate in literature. A published poet and author of *Robert Frost: Contours of Belief*, she is currently working on a study of Frost's inner journey, "Robert Frost: Between the Dotted Stars."

MICHAEL HANCHER is Professor of English and Associate Dean in the College of Liberal Arts, University of Minnesota. Most of his publications concern Victorian poetry and painting, book illustration, and relations between pragmatics and literary and legal interpretation.

ROBERT BERNARD HASS, a doctoral candidate at Penn State, recently annotated Frost's complete poems for Holt's multimedia compendium *Robert Frost: Poems, Life, and Legacy*. He has published articles on Tennyson and Eliot, and his poems have appeared in numerous journals including *Poetry* and *Sewanee Review*. He is currently writing a dissertation on Robert Frost's response to science.

GRALEY V. HERREN teaches twentieth-century American and Anglo-Irish literature, with an emphasis on drama, at Florida State University. He is also the Assistant Editor for the *Journal of Beckett Studies*.

WM. THOMAS HILL is Foreign Visiting Professor of Modern British and American Literature at Tsukuba University in Japan.

TYLER B. HOFFMAN is Assistant Professor of English at Rutgers University at Camden. He has published an essay on Emily Dickinson and the Civil War in the *Emily Dickinson Journal* and is a regular reviewer of American poetry criticism for *South Atlantic Review*. His book *Robert Frost and the Politics of Poetry* is being published by the University Press of New England, fall 2001.

JASON G. HORN is Assistant Professor of English and Chair of the Division of Humanities at Gordon College in Barnesville, Georgia. He has published several articles on late nineteenth- and twentieth-century American literary figures and is author of *Mark Twain and William James: Crafting a Free Self*. He is currently at work on a book that traces the effect of William James's thinking upon a wider range of poets and novelists, including Frost, Stevens, and Wharton.

DIANE N. HULETT is a doctoral candidate in American literature at the University of Kentucky, specializing in twentieth-century Southern and African American literature. Her dissertation examines Robert Penn Warren's views on the civil rights movement in *Who Speaks for the Negro?* and other nonfiction works.

EDWARD J. INGEBRETSEN is Associate Professor of English at Georgetown University, Washington, D.C. He is the author of numerous articles and reviews on Robert Frost, including *Robert Frost's Star in a Stone-Boat: A Grammar of Belief*. Other publications include *Maps of Heaven, Maps of Hell: Religious Terror as Memory from the Puritans to Stephen King*. Recently, he was a Fulbright Scholar in Bergen, Norway.

JAMES A. INMAN is Spencer Fellow at the University of Michigan. He writes regularly on the impact of technology on English Studies, especially as identified in writing studies and American literature. His current projects include coediting an essay collection called *Taking Flight with OWLs: Examining Electronic Writing Center Work*, which explores the role of technology in writing center practice and development, and authoring an essay on Robert Frost's critique of technology.

LARRY R. ISITT is Assistant Professor of English at College of the Ozarks. He has published on Frost, Milton, and Restoration theater.

SARAH R. JACKSON teaches in the Department of English at Stephen F. Austin State University in Nacogdoches, Texas. She has published articles on Robert Frost and his poetry in the *Robert Frost Review*, the *Explicator*, the *Dartmouth College Library Bulletin*, the *Worchester Review*, and *English in Texas*. She has created a Robert Frost Web site: "Robert Frost in Cyberspace: Introducing Robert Frost to a New Generation."

NANCY CAROL JOYNER, Professor of English at Western Carolina University, specializes in modern American poetry and Appalachian literature. She has published *Edwin Arlington Robinson: A Reference Guide* and numerous articles on twentieth-century poets and novelists.

MICHAEL KAROUNOS is a graduate student at Vanderbilt University and a faculty member at Free Will Baptist Bible College.

SANDRA KATZ is Professor of English at Hillyer College, University of Hartford. She is the author of *Elinor Frost: A Poet's Wife*.

KATHERINE KEARNS is the author of three recent books, *Robert Frost and a Poetics of Appetite, Nineteenth-Century Literary Realism: Through the Looking Glass*, and *Feminism, Psychoanalysis, and Historiography: The Search for Critical Method*. She has taught at Yale University, where she was also the Associate Director of the Whitney Humanities Center and the Director of the Teaching Fellow Program in the Graduate School.

L. TAMARA KENDIG is a doctoral candidate in twentieth-century American literature at Lehigh University.

CHRISTOPHER KRENTZ is completing his Ph.D in English at the University of Virginia.

DIANNA LAURENT has a Ph.D. from the University of Mississippi and teaches in the English Department at Southeastern Louisiana University. She has many publications, the most recent a book on research methodologies using the Internet.

ERIC LEUSCHNER received his M.A. from Oklahoma State University, writing his thesis on Stevens and metonymy. His article on "Peter Quince at the Clavier" appears in the *Wallace Stevens Journal*.

TODD LIEBER is Professor and Chair of the English Department at Simpson College, Indianola, Iowa. His article "Robert Frost and Wallace Stevens: What to Make of a Diminished Thing" appeared originally in 1975 in *American Literature* and has been reprinted many times. He has also reviewed several books on Frost.

GEORGE LOPEZ is a graduate student in the English Department at the University of South Carolina.

PAOLA LORETO has published a number of articles and essays on Canadian, Caribbean, and U.S. literatures and is now completing a book-length study on Emily Dickinson.

LINDA LOVELL teaches English at Northwest Arkansas Community College and was the recipient of the Daisy Bates Nonfiction Award from the University of Arkansas Press for her essay "Robert Frost: A Constant Conservative."

ROLAND H. LYFORD is Professor of English at the University of Texas—Pan American, Edinburg, Texas. He received his B.A. and M.A. at Middlebury College, Vermont, where he attended the Bread Loaf School of English and became acquainted with Robert Frost. His doctoral dissertation was entitled "Grammatical Categories in Robert Frost's Blank Verse: A Quantitative Analysis."

JACQUELINE B. MCCURRY is Assistant Professor of English and Director of Dramatic Arts at Saint Joseph's College of Maine. Her essay " 'But all the fun's in how you say a thing': Robert Frost's Influence on Paul Muldoon" appeared in the *Robert Frost Review*.

DAVID MESHER is Professor of English and American Studies and Coordinator of the Jewish Studies Program at San Jose State University. He is also the creator of "Mission: Critical," a critical thinking tutorial on the World Wide Web.

CHRISTOPHER R. MILLER is a Teaching Fellow in English Literature at Harvard University, where he is finishing his doctoral dissertation on British Romantic poetry.

CLAUDIA MILSTEAD is an Instructor at the University of Tennessee.

CRAIG MONK is Assistant Professor of English at the University of Lethbridge in Alberta, Canada. His work has appeared in *American Studies International, History of Photography*, the *Journal of American Studies*, the *Journal of Modern Literature*, and a number of essay collections. He is currently completing a book on American expatriates and the modern little magazine movement.

GEORGE MONTEIRO is a member of the Departments of English and of Portuguese and Brazilian Studies at Brown University. Among his publications on Frost is his *Robert Frost and the New England Renaissance*. He is also the author of *The Blue Badge of Stephen Crane*.

HOWARD NELSON is Professor of English at Cayuga Community College in Auburn, New York.

JUDITH OSTER is the author of *Toward Robert Frost: The Reader and the Poet* and has published articles on Frost in the *Robert Frost Review* and the *South Carolina Review*. She serves on the editorial board of the *Robert Frost Review*. She has also published and presented papers on ESL (English as a Second Language) composition and cross-cultural literature.

MATTHEW PARFITT is Associate Professor at the College of General Studies, Boston University. He has published in the *Robert Frost Review* and elsewhere.

JAY PARINI is Axinn Professor of English at Middlebury College. A poet and novelist, his books include *The Last Station* and *Benjamin's Crossing*. He recently published a biography of Robert Frost.

JASON PEARCE is currently a graduate student in Archival Studies at the University of British Columbia. His research interests include Canadian regionalism, American Modernism, and archival ethics.

JOE PELLEGRINO is Assistant Professor of English at Eastern Kentucky University, where he teaches courses on modern and contemporary poetry, fiction, and cultural studies. His research interests address the connections between literature, philosophy, and music. His published work includes articles on Frost, Yeats, Eliot, and other figures in twentieth-century poetry.

CHRISTIAN L. PYLE is a Ph.D. candidate in English at the University of Kentucky. His dissertation analyzes the Modernist vision of cartoonist George Herriman as expressed in the poetic, indeterminate world of *Krazy Kat*.

GERARD QUINN is a College Lecturer at University College Dublin, Ireland, where he lectures in European and American Modernism and teaches graduate courses in poetry and philosophy. He has specialized in Frost's synecdochic allusions to literature and philosophy.

MARK RICHARDSON teaches American literature at Western Michigan University. He is author of *The Ordeal of Robert Frost* and coeditor, with Richard Poirier, of *Robert Frost: Collected Poems, Prose, and Plays*.

JUDY RICHTER lives and works at Coker Farm in Bedford, New York.

KENNETH RICKARD grew up thirty miles north of Boston. He is completing a doctoral fellowship at the University of Arkansas, concentrating on American literature, 1840–1940.

JOHN RIDLAND has taught Frost, Chaucer, and other poets and poetry writing classes in the College of Creative Studies and the English Department at the University of California, Santa Barbara, since 1961. He has published several books of poems and articles and reviews on Frost in the *Southwest Review*, the *Los Angeles Times Book Review*, and the *Robert Frost Review*.

JEANNETTE E. RILEY is Assistant Professor of English at Kent State University, Stark Campus. Much of her work focuses on contemporary poetry, especially poetry by women, and post-1945 American fiction.

GARY ROBERTS is a doctoral candidate at Brandeis University and is writing his dissertation on vulgarity and poetic diction in modern poetry. His publications include articles on the early history of urban poetry, the poet Jane Kenyon, and the poet Allen Grossman.

AUDRA ROUSE is a Ph.D. candidate at the University of South Carolina, where she is studying American literature.

JOHN P. SAMONDS is an Instructor at the University of Mississippi. His field of study is American literature, particularly Modernist American poetry.

DAVID SANDERS is Professor of English at St. John Fisher College in Rochester, New York, where he teaches English, American, and biblical literatures. He is active in the Frost Society, has published most recently in the *Robert Frost* and the *Yeats-Eliot Reviews*, and is currently writing (when life permits) on Twain, Wordsworth, Elizabeth Bishop, and Robert Frost. Among other works-in-progress are a son and daughter, aged twelve and ten, and a few small stone walls.

SABINE SAUTTER-LEGER is currently finishing her Ph.D. in Modernism at McGill University, where she has taught modern and contemporary poetry and prose. She has published on recent developments in literary theory as well as different aspects of twentieth-century novelistic writing.

GAVIN SCHULZ received his Bachelor's in Mathematics and his Doctorate in American Literature from the University of Southern California. He is currently in Texas participating in the social experiment called Adjunct Teaching.

ROBERT W. SCOTT received his M.F.A. in Creating Writing from American University in 1996, where he is Instructor in the College Writing Program.

GEORGE S. SCOUTEN is a doctoral candidate at the University of South Carolina.

LISA SEALE is Associate Professor of English at the University of Wisconsin, Marathon County in Wausau. She writes on Robert Frost's later work, including his public talks and readings.

DONALD G. SHEEHY teaches in the English and Theatre Arts Department at Edinboro University of Pennsylvania. He has published articles on Frost in *American Literature, New England Quarterly, Texas Studies in Literature and Language, South Atlantic Review, Robert Frost Review*, and other journals. He is, most recently, the General Editor of *Robert Frost: Poems, Life, Legacy* (a multimedia CD-ROM).

MELISSA SIMPSON teaches upper school English at Pulaski Academy in Little Rock, Arkansas.

NEWTON SMITH is Assistant Professor at Western Carolina, where he teaches modern poetry, American literature, Southern literature, Appalachian literature, professional writing, and technical writing. He is a contributor to the upcoming *Encyclopedia of American Literature* and the editor of a reissue of Jesse Stuart's *Mr. Gallion's School*.

SCOTT ROBERT STANKEY is currently a Teaching Professor of English at Anoka-Ramsey Community College in Coon Rapids, Minnesota, where he teaches developmental and college-level writing, contemporary fiction, and American literature. His master's thesis examines William Wordsworth's and Robert Frost's prose statements on the organic creation of poetry.

PETER J. STANLIS is Distinguished Professor of Humanities, Emeritus, at Rockford College, Rockford, Illinois. Among his many contributions to Frost scholarship are *Robert Frost at Bread Loaf* and *Robert Frost: The Individual and Society*.

DERRICK STONE is a poet and has recently completed his master's degree from Memorial University of Newfoundland.

SUSAN M. STONE is a Ph.D. candidate at the University of South Carolina, where she is specializing in nineteenth-century American literature and women's studies. She has published a book review on Catharine Maria Sedgwick's *New-England Tale* and has written articles on Lucretia Peabody Hale, George Ripley, and Sylvia Ashton Warner.

CHRIS-ANNE STUMPF is a doctoral student in English and folklore at the University of Newfoundland.

MARK SUTTON is a graduate student at the University of South Carolina.

NANETTE CUMLEY TAMER is Assistant Professor of English Language and Literature at Villa Julie College near Baltimore, Maryland. She has published essays on the use of classical texts by seventeenth- and eighteenth-century English and American poets.

WELFORD DUNAWAY TAYLOR holds the James A. Bostwick Chair of English at the University of Richmond. His most recent books are *Robert Frost and J. J. Lankes: Riders on Pegasus* (1996) and *Woodcut Art of J. J. Lankes* (1999).

DOUGLAS M. TEDARDS, Associate Professor of English at University of the Pacific, currently teaches courses in American literature and advanced composition. He recently published "Journal Writing and the Study of Poetry" in Art Young and Toby Fulwiler's *When Writing Teachers Teach Literature* and has published his poetry in such periodicals as the *Georgia Review, San Fernando Poetry Journal,* and *Mind in Motion.*

JOHN H. TIMMERMAN is Professor of English at Calvin College and the author of several books, including *John Steinbeck's Fiction* and *T. S. Eliot's Ariel Poems,* and many articles on American literature. He is working on a book entitled *Robert Frost's Poetry: The Ethics of Ambiguity.*

GARY TOTTEN is Assistant Professor of English at Ball State University. His research interests include late nineteenth- and early twentieth-century American literature, the American road book, and the nonfiction novel.

NANCY LEWIS TUTEN is Professor of English at Columbia College in Columbia, South Carolina, where she has taught since 1988. She edited *Critical Essays on Galway Kinnell* (1996) and has published essays on American Writers, including Kinnell, Alice Walker, Robert Frost, Walt Whitman, and Theodore Roethke. From 1988 to 1991, she served as associate editor of *Studies in Short Fiction,* and since 1989 she has been a consulting editor for *The Explicator.* In 1996 the South Atlantic Association of Departments of English honored her with an award for outstanding teaching.

NANCY VOGEL is the author of *Robert Frost, Teacher* and "A Post Mortem on 'The Death of the Hired Man.' " Professor of English and former board member of the Kansas Humanities Council, Vogel is a recipient of the President's Distinguished Scholar Award at Fort Hays State University. She has also published in young adult literature, especially on Maureen Daly. An "earner, learner, yearner," Vogel attributes some of her affinity for Frost's work to having grown up on her family's farm in Grant Township near Lawrence, Kansas, a university town with a New England heritage.

RICHARD WAKEFIELD is the author of *Robert Frost and the Opposing Lights of the Hour.* He has written on American literature for many magazines and journals, and he teaches at Tacoma Community College and the University of Washington, Tacoma.

STEPHEN D. WARNER teaches American literature at the State University of New York at Fredonia.

MARLEY NICOLE WASHUM received her M.A. in English from the University of Central Arkansas, where she wrote her thesis on Frost's influence on the poetry of Seamus Heaney.

DOUGLAS WATSON is Professor of English and Director of the Honors Program at Oklahoma Baptist University, where he has taught since 1980.

EARL J. WILCOX, Director of the Robert Frost Society and Founding Editor of the *Robert Frost Review*, has edited two books and published several essays on Frost. He is Executive Director of the College English Association, President of the Jack London Society, and a founding member and officer of the Southern Region Honors Council. He organized and directed the Robert Frost International Conference at Winthrop University in September 1997.

C. P. SEABROOK WILKINSON is a Graduate School Fellow at the University of South Carolina, completing a dissertation on Washington Allston.

JOHN R. WOZNICKI is Assistant Professor of English at Fairmont State College in Fairmont, West Virginia. His primary area of interest is modern American and British literature, and he has published an essay on Wallace Stevens in the *Explicator*.

LORI M. YATES is a graduate student in rhetoric and composition at the University of Oklahoma.

JOHN ZUBIZARRETA is Professor of English, Director of Honors and Faculty Development, and Dean of Undergraduate Studies at Columbia College. A Carnegie Foundation/C.A.S.E. Professor, he has published widely in numerous books and journals on modern American and comparative literatures, pedagogy, and teaching improvement and evaluation. He has been an assistant and consulting editor for diverse academic journals, and he serves on the executive boards and committees of several professional organizations, including the Robert Frost Society, which has published some of his essays on Frost in *The Robert Frost Review*. When the academic life becomes too hectic, John is an avid telemark skier and fisherman, a six-time national champion in whitewater canoe competition, and the adoring father of two girls who keep him busy outside the ivied walls.